ROMAN POLITICAL THOUGHT

From Cicero to Augustine

DEAN HAMMER

Franklin & Marshall College

CAMBRIDGE
UNIVERSITY PRESS

CAMBRIDGE
UNIVERSITY PRESS

University Printing House, Cambridge CB2 8BS, United Kingdom

One Liberty Plaza, 20th Floor, New York, NY 10006, USA

477 Williamstown Road, Port Melbourne, VIC 3207, Australia

314-321, 3rd Floor, Plot 3, Splendor Forum, Jasola District Centre, New Delhi - 110025, India

79 Anson Road, #06-04/06, Singapore 079906

Cambridge University Press is part of the University of Cambridge.

It furthers the University's mission by disseminating knowledge in the pursuit of education, learning and research at the highest international levels of excellence.

www.cambridge.org
Information on this title: www.cambridge.org/9780521124089

© Dean Hammer 2014

This publication is in copyright. Subject to statutory exception and to the provisions of relevant collective licensing agreements, no reproduction of any part may take place without the written permission of Cambridge University Press.

First published 2014
Reprinted 2016
First paperback edition 2018

A catalogue record for this publication is available from the British Library

Library of Congress Cataloging in Publication data
Hammer, Dean, 1959–
Roman political thought : from Cicero to Augustine / Dean Hammer.
pages cm
ISBN 978-0-521-19524-9 (Hardback) – ISBN 978-0-521-12408-9 (Paperback)
1. Political science–Rome–History. I. Title.
JC83.H37 2014
320.0937–dc23   2014000401

ISBN 978-0-521-19524-9 Hardback
ISBN 978-0-521-12408-9 Paperback

Cambridge University Press has no responsibility for the persistence or accuracy of URLs for external or third-party internet websites referred to in this publication, and does not guarantee that any content on such websites is, or will remain, accurate or appropriate.

To my mentors, Dewayne Barnes, Aaron Wildavsky, and Kurt Raaflaub, who, at very different points in my life helped me realize what I never imagined as possible. I only hope I am able to touch others in similar ways.

CONTENTS

Abbreviations for classical texts • xi
Acknowledgments • xvii

Introduction • 1
Polybius, Roman republican political institutions, and culture • 7
The principate • 19

1 Cicero: To save the *res publica* • 26
What to call the *res publica* • 30
The best state • 31
Law, justice, and society • 36
The Stoics and natural law • 36
Cicero, natural law, and social duty • 38
Cicero, social duty, and justice • 39
Cicero, social duty, and the other virtues • 43
Coetus utilitatis communione societus, partnership, and property • 46
The mixed constitution and the negotiation of power • 48
Potestas and imperium • 50
Auctoritas • 51
Libertas • 52
The role of the people • 58
Property and the function of the state • 59
The breakdown of trust • 62
The *senatus consultum ultimum* • 67
Rhetoric and embodied discourse • 69
The ideal statesman and the "Dream of Scipio" • 76

Tusculan disputations: philosophy, care, and the limits of Stoicism • 79
Cosmopolitanism and empire • 87

2 Lucretius: The poetics of power • 93
Epicurus • 96
Atomism and the constituents of pleasure • 97
Consciousness and the philosophic life • 100
Community • 105
Epic poetry and Lucretius' method of thought • 107
Rome's place • 114
The naturalization of politics: sovereignty and power • 120
Social development and the surrender of sovereignty • 126
Pietas • 129
The majesty of nature and the possibility of politics • 133
The plague • 137
Lucretius and the limits of politics • 143

3 Sallust: Giving endurance to memory • 145
Metus hostilis and the organization of desire • 148
The War with Catiline and the subversion of politics • 155
Cato, Caesar, and memory • 161
The War with Jugurtha and the rise of the new men • 165
Marius and the path to power • 171
The role of the historian • 174

4 Virgil: Politics, violence, and memory • 180
Augustus and ideology • 184
Pastoralism and the Golden Age • 186
Virgil, Lucretius, *labor*, and memory • 193
Labor and *cultus* • 200
Violence • 203
Pietas and culture: The (il)logic of founding • 212
Family, state, and affection • 215
Labor • 223

5 Livy: Political thought as *remedium* • 229
The physiology of thought • 234
Founding • 239

The Tarquins and Lucretia: Inciting liberty • 242
Political corruption and publicness • 249
The *decemviri* and the return of tyranny • 253
Camillus: Reanimating political vision • 258
Securing an imperial landscape: Myths of inclusion • 262

6 Seneca and jurisdiction • 271
De clementia and jurisdiction • 278
The formation of character and the making of madness • 286
Despotism: Creating insanity • 293
Brutishness: The politics of entertainment • 296
Aversion: Hiding from the world • 301
Ungoverned desire • 303
Restoring jurisdiction • 307
Citizenship and community life • 315

7 Tacitus: The political psychology of despotism • 321
Primitive societies • 325
Unmediated politics • 331
The mutinies: The breakdown of trust • 334
Back at home: Fostering servility • 339
Despotic equality and political spectacle • 343
The psychology of terror • 345
Political thought and the restoration of sanity • 353

8 Marcus Aurelius and the *Cosmopolis* • 358
Epictetus • 360
Freedom and manliness • 366
Contemplation • 371
Contemplation and time • 373
Contemplation and space • 375
The *daimōn* • 380

9 Augustine: Political thought as confession • 382
Desire and attachment • 386
The limits of *virtus* • 393
Augustine's critique of Rome: The organization of desire • 397
The human condition • 403

CONTENTS

Wisdom and *caritas* • 408
The desire for the corporeal: The trinity of sensation, perception, and attention • 410
The desire for the incorporeal: The trinity of intellect, memory, and will • 411
The desire for God: The trinity of wisdom, eternity, and happiness • 412
The transformation of desire: Grace and caritas • 415
Roman resonances in Augustine's political thought • 416
Wandering • 419
Dominion • 421
Justice • 423
The affective bonds of community life • 425
Politics as confession • 428

Bibliography • 431
Index Locorum • 505
Index • 547

ABBREVIATIONS FOR CLASSICAL TEXTS

Aelius Aristides

Panath. *Panathenaic Discourse*

Appian

BC *Bellum civile (The civil war)*

Aristotle (Arist.)

De An. *De Anima (On the Soul)*
NE *Ethica Nicomachea (Nicomachean Ethics)*
Pol. *Politika (Politics)*

Augustine (Aug.)

Conf.	*Confessiones (Confessions)*
Contra acad.	*Contra academicos (Against the Sceptics)*
De beata vita	*De beata vita (The happy life)*
Civ. Dei.	*De civitate Dei (The City of God)*
De doc. Chr.	*De doctrina Christiana (Christian doctrine)*
De urb. exc.	*De excidio urbis Romae (On the sack of the city of Rome)*
De fid.inv.	*De fide rerum invisibilium (On faith in the unseen)*
De lib. arb.	*De libero arbitrio voluntatis (On human responsibility)*
De mag.	*De magistro (On the master)*
De mus.	*De musica (On music)*
De ord.	*De ordine (On order)*
De trin.	*De Trinatate (On the Trinity)*
De ut. cred.	*De utilitate credendi (On the usefulness of belief)*

xi

ABBREVIATIONS FOR CLASSICAL TEXTS

De vera relig. *De vera religione* (*On true religion*)
En. Psalmos *Enarrationes in Psalmos* (*On Psalms*)
Ep. *Epistulae* (*Letters*)
Solil. *Soliloquia* (*Soliloquies*)

Augustus

RG *Res gestae* (*Things accomplished*)

Unknown author

Bell. Afr. *Bellum Africum* (*African War*)

Caesar

BC *De bello civile* (*The civil wars*)
BG *De bello gallico* (*The Gallic wars*)

Celsus (Cels.)
Cicero (Cic.)

Acad.	*Academica* (*Academics*)
Att.	*Epistulae ad Atticum* (*Letters to Atticus*)
Balb.	*Pro Balbo*
Brut.	*Brutus*
Caec.	*Pro Caecina*
Cat.	*In Catilinam* (*Against Catiline*)
Cluent.	*Pro Cluentio*
De amic.	*De amicitia* (*On Friendship*)
De div.	*De divinatione* (*On divination*)
De fato	*De fato* (*On fate*)
De fin.	*De finibus* (*On ends*)
De Imperio Cn. Pompei	*On the appointment of Gnaeus Pompeius*
De inv.	*De inventione* (*On invention*)
De leg.	*De legibus* (*On laws*)
De nat. deor.	*De natura deorum* (*On the Nature of the Gods*)
De off.	*De officiis* (*On duties*)
De orat.	*De oratore* (*On the orator*)
De rep.	*De re publica* (*On the republic*)

ABBREVIATIONS FOR CLASSICAL TEXTS

Fam.	*Epistulae ad Familiares* (*Letters to Friends*)
Flac.	*Pro Flacco*
Font.	*Pro Fonteius*
Leg. agr.	*De lege agraria* (*On the agrarian law*)
Marc.	*Pro Marcello*
Mil.	*Pro Milone*
Mur.	*Pro Murena*
Orat.	*Orator* (*Orator*)
Par. stoi.	*Paradoxa stoicorum* (*Stoic paradoxes*)
Phil.	*Philippics*
Q. Fr.	*Epistulae ad Q. Fratrem* (*Letters to his Brother Quintus*)
Quinct.	*Pro Quinctio*
Rab.	*Pro Rabirio*
Rosc.	*Pro Roscio*
Sest.	*Pro Sestio*
Top.	*Topica* (*Topics*)
Tusc.	*Tusculanae disputationes* (*Tusculan disputations*)
Ver	*In Verrem* (*Against Verres*)

Dio Cassius (Dio)
Diogenes Laertius (DL)
Diogenes of Oenoanda (Diog. Oen.)
Dionysius of Halicarnassus (Dion. Hal.)

AR	*Antiquitates Romanae*

Epicurus (Epic.)

Her.	*Epistula ad Herodotum* (*Letter to Herodotus*)
KD	*Kuriai doxai* (*Principal Doctrines*)
Men.	*Epistula ad Menoeceum* (*Letter to Menoeceus*)
Pyth.	*Epistula ad Pythoclem* (*Letter to Pythocles*)
Vat.	*Vaticanae sententiae* (*Vatican Sayings*)

Epictetus (Epict.)
Eusebius

Praep. Evang.	*Praeparatio Evangelica*

Gaius

ABBREVIATIONS FOR CLASSICAL TEXTS

Inst. *Institutiones (Institutes)*

  Galen (Gal.)

De plac. *De Placitis Hippocratis et Platonis (On the doctrines of Hippocrates and Plato)*

  Horace (Hor.)

Ep. *Epistles*
Odes *Odes*

  Lucretius (Lucr.)

De rer. nat. *De rerum natura (On the nature of things)*

  Marcus Aurelius

Medit. *Meditations*

  Philodemus (Philod.)
  Plato

Phaed. *Phaedo*
Phaedr. *Phaedrus*
Rep. *Republic*
Theaet. *Theaetetus*
Tim. *Timaeus*

  Pliny

Ep. *Epistulae*
NH *Naturalis Historia (Natural History)*

  Plutarch (Plut.)

Cato Mai.	*Cato Maior*
De comm. not.	*De communibus notitiis (On the common notions against the Stoics)*
De stoic. rep.	*De stoicorum repugnantiis (On the self-contradictions of the Stoics)*
De tranq. an.	*De tranquillitate animi (On tranquility of mind)*
De virt. Alex.	*De Alexandri magni fortuna aut virtute (On the fortune or the virtue of Alexander)*

ABBREVIATIONS FOR CLASSICAL TEXTS

Non posse suav. *Non posse suaviter vivi secundum Epicurum* (*That Epicurus actually makes a pleasant life impossible*)
Tib. Gr. *Tiberius Gracchus*

  Polybius (Polyb.)
  Quintilian (Quint.)

Inst. *Institutio oratoria*

  Sallust (Sal.)

Cat. *Bellum Catilinae* (*The War with Catiline*)
Hist. *Historiae* (*History*)
Jug. *Bellum Jugurthinum* (*The War with Jugurtha*)

  Seneca (Sen.)

Cons. Helv. *De Consolatione ad Helviam Matrem* (*On consolation to Helvia*)
Cons. Marc. *De Consolatione ad Marciam* (*On consolation to Marcia*)
De ben. *De beneficiis* (*On benefits*)
De clem. *De clementia* (*On clemency/ mercy*)
De cons. sap. *De constantia sapientis* (*On the firmness of the wise man*)
De ira *De ira* (*On anger*)
De ot. *De otio* (*On leisure*)
De prov. *De providentia* (*On providence*)
De tranq. *De tranquillitate animi* (*On tranquillity of mind*)
De vita beata *De vita beata* (*On the happy life*)
Ep. *Epistulae morales ad Lucilium* (*Epistles*)
Her. *Hercules*
Nat. quaest. *Naturales quaestiones* (*Natural questions*)
Thy. *Thyestes*

  Sextus Empiricus (SE)

Adv. math. *Adversus mathematicos* (*Against the mathematicians* [*logicians*])
Pyr. *Pyrrhoniae hypotoposes* (*Outlines of Pyrrhonism*)

Stobaeus (Stob.)
Suetonius (Suet.)

Dom. *Domitian*
Tib. *Tiberius*

Tacitus (Tac.)

Agric. *Agricola*
Ann. *Annales* (*The Annals*)
Dial. *Dialogus* (*A Dialogue on Oratory*)
Germ. *Germania*
Hist. *Historiarum* (*The Histories*)

Thucydides (Thuc.)
Varro

Ling. *De lingua latina* (*On the latin language*)

Virgil (Vir.)

A   *Aeneid*
E   *Eclogues*
G   *Georgics*

Abbreviations of Modern Sources

LS   Long, A.A. and D.N. Sedley. 1986. *The Hellenistic philosophers*. 2 vols. Cambridge University Press.
P   Didymus, Arius. 1999. *Epitome of Stoic Ethics*. Edited by Arthur Pomeroy. Atlanta: Society of Biblical Literature.
Sk   Skutsch, Otto. 1985. *The Annals of Q. Ennius*. Oxford: Clarendon.
SVF   *Stoicorum Veterum Fragmenta*. 1964. Edited by Hans von Arnim. Stuttgart: Teubner.
Usener *Epicurea*. 1887. Edited by Hermann Usener. Leipzig: Teubner, 1887.

ACKNOWLEDGMENTS

This project has been developed over several years as I have become increasingly fascinated by Roman conceptions of politics. Along the way I have benefitted from a great deal of feedback that has helped to both stimulate and focus my thinking. Special thanks to Malcolm Schofield, Michèle Lowrie, Kurt Raaflaub, Daniel Kapust, Ted Lendon, Valentina Arena, Kerry Whiteside, Tom Banks, John Marincola, and Michael Kicey for their helpful comments, as well as to audiences at the American Political Science Association and a symposium on the Roman senate held at the University of Glasgow. I also wish to thank Sara Lupolt for her research assistance and Kristen Marinaccio and Kaitlin Kines for help in compiling the bibliography.

INTRODUCTION

In an influential book that indicated the direction that interpretations of Roman political thought were to take for decades to come, Sheldon Wolin summarized the failure of the Romans to provide a vision of politics. Of Roman thinking in general, Wolin offered the observation that "the student of political ideas must deal with a period notoriously lacking in great political thinkers."[1] The "little there was in the way of systematic theory proves on closer analysis to be more often Greek than Roman in origin."[2] Cicero, according to Wolin, defined a set of Roman principles that diminished politics to "nothing but the pursuit of interests."[3] The historians were content "to report the drift of events rather than to master them, and to resign [themselves] to a world ultimately unconquerable."[4] The philosophy of Seneca was reduced to "groveling helplessness" in the face of absolutism.[5] And political philosophy had "exchanged its political element for a vapid moralism."[6] Possessing neither the seductive appeal of Athenian democracy nor the theoretical originality of Plato and Aristotle, the Romans seemed to have little to say to the student of political thought.

The Romans did not always help their case. So concerned was Cato the Censor with the arrival of an embassy of the three heads of the major

---

[1] Wolin 2004 (orig. 1960), 65.   [2] Wolin 2004, 65.   [3] Wolin 2004, 81.
[4] Wolin 2004, 77.   [5] Wolin 2004, 84.   [6] Wolin 2004, 85.

Greek philosophic schools in 155 BCE (to appeal a Roman fine) that he sought to have their business sped up so that they could return to Greece.[7] Sallust felt the need to justify writing about history and Cicero about philosophy when they could no longer take part in politics (Sal. *Cat*. pref. 3; Cic. *Tusc*. 2.1).[8] Virgil has Anchises, the father of Aeneas, tell his son to remember that the Roman art is ruling, not the Greek accomplishments of science, art, craft, and oratory (*A* 6.847–53). Seneca the Younger was prohibited from teaching philosophy to Nero since it was contrary to the upbringing of a ruler (Suet. *Nero* 52). And Tacitus notes in his biography written upon the death of his father-in-law, Gnaeus Julius Agricola, that Agricola would have pursued philosophy with more zeal than is appropriate for a Roman had not his mother moderated his disposition (*Agric*. 4, which is similar to Ennius' warning reported in Cic. *Tusc*. 2.1). Attitudes toward philosophers played out in severe ways. Under Nero being a Stoic could be used as a criminal charge.[9] Later emperors, starting with Vespasian around 74 CE, also executed or expelled philosophers. This period reached its darkest moments under Domitian in 93 CE with the treason trials of two biographers of Stoics, Thrasea Paetus (ordered to commit suicide under Nero) and Helvidius Priscus (executed under Vespasian), and the mass expulsion of philosophers. At the heart of these concerns was a suspicion of philosophy as undermining authority and the practice of traditional virtues.[10] Plutarch explains how Cato feared that the youth would come to value a reputation based on words rather than the disciplined and communal virtues of the farmer-soldier (Plut.

---

[7] Cato the Elder's motion was precipitated by the arrival of a Greek embassy of three philosophers representing the three major schools (155 BCE) – Carneades, the head of the Academy, Diogenes the Stoic, and Critolaus of the Peripatetics – to appeal Rome's decision to fine Athens for the destruction of Oropus (Plut. *Cato Mai*. 23.1). Particularly upsetting to Cato the Elder was when Carneades argued in defense of the virtue of justice in a rhetorical demonstration and then the next day spoke as convincingly, before an admiring crowd, in defense of injustice (Plut. *Cato Mai*. 22.4–5). On the episode, see Gruen 1996, 175–77. For helpful discussions of the Roman encounter with Hellenistic thought and culture, see Gruen 1992; 1996, 158–92; Wallace-Hadrill 2008.

[8] See Baraz 2012 on Cicero's use of his prefaces to justify his philosophic project.

[9] Griffin 1976, 363.   [10] On the Roman suspicion of philosophy, see Griffin 1997a, 18–22.

Cato Mai. 22.4).[11] And Seneca recalls how the philosophers were expelled as corruptors of youth (*corruptores iuventutis*) (Sen. *Cons. Helv.* 10.8).

It is testimony to the persistence of the view of the Romans as uncritical, even anti-philosophic, that no contemporary work exists that looks comprehensively at their political thought.[12] This book challenges these assumptions, arguing that the Romans were engaged in a wide-ranging and penetrating reflection on the meaning of their political existence. In these reflections, the Romans did not create utopias; they did not imagine another world. Their writings about politics were continually, almost relentlessly, shaped by their own experiences: the ubiquity of violence, the enormity and frailty of power, and an overwhelming sense of loss of the traditions that oriented them to their responsibilities as social, political, and moral beings. However much the Romans are known for their often complex legal and institutional arrangements, or for the extensive work of their jurists in interpreting law[13], ultimately the power of their political thought lies in their exploration of the extra-institutional, affective foundation of political life: tradition, trust, duty, friendship, kinship, and love. In this affective foundation one can identify the core contribution of Roman political thought: political concepts like liberty, power, and authority are neither born from the mind of the philosopher nor shaped by the tidiness of reason but forged in collective experiences that are messy, often ugly,

---

[11] See also Gildenhard 2011, 75–76 on Cato the Elder's view of rhetoric.

[12] On the neglect of Roman political thought, see Hammer 2008, chapt. 1. There has been renewed interest in the political thought of the Romans, upon which this book builds. See Schofield 1995a; Asmis 2004; 2005; Connolly 2007; Hammer 2008; Garsten 2009; Kapust 2011; Lowrie 2009; 2013; Arena 2012.

[13] The jurists, such as Gaius and Ulpian, reflect a development in Roman society in the second and third century CE of legal specialists who wrote extensive legal commentaries as well as advised private parties and magistrates. We know many of the jurists by way of what becomes known as the *Corpus Iuris Civilis*, a collection and codification of law by Justinian. The work is comprised of a collection of juristic writings (*Digesta* in 533 CE), an attempt to unify them as the Code (*Codex* in 534 CE), and a textbook meant for students of law (*Institutiones* in 535 CE). Valuable discussions of the jurists and the Roman legal tradition include De Zulueta 1953; Daube 1969; Bauman 1983; 1985; 1989; Frier 1985; Ando 2011 (on the use of fictions to extend and adapt law). For approaches that attempt to reconstruct and read the jurists as original texts of Roman thought and philosophy, see Honoré 1981; 1982.

and, even with the careful juridical thinking that shows up with the later jurists, ambiguous.[14]

There are several choices I have made in organizing this book, guided by the aim of communicating the diversity, depth, and excitement of Roman political thought. First, the phrase "political thought" conjures a variety of overlapping approaches and goals, ranging from historicist to philosophic.[15] For some, political thought is akin to political history, using texts to reconstruct institutions, practices, and social relations or to explore traditions of language and ideas.[16] Others see political thought as an ongoing process in which individuals and groups are engaged in negotiations about cultural meanings and relations of power. Texts (as well as other aspects of material culture) emerge as sites of performance that play out assumptions, tensions, and criticisms of political, social, or cultural practices.[17] Political thought can also be seen as contributing to a more systematic analysis of political phenomena[18] or as identifying enduring questions about what it means to be a

---

[14] Ando points out that the bulk of jurists' texts that have been handed down to us "were systematically edited so as to provide or conduce the formulation of decision rules," excising discussions of "problems of justification, legitimation, or implementation" that arose from different sources of law (the praetor and emperor), different legal traditions, and evolving social, economic, and political concerns (2011, 20). What the jurists did was draw on "the metaphorical association of soil, system of law, and affective bond as mutually implicated ways of articulating members in a Roman political community" (2011, 26).

[15] On the range of approaches to the study of politics in the ancient world, see Hammer 2009.

[16] Institutions and constitutional structures: Mommsen 1887–88; Talbert 1984; Lintott 1999; prosopography: Münzer 1920; Gelzer 1962; social power: Syme 1939; social history: Raaflaub 2004; Hölkeskamp 2010; class structure and relations: De Ste. Croix 1981; legitimacy: Ando 2000; language traditions: Pocock 1972; Skinner 1988.

[17] There are a variety of inspirations for these approaches, including cultural anthropology (e.g., Victor Turner), sociology (e.g., Erving Goffman; Pierre Bourdieu), semiotics (e.g., Mikhail Bakhtin), linguistics (e.g., J. L. Austin), phenomenology (e.g., Hannah Arendt), philosophy (e.g., Friedrich Nietzsche; Michel Foucault; Giorgio Agamben), literary analytic approaches of New Historicism and cultural poetics (e.g., Stephen Greenblatt), narratology (e.g. Gérard Genette), and feminist theory (e.g., Judith Butler). Explanations and applications of these approaches can be found in Parry 1963; Putnam 1970; Hammer 2002b; Connolly 2007; Lowrie 2009.

[18] For example, Sabine 1937; Morgenthau 1950.

political being.[19] Finally there are theorists who uncover in these texts notions of truth and virtue that transcend the historical time.[20]

In my approach, I have paid serious attention to the historical and cultural contexts that frame the concerns and arguments of the Roman writers analyzed in this text. In doing so, I have tried not to impose on these quite different texts – ranging from philosophic to historiographic to poetic – a singular conception of what political thought looks like or in what form it should appear. Instead, I have approached these writings as practices of thought. In using the term "practice" I am suggesting that the discourses by which political ideas are articulated contain layers of their own past as they are formed through a history that is both learned and experienced. And through these discourses, new practices, purposes, and meanings are generated as participants encounter and communicate different experiences and opportunities. The political thought that emerges does not always (in fact, rarely) exhibit the logic of a philosophic system. Instead it exhibits the logic of practice[21]: the assimilation of different practices, interests, and experiences into symbolic systems that orient how one makes sense of and responds to the political world. What constitutes this political world goes beyond the formal institutional arrangements and functions of the state, encompassing a range of questions that includes, but is certainly not limited to, "What do we value and how are these values expressed in the goals of community life and organization?"; "What binds us together?"; and "On what basis are social relationships, including issues of power and authority, organized?" Where I depart from solely historical approaches is in the reason for engaging with this past. The Roman struggle to make sense of their political world gives us insight into what it meant for them, and can mean for us, to be political beings.

A second choice involves defining what even counts as Roman since Rome was a multi-ethnic empire that grew up alongside, enveloped, and variously appropriated a variety of intellectual and cultural traditions.

---

[19] See, for example, Arendt 1958; 1963; 1968; Wolin 2004.
[20] Classic statements of this approach can be found in Voegelin 1952; Strauss 1964.
[21] The language is from the title of Bourdieu 1990, though I am not adopting Bourdieu's approach.

I have defined the Romans geopolitically, focusing on writers who were involved in or connected in some way to Roman governance (Cicero, Sallust, Seneca, Tacitus, Marcus Aurelius, and Augustine) or who wrote in Latin for a Roman audience (notably Lucretius, Livy, and Virgil). I have also included discussion of those under Roman rule whose writings informed these primary authors (such as Polybius and Epictetus).

A third choice I have made relates to different ways to organize the texts, either by particular authors or by themes and schools of thought. Both methods have a great deal to recommend them. Thematic organization allows the reader to see the development, continuities, and discontinuities of particular ideas or activities across time. One could imagine a number of fascinating themes by which to organize Roman thought, some of which have already been done: rhetoric, law, imperialism, cosmopolitanism, the people, power, authority, liberty, virtue, spectacles, and Stoicism, as examples. I have chosen to organize the chapters by author and text. Although the organization of political thought by author is traditional, it is surprisingly less common in talking about the Romans.[22] The tendency among political theorists, instead, is to mine Roman texts for particular themes, concepts, or practices with the result that the arguments developed by these Roman authors are treated less seriously. I want the Romans to speak for themselves as important thinkers grappling with their own political world. For that same reason I have not explored the legacy of the Romans, a wide-ranging and long-standing influence on such thinkers as Grotius, Machiavelli, Montaigne, Montesquieu, Rousseau, Weber, Arendt, and Foucault as well as on traditions of monarchical theory, constitutionalism, and international relations and law.[23] There are themes that emerge, though, that connect

---

[22] See Hammer 2008, chapt. 1.
[23] Discussions of this legacy can be found in Carlyle and Carlyle 1950 (medieval); Pocock 1975 (republicanism); Schellhase 1976 (Tacitus and republicanism); Canning 1996 (medieval); Skinner 1998 (republicanism); Coby 1999 (Machiavelli); Millar 2002 (constitutional thought); Hammer 2002a (Arendt); 2008 (Machiavelli, Montesquieu, Arendt, Foucault); Stacey 2007 (monarchical theory); Kinsbury and Straumann 2009 (Grotius); Straumann 2011 (constitutional thought). As I argue in Hammer 2008, even though scholars recognize the importance of the Romans to such modern thinkers as

author to author, that speak to us today, and that lead us to understand what is Roman about Roman political thought.

Finally, I have let the Romans speak in their own terms rather than view them through the lens of contemporary theoretical approaches.[24] Of course where we stand always influences what we see. But it is important to avoid an abstractness that the Romans never imagined because context plays such a vital role in their thought. To the contemporary political theorist steeped in abstraction, Roman political thought seems mired in a hopelessly complex array of names, places, laws, and events. But in this complexity we can locate the conceptual core of Roman political thought. For the Romans, the human artifacts that surrounded them provided a foundation, like Livy's *Ab urbe condita* ("From the founding of the city," the modern title of Livy's *History*), by which they related not just to those things, but also to each other.

POLYBIUS, ROMAN REPUBLICAN POLITICAL INSTITUTIONS, AND CULTURE

For many (certainly for his contemporaneous Greek readership), Polybius (ca. 200–118 BCE) serves as the entrée into Roman political thought. He is emblematic of the complex relationships that developed in this Roman imperial world. A rising leader in the Achaean League, Polybius was rounded up along with a thousand other Achaean elites and held prisoner in Rome for suspicion of being opposed to Roman rule of Macedonia. Held for seventeen years, he became a companion of Scipio Aemilianus, who would emerge as one of the most powerful Roman statesmen of the time. Polybius was given access to the highest levels of Roman society, remaining in Rome even when released. He was not just a Greek in a Roman world; he was a Greek theorizing about a Roman political system

---

Machiavelli, Montesquieu, Arendt, and Foucault, that importance is often downplayed or misunderstood.

[24] I have nothing against this approach. In an earlier book, for example, I viewed the Romans by way of a series of modern thinkers (see Hammer 2008).

that had already achieved empire.²⁵ For Polybius, Rome's ability to bring "the whole world under their sway" (Polyb. 6.50.6) while also preserving liberty lay in large part in its political system, which naturally grew or evolved over time (see Polyb. 6.5–9; 6.43.2; 6.51.5–6; 6.57.1). That mixed system of government contained aristocratic (the senate), democratic (the people), and monarchical (the consuls) elements.²⁶ Political power, according to Polybius' well-known formulation, was distributed among different parts of the state so that no one institution held power. Each part brought to the system its own inclinations and interests and each required the cooperation of the other in order to get something done. In times of emergency, the state acted "in concord and support" (6.18.2). In times of peace, the efforts of one part toward supremacy – a fact of human nature – could be "counterworked and thwarted" by the others (6.18.7). For Polybius the mixed constitution worked both to provide stability in any given moment because no group could act without restraint and to slow down the process of *anacyclosis*, the tendency of states to follow a cycle of degeneration.

Polybius is, of course, talking about the Roman republic (ca 509–31 BCE), a period whose beginning is shrouded in myth and end dissolves in violence. Though it is difficult to assess his impact on Roman thought, he found his way into Cicero's discussion (and re-imagining) of the mixed constitution and was certainly read by Livy. And in many ways,

---

²⁵ See Champion 2004 on how Polybius variously represents Rome as possessing both Hellenic virtues guided by reason and barbarian characteristics of irrationality and passion.

²⁶ There is an extensive tradition that views Roman politics by way of its constitutional aspects: by its institutions, procedures, rules of participation and election, offices, formal powers, and relationships between offices. See especially Mommsen 1887–88; Rainer 1997, 9; Millar 1998, 15, 99, 208ff; Lintott 1999; Straumann 2011. For a critical view of these constitutional approaches, see Hölkeskamp 2000. Meier uses the term "organic constitution" (1980, 56). Wieacker views the constitution as an ongoing political process (1988, 353–54). Interpretations of Polybius' view of the Roman constitution vary: Polybius as classifying Roman constitution as aristocratic: Nicolet 1983, 18–22; Nippel 1980, 151; Lintott 1999, 22; Polybius as recognizing broader role of the people: Walbank 1992, 224–30; Millar 1998, 24 (on role of people in Polybius' account); Arena 2012, 92–93 (role of the people but with an aristocratic bias). On Polybius' account of the role of the people, see 6.14.1–12.

Polybius saw the difficulty of easily categorizing the Roman political system. It was not quite the closed oligarchy that would assume near consensus in scholarship, a tightly knit network confined to the major families who competed and controlled the highest offices.[27] Nor could Rome qualify as a democracy, if by that we mean a fundamental equality of everyone to participate in the governance of the community.[28] Rome's political institutions were a complex array of hierarchically organized units, created at different times and for different purposes through their history. These hierarchies were incorporated structurally into Roman politics through a census that differentiated expected contributions to the state by ranks of wealth and accordingly allocated voting on the principle that those who had the most property should also have the most say.[29] Polybius gives us insight, and I will reference those observations, but an understanding of the system requires that we move beyond him.

The sovereignty of the people, the *populus Romanus*, was perhaps the most fundamental (and most difficult to grasp) principle of the Roman republic. We must be careful when we apply this single term to ancient Rome. Sovereignty is a modern concept, datable to the sixteenth century, referring both to the control a state has over its own territory and to a supreme authority within a state.[30] Something like sovereignty clusters around two different, though overlapping, concepts: *libertas*, which is

---

[27] Earlier scholarship argued that Roman politics was controlled by a small number of wealthy families who maintained their power through patron-client relationships and alliances. See Münzer 1920; Syme 1939; Taylor 1949; Badian 1958; Gelzer 1962; Scullard 1973.

[28] Recent scholarship has pointed to considerably more turnover and competition within the elite. The argument of democratic aspects of the Republic is made most notably by Millar 1998. For summaries of the debate, see Ward 2004 and Hölkeskamp 2010, 10, fn 35. Scholars noting turnover and competition but not democracy include Brunt 1965; 1971b; 1988, 351–502; Meier 1980, 15, 163 on plurality; Wiseman 1985; Develin 1985; Gruen 1995; Yakobson 1999; Mouritsen 2001; Morstein-Marx 2004; Hölkeskamp 2010, 36–39.

[29] Dumézil argues that the Latin root *cens-* (as in *census*) is cognate with a Sanskrit root for praise (1969, 103–24). The census, in this sense, is a public recognition of merit.

[30] For the difficulties of the use of the term for ancient Greece, see Davies 1994.

premised on the people being the source of authority for the internal affairs of the *res publica*, and *imperium*, the power of command held by the Roman people and surrendered to their magistrates.³¹ The importance of the people, at least as equals to the senate, is captured in the acronym associated with the state, SPQR (*Senatus Populusque Romanus*), which would show up on coins and inscriptions. More suggestive of something like sovereignty is the formal designation of the state as *res publica populi Romani Quiritium*, "the *res publica* of the citizens of the Roman people" (Varro *Ling.* 6.86).³² The people were the sovereign body in the sense that their decisions were needed to legitimate political processes, including electoral outcomes, judicial outcomes (the people could pardon those who might appeal to them as well as determine capital charges), and legislative outcomes (including approving measures and being able to restrict some aspects of traditional senatorial prerogative).³³

This sovereignty gained institutional expression through a complex, ongoing battle by plebeians (those who were not part of the original, ruling patricians) for both political protections and expression, including access to political and religious offices. This struggle is often referred to as the conflict of the orders (though virtually no contemporaneous evidence survives).³⁴ The conflict is marked by an initial secession of the plebs in 494 BCE (Livy 2.23–24, 32–33), what was in essence a strike or withdrawal from the city by the plebs, that resulted in the creation of the *concilium plebis*, an assembly open only to plebeians, and the establishment of plebeian magistrates called tribunes. Tribunes were deemed inviolable (*sacrosanctus*), which meant that there were penalties for physically harming or interfering with them. They had the power to convene the *concilium plebis* (*ius agendi cum plebe*), intercede or appeal on behalf of plebeians against coercion by other magistrates (*auxilium*), and veto any action or decision by a magistrate (*intercessio*). The *concilium plebis* was usually presided over by a tribune. In addition to passing

---

³¹ Ando 2011, 73–74.
³² See Williamson 2005, 66; Straumann 2011, 285; Schofield, in Hammer (forthcoming).
³³ Brunt 1988, 338–39.
³⁴ On the complexity of sorting out the historical evidence of the nature of the conflict between patricians and plebs in the early Roman republic, see Mitchell 1986; 1990; Raaflaub (ed.) 1986a; 1986b; Richard 1986; Momigliano 1986; Cornell 1995.

plebiscita (resolutions originally binding only on the plebeian population), the body also elected its own officials (the tribunes, ultimately totaling ten, and two aediles responsible for plebeian religious festivals) and held some lower level, non-capital trials. The struggles would also eventuate in the formalization of legal protections[35], the establishment through the *leges Liciniae Sextiae* in 367/6 of consular elections that included plebeian candidates (possibly even setting aside a consular representative from the commons) (see Livy 6.37.4; 6.42.9–11), the opening of membership in religious offices to plebeians in 300 BCE, and the passage of the *lex Hortensia* (c. 287) which made *plebiscita* (resolutions of the *concilium plebis*) binding on the Roman people

In addition to the *concilium plebis* was the *comitia tributa* (assembly of tribes), created later and open to all citizens.[36] People were organized by way of the census into thirty-one rural tribes (*tribus*) and four urban tribes, which were essentially divisions or districts, each tribe receiving one vote (determined by the majority vote of members of the tribe). There were a variety of effects from this organization: larger groups, particularly the plebs crowded into the fewer urban tribes, had a disproportionately smaller vote, though were more able to attend the assembly; as citizenship was extended up and down the Italian peninsula, those farther away would be less likely or able to attend; and wealthier landholders would have greater opportunities for influence since they were distributed across the larger number of rural tribes and were more able to attend these tribes' assemblies.[37] The primary function of the *comitia tributa* was to vote in support or rejection of

---

[35] We take for granted what it means to have legal protections. For a provocative discussion of the development of the concept of law in Roman politics that involves not just procedures but also organizing content, see Schiavone 2012.

[36] There has been some controversy about whether the *concilium plebis* and *comitia tributa* were, in fact, the same assembly. For a discussion and conclusion that they were distinct assemblies (or at least insufficient evidence that they were not distinct assemblies), see Farrell 1986; Lintott 1999, 53–54; Williamson 2005, 22–23. On Roman assemblies, see Taylor 1966; Lintott 1999, 40–64; North 1990a; 1990b.

[37] The tribes were organized to give disproportionate weight for and against particular groups, so the urban plebs were organized into only four tribes, along with freedmen, giving disproportionate weight not just to rural tribes (since few could spend the time to come into Rome) but to landowners who resided in Rome

legislation (*suffragium*) (though those attending could not initiate, amend, or discuss it in assembly).

The *comitia centuriata* (assembly of centuries), an older assembly, was based on the organization of the archaic army. Citizens were divided into 193 units (or centuries) according to the census class (based on wealth). Those with less wealth were grouped in larger numbers into particular centuries than those with more, giving disproportionate weight to wealthier classes.[38] Voting occurred in the order of the centuries, ending when a majority was reached. The assembly had been the original legislative body, but this power shifted over time to the *concilium plebis* and the *comitia tributa*. The *comita centuriata* had also served as the court for capital cases involving Roman citizens, later acting as a court of appeal for some capital cases (after these functions had been transferred to permanent courts). The assembly retained its authority to declare war, vote on peace treaties, and elect praetors and consuls (who possessed *imperium*, or the right to command an army).

Less formally, though perhaps as important as any institution in Rome as a forum for popular expression, were the *contiones*, or nonvoting public assemblies, called by a magistrate (including tribunes). In a *contio* elites addressed the people (rallying support, attacking another, defending oneself) or presented legislation that was required to be before the people, though not necessarily in a *contio*, before it could be voted on.[39] There is

---

(see Mouritsen 2001, 80). Tatum argues for significant representation by the urban masses (see Tatum in Hammer [forthcoming]).

[38] See Dion. Hal. *Ant. Rom.* 4.19.2–3; 21.2; Cic. *De rep.* 2.22.39–40; Livy 1.43.10. Distribution of voting: assembly consists of 193 groups (centuries): wealthy distributed in 18 groups of knights (*equites*) (comprised of the senatorial class and a non-senatorial class who owned property that would come to form a distinct class and be referred to as the *equites*), 70 groups of the first class, and joined by a group of carpenters; poor distributed in 104 groups (*De rep.* 2.22.39–40). The two lowest classes were grouped into 30 *centuriae*, and the *proletarii* into one (Mouritsen 2001, 94). The first vote (at least in elections) was cast by a century from the first class juniors, the younger members, chosen by lot. The wealthiest classes did not control a majority of the vote but would have required the support of some other centuries.

[39] See Morstein-Marx 2004; also forthcoming (in Hammer); Pina Polo 1996. On the composition of the crowd at these *contiones*, see Meier 1965, 560, 614 and Tan 2008, 173–5 (shopkeepers, but representative of the urban *plebs*); Vanderbroeck 1987,

considerable debate about whether the *contiones* served to challenge elite claims or largely reinforced political inequalities.[40]

The people also served as the audience in law courts, a public realm of elite competition and display, conducted before a jury of senators or equestrians. There were public spectacles, such as games, in which the crowd could express their approval or disapproval of individuals and measures.[41] And any person campaigning for office needed to show wide support: a large retinue attending the candidate in public, the support of the urban *collegia* (neighborhood societies of artisans and shopkeepers), the widespread placing of placards and advertising, and people packing venues where the candidate appeared.[42] In short, the people had power to assert themselves and maintained a role in legislating on important issues, meeting more frequently during times of crisis and dealing with such matters as appointing commissions, suspending or circumventing law for particular offices (e.g., for eligibility for office), selecting commanders, declaring war, issuing triumphs or honors, broadening civil or citizen liberties, extending citizenship, distributing grain and land, settling debts, regularizing market conditions, and extending or abrogating *imperium*.[43]

We see a striking example of the complex role of the people with the proposal of the *lex Sempronia agraria* by Tiberius Gracchus in 133 BCE, legislation designed to redistribute some public land held by the rich to the poor. Tiberius, as tribune, chose to propose the law through the plebeian tribal assembly, attracting crowds comprised of voters and non-voters on the day the voting assembly would meet. The senate was able to convince Marcus Octavius, another tribune, to block the legislation, using his right to veto just as Tiberius had ordered the final reading of the proposal before calling the assembly to vote

---

161–65 (politically active plebs); Fantham 2004a, 224 (the urban unemployed and clients); and Mouritsen 2001, 43–44 (wealthy non-office holders).

[40] Millar 1998 argues for the assertion of the people in these forums; Hölkeskamp 1995; 2004; 2010; Pina Polo 1996; and Morstein-Marx 2004 argue that the *contiones* were a forum for advancing elite agendas. Tan 2008 identifies a *popularis* bias in the crowd and use of the *contiones*.

[41] See Millar 1998; Morstein-Marx 2004.   [42] See Tatum (in Hammer [forthcoming]).

[43] See North 1990a; 1990b; Millar 1998; Yakobson 1999, 18–19; Williamson 2005.

(Plut. *Tib. Gr.* 10.2). Accounts vary: Some accounts hold that another voting assembly was convened and when the first eighteen (of thirty-five) tribes unanimously voted to remove Octavius from office for not supporting their interests, Octavius slunk away (Appian. *BC* 12); others that Tiberius had Octavius physically removed (Plut. *Tib. Gr.* 12.1–44).[44] The assembly then voted to accept the legislation, which the senate had to recognize (though they provided limited funding to the agrarian commission). What is noteworthy in the account is that the people could and did express their will. As significant, though, is the end of the story: Fearful of Tiberius' power, both in removing Octavius and in seeking a second consecutive term, the newly elected *pontifex maximus* led the senators and their supporters to beat Tiberius and his followers to death. The people did have a say, but it was constrained by the specter of violent reprisals, limited venues for popular expression, no ability for the people to initiate legislation, and no real efforts to expand participation, even as Roman citizenship nearly doubled with the inclusion of the Italians after the Social War.[45]

The people may have held formal sovereignty but Roman political life was dominated by a political elite, comprised of wealthy patricians (descendants of the original elite families) and plebeians (and eventually what were called "new men"). They competed for the fewer and fewer positions as they ascended the *cursus honorum* (formalized in 180 BCE), a schedule of the order of the elective offices and the age one had to be to pursue them. The two annually elected consuls, the highest elective office, possessed both *imperium* (the power of command) and *auspicium*

---

[44] See Williamson 2005, 5–6.
[45] Mouritsen (2001, 32–35) estimates that somewhere around 1 percent of the eligible population would have participated in politics, both because of logistical constraints (the size of meeting places, transportation from outlying areas, economic sacrifices) and legal constraints (the *leges Aelia et Fufia* [ca. 150] required that assemblies could not be held within three days before a market day, expanding a law from 256 BCE that prohibited assemblies from being held on market days; weighting of voting made the votes of a majority of the people, but a minority of the census classes, essentially irrelevant). Macmullen estimates about 2 percent of the eligible population voted (1980).

(the right to consult the gods on matters of the state).[46] But it was the senate – a body that had limited formal powers, had to be called by a magistrate, existed in principle to provide advice to magistrates, and could only authorize action but could not enforce it – that controlled the political agenda and the treasury and served as the forum where debates were conducted and decisions made. As Hölkeskamp points out, because the senate "assembled all (former) magistrates, priests, commanders, and patrons of peoples, cities, and colonies," it ended up with "a permanent accumulation and exclusive concentration of expertise and experience" to deal with the vast array of political, diplomatic, legal, administrative, and religious issues required in ruling Rome.[47] The power of the senate lies in its *auctoritas*, an influence derived from a respect for its words and actions. The force of *auctoritas* does not come from any ability of the senate to command or coerce (or even enforce) but is connected to a view of the senate as augmenting (*auctoritas* is related to *augere*, to augment or increase) the foundation of Rome by acting according to the precedents and traditions of the ancestors.[48] The designation of members of the senate as *patres* makes explicit the view of the body as descended from these ancestors.

The extraordinary importance of *auctoritas* as a form of authority that did not have coercive force points to a fundamental aspect of Roman politics. Although we know Rome politically through its institutions, ultimately what held the system together – or at least what regulated competition and steered it toward public ends for a while – was an abiding sense of tradition. One of the central concepts of Roman political life was the *mos maiorum* (the custom, or *mores* in the plural, of the ancestors).[49] A simple translation does not do justice to the power of the term. When Ennius, the first great Roman poet, wrote, "On ancient customs and men the Roman state stands" (*Moribus antiquis res stat Romana virisque*) (fr. 156 Sk; my translation; also Quint. *Inst.* 55.10.13),

---

[46] Drogula has recently developed the argument, against the consensus of scholarship, that *imperium* should be understood in its technical sense solely as limited to military command and not including domestic power (2007; also Daube 1969, 3–4).

[47] Hölkeskamp 2010, 30; also Tatum (in Hammer [forthcoming]).

[48] Arendt 1968, 120–28.

[49] On the *mos maiorum* generally, see Arena (in Hammer [forthcoming]).

he was not referring to a particular legal or constitutional framework but to a relationship and attitude toward the past. "The *mos* was the standard to which appeal could be made, the inheritance of custom, procedure, and attitude representing the settled assumptions of shared life."[50]

The *mos maiorum* oriented Roman citizens through *exempla*, stories of individuals and actions, that were reinforced by visual reminders (ancestor masks, busts, and monuments), public ceremonies and celebrations (such as funeral processions and the awarding of military honors, including triumphs), and orations that prescribed and proscribed what it meant to act with virtue (*virtus*), as well as defined the foundation, limits and responsibilities of power and authority.[51] As Flower writes, in describing the funerals of office-holding families, "This pageant of Rome's past – a vital element in republican political culture, as Polybius attests in the mid-second century – created a timeless memory world in which deceased relatives from every previous age processed and spoke and sat together."[52] The image captures something elemental about the operation of the *mos maiorum:* The internalization of these norms relied on the gaze of real and imagined others. Those norms, in turn, manifested themselves in the *decorum* of the speaking and acting subject: not only in one's dress, mannerisms, words, and actions, but also in the *dignitas* (or standing) of one's family, around which a reputation was built.[53] Through emulation of the habits and virtues of one's ancestors, one carried forward the image of one's family and of what it meant to be Roman.[54] As Pittenger writes of triumphal processions, "For the commanders and their critics, the shared project of telling their stories to each other and then transmitting their consensus to the rest of the community served a vital function. In it they found the best of what it meant to be a Roman, to live up to the highest expectations and ideals of their society; and through it they also secured a position

---

[50] Minyard 1985, 6.
[51] See Wieacker 1988, 353–54, 374–76, 502–6; Pittenger 2008, 127–47 (on triumphs); Roller 2009; Hölkeskamp 2010, 17–19; Bettini 2011, esp. 87–130.
[52] Flower 2010, 5; also Stemmler 2000 (on rhetoric); Hölkeskamp 2004, 57–72 (ceremonies); and Sumi 2005, 7–13 (on ceremony); also Polyb. 6.53.
[53] Treggiari 2003 (on ancestral virtues). See, for example, Cic. *Pis.* 1–2; *Mur.* 66.
[54] Treggiari 2003, 153.

for themselves, collectively, as the body within their society empowered to set those very same expectations in line with their own needs and ambitions."[55]

The past not only guided but also motivated. In the competitive culture of Rome, one's ancestors defined one's goals. Driven by the desire for glory, one strove to equal or surpass the achievements of one's forefathers through service to the state.[56] The success of one's ancestors also defined the status of future generations. At first it was birth that secured one's status. But an outcome of the struggle for access to political and religious offices was the emergence of a new political class, the *nobilis*, that was defined by achievement in office-holding. Although the boundaries of the group were neither static nor always clear-cut, one became *nobilis* by attaining a consulship, the highest elective office, but the rank of *nobilitas* then applied to all descendants of the family.[57] The ideology of this group consisted of a "total concentration on, and uncompromising commitment to, politics and war" that was "inseparably linked with the ambition of aristocrats to receive recognition and reward for distinguished service in the form of rank and reputation, authority and influence, and, above all, *honores* and ever more *honores*."[58] The achievement of office in this highly competitive atmosphere required wealth and support, whether from *amicitiae* (friendships and alliances with important families in Rome and the territories), *clientelae* (supporters cultivated through the offer of material benefits and protection), or the ability to mobilize groups. It should be noted that the view of Roman politics as operating through stable ties of friendship and clientage has given way to a view of a much more fluid atmosphere in which relationships and support were neither enduring nor stable.[59]

---

[55] Pittenger 2008, 145. Also Corbeill 2004 (on physicality); Kaster 2005, 12–27 (on *verecundia*); Connolly 2007, 131 (internalization of gaze).
[56] See, for example, Cic. *De off.* 3.2.6; also Connolly 2007, 131.
[57] On the development of the *nobiles*, see Brunt 1982; Wiseman 1971, 2; Shackleton Bailey 1986; Hölkeskamp 1987; 1993; Burckhardt 1990; Goldmann 2002; Forsythe 2005, 276. Later in the second century one became *nobilis* by achieving any curule magistrate, including praetorships, censorships, and curule aedileships.
[58] Hölkeskamp 1993, 26.
[59] See Brunt 1988, 443–502; also Lintott 1999, 176–81.

This competition was expensive, though, keeping *nobilitas* as the province of the rich: patricians or very wealthy plebeian families.

Rome was a community of tradition, but hardly of consensus. The conflicts that inhered in the Roman republic ran deep, and were frequently organized around contending claims about the meaning and inclusiveness of these ancestral traditions.[60] To be able to claim an inheritance, on whatever terms, vested one with authority, access to power and resources, and, at the very least, a say in the governance of Roman political life. The conflicts were numerous: struggles between patricians and plebs for both protections and inclusion; between the propertied and unpropertied classes; between enfranchised Romans and disenfranchised Italians; and, beginning in the second century BCE, between elites who divided (or were categorized by others) broadly as *populares* ("populists") and *optimates* (the "best," sometimes referred to as the *boni*).[61] The names were often more useful as forms of invective or praise than descriptions of a consistent political program or even of stable alliances.[62] Nonetheless, the terms locate an important fissure in Roman political life.[63] The *optimates* used the senate, the most conservative political body in Rome, to protect property and elite privilege. The *populares* invoked the power of the people, often by way of the tribunes, or the advocates of the people, to address problems of debt, poverty, and landlessness.

Added to this competitive Roman landscape was the emergence of the *novi homines*, or new men rising to top positions. They did not have an illustrious Roman ancestry nor were they born of wealthy plebeian families; they had achieved economic, political, or military

---

[60] On the fluidity of the *mos maiorum*, see Arena (in Hammer [forthcoming]), as well as Chapter 3: Sallust.

[61] See Brunt 1971, 94–95; also Taylor 1949; Earl 1967; Wirszubski 1968, 31–65; Tatum (in Hammer [forthcoming]). Also Cic. *Sest.* 45.96–98 with Seager 1972.

[62] On the cross-cutting alliances that get formed, see Gruen 1995, 47–50. I think Gruen understates the political valence of the terms, though, when he suggests that the term *optimates* "was no more than a means of expressing approbation" (1995, 50). That is true, but there are different characteristics and criteria by which individuals assign praise and blame.

[63] See especially Wiseman 2009, 5–32, who puts ideological content back into these categories; also Arena 2012, 80–81, 116–68.

success in Rome's expanding empire and were now demanding access to the highest sources of political power.[64] The *novi homines* could refer to consular candidates whose ancestors had not attained the consulship, but more commonly it referred to a senator who came out of the equestrian class but whose ancestors never entered the senate. The *novi homines* challenged the political order by articulating a notion of excellence as an attribute of character, rather than as a legacy of one's ancestors, that anyone (though not everyone) could possess (see, for example, Cic. *Leg. agr.* 2.1.3–2.2.5). In particular, the *novi homines* wanted access to the consulship, which had been closed informally (though formally open since the reforms of 367/6 BCE) to them.[65]

THE PRINCIPATE

The Republic would eventually be exhausted in the last century BCE by dynastic competition, tumultuous violence, naked self-interest, hypocrisy, corruption, and terror until Octavian, the adopted heir of Julius Caesar, finally emerged as sole ruler with the defeat of Antonius in 31 BCE. Octavian's rise marked the consolidation of the formal power of the state: He retained the autocratic power of a triumvir (which he possessed since joining the Second Triumvirate in 43 BCE), was endowed with the sacrosanctity of a tribune in 36 BCE not to be harmed physically, and held the office of consul (31 BCE to 23 BCE). Furthermore, Octavian possessed the other requisites of Roman power: enormous wealth, an extensive patronage network, command over the army, and the name Julius Caesar.

---

[64] On the *novus homo*, see Shackleton Bailey 1986; Wiseman 1971; Dondin-Payre 1981; Dugan 2005, 1–15.

[65] The reforms replaced a board of six military tribunes with officials with differentiated power, to be shared between patricians and plebeians. See Forsythe 2005, 268–76 on the reforms. While inclusion into the Roman elite was tightly controlled, evidence shows considerable turnover and additions of new families. See Hopkins 1965; Gelzer 1969, 50–52; Dondin-Payre 1981, 54–63; Earl 1982, 622; Hopkins and Burton 1983.

INTRODUCTION

In 27 BCE, in what has come to be known as the First Constitutional Settlement, Octavian offered to relinquish his formal powers to the senate, including giving up control over the army and the provinces. The events took place against a great deal of behind-the-scenes maneuvering in which Octavian ultimately forged the terms of his power and the senate's consent to his power. The senate gave Octavian the title "Augustus," from *augere*, to increase, from which *auctoritas* derives. They also called him "Princeps," or "first man," a term used in republican Rome to refer to the most eminent member of the senate. And they named him consul and granted him the power to administer (by way of legates appointed by him) the provinces of Spain, Gaul, Cyprus, Syria, Cilicia, and Egypt for ten years.

In 23 BCE, in the Second Constitutional Settlement, Augustus further consolidated his powers. He resigned his consulship. But he was granted *maius imperium proconsulare*, which placed almost all the military forces under his command and the command of his legates perpetually. It also gave him power to intervene in provinces even if not the appointed governor.[66] As Lintott notes, "This meant that any instruction given to proconsuls by Augustus, whether in person, by edict or by letter, had the backing of his *imperium* and disobedience was treason."[67] The senate also voted that he should possess *tribunicia potestas* for life, which gave Augustus the encompassing authority to speak on behalf of the people.[68] Augustus was also granted the right to judge appeals for capital cases, which under the Republic had been appeals to the people (*provocatio ad*

---

[66] Syme 1939, 336; Jones 1951, 114–15; Millar 1966 (on evolving role of the emperor's power of *imperium proconsulare*); 1973, 63 (on changes in 27 B.C.E.); Campbell 1984, 32; Badian 1986, 81–83; Eder 1990, 106–7; Turpin 1994; Galinksy 1996, 70–71, 365, 377; Bleicken 1998, 326; Kienast 1999, 99–109; Wieacker 2006, 24.

[67] Lintott 1993, 115.

[68] Syme 1939, 337. Also Bleicken 1998, 352–53; Kienast 1999, 104–9. Tacitus describes the tribunician power as the title for the highest power in the Roman world (*Ann.* 3.56.2). Even Eder, who attempts to understand the principate as at least being seen at the time as consistent with republican traditions, admits that Augustus holding the *tribunicia potestas* was "without precedent" and "greatly contradicted the practices of the traditional *res publica*" since tribunician power had always been vested in plebeians (Eder 1990, 109).

populum).⁶⁹ As Jones writes, "Here the emperor seems to have taken the place of the people as the ultimate arbiter of life and death. *Provocatio ad populum* has become *appellatio ad Caesarem*, and the emperor, instead of the people, decides whether to uphold the magistrate's sentence or not."⁷⁰ Augustus famously writes that he excelled all in *auctoritas* even though he held no more official power, or *potestas*, than others (*RG* 34.3). *Potestas* is limited by law; *auctoritas* has no such limit, associated with prestige that "produces itself anew in its exercise."⁷¹ As Galinsky writes, *auctoritas* refers to "the kind of moral and transcending leadership on which true power is ultimately based."⁷² Augustus' cultivation of his *auctoritas* provided him with an overarching power to author change in a way he could never have accomplished with only *potestas*.⁷³

The senate continued to adhere to its procedures and traditions even as it was stripped of its oversight of financial affairs, and military and foreign policy.⁷⁴ Their most visible new role in the early principate, issuing honors to the emperor and members of the family, demonstrated all the more clearly how closely their role had been organized around promoting imperial history and ideology.⁷⁵ Perhaps most damaging was that the *auctoritas* associated with the power of the senate, the authority that derived from esteem or respect, was now held by the *princeps*.⁷⁶ As Wirszubski notes, "once his auctoritas was accepted there was no need to amplify his prerogative or grant him sweeping discretionary powers."⁷⁷ The *princeps* could veto any resolution of the senate and the

---

⁶⁹ Jones 1960b, 52–54; 1960c, 86–98.   ⁷⁰ Jones 1960c, 94.
⁷¹ Lowrie 2009, 287; see also Arendt 1968, 121–22.   ⁷² Galinsky 1996, 18.
⁷³ See Wirszubski 1968, 110; Galinsky 1996, 18–19 (*auctoritas* as ensuring order); Lowrie 2009, 297–99.
⁷⁴ See Talbert 1987, 221–289; Rudich 1993, xx–xxi.
⁷⁵ See Brunt 1984, 423–44; Talbert 1987, 362–64; Wallace-Hadrill 1990, 146–47; Roller 2001, 99–101; Rowe 2002, 41–42, 60–66. As Wiseman observes, "In one sense, the history of the Julio-Claudians is the history of the slow extinction of this tradition [of the competition for individual glory]. The extinction was inevitable, since ultimately an ethos of personal aggrandisement could not co-exist with devotion to the *princeps*; the surprising thing is how long it took to come about" (1985, 8–9).
⁷⁶ See Wirszubski 1968, 112–23 for his excellent discussion.
⁷⁷ Wirszubski 1968, 117.

senate, in turn, was compelled to approve of measures that the *princeps*, by virtue of his *auctoritas*, recommended.

Other groups fared no better. The equestrian order, depleted through heavy capital levies and excluded from politics in the final years of the Republic, was, as Tacitus suggests, simply purchased by giving them a role in the military and administration.[78] The tribunate, now chosen by the senate (with the approval of the emperor), had no connection to the plebs and little interest in or ability to exercise its traditional powers of vetoing, introducing legislation, and representing plebeian claims.[79] Augustus sought to sever the informal relationships of people to their aristocratic patrons and bind the people directly to him by taking on the responsibility of providing relief, establishing low interest loans, providing access to baths and games, and increasing recipients of the dole.[80] The assemblies of the urban plebs also lost their independence, becoming the site for "ceremonials of consensus."[81] Selection and election to office were largely contingent on imperial favor.[82]

Augustus, furthermore, gained control over the army by professionalizing the soldiers through set terms of service and yearlong deployments in the field. By receiving their pay from the treasury, the soldiers owed their allegiance to the *princeps* more than to the senate and

---

[78] Syme 1939, 355; Brunt 1983.   [79] See Rowe 2002, 54–57.
[80] Yavetz 1969, 96.   [81] Rowe 2002, 96. See also Veyne 1990, 383–86.
[82] Transfer of elections from the people to the senate: *Ann.* 1.15.1; 1.81. Tiberius' refusal of senate's request to nominate additional candidates for the praetorship: *Ann.* 1.14.4. Augustus had restored popular elections in 27 BCE, though he continued to exercise influence in the choice of candidates by personally canvassing for a candidate (an act of *suffragatio*) or writing in support of a candidate (an act of *commendatio*). The emperors could officially only recommend candidates; neither the senate nor the assembly of the people was officially required to ratify these choices. The emperor's influence rested on his *auctoritas* (see Jones 1960a; Levick 1967; and Brunt 1984, 429–32). With the change in elections, the ambitious no longer relied on elections for rank but relied more on the emperor's favor. One result can be seen in the change in household architecture. The *atrium*, which had housed the *imagines* (ancestor masks), provided a form of advertising to the public of one's own status. As elections receded in importance and "power came to be exercised by friends and advisers of the emperor who never held traditional senatorial office," the *atrium* was replaced by peristyles and gardens (Flower 1996, 69–70, 193; also 256).

the state.[83] Military oaths of loyalty were sworn to each new emperor, replacing oaths that had once been made to commanders and (before that) to the *res publica*.[84] *Imperator* acclamations multiplied and were directed exclusively toward the emperor and imperial household rather than being acclamations by the troops toward the commander.[85] And the praetorian guard was formed as an elite and well-paid corps whose primary responsibility was to protect the emperor.[86]

Although Augustus thus consolidated power into his person, he also claimed to be returning power and liberty to the people and the senate, a claim that scholars (and some contemporaneous sources) refer to as *res publica restituta*.[87] Even in antiquity the claim was contested.[88] Syme speaks eloquently to this issue: whatever may have been the benefits in ending the horrors of the previous decades of bloodshed, Augustus' rise to power and rule "was the work of fraud and bloodshed" that systematically eliminated all rivals to power.[89] But a number of scholars

---

[83] See Syme 1939, 352–53; Campbell 1984, 158–62; Rowe 2002, 172. See, for example, *Ann.* 1.2.1 and 1.28.

[84] See Campbell 1984, 19–32.

[85] Campbell 1984, 122–33; Talbert 1987, 363–64. Acclamations as *imperator* ("holder of supreme power" [Talbert 1987, 363, n.18]) could be awarded to senators, but only by personal concession of the emperor. The last award to a senator occurred in 22 CE as a concession by Tiberius to Junius Blausus, the uncle of Sejanus (see *Ann.* 3.74.4; Campbell 1984, 127–8).

[86] See Campbell 1984, 109–20; Keppie 1996. As Campbell writes, "In general the Praetorians remained quiescent and loyal to the reigning emperor whether he was a conscientious ruler or a rogue, and, with the exception of the civil wars in 68–9 and the events of 193, they had little direct impact on imperial politics" (1984, 120).

[87] See Augustus, *RG* 1: *vindicare in libertatem*; *Laudatio Turiae* 2.25; Velleius 2.89.3–4. On the language of foundation in describing Augustus, see Lowrie 2010a.

[88] For a helpful discussion that goes beyond categories of pro- and anti-Augustan approaches, see Kennedy 1992.

[89] Syme 1939, 2. Also Rudich 2006, 9: "Rarely in history do we meet a form of government which portrayed itself as exactly the opposite to what it actually was. It was in fact a regime of autocracy based on military power, while pretending to be the *res publica restituta*." Ando suggests that "the People and the Senate of Rome chose to grant by statute powers that emperors could well have arrogated, and in that perspective the *lex regia*, as it became known, should be understood as giving consolidated articulation to a long process of negotiation in which emperors agreed to accept rather than claim powers and so conceded that the source of those powers lay in sovereign bodies other than themselves" (2011, 101).

have begun to take Augustus' claims more seriously. Galinsky, most prominently, argues that Augustus sought a revitalization of the ideas and ideals of the *res publica* by launching a political, moral, and cultural program aimed at reviving "a value system that placed the common good, the *res publica*, ahead of private interests."[90] He invalidated the illegal laws of the triumvirs (28 BCE), compensated returning soldiers for any expropriated property (ultimately ending the practice of expropriation by 13 BCE), and reduced the bloated roles of membership in the senate.[91] He addressed the material needs of the populace, provided a more rational calculation of the cost of conquest,[92] and, most of all, restored order to a state torn apart by faction. Rome, as Ando writes, "possessed an essentially republican form," a statement guided more by criticism of the reality of republican practice than any revisionist appraisal of the principate. It retained republican form in "its authorizing acts — in the constitution of the monarch's power through the agglomeration of traditional Republican offices, and in the awarding to him of those offices, as well as further, extra-magisterial powers, through comitial actions." The *princeps* furthermore came to exercise over his own people, "by virtue of acts describable in Republican language" such as *maiestas* (a notion of the majesty of the Roman people now consolidated in the person of the *princeps*), the domination it once held over others.[93]

Whatever continuities there might initially have been with the Republic, the rise of Augustus forever placed Rome's political fate in the hands of a single, and largely unaccountable, ruler. This environment was marked by the increasingly despotic rule of Tiberius, Caligula, Claudius, and Nero (spanning from 14 to 68 CE), the tumultuous rule of Vespasian, Titus, and Domitian (from 69 to 96 CE), a relief from this despotism with Trajan (98–117 CE) and Hadrian (117–138 CE), culminating in the rule of the Stoic philosopher, Marcus Aurelius (161–180 CE), and the joining of the emperor to Christianity with the conversion of Constantine the Great (306–337 CE). The principate (with memories and

---

[90] Galinsky 1996, 6; also 64. Wirzubski argues, "Under Augustus the essential rights and liberties of Roman citizens remained untouched" (1968, 122).
[91] Eder 1990, 103. See also Lacey 1996, 210 and Nicolet 1984.
[92] See Lintott 1993, 119–20.   [93] Ando 2011, 113.

images of the Republic always present) would provide the backdrop for Virgil's poetry, Livy's interpretation of Rome's republican past, Seneca's essays and letters, Tacitus' historiography, Marcus Aurelius' philosophic exercises, and Augustine's theological writings.

As obnoxiously confident as the Romans were about their destiny, and as varied as they were in their responses to the crises of their ages, the Roman political thinkers extending from Cicero to Augustine were equally consumed by the precariousness of their hold on power and, unlike Polybius, the fragility of their own system. What makes Roman political thought so interesting is that it does not seek refuge in an ideal state or in ideal conditions of politics. Their thought is born from a deep political crisis, an attempt, amidst corruption, violence, chaos, and despotism to reconstitute a *terra recognita* – to make sense of, to know again and to recognize, the political world they inhabit.

1 CICERO: TO SAVE THE *RES PUBLICA*

There are many reasons to begin the study of Roman political thought with Marcus Tullius Cicero (106–43 BCE). His work comprises the earliest, most complete set of Roman texts we have. He gives us insight into the increasing exposure of the educated Roman elite to Hellenistic philosophy and rhetoric, a byproduct in many ways of Roman conquest.[1] Cicero reveals, as well, the trajectory of the ambitious politician who must be noticed, forge alliances, and, in the violent final decades of the Republic, most of all survive. And he conveys some of the difficulties of the new man (*novus homo*) – the politician with no

---

[1] Helpful summaries of Cicero's intellectual heritage (and the encounter of Roman with Hellenistic culture) are provided by Gruen 1992, 52–83, 223–71; Powell 1995; Horsfall 1996 (on the spread of Hellenistic strands into plebeian culture); Atkins 2000; Zetzel 2003; Gildenhard 2007 (conquest of Greek philosophy). There could perhaps be no more striking illustration of this infiltration of Greek philosophy onto Roman soil than in 84 BCE Sulla keeping for himself as war booty the library of Apellicon, who had likely acquired Aristotle's library (Barnes 1997, 16–17: Aristotle's library inherited by Theophrastus, then Neleus, and purchased by Apellicon). Romans went to Greece (as well as Asia Minor and Rhodes), as Cicero did from 79–77 BCE. There he attended lectures of the Stoic Posidonius in Rhodes and the Academic Antiochus of Ascalon in Athens. And Greeks came to Rome, including Philo of Larissa, the leader of Plato's Academy, to avoid the political instability in Athens that began in 88 BCE when Athens sided with Mithridates, the king of Pontus, against the Romans (subsequently defeated by Sulla).

senatorial ancestors – breaking into the Roman elite. Not only was Cicero born an equestrian, lacking the caché and connections of the senatorial order, but also he had no military credentials (except for a brief stint in his youth and during his governorship of Cilicia).[2] As one biographer writes, Cicero "was an intellectual with few important connections and no influential clients at the beginning of his career. It was never his style to further his political goals by spending money: to begin with, he had no large fortune, and he did not plunder provinces as many other senators did – Caesar prominent among them."[3]

Cicero also provides a personal lens into the tumultuous final years of the Republic. In five years, the legacy of his role as consul in prosecuting the Catilinarian conspirators (63 BCE) changed from acclaim by the senate as "father" and "saviour" of the Republic (*De leg.* 2.17.42; *Cat.* 3.14–15) to exile, his house looted and burned through the state-ratified revenge of Clodius, a tribune (58 BCE).[4] Recalled from exile by the centuriate assembly through the orchestration of friends (57 BCE), Cicero imagined a rejuvenated political career, only to be warned by Pompeius, the powerful and wealthy military commander who had formed an alliance with Crassus and Caesar (known as the First Triumvirate), to remain quiet or face expulsion from Rome. The choice could not have been worse: "speech was his life."[5] Having to choose between political survival and

---

[2] Thus, the emphasis by Cicero on his political courage as akin to military courage (*De off.* 1.22.78; 1.23.79–80; *Cat.* 3.23–27; *De orat.* 1.46.202). Cicero wears a breastplate in the consular election of 63 BCE to emphasize the military-like aspects of his suppression of the Catilinarian conspiracy (see Steel 2001, 162–89). In *On the orator*, Cicero "fashions the ancestors who fashioned him," an inheritance that "washes away Cicero's *novitas*" through his connection with Crassus and other *nobiles* (Dugan 2005, 93, 96).

[3] Habicht 1990, 6.

[4] The question that comes back to haunt Cicero is whether a consul, even guided by the senate's ultimate decree to do what was necessary to protect the Republic (the *senatus consultum ultimum*), can execute a citizen of Rome without a trial authorized by the Roman people, in violation of the *lex Sempronia* established by Gaius Gracchus. The law passed by Clodius, clearly aimed at Cicero, reasserted the illegality of condemning a Roman citizen to death without authorization of the people. The same emergency decree of the senate had been used earlier in Roman history again Gaius Gracchus (121 BCE) and Saturninus (100 BCE), both legally elected tribunes.

[5] Fantham 2004b, 9.

his principles, Cicero at first reconciled himself to the triumvirate of Pompeius, Caesar, and Crassus (publicly in *De provinciis consularibus* in 56 BCE), was even coerced into using his rhetorical skills to defend in court the friends of Pompeius and Caesar who had betrayed him before, until finally standing against Caesar. With the assassination of Pompeius in 48 BCE and Caesar in 44 BCE, Cicero had to face the unpalatable alternatives of Marcus Antonius and Octavian, the whole time seeking political solutions (including negotiating a peace among the parties) in a system torn apart by violence and ultimately subdued by conquest. Cicero's last public defense of the Republic occurred in the *Philippics*, a series of speeches written in opposition to Antonius (the second *Philippic* considered too dangerous to deliver). Cicero paid with his life, his head and hands brought to Antonius and fastened to the Rostra from which Cicero once spoke. Cicero was the outsider who almost became the insider but whose fortunes ended when he no longer had a defender (tellingly, see *Fam.* 3.7.5; Sal. *Cat.* 31.3).

Cicero's intellectual legacy has suffered as many twists and turns as his political fortunes. His historical importance was built on a rhetorical style that no longer suits modern tastes. He emerges as a defender of oligarchy, yet his present day readers are imbued with a political culture steeped in democracy. He speaks with eloquence about protecting politics from violence, yet seems too willing to excuse the violence brought against opponents (pointedly in *Cat.* 3.10; 4.13; *Tusc.* 4.23.51). His proclamations of selflessness smack of vanity (even though he was able to laugh at himself: *Att.* 1.19.10). And his great value as our source for the transmission of Greek ideas to Rome diminishes, in turn, his originality.[6]

Judged by Greek standards, Cicero might disappoint. He possesses neither the theoretical originality of Plato nor the systematizing genius of Aristotle. Sabine, whose work was the textbook of political thought for the middle part of the twentieth century, comments, "In fact, Cicero had

---

[6] For example, Sabine 1937, 161: "The political thought of Cicero is not important because of its originality"; rather, the merit of his works is that "everybody read them." See Striker's thoughtful essay that lends some needed perspective on Cicero's goals (1995).

a really promising plan, if only he had possessed the philosophical capacity to carry it out."⁷ Cicero lacked the ability, though, as Sabine continues, to "strike out a new theory for himself, in line with Roman experience and in defiance of his Greek sources."⁸ But to settle for Cicero's thought as "Greek philosophy in Roman dress," to use Long's phrase, is to fail to understand the stakes of the situation facing Rome, Cicero's diagnosis, and his distinctive solutions.⁹ And to reduce his work to an attempt to solve Rome's crisis (itself praiseworthy) is to miss some of the theoretical originality and systematic underpinnings of his understanding of politics. What Cicero does offer, and what unifies his writings – his orations, political works, philosophic works, and letters – is an ongoing mediation between the eternal order of the cosmos and the contingent expressions of human politics and culture. However much Cicero repeated that our true place is with the gods, he could not imagine a home outside politics. However important reason may be as the distinctive and divine attribute of humans, ultimately our affections for the things we have come to know orient and bind us. Even Cicero's method of thought, modeled after Philo and the skeptical (or New) Academy, underlay his refusal to subscribe to any one doctrine or even affirm the certainty of knowledge, instead requiring that ideas be tested against contenders and be judged by the needs of society to arrive at defensible claims (e.g., *De off.* 1.2.6; 1.6.18; 2.2.7–8; *Tusc.* 5.4.11).¹⁰ The mark of

---

⁷ Sabine 1937, 162.   ⁸ Sabine 1937, 163.   ⁹ Long 1995b, 215.
¹⁰ The New Academy, founded by Carneades (214–129 BCE), rejected the Stoic claim that we can know something to be true with absolute certainty. Although our senses might accurately report the facts, there is no way to assure that the sense-impression accurately corresponds to the object (see Cic. *Acad.* 2.26.84). The New Academy argues for approaching sense-impressions as probable or non-probable (Cic. *Acad.* 2.31.99–32.104; S.E. *Adv. math.* 7.166–89). For recent assessment of Cicero as adherent to the skeptical Academy, see Görler 1995. Some have argued that Cicero changes affiliations from the skeptical Academy (of Philo of Larissa), to the Old Academy of Antiochus, and back (see Glucker 1978; Steinmetz 1989). It is worth recalling that different philosophic schools were not sharply differentiated among contemporaries but continually borrowed from and blended into each other (*De off.* 1.1.2; different schools: *De leg.* 1.13.38–39; 1.20.54; 1.21.55; *De orat.* 3.17.62–3.18.68; also Glucker 1978; Sedley 1981; Tarrant 1985, esp. 127–35). Cicero, for example, understood each of the contemporaneous schools as partial and incomplete formulations of the Socratic ideas that lie at their common origin (*De orat.* 3.19.69–73). And he saw only verbal

Cicero's works, and the poignancy of his diagnosis of Roman politics, lies in his unswerving attachment to, and refusal to ever seek refuge from, the *res publica* that was disintegrating even as he spoke.[11]

WHAT TO CALL THE *RES PUBLICA*

Res publica, or a thing of (or belonging to) the people, is a concept that does not translate easily.[12] Wood has argued, for example, that Cicero refers to the state as the *res* of the people because the Romans "had no abstract notion of the state, thinking of it as the collectivity of citizens in much the same way as the ancient Greeks did with their *polis*."[13] But we should not necessarily assume that Cicero's language points to a theoretical deficiency; rather, we might consider it a conceptual difference. The term "state" directs our focus to institutional and procedural aspects of how a territory is controlled; *res publica*, to an associational conception in which the community, though having institutional aspects, belongs to the people and is bound by affective ties organized by tradition.[14] We will explore the theoretical foundation and implications of this associational notion later, but words that Cicero uses to characterize

---

differences between the Stoic notion that virtue was the only good and the Peripatetic claim that virtue was the supreme good. One then must be careful in ascribing single influences where there may be multiple or creating false puzzles based on assumptions about the consistency of Cicero's adherence to any one philosophic school.

[11] See, for example, comments by Claassen 1999, 110 and Leach 1993, 11 for the depth of his identity as a political being.

[12] On the meaning of *res*, see Drexler 1957, 250–54.   [13] Wood 1988, 125.

[14] See Drexler 1957; Schofield 1995a, 67; 1999, 178–94; Skinner 1989, 112, though Skinner understates the role of procedure, the complexity of authority, and the autonomy of politics in ancient Rome (see especially 109–10). The translation of *res publica* as "regime" is not sufficient either since it does not properly emphasize the critical role of the people in constituting the community. The contemporary connotations of "regime" render it unhelpful as a clarifying device. Furthermore, the translation is limited as an analytic device since it is a more encompassing term than Cicero's. A regime refers to the organization and administration of a territory, without regard to the role or nature of citizenship. A tyranny can be a regime; it cannot, for Cicero, be a *res publica* or a *civitas* (e.g., *De rep.* 3.31.43).

the *res publica* are suggestive. Cicero calls a *res publica* a *res populi*, a thing or property of the people. He sometimes uses *res publica* interchangeably with *civitas*, a term that derives from the word *civis*, or citizen, referring to the organization of citizens into a political body. Further indicative of the associational aspects, Cicero frequently employs synonyms with the prefix "con" to describe community life: *consortium* (*De off.* 3.6.26); *conventiculum* (*Sest* 42.91); *consociatio* (*De off.* 1.28.100; 1.41.149); *conspiratio* (*De off.* 2.5.16); *consensu* (*De off.* 2.5.16); *conciliatio* (*De off.* 1.41.149); and *conjunctio* (*De leg.* 1.10.28; *De off.* 1.17.53, 54; 1.44.157; *Cat.* 4.22).[15]

I will at times translate *res publica* as republic, for reasons related to the obvious etymology. Scholars have shied away from this translation because the modern connotation of a republic, which involves broad citizen participation in the governance of the community, does not comport with kingships or aristocracies, including Rome itself, all of which Cicero includes as examples of *res publicae*.[16] But there is a stronger reason for seeing some similarity between a *res publica* and a republic. As we will see, for Cicero each of the different types of *res publicae* are organized around a notion of the community as a public thing, thus at least bearing some conceptual relationship to the modern notion of a republic. Whatever term we use, it is important to recognize that when Cicero talks about a *res publica*, he has something specific in mind that ties back to the people. With these caveats, I will translate the title of Cicero's *De republica* as *On the republic*. I will also use the Latin, or refer generically to communities, governments, or states when the context is clear.

THE BEST STATE

Cicero, consciously emulating Plato's *Republic* in *On the republic* (54–51 BCE), seeks to craft the best form of government. The frequent translation of *optimus status civitatis* or *optimus status* as "ideal state" can

---

[15] See Asmis 2004. [16] See for example Barrow 1950, 21.

be misleading (*De rep.* 1.20.33; 2.39.66). *Status* refers more to a condition or form of government in this context. Furthermore, the translation suggests a Platonic abstract Form that Cicero specifically rejects. For Cicero, Plato begins "with the assumption of an unoccupied tract of land" and "invent[s]" what one thinks is the best state (*De rep.* 2.11.22). Cicero discounts this approach for two reasons: First, although Plato creates a model of the best state, it is "quite unsuited to men's actual lives and habits" (*De rep.* 2.11.22); second, the pattern is but "a shadow and image of the political body (*umbra et imagine civitatis*)" (a subtle reversal of Plato's allegory of the cave) that cannot compare to "a real and powerful *re publica*" (*De rep.* 2.30.52). The claim says as much about the Roman conception of their own government as it does about the Roman – even Cicero's – reluctance to engage in the sort of abstract philosophizing that they saw as characteristic of the Greeks. But Cicero does not, in turn, embrace what he sees as the contending approach, represented by Aristotle and the Peripatetics, which categorizes different types of states and principles of political bodies (*rei publicae de generibus et de rationibus civitatum*) (*De rep.* 2.11.22). For Cicero, these analyses do not provide "any certain model and pattern" (*ullo certo exemplari formaque*) (*De rep.* 2.11.22, my translation); instead, they give historical examples that correspond to particular typologies.

If the first approach is normative without being sufficiently historical, then the second is historical without being sufficiently normative. Yet it is not clear to scholars what emerges when Cicero combines these methods (*De rep.* 2.11.22). Finley, following Mommsen, sees Cicero as accomplishing neither goal: *On the republic* is as "unphilosophical" as it is "unhistorical."[17] Pöschl argues that while Cicero uses the Roman state as an example, he ultimately idealizes the state to make it resemble a Platonic Form.[18] For Powell, the Roman constitution serves as "an illustrative instance" of "things predicted by the theory."[19] Cornell characterizes *On the republic* as "essentially a theoretical discussion within a historical framework."[20] And for Wheeler, Cicero employs an

---

[17] Finley 1983, 128; Mommsen 1869, 4.728–29.
[18] Pöschl 1936, 99–107; also How 1930. Zetzel (2001) gives that purification a Stoic form.
[19] Powell 2001, 29.   [20] Cornell 2001, 56.

Aristotelian distinction between two different types of ideals: that which is best, and that which is the best for the circumstances.[21]

At first glance, Cicero seems to bear out Wheeler's contention by distinguishing between the ideal as an image of nature (*naturae imago*) and one best achievable by people (*De rep.* 2.39.66). That is, history and circumstances appear to compromise the natural perfection of the ideal. But Cicero's language – of *exemplar* and *forma* – points to a Roman formulation. The Romans thought by way of *exempla*, which are not simply illustrations of ideas, but the logic that one identifies in a set of practices. Nature does not provide a conceptual blueprint that one can attempt to approximate; it provides an impetus that admits of innumerable combinations in practice (see, for example, *De leg.* 1.6.19: *a lege ducendum est iuris exordium*).[22] As Cicero writes, from the "rudimentary beginnings of intelligence" that are "imprinted on our minds" one gives form through speech, "the mind's interpreter" (*De leg.* 1.10.30). The contrast is not between the darkness of the cave and the illuminating brightness of truth. Absent our ability to give form to nature's reason through words, the concepts remain dark and incoherent (see *De orat.* 3.5.19); absent some foundation in nature, though, the concepts one arrives at by way of one's experiences and formulates with words become unstable, lacking normative content (see *De leg.* 1.15.42). Theory and practice are not, then, on opposite poles but, rather, mutually inform – indeed, are necessary for – each other.

What is politically "best," then, for Cicero, are not ideals – the stuff of imagination – but models of action that reason and speech are "striving to make clear" (*De rep.* 2.39.66). The Roman state is not the best achievable in the circumstances provided; the Roman state reveals a model and pattern, perfected in time, of nature's impetus. In fact, the claim can be

---

[21] Wheeler 1952, 49–51; see Arist. *Pol.* 1288b; also Lieberg 1994 (Cicero negotiates between Platonic and Aristotelian approaches); Zetzel 1996, 317–18 (tension between Platonic vision of ideal and historical reality of Roman state).

[22] I think Connolly is getting at this when she writes that for Cicero, "the virtuous self is at once a product of nature and of culture, a bundle of spontaneous impulses that are already scripted from a social code that itself is conceived as the expression of natural law" (2007, 172). The source of concepts for Cicero may, however, be innate. See Tarrant 1985, 123–24; *Tusc.* 1.24.57.

made still stronger: Rejecting Stoicism as too abstract (e.g., *De leg.* 3.6.14, excepting Panaetius) and Epicurean conventionalism as too ungrounded, Cicero suggests that only in society can nature acquire form (see *Sest.* 42.91–92; *De inv.* 1.2.2–3).[23]

We can further clarify the distinctiveness of the relationship between Cicero's best state and nature by juxtaposing it to a Platonic *eidos* (Form) and an Aristotelian *telos* (end). For Plato, the ideal state is brought into conformity with the eternal, immutable Form of the Good by way of the philosopher. If Cicero's founder shares the divinity that Plato associates with the philosopher, it is not in his or her proximity to the Forms but in the ability to authorize ideas: to get others to obey what philosophers have difficulty getting others to even believe (*De rep.* 1.2.3; 1.7.12). Furthermore, the perfection of the state does not derive from the vision of a single lawgiver or legislator who stands outside politics and enforces his will but from the enactment of politics by multiple founders "in a long period of several centuries and many ages of men" (*De rep.* 2.1.2; also 2.21.37).[24] Although Cicero does emphasize the wisdom of Romulus and the other kings more than Livy will later, there is still no person for Cicero who possesses "so great genius that nothing could escape him, nor could the combined powers of all the men living at one time possibly make all necessary provisions for the future without the aid of actual experience and the test of time" (*De rep.* 2.1.2). The claim is striking: Where Plato locates the ideal outside time – thus making time into the enemy of politics – Cicero cannot imagine the perfection of something without the experience that time as history brings.

Cicero's ideal does not exactly map onto an Aristotelian teleology either, though it shares some features. The first cause of human association for Cicero, like for Aristotle, is a natural instinct for association (*congregatio*), a spirit that leads individuals to join together in mutual agreement to form a *civitas* (*De rep.* 1.25.39; also *De rep.* 1.25.40; 4.3.3; *De off.* 1.4.12; 1.43.153; 1.44.157–158; 1.45.159; *De leg.* 1.5.16; 1.7.23;

---

[23] On the influence of Panaetius in making Stoic ethics "less rigorous and more practical," see Morford 2002, 25.

[24] On the Roman notion of founding, seeing Hammer 2002a.

1.13.35; *De fin.* 5.23.65–66). Corresponding to Aristotle's village or Plato's primitive state that exists largely for protection and economic exchange, community life for Cicero begins as dwellings, which he calls a town or city (*urbs*) (*De rep.* 1.26.41; also *Sest.* 42.91). Out of city life customs and laws are established, "and then came the equitable distribution of private rights and a definite social system" (*De off.* 2.4.15). What makes a collection of people into a *res publica*, according to Cicero's well-known definition (as articulated by Scipio Aemilianus in *De republica*), is that it is an assembly of people in large numbers in an agreement with respect to justice and a partnership for the common interest (*De rep.* 1.25.39: *coetus multitudinis iuris consensu et utilitatis communione sociatus*).[25]

Cicero differs from Aristotle's teleology (and it must be remembered that Cicero is likely not acquainted with Aristotle's *Politics*) in arguing that there is neither ineluctability to this movement nor a natural end.[26] In Rome, experiences perfect the original (*De rep.* 2.1.2), institutions and ideas are borrowed and adapted (*De rep.* 2.28.50), authority is variously reasserted, and timely concessions made (*De leg.* 3.10.24).[27] What keeps these successive adaptations from zig-zagging chaotically is not that they unfold according to nature, but that they are built upon the principles that lie at the origin of the community. Different institutions owe their beginning "to the same cause as that which produced the *civitas* itself," which are the associational principles of justice and partnership (*De rep.* 1.26.41; also *De rep.* 2.11.22).[28] The best state is one that gradually perfects the principles of justice and partnership that lie at its origin, even making modifications and accommodations that

---

[25] Intellectual origins of Cicero's definition: Aristotle and the Peripatetics: Frede 1989; Stoic: Asmis 2004. Originality and Romanness of Cicero's definition: Pöschl 1936, 173–75; Drexler 1957; 1958; Kohns 1974, 83 (definition as joining two similar concepts of *consensus iuris* and *utilitatis communio*); 1976, 209–14; Schofield 1995a (Cicero introduces issue of legitimacy of a government).

[26] See Nederman 1988, 5–11 (requires awareness of natural sociability).

[27] See Lintott 1997, 83. Cicero criticizes Cato for speaking as though he is in Plato's Republic rather than Romulus' cesspit (*Att.* 2.1.8).

[28] On the notion of principles in Roman thought, see Arendt 1963, 212–13; 1968, 152–53, though Arendt understates the natural impetus of these principles.

(as Scipio Aemilianus mentions in an aside) seem to defy reason (*De rep.* 2.33.57). From Cicero's seemingly simple definition emerges a distinct understanding of the *res publica*, one that rests, as we will see, on the conceptually rich notions of *consensus iuris* and *coetus utilitatis communione societus*, to which we will now turn.

LAW, JUSTICE, AND SOCIETY

Ius carries a meaning of both law and right that forms the root of the word justice, *iustitia*. There are, in fact, two categories of law employed by Cicero: one natural (*ius naturale*; also *ius gentium*, which is traditionally translated as law of nations) and one civil (*ius civile*) (see *De rep.* 3.4.7; *De off.* 3.5.21–23; *De leg.* 1.5.17; 1.6.18–19; *Pro Sest.* 42.91; also see later juristic rendering by Gaius *Inst.* 1.1).[29] Civil laws are measures specific to particular communities. *Ius gentium* or *ius naturale* is law that is seen as applicable to all nations or all people.

The Stoics and natural law

For the Stoics, from whom Cicero will look for much of his argument about justice (and whose ideas Cicero reproduces in several of his works, translating them from the Greek sources for his Roman audience), the universe is a rational and moral structure in which there are divinely ordered laws (*De nat. deor.* 2.44.115; *De div.* 2.14.33; DL 7.134; 7.136; 7.148–49; *SVF* 1.158, 176; 2.936 [shapes]; 3.32). The Stoics natural law (*lex naturae*; also referred to as *koinos logos*: DL 7.88) describes a set of uniform, impartial processes that operate equally on everyone, whether the movement of the heavens, the mortality of organic beings, or the circumstances of one's life. What it means to be a reasoning creature is to be able to bring clarity to the perceptions and inclinations of the law that nature plants in us (see *De leg.* 1.6.18; 1.9.26–27; 1.10.30; 1.16.44;

---

[29] On the relationship of these terms, Nicholas suggests that *ius naturale* "looks to the origin of this [universal] law in natural reason," and "the term *ius gentium* to its universal application" (1962, 55; also Dyck 2004, 103–4).

1.22.59; 2.4.8–9).³⁰ To act according to these laws is to act morally (*De leg.* 1.6.18–19; DL 7.87–88; Stob. 2.7.5b3 P = *SVF* 3.264; 2.7.6a P = *SVF* 1.179).

Many scholars have read Stoic natural law as resembling a universal law code. Chrysippus, in his opening to *On law*, provides an influential analogy between law and morality: "Law is king of all things human and divine. Law must preside over what is honourable and base, as ruler and as guide, and thus be the standard of just and unjust, prescribing to animals whose nature is political what they should do, and prohibiting them from what they should not do" (Chrysippus *SVF* 3.314, trans. LS 67R, modified). Viewed as resembling a law code, Stoic natural law is seen as being comprised of universal, exceptionless, law-like rules that form moral injunctions.³¹

But natural law, both for the Stoics and for Cicero in his appropriation of Stoicism, appears less as a code prescribing or proscribing types of action and more as the reason of nature. To have reason is to comprehend the relationship of actions to consequences, to make analogies and draw connections, to associate the past, present, and future, and to survey "the course of [one's] whole life and [make] the necessary preparations for its conduct" (*De off.* 1.4.11). Reason guides us in choosing morally right action (*katorthōma* = *perfectum officium*; *recte factum*), the only acts of true value for the Stoics. Such acts depend only on virtue, the disposition of the soul to act in perfect harmony with our nature as reasoning beings: justice (*iustitia* = *dikaiosunē*),

---

[30] On the ambiguities of the term *ius naturale* as regulative and instinctive, see Nicholas 1962, 56.

[31] Those arguing for a legalistic, rule-based approached to Stoic ethics in which the Stoics lay out (like law) universal and binding prescriptions include Mitsis 1993; 1994; Striker 1996; Annas 1993. Others have rejected this approach, seeing the Stoics as providing "substantive moral commands" with a "more procedural understanding of moral 'law'" by which we account for situational differences (Inwood 1999a, 98; also 2005, 97; Nussbaum 1994, 339–40; Vander Waerdt 1994a; Brittain 2001, 256–59; Vogt 2008, 161–216). For a discussion of Seneca's application of Stoic notions of moral law, see Chapt. 6: Seneca. Some argue that the Roman theory of natural law was adopted by the jurists from the Stoics (by way of Cicero): Edelstein 1966, 83; Watson 1971, 232–35; Sandbach 1975, 16; Long 1986, 231. Vander Waerdt disagrees with the association of the Stoic with the juristic conception of natural law (1994a).

wisdom/ prudence (*sapientia/ prudentia* = *sophia/phronēsis*), courage (*fortitudo* = *andreia*), and propriety (*decorum/ temperantia* = *sophrosunē*) as the primary virtues (see Cic. *De fin.* 3.6.21; 3.10.33; *De off.*1.5.15; 2.5.18; *Tusc.* 3.17.36–37; Stob. 2.7.5b1 P = *SVF* 3.262; 2.7.6e P = *SVF* 1.554; also *SVF* 1.202: consistently rational disposition; DL 7.87–89, 97–98). But reason also guides us in making judgments about what the Stoics refer to as an appropriate action (*kathēkon* = *officium*), choices that correspond with our universal nature (as reasoning beings), different contexts, and our particular dispositions (Cic. *De fin.* 3.6.20; *De off.* 1.3.8; DL 7.107–108: reasonable defense can be made; Stob. 2.7.8 P = *SVF* 1.230).[32]

Cicero, natural law, and social duty

The translation of *kathēkon* into *officium* (duty) and *katorthōma* into *perfectum officium* (perfect duty) gives these terms a Roman hue, blurring the distinction between the obligations to moral laws and the deeply held sense of duties that arise from historical traditions.[33] For Cicero, in obeying the laws of nature, we obey ourselves as reasoning beings (*De rep.* 3.22.33).[34] But reason, as Cicero writes in *De officiis*, a work written as a letter advising his son, Marcus, in an elaboration of Panaetius' discussion of duty, directs us to a sense of obligations (*officia*) that are animated by our social instinct, "the deepest feeling in our nature" (*De off.* 1.45.159; also *De off.* 1.4.12; also *De leg.* 1.10.30).[35] There was always a social component in Stoicism. By way of *oikeiōsis*, an inborn

---

[32] It is generally held that appropriate actions are seen by the Stoics as justified by the nature of its doer (see Long and Sedley 1987, 1.365), though challenged by Brennan 1996 who argues that appropriate actions are justified by the content of action. See Stob. 2.7.11e P = *SVF* 3.501–2 for a discussion of right acts (*katorthōmata*). *Katorthōmata* are a perfected form of *kathēkonta* (Kidd 1978, 248–49; Inwood 1999b, 698; White 2012, 109; though it should be emphasized that appropriate actions are not necessarily right actions: see DL 7.88). Stobaeus reports the definition of a *katorthōmata* as a "complete appropriate act" (*teleion kathēkon*) (Stob. 2.7.11a P = *SVF* 3.500). I do not find convincing Vogt 2008, 62, who sees in Stoicism a definitional break so that *kathēkonta* are concerned only with the choice of indifferent goods, not moral ones.

[33] See Brunt 1975, 15–16.   [34] Vogt 2008, 4, 172, 216.

[35] See Schofield 1991, 71 on reason as focused on matters of "*social* morality."

grasp of what is akin to us, we love our offspring and others who share our "common humanity" (*De fin.* 3.5.16–17; 3.6.21–22; 3.19.62–63; also Chapt. 6, 284–86 and Chapt. 8, 378–81). But for Cicero, no doubt influenced by Panaetius, *oikeiōsis* more strongly connects individuals to their social duties and roles. For Cicero, we are prompted "to meet in companies, to form public assembles and to take part in them themselves" (*De off.* 1.4.12).[36] Cicero is careful to note that humans come together not just to provide for the needs of daily life, but because society fulfills the desire for companionship that is in our nature (and that we desire for its own sake) (*De off.* 1.44.158). To withdraw into solitude and never see another human is, as Cicero suggests, to be deprived of life (*De off.* 1.43.153).

Cicero, social duty, and justice

This social instinct organizes Cicero's conception of justice (*iustitia*) (e.g., *De off.* 3.6.28).[37] Cicero develops his position in *On the republic* by way of a response to Philus (who is building his argument around the famous defense of injustice by the Sceptic Carneades in 155 BCE). Philus argues that justice is merely a product of conventions (*De rep.* 3.8.13), conventions that vary from place to place, change over time, and can inflict harm on others (see *De rep.* 3.9.16; 3.10.17; also *De leg.* 1.15.42–43; 1.16.43–44). These arrangements are bargains between the common people and the powerful that arise from mutual fear: "man fearing man and class fearing class" because "no one is confident in his own strength" (*De rep.* 3.13.23).[38]

Cicero, by way of Laelius, responds that natural law is the source of what is just: "True law is right reason in agreement with nature; it is of universal application, unchanging and everlasting; it summons to duty by its commands, and averts from wrongdoing by its prohibitions

---

[36] This aspect is not discussed by Arena 2010, 53–54 and 2012, 261–62, in tracing Cicero's adoption of a Stoic conception of liberty in *On duties*.
[37] See also Schofield 1995b, 201–5.
[38] On the specifically Roman imperial context of Philus' speech, see Zetzel 1996, 301–304, 308.

(*Est quidem vera lex recta ratio naturae congruens, diffusa in omnes, constans, sempiterna, quae vocet ad officium iubendo, vetando a fraude deterreat*) (*De rep.* 2.22.33). As Cicero writes in *De legibus*, echoing Chrysippus, "the origin of justice is to be found in law (*lex*), for law is a natural force; it is the mind and reason of the intelligent man, the standard by which right (*ius*) and wrong (*iniuria*) are measured" (*De leg.* 1.6.19, trans. modified; also *De leg.* 1.15.42; 2.5.11–12). What this language makes clear is that for both the Stoics and Cicero agreements about justice arise not out of fear and weakness, as Polybius (6.5.4–7) and Glaucon (Plato *Rep.* 358e-359b) contend, but out of "a natural impulse for justice."[39]

We can more fully understand the role of justice in Cicero's thought by way of his extended discussion of duties in *De officiis* (connecting it, in turn, to other claims Cicero makes). In this work, Cicero associates two duties with justice: "that no harm be done to anyone" and "that the common interests be conserved" (*De off.* 1.10.21; also 1.7.20; *De fin.* 5.23.65; *De inv.* 2.53.160). The first duty of justice corresponds with the Stoic definition of giving each his due (see *De rep.* 3.11.18; *De leg.* 1.19; also Stob. 2.7.5b1 P = *SVF* 3.262). Asmis, for example, emphasizes this Stoic aspect in Cicero's best state when she identifies "the basic bond" of "natural justice" as an agreement to "[act] fairly with one another."[40] The second duty of justice gives justice a specific social and political role (*De fin.* 5.23.66), connecting it to *utilitas* (interest or benefit).

The *utilitates* of a *civitas*, as Cicero writes in his first treatise on rhetoric, are things that "pertain to the body politic, such as fields, harbours, money, a fleet, sailors, soldiers and allies – the means by which states preserve their safety and liberty – and other things contribute something grander and less necessary, such as the great size and surpassing beauty of a city, an extraordinary amount of money and a multitude of friendships and alliances" that make a city important and powerful

---

[39] Asmis 2004, 584.
[40] Asmis 2004, 589; also Schofield 1991, 72. Also Asmis 2008a, 2: "just as Cicero adopts a Stoic view of natural law, so he uses Stoic theory to forge a connection between natural law and his code of laws."

(*De inv.* 2.56.169). When Cicero says that justice is connected to a common interest, he recognizes that a virtue cannot be instrumental; it must be chosen for its own sake and not because it yields some other benefit (e.g., *De leg.* 1.18.48–49). Cicero, thus, is not replacing *honestas* (moral goodness) with *utilitas* (interest), but is following Stoicism in bringing them into conformity with each other by way of justice (see *De off.* 2.3.10; 3.3.11; 3.4.20, 23; *De leg.* 1.12.33; compatible with Stoicism: see DL 7.148–49 = SVF 2.1132 = LS 43A).[41]

Cicero brings morality into conformity with interest by arguing that justice, which is derived from a social instinct, protects and conserves human interests (*De off.* 3.6.31). He justifies this equation, in part, by arguing that justice is necessary for cooperation (e.g., *De off.* 2.11.40), allows humans to turn inanimate nature into something useful (*De off.* 2.4.13–14), and is the basis for mutual exchange that provides for human wants and makes life worth living (*De off.* 2.4.15). More generally, Cicero argues that the chief end of action, as directed by nature, should be "to make the interest (*utilitas*) of each individual and of the whole body politic identical. For, if the individual appropriates to selfish ends what should be devoted to the common good, all human fellowship will be destroyed (*ut eadem sit utilitas unius euiusque et universorum; quam si ad se quisque rapiet, dissolvetur omnis humana consortio*)" (*De off.* 3.6.26). Justice is not just the ordering of one's own actions; it is a concern with the actions of others and a positive obligation to prevent injury and perform duties (e.g., *De off.* 1.7.23: prevent injustice; *De off.* 1.9.28; 1.10.32; convince others: *De off.* 3.30.110).[42] The function of justice, as Cicero writes, is "to promote and strengthen society" (*ad hominum consociationem*) (*De off.* 1.28.100).

---

[41] I thus disagree with Fott who sees Cicero as introducing (and to some extent disguising) a tension between expedience and right, which for Fott maps onto a tension between politics and philosophy (2009, 161–63). Tensions abound, but I think Cicero was openly working through (even if not resolving or even being critically aware of some of) these tensions.

[42] See Nicgorski 1984; Long 1995b. Nicgorski argues that "inclinations toward the useful are among the sources for the formation of a proper understanding of right" (1984, 563). This is true, but my argument here places emphasis on the role of justice in guiding the social role of utility.

Cicero has traveled far from the Stoic city in his conception of the role of law and justice. For the Stoics, a city is comprised of an organization of men administered by law (understood as nature's reason), a definition that requires that its citizens possess virtue.[43] This community is not the state, as an organization of power and authority, but properly the cosmos.[44] Thus, for the early Stoics, this already existent cosmic city consists of the sages as citizens (and gods as rulers) who are governed by the common law (*koinos nomos*) of their reason in harmony with nature's reason, shed of the contingencies of politics, power, social class, and material condition.[45] Chrysippus, for example, views all laws and constitutions as mistaken (*SVF* 3.324). As Vogt contends, the idea of the cosmic city "is to recognize that actual cities do not ultimately 'live up' to being cities; actual laws are not real laws, and actual cities are not real cities."[46]

Cities and laws are more "real" for Cicero than they are for the Stoics.[47] And Cicero is less concerned with a city of sages that, given the rarity of sage, may at any given time have no citizens. But Cicero's emphasis on the ties that bind a community still has a Stoic resonance. For Cicero society is neither an abstraction nor a complex arrangement of explicit laws (*De off.* 1.10.33); it is people bound together through affection (*De off.* 1.15.49: *benevolentia*; also *De off.* 2.7.23: *diligo*; 2.9.32; 2.20.70: gratitude of poor), recognition of service (*De off.* 1.14.45), and regard for need (*De off.* 1.15.49; 2.8.62).[48] Thus, Cicero sees *beneficentia*

---

[43] See Schofield 1991, 61–84. [44] Schofield 1991, 61–62; Vogt 2008, 65–110.
[45] Gods and sages: Stob. 2.7.11i P = *SVF* 1.587; Eusebius *Praep. Evang.* 15.15.3–5 = *SVF* 2.528 = LS 67L; community comprised only of sages: DL 7.32–33; Cic. *Acad.* 2.44.136; Schofield 1991, 61–62; Vander Waerdt 1994b; Obbink 1999; community comprised of humanity: Plut. *De virt. Alex.* 329a-b; Euben 2001, 265–70; Vogt 2008, 65–66, 76–86, whose argument seems to point more to the notion that nothing from the evidence excludes rather than requires the possibility that others are a part of the city, though not citizens; Vogt 2008, 13.
[46] Vogt 2008, 71.
[47] Ferrary notes, "Cicero's city is neither the city of the wise described by Zeno nor the cosmic city of Chrysippus, even if there are occasional references to the latter" (1995, 68).
[48] Thus I disagree with Nicgorski's contention that for Cicero "the proper ultimate context for justice is the universal rather than the particular community" and that "through decent particular communities ... one approaches the universal one"

42

(kindness) and *liberalitas* (generosity) as aspects of justice. Such acts, as Atkins notes, "take into account what the recipient deserves in respect of his character, the closeness of his relationship and his previous service" (*De off.* 1.14.42, 45), and are thus regulated by the idea of giving what is deserved.[49] Both play a complementary role to justice by "building up *societas*"[50]: *beneficentia* by recognizing and nurturing virtuous behavior that grows out of and supports human fellowship (*De off.* 1.15.46; also 1.16.50) and *liberalitas* by fostering bonds of gratitude. As Cicero writes, one contributes "to the general good by an interchange of acts of kindness, by giving and receiving, and thus by our skill, our industry, and our talents to cement human society more closely together, man to man" (*De off.* 1.7.22; also 2.21.72). The personal nature of the social bond points to why trust (*fides*) is the foundation of justice (*De off.* 1.7.23).[51] Relationships require "truth and fidelity to promises and agreements" (*De off.* 1.7.23). The most contemptible action, and one that plays significantly into his conception of the *res publica* as a form of partnership, is fraud: the person who appears most virtuous while being the most false (*De off.* 1.13.41; criticism of Piso: *Sest.* 9.22). Absent trust, no consensually based form of social organization can survive because it will degenerate into unrestrained expressions of self-interest.[52]

Cicero, social duty, and the other virtues

Our natural sociability underlies and regulates the other three virtues, as well. Cicero acknowledges that wisdom (*sapientia*), or knowledge of the truth, remains the principle virtue (*De off.* 1.6.18; 1.43.153). But in

---

(1984, 564, 565). The universal is important, but one's country remains the most important context.

[49] Atkins 1990, 266. [50] Atkins 1990, 266.

[51] Note Nicholas: "The relationship between partners was treated as an especially personal one...The law therefore left the incidents of the contract to a considerable extent to be regulated by the broad principle of good faith" (1962, 186). Not the least of such oaths kept for 360 years was the guarantee of sacrosanct status of the tribunes and aediles of the plebs, broken (with violent consequences) with the execution of Tiberius Gracchus (see Wiseman 2009, 178).

[52] See Allen 2004, 136–38.

contrast to both the Stoic and Epicurean vision of the *sapiens* (sage) in which public life is an impediment to the pursuit of wisdom (even if, as with the Stoics, the *sapiens* ends up stuck in politics unless there is good reason not to), for Cicero philosophic study is oriented to others, whether in what we study, in our desire to share and communicate with others (*De off.* 1.43.153; 1.44.156, 158; 1.6.19), or in the imparting of moral duties (*De off.* 1.2.5) and political responsibilities that are the result of wisdom (*De leg.* 1.24.62). Knowing about things human and divine is impotent without being put into effect (*De off.* 1.43.153).

Courage (*fortitudo*), the second remaining virtue, can be dangerous without being regulated by the bonds of sociability (*De off.* 1.44.157; 1.15.46; 1.19.63).[53] The greatness of mind associated with courage (and, importantly, with Caesar) has led to an excessive passion for power and glory that has destroyed the community (*De off.* 1.19.62, 64).[54] As Cicero writes, "when one begins to aspire to pre-eminence, it is difficult to preserve that spirit of fairness which is absolutely essential to justice," no longer "constrained either by argument or by any public and lawful authority" (*De off.* 1.19.64).

The final virtue, propriety (*decorum*), which encompasses self-control, reverence (or respect for others), and moderation, has in common with justice the cultivation of character (*De off.* 1.31.111), fulfillment of roles to which, by nature and circumstance, one is best adapted (*De off.* 1.31.114), and not doing harm to others (*De off.* 1.28.99). For Cicero, this sensibility, which enjoins us "to employ reason and speech rationally, to do with careful consideration whatever one does, and in everything to discern the truth and to uphold it," is inseparable from *honestas* (*De off.* 1.27.94).[55] *Decorum* emphasizes not just the internal state of the soul, but (and Cicero is consistent with Stoicism here) how the person looks and acts toward others (*De off.* 1.27.96, 98; 1.28.100–101; 1.29.102; also Sen. *De ot.* 1.1.7).[56] For Cicero, "because society finds its primordial

---

[53] Long characterizes this as a "bold correction to the honour code" by elevating deeds above glory (1995a, 226).
[54] See Gabba 1979, 126.   [55] See Nicgorski 1984, 562.
[56] See especially Dugan 2005, 5–7; Reydams-Schils 2005, 94; Connolly 2007, 142–43; Brunt 1975 on Stoicism and *decorum*. The Stoics "took states of character

ordering principle in the human interaction of speech, the proper regulation of speech (and its attendant bodily behaviors) is the original and essential virtue of civil life."[57] To act as a Roman, to act with *decorum*, is to display social virtue.

The stakes in this grounding of the virtues and interest in a social instinct could not be higher. Caesar's bold rise is but the culmination of decades of an unraveling Roman tradition in which the individual desire for glory and dignity (*Att.* 7.11.1) had long since lost its social motivation.[58] Statesmen no longer saw themselves as assuming a civic body, able to detach themselves from their own personal interests (*De off.* 1.34.124).[59] Cicero carves out a distinctive response. He does not seek recourse in the ideal Stoic community of moral consensus but demands that political thought and philosophy "come down to earth" and "face the urgent claims of necessity and utility" that Stoicism "tended to cloak or to ignore entirely."[60] Nor does Cicero envision Aristotle's citizens who share equally in ruling and being rule. Nor is it Plato's vertically enforced obedience to the authority of reason. As Reydams-Schils points out, Cicero was "deeply suspicious of philosophical values that oppose the social norms to which he adheres."[61] Cicero's best community takes on this Roman cast, as it is characterized by a partnership of hierarchical, differentiated activities and contributions (*De off.* 1.31.110–33.120) in which individuals work with each other toward not just a common goal, but on behalf of a common possession.[62] It is a vision that is organized around the notion of *societas*.

---

to be bodies, and as bodies perceptible" (Schofield 1991, 31; see DL 7.173; also Sen. *Ep.* 11.7).

[57] Connolly 2007, 169.
[58] See Long 1995b, 217; also Cic. *Sest.* 22.49. Cicero's sense of the crisis of his time shows up frequently in his work (see Leach 1993). More generally, Paterson describes the violence of the 80s as the formative experience for "the last generation of the Republic" (1985, 27). See also Mitchell 1984, 32–34. Raaflaub argues that Caesar initially attempted to create a broad coalition before turning to more drastic alternatives (2010).
[59] Reydams-Schils 2005, 96.
[60] Nicgorski 1984, 570. Also Colish 1990, 151; Kries 2003, 392.
[61] Reydams-Schils 2005, 97.
[62] Asmis strikes a similar note: "hierarchical blending of wills" (2005, 406).

COETUS UTILITATIS COMMUNIONE SOCIETUS, PARTNERSHIP, AND PROPERTY

We have explored one aspect of Cicero's definition of a *res publica*, identifying the Stoic foundation of his conception of justice, one (by way of Panaetius) given a prominent social role as it is animated by a social instinct and regulative of our interests. The second part of Cicero's definition of a *res publica* is that it is a partnership (*societas*) for the common interest. *Societas* is sometimes seen as a barely adequate, or misleading, Latin translation of *politikon*.[63] Quite the contrary: *societas* is an intricately textured Latin word that gives context to Cicero's associational conception of justice. *Societas* refers to a range of natural associations, including kinship ties (*De off.* 1.17.54), friendships (*De off.* 1.17.55–56), citizenship (*De off.* 1.17.53, 57), and the universal bond of common humanity (*De off.* 1.17.53; 3.6.28). It is related to *socius*, an ally or partner (e.g., *Verr.* 2.3.50). But the term also has a more legal denotation in Latin, and one that (like the notion of "trust" in Locke's political theory) arguably frames Cicero's understanding of political association: it refers to a type of partnership in which, as de Zulueta writes, individuals "contribute property or work or both to the prosecution of a common aim" (see, for example, *Rosc.* 8.24; *Quinct.* 3.11).[64] In a partnership, as treated later by the jurist Gaius, writing in the context of the burgeoning of Roman law as a formal system, profits and losses must continue to be shared, either equally or in proportion to an agreed upon recognition of differences in service or other contributions (Gaius *Inst.* 3.149–50). A partnership requires that the parties remain "of the same mind" (*in eodem sensu*) (Gaius *Inst.* 3.151). A social partnership fits a particular category of partnership, consensual partnerships, "that are not accompanied by regularly recurring, easily describable, conspicuous

---

[63] Arendt 1958, 27: "profound misunderstanding."

[64] de Zulueta 1953, 2.179. Examples of *societates* include the growth of tax companies (*societates publicanorum*) (see Lintott 1993, 86–91). It has been suggested that Quintus Mucius first articulates the more abstract notion of *societas* (Schiavone 1977; Arena 2012, 162–63). Pangle emphasizes the comparison of "society" to the body (1998, 252), an image that Cicero uses, but is incomplete in characterizing the negotiated, associational, and contractual aspects of a *res publica*.

circumstances."⁶⁵ That is, consensual partnerships are not as formal; rather, a subjective notion of ongoing agreement (more than explicit objective conditions) comes to the fore.⁶⁶

The consent (*consensus*) that makes partnerships possible connects back to the earlier part of Cicero's definition of a *res publica*. *Societas* is not comprised merely of a set of conventional arrangements, a view that Cicero associates with the Epicureans, but is premised on *ius naturale* that arises from "natural reason among all men."⁶⁷ In this context, natural reason means most basically an ability to calculate interest and recognize fairness (see Cic. *Fam.* 1.8.2; Sal. *Cat.* 44.5).⁶⁸ Without the former, there can be no mutuality of agreement but only obedience (like a child or slave) to stated conditions. Without the latter, the agreement becomes nothing more (as Augustine will later observe) than the fleeting arrangements of a den of thieves, prone to deception and violence (see *De rep.* 2.26.48; also *De off.* 1.10.31; 2.11.40: duty to restore trust and fulfill a promise; *Phil.* 2.3.5; 2.4.9). There are limits on the range of actions allowed in a partnership: One cannot be obligated to act contrary to morality (*boni mores*) (Gaius *Inst.* 3.157); one cannot have one's property taken against one's will (3.195); and one cannot reach an agreement to take someone else's property.

Noting the connection to partnerships, Asmis observes, "Like any partnership, the state is a consensual enterprise in which benefits are shared."⁶⁹ But Asmis discounts any association with property, suggesting that *res* refers to a matter or "object of concern" of the people.⁷⁰ Yet, the connection to ownership is hard to dismiss. In ancient law, "*res publicae* were all things owned by the state."⁷¹ Furthermore, Cicero continually works back and forth from political to economic transactions. Notably, in his first definition of justice, Cicero includes as a part of justice the duty "to use common possessions for the common interest,

---

⁶⁵ Daube 1938, 398. ⁶⁶ Daube 1938, 399.
⁶⁷ Gaius *Inst.* 3.154; Daube 1938, 385; also *De leg.* 1.13.35: *societas iuris*.
⁶⁸ See Dyck 2004, 163. Wirszubski sees Cicero's notion of natural law as leading him to a view that the "fundamental laws of Rome ought to be unalterable" (1968, 85). I have suggested here an approach for understanding which laws those are, and why they are important for providing a foundation for a partnership.
⁶⁹ Asmis 2004, 582. ⁷⁰ Asmis 2004, 588 fn. 37. ⁷¹ Watson 1968, 10.

private property for their own" (*De off.* 1.7.20). And Cicero frequently invokes a language of commercial transaction in describing the different types of bonds of fellowship, seeing the model of nature, for example, as captured in the words, "That I be not deceived and defrauded through you and my trust in you" (*De off.* 3.17.70, trans. modified) and "As between honest people there ought to be honest dealing, and no deception" (*De off.* 3.17.70). The slippage is not accidental; it is around this notion of partnership as a form of ownership that Cicero understands the organization, functions, and perfection of the *res publica*.

THE MIXED CONSTITUTION AND THE NEGOTIATION OF POWER

A distinctive aspect of partnerships is that the nature and extent of power is not fixed but is the subject of ongoing negotiation. These negotiations are often seen as operating in Polybian terms, in which the one (monarchy), the few (aristocracy), and the many (democracy) are vested with formal powers, each fearful of the other, each group motivated by (and protective of) the interests associated with their order. The goal of the mixed constitution for Polybius is stability as power contends with power, each group with its particular formal powers preventing the encroachment and concentration of power by the other. To the extent that there is cooperation, it is based on the threat of external danger (see Polyb. 6.18). But that notion is inconsistent with *concordia* and *harmonia*, which is how Cicero imagines the state functioning.[72] Harmony, like in music, occurs from the "proportionate blending of unlike tones" (*De rep.* 2.43.69), so in a *civitas*, concord is produced by "agreement among dissimilar elements" (*De rep.* 2.43.69). It stands in contrast to the Greek *homonoia*, like-mindedness (Arist. *NE* 1167a–1167b; Plato *Rep.* 431d–432a; Stob. 2.7.11b P = *SVF* 3.625; 2.7.5l P = *SVF* 1.68: shared belief about the goods of life).

---

[72] On the differences between Cicero and Polybius' view of the functioning of the mixed constitution, see Lintott 1997; 1999, 222–23. On Cicero's use of Polybius, see Arena 2012, 86–89.

THE MIXED CONSTITUTION AND THE NEGOTIATION OF POWER

We can better understand Cicero's notion of a mixed constitution as a partnership of power, a form of *societas* that functions through the differential expression of power. Those differences are not just different formal powers; they are different types of power. Unlike for the Greeks, where everything from strength to force to rule is contained in the term *kratos*, for the Romans power is not one thing. Rather, there is an extraordinary array of terms that corresponds to different aspects of power, each term with a range of meanings, not reducible to a single measure such as numerical superiority or wealth (*De rep.* 2.22.39). Cicero's mixed constitution is a partnership of three forms of power, each developed over time: *potestas* (including *imperium*), *auctoritas*, and (what I will argue is a third form of power), *libertas*.

The magistrates (expanded to include the tribunes) have *potestas*, which is a jurisdictional power to implement and administer measures, with some magistrates also possessing *imperium*, the power of military command. The senate provides *auctoritas*, an affective form of power that derives from recognition and respect for one's words and actions. *Auctoritas* smooths out the commanding power of *imperium* by giving memory, advice, and continuity to the partnership (*Sest.* 9.21). And *libertas* manifests itself as public choice, not just as a protection from domination, but as a way of collectively and publicly proposing (by way of the tribunes), deciding, and binding each other to the disposition of public things (e.g., *Phil.* 1.7.16; 1.7.18; 1.8.19; 1.10.25; 1.10.26; 2.3.6; 2.42.109). Each of the three forms of power, thus, contributes something essential: *potestas* and *imperium* provide command, *auctoritas* provides continuity, and *libertas* provides choice. But each also requires the recognition of the other: *potestas* and *imperium* must operate within law and precedent; *auctoritas* requires command and recognition by the people; and *libertas* requires the execution of decisions and recognition of (and tempering by) experience and wisdom. At its founding, Rome contains elements of what will ultimately be the three forms of power reflected in the mixed constitution. But the relationship of these elements of power is organized around, and negotiated as, aspects of ownership (moving toward Cicero's ideal state).

Potestas and imperium

The Roman state is initially characterized most prominently by one type of power, the *imperium* of the king, a sovereign, executive power to rule over things, associated with *regnum* (*De rep.* 2.28.50). Kingly power is modeled after divine power: the king, possessed of wisdom and justice, has the absolute authority and ability to issue commands (*De rep.* 2.23.43; 3.25.37). This form of power defines an analogous set of relationships that extends to the household: a god rules the universe, like a king rules his subjects, like a father rules his children, like the mind governs the body (*De rep.* 3.25.37: *sed corpori ut rex civibus suis aut parens liberis*). As Cicero continues (by way of Laelius), "So kings, commanders, magistrates, senators, and popular assemblies govern citizens as the mind governs the body (*sic regum, sic imperatorum, sic magistratuum, sic patrum, sic popularum imperia civibus sociisque praesunt ut corporibus animus*) (*De rep.* 3.26.38). In fact, consistent with this form of power, Cicero conceives of the early Roman community as a large household with a father, extended then to the children who, when mature, comprised the senate (*De rep.* 2.12.23; *De rep.* 2.11.21: raised the people from infancy). Even in this early stage, though, *regnum* contained aspects of partnership: Romulus signed a treaty with the Sabines to make their king "a partner in his royal power" (*De rep.* 2.7.13). *Regnum*, the supreme power of the king, would eventually be invested in the consuls (and other magistrates) as *potestas*, grants of jurisdictional power to carry out their specific civic functions, including administering, summoning, giving judgments, blocking actions, and punishing (see *De rep.* 2.33.57; *Leg. agr.* 2.11.28).[73] Certain magistrates would also be given *imperium*, a political grant of power to raise an army, issue orders, and command in war (*De rep.* 2.32.56; *Leg. agr.* 2.17.45–46).

For Cicero, the problem with the concentration of *potestas* in one man is that it does not have any built in limits to its rule. The *potestas* of a

---

[73] See Drogula 2007, 423–27 on the technical notion of *potestas*. I find Drogula's argument convincing: The *imperium* could not be used in the civic sphere except in exceptional cases, such as by a dictator or under a *senatus consultum ultimum* (2007, 445–51).

master is the "power of life and death" and the possession of "whatever is acquired through a slave" (Gaius *Inst.* 1.52). The association of *potestas* with the household is important because it alters the terms of ownership: the king (as father) can command obedience over his property, eliminating any difference between subjects and slaves (*De rep.* 3.25.37). Part of the problem certainly is that this form of *potestas* depends upon the character of one man so that a community can be quickly destroyed by the vice of the ruler (*De rep.* 1.28.44; 2.23.43; 2.26.47). But even absent the vice of its rulers, a community cannot be a true *res publica* if the people can be owned; if they are not *sui iuris*, or under their own jurisdiction.[74] Cicero points to Syracuse – reputed as "the most beautiful city in the world, with its admirable citadel, its harbours, whose waters penetrated to the very heart of the town and to the foundations of its buildings, its broad streets, its porticoes, temples, and walls – which could not be a *res publica* in spite of all these things while Dionysus was its ruler, for nothing belonged to the people, and the people itself was the property of one man (*nihil enim populi et unius erat populus ipse*)" (*De rep.* 3.31.43). Under the wise king, Cyrus, Persia was not a true *res publica*, either, because the property of the people was "administered at the nod and caprice of one man" (*De rep.* 1.27.43). Even the Massilian people, who were under Rome's protection and ruled by a few leading citizens, were like slaves (*De rep.* 1.27.43). The examples are interesting: Material splendor, even the generosity of the leader, does not constitute a *res publica* as a form of *societas* because the people do not have ownership; they do not have a say in how property is used.

Auctoritas

The *patres*, institutionalized in the senate, provide a different type of power, *auctoritas*. *Auctoritas* is conventionally (and not incorrectly) defined as an influence that derives from respect for one's words and actions as a model of wisdom and virtue (*De rep.* 2.9.15; 2.12.23; 2.28.50; also *De off.* 2.9.33). *Auctoritas* is derived from *augere*, which means to

---

[74] Gaius *Inst.* 1.48; also Skinner 1998, 40–41.

increase or grow, suggestive of how *auctoritas* is not tied to an office or specified powers but "grows on its own power."[75] It is a power that is both enacted, generating influence, and granted by others through their esteem for the individual.[76] But it is not a power that has legal force or is binding on others.

An observation by Heinze is helpful in thinking about what *auctoritas* means from the perspective of *societas*, of a partnership.[77] Heinze suggests that an *auctor* was originally used in legal terminology to refer to a person who, because of his position as seller of something, is responsible for ensuring the validity of the legal transaction or who, because of particular knowledge, is responsible for advice about the transaction.[78] As we have seen, for Cicero the most important aspect of a relationship, including political relationships, is "truth and fidelity to promises and agreements" (*De off.* 1.7.23; 3.70). *Auctoritas*, for Cicero, answers to this concern, not by fixing something permanently in time, but by ensuring the bonds of trust and mutual accountability by which negotiations can occur. The assurance is oriented both to the past, as negotiations occur within a context of precedents, rules, and procedures, and to the future by ensuring that new promises are kept and protections assured.

Libertas

In Rome's beginning, people had the smallest of says, but one that would later prove to be significant in Rome's development: kingship, rather than being inherited, derived from Numa's (the second kind of Rome) consultation with the people (*De rep.* 2.12.23; 2.13.25; 2.17.31; 2.17.32; 2.21.33). This modest concession to the people becomes important for Cicero because it reveals, in its nascent form, how the *res publica* was organized by a sense of a common stake in which *potestas* was granted to

---

[75] Lowrie 2009, 286.
[76] See Galinsky 1996, 12–13; Connolly 2007, 126–27; Lowrie 2009, 279–308.
[77] No Greek equivalent for *auctoritas*: Heinze 1925, 363–64. Lowrie provides a helpful contrast to Greek translations of *auctoritas*, noting how the Greek cannot capture how the authority associated with *auctoritas* is derived from both agency and community (2009, 291).
[78] Heinze 1925, 350–55.

the people and *auctoritas* to the senate (*De leg.* 3.12.28). This *potestas*, which is always understood jurisdictionally as a right to exercise power or carry out one's official tasks, is largely undefined though. In part this *potestas* is transferred or entrusted to the magistrates as a power to command (*imperium*) or implement (*potestas*) (*De rep.* 1.34.51–52; 2.32.56; 3.33.45; *De off.* 1.25.85; 1.34.124). But the power that is most associated with the people is for Cicero what the people know and seek and what balances the *potestas* of the magistrates and the *auctoritas* of the senate, which we can understand as *libertas* (see, for example, *De rep.* 2.28.50; 2.33.57).

Libertas, as has been observed frequently, emerges historically in Rome as a response to enslavement: The "cruel servitude" of the Tarquins (*De rep.* 2.25.46; also 2.26.48), in which people were turned into property, led to the overthrow of kingship and its replacement with two consuls, elected and limited in their term of service. The pressure of debt – that is, of owing without owning – led to the further establishment of two plebeian tribunes (*De rep.* 2.34.59) to counterbalance the power of the consuls (*De rep.* 2.33.58). *Libertas*, thus, becomes associated with a legal status that means that one is not a slave, that one is not subject to the power of another.[79]

Defined simply by its juxtaposition to power *libertas* ends up being conceived in almost wholly negative, and largely private, terms: as not being owned. By that I mean that liberty appears as a response to two questions of ownership: Who owns my property, and who owns me? In answering these questions, liberty is seen as an assertion against the encroaching nature of public power. Connolly, for example, suggests that "Sallust, Livy, Seneca, and later republican thinkers such as Machiavelli joined Cicero in speaking of liberty in primarily negative terms, as defined by the absence of interference guaranteed by law, especially the interference of a magistrate in the free (legal) actions of a citizen."[80] Brunt contends that a "negative sense of liberty was more congenial to the Roman mind than to the Greek," entailing a "mere absence of

---

[79] See Brunt 1988, 283; Pettit 1996: 576–77; 1997: 31–32, 36; Skinner 1998: 38–47; Roller 2001, 220–33.
[80] Connolly 2007, 159.

restraint in a great variety of contexts."[81] Raaflaub suggests that *libertas* is primarily negative and attached to legal and institutional protections from abuse.[82] Pettit tellingly characterizes *libertas* as "antipower."[83] To have liberty is to not be "susceptible" to the power of another.[84] And for Wirszubski, *libertas* appears as almost the surrender or displacement of power; it "is not so much the right to act on one's own initiative as the freedom to choose an 'auctor' whose 'auctoritas' is freely accepted."[85]

It is not that these conceptions of liberty are incorrect; they are incomplete. Connolly, for example, modifies her earlier claim that liberty is something essentially negative, noting that it might better be understood as a "conceptual spectrum, with the poor citizen's freedom from mistreatment by a magistrate at one end and Cicero's notion (the freedom to participate in governing) at the other."[86] But the two ends of the spectrum – of protections from, and participation in – remain conceptually disconnected. By conceiving of the *res publica* as a partnership, though, we can better understand how ownership unites these different aspects of liberty. Like one's body and one's private possessions, the *res publica* is also conceived of as property over which one has jurisdiction. Liberty is a form of power that is organized around the possession and disposal of property, including oneself and public things (*De rep.* 1.31.47; 2.23.43; *De leg.* 3.7.17; *Leg. agr.* 2.11.29).[87]

---

[81] Brunt 1988, 313.

[82] Raaflaub 2004, 266–70; Pitkin 1988, 534–35, following Raaflaub. Roller 2001, 221 argues that liberty has "no conceptual core" but is "merely 'the condition of being not-a-slave.'" Also, "it is incorrect to speak of *libertas* as being a 'political idea' or having a 'political meaning' in Roman culture" (Roller 2001, 232).

[83] Pettit 1996, 577; also 1997, 298; 1993, 19.

[84] See Pettit 1996, 577; Skinner 1998, 41.   [85] Wirszubski 1968, 35.

[86] Connolly 2007, 35; also Brunt 1988, 297, 292 [degrees]; Pitkin 1988, 534: "Rome developed two rival notions of *libertas*."

[87] Brunt and Pettit mention in passing the possible connection of *libertas* to power, but lack a sufficiently differentiated conception of power to develop the case. See Brunt 1988, 312 and fn. 71; Pettit 1996, 589. Pettit writes, "Their antipower gives them the capacity to command noninterference, as we might say, and itself represents a distinctive sort of power" (1996, 589). Pettit never explains what "sort of power" that is.

THE MIXED CONSTITUTION AND THE NEGOTIATION OF POWER

In one sense, *libertas* is a resisting power because it serves no master (*dominus*), acting as a jurisdictional limit to the *potestas* of a magistrate by restricting the ability to arbitrarily act against one's property or person (e.g., *De rep.* 1.32.48; 2.23.43; *Phil.* 3.4.8; 3.5.12; *De orat.* 3.1.4; *Cluent.* 53.147).[88] That is why law is, for Cicero, the beginning point of *societas* (*De rep.* 1.32.49). It is through law that justice is enforced and it is through justice, as we have seen, that the partnership is organized to give each his due and to preserve the common interest, including basic protections of property. Examples of specific laws in Rome include the requirement of a public trial in capital cases and restrictions on the legislating abilities of magistrates, but more fundamentally there must be equality before the law, the right of appeal for each of the partners, and opportunities to attain the highest political offices. Absent such equality, there can be no partnership because there is no jurisdiction over what is owned – neither oneself, certainly, nor the *res publica* (*De rep.* 1.32.49; 3.32.44: without appeal, no protection of liberty; also *De off.* 2.12.41–42: no rights if no equality before law; *De orat.* 1.42.188: common law defined).[89] That is why Cicero associates *libertas* with the recovery of the *res publica* as the property of the people (*res populi*) after the denial by the *decemviri* of the right to appeal (*De rep.* 3.32.44).

In another (and related) sense, liberty is the possession of and power over oneself and one's own property to dispose of according to one's will. By not delineating different notions of power, Pettit understands this ability to dispose of property too broadly, suggesting, "Under the conception of freedom as antipower," which he traces back to the Romans, "I am free to the degree that no human being has the power to interfere with me: to the extent that no one else is my master, even if I lack the will or the wisdom required for achieving self-mastery."[90] The claim is simply untrue in a Roman context with its gradations of domination

---

[88] Pettit 1996, 589, 602 ("denied possibilities of arbitrary interference"); also Pettit 1993.

[89] See Schofield, in Hammer (forthcoming).

[90] Pettit 1996, 578. The difference from Berlin's conception of negative liberty is minimal: for Berlin, negative liberty is freedom from interference (1969); for Pettit, freedom as antipower is freedom from the possibility of interference, which is non-domination (578; also 1997, 24–25).

and control: free women remained under guardianship of a male, any free citizen whose father was alive remained under his will, and subjugated populations would be granted citizenship (though not necessarily the vote) only with their recognition of Roman command.[91] One would be hard pressed to find any ancient, let alone Ciceronian, lineage for this claim of non-interference.

When Cicero asks, in the *Stoic paradoxes*, "For what is *libertas*? the power to live as you will" (*Par. stoi.* 34: *Quid est enim libertas? potestas vivendi ut velis*), he does not go as far as the Stoics in associating liberty with the self-mastery of the sage. Cicero notes (among other things) a political aspect to this freedom.[92] For Cicero (and most of the Roman tradition), liberty becomes license when there is no longer some form of master (*De rep.* 1.42.67). That master is reason, first and foremost, that is given political form in the rule of government, popular assemblies, and the laws (*De rep.* 1.43.67; 3.25.38: popular assemblies, etc., rule like mind over body).[93] Even laws and institutions, thus, are not just protections against interference, as they are in Pettit's interpretation; they, along with *mores*, instill a sense of duty and right that are the requisites of *libertas*.[94]

There is a third way in which *libertas* relates to ownership, and that is its public dimension. Strangely lacking in Pettit's account, no doubt influenced in part by a reaction against the equation of republicanism with positive liberty, is this public dimension. For Pettit, public laws and policy should be aimed at eliminating the possibility of domination by others. That is, public laws protect individuals from being owned. For Cicero, though, *libertas* implies a more expansive notion of public

---

[91] Ando 2011, 90.

[92] I agree with Arena that that there is a Stoic aspect to this idea of liberty, as freedom from enslavement to one's emotions (2010, 52, 55–56). I am not sure that *On duties* reflects a stoicized concept of liberty that is a "radical move" away from his previous notion articulated in *On the republic*.

[93] Schofield argues that the only master in a republic is the laws (1995a, 76). Liberty must recognize authority (of the laws, of reason, and of the senate), which Ferrary recognizes, but overstates (Ferrary 1984, 91–93). Gabba 1979, 132 and Brunt 1988 also associate the call for liberty as senatorial.

[94] Pettit sees the rule of law as consistent with liberty as antipower because it does not allow for power as subjugation (1996, 597).

ownership. Expanding on Schofield and others[95], I will suggest that a *res publica*, as a type of *societas*, is organized around the idea of citizenship as a partnership in the ownership of the state.

What does it mean for a people to own something? Cicero offers a suggestive analogy from Carneades, though in a different context, about how a collective body can own something. In discussing different duties, Cicero asks whether the owner of a ship can dispose of its contents, including the passengers, as he wishes. Cicero responds by stating, "For until they [the passengers] reach the place for which the ship is chartered, she belongs to the passengers, not to the owner" (*De off.* 3.23.89). Cicero says no more, but reconstructing the assumptions may help us understand its political implications, particularly as comparisons of the state to a ship show up in his other works.[96] At the heart of the claim is a distinction between private and public property. The passengers do not have private ownership of the ship. But the ship is not simply private property, either. The ship, as a mode of transportation, becomes common property in the *societas* formed by the agreement between the passengers and owner. In this agreement, there is a common aim (reaching a destination safely), recognition of differential contributions (the passengers pay money, the crew guides the ship), and an entrusting of decisions to the captain.

When Cicero refers to the *res publica* as a *res populi*, he is saying something more than that the people are passengers on a privately owned ship. He is suggesting that the *res publica* is itself a public thing in which the people have a share in determining how that thing will be used. Cicero's formulation, *potestas in populo, auctoritas in senatu*, requires that the people have some ability to make decisions that matter (*De leg.* 3.12.28). *Libertas*, thus, does not just provide walls to stop the encroachment of others; *libertas* entails the ownership of the walls themselves. One suggestive illustration of this assertion of public

---

[95] See Schofield 1995a.
[96] *De rep.* 1.34.51: rejection of entrusting captain by lot; *De rep.* 5.6.8: comparison to favorable course set by helmsman; *Sest.* 6.15: wreckage of ship of state after Catiline; *Sest.* 9.20: leaders at helm of state; *Sest.* 46.98–99: leaders protect common property of the ship; *Att.* 2.7.4: forced to leave helm.

ownership occurs when the people apparently reclaim the Forum in the first half of the second century, reacting to it being filled by aristocratic portrait statues (see also Chapt. 5, 248–49).[97] To be free is to possess a commonwealth, which means, as Schofield notes, that the *populus* "has rights over its [own *res*'] management and use."[98] Law, as Cicero suggests in his etymology, means to choose (*De leg.* 1.6.19; 2.5.11; 3.19.44). To own means to be able to choose the disposition of the item, which requires that one is not only master of oneself and one's private possessions, but that one also shares in being a master of the laws, courts, and treaties, all of which are the mechanisms by which collectivities choose how to allocate public things (*De rep.* 1.32.48).[99]

The role of the people

Making sense of the role of the people in Cicero's work is exceedingly difficult. *Potestas* lies with the people, but (as we saw in the Introduction) it is not the power associated with democracy, a power voiced and then dismissed by Scipio in *On the republic*.[100] The people, for example, cannot propose legislation nor can they even call their own assembly. Cicero's work conveys his own ambivalence about popular participation. In *On the Republic* he gives the primary power of deliberation (*consilium*) to the aristocracy rather than the people, though in the context (as we will see) of a partnership in which the people entrust

---

[97] Wiseman 2009, 49.
[98] Schofield 1995a, 76; also 1999, 188–89. Also Skinner: "if a state or commonwealth is to count as free, the laws that govern it – the rules that regulate its bodily movements – must be enacted with the consent of all its citizens, the members of the body politic as a whole" (1998, 27).
[99] Arena sees this reliance on initiative as replacing an earlier view of laws as guaranteeing liberty (2010, 59). Law remains important in *On duties*, but more importantly, law was never the sole guarantor of liberty for Cicero.
 As I suggest, liberty always required mastery, control, and initiative. And laws always had a foundation in, or were related to, natural law (as seen in *On the laws*).
[100] This contrast is developed in the contributions by Raaflaub (forthcoming[b]) and Fronda (forthcoming) in Hammer. Morstein-Marx 2004 is helpful in balancing the participatory and oligarchic aspects of the Roman republic.

themselves to others (De *rep.* 1.34.51).[101] He at times sees the role of the people as passive – one of affirming authority (*De Imperio Cn. Pompei* 1.2). He is careful to note that the people's desire is not necessarily what is in the interest of the state (*Pro Sestio* 48.103; 49.105; *De leg.* 3.10.23). And he opposed such legislation as the secret ballot (though earlier supporting it) (*De leg.* 3.15.33) and supported limits by Sulla (81 BCE) on the power of the plebeian tribunes to propose laws before the plebeian assembly and to restrict tribunes from seeking higher office, thus making the tribunate no longer a path to power.

Yet, Cicero looks to and draws satisfaction from the approval of the people.[102] He argues for the need to consult the judgment of others to make something better (*De off.* 1.41.147), suggesting as well that indifference to public opinion implies a lack of principle (*De off.* 1.28.99). He depicts the people as entrusting the magistrates with the administration of the *res publica* (*De rep.* 1.34.51–52; 2.32.56; 3.33.45; *De off.* 1.25.85; 1.34.124).[103] He also points to a more active role of the people in granting *auctoritas* and making choices (*De Imperio Cn. Pompei* 24.69). And he seems to defend (or at least assume) the notion that ordinary opinion contains "implicit philosophic knowledge" to which one could appeal and draw on through persuasion.[104] What Cicero did recognize (even if somewhat manipulatively, as in *Leg. agr.* 2.9.22–11.29) is that the legitimacy of the Roman republic rested on the power of the people to authorize actions of the partnership.

PROPERTY AND THE FUNCTION OF THE STATE

Notions of ownership not only inform Cicero's conception of power but also the centrality of property in the functioning (and function) of the

---

[101] See Schofield 1999, 191.
[102] *Sest.* 54.115; 55.117: people support Cicero's return; *Sest.* 56.120–21: people applaud words at show that support Cicero's cause; *Phil.* 1.15.36; *Phil.* 1.15.37: judgment of all ranks is the verdict; *Phil.* 2.34.85: forum; *Phil.* 2.45.115: connected to glory. As Wiseman states, "politics was a spectacle, with the citizens as the audience" (2009, 153–57). On Cicero's use of *popularis*, see Tracy 2008–2009.
[103] See Schofield 1995a, 75–76. [104] Garsten 2009, 159.

state. At a most basic level, and one identified by Wood, among others, Cicero argues that the "chief purpose" (*De off.* 2.21.73) and "peculiar function of the state and the city [is] to guarantee to every man the free and undisturbed control of his own particular property" (*De off.* 2.22.78; also *Caec.* 25.70; 26.73–75).[105] Cicero is negotiating a fine line here. He wants to argue that we are brought together by nature and that it is out of a desire to protect property that we seek "the protection of cities" (*De off.* 2.21.73). The problem, as Cicero recognizes, is that there is no such thing as private property in nature (*De off.* 1.7.21), which one knows by observing how nature provides for other living things. Cicero seeks to reconcile these two arguments by suggesting that although there is no private property in nature, the impetus for the acquisition of property does reside in nature – not as the scramble for power, as Thrasymachus contends, but out of an attachment to oneself and others. Employing the Stoic notion of *oikeiōsis* (= *commendatio* [Cicero], also *conciliari* and the reflexive *sibi conciliari*), which can be translated as appropriation, attachment, or a natural affection for what belongs to oneself,[106] Cicero argues that humans (like all living creatures) are born with an instinct to self-preservation, which includes "procuring and providing everything needful for life – food, shelter, and the like" (*De off.* 1.4.11).[107] The attachment that one has to oneself expands to

---

[105] See Wood 1983; 1988; de Ste. Croix 1981, 426; Long 1995b; Straumann 2011, 291.
[106] *Oikeiōsis* is translated variously as "Zueignung" or "appropriation" (Pohlenz 1948–49, 1.57); "a perception and grasp of what is akin" (Rist 1969, 44, following Plutarch); "well-disposed" (Pembroke 1971, 116); "endearment" (Rist 1978, 263); "a process of taking something to oneself, or accepting or appropriating it or making it one's own" (White 1979, 145); "attachment" (Engberg-Pedersen 1990b, 80–82); a "mental process by which a human being will, if things go rightly, arrive at the true grasp of the good" (Engberg Pedersen 1990a, 119); "affinity" (Erskine 1990, 115–16); "appropriation" or "affective relationships" (Long 1996, 172); "familiarization" (Annas 1993, 262); "identifying with" (Schofield 1995b, 196); "appropriation" (Reydams-Schils 2005, 55).
[107] On Cicero's interpretation of the Stoic relationship to property, see Annas 1997; Schofield 1999, 188–89; Garnsey 2007, 111–18. The Stoics, it should be noted, were not hostile to private property. See, for example, Cicero's reference to Hecaton in 3.15.63. As Long notes, "These thoughts have their basis in Stoicism, no doubt, but it is a secularized Stoicism, which has dropped the edifying but unhelpful talk about a *divine* city shared by gods and men" (1995b, 239).

include others, moving one to accumulate and store things that "minister to his comforts and wants – and not for himself alone, but for his wife and children and the others whom he holds dear and for whom he ought to provide" (*De off.* 1.4.12). Cicero, again following the Stoics, imagines expanding concentric circles of human bonds: kinship, friendships, citizenship, and universal humanity (*De off.* 1.17.53–58).

Property reflects these different relationships: Its acquisition and usage are guided by justice that requires that no one harm another unless provoked by wrong and (as we have seen) requires that men use "common possessions for the common interests, private property for their own" (*De off.* 1.7.20). The law of human society (*ius humanae societatis*) provides for the transformation of common property into private property through settlement, conquest, law, bargain, purchase, or allotment, all except conquest also forms of contract (*De off.* 1.7.21).[108] The securing of property does not conflict with the law of nations (*ius gentium*) and is confirmed by the laws of different communities (*iure civitatum*) (*De off.* 3.5.22–23), which Cicero sees as "a system of equity established between members of the same *civitatis* for the purpose of securing to each his property rights" (*Top.* 2.9).

But the social instinct that is the impetus for the acquisition of property also places limits on the activity. We "are not born for ourselves alone, but our country (*patria*) claims a share of our being, and our friends a share" (*De off.* 1.7.22). There is nothing glorious simply in the accumulation of riches (*De off.* 1.20.68) or the securing of possessions (*De off.* 1.44.158). The acquisition of property must be part of the contribution to common interests (*communes utilitates*): an aspect of "giving and receiving" (*De off.* 1.7.22) rather than the self-regarding motivation of avarice (*De off.* 1.7.24; also 1.8.26; 3.5.22). Cicero, thus, while recognizing that there are those who can contribute to the state

---

[108] The legitimacy of conquest is interesting here. In the Roman law of property, possession cannot be obtained by force (*vis*) (see Nicholas 1962, 108). But the laws regulating the acquisition of property are civil laws, which apply to Roman citizens and not to other peoples. Natural law allows the ownership of property captured from enemies. The property captured can be seen as theoretically belonging to the first occupant to take possession of it, but in practice the property was seen as belonging to the *res publica* and then distributed to individuals (Gaius 2.69; Watson 1968, 63–74).

by managing their own property, lays out the rules: Property must be honestly acquired; it must be increased by "wisdom, industry, and thrift"; and it must be made available to others who are worthy by way of generosity and beneficence (*De off.* 1.26.92; 1.8.25; also 2.24.87: duty to increase and conserve).

The function of the state in protecting property is not to secure privilege (though that is its effect) but to promote the public interest (*De off.* 3.5.23) and foster a social bond (*De off.* 1.7.22; *De off.* 2.24.84: on Cicero's own administration in enforcing payment of debt).[109] Rome's early years, in Cicero's recounting, confirm this function. Numa, the second king, divided the property won by Romulus through conquest, "giving each man a share, and showed them that by the cultivation of their farms they could have an abundance of all manner of possessions without resort to pillage or plunder" (*De rep.* 2.14.26; also 2.18.33). There was, thus, an interest in "peace and tranquility, which enable justice and good faith (*iustitia et fides*) to flourish most easily, and under whose protection the cultivation of the land and the enjoyment of its products are most secure" (*De rep.* 2.14.26). Ancus would similarly divide up conquered property and make the forests along the coast public property (*De rep.* 2.18.33). The ownership of property acts as a stabilizing force in society, which Cicero contrasts with maritime cities in which people are tempted to abandon agriculture (and the homestead) in pursuit of trade and opportunities abroad (*De rep.* 2.4.7–8). For Cicero, the weakness of Carthage and Corinth lay in the "scattering and dispersion of their citizens" because of their "lust for trafficking and sailing" (*De rep.* 2.4.7; also *Leg. agr.* 2.35.95). Property provides a bond that counters the dispersion of the people.

THE BREAKDOWN OF TRUST

The criteria by which Cicero judges the value and success of a mixed constitution are not democratic ones of equality or transparency, but

---

[109] On Cicero's defense of the propertied class, see Rawson 1976; Treggiari 1979; Wood 1983, 745–46 (as a response to a crisis of the landed aristocracy); 1988, 105–15.

whether it provides fairness and stability (*De rep.* 1.45.69). Fairness (*aequabilitas*), a term of Cicero's creation, does not require strict equality in which distinctions are eliminated (*De rep.* 1.27.43; 1.34.53; also *De leg.* 3.9.19).[110] What is fair, from the perspective of *societas*, is negotiated among the partners according to the principle of shared contributions and losses. As we have seen, partners can entrust others, as the people entrust the aristocracy, to make decisions about certain affairs. The mixed form of government advocated by Cicero ultimately institutionalizes the differential contributions of *societas*, one in which "every citizen is firmly established in his own station" (*De rep.* 1.45.69).[111]

The mixed form is not only fairer, but also more stable for Cicero because it prevents excess (*nimius* = beyond measure), which invariably leads to rebellion (*De rep.* 1.44.68; *De off.* 2.7.24). It prevents excess by allowing each citizen a share (*De rep.* 1.45.69), fostering something like political contentment (or tranquility). Absent a partnership of power, a community will soon become subject to the convulsions that arise from *voluptas*, an unrestrained desire for pleasure (*De leg.* 1.11.31; 1.17.47). Under a king the people fear the *voluptas* of an unjust ruler (*De rep.* 2.28.50) who will make his subjects into his property so that they are no longer able to possess or control anything (*De rep.* 1.33.50; 3.31.43). So, too, an aristocracy, desirous of titles and riches, becomes an oligarchy when a faction grabs for title without the acquiescence of the people (*De rep.* 1.33.50). This can lead, in turn, to the overthrow of authority by a mob, and the rise of the demagogue, a popular tyrant who takes away property without deliberation, fairness, or distinction

---

[110] See Fantham 1973, 287. On the philosophic (and specifically Pythagorean) notion of *logismos*, or calculation as informing constitutional arrangments, for Cicero's claim that the mixed system combines both arithmetic equality where everyone has a vote with a geometric equality where those with more at stake (the wealthiest) have a proportionately greater vote, see Arena 2012, 100–116.

[111] Contrast with the more democratic argument (rejected by Cicero) in which people being allowed to vote without being able to hold office is an artificial power because the people "are asked to give to others what they do not possess themselves" (*De rep.* 1.31.47). On these democratic claims that appear in Cicero, see Arena 2012, 119–24.

(*De rep.* 1.34.53; 1.40.62; 1.42.65; 1.43.67; *De rep.* 1.44.68; .3.33.45) until he, too, turns against the people (*De rep.* 1.44.68).

These convulsions suggest the importance of *auctoritas* in protecting against the abrogation of trust by which the negotiation of power can occur. Cicero's positioning of his *Republic* – written as Caesar was ascending to power, but set in 129 BCE in the midst of increasingly fractious, often violent, debates about land reform – points to the two most destabilizing approaches to property for Cicero.[112] One is the acquisition of property by an individual in an attempt to remove oneself from the partnership, including being able to maintain an army (*De off.* 1.8.25, 26). The historical references are to Marius, Sulla, Pompeius, and Caesar. Related to the grab for autocratic power are the extra-constitutional agreements of tribunes, consuls, and military leaders, such as between Clodius (made eligible as tribune by a farcical adoption by a pleb half his age) and the unofficial coalition of Caesar, Pompeius, and Crassus (which we refer to as the First Triumvirate) to parcel out control of money and territory for individual interest (*Sest.* 10.24).

But there is also what in Cicero's mind is the violation of trust with the confiscation and redistribution of property by the state, a concern famously demonstrated by Cicero's disingenuous interpretation and attack on P. Servilius Rullus' agrarian reform bill introduced at the beginning of Cicero's consulship (*Leg. agr.*; *De off.* 2.21.73; 2.22.78; 2.22.79 = theft; 2.23.83; 2.24.85; *De rep.* 1.44.68).[113] Private property, to recall, is not a natural right (since private property does not exist in nature); it arises out of social relationships in which we seek to provide for ourselves as well as for the common good. The violation of property is like a violation of natural law:

---

[112] On Cicero's correspondence regarding Caesar, see Brunt 1986. On Cicero's use of the setting in *On the republic* (and generally) to dramatize contemporaneous events, see Q. *fr.* 3.5.2; Vasaly, 1993; Baraz 2012. This breakdown of trust shapes the experience of Cicero's generation. See Brunt 1971b; 1988; Mitchell 1984, 32–34; Paterson 1985, 27.

[113] See Gabba 1979, 125–33 (Caesar and the Gracchi); Morstein-Marx (in Hammer [forthcoming], on Cicero and Rullus). On Cicero's responses to land reform generally, see Arena 2012, 220–43.

> For a man to take something from his neighbour and to profit by his neighbor's loss is more contrary to Nature than is death or poverty or pain or anything else that can affect either our person or our property. For, in the first place, injustice is fatal to social life and fellowship (*societas*) between man and man (*De off.* 3.5.21).

Cicero draws out the conclusion: "For, if we are so disposed that each, to gain some personal profit, will defraud or injure his neighbour, then those bonds of human society, which are most in accord with Nature's laws, must of necessity be broken (*Si enim sic erimus affecti, ut propter suum quisque emolumentum spoliet aut violet alterum, disrumpi necesse est, eam quae maxime est secundum naturam, humani generis societatem*)" (*De off.* 3.5.21). Attempts to redistribute property, thus, become a violent abrogation of the partnership, a violation of the context through the lawlessness of tribunes (*tribunicia licentia*) in which negotiations can occur.[114] The concern is both historical and personal for Cicero. The dialogue is set right after Tiberius Gracchus introduces a law in 133 BCE to limit holdings of public land that have been taken illegally by the wealthy, thus freeing land to be used by poorer farmers (see Introduction).[115] The events preceding the writing of *On the republic* included, most personally for Cicero, the state endorsed destruction and looting of Cicero's house in 58 BCE, orchestrated by Clodius (*Sest.* 24.54). Throughout his writings, Cicero would associate the violence of the final years of the Republic with attacks on property, including Marcus Antonius' threat in 44 BCE to send slaves to damage Cicero's house for his failure to attend a senate meeting (where Antonius had proposed an additional day of honor for Caesar in all public thanksgivings) (*Phil.* 1.5.12).

Both excessive accumulation and state redistribution of property violate the mutuality by which negotiations can occur (*De off.* 1.7.20; also 3.5.21, 23). They destroy harmony (*De off.* 3.5.22), equity

---

[114] See Gildenhard 2011, 177.
[115] The ideological argument for land reform advanced by Tiberius was that the *populus Romanus* should be given what belongs to them (see Arena 2012, 126–27).

(*De off.* 2.23.83; 2.24.85), and the trust (*fides*) of a partnership (*De off.* 2.22.78, 79; 3.5.23–24; .2.23.81–82). As Cicero writes, making clear the relationship between trust and property, "For there is nothing that upholds a government more powerfully than its credit; and it can have no credit, unless the payment of debts is enforced by law" (*De off.* 2.24.84).

Cicero associates the breakdown of *auctoritas* with the loss of power to stabilize, or, to recall Heinze, to ensure the validity of, negotiations of power.[116] The alternative to *auctoritas* is either stalemate or violence as parties seek or block power so that negotiations do not have to occur. It is in this context that Cicero describes how the "ruling power of the state, like a ball, is snatched from kings by tyrants, from tyrants by aristocrats or the people, and from them again by an oligarchical faction or a tyrant, so that no single form of government ever maintains itself very long" (*De rep.* 1.44.68). The problem of contemporary politics makes the case for Cicero. Cicero's *On the orator*, set in 91 BCE, just before the Social War and the violent proscriptions of Marius and then Sulla, but written as Cicero's own tongue was silenced by Pompeius and Caesar, is tinged with tragedy at the actions against the senate.[117] Cicero's mentor, Crassus, reacting to an assault on the senate by Marcius Philippus, refuses to be silenced by threats against him, asserting his historically constituted power to refute these acts (*De orat.* 3.1.4). Crassus dies of natural causes, avoiding the chaos of the Social War and the fate of the other participants in the dialogue who are executed, driven to suicide, exiled, or who betray others. For Cicero, the powerlessness of claims of *auctoritas* is tied to the loss of politics as a public thing. The Roman people are suppressed by violence (*Sest.* 58.105–8), the voice of the people replaced by hired crowds and mercenary gangs (*Phil.* 1.9.21–22), the senate "abolished," the courts "closed" (*De off.* 3.1.2), and the sentiment of affection replaced by fear (*De off.* 2.8.29). The *res publica*, as Cicero writes at one point, has been "lost forever"; all that remains is to "wait in fear of the most unspeakable crimes" to come

---

[116] Heinze 1925.
[117] For a helpful discussion of the historical context of Cicero's *De oratore*, see Fantham 2004b.

THE *SENATUS CONSULTUM ULTIMUM*

(*De off.* 2.8.29). *Auctoritas*, thus, is closely connected to the *potestas* of the people. Absent a partnership of power, and in particular the central role of *auctoritas* in giving context and continuity to those agreements, the public realm and the power of the people are unsustainable.[118]

THE *SENATUS CONSULTUM ULTIMUM*

The irony, and it is the irony upon which this chapter title has been built, is that the collapse of this public realm begins much earlier, in a tradition developed by the senate in the late Republic where there were not clear laws or procedures to deal with a perceived threat from its own citizens.[119] The decree (*senatus consultum ultimum*) was a statement by the senate advising (though the senate has no ability to compel or invest power in) a magistrate to do what was necessary to protect the *res publica*. Seemingly (and plausibly) a last ditch measure envisioned when the community faces an emergency that is *ultima necessitas* (i.e., most extreme necessity), it becomes a political weapon, adopted in 121 BCE to remove Gaius Gracchus from the protection of law, thus allowing for his assassination by Lucius Opimius, a private citizen (*De orat.* 2.30.132; also 2.31.134; 2.39.164–66; *Cat.* 1.3; *De off.* 1.22.76; *Brut.* 212). The decree is then used against the tribune Saturninus in 100 BCE (*Cat.* 1.4), the tribune Sulpicius in 88 BCE, the proconsul Lepidus in 77 BCE, and most harmfully (for Cicero's own career) to justify the execution of the Catilinarian conspirators without a public trial.[120] Cicero would defend the actions of private individuals to kill magistrates in the public interest:

---

[118] See also Garsten: the orator relied on "the republican institutions of controversy in which the practice of persuasion could be sustained" (2009, 166).

[119] See also Sallust *Cat.* 29.2–3 on the role of custom. On the questionable constitutional status of the decree, including whether the decree located sovereignty in the senate rather than the people, see Lintott 1999, 89–93.

[120] For Cicero's defense of his own actions, see *Cat.* In 63 BCE Cicero defends Rabirius for his possible involvement in the assassination of Saturninus under the *senatus consultum ultimum* issued in 100 BCE On the use of the *senatus consultum ultimum*, see Arena 2012, 200–20. On the symbolic association of Clodius' destruction of Cicero's house with aspirations to kingship, see Roller 2010, 135–36.

Milo against Clodius (*Mil.* 80) like Scipio Nasica, who as a private citizen led the senators in 133 BCE to murder Tiberius Gracchus (*Cat.* 1.3). The justification is to insure the immortality of Rome's rule (*Rab.* 12.33). The problem, using Cicero's own analysis, is that the *senatus consultum ultimum* violates the foundation of stability (even when it attempts to save that stability) by collapsing and subverting the relations of power. As Agamben suggests, the "state of exception" exists in this in-between realm: as a law, since it suspends law itself, which "cannot have legal form."[121] The measure raises more fundamentally the problem of what the thing is that is even being protected since there are no longer distinctions between private and public duties, private and public protections, justified or unjustified measures, and human and inhuman actions.[122] It is not just that Gaius is murdered; it is that the exception becomes a technique of political survival, effectively substituting the power of speech with the speechless force of arms. The range and expressions of power that constitute Cicero's public space become unhooked from any political and legal moorings, the law courts themselves "becoming sites for the enactment of illegal violence" by means of a different type of power, *potentia*, which in this case means illicit sway.[123] The irony is that the solution for this escalating violence could only be found in another longstanding Roman emergency measure: the dictator, now made permanent in the figure of the *princeps*. Rome's recourse to "the emptiness and standstill of law" created by the suspension of all law was to bestow complete power to an individual, and ultimately, to incorporate the state of exception into the *princeps*, an individual who resided both inside and outside the structure of government, whose power, as Augustus himself would write, was based more on *auctoritas* than *potestas* (see Introduction, 19–25).[124]

---

[121] Agamben 2005, 1. Lowrie 2007, 34–44, provides a helpful discussion of the insights as well as limits of Agamben's analysis.

[122] See Agamben 2005, 49: "What is a human praxis that is wholly delivered over to a juridical void?"

[123] Gildenhard 2011, 176, referencing *Pro Quinctio* and the *Verrines*.

[124] Agamben 2005, 48, 69. See also Lowrie who argues that when there was repeated pressure on the structure and traditions of government by repeated uses of the state of exception, "a sovereign emerged" (2007, 55).

The breakdown of *societas* marks the return to a pre-political (or barbaric) state ruled by *vis* (force) rather than *ius* (*Sest.* 36.69; 36.77; 39.84; 39.86; 42.91–92).[125] Cicero did not have to imagine a state of nature; he could watch history unfold. The irony is that he had a hand in that history. In his embrace of the notion that murder could be just if in defense of the safety of the state – both in his decision to execute the Catilinarian conspirators and in his defense of the assassination of Tiberius Gracchus by Nasica (*Tusc.* 4.23.51) – Cicero wed the interests of property to violence rather than law.

RHETORIC AND EMBODIED DISCOURSE

Cicero's discussion of rhetoric and the practice of oratory can be profitably read against the backdrop of this collapse of the public space of politics. Cicero's legacy in ancient times attaches him most fundamentally to his oratorical writings, both the speeches and treatises he wrote. It is only recently, though, that these works have attracted renewed attention in political thought, largely as a response to discursive democratic theory that argues that collective democratic life requires the forging of consensus through reasoned discussion. As Benhabib writes, "practical rationality" has a "culture-transcending validity claim" that has become "the collective and anonymous property of cultures, institutions, and traditions."[126] Oriented by these transcendent "collective rules, procedures, and practices that form a way of life," people, in coming together to exchange views, become aware of other claims, reflect on the reasons for their own claims, and seek a "coherent ordering" of priorities.[127] A hallmark of these discursive approaches is a concern with rooting out all forms of coercive power from political deliberation.[128] Rhetoric, thus, is rejected because it is seen as manipulating the unreasoned

---

[125] See Gildenhard 2011, 216–22 on Cicero's justifications for violence to protect the community.
[126] Benhabib 1996, 69.   [127] Benhabib 1996, 69, 71; also Chambers 1996, 229.
[128] Benhabib 1996, 68–9; Habermas 1996, 146–47; Young 1996, 122–23; Chambers 1996, 99.

emotions, smuggling coercive power back into politics.[129] Rhetoric appears not only to inhibit, but also to undermine, sound judgment.[130]

For some, Ciceronian rhetoric shares features with deliberative claims. Spence sees the development of rhetoric for Cicero as marking "the transition from chaos to order, and from passion to reason."[131] Connolly notes that Cicero put rhetoric forward as "rational and rationalized public discourse" that insists that expressions of authority must "agree with rules of logical argument and a learnable code of proper style."[132] This self-conscious styling, in which the orator is aware of (and responsive to) the traditions and circumstances that shape his and his audience's beliefs, moves rhetoric toward a Habermasian model of communicative competency in which the speaker recognizes "that his beliefs and practices are not fully his own, insofar as they are the products of historical tradition and, more confusingly, the perceptions of others."[133]

Garsten, too, argues that rhetoric can serve judgment. But he places Cicero's stance on rhetoric within the context of his adherence to the skeptical Academy in which one cannot have certain knowledge of truths. For Cicero "opinions contain the seeds of knowledge," which carries three implications for rhetoric. First, by receiving some instruction in philosophy, the orator would be able to craft arguments that were persuasive because they were able "to articulate the element of truth in it."[134] That is, the orator can lead people to better judgments through the persuasive appeal of truth. Second, through contending arguments one could arrive at probable truths based on the partials truths reflected in these different claims.[135] Out of the swirl of opinion, one might be able to acquire more certainty about the status of a particular claim. Finally, through the practice of advocacy, in which the orator must imagine his

---

[129] Benhabib 1996, 83. Young 1996, who argues on behalf of discursive democracy, makes an argument for the role of rhetoric.

[130] Manin 1987: Rousseau opposed rhetoric because the reasoned will of each person has already "deliberated within themselves" (346); Fontana, Nederman, and Remer 2004, 8.

[131] Spence 1988, 16.

[132] Connolly 2007, 67; Keith 2000, 15–16: rhetorical training connected to training in manliness.

[133] Connolly 2007, 144.   [134] Garsten 2009, 159.   [135] Garsten 2009, 160.

own party, the contending party, and the judge (*De orat.* 2.24.102), the orator can learn how "to imagine the point of view of each party," an almost Kantian (and Arendtian) sense of judgment as learning how to adopt and integrate different perspectives (and presumably different elements of truth).[136]

I am sympathetic to these attempts to connect public forms of rhetoric – legal, deliberative, and demonstrative (*De orat.* 3.28.109; 3.29.113) – to reason. For Cicero, the art of rhetoric is not to persuade; it is to persuade rightly. Each form of rhetoric has a particular end to which persuasion aims: the just in forensic speech, the honorable in epideictic speech, and the honorable and advantageous in deliberative speech (*De inv.* 2.4.12; 2.52.157–58). Achieving these ends requires knowledge. Cicero never separates oratory from considerations of different types of reasoning (e.g., by analogy, by deduction), considerations of mitigating and aggravating circumstances, and knowledge of law, history, *exempla*, and even philosophy (*De orat.* 1.5.17–18; 1.12.50–51; 1.14.60; *De inv.* 1.1.1).[137]

Philosophy was never far from Cicero's thoughts, either. As Nicgorski comments,

> Cicero's love and concern for philosophy is not at variance with the life of the statesman-orator but springs in large part from the latter and is to serve this life. The practical perspective is the basis for the elevation of the life of the statesman and persists in informing the judgment of all things by the statesman is Cicero's sure and solid ground. [138]

Gildenhard points to Cicero's "sophisticated use of theoretically informed concepts and categories, the forceful, indeed unconditional endorsement of a civic ethics, and the application of formal techniques that enable untraditional views."[139] But reason alone, shorn of emotion, is not enough. Philosophic knowledge imposes a logical strictness that,

---

[136] Garsten 2009, 161; see, for example, *De orat.* 2.44.185–86.
[137] See Horsfall 1996, 116 on the educational role of oratory for Cicero.
[138] Nicgorski 1984, 572–73; also Zetzel 2003, 130–33 on Roman oratory as a form of public philosophy; Gildenhard 2011 on philosophic aspects of Cicero's oratory.
[139] Gildenhard 2011, 10.

according to Cicero's Antonius, is incompatible with the thoughts and feeling of a community (*De orat.* 1.52.223–53.227; also 2.38.159). Someone like Cato the Younger, for example, about whom Cicero quips to Atticus that he speaks like he is in Plato's republic, emerges as unyielding and singularly ineffective in changing minds (*Att.* 2.1.8).

Philosophy might help the orator, but rhetoric was not the handmaiden to philosophy. In a striking statement, Cicero claims that the orator is a player who acts real life (*De orat.* 3.56.214), an image that recalls the theater more than the philosopher's garden. The orator, like the actor, is able to display emotions. For Cicero, nature has assigned a particular mark for each emotion – a vocal tone and a look (*De orat.* 3.57.216) – so that the orator is able to convey, and we are naturally affected by (*De orat.* 3.50.197; 3.59.223), rhetorical expressions. The difference is that where the actor simply mimics reality, the orator's words and actions correspond with the thoughts and emotions he wishes to convey (*De orat.* 3.59.222; *Orat.* 17.55). That is why the most influential orator is one who is aglow with passion (*De orat.* 2.45.190); the orator must wear the mark of his thought.[140]

The claim can be read, in part, as simply a statement of manipulation. The orator must understand "all the mental emotions, with which nature has endowed the human race" because "it is in calming or kindling the feelings of the audience that the full power and science of oratory are to be brought into play" (*De orat.* 1.5.17; also 1.14.60; 1.46.202; 1.51.223–52.224). It is these sorts of statements that concern the deliberative democrat and not without reason. Rhetoric can become the tool of unprincipled men who, in defending only particular interests or by inciting strife, threaten the survival of the community (e.g., *De inv.* 1.1.1; 1.4.5).

The power of oratory, properly practiced, is not that it can simply manipulate emotions; it is that it is able to communicate the intangible, affective bonds that are born in traditions, history, memory, and experience and that constitute a people's understanding of their relationship to each other. Cicero distinguishes between unreasoned impulse from the

---

[140] See Connolly 2007, 185–91.

passions and emotions and reasoned premeditation (*De inv.* 2.5.17–18). But reasoned premeditation is not contrary to human affection; it is action that is moved by an awareness of affective ties, such as glory, love, and friendship. The arousal of indignation, for example, derives from a sense that a wrong has been committed, either contrary to law or harmful to individuals (*De inv.* 1.53.101–2). Pity becomes possible when the orator gets the audience to contemplate its own weaknesses when looking at the misfortune of another (*De inv.* 1.55.106). The image here is not of pandering or of coercing, but of giving voice to, and amplifying, the goals of justice, honor, and utility that underlie the organization of communities (*De inv.* 1.2.2–3; 1.53.101).

The orator, unlike the philosopher, does not stand outside this network of associations, attitudes, and values but is embedded in the web of community life. The orator is on display (*De orat.* 2.46.192–93), the gaze of the community fixed upon him. The successful orator must employ the "language of everyday life, and the usage approved by the sense of the community," taking his cues, in turn, from the reactions of audience (*De orat.* 1.3.12). But more than that, the orator embodies the culture, making oratory into a "lived practice."[141] Like the legal advocate who must be seen to have impressed (or stamped) on him the feelings of his client (*De orat.* 2.45.189), so the political orator must embody the intangible, animating spirit of community life: the "thoughts, feelings, beliefs and hopes of his fellow-citizens" (*De orat.* 1.51.223). The orator is like the good citizen who serves as a "mirror" to others, "improving and examining himself continually, urging others to imitate him" (*De rep.* 2.42.69).[142] Discipline is required. The orator must learn to regulate his voice, expressions, and movements of the body in a particular way, creating a body that "speaks traditional authority," demonstrates self-control, and conveys its connection to the audience (*De orat.* 1.5.18; 1.34.156–57).[143] But this is not the learning and sheltered practice of arid rules; the orator must launch himself "into action, into the dust and uproar, into the camp and the fighting line of public debate" (*De orat.* 1.34.157). The orator "must have investigated and heard

---

[141] Cape 1997, 176; also Cape 1995. [142] See Skinner 1996, 69.
[143] Connolly 2007, 132.

and read and discussed and handled and debated the whole of the contents of the life of mankind" (*De orat.* 3.14.54). Cicero's language plays upon the affective foundation of community life: "[The orator] ought to feel the pulses of every class, time of life, and degree, and to taste the thoughts and feelings of those before whom he is pleading or intending to plead any cause (*Teneat oportet venas cuiusque generis, aetatis, ordinis, et eorum, apud quos aliquid aget, aut erit acturus, mentes sensusque degustet)*" (*De orat.* 1.52.223).

To draw on a recent image of communities as comprised of strangers, rhetoric plays an important role in giving expression to "the mind and heart, the judgement and the conviction" that accompanies the institutions and arrangements of a state (*Cluent.* 53.146).[144] For Cicero, what rhetoric does that reasoned deliberation cannot is arouse us, move us, and inspire action (and not just agreement).[145] The orator, thus, is present in the beginning, able to organize communities: "to gather scattered humanity into one place" and "to give shape to laws, tribunals, and civic rights" (*De orat.* 1.8.33; *De inv.* 1.2.2). It is only through rhetoric that new patterns of law and justice could be introduced. "Certainly only a speech at the same time powerful and entrancing could have induced one who had great physical strength to submit to justice without violence," to obey others, and even to sacrifice for others (*De inv.* 1.2.3).[146]

The orator is not just an actor, but also a painter of real life. As Cicero (following Simonides) says of Homer,

> it is his painting not his poetry that we see; what district, what shore, what spot in Greece, what aspect or form of combat, what marshalling

---

[144] Strangers: Allen 2004.
[145] Remer 1999, 55; also Vasaly 1993, 27. See, for example, *De optimo genere oratorum* 1.3: move an audience; 5.15: arouse an audience; *De orat.* 3.1.2: Crassus moved to go back to Rome; *De inv.* 2.52.157: honorable things entice and lead us.
[146] We can understand this claim as contrasting with Habermas' attempt to locate law as the motivational source of social integration. As Abizadeh points out, by rejecting any rhetorical force of the law, Habermas is left having to explain how discursive reason, as guided by an attempt to reach understanding, can motivate action (Abizadeh 2007, 457–59; see, for example, Habermas 1996, 27, 147).

of battle, what tugging at the oar, what movements of men, of animals has he not depicted so vividly that he has made us see, as we read, the things which he himself did not see? (*Tusc.* 5.39.114; e.g., *De orat.* 2.43.184: paint character).

Cicero's works never stray far from visualizing this intangibility. Even in one of his most abstract of works, *On laws*, Cicero has Atticus describe how "we are affected in some mysterious way by places about which cluster memories of those whom we love and admire" (*De leg.* 2.2.4). Odysseus, himself, as Cicero recalls, foregoes the promise of divinity so that he may "see" Ithaca once more (*De leg.* 2.1.3). And Atticus comments that in his visits to Athens he delights not only in the buildings and the art but also in the tombs of other great men where he can gaze and imagine the conversations that occurred (*De leg.* 2.2.4). When Cicero describes oratory as a power given by nature (*De inv.* 1.2.2), he is not disassociating rhetoric from reason; rather, he is pointing to the social dimension of reason that moves us and binds us to others.

There is no guarantee against misuse. But there are safeguards. First, the art of rhetoric is part of an art of living that requires the cultivation of both the knowledge and virtue of the orator. Second, oratory, unlike philosophy, "lies open to the view" (*De orat.* 1.3.12). Oratory is concerned, most of all, with public judgment, which for Cicero is the approval of an act by the assent of some publicly recognized, authoritative body: judges, assemblies, or special votes (*De inv.* 1.30.48). Finally, within this public forum, oratory is competitive: claims about the meaning of the past or how we are to respond to an event are open to dispute. The implication is twofold: the public space of politics relies on challenges to keep it from collapsing; and it requires the binding force of rhetoric to keep it from disintegrating. Gurd makes a suggestive connection between Cicero's conception of texts and politics, arguing that Cicero rejected the goal of the perfect text, seeing instead the importance of "collective revision as a means of fostering community."[147] What 91 and 55 BCE (when *On the orator* is set and written) have in

---

[147] Gurd 2012, 51.

common is that they mark the transition from rhetoric to force, from collective revision to dictating, as the binding mechanism of community life.[148]

THE IDEAL STATESMAN AND THE "DREAM OF SCIPIO"

One of the more curious aspects of Cicero's *On the republic* is his discussion of a type of leader: the *tutor* (guardian) or *procurator* (caretaker) who, through his words and actions, will be "truly the guide (*rector*) and pilot (*gubernator*) of a nation" (*De rep.* 2.29.51).[149] Coupled with the final and best preserved book of *On the republic*, "Scipio's Dream," the role of the guide is read frequently as Cicero's call for a strong leader – even a philosopher king or a Stoic sage – who can restore order to the Republic.[150] As one commentator writes, like Plato's philosopher king, Scipio's dream "teaches that it is not ruling, but only thinking, and understanding achieved through thinking, that satisfies the sovereign part of the

---

[148] See especially Fantham 2004b, 305–11. Lowrie argues that Cicero, in his discussion of Caesar (notably in the *Brutus*), shows how rhetoric is threatened as a mode of public presentation and competition (2008). Gildenhard contends that the *Tusculans* marks the claim by Cicero in which there is no longer a public space for oratory but must continue to be taught and practiced in private (2007, 152–55). Gurd suggests in a similar vein that Cicero fashions a "literary republic" in the wake of "the demise of the political public sphere" (2012, 49–50).

[149] Also *De rep.* 1.29.45; 1.34.52; 2.9.15; 5.3.5–4.6; *De leg.* 3.12.28.

[150] Philosopher king: Pöschl 1936, 117–19; Platonic sage: Lintott 1997, 83, n. 39; 84; 1999, 224–25; Stoic sage: Colish 1990, 1.95. The suggestion has been taken still further; namely, that Cicero's *On the republic* was an anticipation of, and became the blueprint for, Augustus' founding of the principate. See Reitzenstein 1917 (Cicero as advocate of Augustus); Meyer 1922, 177–91; renewed by Stevenson 2005, with qualifications (Cicero as advocate of Pompeius). Radford goes so far as to describe Cicero as the "prophet of the Principate" (2002, 71; see also 66). Lind reviews the debate and concludes that there is no connection (1986, 94–5). Wirszubski (1968, 87; 1954, 9) and Galinsky (1996, 74) also reject the connection. Richard Heinze 1924 sees this as an ideal type of statesman, reflective of the traditional senatorial aristocratic values. There is large agreement that the statesman reflects these romanticized aristocratic values as able to stand above party and forge consensus. See How 1930, 41; Wheeler 1952: "enlightened elder statesman"; Ferrary 1984; 1995, 65; Habicht 1990, 42–43, referencing *Att.* 7.3.2; *De leg* 3.14; Powell 2001, 31; Fantham 2004b, 311–19; Asmis 2005, 378.

human soul."[151] Even more strongly (and more contrary to everything we know about Cicero), Pangle contends, "The dream teaches that the sooner the gods allow one to flee from this political life to that other contemplative life, the better."[152] Nicgorski suggests, "Cicero knew and accepted the classical teaching that philosophy for its own sake – search and contemplation – was the highest human activity."[153] From this perspective, the ideal statesman is the philosopher who must compromise the pursuit of truth on behalf of politics, but who will be rewarded with "a heavenly afterlife in the company of the immortal gods."[154]

The "Dream" is styled after Plato's "Myth of Er," making the parallel to Plato enticing to pursue.[155] Furthermore, statements by Cicero about the importance of the philosophic life are not difficult to find (*Tusc.* 1.19.44–45; 1.26.64–65; 1.30.74–1.31.76; 5.23.66, 105, 111, 115; *De rep.* 6.19.20; *De orat.* 1.3.9; 3.17.64; *De fin.* 4.7.17–18). The "Dream," too, suggests this elevation of the eternal over the earthly. As Africanus lifts Scipio into the air, they look back toward the ever-shrinking earth, which now appears insignificant in its place in the cosmos (*De rep.* 6.19.20). Scipio Aemilianus is instructed to scorn the earthly allure of honor and fame (*De rep.* 6.19.20), "For what fame can you gain from the speech of men," asks Africanus the Elder, "or what glory that is worth the seeking?" (*De rep.* 6.19.20). Viewed against the backdrop of the eternal movement of the universe and the divinity of the soul, to be concerned with the testimony of others is to embrace that which is mortal and, consequently, fleeting (*De rep.* 6.19.20; 6.21.23). Furthermore, to vest oneself in earthly things is to relinquish one's happiness to unpredictable and uncontrollable fortune.

But the privileging of philosophic contemplation is incomplete as a characterization of Cicero's ideal. At the very least, Cicero's "Dream" leaves us in a different place than does Plato's "Myth." Perfection, for Plato, lies in the pursuit of the philosophic life that accords a decidedly secondary status to politics. Cicero reverses the hierarchy: The statesman

---

[151] Pangle 1998, 245–46.   [152] Pangle 1998, 246.   [153] Nicgorski 1984, 566.
[154] Pangle 1998, 246; also Penwill 1994, 74: "the ultimate in legitimating ideology."
[155] See Long 1995a. Specific mention is made by Cicero to Er in the beginning of Book 6 (*De rep.* 6.3.3).

not only most resembles the divine in his ability to make a world, but also the political life is superior to the philosophic because it affects more people (*De rep.* 1.7.12; 1.2.3). The statesman, as an orator, emerges as a heroic figure who is able, through eloquence, to "[civilize] men into citizens."[156]

Furthermore, none of Cicero's examples of such ideal statesmen (excepting perhaps the unstated example of himself) would qualify as philosophers or *sapientes* (*De off.* 3.4.16).[157] This leader is good, wise, and skillful (*De rep.* 2.29.51), characteristics that Cicero finds in actual historical examples: Publius Scipio, Gaius Laelius, Lucius Philus, Fabius Maximus, and Manius Curius. They were men with talent, who then cultivated these talents through "the union of experience in the management of great affairs with the study and mastery of those other arts" (*De rep.* 3.3.5). The statesman is a specialist, as Cicero (by way of Antonius) elaborates in *On the orator*: "But if we were inquiring who is he that has devoted his experience, knowledge and enthusiasm to the guidance of the State, I should define him thus: 'Whoever knows and uses everything by which the advantage of a State is secured and developed, is the man to be deemed the helmsman (*rector*) of the State, and the originator (*auctor*) of national policy'" (*De orat.* 1.48.211). However arduous might be the labor, there is no dark cave into which Cicero's statesman (in contrast with Plato's philosopher-king) must be dragged.[158] Rather, the statesman (and Cicero, who thought about casting himself as Scipio, is our best example here [*Q. fr.* 3.5.1–2]), had to be forced into exile from what he would characterize as "the light" of the political world (*Fam.* 2.12.2) and the company of others (*Phil.* 2.44.113).

---

[156] Remer 1999, 54.

[157] See Baraz's recent study that explores Cicero's joining of rhetoric and philosophy in an attempt to provide a conceptual foundation for the renewal of the Republic (2012). Gildenhard suggests a parallel hinted at by Cicero in the "Dream" between Romulus' apotheosis and what should be his. In this reading Cicero pulls back from deification, satisfied with traditional republican immortality (2011, 378–80; also 388–89).

[158] Hamilton, for example, equates Cicero's statesman with Plato's philosopher-king who must "return down to the dark and delusional realm of politics" (2013, 55).

Scipio is directed back to the toils of earthly life where, with his knowledge of the movement of the universe, he is told that care (*cura*) for the country's health is the best exercise of one's eternal spirit (*De rep.* 6.26.29). That is, politics may prepare one for one's departure from earth. But what is less clear, particularly if we take Plato as our cue, is how the philosophic life prepares one for the return to earth. Cicero, it seems, is picking up the strands of an earlier argument in which Tubero makes a defense – seemingly a failed one – of the political relevance of abstract inquiry into the nature of the universe (*De rep.* 1.17.26–29). Inquiry into one does not diminish the other. The statesman does not return with contempt for the traditions and institutions of contemporary society. He does not seek to wipe the "beautiful painting" of the Republic clean (*De rep.* 5.1.2). He does not subordinate political to philosophic goals but is enjoined to preserve, aid, and enlarge the commonwealth (*De rep.* 6.13.13). The statesman does not even stand alone but, as Cicero's language suggests, is a partner in the collective voyage of the ship who must be recognized by, and acts on behalf of, another party.[159] So how does the philosophic life – our contemplation of what "lies outside" – prepare us for our return to earth (*De rep.* 6.26.29)?

TUSCULAN DISPUTATIONS: PHILOSOPHY, CARE, AND THE LIMITS OF STOICISM

We can find an answer to the political role of philosophy in an unexpected place: the *Tusculan disputations* (45 BCE).[160] The immediate

---

[159] Need to recognize: *De rep.* 2.29.51; *Phil.* 2.44.113; Agent: *De rep.* 5.6.8; Gaius *Inst.* 1.19; Cic. *De orat.* 1.58.249; Gaius *Inst.* 4.82, also of tutor; see Fantham 2004b, 316; Guide: *De inv.* 1.34.58; *De div.* 1.14.24.

[160] Cicero considers the *Tusculans* to be one of his great achievements, though scholars have not always agreed. See Douglas 1965, 148; Schofield 2002, 102. Reassessments of the political importance of the *Tusculans* can be found in Gildenhard 2007; Hammer 2008. Gildenhard reads the *Tusculans* as the use of philosophy as a political critique of Caesar and as an effort to educate a "new generation of Roman aristocrats" (2007, 69). Baraz 2012, 93–95 sees the consolatory motives as separate from, and secondary to, the philosophic motives. I am arguing that these motivations are actually related.

occasion for Cicero's writing of the *Tusculans* is the death of his only and beloved daughter, Tullia, in childbirth.[161] Admitting that he had thought about "quit[ting] this world" out of grief for her (*Tusc.* 1.31.76), and returning for the first time to his villa in Tusculum where his daughter had died, Cicero turns in the *Tusculans* to philosophy as therapy: "Assuredly there is an art of healing the soul (*animi medicina*) – I mean philosophy, whose aid must be sought not, as in bodily diseases, outside ourselves, and we must use our utmost endeavor, with all our resources and strength, to have the power to be ourselves our own physicians" (*Tusc.* 3.3.6; see also *De nat. deor.* 1.4.9). The proper treatment for such longing, a remedy that Cicero seeks in (and through the writing of) the *Tusculans*, is to realize "how trivial, contemptible and absolutely insignificant is the object of his desire, how easily it can either be secured from elsewhere or in another way, or else wholly put out of mind" (*Tusc.* 4.35.74; also 4.38.83).[162] As Reydams-Schils states, in what is the generally accepted (and I will suggest incomplete) reading of the *Tusculans*, "the expositions on death, pain, and suffering in the *Tusculanae Disputationes* appear to have no room at all for either Tullia or his sorrow."[163] Cicero recites the Stoic mantra that in the passing of earthly things, nothing unexpected has happened, nothing evil has occurred, and nothing eternal has been lost (see *Tusc.* 3.23.55; 3.29.72; 3.32.77; 4.28.60).

The words emerge as an elaboration of "Scipio's Dream" in which the world appears insignificant from the perspective of the heavens. Philosophy lifts us outside our bodies so that we may see the insignificance of the things we cling to. Through philosophy, we are able to "embrace the whole earth in our survey, its situation, shape, and circumference, as well as both the districts that are habitable and those again that are left wholly uncultivated because of the violence of cold or heat" (*Tusc.* 1.20.45; also 5.25.71). We are able to "[leave] our bodies behind"

---

[161] See *Att.* 12.28.2; *Att.* 12.18.1; *Att.* 12.15; *Tusc.* 3.31.76; 4.29.63; 5.2.5.

[162] On ancient models of philosophy as therapy, see Nussbaum 1994; Erskine 1997; Sorabji 2000; Schofield 2002. For the most thorough treatment of the Stoic aspects of the *Tusculans*, see Graver 2002.

[163] Reydams-Schils 2005, 120.

and finally experience the happiness of the soul freed from envy and desire (*Tusc.* 1.19.44; also *De rep.* 6.26.29). Philosophy empowers one with what Cicero at one point refers to as the foremost virtue, *fortitudo*, which compels one to assume a spirit "that will make you despise and count as nothing all that can fall to the lot of men" (*Tusc.* 3.17.36; *De rep.* 1.2.2). The goal is the Stoic ideal of impassivity (*apatheia*), the complete absence of passions, or of *securitas*, "freedom from care" (*De amic.* 13.47).[164] The *Tusculans* becomes Cicero's therapeutic exercise, his attempt to free himself from earthly longing.[165]

Cicero would reveal in a series of letters to Atticus his unrelieved – even unmanly – grief following the death of Tullia, a sorrow unmitigated by what in Cicero's mind are cold Stoic syllogisms (*Att.* 12.13.1; 12.14.3; 12.15; 12.18.1; also *De orat.* 3.18.66).[166] Cicero even sounds a defiant, anti-Stoic note: "As to my literary consolation of myself, I am not dissatisfied with what it achieved. I reduced the outward show of grief; grief itself I could not reduce, and would not if I could" (*Att.* 12.28.2).[167] In one of his most heartfelt writings, Cicero remarks that philosophy was not placed in the cities of men to teach us "freedom from care" (*securitas*) (*De amic.* 13.47). "In appearance it is indeed an alluring thing," but, as Cicero continues, "in reality often to be shunned" (*De amic.* 13.47). Freedom from care meant indifference to the Republic, a point Cicero

---

[164] See Graver 2002, 83. Although one should be free from passions, one may still have good emotions like "benevolence, mercy, sympathy, and the sober joys of friendship" (Colish 1990 1.42; see Sen. *Ep.* 23.2; DL 7.116: joy, caution, hope). Nussbaum sees Cicero as adopting the Stoic line that one should not have passions, or even "the approved variety of Stoic *erôs*" (2000, 188).

[165] See Hamilton 2013, 51–55, on *securitas* as a sense of elimination (of negative *curae* as well as oneself from politics so that one may practice caring for oneself). Hamilton ends up with Cicero as a Stoic and the *Tusculans* as an unproblematic Stoic exercise.

[166] Unmanly: *Att.* 12.38a.1; 12.40.2; also *Tusc.* 2.21.48; 2.24.58; syllogisms: *Tusc.* 2.18.42; 4.28.61; *De fin.* 4.5–7). Mansfield overstates Cicero's own confidence in the *Tusculans* that "a man," as one who displays fortitude, "is in truth all that he ought to be" (1996, 33).

[167] As Gildenhard notes in discussing Cicero's *De doma sua*, he "turns his overpowering grief into a manifestation of *virtus* by wedding human vulnerability to social commitment" (2011, 37).

frequently returned to in his denunciation of Epicurean and Stoic withdrawal from political life.

Like in "Scipio's Dream," the original flight from earth directs us back to human affairs (*Tusc.* 5.25.70; 5.25.72; compare to *De rep.* 6.24.26; 6.26.28).[168] "As the wise man gazing upon this spectacle and looks upward or rather looks round upon all the parts and regions of the universe, with what calmness of soul he turns again to reflect upon what is in man and touches him more nearly" (*Tusc.* 5.25.71). What touches us is virtue, that which is most divine in us and directs us to perform our duties on earth and to the care of the public realm (*ad rem publicam tuendam*) (*Tusc.* 5.25.72; also *Tusc.* 1.14.32; 4.23.51). *Tueri* means to look at or watch over with the purpose of protecting the object.

What is worth caring for? Cicero provides us with some indication when he compares the Republic to a painting. What Cicero seems to express so much fondness for are the tangible, perishable artifacts of earthly life: music (*Tusc.* 1.25.62), poetry (*Tusc.* 5.4.10), places (*De leg.* 2.1.3; *Orat.* 34.120), monuments (*De leg.* 2.1.3; 2.2.4), government (*Tusc.* 4.1.1; 5.2.5), and laws (*Tusc.* 1.14.31). Cicero notes the paradox. If on our death we may ascend to our "proper home and permanent abode" (*De rep.* 6.26.29), Cicero asks, what is it that we fear will be lost with the disintegration of the commonwealth? Why, too, if "the creature which has existed has become nothing," Cicero inquires, "should Camillus have felt pain, had he thought that some 350 years after his lifetime the present troubles would come, and why should I feel pain if I should think that some nation would get possession of our city at a date 10,000 years hence" (*Tusc.* 1.37.90)?

Cicero provides, in part, a Stoic explanation for our attraction. The answer lies in how the soul longs for immortality (*Tusc.* 5.25.70). Contemplating the gods and feeling our "union with the divine mind" in turn "kindles the desire for attaining an immortality that resembles theirs" (*Tusc.* 5.25.70). One is prompted by nature to love that which is unchangeable and eternal, which is virtue. The Stoics redefine *eros* from a form of desire to a type of friendship. Love is an "effort toward

---

[168] Also compare movements of the universe: *De rep.* 6.17.17–18.19 and *Tusc.* 5.24.69.

friendliness due to visible beauty" (DL 7.130). One is attracted to the "flower of virtue" (DL 7.130) with the aim that the beloved achieve virtue, becoming a reciprocated love or friendship.[169]

But Cicero's sense of attraction in the *Tusculans* goes well beyond anything Stoic. Although the immediate occasion for the *Tusculans* is the death of his daughter, he is also mourning the loss of the Republic under the dictatorship of Caesar. In fact, the opening lines reference his new freedom from (*liberatus*) "the toils of advocacy and from my senatorial duties," a claim of *liberatus* that plays off of, and could not be more opposite, what is meant by republican *libertas* (*Tusc.* 1.1.1).[170] For Cicero, however, the wonder of the soul – its ability to discover and understand – is continually expressed as a set of earthly accomplishments. To demonstrate the relationship of the soul to its earthly artifacts, Cicero traces the course of human discovery and progress: the "great men" who first cultivated the earth to provide "an ordered way of life"; those who, under "civilizing and refining guidance," developed the "finer arts"; those who discovered how to combine musical sounds; those who inquired into the movement of the heavens; those who composed poetry; and those who established justice (*Tusc.* 1.25.62).[171] Cicero's ode to philosophy celebrates the earthly accomplishments of the soul: "You have given birth to cities, you have called scattered human beings into the bond of social life, you have united them first of all in joint habitations, next in wedlock, then in the ties of common literature and speech, you have discovered law, you have been the teacher of morality and order" (*Tusc.* 5.2.5). He further credits the "genius" of the Roman people with the establishment through laws and usage of the "direction and organization" of the *res publica* (*Tusc.* 4.1.1). It is not just that the tangible artifacts of the world express elements of the immortal soul; it is also that one's longing for immortality is fostered in the tangibility and particularity of the things one has come to know, things that tie the individual to the past and carry one's own imprint into the future: cultivated lands (*Tusc.* 1.20.45; also *Tusc.* 1.25.62; 1.28.68, 69); homes

---

[169] Schofield 1991, 34–35; also Vogt 2008, 159.   [170] See Gildenhard 2007, 92.
[171] See also *Tusc.* 5.4.10: Pythagoras enriched public and private life of Magna Graecia with "the most excellent institutions and arts."

and property (*De leg.* 2.1.3; 2.2.4; *Orat.* 34.120)[172]; monuments (*De leg.* 2.1.3; 2.2.4); and cities (*De leg.* 2.2.4; 2.1.3). In fact, Cicero suggests that a "deeply rooted presentiment of future ages" is felt most strongly "in men of the greatest genius and loftiest spirit" (*Tusc.* 1.14.33).

The true nature of things – that which might otherwise be invisible to us – appears to us as beauty. For Cicero, an appreciation of beauty derives from an understanding of how that object fits into a more universal order of reasons and causes.[173] One might discern beauty in objects that fulfill a function or purpose: the functional interdependence of the human body, for example. The sensation of beauty can be an organic part of the item: the delight one feels at the smell of a rose. And beauty can lie in objects that represent order, whether the order is created by nature (e.g., the planets) or purposively developed by humans (e.g., agriculture).[174] What distinguishes us from animals, as Connolly remarks, is an aesthetic sensibility "that allows men to perceive the beautiful, the ordered, and the tasteful."[175] It is as beauty that the tangibility and particularity of the things that comprise our world find expression, the true nature of things recognized (*Tusc.* 1.20.47; 1.28.68; 4.13.31), and the fleeting greatness of humankind given some permanence (*Tusc.* 4.2.3).[176]

The problem of Cicero's age is a failure of discernment. Gildenhard argues that in the *Tusculans* Cicero identifies how civil war and dictatorship "must be ascribed to deficits in (Roman) *culture*, or, more specifically, *education*."[177] The comparison of the Republic to a once beautiful painting is a statement both of its perishability and of the need for those who can see and care for its beauty. The inability to recognize and care for the Republic as a work of art appears in another image in the *Tusculans*: people no longer strive after a distinctive likeness of virtue, one that is formed like a statue from a solid substance, but are attracted instead to a vague outline

---

[172] Treggiari points out how Roman law accounted for the sentiments connected to property (1979, 63).
[173] Davies 1971, 163.
[174] On a discussion of these categories of beauty in Cicero, see Davies 1971.
[175] Connolly 2007, 172. See also *De off.*1.35.126; 1.41.146.
[176] See especially Arendt 1968, 208–18.   [177] Gildenhard 2007, 74.

(*Tusc.* 3.2.3).[178] The desire for immortality can blind one so that one is unable to distinguish true glory from "a copy" (*Tusc.* 3.2.4). The copy, the desire for public reputation, is a "counterfeit" that "mars the fair beauty of true honour" (*Tusc.* 3.2.4). People not only choose the wrong thing to admire, but are so driven by the desire for gain and lust of pleasures that they value nothing other than satisfying their own limitless pleasures (*Tusc.* 3.2.4). No longer bound by love or affection to care for that which is immortal, people, instead, view the world as a source of plunder (*Tusc.* 5.25.72: contrast to philosopher).

Philosophy, for Cicero, teaches something more than to shed these attachments; it is intimately tied to cultivation, a sense of preserving and tending to something that is the source of the word "culture" (*colere* = to cultivate).[179] As Hannah Arendt writes, "culture indicates that the public realm, which is rendered politically secure by men of action, offers its space of display to those things whose essence it is to appear and to be beautiful."[180] Like the farmer cultivating the land, philosophers "sow the seed of laws, regulations and public policy" that must then be tended (*Tusc.* 1.14.31). Poems and songs in praise of virtuous men bestow beauty and permanence to greatness (*Tusc.* 4.2.3). Orations, too, and Cicero is our best example here, recall the places, monuments, and institutions that connect past and present and guide future generations.[181] Even when not directly oriented to politics, the life of the mind instills a life of cultured refinement, an aspect of *humanitas* in which one exercises and recognizes genius (*Tusc.* 5.23.66; 5.36.105).

Such cultivation, suggested by Cicero's use of *humanitas* to also include notions of a shared humanity and values, connects us to others.[182] In a famous image, Cicero compares the life of humans to a spectacle in which "the best type of free-born men" view the games, seeking neither "applause nor gain," but coming "for the sake of the

---

[178] Compare to *De rep.* 5.1.2: Republic retains only the form (*verbo*) but not the substance (*vero*).
[179] Gildenhard suggests that philosophy appears as "a means of maintaining public service after Caesar's clampdown on republican politics" (2007, 80).
[180] Arendt 1968, 218. [181] See Vasaly 1993. See also Remer 1999, 41–42.
[182] See Gildenhard 2011, 201–16 for an extended discussion of Cicero's expansion of the conceptual range of the term.

spectacle" to watch "what was done and how it was done" (*Tusc.* 5.3.9; also *De off.* 3.10.42: "stadium of life"). The philosopher teaches how to admire the things of this world without regard to the self (*Tusc.* 5.3.9).[183] But even in contemplation, or in the life of retirement that is captured in the well-known phrase *cum dignitate otium*, the philosopher is ever mindful of the *res publica*.[184] I agree with Wirszubski that *otium* is not an embrace of either "contemplative quietism or disreputable hedonism" but is a "way of life" that is inseparable from the *res publica*.[185] The tranquility of which Cicero speaks derives not from the contemplation of a Platonic "city in speech," but from the satisfaction of having cared for a city made beautiful by its tangibility.[186]

Habinek notes the association of knowledge with discernment, seeing it as an aristocratic attempt to maintain "separation from the common people" based on taste rather than birth.[187] But Cicero locates the recognition of beauty, as a mode of intercourse with the world, in a community sensibility.[188] As Cicero writes in *On the orator*, "Everybody is able to discriminate between what is right and what wrong in matters of art and proportion by a sort of subconscious instinct, without having any theory of art or proportion of their own" (*De orat.* 3.50.195). Such a discriminating sense occurs not only for "pictures and statues," but also "in judging the rhythms and pronunciations of words, because these are rooted deep in the community sensibility" (*in communibus ... sensibus*)

---

[183] Also Arendt 1968, 219.
[184] See *Sest.* 98; *Fam.* 1.9.21; *De orat.* 1.1; also *De off.* 2.2.6. Interpretations differ about the meaning of this phrase: *otium* as public tranquility and as leisure amidst a political career: Wirszubski 1954; Frede 1989, 81–84; and Nederman 2000c, 25; *otium* as contemplative life that Cicero must elevate/ reconcile with the active life when forced into retirement: Boyancé 1941; Balsdon 1960; and Laidlaw 1968; *otium* as evolving term as Cicero seeks to justify his actions with his own sense of duty: Bringmann 1971 and Colish 1990, 77–78.
[185] Wirszubski 1954, 11.
[186] "City in speech" is the well-known term employed by Strauss to describe the Platonic republic (1964, 121). For a discussion of this relationship between Cicero and Plato, see Nicgorski 1991, 234–38.
[187] Habinek 1998, 129; also 126; also Gildenhard 2007, 185: "what Cicero wants to create in and through the *Tusculans* is a new ruling elite consisting of philosopher kings who are as enlightened as Plato's, but not as disaffected from politics."
[188] See also Arendt 1968, 213–15; 1982, 63; McClure 1997.

(*De orat.* 3.50.195, trans. modified). That is not to say that the crowd always gets it right and is able to recognize beauty (*Tusc.* 5.36.103–4). That is the problem of the age; there are no longer public *mores* that instill sensitivity and care for the things of this world. The *Tusculans* is a response to that loss of sensitivity. It is less a method of detachment than a practice of discernment by which one learns how to care for this world.

COSMOPOLITANISM AND EMPIRE

In his own exile, Cicero finds solace in Socrates' claim to be "a native and citizen of the whole world" (*Tusc.* 5.37.108). Narducci suggests that by "withdrawing into the shrine of conscience, the wise man celebrates his victory over the outside world and his exalted independence from every form of submission."[189] The result is not isolation but a sort of depoliticized cosmopolitanism: "The *res publica*, the ideal of one's country and of the *civis* who within it fulfills himself, loses substance and meaning, while the alternative model of a *déraciné* cosmopolitanism takes on a dignity which was previously unthinkable."[190]

The reference is to Cicero's seeming embrace of a form of Stoic cosmopolitanism in which, as Cicero writes, a "whole universe as one *civitas*" transcends conventional political boundaries and status distinctions (*De leg.* 1.7.23; also *De leg.* 1.5.16; 1.11.32; 1.23.61; *De nat. deor.* 2.31.78–79; 2.62.154; *De rep.* 3.22.33; also Sen. *De ot.*). For the Stoics, reason prompts us to enter into relationships with each other in connections that become more universal over time (also see Chapt. 6, 286–90, 315–20 and Chapt. 8, 375–79). Cicero, like the Stoics, conceives of expanding concentric circles of differentiated human bonds: husband and wife, parents and children, relations of extended kin, political communities, and universal citizenship (*De off.* 1.17.53–54; 3.17.69;

---

[189] Narducci 1997, 71. See also Plasberg 1926, 8–9; Clarke 1956, 58, 60; Süss 1966, 68–69; Alfonsi 1961, 182–85; Wood 1988, 58; Colish 1990, 1.141; Douglas 1995, 208, 213, 214, 215 (from political concerns to introverted concerns).

[190] Narducci 1997, 71. Critical assessments of Cicero's cosmopolitanism are made by Nussbaum 1996; 1997; 2000; Pangle 1998.

De fin. 2.14.45; 3.19.64). The highest bond for the Stoics, that of universal citizenship, derives from our proximity through reason to the gods.

Cicero's attachments were never Zeno of Citium's or Diogenes the Cynic's, who is credited with the phrase "citizen of the world." We may be citizens of the world, but for Cicero we are born for our country (*De off.* 1.7.22), our closest connection is citizenship (*De off.* 1.17.53, 57, 58; *De leg.* 2.2.5), we have a greater obligation to those nearest us (*De off.* 1.14.45; 1.17.54–55; 1.17.57), and we occupy a world comprised of both status (*De off.* 1.13.41) and ethnic differences (*Font.* 21; *Flac.* 24–26).[191] Cicero never flinched from empire, either. For Cicero, rule (*imperium*) is not only natural (*De leg.* 3.1.3), but it is also the duty of the leaders to strive "by whatever means they can, in peace or in war, to advance the state in power, in territory, and in revenues" (*De off.* 2.24.85; also celebration of Pompeius in *Cat.* 3.26; *De off.* 1.12.38: war pursued for glory).[192] It is perhaps not surprising that Cicero would say these words. It speaks not only to a pervasive Roman ideology, but also punctuates the mechanism that financed the ascent of Cicero's own equestrian class. Banking, trade, agriculture, provincial administration, and tax collection (by the infamous *publicani*) were all ways to wealth.[193]

If Cicero does not offer us a particularly sanguine, or in Nussbaum's view, a logically coherent, vision of cosmopolitanism[194], he does offer us

---

[191] Nussbaum suggests that for Cicero "nationality in and of itself supplies no sufficient moral argument for a difference of duties" (2000, 202). True to some extent: Cicero differentiates duties within the *res publica*, but there is no attachment greater for Cicero than the *res publica*. Nederman also notes the patriotic attachments by Cicero to the country (2000c, 20).

[192] See Gabba 1979, 120–22, who identifies echoes of Panaetius' defense of imperialism in Cicero. Also Brunt 1978.

[193] Badian downplays the economic motive for empire before the conquest of Asia, though recognizes the financial rewards, particularly those that accrue to the equestrians after their enfranchisement (1967, 18–28, 57–59). Contrarily, see Rose 1995. Cicero notes that revenues are the sinews of the *res publica* (*De Imperio Cn. Pompei* 7.17). The most important revenues come from Asia (*De Imperio Cn. Pompei* 6.14; 7.19). Also, see Cicero's defense of the *publicani* (*De Imperio Cn. Pompei* 7.17–18).

[194] Nussbaum 2000.

a cautionary one informed by the transformation of the Roman republic into a global empire. The Stoic notion of world citizenship was an ideal community divorced from relations of power, both in their acceptance of power relations as given and unimportant to the virtue of the soul and in their articulation of a notion of community that recognized only the power of reason. In contrast, Cicero asks how does one constitute relations between different peoples in a world of power differentials?[195] And in contrast to a Greek conception of global relations as premised on might (as characterized by Thucydides) in which justice extended no further than the borders of the *polis*, Cicero provides a more nuanced conception of both the different relations and the limits of global power.[196]

One type of power is essentially a globalized version of the patron-client relationships that corresponded, though in a much more limited way than once assumed, to aspects of Rome's domestic politics (see Introduction). These power relationships are personal, hierarchical, and reciprocal. The patron, like Rome in its early years for Cicero, acts as a protectorate in the best interests of the clients (*De off.* 2.8.27), providing security, goods, or even access to Roman culture and entertainment. The client, in turn, returns the kindness (*De off.* 1.15.47–48; *Cat.* 4.22), both by recognizing the authority of the patron and by providing revenue and manpower.[197] For Cicero, one must weigh the worthiness of the object of one's benevolence, taking into consideration the individual's moral character, attitude toward the benefactor, intimacy of relations to the benefactor, common social ties, and services to one's interests (*De off.* 1.14.45). A whole range of relationships of *beneficium* becomes

---

[195] The Stoic acceptance of material conditions is noted by Nussbaum 2000, 190–91.
[196] The profoundly undemocratic aspects of the global dimension of Athens' conception of its *polis* is missed when Euben calls for a "parallel polis with its Greek resonance" as a necessary condition "for the revival and extension of democratic politics" (2001, 282). On the importance of Cicero's extension of justice in global relations, see Nederman 1993; Kinsbury and Straumann 2009. On the flexibility of Rome's administration of conquered territories, including their ability to work through existing institutions, see Lintott 1993. For discussions of Roman integration, see Mouritsen 1998; Jehne and Pfeilschifter (ed.). 2007; Ando 2000 and 2011 (extending beyond republican times); Roselaar (ed.) 2012.
[197] See Champion in Hammer (forthcoming).

possible, extending from alliances to grants of citizenship to groups or individuals in return for service (e.g., *Balb.* 2.6).[198]

The distance, the personal relationships, and the small number of people actually in charge in these relationships made the temptations for corruption irresistible. Patron-client relations, which were always transactional, became vicious and exploitative when no longer bound by any limits, such as notions of duty or propriety (see *De off.* 2.8.27; *De Imperio Cn. Pompei* 5.13). It is in this context that Steel is correct in suggesting that Cicero "is operating, in the speeches, with a concept of empire which depends not on territory, but on the power wielded by individuals, and that this in turn means that the problems which arise in the running of empire can be presented as the result of personal failings rather than endemic to the structures of government: questions of morality rather than administration" (see *De off.* 2.8.28–29; *De Imperio Cn. Pompei* 13.36–39; 14.40–41).[199]

A second type of arrangement, and one meant to mitigate the exploitative excesses that arise from power differentials, is a more legalistic one in which both parties have rights and duties that can be adjudicated. This approach, which has its origins in a Roman conception of the law of nations, is most extensively outlined in *On duties* where Cicero writes that the rights of war (*iura belli*) must be observed (*De off.* 1.11.34): that the only reason for going to war "is that we may live in peace unharmed" (*De off.* 1.11.35), that war can only follow once an "official demand for satisfaction has been submitted" (*De off.* 1.11.36), that protection must be ensured to those who lay down their arms (*De off.* 1.11.35), and that any promises to foreign peoples must be kept (*De off.* 1.13.39).[200] This approach is also the basis of the *leges de repetundis*, which were civil laws aimed at controlling the corruption and excesses of provincial administrators. These laws (and the extortion courts comprised of juries

---

[198] See Steel 2001, 96–97, 108–12. On foreign client relations, see Badian 1958; Lintott 1993, 32–36, 168–74.

[199] Steel 2001, 4. See Edwards 1993, 4; also Kaster 1997, 17–18 on the operation of *pudor* as resting on face-to-face interactions.

[200] On just war and empire in Cicero, see Brunt 1978, 175–78; Pangle 1998, 255–61. On the importance of *On Duties* for moral theories of international justice, see Nussbaum 2000, 176–81.

of knights) themselves became the mechanism of corruption; a lucrative form of extortion in its own right as well as a forum for political vendettas.

A final approach involves wholesale incorporation through broad grants of citizenship, such as the near doubling of the number of Roman citizens with the inclusion of the Italians after the Social War. Power is nominally equal, spanning vast geographic areas and ethnic groups. In its sheer breadth it begins to approximate in actuality the world citizenship that the Stoics imagine philosophically. Nussbaum, in frustration with Cicero's anti-cosmopolitan sentiment that relations in the Republic are different from "other more distant associations," questions the validity of his argument "since already Rome had complex civic and political ties with many parts of the world."[201] I think that experience is precisely what haunts him: for Cicero the extension of citizenship, like the expansion of empire, made citizenship into an abstraction, altering the partnership of power that gave cohesion to the *res publica*. The problem of cohesion for Cicero is not the problem of the integration of different groups with different histories and orientations. Rome's founding legend, after all, is premised on unity being forged from difference (see Chapt. 5, 239–42). The problem of cohesion is, instead, a problem of power.

For Cicero, globalism comprises two images of power.[202] The power of the *res publica* is political, exemplified in the public space of Forum. It is a notion of power as a binding force that is built on, and organized by, affective relationships that are fostered by recognition: recognition of origins, of reciprocal obligations, of generosity, and of merit. The power of empire, however, is organized around *vis*, or might, exemplified in triumphal conquests by powerful military leaders (*Cat.* 4.22–23). The administration of empire required extended commands that concentrated power in the hands of military leaders (*De Imperio Cn. Pompei* 11.31–32). But even without conceiving of globalism in military terms, the vastness of global citizenship altered the affective basis of power. The extension of citizenship, as Rose notes, had revealed to Cicero the problem of "disaffected masses," whose loyalty could be purchased,

---

[201] Nussbaum 2000, 204.   [202] Steel 2001, 168–70.

whose quiescence could be enforced by fear, and whose supremacy in bestowing honors could be ignored (*De off.* 2.8.28).[203]

In developing her own version of cosmopolitanism, Nussbaum ends up constructing a world essentially devoid of power relations, not just power as command, but the more challenging notion of an affective basis to power – of what holds us together. Rejecting the sense of duty that derives from intimacy, Nussbaum suggests that families are just "arrangements" that, more than anything else, are useful in organizing care and resources.[204] For Cicero, though, the bonds of family derive from intimacy. The point for Cicero is that the more abstractly we understand our relations to each other, the less meaningful those relations become.[205]

Sandel, in responding to the abstractness of global citizenship, suggests at one point, "The hope for self-government lies not in relocating sovereignty but in dispersing it. The most promising alternative to the sovereign state is not a one-world community based on the solidarity of humankind, but a multiplicity of communities and political bodies – some more, some less extensive than nations – among which sovereignty is diffused."[206] The potential problem of dispersed autonomy, as Cicero's analysis suggests, is how it displaces, or replaces, one type of power with another. As the foundation of power shifts, from local affections to dispersed attachments, from the Forum to the provinces, from concrete citizenship to abstract fellowship, the risk is that politics, as public ownership, gives way to the public realm as a private possession.

---

[203] Rose 1995, 388.   [204] Nussbaum 2000, 203.
[205] Critiques of this notion of cosmopolitanism are developed by Sandel 1996, 341–49; Euben 2001.
[206] Sandel 1996, 345.

2 LUCRETIUS: THE POETICS OF POWER

Lucretius (Titus Lucretius Carus, ca 99 – ca 55 BCE), in *On the nature of things* (*De rerum natura*), provides a dramatically different perspective on Roman politics. He looks outside Rome: to nature, generally, and the Greek Epicurus, specifically, to provide a philosophic language for his Roman audience (see 1.136–39; 5.336–37).[1] But Epicureanism, as it enjoined the rational person to avoid political involvement (unless an emergency demanded it), appears as less an answer to, and more a flight from, politics. Politics appears as a "dangerous business founded on a false view of how security," the principle human motivation for the Epicurean "is to be attained."[2] One's most important social relationships do not lie in politics but at most in friendship. As Gillespie and Hardie write in their introduction to *The Cambridge Companion to Lucretius*, the Epicurean message of Lucretius "is that one should withdraw from political life to pursue the philosophical goal of happiness: the small circle of friends, rather than the larger structures of city and state, is the best context for this."[3] Lucretius' language seems in keeping with

---

[1] On Lucretius' relationship to Greek philosophy, poetry, and history, see Bayet 1954; Clay 1983, 13–53; Schrijvers 1996; Gottschalk 1996; Sedley 1998; Warren 2007.
[2] Schofield 2005, 441. For a helpful and balanced discussion of Epicurus' attitude toward politics, see Fowler 1997, 123–26.
[3] Gillespie and Hardie 2007, 9.

this sense of detachment when he characterizes the philosopher as "possess[ing] lofty sanctuaries serene," able to "look down upon others" while both new men and the nobility scramble to reach the summit of riches and power (2.7–14).[4] The sweetness of the philosophic life stands in sharp contrast to the toil, pain, and futility of this struggle. What the philosopher sees that those clamoring for power do not is that nature directs "that pain be removed away out of the body, and that the mind, kept away from care and fear, enjoy a feeling of delight" (2.18–19).

It may not be surprising that Epicurus' emphasis on withdrawal from public life would resonate with individuals who, with the rise of the Hellenistic kings in the late fourth and third centuries BCE, no longer had outlets in public life.[5] But the translation of Epicureanism into a Roman context was not so easy for two reasons. First, Roman life was steeped in politics. We get a taste from Cicero of how politics was not just a highly competitive path to respect, fame, and power, but also an expectation of the elite and the primary source of public identity. This expectation had certainly diminished a little in the last decades of the Republic, as members of the elite opted out of the increasingly dangerous business of politics. But we have to wait another half century until Rome's version of Hellenistic kings, *principes*, would make withdrawal from political life an enticing alternative. Second, the Romans had a long-standing distrust of the corrupting influence of philosophers: Epicureans were not included in the Athenian embassy of philosophers sent to Rome in 155 BCE (see Introduction, 2). Cicero frequently criticized Epicureanism for its hedonism. And Lucretius probably was not particularly influential in his time (though important for Virgil). Yet, those associating themselves with Epicureanism played a role in Roman politics, counting among their ranks those who fought for and then against Caesar (and included Caesar).[6]

---

[4] On the interpretation of this passage, see especially Fowler 1997, 134–35. Jope sees Lucretius' poem as designed to teach this sort of philosophic detachment (1989, 20; also Colman 2012). I take up this issue later. Translations for Lucretius are from Rouse 1992 unless otherwise noted.

[5] See discussions by Festugière 1956, 9–17; Foucault 1990b, 3.37–68; 1997, 207–51.

[6] See Momigliano 1941, 151–55 (though many of the associations are difficult to verify); Classen 1968, 114; Bourne 1977, 418; Minyard 1985, 18. Bourne argues that the

How well we can reconstruct the different philosophic genealogies of political actors, or map Epicureanism onto the complexities of political allegiances, is difficult to say. Epicureanism certainly did not translate into a static or consistent political program. The Epicureans demonstrated a remarkable ability to adapt to different environments, including their coexistence with Hellenistic kings around the Mediterranean.[7] But in a Roman context Epicureanism did not merely translate into coexistence either. Cassius invokes Epicureanism in expressing his opposition to Caesar (Cic. *Fam.* 15.19.2–216.2 [Bailey]; 12.12.1–387.1 [Bailey]). And we can discern lingering Roman sensibilities in Lucretius' own allusion to the crisis of Roman society that both unsettles his soul and calls Memmius, his addressee, into politics (1.40–43). How we contextualize the crisis depends on the date we assign to the poem, which ranges from 55 BCE to 49 BCE. The threat to peace may be a sense of foreboding (if dated 52 BCE or before), the imminent outbreak of war (if dated 50 BCE), or Civil War itself (if dated 49 BCE).[8] The closer to the Civil War we situate the poem, the more urgent its appeal. But the date of the poem does not change the power of the message, particularly when set against the decades of strife that formed the backdrop to Lucretius' own upbringing: Marius and Cinna's retaking of Rome, the proscriptions of Sulla, and the struggle for power among Pompeius, Crassus, and Julius Caesar. Despite the continual admonition that nothing is permanent, Lucretius' work is, in Momigliano's words,

---

Epicurean notion of justice, as well as the emphasis on prudence and utility, actually allows for much greater political flexibility to negotiate and accommodate, as evidenced in Caesar (1977, 424). Cicero seems to suggest the influence of Epicureanism in Caesar's camp (*Fam.* 7.12). Caesar, for example, employs Epicureanism in his debate with Cato (Sal. *Cat.* 51.20).

[7] See Norman DeWitt 1954, 183–84. On the relationship to, and possible sympathy for, kingship, see Fowler 1997, 129–30. At a minimum, governments may be important to Epicureans in providing the security necessary for pursuing a good life (Epic. *KD* 6).

[8] On the sense of emergency in Lucretius, see Green 1942, 59; Bignone 1945, 2.114–21; Hutchinson 2001, 150–52. On dating the poem, see Sandbach 1940 (late 55/54 BCE); Bailey 1947, I.3–4; Herrmann 1956 (dating between 52 and 50); Giancotti 1959, 147–48 (dating 62 BCE, references to Catiline conspiracy); Fowler 1997, 121 (55/54 BCE); Sedley 1998, 1 (around 54 BCE); and recent challenges that move the poem closer to the outbreak of the Civil War by Canfora 1993, 49–51 and Hutchinson 2001.

"a vigorous invitation to work and fight for high ideas," a legacy that would excite, at least momentarily, a defense of the Roman republic and liberty in its dying days.[9]

Momigliano likely overstates the case, but he pushes us to ask what in Lucretius' poem could be so politically exciting. Lucretius certainly does not build a political system, or even provide a particularly viable vision of political life. And it is decidedly unclear what the "high ideas" would be. What Lucretius does offer is a poetics of power that resists what he sees as false claims to authority. Of power, Lucretius announces Epicurus as the first who dared to stand against the despotic grip of religion (1.66–67). Emboldened, Lucretius dismantles the meaningfulness or usefulness of categories associated with the *mos maiorum* (the custom of the ancestors): notably, *pietas* and *imperium*. But through his poetry he also seeks to restore "a feeling (*sensus*) of delight" (see 2.19, trans. modified), which he does by relocating the authority of sensation from society to nature and from social convention to individual apprehension. The effect is to give power and authority, terms that are exceedingly rich in Latin, a basis in nature and in turn a foundation in our senses.

EPICURUS

Of Lucretius we know surprisingly little. We do not know his birthplace, his politics, his social status, or even exactly when he dies. Attempts to read Lucretius' personality or psychological state (including possible insanity) from his poem come across as methodologically ill-conceived at best.[10] We are not sure when *De rerum natura* was composed. And specific references in his poem to Roman politics are

---

[9] Momigliano 1941, 157; see also Bignone 1945, 2.84: "ha sentito l'aura della nuova democrazia" (he has felt the breath of the new democracy).

[10] See list in Classen 1986, vii. The evidence of insanity or depression, which begins with St. Jerome, is questioned in Kinsey 1964, 115–30. The reader will note substantial footnoting for this section on Epicurus. My interest is to direct the interested reader to a substantial, and frequently quite technical, discussion of specific aspects of Epicurus' philosophy.

illusive.[11] What we do know about Lucretius places him as a brilliant interpreter of Epicurus (341–270 BCE), a Greek philosopher and founder of schools around the Mediterranean, including in Athens. A brief discussion of Epicurus' philosophy and some of the technical language associated with his philosophy will help us understand the foundation of Lucretius' thought, though in no way does it capture the brilliance, power, or novelty of the poem.[12]

Atomism and the constituents of pleasure

The close connection between physics and philosophy in Epicurean thought may strike contemporary ears as odd, or oddly familiar. Writing in a tradition of atomism, dating back to Leucippus (fifth century) and Democritus (ca 460–370 BCE), Epicurus posits a non-teleological, kinetic, infinite universe comprised of two elements: solids, which account for substance, and the void, which allows for motion (Epic. *Her.* 39–40; Lucr. 1.335–39, 420, 995–97).[13] Solids consist of atoms (*atomoi*, sing. *atomos*, literally uncuttable) that are indivisible, unalterable, and material (Epic. *Her.* 40–41; Lucr. 1.526–39, 600–614). Atoms join together into compounds and in turn dissolve back into the universe. The formation of compounds is not governed by any larger design or purpose but by a virtually infinite array of chance encounters, capable of producing different worlds. Everything is not possible; rather, the stability of a

---

[11] See generally Schiesaro 2007b, 53–54; Conti 1982, 31–33, 44–45 n.8.
[12] Clay provides a sustained and, in my mind, persuasive critique of the notion that Lucretius, as a Roman poet (and thus seen as lacking philosophic training or acuity) had to be essentially copying a Greek source (1983, 26–35). The idea of Lucretius as translator shows up in Bailey's contention that there must have been a Greek poem that served as the source of his work (1949, 11). Sedley 1998 argues for the influence of an Epicurean source, *De natura (Peri physeos)*, of which only fragments remain. To avoid repetition, I have included references from Lucretius that parallel claims by Epicurus. I have focused the discussion on Epicurus' words (to the extent that we can know them with any certainty) more than subsequent interpretations and commentary on Epicurus, since Lucretius seems most influenced by Epicurus. That Lucretius was probably not an active member of Epicurean circles, engaged in contemporaneous philosophical debates, is argued by Sedley 1989, 62–93.
[13] On the relationship of Epicurus to the early atomists, see Asmis 1984, 227–350.

compound is related to the compatibility of the properties of atoms (Epic. Her. 42, 45). Any compound is itself a "dynamic entity": atoms change their relationship to each other, atoms are lost, and other atoms may become part of the compound through collisions (nutrition being one example, disease another).[14] Compounds inevitably dissolve as the bonds that hold them together are loosened or broken apart by the impact of other atoms (Lucr. 1.223–24).

Humans are one such compound, consisting of a spirit (*psychē* = *anima*) that is enclosed within a body and dispersed throughout the entire organism. Both the spirit and the body are corporeal (as they are composed of atoms) (*Her.* 63; Lucr. 3.161–62; 5.132–33). The atoms that comprise the spirit consist of a mixture of breath (*pneuma*), heat (Lucretius will add air), and an unnamed component of highly mobile atoms, none of which by themselves can account for life but only as inseparably mixed with each other and diffused throughout the entire body (Epic. Her. 63; Lucr. 2.178–79; 2.262–87, 937–43; 3.136–46; 3.231–35; 3.241–245).[15] Absent the spirit, the body has no ability to act or respond; it cannot move, breathe, perceive, or feel (Epic. Her. 64; Lucr. 5.559–60: comparison to earth and air). Absent the body, spirit would simply disperse back into the universe.

The spirit is intertwined with the uniquely human, deliberative element of the soul (*to logikon* = *consilium*), also referred to as the mind (*nous* = *animus/mens*). The spirit and soul create one nature. The way in which one knows, experiences, and thinks, just like the way one senses, is defined by the physical contact of atoms from other compounds with our own atoms. There are two types of interactions. There are feelings (*pathē* = *sensus*), which for Epicurus are confined to an awareness of pleasure (*hēdonē* = *voluptas*) and pain (*algēdōn* = *dolor*) and tell us what naturally to choose and avoid (DL 10.34; Men. 129).[16] And there are perceptions (*aisthēseis* = *sensus*), which occur when an image or presentation (*phantasia* = *visio*) produced by emanations – a flow of atoms given

---

[14] Long 1986, 39. See Vlastos for a discussion of the mathematics of Epicurus' atomism (1986).
[15] See Kerferd 1971, 89–96; Gottschalk 1996, 232.
[16] See Glidden 1979, 297–98; Asmis 1984, 97; Konstan 2008, 12.

off by the surface of an object – penetrates our sense organs. Where *pathē* consist of our awareness of our sensory condition of pleasure and pain, *aisthēseis* describe what one perceives: not a discordant sound or comforting heat, but a person talking or the sun shining.[17] To think does not require that the object be immediately present; rather, thinking occurs by way of emanations given off by the memory of previous sense-experiences (*Her.* 46–48).[18]

One's *pathē*, or feelings of pleasure and pain, provide the criteria by which one orients one's actions. The beginning (*archē*) and end (*telos*) of the happy life (*eudaimonia*), Epicurus writes, is the life of pleasure (*hēdonē*) (*Men.* 128–29; also 122), a desire that can be observed from birth (*Men.* 129). Epicurus is speaking within a Greek tradition in which *eudaimonia* requires that one's life is lacking in nothing: complete, invulnerable, and self-sufficient. And he is starting from the argument of Aristippus, a student of Socrates and founder of the School of Cyrene, that pleasure is the only good. But he departs from the Cyrenaic hedonism of enjoying the pleasures of the moment. Although pleasure is the satisfaction of desires, Epicurus associates that pleasure with freedom from bodily pain (*aponia = dolorem abesse*) and from mental anguish (*ataraxia = pax*) (*Men.* 131; also *Men.* 128; *KD* 3; Lucr. 2.17–19).[19] That negative formulation tells us a great deal about Epicurean pleasure. It has less to do with "kinetic" pleasures and active enjoyment that involve the active stimulation of bodily feelings since these activities can lead to the type of mental disturbances that ultimately makes us unhappy (DL 10.123–37; *Men.* 132).[20] More emphasis is placed on static or

---

[17] Glidden 1979, 305. Lucretius uses *sensus* to refer to both feeling (*pathos*) and perception (*aisthēsis*). As Glidden notes, "The purely physiological meaning of *sensus* and *sentire* puts into focus the use of these expressions elsewhere in the poem to denote perceptions and corporeal feeling. It is the physiological process which is the necessary prerequisite for perception. This same process provides both the necessary and sufficient conditions for feeling" (Glidden 1979, 170).

[18] See Asmis 1984, 89.

[19] On Lucretius' language for *ataraxia*, see Cook 1994, 196–97.

[20] Mitsis provides a useful discussion of the distinction between dispositional accounts of pleasure and views of pleasure as a "special type of private episode or feeling" (1988, 19–22). Cicero depicts the Epicureans as practicing self-indulgence (*De leg.* 1.13.39).

katastematic pleasures, which involve the absence of pain and the return of particles to a settled state (see DL 10.136–37). As Epicurus writes, "For what produces the pleasant life is not continuous drinking and parties or pederasty or womanizing or the enjoyment of fish and the other dishes of an expensive table, but sober reasoning which tracks down the causes of every choice and avoidance, and which banishes the opinions that beset souls with the greatest confusion" (*Men.* 131). A life governed by pleasure is one characterized by the stable, harmonious motions of the soul, content with what nature provides.

Consciousness and the philosophic life

In Epicurus' atomistic account, the contours of human life seem almost indistinguishable from the material forces that constitute the infinite universe. To the extent that we take our ethical cues from "feelings" that are no different from "the way in which other animals experience corporeal sensations," it is unclear what if any role there is for human choice.[21] How can we choose to do one thing rather than another since life, sensation, and consciousness are all explicable as material processes in which atoms strike the *psychē*? De Lacy, for example, has argued that if we follow the logic of Epicurus' argument in which we are to see ourselves as nothing more than impersonal processes and forces, then the goal of Epicureanism is to "remove the need for making any choices at all."[22] That is, for De Lacy we become truly a part of nature and follow our nature when we become unconscious, when our actions replicate impersonal processes and forces. To what extent then can we understand the operation of consciousness in Epicurean thought?

If by consciousness one means an aspect of the mind that knows something that the senses do not, then that is absent in Epicurus. The Epicureans specifically critique the Platonists for positing a faculty of reason that is not, itself, dependent on sense perceptions. The mind does not have "any special insight."[23] For Epicurus, the foundation of

---

[21] Glidden 1979, 302.   [22] De Lacy 1957, 118.
[23] Asmis 1984, 162. Asmis corrects a frequent interpretation that *epaisthēsis* refers to something like a "mental interpretation or understanding, as opposed to a purely

knowledge, including of human beings and human interactions, stems from an understanding of the material structure of the universe. The method of comprehension – how we know what we know – is empirical. Only what we perceive by the senses, or grasp by mental apprehension, is true (*Her.* 62; also *KD* 23; *Her.* 38; Lucr. 1.304, 422–25, 699–700; 4.478–80, 483–85). Any apprehension not made by the sense organs must be verified by our perceptual organs, either directly by presentations (to verify general opinions) or through reasoning that is based on perceptions (to verify scientific opinions about what may not be apparent).[24]

But Epicurus' discussion of the mental processes by which one comes to form opinions about the world suggests a critical role – both good and bad – for undetermined consciousness. Through opinion, which Epicurus characterizes as a motion that comes from within the individual rather than from the presentation (see SE *Adv. math.* 7.211–16; *KD* 24)[25], one provides features that are different from what is contained in the presentation. Opinions can be confirmed when those features appear or follow logically. For example, I form an opinion that a friend is approaching from the distance, filling in features I cannot yet see. That opinion may be confirmed as the person approaches, or may be found to be false. Or those opinions can mislead us. We can, for example, have empty (*kenos*) emotions, disturbances that have no relationship to anything in

---

    irrational sensory response" (1984, 162). For this traditional interpretation, see Bailey 1928, 420; DeWitt 1954, 205; Long 1971, 130, n. 11. See Epic. *Her.* 52; DL 10.32.

[24] Bailey sees scientific reasoning as a special cognitive process, one that he associates with *epibolē tēs dianoias*, or applications of the mind. Bailey argues that: (1) an *epibolē tēs dianoias* is a "mental apprehension of an image perceived directly by the mind without the intervention of the senses" (1928, 567–68); (2) the object of an *epibolē tēs dianoias* is a concept which is "'intuitively' apprehended by the attentive mind" (1928, 570); and (3) scientific reasoning occurs by way of a linking of these intuitively correct concepts (1928, 570–71). I do not see applications of the mind as a special case of cognition referring to insights into scientific truth but as describing the way in which the mind engages in perceptions, just like the senses. The one is not more real; all perceptions for Epicurus (and Lucretius) show what is real (helpful here is Asmis 1984, 85–91).

[25] Asmis 1984, 146.

the world but lead us to make incorrect evaluations or arrive at incorrect opinions of what is to be desired and feared.[26]

The problem of politics and society is that it teaches empty opinions by alienating the individual from one's sensual relationship to the physical universe, including each other. Religion, for example, encourages the individual to be terrified of natural phenomena, to look to the gods to explain affairs, and to live in terror about what happens after one dies. So too society teaches that happiness lies in the pursuit of one's bodily desires, a pursuit that results in one embarking on an endless and fruitless quest to sate desires that have no natural limits. As Epicurus notes, "The flesh places the limits of pleasure at infinity, and needs an infinite time to bring it about" (Epic. *KD* 20). Even our fear of death arises from a misconception of our sensual nature: We are finite beings who, on our death, will dissipate back into the universe.

But consciousness, by way of philosophy, is also the mechanism by which one transforms oneself, a transformation explicable by way of Epicurean physics.[27] Tranquility lies in one's possession of stable motions of the soul, motions that accord with Epicurus' principles and the laws of nature (*Her.* 82.1–3). By grasping particular principles with precision, holding them in memory, assimilating them to one's actions, and practicing them, one can form firm and replicable pathways of atomic motions. Epicurus' student, thus, could work his or her way

---

[26] Konstan thus contrasts the Epicurean view of the emotions, which are simply awarenesses of physiological processes, with Aristotle's notion of the emotions, which have a cognitive element and correspond to our appraisal of particular objects in the world (2008, 24–25; see also Glidden 1979, 298).

[27] Marković 2008, 24–29. Furley has argued that the weight of atoms offers resistance to blows so that the weight of the atoms of the *psychē* "would prevent them from being knocked into totally new and unrecognizable patterns by the atoms of entering *simulacra*; it would ensure some continuity of behavior in the *psychē*" (Furley 1967, 231). In terms of changing these patterns, two arguments have been offered. In part, the notion of "atomic swerve," in which atoms sometimes veer off course, disrupts the inherited motions of the *psychē* and allows for new ones to be established (Furley 1967, 234; see Lucr. 2.289–93). But this seems too random to be the basis of an ethical theory that depends on the transformation of the soul. More important are the ways in which the individual can work on the self. Kleve, for example, has argued for a notion of the soul that is "able to cope with and utilize the forces of the swerves," which he says is more frequent than suggested by Furley (Kleve 1986, 127).

up through his extensive and difficult writings and lectures. The student could begin by internalizing the *tetrapharmakos*, the "fourfold remedy" that "God presents no fears, death no worries. And while what is good is readily attainable, what is terrible is readily endurable" (Philodemus, *Against the Sophists* 4.9–15, trans. Long and Sedley), gradually incorporating more of Epicurus' *doxai*, and finally being ready to receive the more complex lessons of his lectures.

This process of assimilation and meditation is not, as De Lacy has interpreted it, a form of subjectivism, in which we can only be interpreters of our experience if we separate ourselves from the objectivity of physical processes.[28] To know oneself is to know the physical processes that comprise the self (Epic. *Pyth.* 85–88; *KD* 12; *Her.* 37, 78, 80). Part of that knowledge is simply the recognition of the material sensations of pleasure and pain. The knowledge, though, is also a form of prudence (*phronēsis*), the most important virtue for Epicurus (*Men.* 132), which allows one to make judgments about the long-term consequences of particular choices and to recognize one's "ability to substitute or eliminate" how one satisfies a desire.[29] Through prudence, the mind determines whether avoiding or desiring something can lead to the tranquility associated with *hēdonē*, the absence of pain or freedom from mental disturbance (see *Her.* 83; *Pyth.* 85, 116). The task of philosophy is to form us so that the conscious pursuit of pleasure "governs and unifies all of our rational choices and gives a structure to our lives as a whole."[30]

Although Epicurus speaks within a tradition that associates happiness with reason that is traceable back to Plato, Epicurus departs from this Platonic heritage in a significant way. Whereas Plato places the purity of happiness in the supra-sensual intelligible realm that can only be grasped by the intellect, Epicurus locates pleasure in the sensations. Desires are

---

[28] De Lacy 1957, 120.
[29] Mitsis 1988, 50. Epicurus shares with both Plato and Aristotle the tie between virtue and prudence (*phronēsis*). For Aristotle, all virtues require prudence, though virtues have different noncognitive roots. For Plato and the Stoics, there is a much more rationalist account of virtues. All virtues are instances of prudence. For the Stoics, for example, cognitive and affective states are the same. See Mitsis 1988, 71.
[30] Mitsis 1988, 15.

not made subject to reason; it is by way of reason that one brings oneself, and one's affective states, into conformity with *pathē*, one's natural desires.³¹ Even a concept (*prolēpsis* = *notitia* or *anticipatio*) does not correspond to some *eidos*, but is simply a word (like true and false, or just and unjust) that is formed by memories and logical extensions of perceptions (see *Her.* 50–51).³² Concepts are neither intuitions that would be "immediately understood by his companions" nor the end point of investigation, but "standards of reference" that correspond to words by which one conducts further investigation.³³ Through this relentless stripping away of empty abstractions and a continual testing of thought against experience and reason, Epicurean philosophy is meant to return us to our senses, to "return to the self,"³⁴ so that we can make choices that better accord with nature.³⁵

The ideal here is the sage, the paradigm of self-sufficiency and invulnerability. Through philosophy the sage attains a life that is complete, lacking in nothing, and free from care. Through contemplation the sage internalizes the laws of nature, recognizing him or herself as part of the material ebb and flow of the universe. Through the cultivation of prudence, the sage learns how to live according to what nature provides, knowing that by satisfying one's natural desires, one's life lacks nothing because pleasures have natural limits (*KD* 18, 20). The sage also recognizes the "ability to substitute or eliminate" how one satisfies a desire, rendering him or her less vulnerable to changing circumstances and fully

---

[31] Furley 1986; 1982, 607–8 casts doubt on whether Epicurus and Lucretius are responding to the Stoics.

[32] See Furley 1989, 165; Asmis 1984, 61–66; Long 1971, 119–22.

[33] Intuitions: Cole 1967, 72, 76–77; end points of investigation: Thury 1987, 283, following Bailey 1928, 245–46; standards of reference: Asmis 1984, 100; also Barnes 1996, 210. Compare to Epictetus where *prolēpsis* bears more the sense of an innate, but not formulated or applied, intuition that serves as the basis of our opinions (2.11.3–18; 2.17.9).

[34] Hadot 1995, 103.

[35] I disagree with Nussbaum, as well, who argues that Epicurus is a "foe of nature and nature's limits" and who praises "a bold transgression of limit" (1994, 215; also 1989, 325). The way that I read the passages that Nussbaum cites (including Lucretius 1.70–79), Epicurus is embracing the transgression of limits, such as ignorance, that we place on ourselves.

happy with what nature has provided.³⁶ The sage realizes that what makes us most vulnerable to circumstances beyond our control is time, which is not a thing in itself like matter or space but an accident that arises from motion and rest. The sage, thus, neither projects forward to some uncertain future nor backward to a past that cannot be changed, but exists in the complete happiness of the present. In the practice of death (Epic. *Men.* 124–27), the Epicurean mode of overcoming temporality, the sage achieves independence (*autarkeia*) by freeing him or herself from contingencies or circumstances that one cannot control, including (or especially) one's own mortality (*Men.* 124–25, 130, 133). The sage becomes like an Epicurean god: tranquil, detached, and unaffected by time.³⁷

Community

The Epicurean is detached but not necessarily alone. It is by way of reason and in our relationships with others – a progressive discovery through practice and the experiments of an active mind – that we are able to see and communicate our relationship to something larger. Language itself is shaped by society into an instrument of utility and self-expression from its origin in physiological reactions to pain and pleasure (Epic. *Her.* 75–76).³⁸ The ability to see and define oneself from the

---

[36] Mitsis 1988, 50.

[37] See Diano 1974, 210–52; Puliga 1983, 247–49, 254, 260; Nussbaum 1989, 325–27; Jufresa 1996; Erler 2002, 170–72; also Diog. Oen. fr. 56 (Smith). Gods as models of life, see Lorca 1996, 862–63.

[38] There are two overlapping issues here: one is whether the first sounds constitute language; the second is whether there is a natural correspondence between things and their names. Those who do not see a natural relationship of words to things include De Lacy 1939, 87–88; Chilton 1962, 161–62; Schrijvers 1974 (only initial sounds, not language, is natural; no relationship of words and things); Glidden 1979, 302–3; Barnes 1996. Those suggesting that these first sounds constitute language, and that there is a direct correspondence between things and their names, include Vlastos 1946, 52–54 (initial sounds convey experience of phenomena); Cole 1967, 61–62, 72–74 (words as shared intuitions); Long 1971, 121–28 (correspondence between things and names mediated by *prolēpseis*); Campbell 2003, 16, 292 (correspondence between words and things; initial sounds are words that get crafted into language).

perspective of and as a part of a more universal nature has profound implications, as well: gone are socially erected hierarchies and in their place is an egalitarian ethos. The archetypical social relationship is friendship: individuals who voluntarily enter and get something out of interactions with each other (see *Vat.* 23, 28, 34, 39, 52, 56, 61, 66, 78; *KD* 28).[39] Even more radically, Epicurus' Garden of philosophers was famous for mixing together all groups: men, women, and slaves. And for good reason: In Epicureanism we are all equal as material beings, subject to the same forces, and sharing the same sensations.[40]

What Epicurus provides is a philosophic starting point for thinking, or rethinking, one's relationship to traditional modes of social interactions and institutions. The gods recede into relative irrelevance; social and political forms are emptied of authority except as they contribute to happiness; the striving for power looks like pointless vanity against the backdrop of an infinite universe; and the instruments of social control are rendered superfluous. In short, avoid politics (*KD* 14, 40; *Vat.* 58), with some wiggle room for times of emergency (*KD* 7; Plut. *De tranq.* 465f-466a; Sen. *De ot.* 3.2 = Epic. fr. 9 Usener; Cic. *De rep.* 1.6.10).

As a vision of community, Epicurus offers the here-and-now: pleasures that are experienced, ones that momentarily unite, but ones that cannot be projected easily into the future. Epicurean politics ultimately finds its limit in temporality. If the goal is to transcend time, then one's relationship to politics is one of detachment that one can achieve by retreating or rebelling. But one cannot attach oneself by building. We will find this same tension played out in Lucretius, now placed in a highly charged Roman political context in which detachment is not readily available as a viable cultural alternative. Lucretius, more than Epicurus (or what we know of Epicurus), gestures toward these Roman

---

[39] See, for example, Festugière 1956, 37–42 on spiritual community. On Epicurus' notion of friendship, see Mitsis 1988, 98–128; Konstan 1996; Schofield 2005, 437.

[40] Farrington provides perhaps the most vigorous defense of Epicurus' opposition to previous aristocratic and oligarchic theories (including Plato's) that distinguished between a ruling class and the common people, but a theory aimed at the "enlightenment" of all people (Farrington 1966 (orig. 1939), 171). On the organization of Epicurus' school, see Farrington 1967, 122–27.

attachments, invoking a vocabulary of power and authority, but one that defines the limits more than the possibilities of politics.

EPIC POETRY AND LUCRETIUS' METHOD OF THOUGHT

Against Epicurus' compact, abstract, reasoned prose, stands Lucretius' epic poem. More than just different in style, Lucretius' use of poetry seems to run contrary to the warnings of Epicurus, who views poetry as a source of pleasure but not of knowledge, ostensibly (though never explained) because poetry parades images and uses language that have no empirical or logical foundation.[41] Lucretius' departure from Epicurus has not always been applauded, driven in large part by the question of how one salvages sober philosophy from emotionally-laden poetry.[42] Minyard asks whether we can call Lucretius an "authorized, exponent of doctrine" and concludes that while putting Epicureanism to verse is novel, "it does contradict the history of Epicurean practice," a practice for which there "must have been a reason fundamental to the history of philosophy since Socrates as well as to Epicureanism in particular."[43] Beye writes more adamantly that the "confusions and conflicts which appear" in Lucretius "are the inevitable consequence of giving poetic treatment to a subject that calls for prose. The objective outlines of the thesis which the rational mind controls grow obscured and distorted in

---

[41] See Plut. *Non posse suav.* 1086f-1087a, 1092e-1096c, DL 10.120 (= fr. 563 Usener); 10.121 (= fr. 568 Usener) (no wise man would compose poetry); Asmis 1995 sorts through the evidence. For Epicurus as less hostile to poetry than assumed, see especially Giancotti 1959, 15–90; Long and Sedley 1987, 1.144–49; Asmis 1995; Obbink 1996.

[42] Related to the tension between emotion and reason is what Patin characterizes as an anti-Lucrèce chez Lucrèce (1868), a Lucretius attracted to religion that exists in tension with the Lucretius attracted to Epicurus. Giancotti, for example, argues that Lucretius seeks to convince himself of the need to purge himself of religious conviction (Giancotti 1959, 131–38). Modifications of this tension appear in Townend 1965; Wormell 1965; Schrijvers 1970; Ackermann 1979, 29: "*Poeta doctus* und *poeta furiosus* gehen in ihm eine Synthese, vielleicht sogar Symbiose ein"; Caranci 1988.

[43] Minyard 1985, 34, 58. De Lacy hypothesizes that Lucretius was perhaps "not fully familiar with all aspects of Epicurean doctrine" (De Lacy 1939, 91).

the imagistic freight of the poem, for this springs from a personal, direct and irrational conscious."[44] Nichols tries to explain why Lucretius would forego a "lucid prose explanation," ultimately seeing Lucretius' poetry as a form of deception.[45] Like honey that disguises medicine, Lucretius' poetry disguises truth from those not yet able, or willing, to receive it.[46]

The explanation is psychologically attractive: One can feel smarter than the ancient audience. But Lucretius is hardly coy, Epicureanism is hardly unknown to Rome, and his audience, as Cicero testifies, is hardly unaware of the poem.[47] Furthermore, it seems like unnecessary subterfuge to craft an epic poem to disguise what Epicurus and Lucretius pretty clearly state: namely, that we inhabit a stark universe composed entirely of atoms, in which the gods play no role. Certainly, if it were a secret then Cicero ruined it by reporting the opinion of some that Epicurus really abolished the gods but kept them in his natural framework to prevent offending the Athenian people (*De nat. deor.* 1.30.85).

The surprise that Lucretius chose poetry (rather than the more suitable prose) entails a number of assumptions. First, it assumes that an author selects from a menu of options, each equally viable. But we cannot suppose that Lucretius opted for a particular style, any more than any writer chooses a particular style. Heraclitus wrote in aphorisms, Solon in verse, Plato in dialogue, and Aristotle in prose. Not to oversimplify the case, but Lucretius likely chose poetry because he was a poet – in fact, a brilliant one who could hardly be considered a dilettante. Second, the claim is premised on a remarkably static notion of intellectual progress that equates insight with stylistic emulation. Lucretius makes no such assumption, seeing his contribution to Epicureanism as lying in his ability to extend the doctrine in new, even bold, ways, rather than in copying the style that came before (for example, 1.923, 926–27).

---

[44] Beye 1963, 160. Bailey sees Lucretius as a philosopher – not an "original" one – "hampered by the restriction of verse" (Bailey 1949, 45).

[45] Nichols 1976, 30.

[46] Strauss 1968, 83–84; Nichols 1976, 34, 148–67 (disguise impiety of not believing in the gods); Clay 1983, 46, 167; Colman 2012, 31–32; Variations by Bailey 1949, 4; Campbell 2003, 11, 182–84 (disguises that human society is not a gift of the gods).

[47] On the popularity of Epicureanism in Cicero's youth, see *Tusc.* 4.3.6. Cicero comments on Lucretius, perhaps one of his smaller poems, in *Q. Fr.* 2.9.3.

Lucretius' epic style situates him at the crossroads of three illustrious lineages: the Greek tradition of Homer, the cosmological poetry of Empedocles, and the Roman tradition of Ennius.[48] Lucretius reworks these traditions, announcing himself, as Sedley remarks, as "the great Roman poet of nature."[49] Finally, the claim rests upon a rigid distinction between the epistemological status of philosophy and poetry when, in fact, this relationship was continually being rethought, even in ancient times.[50] The Stoics argue that a poem's sounds and language are useful in conveying thought vividly. Closer to home, Philodemus, an Epicurean, allows that the pleasure of a poem lies in the "thoughts that are interwoven" with sound.[51] Not a ringing endorsement, but not an outright repudiation either. Some efforts in poetry by philosophers had already been made, Empedocles and Philodemus being the notable examples.[52] We should not be surprised, then, when writers contemporaneous with Lucretius seem less concerned with this presumed heresy.

Some scholars have sought to situate Lucretius' poem within a Roman cultural context, akin to the use of rhetoric to enhance the appeal of a philosophic argument.[53] Asmis, for example, places Lucretius in an historical setting in which philosophers saw themselves as needing to

---

[48] On Lucretius' work as a form of epic poetry, see Murley 1947 and further elaboration by Gale 1994, 99–128. Discussions of Lucretius' use of poetic images include West 1969; Gale 1994.

[49] Sedley 1998, 23. Sedley's claim contrasts with Strauss' assertion that "the opening of the poem is not the place to speak proudly, not to say to boast, of the poet's innovation or originality" (1968, 80). Also Gale 1994, 59–75 on influence of Empedocles.

[50] See my treatment of this conflict between poetry and philosophy in addressing Homeric political thought (Hammer 2002b). Asmis writes: "Cicero, Sextus, and, above all, Philodemus show that at the end of the second century and in the first half of the first century B.C., the Epicureans reconsidered the relationship between poetry and philosophy" (1995, 30). Gale attempts to reconstruct Lucretius' poetic theory, drawing on contemporaneous conceptions of poetry (1994, 138–155).

[51] Quoted in Asmis 1991, 15 from Philod. *On Music* 4, col. 18.16–19. Also Asmis 1992, 402; 1995, 30–31; Gale 1994, 16–18.

[52] See especially Sedley 1998, 1–34; Furley 1989, 176–82; Clay 1983, 22–23, 82–110, 253–57; also Lucr. 1.716–41.

[53] Classen 1968, 100–4; also Cox 1986, 227–29; Gottschalk 1996, 238–39 (tradition of didactic poetry); Marković 2008, 47, 51–148 (rhetorical construction of the poem that parallels Epicurus' methods of argumentation).

employ rhetoric to defend their case. "It is not surprising, therefore, that Lucretius should use the resources of rhetoric in order to make his philosophical doctrines more acceptable to the layman."[54] But even these claims, while helpful, often treat poetry as a mode of presentation that is unconnected to – and may even sit uncomfortably with – Epicurean thought.

If we are to understand what Lucretius might have seen as the potential contributions of the poem to Epicureanism (which is a different question than why he chose poetry over something else), we need to place the poem within the context of Epicurean physiology.[55] We can begin with Bailey's attempt to salvage the coherence of *On the nature of things* when he suggests that the "key to the understanding of Lucretius' mind" was "that it was visual rather than logical."[56] We need not seek recourse in the idiosyncratic workings of a mind; the emphasis on the visual is both culturally significant for the Romans and epistemologically significant for the Epicureans. I will focus on the epistemological significance here (for the cultural significance, see, in particular, Chapter 5: Livy).

For Epicureans, the mind thinks and we see by way of images that strike it from outside. An image is produced by a thin film, or emanation, of atoms that streams off the surface of things (*Her.* 46: *eidōlon* = *simulacrum*, sometimes *imago, effigies, figura*). When we perceive a tree, for example, or another person, the atomic film given off by the object penetrates our sense organs. Similarly, when the mind has a thought, "an appearance has been produced by particles that have entered the

---

[54] Asmis 1983, 37; later also arguing that Lucretius saw his poetry (the honey) as providing clarity (more than deception) to philosophical truths (1995, 34). See also Gale: poetry if properly used can serve philosophy through its "attractive quality" and ability to seduce, but is entirely "subordinate" (1994, 47, 49). Also Ackermann 1979, 16–24.

[55] Efforts to provide a picture of how Lucretius' poetic devices are integral to the thought include Friedlander 1941 (close relationship between patterns of sound and Lucretius' philosophical argument); Schrijvers 1970, 38–47, 87–147, 164–74 (who seeks to show how Lucretian poetry reflects Epicurean physical theory); Armstrong 1995 (on the arrangement of letters); Marković 2008, 40 ("verbal presentation of physical phenomena").

[56] Bailey 1940, 280.

mind from outside."[57] As Epicurus writes, "it is on the impingement of something from outside that we see and think of shapes" (*Her.* 49, trans. Long and Sedley). Epicurus is not distinguishing between apprehensions of the mind or sense organs since the physiology is the same: "And whatever impression we get by focusing our thought or senses, whether of shape or of properties, that is the shape of the solid body, produced through the image's concentrated succession or after-effect" (*Her.* 50, trans. Long and Sedley). Lucretius, following Epicurus, describes this fine film given off by the surface of things, or *simulacra* (= *eidōla*), as resembling the "look and shape" of the object (4.50–51; also 4.63–64). The *simulacra*, propelled rapidly through space, strike and excite our sensory organs (4.197; 4.217; 4.244–49) and mind (4.722). For Lucretius, "what we see with the mind [is] like what we see with the eye," both coming about "in a like way" (4.750–51).

We can be wrong when we add opinions to these perceptions, which are additional evaluations or conclusions that we make about the perception (*Her.* 51). For example, one sees an individual struck down with an illness and concludes that it is a punishment from the gods. Lucretius describes the process by which "we draw large deductions from small indications, and ourselves bring ourselves into deceit and delusion" (4.816–17). This can happen "if your mind fails to attend," just like if "the thing were all the while withdrawn and far removed from you" (4.812–13). Lucretius uses the verb *advertere* (to give attention to) as a synonym for *epibolai* (applications), whereby the mind and the senses perceive by directing their attention to that object. That is, we do not perceive everything, even readily visible things, until we turn our attention to it. Furthermore, particular effort may be required to perceive small things, or highly detailed things, or things at a distance. Because there are so many images, so fleeting, and so fine, "the mind cannot perceive any sharply except those which it strains to see" (4.802–3). The image, thus, perishes unless the mind prepares itself (4.804–5).

To get us to perceive what is in front of us, Lucretius must confront the ignorance and fear that he associates with darkness (see, for example,

---

[57] Asmis 1984, 65. Also Bailey 1928, 565: "the act of apprehension by the mind is, as it were, a kind of fine sense-perception."

1.146; 3.39; 3.91). As Lucretius writes, "This terror of mind therefore and this gloom must be dispelled, not by the sun's rays or the bright shafts of day, but by the aspect of law of nature" (1.146–48). This darkness is not simply figurative but physiological. We can get some sense of how Lucretius portrays the physiology of ignorance in this extended passage, portions of which I have quoted the Latin:

> Again we see out of the dark what is in the light, because when the black air of darkness, being nearer, has entered our open eyes first and possessed them, there follows immediately a bright clear air, which as it were purges them and beats abroad the black shades of the first air; for this bright air is far more mobile and made of far more minute elements and more powerful (*qui quasi purgat eos ac nigras discutit umbras / aeris illius; nam multis partibus hic est / mobilior multisque minutior et mage pollens*). As soon as this has filled up again the channels of the eyes with light, and opened them out after being beset by that black air, at once those images of things follow that are in the light, and provoke us to see. But contrariwise we cannot see out of the light what is in the darkness, for this reason, because a grosser air of the darkness follows second, which fills all pores and besets the passages of the eyes, that no images of anything when thrown upon them may move them (*Quod contra facere in tenebris e luce nequimus / propterea quia posterior caliginis aer / crassior insequitur, qui cuncta foramina complet / obsiditque vias oculorum, ne simulacra / possint ullarum rerum coniecta movere* (4.337–52).

Lucretius associates the "black air of darkness" with thicker air that blocks the movement of images (4.313; 4.348–52; also 4.338, 343).[58] We are blocked by our ignorance from seeing the nature of things. In fact, this ignorance gives rise to a pathological fear and anxiety, further altering how our senses respond to stimuli. As a disease, ignorance and delusion throw "the whole body into riot" and alter "the positions of the first-beginnings" so that "the bodies which once were suitable to cause sensation, are so no longer" (4.665–69). Absent a purging, the mind will

---

[58] Segal 1990, 164.

imagine perils that "find their way into us against our will" (5.43–44). In cases in which the senses are in turmoil, "other things are more apt, which in penetrating can engender a bitter sensation" (4.669–70).

Lucretius' reference is to honey, in which both smooth atoms of sweetness and rough atoms of bitterness are commingled.[59] But honey makes an earlier and famous appearance in the poem when Lucretius compares his poem to how a physician administers "rank wormwood" with honey so that the patient "may drink up the bitter juice" of the medicine (1.936–42). The poem is a mixture, a commingling, giving a new twist to Philodemus' claim that poetry interweaves thought and sound. The poem penetrates the mind by mingling the round, smooth atoms of honey (1.936–42; 4.11–25; 2.437: delight; 6.42: weave web) – the elevated style of epic poetry – with the hooked atoms, also contained within honey, but now associated with medicine that are able "to tear open their way into our senses and to break the texture by their intrusion (*vias rescindere nostris / sensibus introituque suo perrumpere corpus*)" (2.406–7; 2.467; 4.671; also 4.622–26; 5.18; 5.44; 6.24; 6.41; 6.68).[60] Like *simulacra* carrying images of things with great speed to wherever they may go, so, as Thury has argued, Lucretius' verses, as they convey both an image and an account of nature (*naturae species ratioque*) (1.148), enter the minds of those who might pay attention (4.176–82).[61] The poem, in its scope, touches everything, offering new aspects of creation to waiting eyes and ears (2.1024–25). Lucretius' poem does more than hold our attention, though, a notion more in keeping with Hellenistic interpretations of Aristotle's discussion of dramatic presentation.[62] Like the innumerable combinations of atoms that create our universe and strike our senses, so the combinations of letters (2.1013–22) presents

---

[59] Lucretius' claim is in line with ancient characterizations of honey. See SE *Pyr.* 2.63.
[60] See Murley 1947 in his discussion of the epic features of the poem.
[61] Thury 1987, 271, 274; see also Kinsey 1964, 126: "His task is to give [philosophy] life, to transform it into a series of living images"; West 1969, 115: "sensory stimuli" of the images and sounds in the poem.
[62] Schrijvers, for example, suggests that Lucretius employs the technique of *enargeia* to create vivid depictions that hold the attention of the reader (1970, 296–308). Lucretius does state that his poetry is meant to "engage the mind" (1.948–50), but that engagement is part of teaching how to see.

nature "in a steady form and rhythm, so that the reader begins to feel it as a shape, and a rhythm, to sense reasoning itself as physical form and movement, as something of art."[63] By way of Lucretius' poem, we are meant to feel nature's reason.

When Lucretius compares his poem to "the sun's rays or the bright shafts of day" (1.147), he is alluding to the goal of thought. As we saw in the earlier passage, Lucretius describes the physiological process by which we see as one in which the "more mobile" and "more powerful" particles of "bright air" fill the channels of the eyes with light and open them out "after being beset by that black air" (4.343–45). This is not the light that Plato's philosophers see in ascending from the cave, an apprehension of a truth or an essence that is only available to the practiced few; it is a return to the authority of our senses.[64] Minyard captures this sensual foundation to reason when he suggests that ideas "begin in feeling: the feelings which are our immediate and instinctive evaluations of our experience of the world."[65] Lucretius' poetry, like Epicurus' philosophic method, are practices of thought meant to shape how we think by sharpening how we perceive. Lucretius embarks on a sensual journey by way of poetry in which one begins to view the world, including the political world, through the lens of nature rather than the blocked, stifling, and oppressive lens of the *mos maiorum*.[66]

ROME'S PLACE

By the first century BCE Rome had firmly established a cosmology that confirmed it as endowed with a special destiny: It is, as Virgil would

---

[63] Minyard 1985, 67. See also Cook 1994, 205–11, who discusses the continued emphasis on visualization in Lucretius' poetry.

[64] On the importance of autonomous reflection for Lucretius, and the connection to an evolving Roman conception of teaching and learning, see Schiesaro 2007, 68–71.

[65] Minyard 1985, 69.

[66] One aspect of this delight is the poem itself. Cook notes that the "superabundance of visual effects...furthers the immersion of the reader in the vividness, orderliness, and at the same time the variousness, indeed the *voluptas*, of the world taken in by his eyes" (1994, 211).

reiterate in announcing the rebirth of Rome, an eternal city, blessed and protected by the gods, whose unique purpose is to rule (Virg. *A* 6.851–53).[67] Lucretius offers no such solace. For Lucretius, the gods did not create Rome nor was Rome (or the world for that matter) created for humans: "the world was certainly not made for us by divine power" (5.198–99). As evidence Lucretius points to the sheer inhospitability of the natural world to human habitation: wild beasts, unyielding soil, horrible storms, and the inability of newborns to care for themselves (5.200–34). Worlds, instead, come into being by the random movement and arrangement of atoms. There is no council (*consilium*), that is, no conscious assembly of agents, assigning order (5.419–20; also 2.120) but only an infinite array of chance encounters: "For so many first beginnings of things (*primordia rerum*) in so many ways, smitten with blows and carried by their own weight from infinite time up to the present, have been accustomed to move and meet together in all manner of ways, and to try all combinations, whatsoever they could produce by coming together" (5.187–91; also 1.814–15; 5.187; 5.422–25).[68] Lucretius is describing a kinetic universe, a "strange storm" of atoms mixed in "discord," like a battle (5.436, 440; also 2.116–22). Atoms are driven by their own weight (*gravitas*) or by contact with other atoms (2.84–85). Atoms of different shapes and dissimilar forms bounce every which way or, if joined momentarily, soon fall apart either because they cannot be secured fully or because the combination could not allow motions suitable for each part (2.85–87; 2.711–17).

The order of the universe is defined by the physical nature of atoms: every combination is not possible but only combinations of like kinds defined by their inner capacities (1.169–73). These capacities also place limits and boundaries on the power of the combination: how it grows, what it can become, what other elements it needs to survive, etc. Although there may be a number of different worlds that can be created through random interactions, once the world is formed there are law-like regularities.

---

[67] See Mellor 1981, 970–71, 973; Gruen 1984, 273–87.
[68] Lucretius employs a variety of Latin words and phrases for the translation of the Greek *atomos*, depending on context. See, for example, 1.58–59.

So, in the world once formed, the behavior of new atoms is limited and governed by the basic structures to which they are assimilated. Stability and order arise not from the intervention of mind but as the necessary consequence of matter in motion. The indestructibility, size, shape, and motion of individual atoms limit the combinations which they can form, and thus in the world as we experience it definite kinds of things are evidence.[69] Once created, organic compounds are reproduced from their seeds, thus giving continuity to forms (1.159–214; 2.584–98; also Epic. Her. 38–39).

Lucretius introduces his Roman audience not only to a world without design or purpose, but also to one that is born and dies (5.66, 95–96, 98, 109, 239, 242–46, 304–17, 829–32). In wonderfully evocative language, Lucretius describes the earth as both the womb and the grave: "Besides, whatever the earth nourishes and increases is given back in its due proportion; and since beyond all doubt the mother of all is seen also to be the universal tomb, therefore you see that the earth is diminished and is increased and grows again" (5.257–60, trans. modified). The statement reveals a fundamental law of the Epicurean universe: that of the balance (*isonomia* = *servare*) between destructive forces (*motus exitiales*) and creative and constructive forces (*motus genitales auctificique*) (2.569–72; also 1.263–64; 2.75–76).[70] Just as birth is a process by which atoms join together, death (or disintegration) occurs because atoms loosen and disperse into space, either because of collisions with other atoms or because the bonds grow weaker with age and the atoms flow out more quickly then they are replenished with new atoms (see 1.221–24; 2.1128–43; 5.357–58). As the compound becomes more porous, it is more vulnerable to the blows of atoms from the outside until finally the compound dies and the atoms disperse back into the void (2.1139–43). Rome's place is not only temporary

---

[69] Long 1977, 82.

[70] Giancotti, for example, sees the opening invocation to Venus and Mars as personifying these balancing forces (1959, 201–17). So, too, this balancing plays out in the contrast between the opening scene of generation and life and the closing scene in Book 6 of suffering and death. See Bright 1971, 623–26.

(5.829–33); the entire earth may be near its end, exhausted with age and unable to replenish itself (2.1150).[71]

The purely material explanation of the course of nature and human events means that the gods, to the extent that they even exist (see below), do not watch over and influence the course of events. However much one may propitiate the gods in hopes of securing one's happiness – gaining political, military, agricultural, and economic success or avoiding punishment – they actually "enjoy immortal life in the deepest peace, far removed and separated from our affairs; for without any pain, without danger, itself mighty by its own resources, needing us not at all, it is neither propitiated with services nor touched by wrath" (2.646–51; also 5.165–69). Poverty and wealth, slavery and liberty, and war and concord are simply *eventa*, outcomes of the combination of bodies in space (1.455–58).

Three aspects of Lucretius' account deserve mention and suggest how we can begin to make out the contours of his political thought. First, although the gods may be indifferent to Rome, Lucretius is not. Addressing Memmius in this time of trouble, Lucretius notes that he can neither possess an "untroubled mind" (*aequus animus*) nor can Memmius' service to the *res communis* be lacking (1.41–43).[72] Lucretius continues in language that is reminiscent of Achilles' speech to Priam, delineating, rather than conflating, the mortal and immortal worlds: "for the very nature of divinity must necessarily enjoy immortal life in the deepest peace, far removed and separated from our affairs (*omnis enim per se divum natura necessest/ immortali aevo summa cum pace fruatur/ semota ab nostris rebus seiunctaque longe*)" (44–46). Lucretius' poetry, however, is motivated precisely by a connection with and concern for "our affairs" (*nostrae res*) and even with Lucretius' own renown (1.923).

---

[71] Klingner (1986) notes that Lucretius emphasizes the mortality of the world more than does Epicurus.

[72] On Memmius, see Clay 1983, 172–73, 212–15. Memmius is likely a Roman nobleman, possibly the same Gaius Memmius who planned the demolition of Epicurus' home in Athens for new buildings and who is disgraced by corruption charges. For Schiesaro, Lucretius' relationship with Memmius reflects a new model for the transmission of knowledge in the Roman republic (2007, 64–71). This model is consistent with my understanding of Lucretius as articulating a new conception of power.

Lucretius admires the gods' sovereignty. But one's ability to ascend, to become more godlike by detaching oneself from the tumult of the world, seems incomplete as a characterization of Lucretius' purpose.[73]

Second, although much of Lucretius' poem, like Epicurus' philosophy, is a meditation on death as a preparation for its inevitability, it is also a call to life. That is to say, the forces of creation and construction are as natural as the forces of destruction. Not coincidentally, Lucretius frames his epic with a hymn both to Venus, the matron of Rome (by way of Aeneas), who represents the forces of creation and to Mars, who represents the forces of destruction.[74] The opening lines burst with images of generation (1.1, 1.11), conception (1.4), springing forth (1.8), affection (1.19), longing (1.20), and origin (1.23). Although employing what would have been familiar images of Venus (as generation) and nature, the poem, as Clay argues, soon gives way to a notion of *natura* as creation and destruction (1.57), and finally to the bleak truths of a barren universe (1.1109–10).[75] The trajectory of Lucretius' poem, thus, is seen by Clay as bringing "the reader to regard with detachment all that is attractive."[76]

---

[73] Certainly Lucretius is not arguing that we become like the gods, and "transgress" the limits of nature (something that the gods do not even do), as Nussbaum argues (1994, 215). Nor, lacking any relation to other persons, does Lucretius appeal "to the fairly remote ideal of the Epicurean gods" and an "escape" from nature (De Lacy 1957, 121, 124).

[74] These hymns and myths, especially the opening invocation of Venus, are variously interpreted by scholars as personifications or symbols of natural forces of creation and destruction (Giancotti 1959, 201–17; Summers 1995, 49–51); as rule of nature (Ackermann 1979, 181–88); as symbol of pleasure (Bignone 1945, 2.427–43; Elder 1954, 88–120); as ultimately displaced (Clay 1983); as placed into "service of detachment" (Strauss 1968, 85); as alternative to Stoic Zeus (Asmis 1982); as political allegory (Cole 1998); as a way to invest Epicureanism with a religious-like wonder (Schrijvers 1970, 50–60); as symbolic of Lucretius' own desire to entice by illuminating nature (Classen 1968, 103–4); and as a "*mixture* of truth and falsehood," containing multiple "verbal echoes," that can confirm symbolically the true account of things (Gale 1994, 4, 223). Sedley provides an interesting argument that the opening invocation to Venus and Mars is Lucretius' claim to a "literary, not a philosophical, heritage," one modeled after Empedocles (1998, 23).

[75] Clay 1983, 106–10; also Clay 1983, 84-5; Gale 1994, 208–223.

[76] Clay 1983, 110.

I agree that Lucretius, by way of mythology, is drawing on poetic and mythical images that would resonate with his Roman audience, images that he in turn revises. But by interpreting the opening as a form of deception or seduction, we end up reading the poem too linearly when, in fact, Lucretius' poem, like nature, always circles back (1.237). That is, the later parts do not replace the earlier parts; destruction is complemented by "renovation" (*novanda*) (5.194). Humanity does not just bow to the ineluctability of death or the barrenness of the universe but must stake out its existence within the contending forces of destruction and construction.[77] For example, having finished showing how everything that is capable of sensation is composed of parts which have no sensations (2.989–90), a series of passages that Clay brilliantly explores, Lucretius begins anew (though Clay breaks off his analysis right before this passage): "Now, I beg, apply your mind to true reasoning. For a mightily new thing is labouring to fall upon your eyes, a new aspect of creation to show itself" (1.1023–25). This new light displaces old forms of wonder born of ignorance (2.1028, 1029, 1035, 1037) with a wonder excited by the freedom of the mind (2.1047; see also 3.28–30; 5.91–103).[78] The claim would speak not only to a primitive notion of nature as genesis, as Clay points out, but also to an audience who had been raised on a conception of Rome as founded and built (by the generation of Venus) from the fiery blaze of a razed city and the disorder of the wilderness (later in Virgil and Livy).[79] If other poets sing only of the ruin of Troy, Lucretius offers a world (seemingly in complete contradiction to his earlier claim that the earth is exhausted [2.1150]) that is "young and new" and whose arts are still in growth (5.330–31).

---

[77] As evidence of his claim that the natural order is "antithetical to ours" in Lucretius, De Lacy emphasizes the comparisons of atoms to "conflict and war" without accounting for the comparisons to compacts and politics (1957, 124). See also Nugent who argues the *"terra mater* does indeed represent both life and death" (1994, 204).

[78] Clay argues that what is revealed in this exploration of the universe beyond the boundaries of this world is this world's "death" (1983, 246). True enough. But overlooked is the animating impulse – the desire to see and, not incidentally, create – that lies at the heart of this Lucretian passage.

[79] Clay 1983, 86.

Finally, and related to these two points, far from being pessimistic, the argument is meant to free us (as it frees nature) from *domini superbi*, proud masters (2.1091; also 1.63; 2.1047; 5.87). The language immediately recalls the Roman experience of despotism, specifically the rule of Tarquinius Superbus, whose overthrow by Brutus led to the end of kingship and the founding of the Republic (see Chapt. 5, 242–49). But there is unfinished business; one is no freer, but still fighting battles, driven by fear, and desirous of others (5.43–48; also 6.15). In following Epicurus, who "vanquished" these powers "by words, not by swords," Lucretius sets out to finish the revolution by returning sovereignty to the individual (5.44, 49–50; also 1.66–67, 70–79).

THE NATURALIZATION OF POLITICS: SOVEREIGNTY AND POWER

What does our new power look like? If we look at the images that Lucretius employs, then at times that power seems to resemble war. Lucretius describes the motions and arrangements of atoms as an "everlasting conflict struggling, fighting, battling in troops without any pause" (2.118–19; also 5.380–95; 5.440–42).[80] Less violent blows are likened to riots (2.956). When describing order, though, Lucretius draws on images of politics. In depicting the transition from disorder to order, for example, Lucretius at one point differentiates between a wandering crowd (2.109) who neither knows each other nor acts together (2.550; 2.920) and people who are brought together in assembly (*consilium*) (see 2.110; 2.552; 5.426). Birth, rejuvenation, and growth all require assemblies (2.563–64; 2.935–36) and pacts (*foedera*, sing. *foedus*) (1.302, 586; 5.57, 310, 924). Indeed, the universe acquires form as an assembly of atoms (*congressus materiai*) (2.1065).

The power of metaphors is that they employ the familiar, in this case Roman politics, to help one understand the unfamiliar, the physical universe. Lucretius even recognizes the limits of the metaphor,

---

[80] On the use of social and political metaphors in Lucretius, see especially Cabisius 1984/1985; Fowler 1997; Schiesaro 2007.

cautioning that atoms do not really make agreements about the motions to be produced (1.1023). In teasing political theory out of Lucretius, scholars often reverse the logic of the metaphor, using Lucretius' images that would have been familiar to his audience to reconstruct the Roman political world. Lucretius thus appears as political by his acquaintance with, more than any argument about, politics.[81] I want to take a different tact and suggest that the importance of Lucretius' language is not that politics is used metaphorically to understand nature, but that politics is naturalized, given a foundation in nature.

Lucretius, employing a typical Roman trope, casts his eye back to the primitive origins of human community, an anthropology that at first glance seems to confirm his vision of sovereignty as an unconscious, primitive innocence in which one folds into nature.[82] No different from wandering beasts (5.932), the earliest humans were content with "What sun and rain had given, and what the earth had produced of her own accord" (5.937–38). Governed by sober empiricism, primitive humans lived their lives by what nature provided, admiring the powers of nature without in turn viewing nature through the lens of superstition (see 5.969–81).[83]

Yet, the image of primitive sovereignty is incomplete. The comparison of early humans to wild hogs (5.969) cannot be the Epicurean vision. Lucretius gives us some hint of the difference between hogs and humans. Formulated entirely in the negative, Lucretius notes that primitive humans "could not look to the common good (*commune bonum*), they did not know how to govern their intercourse by custom (*mos*) and law (*lex*)" (5.958–59). We should not read this statement as we might read Aristotle, namely, that we become fully human only when we fulfill our natural *telos* and live and act in a political community. Humans for Epicureans do not have ends, and things do not come into being for a

---

[81] Others have scoured the images for indications of Lucretius' reactions to particular events, or for suggestions of a political stance. See Conti 1982, 45, n 8; Fowler 1997, 143–44, n. 93. But it is easy to take this approach too far, reading too much into too little.

[82] For the relationship of this account to Greek accounts of prehistory, see Cole 1967, 25–46.

[83] See Konstan 2008, 88.

reason (4.834–42). Humans have desires. But experience and the processes of life can give rise to the creation of things, including associations, for use in securing our most fundamental desire, that of pleasure (4.851–52). The absence of any sort of community, for example, becomes a deficit because "all things grow and gain strength together" (5.820). As Lucretius points out, the human race would soon have become extinct (5.1026–27) if it had not joined together in mating (5.1013–18), alliances (*amicitiae*) (5.1019), and compacts (*foedera*) of justice to pity the weak, which were seen by most people as *aequum*, or fair (5.1025).[84]

Lucretius' discussion of the development of human communities belies attempts to read the trajectory as simply one of degeneration[85] or of progress.[86] Rather, Lucretius continually measures these developments by their affect on sovereignty, a notion that he, in turn, recasts. Sovereignty is neither freedom from constraints nor an ability to do whatever one wants to do; otherwise the hog's life would by idyllic for humans. Nor is sovereignty for Lucretius reducible to individualism or synonymous with invulnerability (though it may have implications

---

[84] Campbell puzzles about why Lucretius claims that the human race would have become extinct if it had not formed agreements (2003, 254). Campbell attempts to explain the origin of justice and its importance to the community by way of game theory (2003, 255–61). Algra argues that in this stage Lucretius plays down the hedonistic basis of friendship and seems to draw on notions of "familiarization" through habit by which we begin to have regard for others close to us. Although similar to a Stoic notion of *oikeiōsis*, the Epicurean version rests on habit, not instinct, and does not contain a teleology (Algra 1997, 148). Schiesaro sees this idea of justice as Lucretius' version of *ius naturale*, or natural law (5.1023) (2007, 47).

[85] See Green 1942, 57–8; Farrington 1953a; 1953b; Blickman 1989. Farrington describes the "political stage" of society as one that Lucretius "condemned" (1953b, 62). For a comparison of Epicurean and Lucretian models of social development to other ancient models, see Cole 1967. Campbell argues that Lucretius' prehistory is simply a way of using the *topos* of the Golden Age as a way of easing his audience into the truth that the gods do not play a role in the formation of society and culture (2003, 11). Gale sees Lucretius' use of Golden Age myths to revise them by pointing to nature, and not gods and heroes, as playing the central role in human affairs and development (1994, 156–82).

[86] Viewed as progress: Taylor 1947. Asmis sees Lucretius as outlining the progress of technology and ideas that often carries with it the escalation of desires (1996). Nugent views the movement from uncontrolled fecundity to stable descent as a male valorization of the earth as "now tamed, like a properly socialized wife" (1994, 184).

for both). Sovereignty, instead, has a foundation in power, which is connected to (and defined by) nature. Simply put, sovereignty is the ability to act according to nature's power. To understand this notion of sovereignty, we need first to identify what for Lucretius are the characteristics of nature's power.

First, all compounds have distinct powers implanted by nature (1.173: *quod certis in rebus inest secreta facultas*; 2.286; 4.489: *potestas*). Lucretius is not saying, as does Aristotle, that each thing has a unique power. Following from the Epicurean proposition that nothing comes from nothing (1.156–57), Lucretius is arguing, instead, that all things are born from something (1.172). Rather than anything being able to produce anything, we see, instead, that like things bear similar capabilities (*facultates*) – horns, for example, or talons – that Lucretius attributes to the notion that things are produced from seeds that bear the material of their first beginnings (1.169–71). That is, capabilities are inherited. In the creation of compounds, "The first beginnings of the elements so interpenetrate one another in their motions that no single element can be separated off nor can its power (*potestas*) be divided from the rest by space, but they are, as it were, the many forces (*multae vis*) of a single body" (3.262–65; also 5.855–78). Lucretius' language is important, and distinctly Roman.[87] Where *vis* refers to something like strength or vigor (corresponding to the Greek *enargeia* or *dunamis*),[88] *potestas* connotes the appropriate or proper exercise of one's power or capabilities, an authority usually specified and circumscribed by law. *Potestas* is associated with jurisdiction, a notion that combines both the power to do something with the authority to do it. Lucretius, thus, gives the political term *potestas* a natural jurisdiction. One's natural *potestas* cannot be alienated from one's body (without there being something approximating death) (3.264–65; 3.674–76). But power is not unitary; it rests on an ability of the different elements of the body to act and grow together (3.283–85; 3.334; 3.558–59; 3.679–85). The more varied the different kinds of

---

[87] It might be added, also gendered in the emphasis on male *vis*, the political language of *potestas*, and the notion of sovereignty.

[88] See Caranci 1988, 61.

elements and shapes, the more different are the powers (*vires*) and abilities (*potestates*) of the compound (2.586–87).

Second, all things have a natural sense of how to use their power (*vis*) and abilities (*potestates*), even before those powers are fully developed (5.1033: *sentit enim vis quisque suas quoad possit abuti*; also 2.586). Once again, Lucretius is avoiding the language of ends – of what fulfills our nature – and is speaking of how nature implants feelings about how to use powers we possess. Goats butt heads before horns have even grown; lions use their paws before they are deadly weapons; animals screech warnings to each other; and humans are compelled by feelings (5.1087) to employ words and gestures and by utility to give names to things (5.1028–29; 5.1087–90).[89]

Finally, all things have their power limited (1.76: *finita potestas denique cuique / quanam sit ratione atque alte terminus haerens*; also 1.595; 6.65–66): limited by natural capacities (1.584–86) and by other matter (1.998–1000). Of the limits imposed by other matter, Lucretius writes, "Lastly one thing is seen before our eyes to be the limit of another: air separates hills and mountains air, earth bounds sea and contrariwise the sea is the boundary of all lands" (1.998–1000). Of the limits on the power nature has given, Lucretius' description of how atoms form bonds (*nexus*, 1.240) through treaties (*foedera*) is instructive. It "stands decreed what each can do by the ordinances of nature (*foedera naturai*), and also what each cannot do" (1.586–87). Lucretius' use of *foedera* to describe both natural and human arrangements is different from Epicurus, who only applies *synthekē* (agreement or treaty) and *nomos* (law) to humans.[90] There is, thus, a correspondence between natural and human arrangements. For the Romans, where treaties had become increasingly elaborate mechanisms by which Rome managed its expanding empire, *foedera* defined the obligations and limitations of each party, which were held together by respect or *fides* (good faith) for the terms of the agreement.[91] Central to the Roman notion of treaties was the idea of the "inviolability" of boundaries (see 1.584–98; 5.87–90;

---

[89] On the development of human language to communicate feelings, see Ernout and Robin 1962, 3.139.
[90] Asmis 2008b, 142.   [91] See Asmis 2008b, 143.

6.64–66).[92] To use Lucretius' language, the behavior of the compound is governed not by some overarching force or agreement once combined, but by the properties that emerge from the combination of atoms. That is, the coming together of atoms, not some sort of rational agreement or reasoning mind, "constitute[s] the natural process."[93] Second, and often overlooked, the Roman conception of treaties – though not always its practice – allowed sufficient motion for the organism to thrive, whether permitting another community to maintain its customs or another element to exercise its power in a compound. That is, the treaty was prototypical of power because it not only defined aims common to the different parts but also limitations on what those parts could do in their relationship to each other.

What emerges from Lucretius' poem is a universe saturated in power. In fact, it is arguably the central and unifying concept of the poem, given considerable force by the array of terms from which Lucretius can choose to describe the different components and expressions of power. Out of the understanding of power emerges a much more complex conception of sovereignty, one defined by a jurisdiction of power: one's ability to act according to the capabilities and within the boundaries provided by nature. This power is developed through mastery of nature's secrets, a mastery that Lucretius associates at times with a male conquest over, and invulnerability from, unstable, dangerous female matter.[94] Thus, far from using politics as a metaphor for nature, he uses nature to redefine the limits and possibilities of political power, as well as to provide a lens through which social development and organization can be interpreted and critiqued.

---

[92] Asmis 2008b, 144.

[93] Fowler 1997, 147; see also Gottschalk: "nature never became an independent force, but remained an epiphenomenon of the mechanical interaction of atoms" (1996, 240). Fowler corrects Cabisius who hypostasizes Nature by making it a party to the treaty (Cabisius 1984/1985, 113).

[94] See especially Nugent 1994, 186, 194–96; Keith 2000, 39–40. "Thus with disease, as we saw earlier with unstable air masses, distinction is drawn between dangers arising from what is 'extrinsic' (*extrinsecus*) and those inhering in the earth itself. The very terms of this opposition posit a sense in which evil occurrences, whether earthquakes or pestilence, are 'intrinsic' to earth; they are implicitly seen as 'natural' to her, rising up from the porous, moist, putrid mass which *is* her nature" (Nugent 1994, 196).

SOCIAL DEVELOPMENT AND THE SURRENDER OF SOVEREIGNTY

Lucretius' discussion of human communities can be read as tracing the various appearances of sovereignty that are then undermined by a violation of one of these natural conditions of power. One alienates one's power (handing it over to someone or something else), confuses one's natural sense of power with a community-created sense of power, or fails to recognize the boundaries of power. Lucretius continually shows how a misunderstanding of power compromises one's sovereignty and, in turn, one's happiness.

When left to one's own in nature, one could not help but perceive and conform to the reality of power: nature's force in the form of cold, heat, lightning, storms, wild beasts, and disease; nature's provisions, such as food, water, fire, and shelter (e.g., 5.925–52); and the ways in which one's natural faculties – one's strength, ingenuity, and beauty – aid one's survival (5.1111; also 5.858). The virtue of primitive existence, if we can call it a virtue, is that one lived within nature's power, which includes one's own power provided by nature. We get some sense of this equation when Lucretius characterizes the exercise of power through a series of reflexive phrases: "Whatever prize fortune gave to earth, they he carried off, every man taught to live and be strong for himself at his own will" (5.960–61). Primitive humans learned to be strong for themselves (*sibi valere*) and to live by their own will (*sponte sua*) (5.961) just as earth produced of her own accord (*sponte sua*) (5.938). Primitive humans survived by the resources given to them by nature: the "wonderful vigor (*mira... virtute*)" of hand and foot that allowed them to hunt (5.966, trans. modified). Primitive humans were content with what nature provided (5.937–38), living by nature's rhythms and laws (5.977–81), encountering its limits (5.1007–8), and acting with the powers bestowed by it.

The establishment of property (*res*) and gold, though, alters one's perception of this equation by substituting the power of natural attributes – beauty, strength, or intelligence (5.1110–11) – with unnatural ones. Wealth and gold "easily robbed both the strong and the handsome of their honour; or however strong and handsome in body, men for the most part follow the party of the richer" (5.1114–16). Lucretius' next sentence at first seems incongruous: to be governed by a true account means to live moderately with a contented soul (*aequus animus*), since "a little is never lacking" (5.1119). But beauty, strength, and intelligence have built into them natural limits. One cannot be more intelligent than one is. There is, thus, contentment in living according to what nature has provided. But with wealth there are no such natural limits (see 5.1432–33). Our perception of nature altered, one senses neither its limits nor one's own and eventually succumbs to a power one has placed over oneself.

Lucretius characterizes this unnatural life as one of terror and anxiety, which he traces to a fear of death (e.g., 3.64; 3.79). For the Epicurean system to hold up, that fear has to be unnatural. It is certainly the case that humans, like other animals, try to avoid dying. For example, primitive humans would flee in terror from approaching beasts, knowing that if they remained they would be killed or maimed (5.982–86). That flight points to a desire for security that, for Epicureans, is the common and most elemental desire of all beings.[95] Primitive humans removed themselves from harm by fleeing from wild animals. That, in the true Epicurean meaning of the term, makes sense. But no longer perceiving nature's limits or one's own, one loses sense of what it means to be secure and clings to the vestiges of what one thinks will protect one's life.

One is moved by the images not of real things but of false opinions. Lucretius captures the desperation of pursuing empty things when he writes, "as when in dreams a thirsty man seeks to drink, and no water is forthcoming to quench the burning in his frame, but he seeks the image of water, striving in vain, and in the midst of a rushing river thirsts while he drinks" (4.1097–1100). One takes one's cues not from one's senses but from what others say (5.1134): from empty sounds (*Her.* 37–38) that do not directly correspond to sensual stimuli.[96] Like the man seeking the *simulacra* of an image and imagining it will quench his thirst, we seek the *simulacra* of an image of security that we have created. "Men desired to be famous (*clarus*) and powerful (*potens*), that their fortune might stand fast upon a firm foundation, and that being

---

[95] See Campbell 2003, 237.   [96] See Barnes 1996, 213–14; Konstan 2008, 105.

wealthy they might be able to pass a quiet life" (5.1120–22). One even desires monuments and fame so that one might live forever (3.78).

Once one's desires are severed from nature, they are both unlimited and unattainable. In this alienation individuals do not know "the limits of possession, and how far it is even possible for real pleasure to grow; and this little by little has carried life out into the deep sea, and has stirred up from the bottom the great billows of war" (5.1432–35). Lucretius' reference to the sea recalls his earlier discussion of navigation, which exemplifies the problem: driven by the desire for more wealth (5.1008), we transgress nature's limits, only to be "dashed on the rocks by the turbulent billows of the sea" that before passed without ruin (5.1000–1).[97]

But like the man who must drink even harder as he tries to quench his thirst with the image of water, so the more one pursues the image of security, the more anxious one becomes because of its sheer unattainability. Envy rather than contentment drives the individual to strive for fame and power; treachery rather than honor defines the path; and exhaustion rather than satisfaction typifies the outcome.[98] One struggles endlessly "to the summit of honour" (5.1123), seeking "to rule kingdoms" (5.1128). Yet, like Sisyphus one treads on ground that is always shifting (4.995–98), treacherous (5.1124), and unattainable. Anxious about not acquiring power, or fearing someone else will, one resorts to ever more drastic measures, turning the things of nature into instruments of false security. The discovery of bronze and iron, metals from nature used to farm the earth, are transformed into increasingly violent weapons of war. Lucretius writes, "the pattern of sowing and the beginning of grafting first came from nature herself the maker of all things" (5.1361–62). But now "Gloomy Discord bred one thing after another, to be frightful in battle for the nations of men, and added new terror to warfare day by day" (5.1305–7). Even animals are turned into weapons. As Nussbaum writes, "In their frenetic search for invulnerability,

---

[97] On the unnaturalness of seafaring in Roman poetry, see Konstan 2008, 34.
[98] Many have noted allusions to the judicial murders undertaken by Sulla (3.70–71), the *invidia* of Catiline, and clandestine war (2.124–32). See Fowler 1997, 138–40; Cabisius 1984/1985, 116.

humans press into service instruments that lead to their own destruction: religious fears, angry desires to harm, ferocious longings for the possession of one another, the thirst for honor and power."[99]

PIETAS

The irony of seeking an imagined power is that one actually relinquishes one's own power. One has the ability (*potestas*) to avoid the "unnerving terror" that fills the forests and mountains (5.41–42); yet, with the mind clouded, "what battles and perils must then find their way into us disagreeably" (5.43–44, trans. modified). In this alienation from one's senses, one is similarly gripped by religious fear.[100] When Lucretius describes *pietas* as a *dominus superbus*, he is pointing to how despotism thrives from the surrender of power by others, a powerlessness fostered by ignorance, fear (5.73; 5.88), and *horror* (5.1165). Religion is a form of misdirected awe born of ignorance: ignorance of the movement of the heavens (5.1183–87), natural causes (5.1218–40; 6.54–55), the form of the gods (5.1169–82), and one's own soul (1.112). Unable to explain the causes of things, one does not just seek refuge in the gods but relinquishes the power of discovery (5.1185–86). The seeming incomprehensibility of the universe diminishes the individual: "Then when the whole earth trembles beneath our feet, when cities are shaken and fall or threaten to fall, what wonder if the sons of men feel contempt for themselves, and acknowledge the great potency and wondrous might of gods in the world, to govern all things" (5.1236–40; also 5.1204–17).

This governing power is in turn manipulated by priests and political leaders who, claiming privileged information to inscrutable truths (e.g., 6.381–82), keep the people groveling in fear (1.151; also 1.65;

---

[99] Nussbaum 1994, 273.
[100] It is in this context of our alienation from our senses that we can read Lucretius' discussion of religion. Blickman, for example, puzzles about the coherence of Lucretius' discussion of religion (4.1161–1240) that interrupts the chronological progression of the stages of prehistory (1989, 157–59). Manuwald (1980) distinguishes between two periods, one in which humans are taught by circumstance (5.925–1104) and the other by reason (1105–1457).

102–3) and crush them by the weight of absolute power (1.63; also 5.1207, an image Seneca uses later). Lucretius joins two images: that of the oppressive force of the tyrant and that of the physiological weight of ignorance and fear that block the movement of atoms, binding us (1.151) and making our minds shrink (5.1218). "What dreams they'll engineer" to "stir up fear" (1.104–5, 107) about the punishments in this life and the next.[101] Driven by fear and guided by false assumptions rather than experiences, one turns one's judgment over to others.[102] Indicative of this self-alienation, *pietas* leads one to commit "impious" deeds (1.83), including human sacrifices (1.84–101), castration (2.614–15), and wholesale slaughter to alleviate the anger of the gods or receive their favor.[103] The problem of *pietas* for Lucretius is that it requires "the humble acknowledgement of reliance on the will of another," a quiet submission to an absolute power that governs us.[104]

Lucretius is speaking both generally about religion and specifically about the permeation of *pietas* into Roman society. The legend that becomes attached to the original temple dedicated to *Pietas* in the second century BCE was of a child who suckles the parent, a legend that is then viewed by Pliny the Elder as distinctively Roman (Pliny *NH* 7.121; Livy 40.34.4–6).[105] The terrain of *pietas* would grow with the Roman state, reflecting the accumulation of practices and cults derived from its own past, the importation and incorporation of different traditions encountered through conquest, the systematization by the state of ceremonies (through the calendar), and increasingly orgiastic cult practices.[106] The ritual calendar, as well as the placement of temples, served as nothing less than a conceptual map of Roman identity.[107] Most fundamentally,

---

[101] The actual nature of these punishments for Romans is provided by Cicero *De leg.* 2.17.44.
[102] See Epic. *Men.* 23–24, who argues that impiety is the application of the opinions of the majority to the gods, opinions premised on false assumptions rather than experiences.
[103] On the contractual nature of Roman *pietas*, see Fowler 1911, 188, 200–8; Summers 1995, 35.
[104] Summer 1995, 41. [105] See Clark 2007, 69–71.
[106] On the "conservative flexibility" of Rome's religious system, see especially Wardman 1982, 3–9 and 22–62 (in the late Republic).
[107] See Clark 2007, 14.

the city itself was a *templum*, demarcated by a sacred boundary within which *auspices*, a form of dedication preliminary to public action, could occur.[108] Temples were also the sites of political activities: The senate sometimes met in the temple of *Concordia* and *Fides*, and debates and speeches were often staged in particular temples.[109]

In Roman society, *pietas* does not refer to religious conviction or private devotional practices but denotes an array of interconnected public obligations to the gods, family, and state: an emphasis on "acts, rather than beliefs" and "cult instead of theology."[110] Lucretius captures the spirit of submission associated with these different Roman devotional practices: "[To] show oneself often with covered head, turning towards a stone and approaching every alter," or "to fall prostrate upon the ground and to spread open the palms before shrines of the gods," or "to sprinkle altars with the blood of beasts in showers and to link vow to vow" (5.1198–1202).

Yet, Lucretius insists that gods exist, a conclusion we can understand less as an attempt to hide truth from the masses or to smuggle in a new theology and more as a result of his empiricism.[111] Perceptions and images come from somewhere. The continual flow of images of the gods, thus, suggests there is something real that has sensations, is immortal and perfect, and rules the heavens (5.1169–87). Whether or not Lucretius is an atheist largely misses the power of his argument. He does not kill the gods; he vanquishes the idols created by that belief and returns divinity to its true source, to that which endowed the divinity with sensation (5.1172), immortality (5.1175), and power (5.1186–87). That source is in part nature. Piety, as Epicurus writes, is the respect due that which has true majesty – i.e., that which is immortal, consistent, and untroubled – and that is nature (Epic. *Her.* 77).[112] In displacing the gods, though,

---

[108] See Wardman 1982, 10; Cic. *De rep.* 2.9.16.   [109] See Clark 2007, 171–77.

[110] Summers 1995, 33; also Fowler 1911, 185–88 and Wardman 1982, 7. Cicero gives a sense of importance placed on memorizing the complex rites (*De rep.* 2.14.27).

[111] On the Epicurean conception of the gods, see Farrington 1967, 93–104; Summers 1995; Obbink 2002.

[112] On Epicurus' conception of piety, see FitzGerald 1951; Festugière 1956; Gale 1994, 45–50. Friedlander argues that the gods are established "as the images and prototypes of the Epicurean sage" (1939, 373).

Lucretius does not displace humans; he does not replace one master with another but locates in humans the source of power and sensation that one has given to the gods. By banishing our idols (and Lucretius is speaking about both *religio*, traditionally understood as the proper worship of the gods, and *superstitio*, the groundless fear of the gods) we vanquish absolute power over us and "we by the victory are made equal to the heavens" (1.79, trans. modified).[113] The image is striking: We become our own gods by returning power to ourselves.[114]

One attributes sensation to the images of gods that appear to us (5.1172), imagining them not only as powerful, happy and secure, but also as ruling the universe and, thus, the source of one's own happiness and security or despair. Lucretius observes that "if men saw that a limit (*finis*) has been set to tribulation, somehow they would have strength to defy the superstitions and threatenings of the priests" (1.107–9). Instead, believing in the unlimited power of the gods, one surrenders one's sovereignty, lacking the power (*facultas*) to resist (1.110). Lucretius' language could not be clearer in identifying the true source of human power: one attributes (5.1172, 1195), gives (5.1175), locates (5.1188), and ascribes (5.1194–95). But in surrendering sovereignty, one trembles (5.1222), shrinks (5.1218–19), and huddles (5.1223) until one despises one's own weakness (5.1236–40). The irony is delicious: out of an imagined fear of a hell in the afterlife, one constructs a hell on earth – one becomes Tityos devoured by anguish and anxiety (3.992–94); Sisyphus seeking power and retiring in gloom (3.995–1002); and Tantalus frozen with "vain terror" (3.980–83).[115]

---

[113] On the distinction between *religio* and *superstitio*, see Cic. De nat. deor. 1.42.117. Summers rightly argues that Lucretius is not distinguishing between *religio* and *superstitio*, as if to save the one by rooting out the other (1995, 55).

[114] Cook suggests, for example, that "Lucretius continually shifts the focal point of truly pious activity away from the holy temples of the gods in a mental sphere" to create a "self-sufficient piety" (1995, 47, 48). See also Erler 1997, 89: "It becomes obvious that praying does not simply mean talking to the god anymore, but visualizing his nature; the goal is not so much the object of worship as the praying person and his disposition."

[115] We need to address where the images of the afterlife come from since for Epicureans all mental pictures are derived from real images, or *simulacra*. Lucretius seems to

THE MAJESTY OF NATURE AND THE POSSIBILITY OF POLITICS

Lucretius' sketch of social life emerges as a devastating critique of the *mos maiorum* as orienting behavior on behalf of the majesty (*maiestas*), or sovereign power, of the Roman state.[116] The *mos maiorum* teaches one to pursue wealth, honor, and dominion (*imperium*), which are nonnatural and infinite desires. One is continually driven to strive for what cannot be attained because there is no natural limit on these desires, nor is there any permanence or durability to what is acquired (e.g., 2.10–13; 5.1276–80). Neither rank nor rule can cure the body of disease (2.34–39); the monuments of men – the artifacts of memory and glory – crumble under the "mighty force of finite time" (5.311, 314–15); nature grinds down the rods and axes of political authority (5.1234–35). The Roman state cannot achieve what it desires: Kings are killed, men destroy those in power that they once feared, civil bloodshed erupts (3.70), murder is sanctioned by law, and each man vies for dominion (*imperium*) until human affairs are reduced to confusion (*turba*) (5.1141).[117] The *mos maiorum* leads one to violate not just the precepts it encourages but also the natural bonds of justice, honor, friendship, and piety (3.83–84).

In place of the majesty of the Roman state is the "majesty of nature" (5.7), but it is not majesty devoid of politics. Political communities are types of natural compounds that are premised on the recognition of natural boundaries, aims, and relationships. The health of a compound requires two things. First, a healthy compound requires that its boundaries be protected against bombardment and its body from depletion.

---

provide a reasonable explanation: The images are derived from images of vain striving in this life (3.378–79, 995–1023). See Konstan 2008, 65.

[116] Monti notes, "The Epicurean idea of the value of political society is then directly opposite to the Roman aristocratic notion. For the Epicurean the political state exists for the benefit of the individual; according to Roman aristocratic prejudices the individual must serve the interests of the state" (1981, 58).

[117] On the parallel of 3.70–71 to Sallust's description of Catiline (*Cat.* 14.1–3) or to the Sullan proscriptions, see Fowler 1997, 138. The discussion of the breakdown of kingship, as Fowler notes, is filled with allusions to Roman politics (Fowler 1997, 143 fn. 93).

Its strength must be continually supplemented and nourished.[118] The problem of empire is that it simply becomes too large and, thus, too difficult to protect and nourish. Lucretius writes, "For whatever you see growing with merry increase, and gradually climbing the steps of mature life, assimilates to itself more bodies than it discharges, so long as food is easily absorbed into all the veins, and so long as the things are not so widely spread open as to let go many elements and to spend away more than their age feeds on" (2.1122–27). But the larger a thing is, the more difficult it is to send nourishment to the whole or to receive nourishment at home (2.1136–37). "With good reason therefore the things pass away, when by the flowing off they have become thinned, and all fall by blows from without, inasmuch as by great age food fails at last, nor is there anything which bodies buffeting from without cease to break up and to subdue with fatal blows" (2.1138–43). Walls crumble and collapse into ruin (2.1144–45).

Second, a compound requires an ordering of internal relations of power that are premised on the recognition of both limits and capabilities. The image of Rome that emerges from Lucretius' account has two features, both of which capture the failure to recognize the boundaries of power. On the one hand is the tyranny of religion that controls and dominates us like a master. But, as Lucretius notes, life is not given for possession (*mancipium*) but for everyone to use (3.971). The language here is legal: *mancipium* is the process by which ownership of property and slaves is transferred. Nothing in nature allows a life to be possessed in this way. On the other hand, Rome is beset by clandestine motions, language that parallels Cicero's description of Catiline (2.126–27; also 2.944–62; Cic. *Cat.* 2.26).[119] Lucretius connects civil turmoil (3.70) to avarice and the lust for distinction, which causes individuals to transgress the boundary of right (*finis iuris*) (3.59–61). In betraying one's "fatherland," like betraying one's parents and friends, individuals overthrow true piety (3.83–86). The agitation and "violent mischief" throws the body into such a riot that "no place is left for life" and the particles of spirit "flee abroad" (3.253–55; also 4.663–67: note that natural sensations

---

[118] Segal 1990, 96.   [119] See Cabisius 1985, 116.

are altered). In Lucretius' account, and it is distinct among extant Epicurean accounts, the response to *turbatio* is a republic in which men create magistrates and establish right (*ius*) and law (*lex*) (5.1143–44; also 6.1–3 on Athens) that everyone submits to by their own will (*sponte sua*) (5.1147).[120]

Justice, for Epicurus, emerges as an arrangement "over not harming or being harmed" that frees social life from disturbance (Epic. *KD* 32–33, 36–38; also *KD* 5 in Cic. *De fin.* 1.18.57–58).[121] Justice is not simply social convention or a form of compromise as it is for the Sophists. Nor is justice a form of natural right that is inherent in nature. Justice, though, does have a *prolēpsis* (preconception): it is a concept that is meaningful as it derives from human experiences about what is useful in human relations (*KD* 36–38).[122] The specific content of justice may be "different in different places and for different individuals" and it "changes over time, in relation to the same place and the same individuals, in so far as a particular circumstance changes in time."[123] Thus, as Alberti points out, Epicureanism distinguishes relativism from conventionalism and skepticism: Justice is relative to time and circumstance but contains an objective criterion of utility by which one can measure the "truth of the forms of the just and the good."[124] Important for us here is the connection of justice to equality and power. Justice does not arise from an equality of condition (in fact, as Lucretius elaborates, people join together out of the sense that it is fair to pity the weak), but an equality of both capacity (the ability to agree) and outcome (the goal of utility and pleasure).[125]

---

[120] See Momigliano 1941, 157; also Schrijvers 1996, 223; DeWitt 1954, 184 (minimal government).

[121] The term is likely invented by Epicurus and is employed (with revisions) by the Stoics. For the Epicureans, it is a common image under which other images can be subsumed. On *prolēpsis* see Asmis 1984. I disagree with Vander Waerdt who argues, "the content of justice is entirely derivative from the compact of advantage embodied in the positive legal order" (1987, 409). It seems possible, maybe even desirable, for an Epicurean community to be just, without necessarily having an array of laws.

[122] See Vander Waerdt 1987, 419; Alberti 1995, 186–87.

[123] Alberti 1995, 187–88.   [124] Alberti 1995, 189.

[125] See Mitsis 1988, 84 (on justice as coordinating relationships); Armstrong 1997, 331–33 (justice as instrumental); Vander Waerdt 1987, 418 (as a reply to Glaucon's challenge in the *Republic*).

Lucretius points out that with the creation of law, individuals live with a fear of punishment that "taints the prizes (*praemia*) of life" (5.1151). This passage, and similar suggestions by Epicurus, have led to questions about the internal consistency of Epicurean doctrine (or, at the very least, its incompatibility with social institutions). The issue is simply this: A happy life cannot also be a fearful one, yet it is precisely through fear that laws seem to function and injustice – as a fear of detection – seems to operate (Epic. *KD* 34).[126] It may be, as some have suggested, that legal punishment is seen by Epicureans as a necessary, albeit limited, deterrent to control aggressive or unjust behavior.[127] Or laws may be a necessary accompaniment to a fallen society or a temporary measure on the way to a just society in which no such penalties would be necessary.[128]

Two points are worth mentioning about the role of justice and law in Lucretius. First, I read Lucretius as being ironic about the prizes of life. The prizes to which Lucretius refers also bear the connotation of the spoils of theft, which have created the anarchic violence in the first place. Second, the fear that Lucretius is referring to is not the same as the fear of the gods (for example), which is also used as a mechanism of social enforcement (5.1218–25). Rather, the fear that Lucretius is describing is a fear that arises out of acting contrary to something more natural. Law,

---

[126] See Blickman 1989, 160, 175. An ancient (and modern) argument asks what keeps a sage, not governed by fear, from acting unjustly. The answer would seem to be that these sorts of actions would not be conducive to the goal of happiness nor consistent with the disposition of the sage. A second, and more problematic, issue is how the sage (or any individual) is to act when the most basic conditions of justice are reflected imperfectly in the laws and morals of the community. Konstan, following Philippson, suggests that the sage should "obey the precepts of common morality in whatever place and at whatever time he or she may be living" in order to lead "a life free from disturbance" (Konstan 2008, 124; Philippson 1910, 302–3; DeWitt 1954, 184).

[127] Philippson 1910, 298–99. Strauss' suggestion that for Lucretius "religion is of a utility which is not altogether negligible" because it creates fear in potential criminals carries the unsupportable implication that Lucretius would support religion and religious fear as still operating among society (though not operative on the philosopher) (1968, 127).

[128] Necessary for fallen society (though "just state" can be reclaimed through Epicureanism): Campbell 2003, 14; law to protect from aggression but absent in ideal community: Armstrong 1997, 326.

for the Epicureans, makes "both explicit and obligatory a rule of useful conduct," a usefulness that is "a real state of the world."[129] Law "instructs people to do or not to do under threat of penalty ... the same conduct to which the members of the collectivity already adhere spontaneously."[130] The fear created by law, thus, is not necessarily unnatural. The fear of breaking a law arises from knowing that one has acted contrary to a set of natural agreements, a violation that leaves one in an unnatural state.

Some confirmation of the natural basis of agreements about justice and law lies in observing when Lucretius first uses *foedera* to talk about politics in his discussion of the establishment of a republic. Up to this point *foedera* has been used exclusively to describe the natural associations of atoms (the previous mention is at 5.924: *foedere naturae certo*). Now, however, it is used to describe the "bonds of the common peace" (5.1155), a bond that if violated renders the life of the wrongdoer unhappy. It is an unhappiness, as I will argue in the next section, that underlies Lucretius' depiction of responses to the plague. My claim here is that *foedus* in this context is not meant to refer exclusively to a conscious human activity of agreement but is meant to carry with it the by now accumulated meaning of combinations that occur in nature. The quiet and peaceful life (*placidam ac pacatam ... vitam*, 5.1154), as it plays itself out politically, is a result of individuals naturally coming together to rule themselves.

THE PLAGUE

The final book of *On the nature of things* ends with one of the most debated sections of the poem: Lucretius' graphic reinterpretation of

---

[129] Alberti 1995, 166, 171. Alberti argues that justice and law are not connected for the Epicureans: "law's content and its field of operation, its nature and *raison d'être*, lie not in justice, but in utility in general and that the law reflects norms of justice and aims to permit their operation only to the extent that justice is part of the class of useful things and is one way of realizing utility" (1995, 169). I agree that justice is not obedience to law, nor is law simply rationalized justice. They are connected though, as Alberti continues, since justice provides the criterion to decide whether laws are just or unjust (189).

[130] Alberti 1995, 173.

Thucydides' account of the Athenian plague.[131] Lucretius signals the focus of Book 6 when he describes in the first line how Athens spread abroad the "fruit bearing crops amongst suffering mankind" (6.1, trans. modified). The juxtaposition not only echoes the motif of birth and death that frames the poem, but also anticipates Athens' role in this story. Athens gave seeds of life: food, laws, and Epicurus, who through his "truth telling words" (6.24) brought light to darkness (also 3.1). Lucretius, too, has sought to teach his audience to see (1.950); only now he reveals to his audience not what lies hidden in the dark but what lies before us in the light (6.36). Epicurean physics is made into human drama as everything we see is taken away. As Lucretius writes:

> Therefore let them believe as they please that earth and sky will remain incorruptible, given in trust to life-everlasting; and yet sometimes the very present force of peril applies this goad of fear also from one part or another, that the earth may be suddenly withdrawn from under their feet, and fall into the bottomless pit, followed by the whole sum of things utterly giving way, and then may come the confused ruin of the world (6.601–7).

---

[131] I say reinterpretation in contrast to earlier and now largely rejected scholarship that saw Lucretius as (mis)translating the Thucydidean section (e.g., Bailey 1947, 3.1723, 1737, 1740–41). Bright catalogues deviations from Thucydides and offers explanations as to why (1971, 607–20). Commager, in his influential interpretation, sees Lucretius as departing from Thucydides' more practical purpose of providing "aid to future generations" through his description of the physical symptoms of the plague, and focusing, instead, on the "psychic plague of fear and desire" (Commager 1957, 113, 106, 111; also Erler 1997, 83–84). Bright notes that Lucretius' account "turns on the reactions of the sufferers rather than on the suffering itself" (Bright 1971, 619). Schrijvers points to the use of *enargeia* to make vivid the horror (1970, 296–308). Segal identifies this final episode as playing the form of myth, not unlike Plato's "Myth of Er," one conveying an image of bad death in which individuals are overwhelmed by its terrifying, almost surreal, aspects (Segal 1990, 44–45; 191–92, 226, 228–37). On a more political note, Schiesaro views the plague as an expression of distress that arises from politics, comparing the language to Lucretius' earlier descriptions of the scramble for power and fame (Schiesaro 2007, 55–58; 6.1158–60; compare to 2.12–13, 3.62–63, 6.12–16).

No longer coined in Epicurean physics, the passage is perhaps the most explicit depiction thus far in the poem of not just human temporality, but of the destruction of everything we know.

Lucretius starts big, or at least he seems to, by providing accounts of natural disasters, including earthquakes (6.535–556; 6.667), hurricanes (6.557–76;6.668), and volcanoes (6.639–41; 6.669). Initially, Lucretius is making a point about magnitudes. One looks at these natural disasters and trembles in fear at their seeming enormity when they are, in fact, an infinitesimally small part of the "whole universe" (6.651).[132] "If we should keep this steadily before your mind, comprehend it clearly, see it clearly, you would cease to wonder at many things" (6.653–54). But then Lucretius reverses our gaze: Though we are insignificant in comparison to great natural forces, and these great natural forces are insignificant when measured against an eternal cosmos, we should no more wonder at why the earth trembles than we should that someone falls ill (hinted at in 6.652).

When Lucretius pivots to disease, he is initially making a point about equivalencies: Disease is like a natural disaster, not only in its relative insignificance, but also in its cause. The earth and the sky produce "noxious disease" (6.663). "For the foot suddenly swells, a sharp aching often seizes the teeth, or invades the eyes themselves, the accursed fire appears, creeping over the body and burning each part it takes hold on, and crawls over the limbs, assuredly because there are seeds of many things, and this earth and sky produce enough noxious disease that from it may grow forth an immeasurable quantity of disease" (6.657–664). Lucretius moves back to a recounting of natural disasters: "In this way therefore we must believe that a supply of all things is brought up from the infinite to the whole heaven and earth," enough to make earthquakes, hurricanes, and volcanoes (6.665–72). The earth, as Lucretius concludes, is comprised of "elements of every kind of thing" (6.770, 1093–96) that continually "flow and discharge" (6.922). Like the rest of nature, human bodies are mixed with void, allowing elements – food, moisture, heat,

---

[132] See Jope 1989, 21–22 for ways in which Lucretius takes the wonder and fear out of natural phenomena.

cold, and disease – to seep in and out. Disease is simply part of the natural equation (6.769–72; 6.1236).

But this is not disease in the abstract; it is disease played out in the most horrifying way imaginable, as not only bodily pain incurred by those who have it, but also the sense of impending doom by those yet to catch it. And it is a depiction of near human helplessness: of the plague spreading among herds of animals (6.1245); of corpses lying unburied like dogs along the road (6.1222–23); of listlessness as one's mind becomes consumed by the fear of death (6.1230–34); of a community in disarray (6.1278–80); and of individuals deserting the dying because of fear for their own life (6.1239–41).[133] It is disease that can hit anyone anywhere at anytime.

But why end on this terrifying and graphic note? Two general answers have been provided. Some cite the abruptness of the ending as evidence that the poem is unfinished.[134] Others point to the scene as a culmination of a point Epicurus and Lucretius are making: The remedies provided by civic institutions, even by as admired a place as Athens, are exposed as unhelpful precisely because they are founded on ignorance of the nature of things. The final scene, as Bright rightly points out, brackets the opening scene, showing how "the gods, nature and life are balanced by equal but opposite situations of man, society and death."[135] The audience, like the victims of the plague, must navigate their way through this horror and make choices that accord with happiness.[136] By the end, "man is left to himself and fails" because of his "inability to control his response" to the plague, reacting with the same sort of fear

---

[133] Bright notes, for example, how Lucretius deviates from Thucydides to "intensify the horror of the disease's advance" (1971, 612).

[134] Talking generally of the poem, see Sandbach 1940, 75; specifically about the final plague scene, see Bignone 1945, 2.322; Sedley 1998, 160–65, arguing for a reorganization of the final lines.

[135] Bright 1971, 626; Gale 1994, 226–27.

[136] Müller 1977, 217–21 (final test for the audience); Kelly 1980 (price of ignorance); Jope 1989 (designed to lead reader to detachment); Minyard 1985, 60–61 (as a "satire" on Athenian civic responses, before Epicureanism, to disease and death). Strauss doubts that philosophy "has any remedy against the helplessness and the debasement which afflicts anyone struck by such events as the plague" (1968, 82).

that infects society.[137] Only Epicurus can make the pain endurable by teaching how to approach suffering "with *the right frame of mind* – a frame of mind which will enable us to eliminate fear and to tolerate pain cheerfully if it should come our way."[138]

One trajectory, suggested by Jope (among others), is to view the final book as instilling the frame of mind that parallels the opening of Book 2 in which the philosopher looks down from his or her "lofty sanctuaries serene" at the strife and toil of those below (2.7–19). There is, to be sure, a Hellenistic impulse in *On the nature of things* that associates philosophy with detachment: freedom from necessity, from cares, and from wonder.[139] Lucretius' celebration of Epicurus resonates with these Hellenist tones: Epicurus is like a god and nothing prevents us from "living a life worthy of gods" (3.322). Lucretius lends some sense of the grandeur of his own perspective when he writes that true piety is "to be able to survey all things with a tranquil mind" (5.1203). To that extent, Lucretius can be understood as moving his audience toward a notion of philosophic detachment in which, as Jope writes, "man's fears are viewed collectively and impersonally, with the moral distance of one who comprehends their unreason."[140] After reading about detachment in the abstract, and then working through the arguments for the inevitability of destruction, the reader, as Jope concludes, "is challenged by the grim conclusion to look at concrete human suffering...with the same detachment."[141]

I want to suggest a different reading of the final book, one that does not seek refuge in lofty sanctuaries but contains within it a civic dimension. In times of trial, Lucretius notes, we see the real character of a

---

[137] Bright 1971, 628.
[138] Sedley 1998, 165. Also Klingner 1986, 408–9; Gale 1994, 228; 2000, 22–23.
[139] See Jope 1989, 25 (on wonder); Erler 2002 (on Greek tradition of living like a god, though for Epicurus and Lucretius one accomplishes this by focusing on the mortal, not immortal, aspects of the self). Greek sources: Plato *Tim.* 41d–47c, 90c–d; *Rep.* 500c–501b, 613a–b, *Laws* 716c–d, *Phaed.* 81a–84b, *Phaedr.* 245c–249a; Aristotle *NE* 1177b; Stoics, see Cic. *De nat. deor.* 2.59.147; 2.61.153; Zeno *SVF* 1.179. Roman context, see Horace *Ep.* 1.6; Cic. *Tusc.* 3.14.30 (free from wonder), 5.28.81 (unaffected by any occurrence); Piso in Cic. *De fin.* 5.4.11
[140] Jope 1989, 33. [141] Jope 1989, 34; also De Lacy 1964, 55; Morford 2002, 125.

person (3.55–58). That character is not the unambiguous vision of the sage, though, but something much more ambivalent, and at the core of Lucretian thought. The heroes of the story are not detached.[142] Lucretius suggests that for those who deserted the bodies, "avenging Neglectfulness ... would punish" (*poenibat ... incuria mactans*) them not long after by consigning them to die a lonely death (6.1240–41). The statement seems surprising: Why and how would nature punish such action?[143] Strauss, for example, suggests that although Lucretius "does not speak of divine punishment, he suggests it."[144] But Lucretius earlier provides us with a natural analog in describing the "faithful" (*fides*) dogs that yield to death reluctantly (6.1222). So too the "noblest" (*optimus*), moved by both sympathy and reproach, stayed with those who were suffering and cared for the bodies (6.1246).[145] Faithfulness, thus, resides in nature. Trickier is the issue of punishment. But even that becomes explicable within an Epicurean transactional notion of justice. Lucretius' statement that shame and reproach compel those who remain to bury the dead (6.1243–44) recalls Epicurus' suggestion that injustice is something bad because of the impossibility of knowing with certainty that one can escape the notice of others. Neglect punishes not through active agency but by the troubles or afflictions one bears in avoiding one's agreed upon responsibilities. In a system of justice created for mutual advantage, one is punished for neglect by in turn being neglected.

Lucretius' poem opens and closes on the same question: Is there a difference between detachment and abandonment? The final book completes the movement of the first. Lucretius, like Memmius, is drawn down into the world of human affairs for similar reasons: They cannot watch the turmoil and suffering without being affected by it. The final book completes that trajectory. We are not gods, indifferent to what is around us. Nor do we have recourse to a refuge. We are in the world, and we are – by the nature of things – of the world (a formula that Augustine

---

[142] In fact, Jope makes no mention of Lucretius' seeming praise of those who did not abandon the sufferers (1989).
[143] As un-Epicurean, see Bailey 1947, 3.1737.   [144] Strauss 1968, 82.
[145] See Bright 1971, 614: Thucydides only mentions shame as the reason for visiting the dying.

will later revise). Lucretius' poem, thus, shows us not how to ascend, but descend; it shows us how to be in a world with others.

LUCRETIUS AND THE LIMITS OF POLITICS

One of the enduring paradoxes of Epicureanism, generally, and Lucretius' poem, specifically, is how frequently their writings and ideas are invoked by political actors and thinkers. From the anti-Caesarian elements at the end of the Roman republic to the American revolutionaries at the beginning of the American republic (with later stops at Marx [for Epicurus] and Nietzsche [for Lucretius]), history may give us some perspective on the contours of Lucretius' political thought. At a minimum, it seems rash to simply dismiss Lucretius' importance as a political thinker. But we go equally awry in imagining that Lucretius articulates a vision of a political system. Lucretius' importance in political thought lies elsewhere: namely, in the language he provides to address the limits of politics.

It is in his uncompromising battle with the forces of tradition, undertaken with an evangelical zeal, that we can appreciate the immediacy of Lucretius' thought. Against the backdrop of an infinite and eternal nature, the claims of kings cannot help but be diminished. And against the ineluctable forces of a universe in motion, the seemingly invincible power of tyrants is dealt a blow. The "hidden power" (*vis abdita*) of nature tramples on the "noble rods and cruel axes," holding these images of Roman power and authority in derision (5.1233–35). Lucretius punctures the claims to authority that accompany tradition-based esteem (*auctoritas*) and strength (*vis*). He gives the armature of truth to the quest to recover one's natural power.

The problem of Lucretius' poetics of power is that it is unable to reconcile a life in rhythm with the eternal laws of a timeless universe with a life occupied by the temporal concerns that govern politics. Time for Lucretius is not an attribute of atoms or of the universe; it is a marker of the passage of events (1.459–63). Events come and go, but have no existence in themselves (1.465–66). In important ways, Epicureanism seeks to defeat the grip of time by teaching how to exist in the happiness of the moment. But politics is not about the moment; it is invariably about the future, about how a community defines a shared destiny. Lucretius' poetry works as a politics of defiance because it so easily demonstrates the falsity and fleeting nature of the bonds of community life; it does not work as a politics of construction because it cannot, perhaps it dares not, project a community forward in time.

Epicurus was adamant that any doctrine cannot forget the past and must leave room for hope, which is an interesting nod to the ways in which temporal creatures plot out their lives (Epic. *Men.* 127; Cic. *Tusc.* 3.15.33). But imagining, or even building, a political community needs more than hope; it requires that we anticipate some future place that may lie outside our ability to actualize; it requires living with imperfection; and it requires structures that invariably demand compromise. Epicurus' Garden, like Thoreau's Walden, thrived as a refuge from, more than an image of, political life. But they similarly challenge us by questioning what we take for granted, denaturalizing what we assume is unassailable, and making us accountable for the trajectory of our lives. In that accountability lies explosive political potential.

3 SALLUST: GIVING ENDURANCE TO MEMORY

Sallust (Gaius Sallustius Crispus, 86?–35/34 BCE), in introducing *The War with Jugurtha* (*Bellum Jugurthinum*), employs a trope common in Roman historical writing: the role of the historian recording the events of the past so that they can be remembered and individual deeds imitated or avoided (*Jug.* 4.1). To some extent the language reads as an apology that is as familiar to the Romans at it would be unfamiliar to the Greeks. Intellectual pursuits are contrasted with practical ones; inactivity (*inertia*) with industriousness (*industria*) (*Jug.* 4.3). Sallust justifies his new occupation in part by pointing to his own time in office. Sallust, like Cicero, was a *novus homo*: an Italian of equestrian origins, he rose to tribune of the plebs, senator, praetor, and provincial governor under Caesar.[1] But he also points to the service his history will provide by illustrating *exempla* that kindle the desire to imitate the virtue, and equal the fame and glory, of one's ancestors (*Jug.* 4.5–6; also *Cat.* 8.5).

---

[1] On Sallust's life, see Syme's lively account (1964, 29–42). Sallust's political career: tribune of the plebs (52 BCE); expelled from senate by the censor, Appius Claudius, possibly in retaliation for his speeches against Cicero and Milo (50 BCE); sent as praetor by Caesar to suppress a mutiny in Campania (47 BCE); chosen by Caesar as first governor of Africa Nova (which included annexed portions of Africa and Numidia) (46 BCE); accused of extortion and allowed, likely with Caesar's intervention, to retire (45 BCE).

Sallust has not been the subject of much attention as a political thinker, receiving only passing attention, for example, in the comprehensive *Cambridge History of Greek and Roman Political Thought* and no treatment in the *Blackwell Companion to Greek and Roman Political Thought*. Sallust's political thought is often assessed as a form of *popularis* propaganda,[2] a fairly simple (and historically questionable) analysis of the emergence of Roman corruption with the defeat of Carthage, or both. Earl, whose work remains the fullest discussion of Sallust's political thought, characterizes Sallust as clinging to an "artificial and unhistorical view."[3] And Paul comments that Sallust's "view of the past is idealistic and schematic" and a discredit to sober history.[4]

There is good reason for the student of political thought to pay attention to Sallust, though, if for no other reason than because of how he problematizes the central concept of Roman political life: the *mos maiorum*, or the custom of the ancestors (see Introduction, 15–18). The memory of one's ancestors oriented political, military, and social action, serving to channel desire by prescribing and proscribing conduct. But when Sallust looks to the past, he is less idealizing than exploring the problematic genealogy of political concepts forged in memory. The paradox of memory is that it is always only present – it only exists as it is remembered and practiced and it changes the moment it is recalled or enacted differently.

The conceptual map that orients Roman political life does not have an ontological status that accords with some reality. Nor did the *mos maiorum* exist as a rigid set of rules in which one could point to binding words or coerce through a judicial apparatus. In fact, as Arena has suggested recently, the *mos maiorum* was not only "open to continuous variations and interpretations," but also that the normative force of these

---

[2] Sallust as biased: Mommsen 1869, 3; Schwartz 1897; von Fritz 1943; Waters 1970; Parker 2004: "Anyone writing the prehistory of the Jugurthine War on the basis of these facts would produce an account very different from Sallust's" (422). More balanced appraisals of Sallust's account are provided by Schur 1934; Syme 1964; MacQueen 1981, 14–21; Schmal 2001, 54–57. The most thorough attempt at constructing the legal issues is provided by Drummond 1995.
[3] Earl 1961, 42.   [4] Paul 1984, 5; also Laistner 1947, 53.

claims was performative.⁵ The force of any assertion about rights, duties, or practices rested on its recognition and acceptance, a cultural negotiation not just among the elite but requiring "the consensus of the people at large."⁶ There are no clear criteria to differentiate the regeneration of paths from their degeneration, nor is there anything to distinguish between a "proper" and "improper" path since the map is the path that one invokes and others recognize.

When Sallust looks back, he is tracing an inheritance that can no longer be relied upon to provide any orientation beyond the immediacy of one's desires. In Sallust's formulation, under the pretense of *bonum publicum*, individuals sought their own *potentia*, or might (*Cat.* 38.3). Hardly simply a "hackneyed" portrayal of the loss of virtues that had become "commonplaces alike of rhetoricians and philosophers," as Laistner contends, Sallust's works address a more nagging question, and one central to political thought: if words or, more generally, social norms and values acquire meaning in practice, then on what basis can one favor one meaning over another? Or more specifically, by what criteria does one decide how desire should be organized?⁷ Sallust answers not by reference to how well the map accords with some truth or reality but by reference to the performative question of why make a map in the first place. At the heart of Sallust's answer is a concern with giving endurance to memory. For Sallust, the loss of the orienting force of the past risks creating a map that has no meaning, goal, or reference beyond oneself. In transforming the Roman past into a treasure map, individuals enrich themselves but risk leaving nothing enduring behind. What is so compelling about Sallust's argument is that he does not seek to reorient Roman politics by way of Greek concepts or philosophic truths. He does

---

⁵ See the excellent discussion by Arena of the flexibility by which the *mos maiorum* operated in Hammer (forthcoming).

⁶ Drummond 1995, 87.

⁷ Arena in Hammer (forthcoming); also Laistner 1947, 171 fn 21, 47. Sklenář explores this question of meaning by way of Saussure and Thucydides, suggesting a distinction between a Thucydidean view (which influences Sallust) of meanings as based on consensus (like Saussure) and needing stability versus Sallust and Cato's view of meanings as anti-Saussurean because they argue that meanings should be attached to particular words (1998, 216–17). See also Büchner 1983, 260; Minyard 1985. 21–22.

not create a city of words by wiping away memories and organizing the community by the logic of philosophy, as does Plato, but summons a political world that makes sense – and has stopped making sense – as accumulated memories and practices.[8]

METUS HOSTILIS AND THE ORGANIZATION OF DESIRE

The centerpiece of Sallust's political thought is seen frequently (and perhaps unfortunately for his legacy) as lying in his theory of *metus hostilis*, or fear of the enemy. The claim is that absent the fear of an enemy, a state loses its discipline and civic mindedness and degenerates into self-interest, faction, and luxury. The idea was commonplace in ancient discourse. Aristotle, for example, describes how military states "lose their edge in time of peace" (*Pol.* 1334a6–8). And Polybius notes how threats from other states compel a community to "act in concord and support" (6.18.2; also 6.57.5; 31.25 on Cato; 32.13.6). Sallust probably gets his cues, as well, from a Roman tradition that poses a debate between Cato the Elder (Cato the Censor) and Scipio Nasica about whether Carthage should be destroyed.[9] For Earl, "Sallust's choice of the destruction of Carthage as the turning point in Roman history set a fashion," followed by Pliny (*NH* 33.150), Velleius Paterculus (2.1.1), Florus (1.33.1; 1.34.18; 1.47.2), Augustine (*Civ. Dei.* 1.30, 31; 2.18), and Oros (5.8.2).[10] According to Earl, what stands out in Sallust's account is that the destruction of Carthage in 146 BCE did not just intensify a set of earlier trends, but was "the moment" when the decline in public morality began.[11] Although we do not know if Sallust set this fashion (since discussions of decline were pretty common in Rome), the importance of Carthage looms large in Sallust's account (though, as I will argue, not quite in the way it is frequently understood). As Sallust

---

[8] On Rome as an "affective universe," see Vasaly 1993, 60.
[9] See Earl 1961, 47; Astin 1967, 272–81; Plut. *Cato Mai.* 27; Polyb. 38.21–22. On the ancient use of fear generally, see Wood 1995; Kapust 2008.
[10] Earl 1961, 47.   [11] Earl 1961, 49.

writes, without an enemy to fear the community was "torn to pieces" by contending factions (*Jug.* 41.5). "Thus," Sallust notes, "by the side of power (*potentia*), greed arose, unlimited and unrestrained, violated and devastated everything, respected nothing, and held nothing sacred, until it finally brought about its own downfall" (*Jug.* 41.9).

As a theory of social change, Sallust's account has been criticized for ignoring or downplaying earlier episodes of discord and resting on an overly rigid conception of historical decline.[12] As an exploration of political virtue, Sallust's analysis, according to Earl, does not explain "how or why" corruption occurs with the loss of an enemy since "true" *virtus* "should surely be independent of external compulsions."[13] "Vague references to fortune and to 'peace and the abundance of those things which mortals consider of first importance' do not provide an intellectually compelling explanation."[14] Along these same lines, Sklenář suggests that Sallust's "presentation of ancestral *virtus* departs from the purely rationalistic conception of the preamble."[15]

It is certainly the case that if we understand *virtus* as a form of abstract morality, then the attribution of Rome's decline to the destruction of Carthage and the influx of foreign luxury cannot help but look "artificial and mechanical."[16] But the beginning point of Sallust's analysis is not reason or virtue; it is (like so much of Roman political thought) desire. Humans for Sallust are naturally disposed to be "greedy for power (*avidus imperi*) and eager to gratify its heart's desire (*animi cupido*)" (*Jug.* 6.3; *Hist.* 1.8, McGushin). But desire is also critical to the creation of a competitive ethos that drives Rome toward greatness. The deeds of one's

---

[12] Contending views of corruption in early Rome are discussed by Lintott, who suggests that ascribing "the failure of the Republic to moral corruption derived from wealth and foreign conquest" is the result of propaganda from the Gracchan period (1972, 638). Earl traces the stages of decline as *virtus* to *ambitio* and *avaritia*, and finally, with Sulla, to *luxuria* (1961, 42, 15). Conley modifies the reading of Sallust to suggest that there are only two stages of decline: *ambitio*, and then *avaritia* and *luxuria* together (1981, 380). Lintott argues for a less schematic understanding of the relationship between *ambitio* and *avaritia* in Sallust (1972, 627–28).
[13] Earl 1961, 51–52; also 1982, 629. [14] Earl 1982, 630.
[15] Sklenář 1998, 211; also 209: "The *virtus* responsible for all human accomplishment is intellectual."
[16] Earl 1982, 629.

ancestors, for example, do not speak to reason but are supposed to inflame the heart to equal the fame and glory of one's forefathers (*Jug.* 4.5, 6). It is the cultural equivalent of playing with fire. So a necessary question that Sallust asks is how Rome early on controls the flame.

Sallust is exploring how communities organize desire. In fact, he is making exactly the claim that Earl dismisses: The coherence of a community – what holds it together as something more than an aggregate of individual desires – requires a force powerful enough to shape and constrain those desires. Sallust's discussion of early Rome traces the mechanisms by which the organizing principles of Roman life are given shape. Carthage is important, not only because its destruction removes an important constraint, but also because the prosecution of the war and the expansion of Rome's empire alters the constellation of constraints that forms Rome's political inheritance and shapes individual dispositions.

We make a mistake if we see Sallust as imagining early Rome as reflecting a pristine record of what Earl describes as "unbroken *concordia, boni mores* and *virtus.*"[17] Sallust does use the language of *concordia* in describing Rome's founding: "After these two peoples [the Trojans and Latins], different in race, unlike in speech and mode of life, were united within the same walls, they were merged into one with incredible facility, so quickly did harmony change a scattered and wandering band into a commonwealth (*Hi postquam in una moenia convenere, dispari genere, dissimili lingua, alii alio more viventes, incredibile memoratu est quam facile coaluerint; ita brevi multitudo dispersa atque vaga concordia civitas facta erat*)" (*Cat.* 6.2, trans. modified; also *Jug.* 10.6 on advice by Micipsa to his sons). *Concordia* is frequently translated here as "harmony," which is misleading (and historically false by Sallust's own account). In this context we can better translate *concordia* as "coming together," a sense of common or public purpose that is more than a sum of individual and inchoate private desires. Thus, Sallust

---

[17] Earl 1961, 41; also Earl 1982, 627; Paul 1984, 5.125; Kapust 2008, 365; summarizing scholarship, see Vasaly 2009, 253. Sallust says there was minimal avarice in *Cat.* 9.1. Accounts of earlier discord include *Hist.* 1.10 = Aug. *Civ. Dei.* 2.18; *Hist.* 1.3 = Aug. *Civ. Dei.* 2.18; also Wood 1995, 179–81.

juxtaposes the *concordia* of a *civitas* with *dispergere* (scattering) and *vagus* (wandering), images of entropic desire.

Concordia, thus, comes about as organized desire, though what organizes it undergoes some modifications. Wisdom (*sapientia*), which is associated with knowledge and judgment about worldly affairs and identified originally with the king and fathers (*patres*) (*Cat.* 6.6), plays a part. So, too, the people invest their whole "energy" in martial excellence, or *virtus*, on the battlefield to avert danger to "their liberty, their country, and their parents by arms" (*Cat.* 6.5). But the forces of wisdom and *virtus* undergo change. Absent constraints on desire, the wisdom associated with kingship gives way to arrogant tyranny (so much for the so-called "unbroken" record of *concordia*) (*Cat.* 6.7).

When the kings are replaced with consuls and the Republic established, both *virtus* and *sapientia* become more generalized characteristics of citizenship, taking on an increasingly political connotation (*Cat.* 7.2).[18] Where talent had been inhibited by the natural suspicion of kings

---

[18] On a conception of *virtus* encompassing a broad set of political and military qualities, see Pöschl 1940, 12–26; Earl 1967, 21; Badian 1967, 13; Eisenhut 1973, 48–57; Scanlon 1980, 29–30; Hock 1988, 21, 23–24; also Earl 1960 (in Plautus) and 1962 (in Terence). McDonnell rejects the original association of *virtus* with a "unified political-ethical concept," limiting its early Roman meaning to associations with martial qualities that then gets expanded through borrowings from the Greek *aretē*, or excellence (2006, 363; also 293–95). Pöschl rejects any Greek influence, seeing Sallust as articulating a distinctively Roman concept (1940, 17–26, 46–47); McDonnell argues for it (2006, 72–141, 369; also Schmal 2001, 115, with qualification). Wood, too, argues that Sallust's emphasis on the relationship between fear and virtue derives from Sallust's recognition of Rome as a military state (1995, 181–82). McDonnell's argument is important, and I will draw on it. But I think McDonnell at times too rigidly separates the different meanings of *virtus*, suggesting, for example, that "Sallust presents two different kinds of *virtus*," one Roman and the other Greek, one without ethical coloring the other ethical, and "confined" to different parts of the narrative (2006, 356). McDonnell at times tempers his claim, conceding that "martial *virtus* on occasion carries an ethical connotation" in Sallust's narratives (2006, 356; also 128 on the possibility that *virtus* always contained some ethical sense). In a somewhat surprising claim, Farron suggests that "Vergil's contemporaries did not regard military preeminence as the ultimate Roman virtue" (1981, 100). I am not sure from the context what "ultimate" means here, but one would be hard pressed to identify another Roman activity around which so much energy was expended, so many honors bestowed, and so many ethical terms employed.

toward the merit of others (*Cat.* 6.2), in the Republic "every man began to lift his head higher and to have his talents (*ingenium*) more in readiness" (*Cat.* 7.1). The "thirst for glory" (*cupido gloriae*) associated with the martial aggressiveness of *virtus* now extends into the political arena and includes more men (*Cat.* 7.3).

The battlefield remains the primary training ground of desire. As soon as young men can endure hardship, they are taught endurance, fearlessness, and discipline and compete with each other to be seen performing great military deeds (*Cat.* 7.3–6).[19] But the aggressiveness associated with *virtus*, once it is extended to politics, has to be tempered by laws and *mores*, qualities associated with the good man (see *Jug.* 64.1).[20] Soldiers act not just with boldness (*audacia*) but also learn to restrain this boldness through right (*ius*) and equality (*aequitas*). Orders are enforced, placing limits on actions in war. And in times of peace alliances are governed by kindness rather than fear and forgiveness rather than vengeance (*Cat.* 9.1–5; also 6.5). The state thrives as men are recognized for, and allowed to practice, their good talents (*ingenium bonum*) – a phrase revealing of Sallust's embrace of the ideology of the new man – while restrained by both laws and *mores* (*Cat.* 10.5).

It is worth noting that we have talked about moments in Rome's history in which desire is unleashed without yet mentioning Carthage. That is because the role of Carthage flows out of this analysis (rather than being injected into it). Carthage is one constraint that, like earlier enemies, gives public organization to desire. The looming presence of Carthage, transmitted over decades to the Roman people through images of heroic successes and humiliating losses, serves as a continual reminder of what Romans desire. The existence of enemies, early in Rome's history and later with Carthage, has an extraordinary ability to focus the community because the goal (defeating the enemy) is clear, the means of achieving the goal (discipline and sacrifice) are inculcated

---

[19] See McDonnell 2006, 181–85 on the relationship between citizenship and military preparation.

[20] See Levick 1982 on the tension between ambition and equality, and ambition and *virtus*, in Roman politics. Also Long: an ideology based on glory "is always at risk of deriving ethical worth from material status, and of using the glory and wealth that accrue to the powerful as absolute standards of their actual merit" (1995b, 217).

from an early age and practiced, and the cost of not achieving the goal (survival) is dramatic.

The final defeat of Carthage weakens the martial impetus that lies at the heart of the Roman conception of *virtus*. And the absence of any real threat alters the calculus of action. But the importance of Carthage does not lie simply in the removal of the constraint of fear. It reveals how Rome's foreign ventures have implications for the institutional organization of desire. Rome's empire had grown so large and so complex that its maintenance required that the people relinquish their power, delegating the administration of the empire to the provinces (who are ruled by designees of the senate) and to turn their authority to decide foreign matters over to the senate.[21] As Sallust writes:

> Affairs at home and in the field were managed according to the will of a few men, in whose hands were the treasury, the provinces, public offices, glory, and triumphs. The people were burdened with military service and poverty. The generals divided the spoils of war with a few friends. Meanwhile the parents or little children of the soldiers, if they had a powerful neighbour, were driven from their homes (*Jug.* 41.7–8).

That meant that power becomes more concentrated, but not necessarily more unified, in a few hands.[22] Victory goes to the individual who amasses the most resources, most telling armies. Absent the dispersion of power, there are no checks or limits on how those resources are acquired or how they can be employed. It is in this altered context that we can understand how the practice of plundering, learned on the battlefield, could have such free reign at home.

When Sallust uses the verb *miscere*, or to mix, to characterize Roman culture, he is describing the confusion of a concept whose organizing and orienting power now rests on an ill-defined inheritance (*Cat.* 10.1).

---

[21] Keaveney 1982, 2; Hölkeskamp 1993, 33–35.
[22] If Badian's argument is correct that the senate resisted the expansion of empire (1967, 29–40), then Sallust's analysis is all the more striking because it suggests the inability of traditional institutions to restrain the actions of a powerful few. Badian confirms this analysis, pointing to the loss of constraints or the ability to control "the ambition and greed of individual nobles" (Badian 1967, 48).

Released from any sorts of institutional or traditional constraints (*Jug.* 41.3), human desire – in a Roman context, the desire for prestige (*dignitas*) and glory – runs like water over a broken levee: Separate streams dig divergent channels in which more water would follow. At first, the water rushes toward the same outlet – glory, honor, and power (*imperium*) – but not by way of the true path (*vera via*) (*Cat.* 11.2). Sallust calls that *ambitio*, an excessive desire to be recognized that employs craft and deception (*Cat.* 11.1–2). But the continual rush of water soon finds the easiest path, one directed not toward glory but by the immediate desires of the body. Motivated by avarice (*avaritia*), the desire for money transforms glory, honor, and power into commodities valued for the price they can bring (*Cat.* 10.4; also 12.1; 30.4; *Jug.* 31.12; 35.10; *Hist.* 1.14 = Arusianus Messius 484.19). But probably most dramatically, and captured in the image of streams of water digging their own paths, the destruction of Carthage (and of Corinth) and the conquest of Asia that heralds new sources of untold wealth for the taking,[23] are the catalysts for the breakdown of consensus and of the mechanism by which both domestic and foreign agreement might even be reached: not just discord, but the assassination of opponents; not just factions, but armed gangs suppressing opposition; not just tyrants, but wealthy dynasts who could finance their own armies; not just the struggle for inclusion, but a protracted and exhausting war that will ultimately span the Roman world.

Sallust is not saying that something changes in human nature; he is saying that something changes in the structures of constraint. If individuals before Rome's founding possess a diffuse energy, and if the early Republic reflects a concentrated and purposeful energy, then Rome after the destruction of Carthage suffers from this energy now uncontrolled and turned against itself. The problem is not that there are no longer the orienting forces of tradition and memory; it is that they orient in the

---

[23] The destruction of Carthage and Corinth is seen by some as reflecting an imperial strategy pursued less through colonization and more through demonstrations of force and terror. See Astin 1967, 272–76; Purcell 1995; Morstein Kallet-Marx 1995, 84–94 (on the razing of Corinth in 146 BCE); Flower 2010, 70–71; also Cic. *De off.* 2.8.27. On the importance of Asia's wealth in altering Roman incentives to annex and exploit territories, see Badian 1967, 42–45.

wrong way. For good reason, Sallust, in his two extant works, *The War with Catiline* and *The War with Jugurtha*, explores the political genealogy of this corrupted inheritance: The new man, Marius, begets the corrupt patrician, Sulla, who acculturates the revolutionary patrician, Catiline. And the virtuous patrician, Scipio Aemilianus, begets the ambitious "new man," Jugurtha, who plunges Rome into war. These are the decades from which the Republic never recovers and for which Sallust has no easy answers.

THE WAR WITH CATILINE AND THE SUBVERSION OF POLITICS

Sallust begins *The War with Catiline* (*Bellum Catilinae*, possibly published between 44 and 40 BCE[24]), an account of a conspiracy led by Catiline to overthrow the Roman government (63 BCE), on a conceptual note, one that frames his argument and announces the philosophical importance of his history: Human power (*vis*) lies in the rule of the body by the *animus*, which, as the word denotes, consists of qualities of both the mind and spirit (*Cat.* 1.2).[25] A life dictated solely by the body is one, like the beasts, that is enslaved by the appetites (*Cat.* 1.1). The fate of a life devoted to bodily desires, whether riches or beauty, is to pass through this world in silence, like "mere wayfarers" (*Cat.* 1.1; 2.8), existence made "fleeting and frail" (*Cat.* 1.4), one's life indistinguishable from one's death (*Cat.* 2.8). But a life ruled by the mind brings glory that makes one immortal in memory (*Cat.* 1.3–4). It is easy to dismiss Sallust's

---

[24] See MacKay 1962.

[25] I say that it frames the argument to contrast with views of Sallust's prologues as either independent of or inconsistent with the main text (on scholarship, see Paul 1984, 9–10). Earl notes that Sallust breaks from the Roman tradition of the first sentence announcing the genre by seemingly coupling a philosophic prologue with a work of history (1982, 626). On the connection of the prologue to Posidonius, see Schur 1934; connection to Plato, see Egermann 1932; MacQueen 1981; Schmal 2001, 112–14; to Stoics, see Pantzerhielm Thomas 1936; Hock 1988 (by way of Cicero); to Aristotle (and *Cat.* and *Jug.* as moral treatise), see Earl 1972. Other influences generally: Thucydides, see Scanlon 1980; 1998; Woodman 1988, 126–28; Cicero, see Hock 1988.

claim as a watered down and derivative gloss on Hellenistic rationalism that privileges the life of wisdom and the cultivation of the immortal parts of the human soul.[26] But there is more to his claim. A community in which its members know no language other than the immediate desires of the body risks become fleeting and frail, not only passing but also leaving no trace in the memory of others.[27]

Catiline emerges in the wake of Sulla, to whom Sallust attributes two alterations in Roman political culture: the introduction of luxury and avarice (*Cat.* 11.3) and the institutionalization of political violence. Sulla allows his soldiers to pillage in the foreign arena in order to secure their loyalty (*Cat.* 11.5–7) and then turns that army against Rome's own citizens (88 BCE), identifying through proscription those he characterizes as *hostis*, a foreign enemy to be defeated (e.g., *Cat.* 11.4).[28] Citizens on proscription lists could be legally killed and their property confiscated, a mechanism that for Sallust serves to further "glut" Sulla's followers with riches (*Cat.* 51.34).[29] In emphasizing the devouring aspect of the soldiers who destroy, steal, or consume everything in their wake, Sallust is drawing a contrast with how Rome created the stabilizing structures of empire, at first through war but more enduringly through *amicitiae* that were public, mutually beneficial alliances (*Cat.* 6.5; 11.7; also *Jug.* 8.2). We cannot help but be reminded of Sallust's prologue: Political immortality – the desire to build something that lasts forever – had

---

[26] See, for example, Laistner who states, "the concept that man differs from the other animals because he has a soul or mind to direct him has been formulated by Plato, Aristotle, and Isocrates" (1947, 52); also Scanlon 1980, 34–35; McDonnell 2006, 370–71. Sklenář sees a tension between "Sallustian rationalism" and "nostalgia for a virtuous Roman past" (1998, 208–9). As I argue below, I do not see as clear a split in Sallust's thought.

[27] On associations of slavery and the body, see Hock 1988. I agree with Pantzerhielm Thomas in cautioning against assigning too much theoretical significance, or too specific of a philosophic school, to Sallust's juxtaposition of mind and body (1936, 151). Egermann, for example, associates Sallust's discussion of mind and body with Platonic dualism (1932, 7).

[28] Raaflaub argues that the Pompeians effectively (if not explicitly) characterized the Caesarians as hostile enemies (1974, 192–200, 236–38).

[29] On Sulla, see Volkmann 1958; Meier 1980, 222–28; Levick 1982; Keaveney 2007, 37–38; 1983; von Ungern-Sternberg 1998; Flower 2010, 92.

begun to give way to political insatiability – the desire to sate one's immediate desires that makes any agreement unstable. Rome's citizens, to recall the prologue, are becoming like the beasts who exist only to fill their belly (*Cat.* 1.1).

The picture Sallust paints of Roman society at the turn of the century is one where men and women become habituated to self-indulgence, an orientation to the immediate desires of the body (*Cat.* 13.5; also 13.3). On a slightly autobiographical note, Sallust describes how in his "youthful weakness" he succumbed to an environment characterized by "shamelessness, bribery, and rapacity" (*Cat.* 3.3–4; compare to *Cat.* 14.4–5). But it's not just a general atmosphere. Sallust makes explicit Catiline's political inheritance. Catiline is inspired by Sulla's desire for kingship (*Cat.* 5.6). Furthermore, Catiline surrounds himself with aristocrats who had wasted their inheritance (*Cat.* 14.2; 37.5) and with Sulla's soldiers who had squandered their riches gained from pillaging (*Cat.* 16.4; 37.6). Catiline continues the tradition, educating those attracted to him in vice (*Cat.* 16.1–2; also *Cat.* 14.5).

Sallust's characterization of Catiline as a "madman" (*Cat.* 15.5; also 5.1–5), a person, as Vasaly comments, of a "protean" spirit (*animus*) and "monstrous" desires, only makes worse the ease with which he garners a political following.[30] Catiline plots his route to kingship both by electoral means – seeking a consulship – and by way of insurrection. Scholars have suggested incredulously that the chronology does not make sense; no Roman aspiring to elective office would simultaneously plot the violent overthrow of the government. Whether Sallust's chronology is correct is difficult to determine. But Sallust is making a more telling point: There may in effect be very little difference between these two paths. Catiline may be the leader of an insurrection, but more ominously he is the herald of a new politics in which the language that gives integrity and purpose to processes had already been subverted.

The Republic, as Cato the Younger so poignantly exclaims, had lost the true names of things (*vera vocabula rerum*) (*Cat.* 52.11).[31] For

---

[30] Vasaly 2009, 253.
[31] Also *Hist.* 1.55.24 (Lepidus talking about Sulla); Cic. *Sest.* 34.73.

Sallust that truth is less obvious since the meanings one ascribes to words are forged in history and given form by memory. We can perhaps better understand the truth of words for Sallust as a type of objectivity. Words are objective if they have meanings that are publicly recognized and shared. The contrast is with false words that have no publicly recognizable meaning because they can as easily mean their opposite.

The Catilinarian conspiracy is a study in false words. Catiline, for example, employs the foundational vocabulary of Rome, referring to how the *virtus* and *fides* of his followers had been tested. As Sallust has Catiline say to his followers:

> If I had not already tested your courage and loyalty, in vain would a great opportunity have presented itself; high hopes and power would have been placed in my hands to no purpose, nor would I with the aid of cowards or inconstant hearts grasp at uncertainty in place of certainty (*Ni virtus fidesque vostra spectata mihi forent, nequiquam opportuna res cecidisset; spes magna, dominatio in manibus frustra fuissent, neque ego per ignaviam aut vana ingenia incerta pro certis captarem*) (*Cat.* 20.2–3).

But the foundation of this conspiratorial group – what binds them together and animates their actions – is not manliness but what for the Romans is effeminizing luxury. Sallust, in drawing upon Roman views of the East, traces this inheritance to Sulla, who introduces eastern luxury to his troops as he plunges into Asia. He allows his soldiers "a luxury and license foreign to the manners of our forefathers; and in the intervals of leisure those charming and voluptuous lands had easily demoralized the warlike spirit of his soldiers" (*Cat.* 11.5–6). Soldiers "first learned to indulge in women and drink; to admire statues, paintings, and chased vases, to steal them from private houses and public places, to pillage shrines, and to desecrate everything, both sacred and profane" (*Cat.* 11.6). These habits infiltrate Roman culture to the point where "the passion which arose for lewdness, gluttony, and the other attendants of luxury was equally strong; men played the woman, women offered their chastity for sale; to gratify their palates they scoured land and sea; they slept before they needed sleep; they did not await the coming of hunger or thirst, of cold or of weariness, but all these things their self-indulgence anticipated" (*Cat.* 13.3; also Cic. *Cat.* 2.22).³²

These passions reflect a different orientation of desire than the virtues associated with manliness. Rome marshals the passions so that their satisfaction – the testimony of others – can be achieved only through active displays of strength, courage, prowess, and competitiveness. The new passions depend only on the testimony of one's own body, achieved by yielding to its every wish. There is an important political implication to this gender inversion: It points politically to the replacement of a public with a private realm, a realm of hidden desires in which action is governed by private want. Cato the Younger, for example, admonishes the senators for valuing "your houses, villas, statues, and paintings more highly than your country" (*Cat.* 52.5). Not by accident does Catiline bypass the Forum and address his followers in a "private room" that excludes "all witnesses" (*Cat.* 20.1). It is the portrait of people whom, like the image of women in Roman society, are both hidden from public view and dominated by private appetites. Cato makes the connection explicit: "When each of you schemes for his own private interests, when you are slaves to pleasure in your homes and to money or influence here, the natural result is an attack upon the defenceless republic" (*Cat.* 52.23).

The sobering reality is that Catiline's language of politics really does not stand out. Sulla had already circumscribed opportunities for public speeches. There is no public language to which words and actions are accountable, but only private desires. As Earl notes, "The real nature of Roman politics is laid bare as a struggle for power disguised under fair names, in which both the senate and its opponents were equally concerned and equally devoid of the high principles they professed."³³ Catiline's followers, for example, represent a cross-section of Roman society or, more accurately, an alliance of debtor classes: plebs, slaves, senators, equestrians, and noblemen from the provinces and free towns

---

³² For a helpful overview of the effects of the influx of wealth into Rome, see de Ligt in Hammer (forthcoming). On Roman attitudes toward the introduction of foreign luxury, see Gruen 1992, 52–83 (on Cato and Hellenism) and 84–130 (on the introduction of foreign art). On Sempronia and gender inversion in Sallust, see Boyd 1987. On the theme of servility in Sallust, see Hock 1988.

³³ Earl 1961, 93.

who were united by the grip of debt (and political opportunism) (*Cat.* 17.2, 5; 20.13; 21.2).³⁴ Catiline refers to them in the language of political association. They are brought together by friendship (*amicitia*) (*Cat.* 20.4), which forms the base of a politician's core support. And his followers exhibit, in Catiline's words, *fides* (*Cat.* 20.3), or good faith, which is a sense of obligation born of loyalty or promises to others that gives stability to political associations and alliances. But the nature of the alliance is different: not a public agreement, but one hatched in private (*Cat.* 20.1). And it is an alliance in which the benefits are not just the traditional gifts that come with power, but also, taking his cue from Sulla, "all the other spoils that war and the license of victors can offer" (*Cat.* 21.2). Only now friendship and loyalty turn against Rome. The spoils of war are not going to be won from an external enemy but in this case from Rome's own citizens.

Perhaps most dramatically, Catiline, though a patrician, adopts the language of a *popularis*, characterizing the cause as emancipation from oligarchy:

> All the rest of us, energetic, able, nobles and commons, have made up the mob, without influence (*gratia*), without authority (*auctoritas*), and subservient to those to whom in a free state we should be an object of fear. Because of this, all influence, power, rank, and wealth (*omnis gratia, potentia, honos, divitiae*) are in their hands, or wherever they wish them to be; to us they have left danger, defeat, prosecutions, and poverty (*Cat.* 20.8; also 20.13; 58.11).³⁵

Earl points out that Catiline's invocation of the cause of *libertas* (*Cat.* 20.6) seems hard to distinguish from Pompeius' justification for raising an army (*Bell. Afr.* 22.2) and Caesar's own justification for entering Rome (*BC* 1.22).³⁶ But *libertas*, which Catiline invokes initially and traditionally as emancipation from domination, now broadens into a more wholesale

---

³⁴ See Yavetz 1963, 488–91, 497–98.
³⁵ A similar claim, and misuse of language, is employed by Philippus on behalf of Sulla and the senate (*Hist.* 1.77.3).
³⁶ Earl 1961, 55.

freedom from the past. Catiline's political slogan, *tabulae novae* (*Cat.* 21.2), which is aimed at the abolition of debt, now speaks tellingly to the desire to wipe the past clean.

CATO, CAESAR, AND MEMORY

Cato the Younger and Caesar are seen most frequently as the two alternatives to Catiline (though how those alternatives are understood differs dramatically). The encounter between Cato and Caesar occurs in the senate in a debate about whether the conspirators, both those already caught and those yet to be caught, should be sentenced to death. Sallust introduces Cato and Caesar as "two men of towering *virtus*" who emerge at a time when so few great leaders exist (*Cat.* 53.5; 54.1).[37] Making sense of this pairing of individuals so divergent in their conduct and principles, Syme offers the argument that "their qualities could be regarded as complementary no less than antithetic. In alliance the two had what was needed to save the Republic."[38] Batstone suggests that through this exchange Sallust does not point to the complementarity of these men but "reveals in his antithesis a fragmentation of varying dimensions which is the result of virtues themselves in conflict with each other and an underlying conceptual failure which produces an opposition between the traditional Roman virtues of action and the traditional intellectual categories by which those virtues are known, named, and understood."[39] Sklenář posits a split in Sallust's own thought between the rationalism of Caesar and the moralism of Cato, one that ultimately seeks recourse in a pristine state of ancestral customs that Sallust's own analysis undermines.[40] And McDonnell rejects any sort of tension or ambiguity, seeing Sallust as siding with Cato in arguing for a "self-sufficient, ethical type of *virtus*" in opposition to "traditional martial *virtus*."[41]

---

[37] Perhaps as important, as McDonnell suggests, is that Pompeius, a military general most associated in the Roman mind with *virtus*, is not included (2006, 295–300).
[38] Syme 1964, 120; also Scanlon 1980, 107–8 and Kapust 2011, 76–77: constructive tension that forges consensus.
[39] Batstone 1988, 2. See also Levene 2000, 181–190.
[40] Sklenář 1998, 217–19.   [41] McDonnell 2006, 377; also 379.

I do not see Sallust as positing a confrontation between rationalism and moralism, or between a self-sufficient morality (ethics, in McDonnell's language) and a historically constituted ethic. Sallust is exploring how one uses the past, a question made salient (perhaps even urgent) by the loss of any consensus about what that past means. There are a number of questions taken up in this exchange: What examples from the past does one privilege? How far in the past does one go? And how does one decide?

Caesar's opening reference to the importance of the mind in deliberating on action (*Cat.* 51.1–4) is seen by Sklenář as evidence of Caesar's "rationalist doctrine," in contrast to Cato's nostalgia (and revealing of Sallust's conflicting agenda).[42] But Caesar begins in the same place where Sallust and Cato do (compare *Cat.* 1.1–4 to 51.1–4): on the terrain of history. Sallust writes a history of the deeds of the past that are "worthy of memory" (*Cat.* 4.2; also 3.2). Caesar reminds his audience of "times when our forefathers (*maiores*), resisting the dictates of passion, have acted justly and in order" (*Cat.* 51.4). The claim is not wholly different from Cato's own reference to how the *maiores* "raise our country from obscurity to greatness" not just by force of arms but by a broad set of qualities, including justness and an "independent spirit free from guilt or passion" (*Cat.* 52.19, 21). Success for both Caesar and Cato comes, as Cato says, from "wisdom in counsel" (*Cat.* 52.28).

The argument is not about reason or the intellect but about how one uses the past to make judgments in the present, a use that turns on divergent conceptions of memory.[43] For Caesar, memory only goes back so far. "Most mortals," Caesar exclaims, "remember only that which happens last" (*Cat.* 51.15). History, thus, is a continually evolving and flexible record of responses to particular exigencies and experiences. Caesar, for example, references the Porcian laws passed later in the second century that forbade the flogging and execution of Roman citizens

---

[42] Sklenář 1998, 208–9.

[43] Thus, the issue is not how many precedents Caesar and Cato invoke, or the surprise that Cato only refers to one, as Levene argues (2000, 182–83), but the way the past is understood. See Connolly 2009, 186–87, on the use of the past in the encounter between Cato and Caesar.

(*Cat.* 51.21–23; 51.39–40), a response to the oppression of one group by another (*Cat.* 51.40). He mentions, as well, the willingness of Rome's ancestors to adopt and imitate foreign practices and institutions that were useful (*Cat.* 51.37–38). The propensity to judge by the moment enables the ready modification of precedent, but also more ominously makes easier the misuse of precedent. Caesar notes, "All bad precedents (*exempla*) have originated in cases which were good; but when the control of the government falls into the hands of men who are incompetent or bad, your new precedent is transferred from those who well deserve and merit such punishment to the undeserving and blameless" (*Cat.* 51.27). Caesar's reference is to the Sullan proscriptions, but the statement is drenched in irony: It is under Caesar's authority later that this new precedent will be carried out and Roman citizens executed.[44]

Cato, on the other hand, refers to a more distant past: the original ancestors who raised Rome from obscurity (*Cat.* 52.19). In calling for the execution of the conspirators "after the manner of our forefathers" (*Cat.* 52.36), Cato goes back almost three centuries, to the example of Manlius Torquatus ordering the execution of his own son for disobeying orders (*Cat.* 52.30–31). For Cato, memory is, ironically enough, a bulwark against time: not as a record of adaptation but of firmness to "forestall" the changing desires of the moment (*Cat.* 52.4, 9). Cato's principle of decision is clear: "Once a city has been taken nothing is left to the vanquished" (*Cat.* 52.4). The razed city of Carthage looms as a visual artifact of the irretrievability of a lost past.

For Cato – and Sallust – time erodes even the ability to make distinctions because memories can be lost and precedents manipulated. Caesar may be the man for the times, though that is not because one is a statesman and the other more doctrinaire, as Schur suggests.[45] Caesar is probably correct: Memory does not go back very far but responds to the exigencies of the moment. And he is more adaptable as a result,

---

[44] See Levene 2000, 190.

[45] Schur 1934, 199–201. Batstone seems to follow this idea, as well (1988, 15). Suggestions of Cato's political shrewdness are provided by Gruen 1995, 54–55, 91–92; Meier 1980, 270–88.

able to replace old memories with new by lavishly "giving, helping, and forgiving" (*Cat.* 54.3).[46] In fact, if Caesar is willing to do anything, Cato by this point stands more as a force of obstruction than of reformation. But the reader cannot miss the criticism of Caesar, coming at the end of a series of juxtapositions, in which Sallust remarks that Cato "preferred to be, much rather than to be seen as, good (*bonus*)" (*Cat.* 54.6, trans. modified). McDonnell and Sklenář read into this statement a Hellenistic influence which elevates a self-contained, philosophic morality over a culturally constituted, historically derived ethic. But this places a large and unnecessary burden on the text. The difference between Caesar's view and Cato's is not an ontological distinction between reason and history, but a statement about what claim time makes on us.

Cato's virtue is attributable to his *integritas vitae* (*Cat.* 54.2), which is defined as an undiminished condition of living. Cato's *integritas* is strangely immune from the exigencies of the moment: It steadfastly refuses the enticements of the occasion, stands apart from the corruption of the times, and does not even bow to affective ties born in time, such as between father and son. Cato has *integritas* because he affirms a standard that is rooted firmly, and in the right way (to recall his earlier invocation of *vera*), in history. The past authorizes how one judges the present, rather than present circumstances affecting how one interprets and uses the past. Absent *integritas*, the virtue associated with Cato, the "giving, helping, and forgiving" of Caesar may be indistinguishable from bribery and generosity from wasteful squandering (*Cat.* 54.3). For Cato, "we have extravagance (*luxuria*) and greed (*avaritia*), public poverty and private opulence. We extol wealth and foster idleness. We make no distinction between good men and bad, and ambition (*ambitio*) appropriates all the prizes of merit (*virtus*)" (*Cat.* 52.22). The problem with Cato's claim is its absoluteness: It admits of no debate, no compromise, and ultimately possesses very little political currency. Cato's most memorable act poignantly reveals the speechlessness of a truth that no one cares about anymore: He commits suicide

---

[46] See also *Hist.* 3.48.3: "I know how much more secure a faction of wicked men is than an upright man alone."

in 46 BCE, protesting Caesar's dictatorship and what he saw as the loss of the Republic.[47]

The danger of words losing their ability to orient action – of *virtus* effeminized, of squandering called *liberalitas*, and of recklessness called courage (*fortitudo*) – is that the Republic is reduced "to extremes" because there are no longer limits on, or even distinctions between, good and bad (*Cat.* 52.11). By the end of *Catiline* we have a sense of how these extremes play out in the Roman republic. Written amidst a decade long Civil War, *The War with Catiline* ends, similarly, on an image of civil war: soldiers turning over the bodies of the dead to find "now a friend, now a guest or kinsman; some also recognized their personal enemies. Thus the whole army was variously affected with sorrow and grief, rejoicing and lamentation" (*Cat.* 61.8–9). On the battlefield are the remains of an exhausted city (*Cat.* 39.4), fertile ground for "a more powerful adversary" to establish *imperium* and take away liberty (*Cat.* 39.4). The complementary pair, to recall Syme's formulation, may not be Cato and Caesar, but Caesar and Catiline, both striving for power and glory, one who is reckless in *liberalitas* and the other in *fortitudo*. But power (*imperium*) and glory (*Cat.* 52.10) in a community that has lost the true name of things may be nothing more than the fleeting desire for riches, secured by arms (recall *Cat.* 1.3–4), that leaves nothing more lasting than tears behind.

THE WAR WITH JUGURTHA AND THE RISE OF THE NEW MEN

In his second monograph, *The War with Jugurtha* (generally seen as written in the 40s after *The War with Catiline*), Sallust moves back in time and broadens the scope (to interactions outside Rome) to understand the conditions that gave rise to Sulla and Catiline. The history provides perspective on the tumultuous decades dating roughly from the Gracchi to Sulla, a period in which pressures at securing the empire would have

---

[47] A standard and reputation, it should be noted, that is recognized by others (see *Cat.* 54.3, 6; also *Hist.* 2.47.5).

repercussions at home in maintaining the Republic. This tumult, which played itself out in fierce, aristocratic rivalries, was fueled by increasing impoverishment, landlessness, and indebtedness of Roman citizens; the desire for access to power by a growing class of businessmen, political functionaries, and traders; demands for enfranchisement among Italian allies, or *socii*, especially among an emerging wealthy class (erupting in the Social War of 91 BCE)[48]; the plight of returning, landless soldiers; and the poverty of the urban poor crowded into the city.

Against this chaotic and corrosive backdrop, Jugurtha (160–104 BCE), as Earl points out, "recalls the Roman youth of the early Republic": physically strong, energetic, intelligent, handsome, disciplined, and trained not in rhetoric but in athletic and military activities (*Jug.* 6.1).[49] He displays *virtus* through the exercise of strength and endurance (see *Jug.* 1.3). Even alongside Romans, Jugurtha stands out. He earns military glory through valor in war and wisdom in counsel, winning the friendship of the patrician, Scipio Aemilianus (just as Masinissa, Jugurtha's grandfather, befriended Scipio Africanus) (*Jug.* 7.5).

Jugurtha plays out the tension in Roman political culture between glory and ambition. Public glory, like private ambition, springs from desire (recall *Jug.* 6.3). In the early Republic, desire is directed by the memory of great deeds that "kindles in the breasts of noble men this flame that cannot be quelled until they by their own prowess have equalled the fame and glory of their forefathers" (*Jug.* 4.6). Memory directs desire toward virtue. As Sallust remarks, "I have often heard that Quintus Maximus, Publius Scipio, and other eminent men of our country, were in the habit of declaring that their hearts were set mightily aflame for the pursuit of virtue whenever they gazed upon the masks of their ancestors" (*Jug.* 4.5). These references, as Grethlein notes, point to a "naming system [that] mirrors a concept that sees history as a continuum dissolving the perilous forces of change."[50] Jugurtha does not stand outside this system: Though of inferior birth, Jugurtha develops

---

[48] On the association of *libertas* with the demand for Roman citizenship by the Italians, see Wirszubski 1968, 66–70.
[49] Earl 1961, 62.   [50] Grethlein 2006, 137 fn. 10.

important ties through "intimate friendship" (*familiaris amicitia*) with important Roman leaders (*Jug.* 7.7).[51]

But this desire is unleashed in a period in which memory is altered as both the established aristocracy and new men "make their way to power and distinction (*imperia et honores*) by intrigue and open fraud rather than by noble practices" (*Jug.* 4.7). Scipio Aemilianus, wary of the two paths desire can take, advises Jugurtha to cultivate *amicitiae* among the Roman *populus* and not, by way of bribery, with particular individuals. The suggestion is that such friendships do not serve public ends but, like the *amicitiae* of Catiline, use public resources to achieve private ends (*Jug.* 8.2). Scipio Aemilianus, speaking to the instrumentality of *ambitio*, warns Jugurtha of the danger of "buy[ing] from a few what belonged to the many" (*Jug.* 8.2). So too his father (by adoption) advises Jugurtha, "Neither armies nor treasure form the bulwarks of a throne, but friends (*amici*); these you can neither acquire by force of arms nor buy with gold; it is by devotion and loyalty that they are won" (*Jug.* 10.4). Even, or especially, in a transactional society like Rome, there has to be boundaries between legitimate and illegitimate forms of developing the networks that underlay power. But neither Scipio Aemilianus' words nor his actions as a model of *virtus* can compete with the pervasive, habituating, and enabling corruption of the community. Both new men and nobles in the army, "who cared more for riches than for virtue and self-respect" and operated by way of faction at home, "fired Jugurtha's spirit" by telling him that he could become the sole king of Numidia with the death of Micipsa (*Jug.* 8.1, trans. modified).

Echoing Scipio Aemilianus, Micipsa speaks in the language of old Rome, appealing on his deathbed for Jugurtha to develop *amicitiae* by duty (*officium*) and trust (*fides*) and to rule with his brothers through *concordia* (*Jug.* 10.4, 6). But in the new politics animated by ambition, friends are won by largesse and agreements secured by bribes. After plotting the murder of Hiempsal and moving to seize Numidia, Jugurtha fears only the reaction of the Roman *populus* for his broken promises and

---

[51] Raised in the household of Micipsa, the king of Numidia, Jugurtha was Micipsa's brother's son who was left a commoner in Masinissa's will (the father of Micipsa and previous king of Numidia) because he was born of a concubine (*Jug.* 5.7).

aggression (*Jug.* 13.5). Placing his faith in the avariciousness of the Roman nobles, Jugurtha sends his envoys to Rome where he directs them "first to load his old friends with presents, and then to win new ones – in short, to make haste to accomplish by largess whatever they could" (*Jug.* 13.6). Jugurtha's envoys are successful in changing the sentiment of influential senators against strong actions opposed to Jugurtha in advance of Adherbal's appeal (*Jug.* 13.7).

Adherbal's address to the senate emulates both the language and themes of Roman republican rhetoric, which are nothing less than the broad cultural arrangements that made agreement possible. He recalls the close alliance (*amicitia*) of Numidia with Rome, including the aid they gave to Rome in the war with Carthage. He refers to his own tragic plight in which he has been rendered destitute by crime (see *Jug.* 14.7, 17, 23).[52] And he appeals to right (*ius*), which appears here as a form of recognition and reciprocity (a payment of debt) by the Romans for the loyalty and sacrifices of the Adherbal line (*Jug.* 14.1, 4). Most of all, Adherbal summons memory, an appeal he repeats in a later desperate letter to the senate (*Jug.* 24.10). In a pointed comment, suggestive of the way Roman memory is being altered, Adherbal laments that he will become a "monument to Jugurtha's crimes," a record not of virtue but of what Rome had become.

The exchange is instructive and jarring because of its ineffectiveness. Adherbal speaks truth when he states that goodness (*probitas*) cannot protect itself; it requires power (*Jug.* 14.4). But power is no longer publicly visible; it does not need to be defended through language but now lies disguised, curbed only by the fear that it will be exposed (see Chapt. 5, 249–58, on this notion of corruption). Senators bribed in private assail Adherbal, "exerting their influence, their eloquence, in short every possible means, they laboured as diligently in defence of the shameful crime of a foreigner as though they were striving to win glory" (*Jug.* 15.2, trans. modified). Aemilius Scaurus is the barometer of ambition: He joins in the praise of the *virtus* of Jugurtha until, fearing that "such gross corruption would arouse popular resentment, he curbed his

---

[52] See Dué 2000 on the tragic roots of Adherbal's speech.

THE WAR WITH JUGURTHA AND THE RISE OF THE NEW MEN

habitual cupidity" (*Jug.* 15.5). The senate opts to appoint ten commissioners to divide the land between Jugurtha and Adherbal. But the commission is as easily corrupted as the senate. Lucius Opimius, a noble who had brought about the death of Gaius Gracchus and Marcus Flavius Flaccus, and who is appointed to head the commission to divide the lands between Jugurtha and Adherbal, chooses gold over honor (*Jug.* 16.2–3). Soon enough the commission divides the lands, giving Adherbal the part that is "preferable in appearance rather than in reality," a comment by Sallust that serves to reinforce the disjuncture between being and seeming (*Jug.* 16.5). And Jugurtha continues to employ the public language of the new men, referring to his "merit" that led him to win approval from "all good men," including Scipio Amelianus (*Jug.* 22.2), even while seized by fervor (*Jug.* 20.6). The disjuncture between words and deeds is revealed when Jugurtha ultimately tortures Adherbal to death, massacres Numidians and traders that he encounters, and seizes Africa and Numidia (*Jug.* 26.3).

Even when Rome learns of this "outrage" and brings the matter up for discussion in the senate, public speech is used not to clarify but to obfuscate. By "interrupting the discussions and wasting time, often through their personal influence, often by wrangling," these *ministri* of Jugurtha, a term that suggests how bribery had turned the Roman senators into instruments of Jugurtha's ambition, "tried to disguise the atrocity of the deed" (*Jug.* 27.1).[53] Only Gaius Memmius, a tribune hostile to the nobles, exposes the tactics to the Roman *populus*. Fear, in this case of the people, works: The senate, aware of the potential reaction of the people, assigns two consuls who were to be elected to lead armies in Numidia and Italy (*Jug.* 27.3). But the consul to Numidia, Lucius Calpurnius Bestia, surrounds himself with nobles with a "strong party spirit," including Scaurus, who are governed most of all by avarice (*Jug.* 28.4–5). Jugurtha, through the "power of money," is able to turn Calpurnius and Scaurus from the public purpose of waging war to private arrangements with the king (*Jug.* 29.1, 5).

---

[53] Cicero similarly describes the actions of the senate is debating his recall in 57 BCE (*Sest.* 35.75).

The thorough permeation of Roman politics by instrumentality, in which money and not memory orients political action, provides the backdrop (and context) for Memmius' appeal to memory – the memory not of the nobility but of the commons.[54] As Memmius reminds his audience, "I shall make use of the freedom of speech (*libertas*) which is my inheritance from my father" (*Jug.* 31.5). Memmius' speech, directed more to the *populus* than to the *nobiles*, reminds his audience of the oligarchical counter-reaction in which "during the past fifteen years you have been the sport of a few men's insolence; how shamefully your defenders have perished unavenged; how your own spirits have been so demoralized because of weakness and cowardice that you do not rise even now, when your enemies are in your power, but still fear those in whom you ought to inspire fear" (*Jug.* 31.2). *Maiestas*, or the majesty of the people, had been stolen. This majesty, which was more a rhetorical expression than a legal principle, was nonetheless an important underpinning of republicanism, identifying the people as having the sovereign power to confer honors and judge the actions of officials.[55] But now, as Sallust writes, priesthoods, consulships, and triumphs are paraded before the people as if they are honors rather than stolen goods (*Jug.* 31.10). Soldiers compete not for honor but for plunder, which they then barter (*Jug.* 44.5). Moreover, the attributes that are held most dear to Roman citizens – loyalty, reputation, and piety (*fides, decus, pietas*) – are sought as a source of gain (*Jug.* 31.12).

Memmius points to the transformations in political language. The common purpose that unites people into political friendship (*amicitia*) is transformed into *factio* as individuals are brought together for plunder. Gain replaces honor (31.12). Servility replaces power (*imperia*) (31.11). Cowardice replaces vehemence (*Jug.* 31.14, 17). And *libertas* now finds expression as unbounded passion. To the extent that the commons respond (they may be the last hope), they too succumb to hatred of the nobility and party passion rather than love of the *res publica* (*Jug.* 40.3).

---

[54] As Kraus notes, "For money not only corrupts, it confuses as well. In its ability to erase meaning, or to replace one meaning with another, it is a fitting tool for someone who is himself polyvalent, shimmering, impossible to pin down" (1999, 223).

[55] On *maiestas*, see Brunt 1988, 338–39.

MARIUS AND THE PATH TO POWER

If Memmius recalls the rise of the new men, Marius points to their future path to power. Characteristic of a new man, Marius "had in abundance every qualification except an ancient lineage: namely, diligence, honesty, great military skill, and a spirit that was mighty in war, unambitious in peace, which rose superior to passion and the lure of riches, and was greedy only for glory" (*Jug.* 63.2). Trained (like Jugurtha) in military exploits rather than rhetoric, Marius rises through a succession of offices, beginning as military tribune. Only the consulship seemed closed to him since "nobles passed the consulate from hand to hand within their own order," considering no new man worthy of that honor (*Jug.* 63.6–7). In fact, responding to Marius' request for a furlough so that he could canvas for consul, Metellus answers in the way typical of the nobility: Marius should not "entertain thoughts above his station" (*Jug.* 64.2).

Marius not only entertains these thoughts but he also shows how to put them into action. He plays to the dissatisfaction of both *equites* (equestrians) and plebs. He stirs up the traders in Utica, hurt by the protracted war, by suggesting that Metellus was purposely prolonging the war out of his desire for power (*Jug.* 64.5–6). He incites the Roman knights to write letters in criticism of Metellus' handling of the war (leading to support for Marius' canvass for his consulship) (*Jug.* 65.4–5). More ominously for the future of Rome, though, and in contrast to the discipline imposed on the army by Metellus (*Jug.* 45.2–4), Marius showed the path to military dictatorship and to a new wave of urban violence by creating a client army of landless recruits (a necessary response to manpower shortages) loyal to him, originally intended to enhance his *auctoritas* by increasing his *clientelae* across Italy and into Africa, but ultimately, when employed by Sulla, to terrorize opponents.[56]

---

[56] See Keaveney 2007, 23–25: recruits as response to manpower shortage. There is some dispute about how different is the composition or attitudes of post-Marian armies. Those arguing against any significant change in loyalty toward the Republic include Brunt 1988, 240–80 and Gruen 1995, xvii–xviii, 366–68. Contrarily, others point to the tie between political disaffection and violence. See Sherwin-White 1956, 4–5

Marius' consular speech before the senate provides a striking recasting of history. The point of pride for the new man is that he stands outside history. His virtue is uninherited (*Jug.* 85.38). Family portraits mean nothing (*Jug.* 85.29–30); he cannot rely on the deeds of his ancestors but only on himself (*Jug.* 85.4). In fact, to recount the deeds of one's ancestors serves only to delude one into believing oneself more glorious (*Jug.* 85.21). Moreover, in contrast to many nobles who turn to histories and treatise to learn how to be consul, Marius' own skills are honed in the battlefield (*Jug.* 85.12, 14). Marius is taking aim not just at the nobility, but also at what is seen as the "Hellenic over-refinement" of the aristocracy that had resulted in incompetent military leadership.[57] Marius seems like a possible model for the recovery of Roman *virtus*, aligning himself with the traditional martial prowess of the Roman soldier by eating, sleeping, leading, and at times fighting alongside his men.

But what is power without history? For Sallust, as for the Romans, power (*imperium*) is not an abstraction but is given shape and life in history: in *leges* and *mores*. Metellus, for example, as consul elect, takes over an army (just defeated under Aulus) that is "weak, cowardly, and incapable of facing either danger or hardship, readier of tongue than of hand, a plunderer of our allies and itself a prey to the enemy, subject to no discipline or restraint" (*Jug.* 44.1; also 44.5). As *imperator*, Metellus imposes the discipline and training of the *maiores* (*Jug.* 44.3). He limits indulgence and luxury by ending the sale by soldiers of plundered goods for foreign luxuries, the ability of soldiers to have slaves or pack animals, and replaces idleness with daily marches (*Jug.* 45.2). For Marius, though, upon finishing his speech and true to a notion of power without history, he begins to enroll soldiers based not on *mos maiorum* but by allowing anyone, even those without property, to enlist (*Jug.* 86.2). And he secures the loyalty of his men by giving them the spoils of war (*Jug.* 87.1; 84.4).

(as *clientelae*); Badian 1962, 219, 228 (use as *clientelae*); Brunt 1962, 75–76 (changes in loyalty); Morstein-Marx and Rosenstein 2006, 625–37 (violence and fragmentation); Keaveney 2007, 28 (landless desire what their comrades desire), 37–55 (politicized by Sulla). Note also the enrollment of thugs into clubs by Clodius to terrorize Rome in 58 BCE (Cic. *Sest.* 15.34).

[57] McDonnell 2006, 273.

Sallust ends on an ironic note: In a short time the raw soldiers fight with the same courage as the old soldiers (*Jug.* 87.1–3). Absent history, the equality of human nature, a beginning point for the claims of the new men (*Jug.* 85.15), expresses itself as both virtue and untempered desire. The proof of the new genealogy, and the paradox of Marius' legacy for Sallust, is to teach both Sulla and Caesar how to develop a basis of power by appealing to desire. Sallust, thus, ends where *Catiline* picks up: Sulla, a patrician whose family had been almost extinguished by obscurity (*Jug.* 95.3), ultimately vanquishes Marius, oversees the execution of opponents across Italy, strengthens the power of the senate and brings in people loyal to him, limits the power of the tribunate and the *comitia tributa* by eliminating its ability to initiate legislation or veto senatorial actions, restricts the actions of the *concilium plebis* to electing tribunes, and requires that only the *comitia centuriata*, the assembly dominated by property owners, can vote on laws.[58] Named as dictator, Sulla has the power to make laws, alter the constitution, confiscate property, decide on life and death, establish colonies, found or destroy cities, decide on whether there would be war, and take away or give kingdoms to client princes.[59] Caesar, also born of a patrician family, reverses the pro-senatorial course, but not the means, elevating himself to dictator.

Like in *Catiline*, *Jugurtha* speaks to the problems of desire without history. In *Catiline*, desire exercises power by force of arms. In *Jugurtha*, Rome also appears as a city without a history, one in which nothing is respected or held sacred (*Jug.* 41.9) but valued only as it can be bought and sold. As Jugurtha is purported to have commented while looking back at Rome, "A city for sale and doomed to speedy destruction if it finds a purchaser" (*Jug.* 35.10). Jugurtha, as it turns out, was not its purchaser; Caesar was.

Yet, even as Sallust decries the corruption of Roman politics, he paints a vivid picture of political life: of appeals to the senate and the people, and of arguments that draw their authority from precedent, traditions, or the needs of the situation. What Sallust's analysis foregrounds – and this

---

[58] On Sulla's violence against opponents, see Keaveney 1982, 149–60; on Sulla's revisions to the constitution, see Keaveney 1982, 72–74. Also Mackay 2004, 131.
[59] See Keaveney 1982, 161.

is reflective of Roman political thought generally – is the thorough permeation of politics into life: how every position or claim can be contested and must be defended. Sallust does not offer solace by locating politics in abstractions, objective laws, or truths. Rather, politics is located in the people who, whatever their limitations, provide the last check on tyranny in jealously protecting their liberty (*Jug.* 3.2–3).[60] Absent the people, communities are transformed into the instruments of the few who plunder for their own gain.

THE ROLE OF THE HISTORIAN

Sallust describes the work of the historian as recalling the memory of great deeds (*Jug.* 4.1, 6), *exempla* that once inflamed the spirit of subsequent generations to imitate the deeds of the past (*Jug.* 4.6).[61] The problem, as Sallust continues, is that the past no longer inspires. Grethlein, for example, reads Sallust's account of the *imagines maiorum* (*Jug.* 4.5), or masks of one's ancestors, not as a parallel to historiography, but as a contrast: "The historiographical work of Sallust gains its relevance from the failure of the *imagines maiorum* to maintain the *commodum historiae*."[62] But Sallust seems to hesitate in claiming that his history can provide alternate *exempla* (see *Cat.* 3.2; *Jug.* 4.1, 4.6–7). The inheritance of the past had become so confused that it no longer functioned to provide true standards by which subsequent generations can measure themselves. Instead, a perverse competition had ensued in which individuals sought to rival their ancestors "in riches and extravagance rather than in uprightness and diligence" (*Jug.* 4.7). Not surprisingly, then, what one discovers are *exempla* that are as unclear as the time. As evidence, one need only note scholarly disagreement about whether Cato the Younger, Caesar, both, or neither are to be praised. Metellus, a more prudent version of Cato, does not serve as a model, either.

---

[60] Modifying the view of Sallust as having disdain for the crowd; see Scanlon 1980, 59.
[61] Scanlon places Sallust's work in a tradition that emphasizes the "civic function" of historiography (1998, 194–96 on Asellio and Polybius).
[62] Grethlein 2006, 139 n. 20.

He successfully brings order back to the troops in Africa through old-fashioned Roman discipline (*Jug.* 45.1–3). But he succumbs to the guerilla tactics of Jugurtha, unable to get his men to "keep their ranks" (*Jug.* 51.1), until "chance held sway everywhere" (*Jug.* 51.1). Marius, who replaces Metellus and defeats Jugurtha, does not work either. He becomes a Caesar-like character, gifted at manipulation and deceit, but also the model for Sulla.[63]

Sallust's style, which is seen as mirroring the "restlessness" and "discordancy" of the time, further complicates the problem of identifying *exempla*.[64] It may be the case, as Kraus suggests, that "disorder and corruption" threaten Sallust's task of writing history by making it impossible to organize a true account of things.[65] The levels of dissimulation and falseness make it impossible to identify true and false accounts, as well as true and false causes. Or it may be that by the time Sallust is writing in the midst of civil war there are no longer viable alternatives: Who does one choose as the heir to the Republic once party strife (*factio*) degenerates into violent civil war between men struggling for dynastic power? Or perhaps more poignantly, what is the point in choosing at all?

In casting about for a solution, Sallust looks neither to the patricians nor the new man, both of whom have succumbed to this corrosive environment, their inheritances now inextricably linked. Rather, Sallust crafts an alternate genealogy, one that emphasizes the *populus Romanus* as the heirs of the founding of the Republic. We have already seen hints of this throughout Sallust's two shorter works. Sallust characterizes the Gracchi as beginning "to assert the freedom of the commons and expose the crimes of the oligarchs" (*Jug.* 42.1). He announces the reason for writing *The War with Jugurtha* as "the first time resistance was offered to the insolence of the nobles" (*Jug.* 5.1). And he identifies the people's jealous embrace of their liberty as checking the corruption and complicity of the nobility (*Jug.* 3.2–3). In the surviving fragments of his *History*

---

[63] See Kraus 1999, 240.
[64] Paul 1966, 105. See Syme 1964, 257–67; Earl 1982, 640; Woodman 1988, 120–24; Kraus 1999, 244–45.
[65] Kraus 1999, 245–46.

we see the genealogy articulated explicitly. Macer, tribune to the plebs (who would later, and suggestively for the claim here, write a heroic history of past plebeians), links the manly (*virilis*) deeds of the ancestors to the struggle to gain the tribunate for the commons, to open the magistracy to plebeians, and to gain the secret ballot (*Hist.* 3.34.15, McGushin; also 3.34.1).[66]

Sallust is not making a radically democratic argument. Without the *populus Romanus*, there can be no *civitas*, a term (like the Greek *koinon*) that denotes a united body of free citizens (e.g., *Jug.* 3.2). The term *populus Romanus* itself is ambiguous, denoting both the entire Roman citizenry (e.g., *Cat.* 4.2; 8.5; 34.1; 36.4; 52.10; *Jug.* 5.1) and a group of people who defined itself in opposition to the senatorial aristocracy (e.g., *Cat.* 38.3; 51.43; *Jug.* 5.1; 9.2; 21.4; 27.2; 27.3; 30.3; 34.2; 40.1; 41.2; 41.5; 63.4; 84.1; 111.1; 112.3).[67] Sallust captures this ambiguity, pointing both to the *concordia* of the Roman people in the early days, and the increasingly bitter divisions between the commons and aristocracy later. What Sallust continually recalls is the role of the people as the critical arbiter of aristocratic competition: a necessary bearer of the criteria by which honor is bestowed and contributions recognized.[68] The people give power to the consul (*Cat.* 29.3), confer gifts and titles (*Jug.* 5.4; 14.8; 65.2), extend treaties (*Jug.* 39.3), and provide a check on excessive behavior (*Jug.* 13.5; 27.3). Yet, the laws and customs that framed the competition gradually gave way to an increasingly fierce competition to frame the laws and customs until the winner emerged by becoming in effect the state: able to declare what is legal and illegal, who are friends and who are enemies, and who shall live and who shall die.

The *populus Romanus* is not without its problems. If excessive ambition and avarice mark the failure of the rulers, then excessive excitement (*Jug.* 33.3; 66.2) or weakness and inaction (*socordia*) seem to be the moniker of the commons (*Hist.* 1.48.20, McGushin; 4.48.8: weakness and inactivity; 3.34.26: lethargy; *Jug.* 31.1: spirit of submission). Lepidus, crafting his message to those excluded from, and oppressed by, Sulla's reign, provides a diagnosis of how oligarchic corruption

---

[66] On Macer's *History*, see Wiseman 2009, 19–20. [67] See Ferrary 1982, 748.
[68] See Hölkeskamp 2004, 88–91.

persists in the absence of any resistance: "inaction" will allow Sulla's allies "to continue on a course of robbery with violence and to appear fortunate in proportion to one's audacity" (*Hist.* 1.48.20, McGushin). This inactivity is the byproduct, in part, of the instrumentality of politics in which silence can be purchased (*Hist.* 3.34.19). But this weakness seems to be reinforced, as well, by the corruption of language in which cowardice is called peace, liberty is called treason, and illegality is called virtue (*Hist.* 3.34.13; see Philippus' use of language, as well: *Hist.* 1.77.1). Sallust notes that with the defeat of Carthage, "the terms 'good' and 'bad' were applied to citizens, not on the yardstick of services rendered or injuries inflicted on the state, since all were equally corrupt; any individual of outstanding wealth and irresistible in his lawlessness was considered 'good' because he was the preserver of existing conditions" (*Hist.* 1.12, McGushin = Gellius 9.12.15, Augustine *Civ. Dei.* 3.17). We see this corruption of vocabulary not only in the appropriation of the language of the commons by the patrician, Catiline, but also in the speech of Philippus (against Lepidus) denouncing opposition to oligarchy as "overthrowing our liberty" (*Hist.* 1.67.3, McGushin). As Macer enjoins the people in 73 BCE, on behalf of tribunician reform, "Do not change the names of things to suit your own cowardice and give to slavery the title of peace" (*Hist.* 3.34.13, McGushin). Memmius, too, comments ironically on how returning land to the plebs is a form of kingship while political assassinations against plebeian leaders are legal acts (*Jug.* 31.8).

Only by craft (*dolus*) can a minority prevail against the people (*Hist.* 3.34.21). The people, therefore, must be roused (*Hist.* 1.48.7; 1.48.27), not in a demagogic frenzy but by way of a restoration of founding principles. To do that, though, if we are to follow the logic of Sallust's argument, requires an enemy. If Sallust traces the loss of Rome's external enemies, he also reveals the emergence (or reemergence) of internal enemies: kings who become tyrants; Catiline, a false prophet of the commons; and political leaders like Sulla (and now Caesar) whose dominion is paid for at the price of liberty. Lepidus speaks a truism of Sallustian politics: "One must feel fear or inspire it" (*Hist.* 1.48.10, McGushin). In fact, the two claims are linked: The problem of the commons is that they do not realize their survival is at stake and thus succumb. This is not just faction; it is like war against what has become an enemy that gained strength as Rome's external adversaries lost theirs. Thus, Sallust's language continually recalls images of an internal war against the *populus*: of gaining the state by arms (*Cat.* 11.4); of citizens as victors turning on other citizens (*Cat.* 11.4); of the nobility as enemies turning on the commons (*Jug.* 31.3); of enslavement by one's own people (*Jug.* 31.11; 31.20); of the surrender of sovereignty (*Jug.* 31.9); and of the commons as the vanquished (*Jug.* 42.4–5; *Hist.* 3.34.27). Sallust is not exaggerating for effect: Rome in the age of Marius and Sulla had been transformed into "a landscape of extreme urban violence," in which groups turned to arms to overturn or influence political outcomes.[69] In invoking this language of fear, Sallust is reminding the people of what is at stake, of what is being lost.[70]

But the path to the restoration of the Republic cannot lie in the assertion of one faction over another (*Jug.* 42.4) any more than in civil war.[71] It requires steering a course: between indulgence and severity (*Jug.* 45.1), between animation and obstruction (*Jug.* 40.2), and between honor and resentment (*Jug.* 44.4–5). Most of all, in recalling the genealogy of the Republic, Sallust is identifying four features that have been lost: decisions are made in public; leaders are accountable; laws are equal; and the people have a say in the governance of the Republic, including by way of access to office. The importance of these conditions for Sallust is that they are the basis by which differences can be settled, ambition channeled, and agreements reached.

What is required is history. In saying this, I depart from efforts to collapse Sallust's works into forms of rhetoric that deconstruct the ground upon which they stand. As Lendon points out: "In a world suffused with rhetoric, the ancient historians were, perhaps, trying to do something different and interesting."[72] Lendon probably draws too rigid of a line between history and rhetoric, but the point is well taken: Sallust is not engaged in a meta-discourse about rhetoric; he is pointing to

---

[69] Flower 2010, 90.
[70] See also Kapust 2011, 55–61 on the role of antagonistic rhetoric in Sallust.
[71] In fact, if we are to follow Wood's insight, the challenge is in transforming what is primarily a "military axiom" of *metus hostilis* into a civic aim (1995, 183).
[72] Lendon 2009, 58. That "something" is to accurately narrate events.

the consequences of politics without history. The *exempla* that Sallust provides, thus, are not of particular individuals performing great deeds but of the consequences of forgetting these conditions and of the moments in which these principles are reasserted. Sallust provides us with snapshots of politics that had become the training ground of a generation of leaders who saw the Republic as their possession. What bound people to leaders and made them complicit in their own enslavement was their imagined enrichment. Sallust, in writing his histories, is not just recalling these events; he is identifying the people as the only force powerful enough to constrain the increasing might and assertiveness of individuals who see the Republic as for sale.

4 VIRGIL: POLITICS, VIOLENCE, AND MEMORY

Virgil's (Publius Vergilius Maro, 70–19 BCE) poetry raises a fundamentally different interpretive question for political thought than does Lucretius'. Both engage in an ongoing dialogue with Greece: Lucretius with Epicurus; Virgil with an entire epic tradition, most notably Homer. Although making very few historical allusions, Lucretius' political thought undertakes a sustained critique of the vocabulary of Roman politics. Virgil's poetry, on the other hand, is overtly political, comprised of numerous allusions to political actors and events.[1] If Lucretius' stance toward Roman politics is openly critical, Virgil's position is less clear. He seems variously – or is seen variously – to be an imperial enthusiast[2] and

---

[1] See discussions of references in Virgil to the destruction of Carthage: Harrison 1984; the destruction of Alba Longa by Rome: Hardie 1986, 348; the assassination of Caesar: Tarrant 1997, 173; Caesar's star that reportedly appeared during Octavian's games in honor of Caesar: Perkell 2001, 79; the war between Octavian and Pompeius: Zetzel 1989, 271; the struggle between Octavian and Antonius and Octavian's victory at Actium: Hardie 1986, 350–54; R.D. Williams 1990, 25; Gurval 1995, 209–47; R.D. Williams 1981; land confiscation and eviction: Boyle 1986, 16; Wilkinson 1966; Perkell 2001, 74–75; proscriptions; Farron 1981; the consulship of Pollio and the pact he negotiates between Antonius and Octavian: Tarrant 1997, 173; and Virgil's own relationship to Maeceneas, his patron and one of Augustus' closest advisors.

[2] Celebration of the Roman (and Augustan) imperial ideal of the triumph of civilization and peace: Büchner 1956, for example, 438–41; Klingner 1967, for example, 361–63; Pöschl 1962; Getty 1950; Ryberg 1958; MacKay 1963; Wilkinson 1963; McGushin 1964;

detractor[3]; a Stoic[4], Epicurean[5], and pragmatist[6]; and as hopeful[7] and melancholy.[8] However divergent the views, though, there is agreement: Whatever his debts to Homer and the Greek epic tradition, Virgil is profoundly Roman, and whatever his attitude toward Augustus, he is deeply political.[9] As Hannah Arendt remarks at one point, Virgil expresses the Roman political experience in its "purest form."[10]

Arendt never explains what she means. But we can begin to understand the claim by thinking about the alternative approaches to political thought available to Virgil. One alternative is the Greek (specifically Homeric) epic tradition, which privileges the greatness of the individual warrior. A second alternative is recourse to an ideal community, whether Plato's republic, Epicurus' community of sages, or even Cicero's *res*

Camps 1969; Johnston 1980; Buchheit 1963; 1972; Wallace-Hadrill 1982; Wilhelm 1982; Jenkyns 1985; Hardie 1986, for example 172; Cairns 1989; Toll 1991; 1997 [national idea]; Powell 1992; Gurval 1995, 209–47 (shield: victory of Augustus "assures the universal order" and creates a poetic interpretation of Actium as a "victory over barbarian foes," but "could not forget the misery and loss inflicted in the still recent past," 238, 246, 244); Galinsky 1996, 93–100; Balot 1998, 92–3; Morgan 1999, 105: "dissolution and rebirth"; Bell 2008. As didactic: Miles 1980; Morgan 1999; Gale 2000. As creator of an Augustan "intellectual and aesthetic order": Johnson 1976, 136.

[3] Parry 1963; Clausen 1964; Quinn 1968; Boyle 1972; 1979 (discrepancy between imperial ideology and its reality); Putnam 1979; 1995; Miles 1980; Farron 1981; 1982; 1985; 1986; Thomas 1982; 1988; Feeney 1984; Ross 1987; Harrison 1990; Martindale 1993; Quint 1993; O'Hara 1994; Zetzel 1996; 1997; Thomas 1988; 2001; 2004–5; Tarrant 1997; Batstone 1994; 1997; Perkell 1989; 2001; 2002; Connolly 2001.

[4] As the realization of a Stoic ideal of self-control, piety, and reason: Bowra 1933; Edwards 1960; Otis 1963, 219–20 (humanizes Stoic ideal); McGushin 1964, 235; Pöschl 1962; Bonds 1978; Horsfall 1976, 77–82, with qualifications; Heinze 1903, 266–73; Lyne 1983, 191; Gill 2006, 435–61.

[5] Johnson 1976, 150–54. [6] Stewart 1972; Stahl 1981; Lyne 1983.

[7] Otis 1963; Wilkinson 1969.

[8] Jenkyns 1985, 75. Pessimistic about power of poetry: Putnam 1970, 339; Hubbard 1998, 122; Boyle 1986, 32–35 (*Eclogues*).

[9] Homeric traces: see Knauer 1964 (also language of Ennius and the Roman epic: 70–71, 74–76); 1989, 177–248; Lyne 1987; Dekel 2012; Apollonius of Rhodes: Otis 1963, 9, 18, 24; Ziegler 1966, 15–23; Briggs 1981, 948; Roman tragedy: Wigodsky 1972; Greek tragedy: Lyne 1987; prophecy: Horsfall 1991, 206; aetiological poetry: Horsfall 1991, 206–9.

[10] Arendt 1978, 1.152.

publica. A final option is a form of political escapism, a flight from the public world to an increasingly private and interior one.[11] Virgil variously draws on each of these strands: in his creation of a post-Troy epic tale, in his invocation of the Golden Age, and in his pastoral poetry. But Virgil's thinking never seems to find solace in these alternatives. His thought, instead, continually arises from, and returns to, the experience of action in the world, a world that is conveyed as less romantic than Homer's, less perfect than Plato's, less tidy than Aristotle's, less natural than Lucretius', less reasoned than the Stoics', less private than the elegiac poets', and certainly less republican than Cicero's.

With Virgil we are witnessing the transition from the Republic to the principate, a state organized by political forces that seem as powerful and as abstract as any divine forces (see Introduction). Born into a Roman province in Italy, the Rome Virgil knew was one marked almost exclusively by faction and violence: a young boy when Cicero was elected consul, a teenager while Cicero was composing his philosophic works against the backdrop of the increasingly naked struggle for power between Caesar, Pompeius, and Crassus who comprised the informal coalition known as the First Triumvirate. Virgil's twenties were witness to Caesar crossing the Rubicon, thus beginning decades of bloody civil war; Caesar's assassination and the legal establishment of the Second Triumvirate (the *Triumviri Rei Publicae Constituendae Consulari Potestate*, or "Triumvirs for Confirming the Res Publica with Consular Power"), essentially a dictatorship shared by Octavian, Marcus Antonius, and Lepidus; another round of proscriptions, including the assassination of Cicero; and a war that spread to the east as Marcus Antonius and Octavian's forces defeated Caesar's assassins, Brutus and Cassius, and their armies at the battle of Philippi (42 BCE). Virgil writes his *Eclogues* in the late 40s and early 30s after the initial settlement of peace between Octavian, Antonius, and Lepidus that divided the empire into spheres of influence (with the Treaty of Brundisium in 40 BCE). It was a peace that did not hold. He writes *Georgics* in the years after Octavian's final victory over Antonius at Actium in 31 BCE, and he composes the *Aeneid*

---

[11] Snell 1960; Putnam 1970, 8–15; Wolin 2004, 70–75, Foucault 1990, 3.39–68.

between 29 and 19 BCE during the consolidation of Octavian's (to be Augustus') reign.

Yet, even while keeping in mind these dramatic events I want to resist the tendency to read his poetry as allegorical, looking for contemporaneous analogs to his characters and events. Not only does Virgil's poetry resist such a mapping, but also such an approach makes for bad poetry and equally bad political thought. Only at great peril do we rest our interpretation of Virgil's poetry on the little we actually know of his relationship to Augustus, his attitudes toward empire, or the impact of historical events on his ideas. But this history is instructive nonetheless because it provides some context for understanding the range of possible influences on Virgil. Images of the *res publica* linger although the salience of such institutions as the consuls, senate, tribunes, and assembly is gone.[12] In its place is the language of *imperium* that is as global in its scope as the *princeps* is absolute in his rule: command that, as Virgil puts in the mouth of Jupiter, will have "no bounds in conditions (*rerum*) or time" (*A* 1.278, trans. modified), one in which the whole world will be transformed to be governed at Rome's feet (*A* 7.100–1; also 7.258).

The haunting issue that underlies Virgil's poetry is whether the new age (*saeculum*) that marks the beginning of a new century (approximately) and falls at the beginning of Augustus' reign signals a continuation of or a break from the division and bloodshed that has shaped the only political memories Virgil could have.[13] In Virgil's works, memory dislocates. But if there is a future, if communities are to share a common destiny, it has to lie in the ability of memories to also relocate. This occurs not by way of reason but by the transfer of memories into affections that orient and direct human action. Virgil's poetry does not stand impotently outside Roman politics to either valorize or critique it. Instead, as an act of poetic building,

---

[12] Senate in Lavinium (*A* 7.174: curia); ancestor images in Lavinium (*A* 7.177); assembled nations (*A* 7.247); Senate and people on shield (*A* 8.679; 9.192); *concilium* (*A* 9.227; 11.304; 11.460); liberty (*A* 11.346); senate (*A* 11.379).

[13] See Lowrie 2010a, where she argues that the challenge the *Aeneid* poses to Augustus is whether Rome's history will move forward or be mired in violence.

Virgil re-members, bringing something new into the world from the ruins of a civilization.[14]

Hardie has suggested that the "Virgilian version of history" is one in which "history effectively stops."[15] But reading what Virgil has built as exalting a perfected and changeless city[16] or as an affirmation of impersonal duty makes the same mistake as interpreting him as defending some ideal of universal peace or non-oppression (toward each other and toward nature). Both approaches turn Virgil's thought inside-out, placing his poetry in service to an abstract ideal. I think Connolly is largely correct in suggesting that Aeneas "is neither simply a Republican exemplum nor a kingly or imperial one; he is, rather, a figure of disconnected and resistant sensibility whose acts and words call into question the logic of exemplarity itself."[17] Aeneas is not a model of perfection or completeness. He is not a finished product. But neither are *exempla* for the Romans as they are constructed from the tangibility and particularity of human experiences. In such incompleteness lies an ability to recognize the shortcomings of even those one praises (as Sallust does with Cato the Younger and Caesar) as well as to continue to build on the incompleteness of the past, as one sees in notions of Rome's continuous founding for Cicero and Livy. That incompleteness may be Virgil's point. However large, however abstract may be the principate, it is a world, like Virgil's own poetic world, that is always being built. And however grand the ideals of *gloria*, *pietas*, and *pax*, Virgil reveals their human dimension in the experiences of memory, affection, and loss. It is the mark of human achievement that around those experiences communities can be built.

AUGUSTUS AND IDEOLOGY

One of the more profound changes that occurs with the rise of Augustus, as Zanker and Galinsky have demonstrated, is the importance of one person in constructing not just an image of himself, but an ideology of

---

[14] On the diverse and inconsistent traditions from which Virgil built his epic, see Bickerman 1952; Horsfall 1990.
[15] Hardie 1992, 60.   [16] Hardie 1992, 60.   [17] Connolly 2010, 406.

the principate.[18] Augustus was relentless in promoting himself: holidays, thanksgivings, games, public buildings, monuments, coins, rituals, his own *Res Gestae*, and the cultivation of a literary circle of friends, Virgil among them. Having said that, though, ideologies are not univocal constructions, and the old image of Virgil as the mouthpiece of imperial propaganda, a viewed shaped in scholarly interpretations by the experience of fascism, is no longer in vogue. It is possible, though no actual evidence exists, that Augustus would have suggested to Virgil, by then having established a close friendship, to write an epic.[19] Donatus tells us that Virgil read the second, fourth, and sixth books to Augustus. But I agree with White that it is unlikely that Augustus had any direct say in its content or direction, nor did he need to.[20] Ideologies exert their influence more subtly by organizing the logic of discourse: privileging particular values and concerns, organizing juxtapositions, and veiling alternate claims.[21] As we will see, Virgil reflects (and is reflecting on) an age that Augustus played a large part in defining, one that altered the possibilities and promises of political life.

Even though Augustus is careful to maintain the semblance of republican institutions and ideology, those institutions play little role in Virgil's poetry. In talking about imperial poetry, White contends, "The emphasis on empire had the effect of suggesting that Augustus' political mandate was defined not at the level where power was regulated by established institutions, but at a level above and beyond the state, where it was not regulated at all."[22] I am not sure I would go that far for two reasons. First, institutions were never very helpful guides to the operation of power in Rome, as the previous chapters have suggested. Second, power for Virgil is very much a human enactment, both in its obliterating form as violence and in its productive form as agreement. Virgil's poetry is not about institutions any more than it is about Augustus. Although Augustus is celebrated (e.g., *E* 4.49, 51; *A* 6.782, 794–805) and images of civil war leave their mark on his poetry (*G* 4.67–87), Virgil's poetry is

---

[18] Zanker 1988; Galinsky 1996.   [19] White 1993, 115.   [20] White 1993, 116.
[21] More complex approaches to the operation of ideology in Augustan Rome are developed by Zanker 1988; Kennedy 1992; White 1993; Galinsky 1996.
[22] White 1993, 167.

ultimately an attempt to re-imagine community – to restore tangibility – in the age of the principate.

PASTORALISM AND THE GOLDEN AGE

Virgil begins the *Georgics*, his farming poem, with an invocation that orients the reader to a world that is both unfamiliar and prior to Rome's founding. In the words of one Virgilian scholar, "Virgil makes the very beginning of his poem address what we might call 'the problem of beginning', namely that one is always beginning and that one's beginnings are always already in another context."[23] Prior to the founding of the city is the Golden Age of abundance under the reign of Saturn (*G* 1.125–28; *A* 7.46–49, 202–4 under Latinus; 8.314–25). As Virgil writes, "Before the reign of Jove no tillers subjugated the land: even to mark possession of the plain or apportion it by boundaries was sacrilege; man made gain for the common good, and Earth of her own accord gave her gifts all the more freely when none demanded them" (*G* 1.125–28). This is the race of the Latins, descended from and ruled by Saturn, that preceded Aeneas' arrival and conquest: a Golden Age of perfect peace (*A* 8.324–25) in which the people were "righteous, not by bond or laws, but self-controlled of their own free will" (*A* 7.202–4; 7.46–49: Latinus as descendant of Saturn).

Virgil's image of the Golden Age is one of natural harmony among an almost limitless number of species and varieties of plants and animals – without, it might be added, the pains of cataloguing this diversity (*G* 2.103–4). The earth uncultivated "pour[s] forth" its bounty (*E* 4.18–19; *G* 1.127–28); the goats unbidden "bring home their udders swollen with milk" (*E* 4.21–22); animals do not fear or prey on other animals or humans (*E* 4.22; 5.60; 8.28; 8.52; *G* 1.130; *A* 7.483–92); venomous snakes and plants do not threaten (*E* 4.24–25; *G* 1.129); wild brambles bear grapes (*E* 4.29); the oak gives honey (*E* 4.30) and apples (*E* 8.52–3); the shepherds, along with Pan and the woodland nymphs,

---

[23] Batstone 1997, 131; also Arendt 1963, 210; 1978, 2.212–14.

pass the days in pleasure (*voluptas*) (*E* 5.58) and leisure (*otium*) (*E* 5.61); the woods are filled with song (*E* 5.62–63); and people, under the rule of Saturn, live in perfect peace (*A* 8.325), do not subjugate the land or mark it with boundaries (*G* 1.125–27), make gain for everyone (*G* 1.127), and live justly (*G* 2.474). Those who inhabited this land, as Virgil writes, lived a life of purity, knowing the rural gods and remaining unaffected by concerns of honor, the rule of kings, the envy of the rich, the rigors of law, and the madness of the Forum (*G* 2.490–512).

There are by this time fairly established poetic traditions that told of human corruption and decline, from virtue to vice and from abundance to labor, prominently (and differently) articulated by Hesiod, Aratus, Lucretius, and Jewish messianism.[24] These traditions are contemporaneously expressed by Catullus (greed of race of heroes corrupts simplicity of farming life) and Horace (in his sixteenth Epode). "The dominant cultural metaphor throughout Virgil's poetic corpus inherited from the Greek and Roman anthropological and poetic traditions," Thomas notes, "frames human change in a movement from Saturnian to Jovian, from an age of gold to one of iron."[25] Images of rustic life, which recall the Golden Age, had become by this time in Rome "a major literary mode of commentary on contemporary events and the larger speculations they provoked about the nature of civilization and the human condition."[26] But to what purpose?

There is probably no ancient writer, and certainly no ancient Roman writer, who has invited such a vast array of seemingly contradictory interpretations. In part, that is the mark of great literature: We are able to continually see new things as the work takes on some of the hues of contemporaneous concerns or interpretive stances. But it may also be due

---

[24] Hesiod: degeneration of humanity consigned now to wretched toil, but rustic piety of work; Aratus: city of just men with agriculture central in which *Dikē*, herself, wielded the plough; Lucretius: corruption of primitive life because of natural processes, but hardship brings invention; and Jewish messianism: Golden Age returns. See Wilkinson 1963; Wilkinson 1969, 56–65; Johnston 1980, 15–61; Wallace-Hadrill 1982, 21; Farrell 1991.

[25] Thomas 2004–5, 122. See, for example, *G* 1.121–35.

[26] Miles 1980, xii; also Smolenaars 1987 on the relationship between the Golden Age and rustic life.

to a tendency to read Virgil through a series of dichotomies: poetry or politics, nature or labor, pastoral or urban, subversion or propaganda, imperial critic or apologist, passion or reason, individual or community, optimism or pessimism, innocence or guilt, peace or violence, just or unjust, or humanism or chauvinism. What is even more striking is that these dichotomies do not even align in the same way for any given interpretation. For example, he is seen as pro-Augustan because he celebrates a Golden Age of innocence, because he rejects a Golden Age of innocence, because he justifies vengeance in the name of empire, because he argues on behalf of *clementia* in the name of empire, because he aligns himself with an Augustan ideology of reason, because he aligns himself with an Augustan celebration of emotion, because he champions *pietas* as the foundations of cosmopolitan attachments, and because he celebrates *pietas* as the basis of a national identity. Something has to give, not the least of which is the tendency to think in dichotomies. But helpful in charting an interpretive path is having a sense of the options.

On one end of the interpretive spectrum is a romantic privileging of the spirit over and against the intrusion of politics. Snell famously attributes to Virgil the western invention of Arcadia, an expression of the soul's "longing for peace and a home," including the hope of a return of the Golden Age under the reign of Augustus.[27] Although there are political notes, Virgil's pastoral and farming poems, according to Snell, are meant most of all to be appreciated as an aesthetic experience.[28] Putnam similarly describes "the landscape and its inhabitants" as "a realization in tangible form of the poetic mind at work," specifically the "search for freedom to order experience."[29] The *Eclogues* emerge as a reaction against "the artificiality imposed on life by society as it grew."[30] And the *Georgics* read as a "methodology to cope with the external world," one in which "control and chaos are locked in a struggle for victory over man and his world."[31]

---

[27] Snell 1960, 292; also 294–95: applied to *Georgics* and the *Aeneid*.
[28] Also Wilkinson 1969, 11, though recognizing a broader social and philosophical purpose (e.g., 48); Jenkyns 1998.
[29] Putnam 1970, 8.   [30] Putnam 1970, 11.
[31] Putnam 1979, 15; also Smolenaars 1987.

Rejecting this vision of Virgil's poetry as an evocation of a spiritual (more than a political) landscape, others see Virgil's poetry as an ideological expression of (even contribution to) an Augustan ideology.[32] Wilhelm views Virgil as exalting an age in which Saturn, now celebrated by Augustus, establishes the "essence of Italian civilization": farming, law, order, and peace.[33] Others reject any yearning for some Saturnian bucolic age, seeing instead the expression of a new Golden Age of Jupiter that will bring law, civilization, the progress of the arts, and peace.[34] In Otis' influential interpretation, the *Georgics* emerge as a theme of resurrection (in the story of the *bugonia*, the ritual of regenerating life) and Aeneas' journey as akin to a pilgrim's progress: from the Homeric warrior to the civilized, pious, and self controlled Augustan (and sometimes Stoic) individual.[35] Ryberg understands Virgil's pastoralism as developmental, not unlike how the primitive, irresponsible innocence of childhood necessarily matures into the more complex wisdom of adulthood.[36] The Golden Age of Augustus has elements of this innocence – the Romans are heirs of Saturn, by way of Latinus – but has now progressed to a "state ideal" in which the Roman people (led by their ruler) accept their responsibility to ensure peace and justice in the world.[37] Wallace-Hadrill gives perhaps the strongest take on Virgil's contribution to an imperial ideology. Tainted by *scelus*, sometimes translated as sin or an offense against the gods, Rome must seek expatiation in a savior. "The fourth *Eclogue*, written at a moment of acute political instability, is a poetical realization of a widespread attitude, that the solution lay no longer in republican institutions, but in a Messiah."[38]

---

[32] The most cautious expression of this is Galinsky, who identifies Virgil's "own attentiveness to the Augustan ambience" (1996, 251).

[33] Wilhelm 1982, 215.

[34] Jenkyns 1985; 1989: rejection of Snell's notion of Arcadia; Getty 1950, 12; Wilkinson 1963, 83: Golden Age idyll as "inconsistent" with the tenor of Virgil, more "a dream of a literary townsman"; Boyle 1979, with considerably ambiguity; Balot 1998, 92–3; Morgan 1999, 105: "dissolution and rebirth"; Buchheit 1972, 161–73.

[35] Otis 1963, 188–90, 219, 222–23.   [36] Ryberg 1958, 122–23.

[37] Ryberg 1958, 130.

[38] Wallace-Hadrill 1982, 36. The theme of the return to the Golden Age "became a recurrent topic in poetry, imperial panegyric and the official coinage, and it continued to fertilize the imperial ideal long after the classical period" (Wallace-Hadrill 1982, 22).

A variant of these ideological interpretations focuses more on the didactic elements of the poems, though the range of different interpretations suggests that Virgil was either not particularly good at teaching lessons or was engaged in a different (or additional) task. The lessons vary markedly, including teaching that active labor is superior to contemplation[39], that the "farmer's way of life" is "the cornerstone of civilized existence,"[40] that the dreary inevitability of human labor makes empire possible,[41] that an "elite traumatized by civil war" should welcome Octavian,[42] and that Octavian should emulate the farmer, the "toiling and suffering ideal monarch,"[43] or Jupiter, who is coextensive with the universe.[44]

A more critical, even pessimistic, reading of Virgil's image of the Golden Age emerges against the backdrop of Vietnam, led by what has become known as the Harvard School. In his important essay, Parry points to the contrast between the explicit message of the poem that the expansion of Rome had brought about "a happy reconciliation of the natural virtues of the local Italian peoples and the civilized might of the Trojans who came to found the new city," and a different suggestion in the final books "that the formation of Rome's empire involved the loss of the pristine purity of Italy."[45] For Clausen, Virgil celebrates Rome's achievements, "yet he remains aware of the inevitable suffering and loss: It is this perception of Roman history as a long Pyrrhic victory of the human spirit that makes Virgil his country's truest historian."[46] Rome's history is one of "lost ideals and forgotten aspirations,"[47] of *clementia*

---

[39] Schiesaro 1997.
[40] Miles 1980, 62–63, 69. Also Johnston 1980, 129: A renewed Golden Age will be based on the farmer who "can apply his restorative art to the ravaged fields, and ultimately to the ravaged society"; also Galinsky 1996, 93–100.
[41] Gale 2000, 157.   [42] Morgan 1999, 128.
[43] Cairns 1989, 32.   [44] Nappa 2005, 19.
[45] Parry 1963, 68; also Nethercut 1971–1972; Rosivach 1980; rejected by Moorton 1989.
[46] Clausen 1964, 146.
[47] Boyle 1986, 16; also 1972, 71: "the indigenous sanctity and values of a free, pastoral Italy are being pushed aside by the exigencies of the imperial process." For Griffin, Rome trades "the life of pleasure, of art, and of love" for its "austere and self-denying" destiny (Griffin 1979, 68; discussing both *Aeneid* and the Fourth *Georgic*).

giving way to *furor*,[48] and of how "knowledge, science, [and] the *artes*" are "won by violence and lead inevitably to death."[49] More than just commenting on Roman culture, Virgil, in Thomas' argument, "saw what was going on" by associating "the deceptive Jupiter and the deceptive Aeneas" with Augustus who, in the next decades would succeed "in perpetrating the greatest political fiction of the West, that an absolute monarchy was in fact a pure republic."[50]

A final group of scholars influenced by New Historicism and reader response theory, while noting the tensions in Virgil's depiction of the Golden Age, see him as emphasizing the indeterminacy of interpretation. Batstone summarizes this approach in describing how in the *Georgics* "there is interdependence and discontinuity in both the object and the interpretation, and here we find the space which the poem opens for thought and feeling as its tensions, contradictions, and mysteries impinge on the project of knowing-and-doing."[51] For Perkell, the *Georgics* move "from didactic, which presumes to know, to tragic, which does not."[52] What emerges from Perkell's reading is a sharp contrast between the non-material, non-instrumental, non-violent values of poetry (that are in harmony with nature) and the material, instrumental, violent values of the farmer and Iron Age humans (that are incongruous with nature). Reading Virgil's depiction of the relationship of Aristeaus to Eurydice, for example, Perkell argues, "If one sees rape as an act of domination, it becomes clear that rape is the paradigmatic gesture of productive man to nature."[53] The reader is presented with the "disparity between the present, as the poet sees it, and an ideal vision of alternative moral values," a disparity that the reader is left to resolve.[54]

I agree that there is considerable ambiguity in Virgil's image of the Golden Age. It seems variously to be a period of effortless abundance and sloth, natural harmony and helplessness, a contented but irrelevant life, cultivation and destruction, and the starting point for both

---

[48] Putnam, 1995, 148; also 2011.   [49] Ross 1987, 233.   [50] Thomas 2004–5, 146.
[51] Batstone 1997, 125–26.   [52] Perkell 1989, 19.   [53] Perkell 1989, 71.
[54] Perkell 1989, 90. For Connolly, the shifting and ambiguous references to places and people in Virgil's *Eclogues* not only "mirrors the indefinable quality of the whole landscape" but also "oblige[s] us to face, and critique, our own expectations of land as stability" (Connolly 2001, 112, 113). See also Gale 2000, 56.

human corruption and technological progress. I am less sure that this ambivalence is meant, as these interpretations suggest, either to "deconstruct" the myth of the Golden Age and signal that Jupiter's age is superior to Saturn's[55] or to offer an alternative to domination and conquest by putting in its place a recognition of "the humane value of community."[56] Although I find attractive Perkell's suggestion that the function of Virgil's use of the Golden Age is "to keep alive the continuing moral question: what *is* the Good?"[57], that question seems rather more Greek than Roman, more Plato than Virgil, and more philosophical than poetic.

The ambiguity of Virgil's accounts of the loss of the Golden Age – as a punishment for Prometheus' theft from the gods (*G* 1.61–62), as stages of human corruption, and as an activation of the mind and a mechanism for introducing *artes* by Jupiter – seems to blunt its moralizing or didactic function. By evoking the Golden Age, Virgil is less conveying a sense of any past or future vision of society and seems more to be situating humans amidst nature's "laws and eternal covenants (*leges aeternaque foedera*)" (*G* 1.60). These laws encompass the deathless/ timeless rhythm of the seasons (e.g., *G* 1.71), the indifference to life and death (*G* 3.349–83; 3.478–514; 4.471–80; 4.489), and a barely contained (by covenant) violence, chaos (*A* 1.50–63), and entropic decay (*G* 1.197–98).[58] As this language suggests, Virgil is, in Klingner's words, engaged in an inner conversation with Lucretius.[59] Though there are moments, such as the tenth *Eclogue*, where Virgil seems to affirm a human acceptance of the limitations of living in what resembles an Epicurean cosmos, he does not offer an Epicurean vision – or a Stoic or pastoral one – in which human life can be brought into accord with nature.[60] Nor, I might add, does he provide "two different views of the way things are," as has been

---

[55] Nappa 2005, 158; also Thomas 2001, 143.
[56] Perkell 2002, 33, 22.   [57] Perkell 2002, 35.
[58] Ross argues that for the Romans, "'Nature' is agricultural, is inconceivable without man, and is his creation" (Ross 1987, 23). If that belief existed before Lucretius, it certainly could not have survived after.
[59] Klingner 1967, 198; also Hardie 1986, 157–240; Gale 2000; 2003.
[60] Epicurean aspects: Conte 1986, 129; Stoic aspects in the *Georgics* (providence): Miles 1980, 93–98.

argued, one Lucretian and one more traditionally Roman, so that we are "left to resolve the apparent contradictions for ourselves."[61] Virgil rehumanizes Lucretius' bleak, indifferent cosmos by showing how the introduction of memory alters the terms by which one comprehends the natural landscape. A humanized landscape is an incongruous one: one in which the attempt to forge memory must cut a linear path, often violently and invariably incompletely, across the ceaseless rhythm of nature. Virgil does not leave us poised between the contradictory impulses of Golden Age poetic communion and Iron Age agricultural rapaciousness, though, but negotiates these polarities by suggesting an attitude of cultivation.

VIRGIL, LUCRETIUS, *LABOR*, AND MEMORY

In his discussion of the human relationship to nature Virgil invites a comparison to Lucretius, signaling his relationship when he describes the power of the Muses to reveal to him the distant forces and causes of the universe, only to suggest the limits to the quest: "But, if the chill blood about my heart bar me from reaching those realms of nature, let my delight be the country, and the running streams amid the dells (*sin, has ne possim naturae accedere pratis, / frigidus obstiterit circum praecordia sanguis, / rura mihi et rigui placeant in vallibus amnes*)" (G 2.483–85). Dyson interprets this passage as suggesting that "in fear" Virgil turns to supernatural explanations rather than scientific ones.[62] The interpretation not only equates cold blood with fear, which may be erroneous, but identifies fear as Virgil's point of departure from Lucretius.[63] I think the point of departure is subtler, having to do with the relationship of memory to nature. In contrast to approaches that argue that Virgil attempts to restore (or laments the loss of) harmony with nature,

---

[61] Gale 2000, 24, also 273; Gale 2003; Dyson 1994; 1997; also comparable to skeptical methodology: Gale 2000, 271.

[62] Dyson 1997, 451.

[63] Wilkinson notes that Virgil refers to the ancient notion that blood around the heart conditioned thought (1969, 134).

I suggest that memory necessarily opens a gap between humans and nature. To not have memory is to not be human. Virgil's exploration of how to reconcile that gap in the *Eclogues* and the *Georgics* serves as the foundation for the political thought of the *Aeneid*.

Virgil concedes that the person may be happy (*felix*) who succeeds "in learning the causes of nature's working" so that there is no fear of nature's inexorable fate or "the howl of insatiable Death" (*G* 2.490–92, trans. modified). But for those who cannot penetrate the dark mysteries of the cosmos, there may also be happiness in the timeless delight of nature's song (*G* 2.493–94). Virgil, in fact, begins the *Georgics* on this note of joy: He will sing of "what makes the fields happy" (*laetae*) (*G* 1.1, trans. modified). Happiness, more than fear, are the shared motivations. But more than that: What Virgil's rustic world has in common with Lucretius' cosmos is that neither exists in time.[64] By that I mean that there is neither a past nor a future, neither memory nor more than the fleeting fame that a grape brings to the vine or corn to a stalk (*G* 2.486; *E* 5.32–34). And though Virgil characterizes this bucolic world as one of carefree happiness and pleasure, it is one that is as inhuman as Lucretius' universe, if by that one means that humans are in no way important to this vision. We catch glimpses of this inhuman nature, even the happiness that seems to attend this life. In the featureless landscape of the North, the inhabitants live at ease (*otium*) (*G* 3.377; compare to *G* 2.486–89, 526–31), beneath the ground in caves, "but far and wide earth [that] lies shapeless under mounds of snow and piles of ice" (*G* 3.354–55). Humans similarly leave no mark on the Libyan landscape where herdsmen roam on a vast, featureless plain with no shelter (*G* 3.342–43).

Humans are for Virgil a part of, even indistinct in ways from, nature. Virgil employs terms and descriptions that universalize the activities and dispositions of all living things: love (*G* 3.242–44); home (*G* 1.182; 4.153–57); agreements (*G* 4.158); division of labor (*G* 4.158–68); love of gain (*G* 4.177); fear of age (*G* 1.186); battle (*G* 4.1–7; 4.67–87); community (*G* 4.1–7); sacrifice (*G* 4.203–5); character (*G* 4.95); even glory (*G* 4.6; *G* 4.205, 218; *E* 5.32–34), which is an attribute of all organisms.[65]

---

[64] See Arendt 1978, 2.214–15.
[65] See, for example, Otis, who sees the anthropomorphizing as meant to identify "the nature," including the feelings, "common to both animal and man" (Otis 1963, 153).

Glory is instructive here because it reveals gradations from Golden Age organisms to Iron Age humans, gradations that distinguish humans from nature. The glory associated with the Golden Age is both effortless and unconscious; it is the culmination of natural fruition, like the blooming of a flower or the ripening of fruit. But the glory of a bee, in Virgil's extended discussion of the community of bees, does not seem quite the same. Bees, it is worth recalling, were made cooperative and passionless by Jupiter as a reward for feeding him in his infancy (G 4.149–50). They not only share Iron Age modifications with humans, but they may also have a share of divine intelligence (G 4.220). The glory of bees is different from Golden Age organisms, though, both in how glory is won and what it achieves. Where the glory of a flower is simply the culmination of natural and self-contained processes of growth and decay (see, for example, G 1.127–28), the glory of bees is won by *labor* – the activity of work and toil, introduced by Jupiter, by which one must extract resources from the external world (G 4.158–69; generally of the introduction of *labor* by Jupiter, see G 1.118–46; G 1.145–46: *labor improbus*).[66] And where the glory of a flower is fleeting, its beauty experienced in the moment, the glory of bees resides in what they have built, cared for, conquered, and sacrificed in order to leave something for future generations. The glory of bees lies not just in their devotion to, and willingness to sacrifice for, the community, but in leaving behind something tangible, something that would not exist except for their labor. "Therefore, though the limit of a narrow span awaits the bees themselves – for it never stretches beyond the seventh summer – yet the race abides immortal, for many a year stands firm the fortune of the house, and grandsires' grandsires are numbered on the roll" (G 4.206–9). There is, as Gale suggests, a kind of immortality that redeems Lucretius' vision of death by building something that appears as more than recycled matter.[67]

Humans, like bees, must similarly labor to leave their mark on the landscape. *Labor*, as has been recognized frequently, is central to the

---

On the philosophic backdrop to different ancient conceptions of animals, see Gale 2000, 94–105.

[66] Miles 1980, 85: *labor* as unrelenting toil.   [67] Gale 2000, 49–50.

Roman value system, connected to military exploits and agricultural efforts, related to *cura* (concern), associated with virtues like *diligentia*, *ratio*, and *consilium*, and seen as "essential to the pursuit of *dignitas* ('rank') and *gloria* ('prestige')."[68] As Virgil writes, in suggesting the relationship of fame to *labor*: "Here is toil, hence hope for fame" (*G* 3.288). Human *labor*, like that of bees, is extractive, altering the shape of nature and thus always containing elements of violence and subjugation (e.g., *G* 1.125). Like Aristaeus who must forcibly subdue Proteus to acquire the secrets of the Underworld (*G* 4.398, 405–14), so the farmer, through *labor*, must carve out the soil, clear trees, root out weeds, and battle disease and intruders. Not surprisingly, then, and to the considerable consternation of modern critics, Virgil often mingles agricultural and military images (*G* 1.155, 160).[69]

There are two important differences between bees and humans, though. First, humans must learn to read nature (including bees) (e.g., *G* 1.424–26; 1.439: *signa*; 4.106–7) whereas other animals (including bees) sense changes (*G* 1.420). Thus, the *Georgics* describe how to recognize types of soil, how to raise the appropriate crops and herds, how to tend to them, and how to identify potential threats (e.g., *G* 2.35–36; 2.226–56; also *G* 1.424–26, 438–39, 464–65). To read the *Georgics* as an instructional manual or a paean to rustic life is to miss the larger conceptual point: With each instruction, the gap between human comprehension and natural processes is made more apparent.[70] Unlike in Lucretius, where knowledge of natural laws provides "unlimited epistemological potential," for Virgil such comprehension will always be incomplete.[71]

---

[68] Gale 2000, 145. On labor, see Lau 1975; Gale 2000, 143–95.
[69] See, for example, Bradley 1969: farmer at war with nature.
[70] This argument is consistent with Schiesaro's claim that in the *Georgics*, knowledge is a divine possession. To acquire knowledge "is a tortuous and indirect process in which every stage is inevitably charged with complex relations" (1997, 67). Spurr 1986, in placing the *Georgics* in an agricultural handbook tradition, provides some useful correctives to symbolic readings of the poem.
[71] Schiesaro 1997, 71, who also develops the intertextual connection between the *Georgics* and Cicero's *De divinatione* that seeks to assimilate rational and religious modes of knowing.

Second, unlike bees, humans introduce memory to the timeless landscape. The opening verse of the *Eclogues* is premised on memory of place that only humans would know: to be exiled from one's "country's bounds and sweet fields" (*E* 1.3). Even the rule of Octavian, celebrated as the return of a Saturnian Golden Age (*E* 4.4–25), is accompanied with stories of the "glories of heroes" and one's "father's deeds" so that one may learn of *virtus* (*E* 4.26–27). In fact, those deeds are manifested as the artifacts of war, the weapons that are now part of, but still standing out from, the soil. In a wonderfully evocative verse, Virgil, in recalling the battles of Octavian, writes, "Yes, and a time will come when in those lands the farmer, as he cleaves the soil with his curved plough, will find javelins corroded with rusty mould, or with his heavy hoe will strike empty helmets, and marvel at gigantic bones in the upturned graves (*Scilicet et tempus veniet, cum finibus illis / agricola incurvo terram molitus aratro / exesa inveniet scabra robigine pila, / aut gravibus rastris galeas pulsabit inanis, / grandiaque effossis mirabitur ossa sepulcris*)" (*G* 1.493–97; see also *A* 7.526; *A* 7.551). The passage is fraught with ambiguity: Stories are mortal fixtures in an immortal landscape. Time, of no consequence to nature, robs humans of memory, even the memory of songs once sung about timeless nature (*E* 10.51–52). Memories, thus, invariably invoke loss: the passing of a loved one (Orpheus), the destruction of the products of one's *labor* (the plague), and, as we will see, the displacement from one's home (Aeneas). There is, in fact, always a gap – always an incongruity – between the timelessness of nature and the efforts through memory to make human *labor* similarly timeless.

The question that haunts Iron Age humanity, and one centrally Roman, is this: How does one respond to the gap between the desire to make permanent the products of human toil and the realization of nature's memoriless eternity? Virgil presents us with several options, which, as I will suggest, he returns to in the *Aeneid*. One response is to close the gap by attempting to make the *gloria* achieved through *labor* as eternal as nature, seeing in *labor* the ability to reverse the process of decline from the Golden Age.[72] For Virgil, though, what begins as a

---

[72] Stehle 1974, 350, 355; also Bradley 1969, 352: "the idyllic existence of the Golden Age is made accessible via a productive relation to nature."

subjugation and invention necessary to shape nature, triumph over want (e.g., *G* 1.125; 1.145–46; 1.155–61; 1.168; 2.61–64, 279–87), obtain fame (*G* 2.486; 3.46–48), and rule (*G* 3.16–39) turns into a Lucretian scramble for immortal power that cannot be obtained (see, for example, a Lucretian sensibility in *G* 2.461–68). In Virgil's entropic universe, all things "speed towards the worse and slipping away fall back" (*G* 1.199–200). Thus, Virgil recounts the plague that renders useless all human arts (*G* 3.378–565). Paradoxically, in the attempt to immortalize one's accomplishments through glory and earthly triumphs (*G* 1.504), one risks unleashing strife (*G* 1.511), undoing the products of labor by leaving the world in ruins (*G* 1.500; 2.505–12). The images recall the decades of civil war alluded to in Virgil's passages on the bees: of two kings leading a divided people (*G* 4.67–70), as well as the references to Egypt. Egypt figured in civil war in two ways: first between Pompeius and Caesar (where Pompeius sought refuge in Egypt) and then between Octavian and Antonius (who through his alliance and intimate relationship with Cleopatra becomes associated with Egypt and the Oriental East in Octavian's propaganda) (*G* 4.210–18; depictions of Antonius in *A* 8.685–88).[73] In fact, Virgil draws on a discourse that already appears in Cicero (and appears as well in Horace), that of the security of the community resting on the safety and *auctoritas* of the leader (see *G* 4.210–18; *A* 1.151: *pietate gravem*; Cic. *Marc.* 22; *Brut.* 56; Hor. *Ode* 3.14.13–16; 4.5.25–8). Absent a king, a "guardian of their toils" (*G* 4.215), the bees rip apart what they have built, their hives, though the solution alludes to an eastern form of despotism so anathema to Roman ideology.[74] The "mindless and passive loyalty to their king" that the Romans associate with the East strikes dangerously close to home as a solution to civil war.[75]

A second option to closing the gap between humans and nature is the erotic love of Orpheus who is generally seen as achieving a fusion with nature. Orpheus' elegiac language is nostalgic: a song of mourning for his

---

[73] On discussions of the analogies between bees and Roman society, see Wilkinson 1969, 180–81; Perkell 1978; Batstone 1997; Morley 2007; Lowrie (forthcoming).
[74] See Galinsky 1996, 20–24: multiplicity of meanings that draw on exemplary past; Lowrie (forthcoming): Eastern resonance.
[75] Perkell 1978, 213; Lowrie (forthcoming).

departed wife, Eurydice, who is killed by a snake as she runs from Aristaeus' attempt to rape her. Through the beauty of his music, Orpheus is able to move nature to allow him to retrieve his wife from the Underworld. But just before reaching the light of the upper world, Orpheus is gripped by a "sudden frenzy" of love, violates the agreement, and looks back at Eurydice (G 4.488).[76] Thus was undone all the *labor* of the journey; Eurydice vanishes again and Orpheus is left only with the singular memory of his twice lost love. "For the lover retains a memory only of his beloved and forgets everything and everyone else, indeed, as the limit, even himself."[77] It is a memory woven into a continued lament that is so beautiful that it moves the oaks, but its singularity – indeed, its naturalness – pushes Orpheus out of human surroundings, condemning him to roam the featureless, frozen northern landscape. His unyielding lament ultimately collides with rituals (though the nature of those rituals is unclear), the human form given to nature and the divine, leading the northern women, perhaps out of scorn for his devotion to Eurydice and not to them, to tear Orpheus apart and scatter him around the land. Orpheus may provide the poetic voice by which humans can reconcile themselves to their own mortality.[78] But Orpheus' poetic immortality emerges as a macabre timelessness, his body mutilated and spread across the earth, his "disembodied voice and frozen tongue" echoing along the stream (G 4.525). Disembodiment is the price of one's fusion into nature's timelessness.[79]

The untenability of either *labor* or poetry as solutions to the gap between human memory and nature's timelessness has led scholars to see not a solution but a tragic dimension to human action. Suggestive is Virgil's original treatment of Orpheus and Aristaeus, bringing into collision a poetic and cultural hero, both made gods, one for his gift of music, the other as a patron of technical arts (such as beekeeping). The collision has been interpreted as arising from two different modes

---

[76] Otis sees Orpheus' failure as a failure to control his passions through reason (1963, 212); also Putnam 1979, 304, 315–16. The evidence is unclear about whether in other, earlier variants, Orpheus was successful in restoring Eurydice to life. See Bowra 1952; Heath 1994; Gale 2003, 333–34.
[77] Most 2001, 158; also *E* 2.68; 8.85–89.   [78] Stehle 1974, 367; Parry 1972, 51–52.
[79] On this tension between spirituality and physicality, see especially Putnam 1979, 316.

of truth: the poet's truth and farmer's truth.[80] The farmer's mode, it is argued, is to "vanquish nature through his technology"[81] and impose "rigid order"[82] through reason, "violence and destruction."[83] In contrast is the poet's mode, which is seen as blending with nature and yielding to inspiration and passion. I will suggest that for Virgil the response to the gap between humans and nature is reducible neither to domination nor to surrender, but is characterized by an attitude of *cultus*, cultivation (G 1.198. 2.35; also A 8.316), which is the basis of the word "culture." It is an attitude that connects Virgil's *Aeneid* to the *Eclogues* and the *Georgics*.

LABOR AND *CULTUS*

Virgil signals the importance of *cultus* in the opening verses of the first and second book of the *Georgics* (G 1.3; 2.1). *Cultus* is associated with building and caring for something (e.g., G 2.48, 55; also A 3.505). The care, a tending to something, is akin to a form of education or upbringing by which something is ordered from disparate wildness and made to flourish (e.g., G 1.95; 1.153; 2.77). Thus, one must "learn the proper *cultus*" for different kinds of plants and animals (G 2.35) and, in turn, train them. Under constant *cultus*, the thing will shed its wild spirit and "readily follow" the *artes* one would have them learn (G 2.51–52; also 2.61–62). *Cultus* is associated with elements of subjugation, conquest, and control (e.g. G 2.114), even violence.[84] One must cut off an ulcer (G 3.452–56), for example, or remove portions of a hive (for bees to work harder) (4.239–50; E 2.38–39: orchards call out to have fruit plucked). Even the odd story of the ritual of *bugonia* suggests how regenerated life can exist alongside, even arise from, violence and rot (G 4.555–56), not unlike the birth of Rome from the fires of Troy and

---

[80] Perkell 1989, 139–90.   [81] Perkell 1989, 34.
[82] Gale 2000, 274.   [83] Gale 2000, 54.
[84] Morgan points to a Stoic cosmological model of destructive violence that makes possible renewal (Morgan 1999, 86; also on sacrifice, see 112–16).

the new birth of Octavian that can arise from the desolation of Italy (*E* 4.8; *G*. 4.560–61).[85]

The attitude that engenders *cultus* does not rely on vanquishing, and thus is not driven by the need to eliminate the gap between humans and nature. In fact Virgil reopens this gap by way of mystery.[86] Strikingly, in the *Georgics*, which describe how humans can begin to know nature, Virgil ends on two notes of mystery. The first is the Corycian gardener who is somehow able to fill his table with food from unclaimed land that is not suited for crops, vines, or pasturage (*G* 4.116–48).[87] The second, by way of a journey into the Underworld, is the practice of *bugonia*, Egyptian in its origins, in which a new generation of bees is born from the rotting carcass of an ox. I disagree with Stehle who argues that the *bugonia* "symbolizes man's complete understanding of and control over nature."[88] It would be an odd symbol of control, a rite cloaked in mystery in which no rational explanation of how it works is given. On the way to learning this mystery, Aristeaus, for example, our seeming symbol of mastery, gazes in wonderment at his mother's undersea world (*G* 4.363–67).

Cultus modifies, as well, what Gale depicts as Virgil's use of the "Lucretian triad *metus/ cura/ labor*," where *cura* is suggestive of misery, anxiety, and distress.[89] There is no doubt that *cura* invites a certain anxiety: One is taking care of something that may succumb to disease or predators or may become smothered in a tangle of weeds (see, for example, *G* 2.415–19). But by connecting *cura* to *cultus*, we can round out our understanding of *cura* (e.g., *G*. 1.3; 2.415). *Cura* is not endless misery and drudgery, nor does it culminate in anything like *metus*, which is used infrequently by Virgil (*metus* appears twice; *metuere* eight times).

---

[85] *Bugonia* as redemptive: Farrell 1991, 263–84; Dyson 1996, 281; Morgan 1999, 136–38 (as miracle, like Octavian's emergence from the final destruction of Antonius in Egypt); as distancing from Egypt: Habinek 1990.

[86] See, for example, Perkell 1989, 146.

[87] Perkell argues that the garden serves "as an image of beauty that is nonmaterial, nonproductive, nonprofitable, and thus in opposition to the farmer's work, which is material and answers to physical needs" (1989, 132). But the garden feeds him. Wilkinson views the old man as a pirate (1969, 174–75).

[88] Stehle 1974, 369.   [89] Gale 2000, 159, 146–54.

There is anxiety, certainly failure, but it is more like the anxiety of raising a child: Things may not turn out well, but if done properly, and fortune is on one's side, the child serves as testimony to the product of one's labor, something to which one has tended and for which one has a certain affection.

The attitude of cultivation joins together the image of the farmer with that of the poet and the political leader.[90] Each, as Putnam notes, is a framer of order.[91] The fields, like cities, are monuments to human *labor* (*G* 2.155). And the task of the poet is to build (*condere*) a story (*E* 6.7).[92] Virgil is not shy in fusing the poetic and political: he identifies himself as a sculptor and builder of a temple to Octavian (*G* 3.26–39; also Hor. *Ode* 4.15).[93] It is by no means obvious what image of politics guides Virgil's efforts. I tend to agree with Galinsky that a feature of Virgil's poetry is that one "cannot go home again," neither humans to the Golden Age, Aeneas to Troy, nor Rome to its Republic.[94] That is, Virgil's vision of politics is not oriented to the past. Nor is Virgil particularly interested in institutional forms. Virgil's poetry comes to us less as a solution than as an exploration of the conditions and struggle upon which a future community can be built. It is in identifying those conditions that Virgil's *Georgics* end as they begin, on a note of cultivation: he sings of the *cultus* of the fields, cattle, and trees as well as of Octavian who gives laws to willing nations (*G* 4.559–62).

---

[90] See Gale 2003, 331: "Throughout the poem, then, Virgil offers us a series of different and conflicting models for the relationship between poet and *princeps*, or between the active and the contemplative life. Sometimes it is suggested that the two can cooperate harmoniously, sometimes they are mutually opposed. The statesman is represented in some parts of the poem as the source of political violence, but portrayed elsewhere as a restraining force that, like the shaping hand of the farmer, will impose order on the unruly passions of his subjects. Similarly, the poet is linked now with order, now with disorderly passion." Boyle sees a conflict of the poetic and political world in the *Eclogues* (1986, 38–39) that is possibly overcome in the *Georgics* (1986, 42–43, 76–84).

[91] Putnam 1979, 321.   [92] See esp. Putnam 1979, 321.

[93] Balot 1998, 89, following Pindar's epinician themes; Boyle 1979, 74–75. In my mind, Perkell draws too sharp of a distinction here between the aggression of Octavian and the achievement of the song without aggression (1989, 62). It seems unlikely that Virgil is singing of Octavian's achievements in order to condemn them.

[94] Galinsky 1996, 123.

VIOLENCE

As one moves from the *Georgics* to the *Aeneid*, one can almost watch as the farm tools are shaped into weapons (*A* 7.635–36). One of the curiosities, certainly one of the interpretive challenges, of Virgil's *Aeneid* is what we are to make of the violence. The *Aeneid* is steeped in violence.[95] The epic's first word is *arma*. It begins with the destruction of Troy and is driven by Juno's wrath toward the Trojans (*A* 1.25–33). The love story with Dido ends with her suicide (and the promise of more violence). The killing of Silvia's trained stag, an image of the Golden Age, reveals a rustic people easily moved to "savage rage" who turn the fields into "a dark harvest of drawn swords" (*A* 7.510, 526). The later books are comprised almost entirely of the conquest of Latium. And the poem culminates with what some see as Aeneas' cold-blooded, even pointless, slaughter of Turnus. Nothing – neither nature nor culture, neither innocence nor guilt, neither piety nor impiety (e.g., *A* 2.430) – is untouched by violence. And what is perhaps the most striking feature is how little the violence plays in defining heroic action.

Here is what I mean. In classic American westerns, for example, or spy movies (or the current trend in superhero movies) there is a lot of violence, but the hero is either able to maneuver through the violence (through craftiness) or master the violence (by being better with his weapon). So, too, to some extent we see the same skills in the Homeric epics: Odysseus maneuvers, Achilles masters. Aeneas does neither. Nor does any other character. Nor, and this is Virgil's point, can any other character. Rather than mastering or maneuvering, Aeneas experiences only the dislocating effects of violence: the chilling dread (*A* 1.92), feigned hope (*A* 1.209), stifled anguish (*A* 1.209), and the almost unbearable sorrow of loss (*A* 1.460–63) that accompanies exile (*A* 1.1–2) and wandering (*A* 1.32). In Aeneas' first act of narratively reconstructing the

---

[95] The argument here is consistent with Pöschl's suggestion that Virgil's poetry is built around an aesthetic principle of light being framed by darkness (Pöschl 1961, 296). See Lowrie 2005; 2010c for attempts to categorize the different aspects of violence in the *Aeneid*, recognizing the overlapping uses of and justifications for violence that go beyond law or reason.

past, a scene that is modeled after Odysseus' tale to the Phaeacians, Aeneas tells not of heroes but of victims, and not of great deeds but of terrifying chaos and brutalizing violence: the distant sounds of the city ablaze (*A* 2.298–308), the frantic desire to rush into (and die in) battle (*A* 2.314–17), the vision of a desecrated Hektor (*A* 2.270–80), the "shrieks and woeful uproar" of Priam's house in confusion (*A* 2.486–87), the lasting vision of corpses strewn about the streets (*A* 2.363–66), the former king now a "corpse without a name" (*A* 2.558), a desperate escape through the labyrinthian streets, and the realization that "we Trojans are no more" (*A* 2.325). As if to secure the memory in the mind of his audience, Virgil returns us to the destroyed city for Aeneas' last, futile embrace of the ghost of his wife, lost and killed in the flight from Troy (*A* 2.793).[96] It is a scene of almost desperate unintelligibility: a city rendered unrecognizable, sounds indistinguishable, paths impassable, and action foreclosed by an incomprehensible destiny.[97] The images repeat later in the epic: a "maze inextricable" that is recalled in the story (and crafted images) of Daedalus (*A* 6.27) and the "tangled path" that Nisus must navigate (unsuccessfully) to retrieve Euryalus (*A* 9.390–91), who remains unburied in a foreign land (*A* 9.485) and whose mother laments where to go.

We see similar scenes of violence and confusion in Homer. But Homer reverses the effect of the violence, restoring the warrior in the memory of the community. There are no beautiful deaths in the *Aeneid*, though.[98] "How changed he was," Aeneas recalls in his encounter in his dream with Hektor: black with bloodied dust, ragged hair, beard matted with blood, covered in wounds, torn by the chariot (*A* 2.271–79). For Deiphobos, whom Aeneas spots in the Underworld attempting to hide his mangled faced with his handless arms (*A* 6.494–99), "memory is shame and pity."[99] Whatever memorial to Deiphobos that may have existed is now gone; all that remains, again reversing the Homeric record, are the mutilating scars earned not through one last great deed (to recall Hektor),

---

[96] On the comparison of Aeneas' descent to Orpheus', see Gale 2003, 337–39.
[97] On this general theme of "darkness visible," the incomprehensibility of human thought, action and perception, see Johnson 1976, 75–99.
[98] The language is from Vernant 1991, 50–74.   [99] Bleisch 1999, 203.

VIOLENCE

but by treachery.[100] There are those who remain alive, such as Achaemenides, who is left behind with the Cyclops (*A* 3.613–14): miserable, forgotten, (*A* 3.590–92), no longer among (or able to be killed by) men (*A* 3.606). And there is Palinurus (a steersman who is tossed overboard), who swims unburied (*A* 6.337–71), a sight that recalls the throng of unburied (*A* 6.305) that Aeneas first encounters in the Underworld. Even Virgil's poetic memorial to Euryalus and Nisus is followed by the wailing of Euryalus' mother that her son will "lie in a strange land, given as prey to the dogs and fowls of Latium" (*A* 9.446–49, 485).

Even (or especially) the crafted images of the Trojan War that Aeneas sees on the Temple of Juno in Carthage underscore the irreversible memories of violence. The "wondrous sights" of battle might seem to compensate for violence by providing *fama* (*A* 1.494). But these pictures are ultimately *inanis* (empty) (*A* 1.462–64, 494), unable to undo (and in fact heightening memories of) the violence suffered by the Trojans. The panels include Rhesus being killed in his sleep by Diomedes, Troilus being dragged unarmed by a chariot, Athena who is silent before the supplication of the women of Troy, and Achilles ransoming the body of Hektor. There are no "joyful memories of those ancient ills" (*A* 11.280), even by the victors, Diomedes recalls in refusing the appeal by Venulus, the envoy sent by Turnus, to create an alliance against Aeneas.

This early portrait of Aeneas – both his mad rush to take up arms (*A* 2.316, 355, 594–95, 771) and the crushing weight of his memories – is often read against a narrative trajectory that privileges the movement "from nostalgia to forgetfulness of the past and anticipation of the future," emotion to reason, vengeance to forgiveness, individual attachments to the recognition of "impersonal duty," and mortality to divinity.[101] For Bowra, who reads the *Aeneid* through a Stoic lens, "Aeneas is a Stoic, but like all Stoics he has to go through a period of probation, and during this his temptations and difficulties are often too much for him,

---

[100] Bleisch 1999, 205–6.
[101] Gale 2003, 342: forgetfulness; Gale 2003, 347: impersonal duty; Bacon 1986: divinity. Also Bowra 1933, 12–13; Otis 1963, 305–7; Williams 1964, 52; Cairns 1989, 29–30; Quint 1993, 63–4; Gill 2006, 460: how close Aeneas comes to "very demanding normative standards of rationality and virtue, those of Stoic-Epicurean wisdom."

and he fails."[102] What is emphasized in these readings, in particular, is Aeneas' gradual recognition and embrace of his fate that requires that he shed his personal memories so that he may soberly and steadfastly fulfill his duty to something much larger.

The analog is often to Octavian who is seen by some as plotting a future that requires forgetting the past decades of fierce rivalries, civil war, and unremitting violence.[103] As Quint argues, the end of Book 6 and Book 12 "suggests that the need for the survivors of the Trojan war and later of the poem's Italian wars – and for the survivors of Rome's own civil wars – to forget the tragic memories of their past is as deep-seated as life itself, part of the basic processes of the psyche. Both a fresh start in Italy under Aeneas and the national revival fostered by Augustus require the same collective act of oblivion that the souls undergo in order to be reborn."[104] As Most contends, through his endorsement of *clementia* Octavian "urged one to forget the murdered Caesar."[105] For Aeneas to choose *clementia* "requires that Aeneas forget Pallas and forgive Turnus."[106]

But forgiveness arises precisely because one cannot forget. And just as there is no one who is not bathed in violence, so there is no one in the *Aeneid* who forgets. In fact, each character is entangled in the realization that there is no forgetting; that the past cannot be undone. In the face of Aeneas' rejection of her, Dido seeks to "release" herself from love (*A* 4.479; also *A* 4.652): wishing the Trojans had never landed (*A*. 4.658), "destroy[ing] all memorials" of Aeneas (*A* 4.498), and then seeking vengeance through a curse. Precisely because it is impossible to undo history, Dido knows that even if the curse works she will die "unavenged" (*A* 4.659). Euryalus' mother, who chooses to follow her son to this *terra ignota* (unfamiliar land), cannot retrace her steps: There is no "last farewell" (*A* 9.482), no place to go to (*A* 9.490), nothing to hope for but to "break life's cruel bonds" (*A* 9.497). Aeneas, too, closes the epic on a final act of violence spurred by the sight of the slaughtered Pallas' belt, a "memorial of cruel grief" (*A* 12.946). Aeneas' departure

---

[102] Bowra 1933, 11. [103] Quint 1993 53–65; Zetzel 1989, 282–84; Gale 2003, 341.
[104] Quint 1993, 64. [105] Most 2001, 167; *clementia* as forgetting, also Putnam 1995, 4.
[106] Most 2001, 168.

from Stoic "rationality and virtue," a psychology that Gill sees as operative in the *Aeneid*, arises not from a failure to live up to this standard but from a view of individuals as unable to free themselves from their past.[107] His eschatology makes clear the ubiquity of memory: Even in death the "pangs [of love] leave them not" (*A* 6.444). Only after the taint of the body is removed by being hung out in breezes, or scrubbed, or exposed to fire can a soul, after a thousand years, be returned to its original state without memory (*A* 6.715, 730–47, 750).

Virgil's poetic task is one built largely around memories, as Virgil announces in the opening lines: "*Musa, mihi causas memora*" (Muse, tell me [remind me] of the causes) (*A* 1.8).[108] Virgil's poetry, as Pöschl notes, is organized around moments of departure, which is "the moment when memory reaches a climax of intensity."[109] So if not forgetfulness, what does the *Aeneid* do? Ross, joining a number of other scholars, suggests that Virgil, in depicting the savagery of Troy (and Rome's) past, concludes that the heroic ideal ends in brutality, bloodiness, and pointlessness.[110] So too, Boyle argues that the quest for fame, including Aeneas' own actions, are "portrayed in terms of futile, violent heroism."[111] But that places too much normative weight on the violence, as though it needs to be – or, perhaps more accurately, can be – justified. Violence is not joined with courage, as it is for Plato. It is not justified by power, as it is for the Athenians (by way of Thucydides). It is not redeemed by righteousness, as it will be later by Augustine. The power of Virgil's conception is that violence simply is; it is a part of Rome's founding, a fact of Augustus' rise, and a ubiquitous aspect of political life.[112]

Violence does have an effect, though; it traumatizes. The poetic act of remembering is one of renewing (*A* 2.3), making present (and painful) the past (*A* 2.12). The process is selective, the poet framing what to remember and how to remember it, creating a narrative that

---

[107] Gill 2006, 460. [108] See Reed 2007, 170–71; Seider 2013, 11–12.
[109] Pöschl 1961, 298. [110] Ross 1998. [111] Boyle 1972, 75.
[112] This is contrary to Arendt's reading of the *Aeneid* in the context of America's founding that minimizes violence in the epic (1963, 213–14). On images of violence and sacrifice associated with Augustus, see Dyson 1996.

transforms trauma into a narrative that connects past to future.[113] Virgil's poetry implicates his audience in the disorienting confusion and staggering sense of loss, whether of the fall of Troy or the war with the Latins, in which by the end it is impossible to distinguish in any meaningful way between vanquisher and vanquished, innocent and guilty, and who will suffer and who will not. What is seared into Roman consciousness by way of Virgil is that they, however paradoxically, are connected through the dislocating effects of violence. From the "shock [that] nations should clash," as Venulus states, there is the possibility of "everlasting peace" (A 12.503–4). The *pax* of which Venulus speaks does not derive from a new Augustan age of reason and civility. It is not the defeat of *furor* by reason. Rather, in recognizing the horror of boundless violence, leaders are able to tame the passions and soothe the rage of their people (A 1.57, 153), reestablishing limits and engaging in the cooperative task of rebuilding. Stated slightly differently, violence forges a common plight; treaties and agreements form a common future.

For Virgil, the principle force that is antithetical to treaties (and to politics) is a private, unbounded love (and longing) that intrudes on public life. As Dunkle notes, for the Romans "the opposite of *libido* was *lex*."[114] The archetypical case is Dido, presented (as Cairns argues) as an elegiac lover.[115] The private, exclusive aspect of Dido's and Aeneas' love is made clear: in their *cupido* they are "unmindful of their realms" (*regnorum immemores*) (A 4.194). In the denial of her love, Dido prays that "no love or treaty" may "unite" the Italians and Trojans into one nation (A 4.624).

There are other cases, as well, of private emotions blocking public agreements. There is Juno, who ascribes her nearly uncontrollable and unbounded (A 10.106) anger toward the Trojans to her inability to forget Paris' slight (e.g., A 7.290–300; 7.308–22).[116] Juno seeks public

---

[113] On the role of trauma and memory in the *Aeneid*, see Seider 2013.
[114] Dunkle 1967, 168.
[115] Cairns 1989, 136–50; see 147–49 for a catalog of uses of *amor* in describing Dido.
[116] A contrary reading is provided by Spence: Juno's voice, the voice of the irrational, is the embodiment of what is oppressed in a humanistic world (1988, 23).

vengeance, aiming not at individuals but at nations (*A* 7.316). And she plots her final revenge by similarly playing upon the private emotions of the household, calling on the savage and divisive Allecto (*A* 7.323–40), one of the Roman Furies, to inflame Amata, "who, with a woman's distress, a woman's passion, was seething with frenzy over the Teucrian's coming and Turnus' marriage" (*A* 7.344–45, 341–405). Amata, driven by frenzy, not only hides her daughter, but calls out to the mothers of Latium, "If in your loyal hearts still lives affection for unhappy Amata, if care for a mother's rights stings your souls, loose the fillets from your hair, join the revels with me" (*A* 7.401–3). Allecto is able to shatter "the pact of peace" and "arm for strife brothers of one soul" (*A* 7.339, 335).[117]

The gendered aspects of political order as they are reproduced in the *Aeneid* have been frequently noted.[118] Against the male virtues of strength, patience and endurance are the female powers to seduce (Dido toward Aeneas, Venus toward Vulcan), to bring into being through birth, and to destroy.[119] As Keith suggests, "the men who wage war in the *Aeneid* emerge as the proponents of peace, while the advocacy of war is displaced onto a series of militant women."[120] I think this understates how easily everyone succumbs to violence. But there is another related aspect that these emotions represent, and that is a privileging of the purity of blood-relationships. Amata jealously protects the household, reminding Latinus of his love and loyalty to his blood-kin (*consanguineus*) (*A* 7.366) and opposing the impurity of foreign marriage to the end (*A* 12.54–63; also 7.365–66: love for your own). But so does Turnus, whom Allecto also infects with the anger (*A* 7.462) at being denied to a foreigner "the dowry your blood has won" (*A* 7.423–24). Turnus "[profanes] peace" (*A* 7.467), inciting his followers to frenzy at the prospect of

---

[117] As Keith notes, "Civil discord in particular is frequently mapped onto the gender system" (2000, 69).
[118] See Keith 2000, 18–35.
[119] Keith 2000, 25–26 (on Dido); Putnam 2001, 177, 183; Connolly 2010.
[120] Keith 2000, 77. Keith connects Virgil's imagery of militant women with both Augustan propaganda against Cleopatra and the "unprecedented visibility of upper class Roman women in the political upheavals of the decade after Caesar's assassination" (Keith 2000, 78).

the foreign Aeneas marrying Lavinia: "Teucrians are called to reign; a Phrygian stock mingles (*admisceri*) its taint" (*A* 7.578–79). Suggestive of his disdain for any such agreement, in his final battle with Aeneas, Turnus even uses as a weapon a boundary stone that functions to prevent disputes in the field (*A* 12.897–98).

Cairns notes that the implication of a compounding set of images – of Hercules killing Cacus and of Octavian killing Antonius – bears "the unmistakable implication" that "Aeneas, like Hercules and Augustus, must end discord by destroying its cause."[121] But Virgil is making a larger political point. The choice is not between Golden Age innocence and Iron Age corruption, nor between reason and passion, nor even whether violence can be destroyed by violence. The choice is actually about the political implications of action in a violent world. On the one hand is someone like Mezentius, who is given shelter by Turnus. Virgil's description of Mezentius as *superbus* recalls Tarquinius Superbus, the last of the Roman kings, who based decisions on personal favor rather than law, made judgments in private rather than public, held power perpetually, and recognized no boundaries on the exercise of power until forced to flee the just (*iustus*) outrage of the people (*A* 8.489–94).[122] Rome, as Anchises enjoins Aeneas, is to vanquish those who are *superbi* (*A* 6.853). Mezentius' arrogance, like the broken treaty, and like Juno's anger, threaten to engulf the world again in flames: Lavinium now burns like Troy once did (*A* 12.596). The alternative requires agreement, whether the agreements of friends, patrons and clients, marriages, or treaties and alliances by which discord is made into peace.[123]

Agreements are humanly fabricated moments, carved out of nature, a point made in Virgil's description of Latinus' scepter, which "shall never sprout with light foliage into branch or shade, now that, once hewn in the forest from the lowest stem, it is bereft of its mother, and beneath the steel has she its leaves and twigs; once a tree, now the craftsman's hand had cased it in fine bronze and given it to the elders of Latium to bear" (*A* 12.206–11). In a striking reversal of Book 1 of the

---

[121] Cairns 1989, 102.   [122] Dunkle 1967 and 1971 on how tyrants were characterized.
[123] On the theme of concord and discord in the *Aeneid*, see Cairns 1989, 85–108.

Iliad when Achilles throws his scepter to the ground in response to the broken agreement, Latinus swears that "no time shall break this peace and truce for Italy, however things befall; nor shall any force turn aside my will, not though, commingling all in deluge, it plunge land into water, and dissolve Heaven into Hell (*nulla dies pacem hanc Italis nec foedera rumpet, / quo res cumque cadent; nec me vis ulla volentem / avertet, non, si tellurem effundat in undas / diluvio miscens caelumque in Tartara solvat*)" (*A* 12.202–5).[124] Turnus does not have a place in this world (*A* 12.695), nor does Mezentius,[125] nor does Juno in her wrath (*A* 12.808–842).[126]

In Aeneas' visit to the Underworld, the harshest punishments await those who break the bonds of trust: whether client relationships, marriages, allegiances to a master, or treason (*A* 6.608–13). As Zetzel notes, "In a sense, Virgil's mythology is demythologized. There are no miraculous interventions, there is no divine vengeance; although there is a divine order which ensures ultimate justice, humans are left to make their own decisions – and to live for all time with the results."[127] When Priam asks "if in heaven there is any *pietas* to mark" the outrages of Achilles, his appeal will go unanswered (*A* 2.536). It is Aeneas, identified as *pius* in these moments, who must assert (and then enforce) the terms of a treaty of what is due (*A* 12.175–94; 12.311–17).

---

[124] On this scene in the *Iliad*, see Hammer 2002b, 86, 132.

[125] I find Putnam's claim unconvincing that Aeneas should have recognized *pietas* in Lausus' protection of his father, Mezentius, and thus should have spared him (Putnam 1995, 134–51).

[126] Contrary readings are provided by Bowra 1933, 21: lament for no room for the "high confidence" of Turnus and the "absorbing passion" of Dido in "the uniform Roman world" of Augustus; Anderson 1969, 100; Boyle 1972, 85; Farron 1981; 1982; 1985; Dyson 1997, 456: surrender to fury; Johnson 1976, 117: end of epic designed around *devotio* of Turnus (to country) and *evocatio* of Juno (12.834–40); Lee 1979, 140–43: confuses vengeance with *pietas*; Spence 1988, 37–38: with killing of Turnus, Virgil ends with voice of the oppressed; Cairns 1989, 67: Turnus as bad king; Putnam 1995, 24, 45: narrow peace founded on ethics of revenge rather than *pietas*; Lowrie 2005, 964: moment of sacred or sovereign violence; Gill 2006, 458–61: failure to meet Stoic standard of rationality and virtue; Reed 2007, 44–72: Turnus as orientalized.

[127] Zetzel 1989, 283. I agree with Feeney who argues that Virgil ultimately denies the audience of any Platonic consolation in the afterlife that directs one away from this world (1986).

The gods can muck things up: What is in essence a civil war (*A* 7.545; 8.29), a *triste bellum*, can come to an end only when Juno reaches agreement with Jupiter (*A* 12.818–42). But the fulfillment of that end requires human agreement, an agreement born of the knowledge of the potential limitlessness of human violence if uncontrolled by *leges* and *mores*.[128]

PIETAS AND CULTURE: THE (IL)LOGIC OF FOUNDING

In Plato's autochthonous myth, a people are constituted from the earth. Their common identity, since they are born of the same mother, precedes any historical memory. For Virgil (and for the Romans generally) the problem of founding, of forming a community, poses a more complex relationship to memory. Virgil does not start from the clean canvas of Plato but from the nearly incoherent memories of the past, in lands already occupied by others. And Rome is not a philosophic experiment; it already exists and is foretold in the poem as a nation destined to *imperium*. Those who point to Aeneas as either recognizing or failing to recognize his duty in subordinating his emotions to fulfill this higher destiny miss an important point. However fated and however favored, Rome is not an abstraction; it is, as we saw developed by Cicero before (and will see with Livy later), a city and a culture built on *pietas*: on a concrete and affective sense of obligations to family, companions, the community, and the gods.[129]

And therein lies the problem. If the last century of Roman politics demonstrates anything, it is the ability (as we see in Sallust) of political and military leaders – not the least Octavian – to rise to power by creating a strong and exclusive sense of obligation among their followers. *Pietas* in Rome works in two ways: It serves as a form of collective memory by reinforcing familial, communal, and religious obligations through a respect for ancestral tradition (*mos maiorum*) and can create exclusive and divisive loyalties that conflict with each other. The

---

[128] See, for example, Moorton 1989, 128.   [129] See Burgess 1971, 48.

political questions that Virgil takes up in the *Aeneid*, and one informed by what were in essence two bloody civil wars – the Social War (*Bellum Sociale*) over the demand for inclusion by the Roman *socii* (allies) and the decades long battle for supremacy by Pompeius, Julius Caesar, Marcus Antonius, and Octavian – are these: To whom does one owe *pietas*? Upon what memories are those obligations created? Or asked slightly differently, on what basis does Aeneas deserve the moniker *pius*?

The variety of answers suggests the ambiguity of the concept. Aeneas is seen by some as *pius* because of his integration of his sense of obligation to both his past (Troy, his family, his companions) and his future (obedience to the gods and Fate) or (less plausibly) because of his realization of a "universal brotherhood outside this world."[130] For others, the poem seems more to reveal the problematic nature of *pietas*: how excessive nationalism or obligations of friendship lead to acts of savagery, vengeance, and suffering.[131] As Burgess writes, "the Roman mission," which Aeneas fulfills through *pietas*, "is incompatible with humanity."[132] Finally are those who see Aeneas as having failed to achieve a more expansive notion of *pietas* that incorporates both a duty to friends and family and a humanistic care of others.[133] For Boyle, the ideology of the Roman empire is based on the "manifestation of *pietas*" as a sense of both duty and compassion (pity), an ideology that degenerates in the end as Aeneas succumbs to *furor*.[134] For Johnson, "Aeneas begins in *pietas*, struggles heroically to maintain all the claims of *pietas* in the teeth of hell and ruthless heaven; but he ends in anger. Turnus is, at last, not a guilty criminal destroyed by holy anger but a pharmakos; but of the two, killed and killer, it is difficult to say which is the more tragic: Aeneas kills Turnus out of despair."[135] For Putnam, *pius* Aeneas is continuously implicated in personal, "self-serving" actions of violence motivated by anger (as in his killing of Lausus while he protects his father).[136] As

---

[130] See Bowra 1933, 11; Otis 1963, 307–8; McGushin 1964, 252; Lee 1979, 45; Bacon 1986, 312–13.
[131] Clausen 2002, 100; also Knox 1997; Burgess 1971, 49; Pavlock 1985, 222; Most 2001, 168
[132] Burgess 1971, 50.
[133] *Pietas* linked to compassion: Johnson 1965, 361; Camps 1969, 24–25; Boyle 1972; Pavlock 1985, 221; Putnam 1995.
[134] Boyle 1972, 64, 73.   [135] Johnson 1965, 363.   [136] Putnam 1995, 136.

Putnam suggests, "our respect is undermined for Aeneas who is brutalized by an inability to respond sympathetically to his own supposedly characteristic virtue in the operations of others."[137] Aeneas' act is "the final *impietas*," a failure to recognize and be compassionate toward the fulfilling of filial duty by others.[138]

These radically different interpretations of *pietas* arise in no small part from a two thousand year intervening history that has imposed on Virgil a very modern sensibility. We flinch at the savage violence, but there is little to suggest that for Virgil or his contemporaries *pietas* is compromised by violence, or even anger. Rome is a state, after all, founded in murder and rape, its spectacle entertainments brutal, its punishments included public crucifixions and (in the military) being beaten to death with sticks, and its practice of victory included displaying the heads of those who had been conquered. And within the *Aeneid*, Ilioneus describes Aeneas as being just (*iustus*), *pius*, and accomplished in war and arms (*bellum et arma*) (*A* 1.544–45; also 6.403, 769, 878–79). As Galinsky points out, "To the contemporary Greek and Roman, then, the picture of the avenging Aeneas, who is stirred to anger and meting out punishment in proportion to the crime, would have looked anything but odd or out of place."[139] As to the universality of the notion, Aeneas certainly respects the filial *pietas* of Lausus (*A* 10.824). But to suggest that this recognition militates against violence imposes an unwarranted post-Kantian moral sensibility. Aeneas honors Lausus by returning his arms to him; he is not compelled by *pietas* to save or forgive him. Any comparison of Aeneas to Caesar and Octavian's elevation of *clementia* as a virtue is even less plausible: At its best, *clementia* was a political expedient. Finally, it is hardly surprising that there would be tensions in the concept of *pietas*. Neither for Virgil nor for the Romans (nor for us) does it acquire philosophic consistency; it is a performative concept that acquires the logic of centuries of practice.

---

[137] Putnam 1995, 136; see also Putnam 2011.   [138] Putnam 1995, 162.
[139] Galinsky 1988, 327; see also Cairns 1989, 83: distinction between moral condemnation of *furor* and less condemning of *furiae*; Stahl 1981, 166–69: "community-oriented *furor*."

I do not mean to understate the complexities of the concept, particularly given the exhaustive treatment *pietas* has received in studies of Virgil. Virgil's interest in *pietas* is not as a philosophic concept, though, nor as a critique of the principate, but as a cultural practice that defines Romanness. By that I mean that the matrix of obligations that defines the practice of *pietas* does not derive from reason and is not universal; it is organized around an affective sense of what is revered and why it is revered.[140] The importance of *pietas* as a Roman cultural concept lies in the creation of a collective sense of continuity between past and future (like one sees in the *mos maiorum*), a continuity that requires the transfer of affections from local attachments to a multi-ethnic, geographically expansive, and fragmented Roman state. Virgil accomplishes that transfer in the *Aeneid* in two ways, both of which answer to the human predicament of violence and memory. First, Virgil makes the disorienting violence of wandering and exile into the foundation of a common inheritance. Second, Virgil orients action from a world destroyed to a world built. These two aspects of *pietas* do not replace the family and the gods; rather, they are complementary to, and help to orient, these other aspects of *pietas*.

Family, state, and affection

The most immediate and salient aspect of *pietas* is filial. Aeneas leaves Troy physically carrying his father (*A* 2.707–9; also 6.110–14: as partner), holding the hand of his son, Iulus (*A* 2.723–24), and bringing with him the "sacred emblems of our country's household gods (*penates*)" (*A* 2.717; also 5.94: renew the uninterrupted rites of his father). The reappearing image of his father (*A* 6.687–88, 695–96), an image now that he vainly tries to hold (*A* 6.701–2), as well as the longing by his father to hear Aeneas' familiar tones (*A* 6.689), serve as reminders of the intimacy that underlies these filial connections. Euryalus pleads to the community to watch after his mother (*A* 9.293–302). And Virgil even has to admire how

---

[140] I disagree with Lee who argues that *pietas* "has nothing to do with the emotions [one] feels" (1979, 20; also 47).

Lausus dies protecting his father, even though his father is the terrible tyrant, Mezentius (*A* 10.790–812).

But the family cannot "properly exist without a *patria*."[141] That is the reason, as Otis argues, why Anchises leaves Troy only when he is persuaded that there will be a *patria* that replaces it (see *A* 2.701–4). But Virgil recognizes that loyalties are not easily replaced. The *Aeneid* becomes an exploration, and in fact takes part in the construction, of the affective basis of *pietas* for the new *patria*. From a genealogical perspective, the founder is like the parent so that attachment to the state rests on the transfer of household intimacy. For good reason, Aeneas is referred to as both *pius* and *pater*.

In a political culture in which the *mos maiorum*, more than any specific laws, defines the expectations of the community, it is not surprising that Virgil pays so much attention to genealogy.[142] Family lineages are important to the Romans for a number of reasons: They instill habits, suggest dispositions, provide status, and legitimate authority. As Horsfall notes, "Virgil turns repeatedly to the importance of the gens and the values (or dangers) it transmits: Tarquinii (6.817), Decii and Drusi (6.824), Gracchi and Scipiones (6.842–3), Fabii (6.845). The plurals are not ornamental; they point straight to continuity."[143] So Virgil constructs lineages that trace back to Troy: Augustus' own descent from Aeneas (and Venus) (*A* 1.286–88); the continuity of Trojan and Italian family lines (*A* 5.116–23); and, of course, the origin of the Trojans from its founder, Dardanos, who comes from Italy (first told by the *penates* at *A* 3.167–68). Inheritance is also important in establishing resemblances, in physically instantiating continuity. In the parade of youths before the equestrian display at the funeral games, led by Polites, Atys, and Iulus, the spectators look with joy "to recognize the features of their departed fathers" (*A* 5.576). Andromache, too, sees in Aeneas' son, Ascanius (Iulus), the "sole surviving image of my Astyanax" (*A* 3.489). Not by accident are

---

[141] Otis 1963, 245.
[142] Bacon argues that the blurring of past and future reinforces a notion of timelessness (1986, 325). We can better understand this blurring as a claim of continuity, both historically and between the human and divine world.
[143] Horsfall 1991, 204.

PIETAS AND CULTURE: THE (IL)LOGIC OF FOUNDING

some of the early cities imitations of Troy: Pergamum in Crete, in which the people rejoice in the familiarity of the name (*A* 1.132–34), a little Ilium and Troy in Sicily for those exhausted from the journey (*A* 5.755–58), and a small copy of Troy in Buthrotum (*A* 3.335–36, 349–51), built by Helenus, son of Priam.

The unsuitableness of these little Troys, which requires that Aeneas must continue his journey, marks an important redefinition of resemblance (and genealogy), away from simply romantic versions of Troy or membership based on ethnic purity. The Trojans are now scattered all over the world (*A* 1.602). And what is assembled in Rome is not Troy imitated; it is a city of strangers, foreigners, conquered peoples, rivals, and diverse traditions (*A* 12.823–29, 834–35). Certainly, as we have seen, the Trojans establish their lineages. But what is celebrated in the end is "a race, blended (*mixtum*) with Ausonian blood" (*A* 12.838).

If inheritances are important in providing a sense of resemblance, than what does a Roman look like? The narrative of Roman identity (and we will see this developed by Livy, as well) is neither one of purity nor pluralism; it is one of incorporation, assimilation, and acculturation, a myth that served imperial ends since no one was beyond Rome's global reach. But the legend of founding may also speak to real anxieties about identity in the aftermath of both widespread enfranchisement among people whom did not necessarily have much in common with each other (Virgil himself born in a province) and decades of division with the community torn apart by civil war.[144] We see some of these anxieties played out in Rome's connection to Troy. Troy brings with it the guilt of Laomedon for having cheated Apollo and Poseidon (civil war being the expiation for that wrong in *G* 1.501) as well as the habits of luxury and indulgence that Rome had come to associate with the eastern Other (see *A* 9.617–20: 4.206–8).[145] The lingering association of the Trojans with effeminizing luxury appears in Aeneas' recovery of wealth and dispensing of largesse (*A* 3.354–55; 5.111–13, 250–51).[146] And it shows up in

---

[144] See Toll 1997 on concerns about "Roman-ness." Also Syme 1939, 286.

[145] Keith 2000, 21: "The Trojans' clothing is culturally coded in ancient Rome as quintessentially female."

[146] See Reed 2007, 98–99.

Numanus' battlefield boast to Ascanius, Aeneas' son, in which he contrasts the "hardy stock" of Italians with the Trojans (A 9.603), employing language that will come to characterize Romanness: hardened in youth, trained to use the bow and arrow, "patient of toil, and inured to want, our youth tames earth with the hoe or shakes cities in battle" (A 9.607–8). The Trojans, on the other hand, appear as "Phrygian women" who delight in wearing "embroidered saffron and gleaming purple" (compare to Dido's clothing: A 4.137–39) and whose joy is "sloth" (A 9.614–15).

These origins are mitigated to some extent by the Italian origins of Troy's founder, Dardanus. And they are slowly divested of certain cultural characteristics associated with this past as Aeneas confronts and defeats images of eastern luxury and femininity: Dido, most prominently, as well as the depiction of Cleopatra on Aeneas' shield in her battle with Octavian (A 8.696–713).[147] So too, Aeneas' son answers Numanus' taunt by driving an arrow through his head. Ultimately Juno is reconciled to the defeat of the Italians only if the Latins do not "become Trojans" or "change their language and alter their attire" but are a people of "Roman stock, strong in Italian manliness (*virtus*)" (A 12.823–28, trans. modified).

But from where does this Roman identity come? If not ethnicity then what unites this mixed race? Virgil's response is to craft from this scattered people a distinctive Roman identity (and, as I will suggest later, its habits of *labor*) from the experience of exile (A 1.602).[148] The experience not only connects the Trojans to aboriginal Italy (who are themselves ethnically diverse),[149] but also multiplies in Rome's own history: Aeneas founds Rome on the land of the exiled Saturn (A 8.319–20); the

---

[147] On the ambivalence of invocations of Troy, see Cairns 1989, 127–28: "taint of Troy" that diminishes with italianization of Trojans; Feeney 1984, 192–93: "degeneracy and moral shabbiness" in which the Trojan past "dwindles while the epic progresses" though still expressing anxiety about the integrity of the state; also Feeney 1991, 131–32. On Virgil's construction of nationality by way of provisional and fluid oppositions, see Reed 2007 as well as discussions of Dido (73–100), Camilla (19–20, 22–24, 40–43), and Turnus (44–72).
[148] On efforts of characters to draw comparisons, see Seider 2013, 60–63, with an intersting discussion of E 1.19–25.
[149] See Moorton 1989, 119.

exiled King Evander (*A* 8.333) shows Aeneas Pallenteum, the future site of Rome (*A* 8.323); and Rome is peopled by exiles under Romulus (*A* 8.342). The experience is framed by Virgil as a component of a shared past. Some sense of this is expressed by Aeneas in departing from Buthrotum: "Hesperia allied to Epirus – who have the same Dardanus for ancestor and the same misfortune (*casus*) – of these two we shall make one Troy in spirit" (*A* 3.503–5, trans. modified).

We see other exiles: Dido, Mezentius, and Camilla. It is around these other experiences of exile, though, that the boundaries of Roman identity are brought more clearly into relief. For Dido, who must flee from her tyrannical brother, Pygmalion (*A* 1.335–71), the rupture leaves the mark of loneliness and unresolved loss, a "vanquished soul" (*A* 4.434) that makes her susceptible to unrelieved longing (*A* 4.1–5, 17–33, 467–68).[150] Aeneas, too, succumbs to *amor*, his soul shaken by his love (*A* 4.395). This private love joins them "in wanton ease together," an allusion to images of eastern luxury, "heedless of their realms and enthralled by shameless passion" (*A* 4.193–94).[151] The danger is that Rome will never be founded, instead merged into Carthage, their identities blurred (*A* 4.101–104).[152] His most important *amor* cannot be to Dido but to his *patria* (*A* 4.347, also 4.341–43: *cura*), to a love for Rome's future and "the glory that was to be" (*A* 6.889; also 6.822–23: Brutus executes own sons out of love of country).[153] He feels agony but "his mind stands steadfast" (*A* 4.449) and a "resolve now settled in his soul" to leave her (*A* 5.748).[154] Aeneas, thus, is not caught in the private longing of Dido (or Orpheus) but is able to make his love into a public (and ultimately manly) thing.[155]

---

[150] Cairns suggests that Virgil treats Dido as an elegiac character, which is a private as opposed to public form of poetry. She can be a sympathetic character with the faults of a lover (1989, 149). Gill views Dido through the lens of Stoic madness (2006, 442–48).

[151] On Dido's association with the east, see Reed 2007, 73–100.

[152] Reed 2007, 92–95.   [153] Reed 2007, 184–86; 2010, 73–74.

[154] See, for example, McLeish 1972, 130: Dido is un-Roman vs. Aeneas who is Roman ("calm, quiet and decisive" vs. impulsive, exotic, luxuriant).

[155] Perhaps there is an analogy in Virgil's description of the way a branch is taken from its mother to be made into an artifact (a scepter) of male, political authority (*A* 12.209; Putnam 2001, 164–65).

Mezentius' exile is the result of him having to flee from his own people (A 8.481–93). The association of Mezentius with the Tarquins (see Chapt. 5, 242–49) makes the Trojans resemble more the "exhausted citizens" who forged a republican identity under the tyrant (A 8.489; see, for example, A 1.178; 3.145, tied to *labor*). Moreover, the distinction serves to further differentiate Turnus from the Trojans. Turnus is not only Greek (A 7.371–72), an inheritance that by itself is not disqualifying (examples include Evander; treatment of Diomedes [A 11.252–95]; the Sicans, Salius, and Patron, who become naturalized Trojans[156]), but he harbors Mezentius (A 8.493). Turnus, thus, becomes implicated in monstrous injustice (A 8.494), an impiety toward the people and the gods that Turnus will repeat toward the Trojans (A 7.595–97; 9.133; contrast to the Trojans' piety: A 8.184–89).

Camilla is an interesting case, a liminal character at the margins of society, described more in immortal than mortal terms (A 11.507: *horrenda*; 11.664: *aspera*; 11.657: *dia*), compared to male fighters (7.805: *bellatrix*; 11.711: *interrita*), even overshadowing Turnus in Virgil's description (7.912–17).[157] As an infant she is brought up by her father in exile in the wilderness, no city willing to accept her tyrannical father (A 11.539–69). She shares the attributes of manliness with the Romans. Never learning the arts of womanhood, "she cherishes unsullied a lifelong love for her weapons and her maidenhood" (A 11.583–84; also 7.805–6). She even seems to be part of the pastoral landscape, living among shepherds (A 11.569), raised on the milk of a wild mare (A 11.571–72), cloaked in animal skins, and taught as soon as she could hold a spear to hunt (A 11.578–80).[158] Virgil attributes her death to a reckless desire for booty and spoils (A 11.778–82), in this case seemingly the feminine weakness for Chloreus' fine clothing. But Camilla's desire for glory, even her recklessness, hardly distinguishes her from male warriors (compare with Nisus and Euryalus at A 9.357–66).[159] The problem is that she exists outside culture, unable to build a civilization. There is an

---

[156] See Cairns 1989, 227.   [157] See Becker 1997.
[158] Camilla as *bellatrix*, connecting her to the Amazon warrior Penthesilea (A 7.805; 11.662; see Keith 2000, 27).
[159] See Keith 2000, 30; Reed 2007, 24.

obvious gender component: Civilization depends on the domestication of women.[160] The maiden warrior (11.804, emphasized by Virgil in her death) leaves no family lineage behind.[161] That domestication occurs as the Volscians will be incorporated into Rome.

The funeral games become a point of transition in building this civilization.[162] As a form of stylized violence, the games may serve to posit the *mores* by which aggression can be controlled.[163] It should be noted, however, that there is almost no instance of controlled aggression following the games, including Aeneas' final act of rage in killing the defeated Turnus. I think there is a different purpose. Modeled after the funeral games in the *Iliad*, in which the norms and values of the community are reenacted, tensions explored, and community life reaffirmed, the funeral games in the *Aeneid* offer a vision of an imperial community.[164] I understand a community in this sense as a people who imagine some relationship to each other, whether as a result of a shared past, shared affections, shared interests, or shared goals.[165] There are several aspects of these games worth noting. First, the games are meant to be familiar,

---

[160] The claim is tied historically by Keith to an Augustan argument that the "Roman Order is re-established externally through the defeat of Cleopatra and internally through the re-domestication of Roman women" (Keith 2000, 81).

[161] Reed 2007, 40–41.

[162] Different arguments have been made about the place of the games in the *Aeneid* and in Rome: they are patterned after the funeral games of the *Iliad* (Willis 1941, 406–7; Otis 1963, 41–61; Harris 1968–69; Williams 1960, ix–xiii; Camps 1969, 100); they imitate the Phaeacian games of the *Odyssey* and thus fall in the middle of the journey (Cairns 1989, 230–36); they serve as a form of entertainment for the people to relieve their toils (Crowther 1983, 271); they reflect a contribution to a revived interest by Augustus in the games, noting particularly the creation of the Actian games, in which Augustus "grafted" games honoring Apollo onto a local Greek festival (Willis 1941, 404; also Williams 1960, ix–xi; Harris 1968–69, 17–19; Camp 1969, 100–2); and they reflect an interest by Augustus in epinician poetry that functions to make the Trojan competitors heroic (Cairns 1989, 223) and tie the heroes to the gods (Cairns 1989, 222).

[163] See, for example, Anderson: the games provide an "ethical rather than realistic account of victory" with "an accent on the note of vicarious sacrifice in the context of every success" (Anderson 1969, 52); Cairns: there is an association of the games "with peace and concord" (Cairns 1989, 228; also 236–48).

[164] On the funeral games in the *Iliad*, see Hammer 2002b, 134–43.

[165] See Anderson 1983 for the classic conceptualization of "imagined communities."

giving historical continuity to this nascent community.[166] Second, the games reflect the broadening of the affections at a point of transition from Troy to Rome, and from familial to state observance of *pietas*. Aeneas publicly enacts and renews "his father's uninterrupted rites" (*A* 5.94). Virgil further generalizes this continuity, constructing a genealogy that links a series of Trojan competitors to future Roman families (though the choice of families, as is frequently noted, is odd). And the games are organized generationally, the contestants divided (in order of contests) between current leaders and heroes in the ship race, youths in the foot race, older men in boxing, the Sicilian hero Acestes featured in the archery contest, and boys in the equestrian display.[167] Third, the games are multi-ethnic, held in Sicily, including Greeks (Salius and Patron) (e.g., *A* 5.293), amongst an undifferentiated, though hierarchically organized (*A* 5.289–90, 340–41), throng (*A* 5.76; also *A* 8.636).[168] Fourth is the games' spectacular nature, a testament to what Rome will build. Virgil emphasizes on a number of occasions the huge crowd (*A* 5.76, 107, 289, 293) whose applause echoes through the woodland (*A* 5.148–50), and the topographic scale (which get repeated by later historians). The valley that forms a theater (*A* 5.288–89) and the vast sea are the stage for boat races, recalling Caesar's *naumachia*, Octavian's celebration of naval victory at the Actian games, and Homer's chariot races, now made wilder (*A* 5.146–47).[169] Rome does not replace the family with the state (as does Plato) but gives these diverse genealogies a place in which affection for the family is broadened to affection for the state.

---

[166] I think there are certainly Augustan accents in these games, including the *ludus Troiae*. But the games had a long history in Rome. There was a tradition of gladiatorial contests as features of funerals, as well as attempts to incorporate Greek athletic contests into games (for example, 186 BCE by Marcus Fulvius Nobilior; 167 BCE by L. Anicius; 81 BCE by Sulla; 58 BCE by Marcus Aemilius Scaurus; 55 BCE by Pompeius; 53 BCE by Gaius Scribonius Curio for funeral games; 46 BCE by Caesar; 44 BCE by Octavian for Caesar; 29 BCE by Octavian) (Willis 1941, 405; Crowther 1983, 269).

[167] Willis 1941, 407.

[168] On the complex etymologies and blurring of national identities through the names of warriors in the *Aeneid*, see Reed 2007, 5, 129–47; 2010.

[169] On the relationship of the games to Roman conceptions of building, see Hammer 2010.

PIETAS AND CULTURE: THE (IL)LOGIC OF FOUNDING

Labor

A part of a Roman identity is not just a sense of a shared past, but also a shared ethos: dispositions that define what made Rome and what it means to be Roman. At the heart of Virgilian *pietas* toward the Rome to be is an admiration for the world as something built, as the product of *labor*.[170] As Virgil makes clear in the prologue, Aeneas' *pietas* is connected to his *labores* (*A* 1.10) that is directed toward fulfilling the tasks set out by both the gods (*A* 4.393–95) and one's ancestors (*A* 6.687–88). As Virgil announces in the opening of the *Aeneid*, "So vast was the effort to found the Roman race (*Tantae molis erat Romanam condere gentem*) (*A* 1.33).[171] We have already seen the value ascribed to labor in the *Georgics*. As we move from the *Georgics* to the *Aeneid*, the farmer becomes the founder and the fields become cities. Like the farmer, the builder of a city must labor. The physical toil one sees in the *Georgics* is displaced, though, occurring outside the narrative. It is replaced by more psychological aspects of suffering and endurance that serve as a prelude to the making of agreements, the establishment of institutions, and the building of the city. As Jupiter (by way of Mercury) reminds Aeneas, he must labor for his own fame as well as the future of his heir (*A* 4.272–76). There is a continual return to the task of building and crafting: the prophecy that Aeneas' people will set up laws and city walls (*A* 1.264: from *pono*); the Roman people as patient in toiling and taming the earth (*A* 9.607–8; contrasting with Phrygian luxury); the *labor* of flight and founding (*A* 3.160, 458–59) that one must endure (*A* 3.94; 5.769); the exertion (*opera*) of cutting and piling trees for Misenus' altar, as required by the Sibyl (*A* 6.176–84); the building of a memorial hung from a fashioned oak (*A* 11.5, 16); the effort by Aeneas to restore Pergamum by his own hand

---

[170] Arendt 1963, 207–10, though in Arendt's vocabulary what is built is more associated with work. Also Arendt 1958, 108–9.
[171] This connection of *labor* to *pietas* is one of the insights of Otis, though I disagree with the conclusion he draws (Otis 1963). Cairns associates *labor* with the qualities of the "toiling and suffering ideal monarch" who progresses ethically through these labors (1989, 32). McGushin associates it with Stoicism: "the parallels between Aeneas and Hercules lay in its portrayal of the ideal of Stoic virtues — an ideal applied to all who undertook the task of building and guiding Rome" (McGushin 1964, 235).

(*A* 4.344; also hands building a city at *A* 3.498); the working on the walls of Pergamum (*A* 3.132: *molior*); the marking of the boundaries of the city with a plough (*A* 5.755–56: Acesta; also *A* 7.157–59: toiling in the soil to mark Lavinium); and the "craftsman's hand" (*artificis manus*) that shapes the scepter of authority (*A* 12.210).

When Aeneas first arrives at Carthage, he marvels not just at the "massive buildings, mere huts once" (*A* 1.421), but at the human labor: the workmen who "press on, some to build walls, to rear the citadel, and roll up stones by hand, some to choose the site for a dwelling and enclose it with a furrow," others who dig harbors, lay foundations, and "hew out of the cliffs vast columns" (*A* 1.421–28). The vision is a glimpse of what and how Rome will develop from a small village. But there is poignancy in that future as he looks at Carthage. Rome's emergence will result in it not just destroying Carthage, everything Aeneas now sees, but also leaving no trace of the city behind.

Virgil shares with Lucretius an entropic view of time in which all the things we do and have, all the products of labor, are subject to dissolution. Virgil differs from Lucretius, at least in emphasis, on the rebirth of culture.[172] Perhaps not surprisingly, Aeneas' mother is Lucretius' Venus. For Virgil, and unlike Lucretius, from the rubble of the past is a desire to rebuild: The wandering Trojans, as Virgil comments at one point, crave a city (*A* 5.617). The tension is always a part of the *Aeneid*. While Aeneas gazes at "the handicraft of the several artists and the work of their toil" (*A* 1.454–55), portrayals of the devastation of the Trojans on the Temple of Juno, he recalls the fiery destruction of Troy from which a new city will be built (*A* 1.456, 494).[173]

---

[172] See also Hardie 1986, 196: "Looked at in yet another way the *Aeneid*" inverts Lucretius by telling of "a progression from the *destruction* of a city to the *construction* of a city." My interpretation is in contrast to Bacon 1986, 312: "the goal of the hero's *labores* is not in this world but in the world of the spirit." It is also in contrast to Boyle 1972, 76, who sees the visit to Buthrotum as "undermin[ing] seriously" the value of the mission of founding a new city.

[173] See also Stanley 1965, 276–77: "in Vergil's literary and historical perspective, Achilles and Aeneas, Greek and Trojan, Roman and Tyrian are bound to that realm where the rôles of the slayer and the slain are inevitably united by the reversals of time."

The Virgilian landscape is one dotted by new cities that arise from old civilizations: Troy, Tyria, and Arcadia. Dido builds Carthage (*A* 1.418–49). Antenor builds the Trojan city of Patavium (*A* 1.247–49). Helenus, the son of Priam, builds a replica of Troy in Epirus (*A* 3.333–51). Aeneas' descendants, Procas, Capys, Numitor, and Silvius Aeneas will found Nomentum, Gabii, Fidenae, Collatie, Pometii, Fort Inuus, Bola, and Cora (*A* 6.760–78); and Romulus will found Rome (*A* 1.275–78). King Evander shows Aeneas the Arcadian city of Pallanteum (*A* 8.355–58), including where such future Roman sites as the Capitol will rise from the "woodland thickets" (*A* 8.348). And Aeneas founds the cities of Aeneadae in Thrace (*A* 3.13–69), Pergamum in Crete (*A* 3.132–139), and Acesta in Sicily (5.746–61), before finally establishing Lavinium in Italy.

The products of human *labor* provide a sense of continuity between past and future – something enduring and recognizable. Thus, we can recall Virgil's description of both the dislocating effects of the loss of a home and of the desire of a people to refound a city, often in the likeness of what they knew. What Virgil seeks to accomplish through his poetic building, as Bonjour suggests, is a reintegration of feelings, an affective sense of attachment to a built Rome.[174] In a wonderfully poetic scene, as Evander shows Aeneas the Aracadian village that will become Rome, Virgil orients the audience to a city they know by its buildings: the Carmental Gate (*A* 8.338), the Tarpeian house (8.347), the Capitol (8.347), ancient memorials (8.356), the fort of Janus (8.358), the fort of Saturn (8.358), the Forum (8.361), and the Carinae (8.361). In Aeneas' visit to the Underworld, Anchises identifies "nameless places" that will be built in Aeneas' name and "one day be famous names" (*A* 6.776). Aeneas' shield, too, as Williams rightly notes, places considerable emphasis on both the maker and seer of the shield: *fecerat* (8.628, 630), *addiderat* (8.637), *extuderat* (8.665), and *addit* (8.666); also *aspiceres* (8.650), *cernere erat* (8.676), *credas* (8.691), *miratur* (8.730).[175] The shield, of course, recalls Homer. But there is a quite different content. Where

---

[174] Bonjour 1975, 475.   [175] Williams 1981, 10.

Achilles' shield attempts to capture the abstractions of peace and war, Aeneas' shield communicates the foundations of Rome, not as a moment in time but as the experiences that animate its regeneration and augmentation. The shield portrays the multi-ethnic character of the empire: "conquered peoples" who are "as diverse in fashion of dress and arms as in tongues" (*A* 8.722–23). The *imagines* (representations) on the shield (*A* 8.730) make the same statement as the *imagines* that Aeneas encounters in the Underworld (in what is frequently interpreted as emulating a funeral parade).[176] Whether the ancestor busts, the monuments, or the buildings, these representations are, for the Romans, the visual artifacts of *labor* that convey collective hope and sacrifice. One is to behold (*aspicere*) (*A* 6.771) and admire (*mirari*) (*A* 8.730) the strength (*vis*) and civic devotion that was required, and will be required, to build a city (*A* 6.771–72; also 6.660–65) and to rule the world (*A* 6.851). The parade of heroes kindles Aeneas' soul "with longing for the glory that was to be" (*A* 6.889) just as Aeneas raises to his shoulder "the fame and fortunes of his children's children" (*A* 8.730–31). The images recall an earlier scene of *labor* in which Aeneas says to his father, "on my shoulders I will support you, and this *labor* will not weigh me down. However things may fall, we two will have one common peril, one salvation" (*A* 2.707–10). The language speaks more generally of Rome's founding identity: a community forged with "one common trial, one salvation" (*unum et commune periclum, / una salus*) (*A* 2.709–10).

There is an obvious cosmological dimension to Roman *pietas* that is joined with *labor*. Aeneas' *labores* fulfill "Heaven's bidding" (*A* 4.396, 273; 12.177). The final acts of Latinus and Aeneas join human fabrication – the promise of a treaty, symbolized in the artifact of the scepter – with prayers to the gods who sanction treaties (*A* 12.191–92, 200). Aeneas also earlier links the *labores* of the Trojans to some hope in the *pietas* of the gods (*A* 5.688), a sense of what has been earned or deserved (as Aeneas makes clear at 5.692: if I deserve it).

---

[176] Habinek 1989, 236.

There is also conformity of images of Roman life with divine sanction. Bacon sees the Underworld as showing how Aeneas' "election means isolation, loss of community, and surrender of all human ties."[177] What is more striking is how truly Roman the Underworld appears. In his trip to the Underworld, Aeneas sees the future builders and heroes of Rome (A 6.756–892), a desire to construct something that accords with the divine spirit within that longs for life (A 6.721, 724–27). The greatest reward is reserved for those who have built something, served something, or created something, that endures (A 6.663: ennobles life).[178] Although the souls are cleansed of mortal impurities, in the Elysium fields the Romans do what Romans do. They retain their bodily shapes, though in what seems now to be purified ether. They wrestle, compete in sports, dance, sing, play instruments, and take pride and care (*cura*) in their chariots, horses, and arms (A 6.637–59). It is almost as if the Romans could not imagine eternity apart from their particular *artes*, from the tangibility of human affairs. It is certainly the case that Virgil could not.

It is a long way from the *Eclogues* through the *Georgics* to the *Aeneid*, though one that evinces a particular attitude toward the world. There is little room in a violent world for nostalgia; one cannot go back to what no longer exists, whether the Golden Age, Troy, Carthage, or the Republic. Nor, though, can one simply forget. But to move forward requires the act of remembering, of organizing memories to remake a community. Virgil's political thought plays a role in this act of building, not by providing a blueprint of laws and institutions but by narratively constructing the affective foundations of community life. His audience becomes a participant in becoming Roman, sharing in the disorienting

---

[177] Bacon 1986, 317; also Feeney 1983, 219: "pressures and cruelties inflicted upon the individual who embodies in his own person the aspirations and future of a whole nation."

[178] Some see the Elysium fields as a reward for virtuous lives (Williams 1964, 55–56: reward for virtuous lives; Bacon 1986: election). I tend to agree more with Habinek that they are rewards for achievement (Habinek 1989, 234). "What unites these funeral rites and Anchises' grand vision of spiritual migration and homecoming is the notion that the memory of posterity grants the deceased a stable, secure afterlife." (Habinek 1989, 236–37).

experiences of wandering and loss and becoming reoriented through a transfer of affections to what had been built. However paradoxically, the possibility of politics for Virgil lies in the ability of his audience to imagine itself in this poetic past, not as an act of retreat but of recognition of a shared inheritance by which it can foster a common destiny.

5 LIVY: POLITICAL THOUGHT AS *REMEDIUM*

≈≈≈≈≈≈≈≈

Livy (Titus Livius Patavinus, 59 BCE-17 CE) begins the writing of his history at about the same time Virgil begins his *Aeneid*, after the end of the Civil War. If Cicero, Lucretius, and Sallust had witnessed the gathering storm of private armies, heightened aristocratic rivalries, mounting armed and mob conflict, and for Cicero and Sallust the rise and fall of Caesar and the violent reprisals by the Second Triumvirate comprised of Lepidus, Octavian, and Antonius, Virgil and Livy's writing is informed by the next decade of a bloody struggle for supremacy between Octavian and Antonius that spanned the Roman world and ended with the defeat of Antonius at the Battle of Actium in 31 BCE. Livy's Preface sounds an expectedly plaintive note. Although his readers might want to delight in the spectacle of modern times, Livy's diversion, as he writes, lies in escaping to the Roman past: "I myself, on the contrary, shall seek in this an additional reward for my toil, that I may avert my gaze from the troubles which our age has been witnessing for so many years, so long at least as I am absorbed in the recollection of the brave days of old, free from every care which, even if it could not divert the historian's mind from the truth, might nevertheless cause it anxiety" (pref. 5).[1]

---

[1] Following Luce (1965) and Badian (1993, 17–19), the first publication of Book
  1 appeared no later then 30 BCE and the publication of the pentad around 27 BCE. We

Livy's history, though, is anything but an escape into a time without care.² From the beginning Rome is born of strife. As Livy's account progresses heroes are tarnished, lessons are forgotten or misapplied, institutions are corrupted, common identities are questioned, friends become enemies, and political survival exacts a higher and higher price in blood. So what sense are we to make of Livy's political thought? His writings show a variety of influences: an annalistic tradition that chronicled names and events[3]; a Hellenistic historiographic tradition that embellished the past by creating dramatic encounters between characters, inventing speeches, and inferring emotions;[4] and a Roman rhetorical tradition that taught lessons, or *exempla*, by which individuals were to take their cues about character and conduct.[5] But what is missing, as Wiedemann notes in his survey of Latin historical writing, is "explicit theoretical analysis": Livy's "analytical categories are unsophisticated," his "literary intentions" of creating a coherent narrative take priority, and he takes for granted, rather than explains, Roman political and social institutions.[6]

---

cannot tell if the preface was written with Book 1 or with the publication of the pentad. In any case, as Badian writes, "there was no enthusiastic welcome for the *nouus status rei publicae*" (1993, 19).

[2] In contrast with Collingwood's assessment: "From the beginning" of Livy's history "Rome is ready-made and complete. To the end of the narrative she has undergone no spiritual change" (1946, 44).

[3] Walsh 1966, 129. See also Kraus 1994a, 9–13.

[4] Critical assessments of Livy's use of evidence are provided by Badian 1966 (on the early historians); Syme 1959, 28; Ogilvie 1965, 5–7; Rawson 1985, 219–20; and Raaflaub 1986a, 16–22; 1993. More sympathetic assessments that place Livy in a broader rhetorical tradition are provided by Walbank 1960; Walsh 1961, chapts. 5–6; 1966; Burck 1964; Luce 1977; Fornara 1983, chapt. 3; Cornell 1986; Konstan 1986; Ungern-Sternberg 1986; Vasaly 1987, esp. 225; Wiseman 1987, 256–61 (ancient historiography, generally); Pauw 1991; Kraus 1994b; Miles 1995; Jaeger 1997; Marincola 1997, 76–79; Oakley 1997, 72–99; Kraus and Woodman 1997; Feldherr 1998; Chaplin 2000. For a spirited defense of the aim of Roman historiography as aimed at truthful recollections of the past, see Lendon 2009.

[5] On *exempla*, see Chaplin 2000; Matthes 2000, 47; Kapust 2011, 92–99.

[6] Wiedemann 2000, 523. Also Hulliung: Livy substituted analytic insight with "melodrama," content to see Roman grandeur as springing from a natural Roman character (1983, 147).

But in searching for analytic categories in Livy's political thought, we look for the wrong thing. For Livy, political concepts are not comprehensible as theories any more than politics is organized by reason. For Livy (like Virgil), we are oriented to the political world by a range of affective associations that are forged in history, transmitted as cultural memories, and enacted as human practices. These associations operate most powerfully by way of sight, not only in what we see but also in how we remember and think. When Livy takes us inside his historical actors, vividly portraying the "mental and emotional experiences felt,"[7] he is doing more than seeking dramatic affect. His "psychological history," to use Walsh's term, is actually a conceptual history, one in which political concepts acquire form as felt meanings.[8]

By felt meanings I am pointing to the connection for Livy between the conceptual and the phenomenal. The abstractions of political language – terms like liberty, power, and authority – are given form by way of experience: immediate experiences, memories of experiences, and experiences that we inherit. These experiences give particular words or phrases meaning as an interlocking set of affective responses. These affective elements have implications for the political concepts by which one orients oneself politically. Concepts acquire salience – they are seen as belonging to oneself – to the extent that they are felt. And concepts acquire objectivity or meaningfulness beyond oneself when one has a sense that these sensations are aspects of shared experience.

We get some sense of the visual aspects of the felt meanings with the Roman topography, which, as we saw with Cicero and Virgil, becomes a veritable map of Roman political consciousness: Monuments, statues, triumphal arches, buildings, even spaces were the visual markers by which Romans recognized the past. The question that haunts Livy, as he stands between the Republic and the principate, is whether these monuments, after decades of civil war, still have the capacity to summon a set of collective experiences that are different from one's own desires. Can these markers still guide conduct, clarify goals, distinguish best from worst, and, most of all, convey what it means to be Roman? Livy's

---

[7] Walsh 1961, 171. See also Walsh 1966, 129; Burck 1964, 195–233; and Luce 1977, 231.
[8] Walsh 1966, 129.

Ab urbe condita ("From the founding of the city") is about founding, not as creating something new, but as reanimating one's relationship to a political world.

Livy's concern with the animating force of politics is in keeping with the age. In fact, there could be no more pressing question to the political thinker. His writing evinces the traditional republican morality born of his own upbringing in the provincial city of Padua. In a way that we do not see with Virgil, his language points to the loss of the Republic, both in the corruption of civic virtues and in the gutting of the institutional power of the senate and the people. But he also has to appeal to, or at least not anger, the *princeps* who, at best was a powerful patron and, at worst, held the power of life and death. With some justification, then, Livy's political thought has been dismissed as imperial propaganda.[9] Livy does refer to Augustus as a founder (4.20.7). But Livy's stories are not Augustus' monuments, carefully arrayed to yield particular meanings. The monuments of Livy's history, visible reminders of past events that cause the reader "to think" or "to behold" and " to contemplate," tell the story of how the animating spirit of politics is ultimately negotiated in the actions of a community and not the will of one individual.

Livy's *Ab urbe condita* appears to the modern scholar as an alternative to Plato's philosopher-king and Aristotle's model of *phronesis*, both of which ultimately look to reason as the mechanism by which communities can be made to endure.[10] Gone is the philosopher, or even the leader, who can stand outside time and history and craft appearance.

---

[9] See, for example, Taylor 1918, 158–59; Syme 1939, 316–18, 464–65, modified to some extent in Syme 1959; Cochrane 1940, 98–99; Liebeschuetz 1967, 55; Strasburger 1983, 265–66; Joshel 1992, 114; Cizek 1992. Views of Livy as more critical of Augustus: Walsh 1961; Mette 1961; Petersen 1961; Ogilvie 1965, 2–3; Gabba 1984, 79–80; Burck 1991; Badian 1993; Miles 1995, 47–54. Luce sees Livy as able to "lift his eyes from the struggles of the immediate past" and, from the perspective of someone who is a provincial and who did not have a political career, could explain "Augustus' appeal and success" (1977, 298). Some recent scholars have allowed for the independence of Livy's work while noting its similarity to Augustus' project of building a new Rome: Levene 1993, 243–48; Kraus 1994a, 6–9; Galinsky 1996, 280–87; Feldherr 1998; Chaplin 2000, 192–96. For reviews of the scholarship, see Deininger 1985 and Badian 1993.

[10] This argument stands in contrast to Rahe's claim that Livy's notion of the loss of liberty was "like most Roman notions, in its origins Greek" (2000, 284).

Although there may be differences in innate dispositions to understand and respond to situations, the way in which elites and masses make sense of the world is essentially the same. We are phenomenal beings animated by impulse. The emphasis on appearance also suggests shared vulnerabilities. Corruption is not the failure of reason (as it is for Plato); it is the failure of vision, which, more than anything else, is the inability to see – and thus be animated by anything – beyond our own fears, pleasures, interests, or even generalizations.

But the most dramatic implication of Livy's understanding of how political ideas are formed and organized is that elites, no matter how important they may be (or may want to be) in directing the people, are never able to completely define those meanings for the populace. They are never able to fix interpretations. The people, as Livy's *History* makes clear, are continually and vigorously engaged in acts of interpretation that derive as much from their own experiences and conditions as from anything the elite might contrive.[11] Whether begrudgingly recognizing this or not, Livy's psychological history traces the animating role of popular vision in the emergence of liberty and the effects of political blindness by both elites and masses in the corruption of the community.[12] The trajectory of the early books of Livy's *Ab urbe condita* is toward the increasing openness of Roman politics, not out of a principled belief in rights but because the health of the community depends on the shared, though not necessarily harmonious or identical, ability to orient and organize shared meanings. The concern becomes more pronounced as

---

[11] There is a growing scholarship that argues against the view that Roman politics was largely divorced from the attitudes and opinions of the populace. The view of Rome as a largely closed oligarchy is articulated by Gelzer 1962 (= 1912); Münzer 1920; Syme 1939; Scullard 1973. Challenges to this approach (though not agreement) have been made by Meier 1980; Nicolet 1980; Millar 1984, 1986, 1998; Brunt 1966; 1971b: 74–111, 1982, 1988: 4–6, 23–56; Vanderbroeck 1987; North 1990a, 1990b; Badian 1996; Lintott 1999; Hölkeskamp 1994, 11–19, 75–81; Jehne (ed.) 1995; Bell 1997; Yakobson 1999; Morstein-Marx 2004; forthcoming in Hammer; Williamson 2005; Wiseman 2009; Tatum (forthcoming in Hammer). Even Mouritsen, who attempts to demonstrate that politics had little connection to popular interest, notes how leaders competed for popular support (2001).

[12] Kapust, on the other hand, places more emphasis on the "virtuous behavior of elites" that generates goodwill and affection from the community (Kapust 2011, 84).

Livy turns his attention to the periphery of the empire, asking the question in his account of the Second Punic War, "Who will fight for us?" Livy's *History* becomes a reflection on the loss of, and in turn the possibility of renewing, the animating spirit of the Roman politics, even if the terms of that renewal are forever changed.

THE PHYSIOLOGY OF THOUGHT

When Livy diagnoses the maladies of Roman politics and refers, in turn, to the study of history as healthful (*salubris*), he is employing medical analogies that were already well established in Roman discourse, shared by the Stoics, Epicureans, and, to some extent, the Skeptics.[13] The philosopher, like the physician, is portrayed as healing the diseases of the soul. In Livy's adaptation of this image, the historian assumes this therapeutic task, though how is not entirely clear.

Medical knowledge, which included the study of internal (what would now be called "psychological") disorders, was not the province of particular experts but had become a part of intellectual culture.[14] Livy likely would have been aware of some of the debates about the physiological underpinnings of thought and action, given his study and work in rhetoric and philosophy that is generally seen as preceding his writing of his history.[15] The evidence does not allow us to identify Livy with a particular philosophic school, or ascribe to him a specialized, technical vocabulary. Walsh, for example, has attempted to demonstrate Stoic influences on Livy.[16] Although there may be Stoic resonances, Livy

---

[13] Fantham 1972, 14–18, notes the general diffusion of medical imagery in Latin literature. On the close relationship between philosophy and medicine, see Frede 1987. On the prevalence of images of disease in ancient Roman writing, see Woodman 1988, 133; Moles 1993, 133–34; Nussbaum 1994, 13–16, 48–77, 316–58.

[14] For the diffusion of medical knowledge in Rome, see Rawson 1985, 170–84.

[15] See Rossbach 1882, 367, n. 3; Walsh 1958, 355; 1961, 4; Syme 1959, 51; Seneca *Ep.* 100.9; Schindel 1983 takes a more critical look at the nature of this philosophy.

[16] Walsh 1955; 1958; 1961, 46–81; also Ogilvie 1965, 48 (Livy's Stoicism as "polite"). Kajanto 1957, 53–63; Liebeschuetz 1967, 51–53; and Levene 1993, 30–33 provide criticisms of Walsh's argument.

seems rather un-Stoic in his continued appeal to the emotions in his historiography. This resort to the emotions has led some scholars to suggest an Aristotelian influence. Although the actual texts of Aristotle were probably not widely read in Rome, his ideas (and the ideas of the Peripatetics who followed Aristotle) on the arousal of the emotions through vivid description "filtered into wider culture" through a rhetorical and historiographic tradition.[17] And Livy is also seen as influenced by Cicero, who variously transmits (as we have seen) Stoicism, the approaches of the New Academy, and his own works on rhetoric (as well as his orations).[18] These were not strictly demarcated intellectual approaches; different schools had a remarkable ability to incorporate peripheral ideas into any particular approach.[19] My primary interest is to suggest how Livy's appeal to the emotions is more than just dramatic, as is often seen in ascribing an Aristotelian influence on Livy, but is integral to history as *remedium*.

Common to these different approaches, particularly the influential schools of Stoicism and Epicureanism as well as medical thinkers, is a conception of humans as "psychophysical wholes": "reason and emotion or desire" do not "constitute radically separate and potentially conflicting sources of motivation."[20] Except for someone like Posidonius, who retains Plato's tripartite division of the soul, reason, emotion, and desire are not seen as occupying different parts of the soul. They are not only unified aspects of the soul but also constituted by matter and thus integrated (though with distinct capacities) with the physical person.[21] The human body and soul are seen as comprised of *pneuma*, a material substance made up of air and water that moved continually through the body. One part of the *pneuma* is the *psuchē* (= *animus*/ *anima*), which is the animating source of life, responsible for our drives, perceptions, and

---

[17] Levene 1997, 130–31; also Rawson 1985, 289–91. On the influence of Aristotle on Cicero, see Frede 1989 (on *The Republic*); Classen 1989 (on the *Tusculans*) and Rawson 1985 (generally).

[18] On the influence of Cicero on Livy, see Syme 1959, 51, 53; Moles 1993, 146; Vasaly 1993, x, 33, n. 30; 53; Chaplin 2000, 13–14.

[19] See, for example, Shaw 1985 on Stoicism's ability to incorporate peripheral ideas.

[20] Gill 2006, 12.   [21] von Staden 2000, 79–80.

cognitive actions.[22] A key feature of this interaction of soul and body lies in notions of perception, in which external data stimulates the sense organs that transmit what is essentially an image to the mind.[23] Thoughts – how one understands the image – involve combining information about the present object with stored images, including one's memory of past experiences, one's reaction to and evaluation of these experiences, and one's ability to "make inferences and form concepts" from those images.[24]

Disorders of the soul, however defined in the different approaches, were not because of warring parts of the soul but because of imbalances. For the Stoics what keeps the entire body functioning properly is tension (*tonos*) that "characterizes the movement of its cohesive *pneuma*."[25] Proper "tensional movement" of the *pneuma* allows data to be clearly transmitted and in turn evaluated. Galen, drawing on a tradition of the humors, sees the body as comprised of distinct substances: yellow bile, black bile, phlegm, and blood.[26] The balance of these elements is not only related to physical disease but also affects how one sees and responds to particular situations, whether one is easily angered or calm, for example, or hopeful or melancholic. Since these humors are seen as corresponding to the seasons and elements of the earth, one's behavior – the particular proportion of humors – are attributable in part to geography and climate (for example, on the Gauls: Livy 5.33.11; 3.48.3).

But in all of these approaches one's behavior can also be affected by habituation (for example, Livy pref. 9).[27] One learns to value particular

---

[22] On ancient debates about the qualities of *pneuma*, see Rawson 1985, 172–73 and Colish 1990 1.27–28. *Psuchē* may also carry a meaning that accords with *anima*, connoting the immortal part of the soul. *Animus* (the mind) seems more appropriate to Livy's usage.

[23] Epic. *Her.* 46–53; Lucr. 4.722–822; Diog. of Oen. fr. 9; DL 7.45–46, 49–50; Posid. in Gal. *De plac. F.* 164.53–54: thrust before vivid mental picture; 165.26–28; 169.224–17; Plut. *De comm. not.* 1084f–1085a; Cic. *De orat.* 2.87.257; 3.40.160; 3.41.163; Quint. *Inst.* 6.2.29–30. See, for example, Frede 1992, 289; Webb 1997, 117–21.

[24] Long 1996, 247. See Cic. *Acad.* 2.7.21.

[25] von Staden 2000, 100. Also Rist 1969, 86–91; von Staden 1978, 97; Inwood 1985, 164–65.

[26] von Staden 2000, 106.

[27] Gal. *De plac. F.* 164.53–54; see also F 165.26–28, 169.114–17; also Cic. *Tusc.* 3.1.2; 3.5.11.

types of behavior, to associate particular types of actions with good or bad outcomes, and to be moved to act (or restrain oneself from acting) accordingly. Drawing a comparison to diseases and disorders of the body, Cicero writes, the "disturbing effect of corrupt beliefs warring against one another" creates "troubled movement...in the soul" (*Tusc.* 4.10.23; 3.10.23). Sicknesses, or more generally "defects" (*vitia*), arise when, through repeated association of desire and pleasure with a particular object, one comes to value an object as good that is not good (Cic. *Tusc.* 4.10.23–11.27; also Livy pref. 9).

We have seen already the Stoic solution in Cicero's attempt to cure his grief, a gradual stripping away of emotions that grip us by recognizing and accepting what cannot be controlled. But that clearly is not Livy's solution whose *remedium* is charged with emotion. Cicero is helpful here in providing some insight into the therapeutic task of the historian. In talking about Stoic analogies of sickness, Cicero criticizes them for their inability to employ rhetoric to change minds.[28] What rhetoric does, as we saw in Chapter 1, is shape emotions by painting real life.[29] "Truth," as Moles suggests in his discussion of Livy, "is a matter of sight."[30] Action is a matter of sight, as well, for it is by way of these images of what to emulate and what to avoid that we are moved to act. Underlying Livy's *History* is a sense of how the rhetorical formulation of history – the ways in which the past is seen and felt – can change minds.

In directing attention to his history as a "conspicuous monument" (pref. 10), Livy is thrusting before his reader vivid images of the past that are meant to evoke an emotional response.[31] In those responses, Livy trains thought (as suggested by *intueri*, to contemplate) (pref. 10). That training addresses two errors. First, Livy seeks to address what the Stoics

---

[28] See Graver 2002, 84 and Remer 2004.
[29] See Chapt. 1, 69–76; Cic. *De orat.* 2.44.186: rhetorician must recognize malady and dispostion of the patient to provide proper treatment. On the relationship of the rhetorician to the historian, see *De orat.* 2.12.51–16.70. On the influence of *De orat.* on Livy, see Walsh 1961, 42–43.
[30] Moles 1993, 154.
[31] On history as a monument, see Moles 1993; Miles 1995; Kraus and Woodman 1997; Jaeger 1997; Feldherr 1998; Chaplin 2000. On emotional response, see Jaeger 1997, 22; Moles 1993, 153; Vasaly 1993, 26–39, esp. 29–30; and Levene 1997, 139–47.

refer to as errors of hastiness, an attitude that figures prominently in Livy's characterization of the "gradual relaxation of discipline" that has bred a disorder (*vitium*) in Rome, as well as in his own readers (pref. 9; also pref. 4; DL 7.48). Such examples appear frequently with military commanders sizing up the strategic situation, such as in the rashness of Gaius Flaminius (22.3), Gaius Terentius Varro (22.38, 22.39.1), and Marcus Minucius (22.12.11–12) in the Second Punic War. The problem here is that one draws conclusions too quickly to a picture that is either not clear or is the wrong way to achieve a particular goal. We may not be able to control how something initially appears to us, but we can learn to direct the senses to look again, or look more closely, or look from a different angle, to better perceive the object.[32]

The second way in which Livy trains thought is by examining errors of purpose. In talking about the loss of purpose, Livy can sound moralistic. But the more profound significance of his argument is his concern with the loss of common animating dispositions that oriented people toward common ends. Livy can look back and see how the desire for "excessive pleasures" brought ruin to the Republic (pref. 12). But looking forward was every bit as haunting. The problem is not just luxury. Population increases, an expanding empire, and war raise a more fundamental question: what collective purpose animates such a diverse and dispersed people? Livy's political thought, thus, is aimed at recovering (or extending) an impulse toward a collective purpose. When one "choose[s]" what lessons to imitate and what to avoid according to what is "shameful in the conception and shameful in the result" (pref. 10), one learns to associate negative emotions with improper ends (and positive emotions with proper ends). With the repetition of experiences and examples, the images can be stored in memory and combined with other similar images to form concepts.[33] As Vasaly writes, the "constant

---

[32] Jaeger uses the metaphor of the labyrinth in which those making their way through the maze must continually struggle to be attentive to detail: to identify clues, assess the situation, see opportunity, and sort through confusion (Jaeger 1999).

[33] Examples of concept formation can be seen in Cic. *Acad.* 1.11.41: on Zeno; 2.10.30: for Stoics, images united by mutual resemblance; DL 10.32: for Epicurus notions arise from analogy, similarity, confrontation, combination. On how rhetoric contributes to the formation of concepts, see Gildenhard 2011.

reliance on the visual and the concrete was but the Roman gateway to the world of ideas."[34] In seeking to inspire by casting his audience's gaze to the past, Livy points to how concepts are born in time and animated by experience. Through the telling of history as a record of deeds that are "worthy of memory" (7.2.2), what is not just portrayed but also felt are the animating forces of politics: the beliefs, ideas, habits, and principles that move people to act.

FOUNDING

In starting his *History* from the beginning of the city (*a primordio urbis*), Livy signals the centrality of founding to his political thought. Foundings provide identities, indicate purposes, establish boundaries, create authority, portray virtues, and often play out and resolve particular tensions. Rome's earliest founding myths, to the extent that they can be reconstructed, were largely ethnic myths: a people bound by shared origins who created a community together.[35] The Roman founding myth as it evolved, and as it is most powerfully articulated by Livy, is a different type of myth: It is a multi-ethnic myth that makes possible global incorporation. But the myth reveals, as well, Livy's (and a Roman) conception of how communities are organized, not by reason but by desire.

Livy's recounting of Rome's founding contrasts most dramatically with Plato's account in *The Republic* of a visionary founder who wipes the slate clean, establishes a community governed by reason, and imagines a people who spring from the earth.[36] The Greek tradition exercised its own influence on Roman conceptions. Dionysius of

---

[34] Vasaly 1993, 257. On the power of words to affect mental images, see Watson 1988, 215–19; Webb 1997; Quint. *Inst.* 6.2.29.
[35] Wiseman 1995, 89–102 provides a survey of different interpretations of the Romulus and Remus myth. On the Indo-European context for the myth, see Bremmer 1987. Greek conceptions of the Roman founding are discussed in Bickerman 1952. For a discussion of the fixing of the Aeneas myth, see Gruen 1992, 6–51. For a discussion of the relationship between the Romulus and Remus myth and the Aeneas myth, see Cornell 1975.
[36] See Momigliano 1989, 58; Cornell 1995, 60; Dench 2005, 96–117.

Halicarnassus attempts to bring the Roman founding legends into line with Greek ideals, characterizing the original inhabitants as freemen who had fled from oppression elsewhere (*Ant. Rom.* 2.7–29). And Cicero portrays Romulus as a visionary founder more in keeping with Greek notions (*De rep.* 2.2.4). But Livy seems almost to revel in the contrast between the Roman founding and autochthonous myths of pure origins. There are several contrasts worth noting.

First, the primary characteristic of Plato's founder is reason, where for Livy it is desire. Livy's language continually draws on the language of desire. Romulus and Remus are suckled in the wild and gain both strength of body and resolution of spirit by hunting in the wilds, preying not only on wild beasts but also on wild men – bandits (1.4.9). Romulus kills the tyrant, Amulius (1.5.7). The decision of founding is one in which the twins "were seized with the desire (*cupido*)" to locate the city where they had been raised (1.6.3). The establishment of Romulus as the city's founder occurs as he kills his brother in anger (1.7.2). Romulus populates the city by offering asylum, attracting those "eager for new conditions" (1.8.6). And the continuation of Rome is secured by the abduction of the Sabines, driven by Romulus' "resentment" for the neighboring cities refusing to allow intermarriage (1.9.6).

Second, Plato's city is comprised of ethnically homogeneous individuals, the people springing from the land. The idea is not confined to Plato. Long after Livy, Aelius Aristides would praise the Athenians for their pure origins.[37] To make clear his departure from these myths, Livy comments on how founders of cities "pretend that the earth had raised up sons to them" (1.8.5). But Livy's city is multi-ethnic, founded by a Trojan and populated not only by dispersed people of unknown origins in the beginning but depending for its continued growth on the incorporation of surrounding tribes, including the Sabines. As Feldherr comments, Livy presents "an array of conflicting and overlapping national identities, each set in motion by war or sedition and blurred by the process of wandering."[38] Rome, thus, must look to non-ethnic sources for unity.[39] The Sabine story provides the archetype for how Romans are

---

[37] Aelius Aristides *Panath.* (in Oliver 1968). [38] Feldherr 1998, 113.
[39] See Dench 2005, 11–35, 93–151.

made. Initially at war, the Sabine women kidnapped and made the wives of the Romans, *concordia* is achieved through the transformation of the affections of groups from indignation (1.9.14) to begrudged acceptance compelled by visible reminders of strength to reconciliation that arises from recognition of affective ties (1.9.15; 1.10.4–5; 1.13.6).[40] The women are brought into co-partnership (*societas*) "in all the possessions of the Romans" (1.9.14). In Livy's telling, at the point at which Rome is about to defeat the Sabines, the women, who had earlier plotted with the Sabines to seize the citadel, rush into battle, separate the armies, and plead that the opposing armies are now related through marriage so that the women's husbands and sons were facing their parents (1.13.2). This plea for reconciliation, born of a felt connection between the groups, moved both the multitude and leaders, creating a "stillness" and "sudden hush" (1.13.4). In this stillness the leaders agreed to a truce that "made one people out of the two" (1.13.4). Rome fosters these ties in several ways: through its own myths of ethnic incorporation (e.g., the naming of the *curiae* after the Sabine women) (1.13.6), as well as through such mechanisms as colonization, immigration, citizenship, and intermarriage (1.11.2; 1.11.4). There is the promise of assimilation, but one that requires some effacement of identity to the Roman corporate identity (see also later in Tac. *Ann.* 11.24.4). As Livy writes, in the language of Roman incorporation: "They shared the sovereignty, but all authority was transferred to Rome (*Regnum consociant; imperium omne conferunt Romam*) (1.13.5).

Third, Plato's city is hierarchical and the functions of its citizens fixed. Only the gold class, implanted at birth, can rule. But Rome is populated by "an obscure and lowly" (*obscurus atque humilis*) multitude: untutored rustics, on the one hand, and a disordered (*turba*) mob, representing different social classes (including slaves), who flocked to Rome on the promise of asylum, on the other (1.8.2; 1.8.5; 1.8.6). Although hierarchic distinctions are integral to Roman politics, Livy's founding celebrates the self-made, new men (*novi homines*) who are not virtuous because of their noble ancestry, but because of their actions.[41]

---

[40] On the rape of the Sabines, see Hemker 1985; Miles 1995, 179–219; Brown 1995.
[41] See especially Miles 1995, 149–51.

Fourth, Plato's founding is a once-and-for-all affair that occurs at the inception of the community. Rome, however, is built by "successive founders" (2.1.2) who continually shape the animating dispositions and institutions of the Roman people by innovating within the context of a recovered past. Thus, Romulus recovers the land of his grandfather, Numitor, and then builds a new city. Numa gives Rome a "new foundation in law, statutes, and observances" (1.18.4; 1.19.1). And Ancus reinforces this example by ordering the pontifex to copy the religious commentaries of Numa and "display them in public on a whitened tablet" (1.32.2). As Miles notes, "Livy presents an approach to Roman history that explicitly acknowledges the value of change and that denies to the *maiores* and their institutions a universal and timeless value."[42]

Finally, Plato paints on a clean canvas. For Livy, the founder is a builder (from *condere*, "to build") who must work with the materials he has. If the corruption of the political world makes Plato's founder reluctant to enter it, then it is precisely that corruption that inspires Livy's founders to reform it. Livy's notion of founding speaks to an age when there are no longer deserts and wildernesses out of which may be created new communities but only the rubble of the past: populations divided in their loyalties, born of different historical experiences, and oriented toward divergent and opposing ends. Livy's founding legend points both to the promise and the problematic nature of Roman identity in the age of Augustus: What is Roman now that it is comprised of people who are dispersed over a vast empire, who know each other by way of conquest, and who, for the last several decades, were divided against themselves in civil war?[43]

THE TARQUINS AND LUCRETIA: INCITING LIBERTY

The core of Roman identity for Livy is liberty. The kings, as founders, play a critical role in creating political order, directing the animating spirit of a disordered mob, at first moving people by the compulsions of

---

[42] Miles 1995, 119.
[43] On the ideological role of these refugee narratives for empire, see Lee-Stecum 2008.

fear and awe until the principles of authority, law, discipline, and vigor had become internalized (e.g., 1.8.2). But kingship cannot forge liberty. It does, however, provide the experiences and memories against which liberty would be defined. The story of Tarquinius Superbus, the seventh Roman king, points to the threat that leaders pose when they assume arbitrary authority. Gone is any collective affection (*caritas*) (1.49.4). In a description that could as easily be made of the late Republic dictatorships of Sulla and the Second Triumvirate, Livy writes: "To inspire terror therefore in many persons" Tarquinius Superbus tried all capital cases himself and thus "was able to inflict death, exile, and forfeiture of property, not only upon persons whom he suspected and disliked, but also in cases where he could have nothing to gain but plunder" (1.49.5; also 1.51.1).[44] In depriving the senate of its authority, diverting public moneys to build his palace, and making slaves of his own citizens, Tarquinius pressed down the spirit of the people (1.51.1).

But the story also points to the ways in which political concepts like tyranny and liberty are not abstractions but acquire form through their felt effects. At first glance Tarquinius' actions resemble Romulus'. Like Romulus' incorporation of the Sabines, Tarquinius mixes Latins with Romans and places them under his command (1.52.6). Tarquinius also appears like Romulus in his military prowess, extending control over surrounding territories. And, like Romulus' abduction of the Sabines, there is a similar initiation of sexual violence with Sextus Tarquinius' rape of Lucretia.[45] But tyranny alters the animating dispositions of the people. Through visual demonstrations (*documenta*) of the futility and danger of opposition, the tyrant creates one will, but it is one directed toward the lustful desires of the tyrant and those loyal to him and not toward the lawful maintenance of the state (1.52.4).[46] As Livy writes, "in the sweetness of private gain men lost their feeling for the wrongs of the nation" (1.54.10). Desire and fear, rather than affection, are now the animating dispositions that define community life (1.47.6–7; 1.49.4).

---

[44] For a survey of scholarship on the Tarquins, see Cornell 1995, 215–26.
[45] See Matthes 2000, 42–43.
[46] Dunkle notes that for the Romans, "the opposite of *libido* was *lex*" (1967, 168).

In the story of Lucretia we see played out the assertion of political power premised on desire and fear. In discussing the role of Lucretia (and the earlier rape of Rhea in the founding of Rome), Matthes asks the question, "Why are the stories of women's sexual violence simultaneously recalled and then buried in Livy's history?"[47] Matthes interprets the rape of Lucretia as a violation by the tyrant of patriarchal power, a type of familial power that authorizes political power.[48] Although kingship is not inherited in ancient Rome, political power is vested in familial lines. In fact, the Tarquin line arises from a disputed inheritance. Lucumo, the first Tarquin, inherits all of his father's property with the death of his older brother, Arruns. Lucumo's father (Demaratus) does not realize that Arruns' wife is pregnant, and thus does not make provisions for the child, Egerius, to inherit his share of the wealth. Collatinus, the husband of Lucretia and the son of Egerius, is the legitimate, but dispossessed, heir of Demaratus. From this perspective the rape of Lucretia appears as a violent assertion of both patriarchal and political power by making Sextus Tarquinius the father of the Collatinus line.

Lucretia's death seems to confirm the foundation of politics in violence. In founding the Republic, as Matthes write, "Lucretia must die."[49] From this gender perspective, Lucretia must die so that a tyrant's son is not born from her. She must die because "her violation marks the failure of masculinity" to protect her.[50] And she, like all female bodies, must be passive carriers of cultural value rather than participants in the political life of the Republic. Female bodies, like Lucretia's corpse, become "silent signifiers" who symbolize, but do not act.[51]

But Lucretia also signifies, however paradoxically (given her passive role as a dead body), a soul that does not succumb to the disorder inflicted by tyranny. The tyrant rewards timidity (rather than vigor) and private interest (rather than public good). What brings down tyranny, as Livy seems to indicate, is not force per se (though that is

---

[47] Matthes 2000, 24. On differing interpretations of the Lucretia story over time, see Donaldson 1982.
[48] Matthes 2000, 27.   [49] Matthes 2000, 31.   [50] Matthes 2000, 31.
[51] Matthes 2000, 35. For Matthes, the mother is displaced, as well. Brutus, in kissing Mother Earth, both draws on the generative power of the female and gives birth by himself to the Republic (Matthes 2000, 29–30).

certainly necessary) but resoluteness: a decision no longer to acquiesce.[52] The problem is that acquiescence occurs so incrementally and in such a hidden way that citizens cannot perceive themselves becoming slaves. The greatness of Brutus, for example, is that he is able to survive but not succumb, but he can only do so by making himself politically invisible (1.56.7; 1.56.8).[53] The exemplary character of Lucretia is that her soul, too, cannot be moved by the tyrannical will (see 1.58.4). As Livy writes, "They carried out Lucretia's corpse from the house and bore it to the market-place, where men crowded about them, attracted, as they were bound to be, by the amazing character of the strange event and its heinousness (*Elatum domo Lucretiae corpus in forum deferunt concientque miraculo, ut fit, rei novae atque indignitate homines*)" (1.49.3). Her political significance is that she, in her death, is "thrust before" the Roman populace, etching a "vivid mental picture" of a resolute soul: a lifeless body that reminded the Romans of what they once were (1.59.3; 1.59.4).[54]

Livy describes how the body of Lucretia summons an affective response to a set of experiences: "Every man had his own complaint to make of the prince's crime and his violence. They were moved, not only by the father's sorrow, but by the fact that it was Brutus who chid their tears and idle lamentations and urged them to take up the sword, as befitted men and Romans, against those who had dared to treat them as enemies" (1.49.4). I differ from Jed, who argues that Brutus is teaching citizens "to subordinate their emotions to the cause of liberty" and "to isolate interpretive thought from tangible feelings."[55] Brutus, instead, is organizing a notion of liberty around a collective set of felt experiences.

---

[52] The Sabine women, too, in Livy's account, intervene in the battlefield to bring about political *concordia*. See especially Brown 1995, 306–11.

[53] See Ogilvie 1965, 217: "very different in intelligence from the mask which he had assumed."

[54] The quotation is from Posidonius: Gal. *De plac.* F 162.8–9. See Joshel 1992, 125. As Calhoon argues, Lucretia serves as a reminder of how much of Rome had sunk into self-indulgence and idleness, which breeds effeminacy (1997, 154). In Williams' language, Lucretia produces a "shock of *recognition*" when she becomes a "semantic figure" that articulates a widely held experience (Williams 1979, 164, italics in original).

[55] See Jed 1989, 10, 12.

Before the gathering crowd Brutus recreates in words the vivid image of Lucretia's death: the violence and lust of Sextus Tarquinius, the defilement of Lucretia, and the sorrow of the father (1.59.8). Brutus articulates, as well, the meaning of tyranny by recalling a set of experiences: how the king had made slaves of the people, made warriors into artisans, murdered Tullius (the previous king), and how Tullia (the wife of Tarquinius and daughter of Tullius) drove over the body of her father. He recalls the misery of the plebs who were made to toil in ditches and sewers (1.59.9). After recounting these outrages, made still more vivid by the freshness of the death of Lucretia, Brutus "inflamed the people," moving the crowd from lament and complaint to action until they abrogated the king's authority and exiled the Tarquins (1.59.11; also 1.59.4).[56] However terrifying may be the raw power of the tyrant, its strength, whether Sextus' "victorious lust" or his father's reign, rests on the acquiescence of the soul (1.58.5).

Livy is not just engaging in good storytelling. His point is that concepts are not built from air, not born in a moment, and not organized by reason, but are formed through a succession of events that one comes to recognize as related. Through "an affection of slow growth" toward family, place, and soil, the people had become "firmly united in their aspirations" (2.1.6). Liberty acquires conceptual substance in memory, not the least of which is the Roman institution of slavery. The Romans knew well what it meant to be a slave: It meant that one's status was as a possession, which entailed the absence of rights, of redress, or of the ability to possess anything or enter into agreements.[57] Lucretia's body, as Brutus reminds the people, is the culmination of how tyranny enslaves not just the body but the will by subjecting it to another will that is both arbitrary and unbounded. From the experience of subjugation to the arbitrary will of another arises the principle of liberty, in which "laws [are] superior in authority to men" (2.1.1).[58]

---

[56] For Lucretia as ritual scapegoat see Klindienst Joplin 1990 and Calhoon 1997.
[57] Wirszubski 1968, 1.
[58] Klindienst Joplin states, "Memory of the female victim, raped and killed, is hard to sustain. Memory of the tyrant is not" (1990, 51). My suggestion is that the memories are tied together and integral as felt meanings.

There are three aspects to the Roman notion of liberty that we can distill from Livy. First, there is its institutional dimension. Liberty, as it stands in contrast to *servitus* and *dominatio*, said of both kingship and slavery, requires that limits be placed on the exercise of power by any individual or group of individuals.[59] The king is replaced with two elected consuls and the consuls' terms are limited to one year (2.1.7). The number of lictors that the consuls could have is also limited so that "the terror they inspired should not be doubled by permitting both to have the rods" (2.1.8). The senate is restored. Sacrificial ceremonies performed by the king are transferred to a new office. And the people, who were vehement (*avidus*) about their new liberty (*nova libertas*), swear an oath to never allow a king (*rex*) in Rome again (2.1.9; 2.2.5).

Second, liberty is tied to equality. *Aequa libertas* is not a statement about equal participation in the affairs of the state but about an equal application of the law and the protection of particular rights for patricians and plebeians alike (3.31.7; 3.34.3; 4.5.1; 6.37.4; 6.37.11–12; and 38.50.5–8).[60] In the differentiated, hierarchical Roman society, the concern is not with the state as an abstract instrument of power but with the assertion of one group over another. "The Roman citizen sought to assert and safeguard his rights, not against the overriding authority of the State, or the tyranny of the majority, as it is sometimes called, but against other citizens who were stronger than himself."[61] This assertion, as Wirszubski has argued, appears as the conflict between *dignitas*, or a sense of esteem associated with status, and the equality of *libertas* (3.65.11; 4.6.11; 6.37.11; 7.33.3).[62] *Libertas*, thus, is defined in terms of one's status as a *civis*: a juridical equality, more than a range of available choices, that is associated with citizenship and over time comes to include a variety of rights: *suffragium* (the right to enact or reject proposals or magistrates through vote) (see 4.5.2; 6.27.6); the right to *provocatio* (the legal protection against arbitrary punishment by a magistrate) (3.13.4;

---

[59] See Pettit 1996: 576–77; 1997: 31–32, 36; Skinner 1998: 38–47; Brunt 1988: 283; Raaflaub 2004, 266–70; Arena 2012, 14–30.
[60] See Wirszubski 1968, 9–15; Schofield, chapt. 7, in Hammer (forthcoming).
[61] Wirszubski 1968, 16–17.   [62] Wirszubski 1968, 15–17.

3.45.8; 3.55.4; 3.56.5–6; 3.56.10–13),[63] and the protections and powers afforded by the tribunes. These protections and powers include *auxilium* (the right of a tribune to intercede on behalf of an appellant) (2.33.1), *intercessio* (the right to veto actions of a magistrate) (4.48.6; 4.53.4; 6.38.5; 10.37.9), *sacrosanctus* (the inviolability of tribunes) (2.33.1; 3.55.10), and *ius agendi cum plebe* (the right to call the plebeian assembly).[64]

A third aspect of *libertas* relates to initiative. Some argue that in the overthrow of kingship, by vesting political power in citizenship rather than family, the Republic seems to sever the connection between patriarchy and politics, transforming the dependent subject into the independent citizen.[65] Others have identified the unification of the roles of consular and father in the figure of Brutus, which establishes a new relationship to the people that is both political and paternal.[66] Certainly, through the lens of Augustus' rise, consular and paternal powers are joined in the image of the *pater patriae*. And it should not be forgotten that the patriarchical elements of hierarchy and exclusivity remain components of Roman citizenship. But in the early Republic, the people do express their new liberty as initiative. The people's power is carefully circumscribed by Roman law: The assembly has to be convened by a magistrate; the assembly can neither propose candidates nor introduce bills; and the assembly has to vote on the bills presented to it.[67] Nonetheless, there is considerable informal power that the people seize upon immediately. The people demand that Brutus, to his astonishment, exile the Tarquin family, including a current consul (2.2.7). Later, after the death of Brutus, the people begin to suspect that Publius Valerius, who is building his house on the highest part of the Velia, aspires to be king.

---

[63] The primary laws associated with the right to *provocatio* are the *lex Valeria* of 300 BCE, the *leges Porciae* of the second century, and the *lex Sempronia* (123 BCE). The first sets of laws established the right to appeal to the people for sentences of executions, floggings, and heavy fines, increased the penalties for violations of *provocatio*, and extended the application of the right to outside Rome. The *lex Sempronia* prohibited the capital punishment of any citizen without approval of the people (either the assembly or court) (see Arena 2012, 50).

[64] Arena 2012, 29.

[65] See Matthes 2000, 30. On the powers of the father in Roman law, see Roller 2001, 237; Arena 2012, 23.

[66] Feldherr 1997, 153; also Kapust 2011, 99–100.   [67] Wirszubski 1968, 18.

The power of the people is evidently strong enough to initiate concern by Valerius who, in appearing before the people, acknowledges that "the people's majesty (*maiestas*) and power were superior to the consul's" (2.7.7). And he agrees not only to bring his house down from the hill, but also to place it "under the hill" so that "you may live above me" (2.7.11). And the first secession of the plebs (494 BCE), a response to debt bondage and arbitrary actions of consuls and senators, results in the establishment of the *concilium plebis* and the creation of the plebeians' own magistrates, the tribunes, who could not be physically harmed, could intervene on behalf of the plebs, and had the right to convene the plebeian assembly (2.23–24, 32–33). The power of initiation was extended later by opening consular elections to plebeian candidates (through the *leges Liciniae Sextiae*) (6.34–42), a right seen as critical to the exercise of sovereignty by the people (see 6.37.4), and then through the *lex Hortensia*, which made resolutions of the *concilium plebis* binding on everyone. As Arena points out, over time more emphasis was placed "on the people who imparted its command rather than on the magistrate who put forward a legislative proposal" (see 4.30.16; 6.21.5; 6.22.4; 7.19.10; 10.9.1; 21.17.4; 27.5.16; 30.43.2–3; 33.25.7; 38.45.5).[68] The point is that liberty, as a felt meaning, emerges as both an animated and animating concept, one that becomes a part of the conceptual world of Roman politics. It is born of the horror of oppression but serves as a stimulus to action as new experiences are interpreted through these meanings. But memories fade, animosities reappear, and the cause of liberty will be newly contested and dramatically expanded.

POLITICAL CORRUPTION AND PUBLICNESS

For Livy, Roman liberty stands between two poles: tyranny and *factio* (at first between patricians and plebeians, and then between nobles and the people).[69] In one, the political space collapses as opportunities for initiative are compressed into one will. In the other, the political space

---

[68] Arena 2012, 63.
[69] See 9.46.12–13 for the transition between these two factional divides.

disintegrates when groups assume the power to make laws for the community. Human nature only intensifies the problem. As Livy notes:

> So difficult is it to be moderate in the defence of liberty, since everyone, while pretending to seek fair-play, so raises himself as to press another down; while insuring themselves against fear, men actually render themselves fearful to others; and having defended ourselves from an injury, we proceed – as though it were necessary either to do or suffer wrong – to inflict injury upon our neighbour (3.65.11).

In the Roman context, this ongoing strife plays itself out in the conflict of the orders, a struggle for advantage between plebeians and patricians in which when one group practices moderation, the other group seizes the advantage (3.65.7; see Introduction, 10–11).

The sheer destructiveness of strife by the first century BCE suggests why Livy might want to locate Rome's greatness in its "noble *concordia*" (5.7.10; also 2.1.11 on origins of the Republic). Yet, however much Livy may have praised the "civic virtue of *concordia*" as a moderation of spirit,[70] his *History* betrays a deeper and more political truth about the emergence of the Republic: The struggle for access to power reveals a republican culture not of concord but of open competition and compromise (see 2.33.1–2; 6.37.4; 42.9–11; and Introduction). Institutions are important as mechanisms for maintaining a political space, one that limits the encroachment of power while preserving its exercise (as initiative). Neither institutions nor human virtue are sufficient, though, to maintain liberty, particularly since liberty is born from neither of these. Liberty is inscribed in political character as a set of felt meanings, animated by experience and organized by memory. That relationship has a significant implication: One's judgments are affected not only by the experiences that underlie one's own political character but also by one's appraisal and response to the character of another. These are not simply rational calculations: One's decision to trust, be inspired, or be forewarned arises in part from reason but also by the congruence of the idea with the emotions and by one's appraisal of the character of the speaker. The

---

[70] Walsh 1961, 69; also Brown 1995, 315–17. On discord, see Momigliano 1942, 120; Flower 2010, 46–52.

greatest danger to judgment lies not in discord but in a type of political blindness in which one loses one's ability to see or judge the situation or the person. Political blindness alters the visual and experiential cues that animate political character and guide political judgment.

Livy's language suggests the hiddenness of the forces that corrode liberty. Corrupt individuals can attempt to disguise their motivations so that their private goals appear as public ends. So, for example, Spurius Maelius distributes his private grain supplies to feed the people, gaining so much popularity that he begins to aspire to *regnum* (4.13.4). Spurius Manlius Capitolinus, angered by the honors given to Camillus and inflated by his own pride (6.11.6), accuses Camillus and others of hiding the ransom that was to be paid to the Gauls. Or one's imagination might be clouded by resentments or license, replacing public cues with private ones. So in Livy's telling, the soldiers, seduced by the pleasures of Capua, and angered by poverty and debt, "forget their native land" – in effect erasing their own political foundation – and plot (in a scheme hatched in private) to march on Rome (7.38.5–10; 7.39.14–17).

The response to political blindness is publicness: the ability, both in assemblies and in the faculty of public accusation (and in *exempla* and *monumenta*), to make visible through words the aspirations and motivations of others in the community so that judgments can be formed. Required to appear before the appointed Dictator and the people, Spurius Maelius flees and is killed. His desire for kingship and the ways in which he sought to purchase liberty is cast before the community's eyes as a negative monument: Lucius Quinctius Cincinnatus orders that Maelius' house, situated below the Capitol, be demolished and nothing built in its place (4.16.1).[71]

Livy's treatment of Spurius Manlius Capitolinus points even more explicitly to the visual components necessary for the maintenance of liberty. Manlius Capitolinus' charges (like the Catilinarian conspiracy to which it alludes) are so powerful precisely because he plays upon the

---

[71] On the symbolic dimension of house demolition in Rome, see Roller 2010. Lowrie argues that Livy revises earlier versions of the story to place it within "a perfectly legal and well-managed state of emergency against a religious threat" (Lowrie 2010b, 179).

suspicions of the people that the nobility is getting richer while they are being dragged into debt. Manlius is summoned before the people where he is told to "disclose from their hidden (*clandestina*) plunder those men" whom he has accused of stealing from the people (6.15.5, trans. modified). Manlius responds by playing on the idea of sight: "The more you bid us expose your sleight-of-hand, the more I fear you may have robbed us even of our eyes, while we were watching you (*Quo magis argui praestigias iubetis vestras, eo plus vereor ne abstuleritis observantibus etiam oculos*)" (6.15.13).

Despite arrest and later release, Manlius' popularity grows as he calls for a leveling of dictatorship and consulship so that "the Roman plebs may be enabled to lift its head" (6.18.14). When the senate and tribunes meet to decide how to stop Manlius so as not to turn the conflict into a war, the tribunes of the plebs suggest a trial: "Nothing is less popular than kingly power. As soon as the populace, seeing (*viderint*) that our quarrel is not with them, are changed from supporters into judges, and see that the prosecutors are plebeians, the defendant a patrician, and the accusation that of seeking to set up a kingdom, they will not favour any man at the expense of their own liberty" (6.19.7, trans. modified). At first it appears that Manlius will not be convicted since the trial occurs in the Campus Martius, where Manlius is able to fix the people's eyes on the Capitol and Citadel, calling to mind their gratitude for his defense of the city. The tribunes realize that "unless they could also emancipate men's eyes (*oculos*) from the associations of so glorious a deed," no judgment will be possible (6.20.10). So the trial is moved out of sight of the Capitol where "men steeled their hearts" and pronounced judgment (6.20.11).[72]

Even the threat of civil war in the conspiracy against Rome dissipates once fellow citizens "came within sight of one another" and were "at once reminded of their fatherland" (7.40.1). Their anger and frenzy subsequently subsided as leaders on both sides and their men "began to seek for ways to meet and confer together" (7.40.2). Marcus Valerius Corvus, the commander of the defending army, highlights the affections

---

[72] Wiseman argues that given the topography of Rome, the trial could not be held out of sight (Wiseman 1987, 225–43), which suggests even more strongly the importance of sight in recalling the felt meanings that underlie judgment.

that unify the people (7.40.3): The hills that surround the camp are on native soil (7.40.6); he has led them to defeat the Samnites (7.40.6); even as patrician, he (identifying a new set of meanings associated with Roman politics) has defended merit as a basis of position and achievement (7.40.7–8; recall 7.32.14); and in doing battle, the conspirators would be attempting what no past secession of the plebs had attempted (7.40.11–14). The appeal is strong enough to move Titus Quinctius, the leader of the conspirators, to tears, to submit to the authority of Corvus, and to appeal on behalf of the conditions of the plebs.

These cases do not speak particularly well of the plebs, who seem susceptible to demagoguery. Of course, Livy's aristocratic biases show. Landlessness, indebtedness, hunger, and poverty were not simply rhetorical and irresponsible tropes; they were realities of plebeian life. But the masses were not the only ones unable to distinguish between public and private ends. Livy's discussion of the *decemviri* tempers the privileging of the judgment of the *nobiles*. For Livy, the aristocracy probably can judge better, if uncorrupted. But that is a big "if." The *decemviri* episode shows not only how susceptible all groups are to corruption, but also how that corruption can arise from the dissipation of the animating spirit of the community – the constellation of felt meanings. For Livy, political judgment must ultimately rest on publicness: not just open debate, but debate that recognizes a shared (even if disputed) claim to the meanings that orient a community's political life. Absent that claim, the only recourse of judgment is to the hidden desires of the heart.

THE *DECEMVIRI* AND THE RETURN OF TYRANNY

The backdrop to the rise of the *decemviri* is the fragmentation of the shared aspirations that had originally inspired plebs and patricians to cast off kingship. The immediate dangers to the Republic had receded and old animosities had returned. The patricians were driven to harshness by their hatred of the plebs and were divided by private interests that undermined their ability to deliberate (2.29.9; 2.30.2). The minds of plebs were affected, as well, by a "spirit of license" because of "plenty and idleness" (2.52.2). The tribunes in turn used these occasions to rouse the plebs "to madness" with the "poison" of land legislation (2.52.3). Answering to the growing turmoil and threats to the state, in which the tribunes exacted concessions by obstructing the raising of troops, both sides agreed to send a delegation to Athens to copy the laws of Solon and learn about the customs, laws, and institutions of other Greek cities (3.31.8). The Romans then transferred all authority to the *decemviri*, a Board of Ten who would codify the laws of Rome.[73]

Although the beginning of the *decemviri* was by all appearances promising enough – and Livy points to the publicness by which the *decemviri* operated in the first year – the Board, when reappointed with Appius as the head, degenerated into tyranny.[74] The marks of tyranny were ignored because each side was blinded by their excessive desire to destroy the other. The aristocracy was happy to have the tribunes silenced. And the treatment of the plebs by the consuls over the last several decades had replaced one memory with another, leading the plebeians to hate the consuls as much as the kings and thus to favor a continuation of the *decemviri* (3.34.8). The seeds of demagoguery that Brutus feared would agitate the people at the inception of the Republic had taken root (2.1.4; 2.1.9). The perverse way in which tyranny asserts itself into the political realm is suggested by Livy's portrayal of Appius' rise as the inversion of Brutus'. Where Brutus took off his mask to overthrow the Tarquins, as Livy comments, Appius "now threw off the mask he had been wearing," a mask of humility and support for the plebs, and began to act according to his true nature (3.36.1).[75] Not the least of these outrages was the addition of two further tables of unequal (unfair) laws (*iniquarum legum*), to use Cicero's characterization,

---

[73] On the tradition of the *decemviri*, see Ogilvie 1965, 451–89 and Wiseman 1979, 104–12. For a comparative analysis of the Twelve Tables in the context of broader legal and political developments, see Raaflaub 1986b and Eder 1986.

[74] On the publicness of the *decemviri*, see 3.33.8; 3.33.10; 3.34.1. When the *decemviri* completed ten tablets, they made them public so that the proposed laws might be debated and modified before being finally confirmed (3.34.2). A consensus emerged that the *decemviri* should be reappointed to give time for two more tablets to be added.

[75] Livy is reconciling two traditions, one of Appius' achievements in establishing the first ten tables, the other of Appius' tyranny associated with the final two tablets. See Vasaly 1987, 212–16; Ogilvie 1965, 461–62, 503–6. On the historicity of the latter tradition, see von Ungern-Sternberg 1986.

including the prohibition of intermarriage between plebeians and patricians (e.g. Cic. *De rep.* 2.37.63).[76]

In describing the rise of Appius as the head of the *decemviri*, Livy is in part employing the stock image of the tyrant who bases decisions on personal favor rather than law, makes judgments in private, holds power perpetually, and recognizes no boundaries on the exercise of power (3.38.1; 3.36.7–9; 3.37.8).[77] Tyranny operates by destabilizing the markers by which one orients oneself in the public realm. The Forum, the often raucous political center of Rome where laws were proposed and voted on, appeals heard, and magistrates elected was now marked by the rods and axes of 120 lictors (twelve for each *decemvir*), the abolition of the right of appeal (3.36.4), and pronouncements of decisions made in private (3.36.8). The once noisy crowd, inspired now by terror and fear, dared not "pronounce a word in praise of liberty" (3.36.6; also 3.36.5; Livy portrays a similar unaccountability of judges in Carthage: 33.46.1).

But Livy is not just presenting a stock image; he is exploring how tyranny alters the animating dispositions of the community. The people "had lost heart" (*animus*) (3.38.2). And the senators withdrew to their farms, disregarding public affairs in the belief that they would be safe from the *decemviri* (3.38.11). Livy emphasizes how the abandonment of civic engagement further dissipates the shared felt meaning of Roman political liberty. When a crier finally summons the senators because of the need to declare war, "it was like an innovation, so long had they disregarded the custom of consulting the senate" (3.38.8). These felt meanings are given spatial form when we, like the plebs, encounter the stark emptiness of the political space. "Men looked about in every corner of the Forum to discover a senator, and seldom recognized one anywhere; then their glances rested on the Curia and the decemvirs sitting there alone" (3.38.10). When summoned again, additional senators attend but seem more to gesture toward, than embrace, the memory of political liberty. Marcus Horatius Barbatus, for example, calls the *decemviri* "ten

---

[76] See Schofield in Hammer (forthcoming).
[77] Livy employs what Vasaly refers to as the "stock" traits of the "tyrannical personality" (1987, 218). See also Dunkle 1967 and 1971 on how tyrants were characterized.

Tarquinii" and reminds them that his family and the family of Lucius Valerius had been leaders in overthrowing the kings (3.39.3). He even recalls the reasons for the overthrow of the kings: the pride and violence that men had come to hate (3.39.4). But "liberty went no further than speech" (3.41.4). Fearful of the plebs and resentful of the tribunes, the senators accede to the wishes of the *decemviri*.

One of the most politically chilling aspects of Livy's account (and I leave aside the murder of Verginia here) is the way in which institutional forms and processes can becomes fictions (3.44.9) as they provide a public language for executing private desires. Institutions, by themselves, are not guarantors of liberty. Appius Claudius stages a legal abduction of Verginia, a free woman, by having Marcus Claudius, his client, claim her as his slave. To calm the crowd, Marcus Claudius declares that "he was proceeding lawfully, not by force" (3.44.8) and, thus, brings Verginia before the tribunal of Appius, the inventor of the plot. Appius even mimics senatorial language when he accuses Icilius, Verginia's fiancé, of being "a turbulent fellow" who "breathed the spirit of the tribunate" and who sought only to stir up strife (3.46.2).

The staging of the trial serves, more than anything else, as a forum for transforming felt experiences into public meanings. The day before the trial, the crowd could only "murmur" its disapproval when Marcus Claudius claimed Verginia, but no one "dared to stand out" (3.45.4). Only Icilius is able to excite the crowd (3.46.1) by speaking about the hiddenness of Appius' tyrannical desire and connecting his personal grievance to the broader loss of public appeal when the *decemviri* took away the assistance of the tribunes and the right of appeal, "two citadels for the defence of liberty" (3.45.8). It is interestingly the women who articulate the felt experience of tyranny, not through words, but as they wept in silence (3.47.4: *plus tacito fletu quam ulla vox movebat*).

But ultimately it is the sight of Verginia's body, stabbed in desperation by Verginius and held up for the crowd to see, which recalls the animating spirit of liberty that had been dissipated by faction and, consequently, had receded in memory.[78] Unlike the young nobles that

---

[78] For the connection of Verginia to Roman (especially plebeian) liberty, see Syme 1939, 155, 306, 469; Wirszubski 1968, 103–6; Vasaly 1987, 220–21.

THE *DECEMVIRI* AND THE RETURN OF TYRANNY

Appius is able to corrupt through the promise of spoils, Verginia cannot be seduced with money or promises (3.44.4). She, like Lucretia, appears as the soul that is unwilling to bow to tyranny, though with a difference. Lucretia's virtue is her chastity. Thus, Livy emphasizes her refusal to comply with the sexual desires of Sextus Tarquinius. Verginia is also chaste, but the issue is her political liberty. Thus, the events are given a political register. Verginia's status is as a free woman, the seduction appears more as the political act of bribery, the abduction occurs in court, Appius' crime is to sentence a free woman to slavery (3.56.4, 8), and the language of vindication (3.45.11; 3.48.5: *vindicare in libertatem*) parallels, as Vasaly points out, late Republican and early Imperial associations of the defense of *libertas* with the defense "of the *libertas* of the state as a whole."[79] Verginia, thus, sparks a response to the loss of institutional protections associated with liberty, most notably the loss of the power of the tribunes and the right of appeal (3.48.9). The people come to recognize their own vulnerability to the private desires of a few. "The wildest excitement prevailed amongst the people," Livy notes, "occasioned in part by the atrocity of the crime, in part by the hope of improving the opportunity to regain their liberty" (3.49.1). The *populus* and leaders of the *populus* now join together, forcing back the lictors, and drowning out with noise Appius' voice until he is forced to sneak out of the Forum (3.49.6). The reestablished institutional protections become like a "shield," protecting even the weakest from the encroachment of others through the equal application of laws and judgment (3.53.9).

As with Brutus, and suggestive of the historian's task, Verginius in turn arouses those who were not present by telling of the event. Covered in gore, Verginius "drew the attention" of his fellow soldiers back in camp and "aroused greater commotion" than in the city (3.50.2–3). There he warns them that "the lust of Appius Claudius had not been extinguished," and that the calamity should be a warning (*documentum*) to protect against "similar wrongs" (3.50.7). The crowd responds with shouts that they will not fail his suffering or his liberty (3.50.10). Even then, those who come with Verginius go about to the crowd and tell them

---

[79] Vasaly 1987, 221.

how much worse the event would have appeared if they could have seen it instead of just hearing about it (3.50.10). In response, the men arm themselves, abandon the camp, and march on the city to reclaim their liberty (3.50.13).

Two notes follow this episode. First, Livy associates *concordia* with the restoration of tribunician power (3.52.2; 3.54.7). Reacting against the continued authority of the *decemviri*, the plebs secede for a second time (342 BCE). Absent the people, however tumultuous they may be at times, the city is emptied of anything that animates it. With the second secession of the plebs, the city stands as abandoned, desolate, and lonely (3.52.5). The city, thus, is reanimated only with the strengthening of the tribunes and the restoration of the principle of sacrosanctity and the right of appeal by way of the *leges Valeria et Horatia* (3.55.4–7). Second, Verginius opposes the right of Appius Claudius to appeal to the people, claiming that he is beyond the laws of "citizens and men" (3.61.1). But the denial of a public appeal, even when earlier appeals to the people had endangered the Republic, runs contrary to the liberty that is being reclaimed and invites precisely the hiddenness that allows rumors, resentments, and recriminations to go unchecked. The *decemviri* affair becomes a case study in the critical role of publicness in the maintenance of felt meanings. The *decemviri* did not create faction; they gave it private recourse by transforming public institutions into instruments of private desire. The result – and that result plays itself out in the end of the Republic – was the dissipation of the animating spirit of the community.

CAMILLUS: REANIMATING POLITICAL VISION

Both Plato and Aristotle provide compelling, albeit dramatically different, visions of political life. And they also provide insightful analyses of the forces of corruption. But neither of them indicates how to reverse those forces and restore a community. When Plato traces the inevitable decay of his republic, he is left with little recourse except the Myth of Er by which individuals, more than communities, can be redeemed. And while Aristotle points to the ways in which habits of virtue are initially formed through education and cultivated through the activities of ruling and being ruled, he has little to say about how one reverses the trajectory when what is inculcated are habits of corruption.

Livy locates this possibility of restoration in the Roman idea of multiple founders. Romulus is a founder. The subsequent kings are successive founders. Brutus is a founder. And so, too, is Camillus.[80] These successive founders are each engaged in the construction not of a utopia but of a world that is recognized again. They reanimate political vision by building on a past that had receded in memory.

Rome, in Livy's story of the siege of the Capitol by the Gauls, had become unrecognizable. The Romans had become so corrupt that they began to resemble the Gauls whose intemperate disposition was attributable to their damp and cold climate (see 5.33.11; 5.48.3).[81] The reversal of the Gauls and Romans is known well enough: The Gauls display the strategic acumen of the Romans and the Romans become as impatient, rash, and careless as the Gauls once were.[82] The Battle of Allia becomes a turning point in which the Roman army is routed, and the surviving soldiers flee back to the Capitol where they watch as the Gauls ransack the city (likely 387 BCE).

The episode is revealing of the assumptions that guide Livy's political thought. The question is not whether reason rules, but which animating dispositions orient political action: What seizes one's attention? As Ogilvie notes, Livy gives the occupation of Rome "an original treatment by stressing not so much the events as the impression of the

---

[80] So too for Livy, as Miles suggests, is Augustus a founder (1995, 132–33; see Livy 4.20.7). Scholars have generally, and rightly, emphasized the religious aspects of the Camillus legend. See Ogilvie 1965, 626; Dumézil 1980; Feldherr 1998, 79–81. On the fashioning of the Camillus legend, see Gaertner 2008, who rejects a deliberate Augustan refashioning by Livy. On the role of the Camillus legend in the late Republic, especially in Cicero's (and possibly Pompeius and Caesar's) self-fashioning as a second Camillus, see Gaertner 2008.

[81] See Balsdon 1979, 65; Ogilvie 1965, 727–29.

[82] Traditional view of Gauls: 5.33.11; 5.37.4–5, 8; 5.48.3; rashness of Romans: 5.36.1; 5.37.3; 5.37.7; 5.38.1; 5.38.5; 5.38.7–8; temperance of Gauls: 5.38.3–4; 5.39.1; 5.41.4. Luce notes that Livy's account differs from those in Diodorus and Plutarch by emphasizing the guilt of all elements of Roman society, not just the Fabii (1971, 277). On the Gauls as an "ethnographical mirror," following François Hartog, see Kraus 1994b, 279.

participants."[83] For Livy, the grandeur of Rome had become conflated with possessions, glory with greed, and discipline with wantonness. The problem with these dispositions is that they are impatient: They lead one to grab for what immediately feels good or seems good and to avoid that which does not (regarding military training and preparation, see 5.6.2; 5.6.8). The Roman political arena had become a circus in which little is demanded of the participants other than to sate their desires. But now the people are witnesses to "the pageant of their dying country" (5.42.4).

An untrained mind cannot sort out what is important and unimportant and cannot connect impulses or organize meanings. Thus, the Roman minds that are in disarray are unable to grasp (*concipere*) or to "stand fast" (*constare*) (5.42.3) in the barrage of stimuli: the shouting of the Gauls, the cries of lament by women and children, and the burning and crashing of buildings (5.42.4).[84] Turning this way and that, the Romans are unable to grasp all that is happening. But the occurrence of the same events each day conditions the soul so that "like men grown used to grief, they ceased to feel their own misfortunes" and began with resolve to look to their weapons as "their only remaining hope" (5.42.8). All that moved people before – power, wealth, luxury – was in rubble, reducing the animating source of action to one fundamental impulse: liberty, which appeared in its most elemental and visual form, as a hill, "however small and naked" (5.42.8).

In this exercise of endurance that accompanies the blockade by the Gauls, we see the reversal of trajectories as the Romans, reanimated by the sight of plunder, begin to remember their strength and resolve. The Gauls become "careless" with their success, not unlike the Romans before (5.44.6). The Romans who had been "wanderers" since the capture of the city begin to reassemble at Veii, gathering strength in the process (5.46.5). Furthermore, "the place itself reminded men of Camillus," recalling Romulus' own love and place and pointing to a reversal of their thanklessness for Camillus' past services (5.46.6; 5.44.2). Seeking now a leader, the men at Veii consent to recall Camillus from exile. He arrives just as the Romans are about to ransom their lives. Directing their

---

[83] Ogilvie 1965, 727.   [84] Ogilvie 1965, 727. See Williams 1955, 229.

eyes to the temples, families, native soil, and "the hideous marks of war," which recalls their earlier gaze as they watched the city burn, Camillus calls upon them "to defend, recover, or avenge" their loss (5.49.3).

After the defeat of the Gauls, Camillus has to turn his attention to persuading the plebs to remain in Rome rather than migrate to Veii where there is the allure of wealth.[85] Camillus must act as a "second Founder" (5.49.7), not only rebuilding a city but also creating order from disorder by training and reanimating political vision. This vision is constituted by felt meanings, which are tied most obviously to traditions that lend some familiarity and affective relationship to the recollections of places, spaces, objects, legends, institutions, beliefs, individuals, and families. As Viroli writes, in describing Roman patriotism, love of country "is an attachment not to abstract institutions and rights, but to the institutions and the rights that citizens feel as being theirs because they preserve and enjoy them through their service."[86] If Rome were only a place, then the community could as easily migrate to Veii. But Rome is more than a place: It is something formed on sacred foundations (5.51.4) and handed down and reaffirmed through state and family rituals that are tied to the place (5.52.2–3, 7, 8). Playing upon a Roman sense of military renown, Camillus reminds the people that deserting Rome will accomplish what no enemy had been able to do: leave Rome empty and the enemy city full (5.51.3; 5.53.5). Camillus, furthermore, taps into a deeper set of felt meanings that have been overshadowed by interest. Why was Rome defended (5.51.3)? Why were sacred rites observed (5.52.12)? Can you "stomach" the outrage of our enemies inhabiting Rome (5.53.7)?

The city had been made into a wilderness, Camillus observes (5.53.1). But it is a wilderness that recalls the original founding. "Our ancestors, refugees and herdsmen, at a time when there was nothing in this region but forests and marshes, built quickly a new City," Camillus reminds his audience (5.53.9). Thus, Camillus summons to his audience's mind the land that was "familiar" to their "eyes," moving them in their own affection toward the city (5.54.3; also 5.55.1).[87] Like Camillus, Livy

---

[85] On avarice as a theme of Book 5, see Miles 1986.   [86] Viroli 1998, 150.
[87] See, for example, Hölkeskamp 2004, 138–68, on the role of visual monuments in the cultural memory (*kulturelles Gedächtnis*) of the Roman republic.

relentlessly casts his audience's gaze outward – to the bodies of Lucretia and Verginia, to the vacant Forum, and to the ruins of Rome. In the recollection of loss, one may initially react by thinking about one's own private grievances and interests. But individual loss can give way to a greater sense of collective loss as these images summon a set of affections that bind oneself to the city. Felt meanings, most of all, have the power to animate: to overturn tyranny, to establish liberty, to resist corruption, and, like Camillus, to build a city again.

SECURING AN IMPERIAL LANDSCAPE: MYTHS OF INCLUSION

The sacking of Rome raises a fundamental question about the animating meanings that orient and unite the young Roman republic. Camillus' vision of a repopulated Rome rests on addressing the alienation of the plebs from any sense of shared purpose or shared role in the future of the Republic. Livy's account of the Second Punic War (218–202 BCE) fought against Carthage inquires more broadly into the foundation of empire. In the centuries leading up to the Second Punic War, Rome had expanded steadily through its relationships with surrounding territories: a defensive alliance with surrounding cities to form the Latin League; struggles with these cities to establish supremacy; wars and the annexation of the Etruscan territory to the north and west; colonization; the extension of their power through the rest of peninsular Italy through conquests and alliances; and then expansion into Sicily, the Iberian peninsula, and Gaul.[88]

Livy directs his reader in the preface to think about Rome's imperial power (*imperium*), which grew in peace and war (*domi militiaeque*) (pref. 9). *Imperium* means most simply the power to command, though there are two interconnected notions of *imperium* that develop over time. Initially, *imperium* is associated with the civil, military, and religious authority of magistrates: the right to issue orders and command armies

---

[88] See Lintott 1993, 5–6.

and an associated power to ask for and interpret signs from the gods (or *auspicium*).[89] But the meaning of *imperium* also takes on "an increasingly concrete, territorial sense."[90] The two meanings are connected: Rome expands by virtue of the power of individuals to wage war on behalf of the state. But imperial power comes to be vested in more than an individual; it becomes associated after Sulla with the *res publica* and the people of Rome as a form of territorial control.[91]

The boundaries of early Roman *imperium* were uncertain, consisting of provinces directly administered by Roman officials, allied kingdoms, and free cities, each with different forms of administration, relationship to Rome, power, and freedom.[92] However varied may have been the terms of inclusion, the *socii et amici* (allies and friends) were contributors to, more than equal sharers in, Roman power. Thus, in 340 BCE when Annius, recalling the manpower the Latin League contributes to the Roman army, calls for an equal governing share with the Romans (8.5.6), he is met with the outraged reaction of Titus Manlius. Alluding to the religious authority of the magistrate, Titus Manlius, severe even by Roman standards, asks, "Shall you behold, O Jupiter, alien (*peregrinus*) counsels and an alien (*peregrinus*) senate in the consecrated temple, yourself overpowered and taken captive" (8.5.8, trans. modified)? Over a century later, Spurius Carvilius suggests, out of concern with the decimation of the Roman state during the Second Punic War, that citizenship be given to two senators from each of the Latin states, from whom some would be chosen into the senate to replace the deceased (23.22.5). Not surprisingly, the idea is seen as potentially disastrous. Quintus Fabius Maximus admonishes Spurius Carvilius for raising the issue "in the midst of such unsettled feeling and wavering loyalty among the allies" (*suspensos sociorum animos incertamque fidem*) (23.22.8).

The discussion could be suppressed but not the unsettledness (which would come to a violent head in the Social War [91–88 BCE], fought between Rome and the *socii*). At the heart of Roman *imperium* is a tension: Its power, magnified as it extended across the earth, dissipated as it

---

[89] Richardson 1991, 2; Feldherr 1998, 53; Drogula 2007. Also see Chapt. 1: Cicero.
[90] Richardson 1991, 1.   [91] Richardson 1991, 5.
[92] See especially Lintott 1993, 22–42.

radiated outward from the center. Conquering and then defending territories exhausts manpower and wealth (22.32.5). And felt attachments grow weaker the farther from the center one was. This weakness of these attachments manifests itself in two guises: as the questionable loyalty of communities on the periphery and as the waning memory of authority of those in the battlefield. As Rome becomes more enfeebled (22.8.4), it has to face the haunting question: "Who will fight for us and why?" The answer for Livy lies in the creation of myths of inclusion by which (building on earlier Roman traditions) marginal groups are made participants in *exempla* that connect Rome's republican past to its imperial future. As it turns out, the real myth is not whether the events occurred or not, but that the idea of inclusion far exceeded its reality.

Hannibal, the Carthaginian military commander, aims directly at peeling away the periphery by altering the transactional cost of loyalty to the center. In a world defined most of all by honor, Hannibal seeks to contend with Rome for "honour and dominion" so that others will be compelled to "yield to his own good fortune and valour" (22.57.3).[93] He does this variously by terrorizing enemies (22.4.1; 22.6.12; 22.7.6; 22.13.11), disgracing the Romans (22.6.9; 22.14.6), and favorably treating Rome's allies. After the battle of Trasumennus (and later after Cannae), for example, Hannibal frees the captured Latins while keeping the Romans as prisoners (22.7.5; 22.57.1 after Cannae). Hannibal also saves Fabius', the Roman dictator's, house, while razing the rest of the countryside in the attempt to further sow the seeds of discontent (22.23.4). As Hannibal penetrates further into Italy, the allies "wavered" as they "lost all hope of the empire (*desperaverant de imperio*)" (22.61.10).

Even among Roman citizens on the battlefield the memory of authority is losing hold (22.11.6). Fabius, for example, faces near "sedition" from his troops when he refuses to directly engage the enemy (22.14.1). Minucius Rufus, Fabius' surbordinate as master of the horse, fuels the seditious talk: "Violent and hasty in his opinions and of unbridled tongue, he spoke of Fabius – at first in the hearing of a few, but after a time quite openly to everybody – not as deliberate but as slothful, not as

---

[93] On honor as the basis of transactions, see Lendon 1997.

cautious but as timid, inventing faults that neighboured on his virtues; and exalted himself by disparaging his superior – an infamous practice, which has grown in favour from the all too great prosperity of many who have followed it" (22.12.12). Minucius, drawing a negative (and incorrect) comparison of Fabius to Camillus (as well as to Papirius and the Samnites, and to Lutatius and the Carthaginians in the First Punic War), decries the seeming timidity of Fabius to engage in fighting even with the disgraceful spectacle of a colony destroyed (22.14.4–14). If Camillus had acted similarly, Minucius continues, then Rome would have been destroyed by the Gauls. The issue is not just one of a commander becoming over-anxious; it is of authority inverted. Marcus Metilius, tribune of the plebs, calls for Marcus Minucius to share equal power with Fabius. Gaius Terentius Varro, who had risen to prominence by attacking the reputations of better men, seeks to take advantage of Fabius' unpopularity and successfully sponsors a bill to make Minucius' *imperium* equal to the dictator's. And Minucius, having claimed a victory that, in fact, cost thousands of lives and little gain, has become insufferable. Livy writes how Fabius "had by vote of the people been reduced to a level – the superior with his subordinate, the dictator with the master of the horse; and this action, to which history could afford no parallel, had been taken in that very state in which masters of the horse had been used to tremble and shudder at the rods and axes of the dictator" (22.27.3).

The devastating defeat at Cannae brings these issues of a common animating impulse to a head. Despite Livy's hopeful claim that the allies did not waver in their loyalty because Roman rule had been just and temperate (22.13.11), after Cannae the common people in Capua begin to disparage Roman *imperium*, "for which there used to be some respect" (23.4.6). The Sardinians had grown weary of the heavy tribute and requisitions of grain by the Romans (23.32.9). Soldiers on the battlefield betray their own *exempla*, choosing surrender rather than courageous battle. Even the city is beset with "terror and confusion," comparable to the confusion that follows the seizure of Rome by the Gauls (22.54.8; see earlier 22.7.6).

The immediate concern is to impose order within the city. Quintus Fabius Maximus acts immediately to control movement within the city, as well as rumors, incorrect information, and excessive expressions of lamentation (22.55.6–8). As Jaeger notes, "The restoration of order moves outward from the interior of the mourning households to the entire area enclosed by the city walls, for the entire urban population, nor just the women, must be restrained."[94] The task, Jaeger continues, is to control the emotions of panic and fear of those within the walls of the city, and then redirect the memory of Cannae by associating its aftermath with the restoration of civic order.[95] But disorder within the city is not the only problem; continuing the trajectory suggested by Jaeger, Rome must also address the disarray in the periphery resulting from the loss of any common, animating impulse.

We see this loss of felt meanings played out among both allies and soldiers in the field. Among the allies, Capua, a city in Campania, illustrates the tenuousness of extending these meanings beyond the city. Seeing the opportunity to assert its *imperium* on the Italian peninsula (23.6.1), and having their request to share power equally with the Romans rejected, both the people and the senate (led by Pacuvius Calavius) of Capua revolt (23.6.4). The long history of their alliance – originating in Campania looking to Rome for protection against the Samnites in the fourth century, ending with Roman control of Campania after the Second Samnite War (326–304 BCE) (23.5.8), and reinforced through a share of citizenship (23.5.9) and intermarriage (23.4.7) – "seemed to all to have been blotted out (*deletum*)" (23.6.3). Capua thus sends an embassy to Hannibal to establish an alliance that would give Campania complete independence (23.7.1–2). They even seize and kill Roman citizens in the city (23.7.3). Only Decius Magius, recalling the bad *exempla* of the rule of Pyrrhus over the Tarentines, and the son of Pacuvius Calavius, who remains loyal to Rome, reject the alliance and the admission of the garrison from Carthage into the city (23.7.5).

Capua eventually succumbs to a Roman blockade (211 BCE), with Hannibal ultimately abandoning efforts to defend the city. What is interesting is what Rome decides to do: It creates an "unfounding." If we understand the recollection of foundings as aimed at recalling the animating purposes that orient a community, then Rome seeks to undo

---

[94] Jaeger 1997, 101–2.   [95] See Jaeger 1997, 100–3.

that process. They do not do this, as some of the leaders of the revolt fear, by literally and figuratively leveling even its foundations so that no memory of its origins would be remembered, as they do with Alba (and will do with Carthage) (26.13.16). Rome decides to leave intact the "innocent buildings" (26.16.12). Reversing the process of populating a city, Rome scatters the multitude of citizens "with no hope of a return" (26.16.11). Rome peoples the city as a domicile for farmers, resident aliens, freedmen, tradesmen, and artisans (26.16.8), but without a political body (*corpus nullum civitatis*). Lacking a senate, a council of plebs, and magistrates, the people have no shared thing between them (*nullius rei inter se sociam*) and thus would be incapable of agreement (*consensus*) (26.16.10). In this case Rome secures the imperial landscape by imprinting on its allies a memory of the power (*vis*) Rome has in its ability to grant clemency, exact punishment, render helpless its enemies, and unmake a city (26.16.13).

Vis, as a form of power, is incomplete. *Vis*, which is associated with Roman vigor, is a mechanism by which Rome conquers territories and enforces its will on others. That there is something more is suggested by what Rome seeks to destroy in Capua: namely, the political institutions by which collective power and purpose are fostered. And as it destroys the public things that people share in Capua, thus depriving politics of its animating source, so it must also restore and extend those things so that new groups will share in the felt meanings of Rome. The debate about what to do with the armies in the aftermath of Cannae reveals the struggle to define and extend a different type of power, one that generates belief in what it means to be Roman.

Livy reveals both the loss of and the possibility of renewing and extending the animating meanings of Roman politics in the debate about whether to ransom back the surviving soldiers of Cannae. The leader of the envoy to the Roman prisoners captured at Cannae, pleading to the senate to ransom them from Hannibal, recalls the examples of the Roman ancestors ransoming prisoners from the Gauls and from Pyrrhus in the Pyrrhic War (280–75 BCE). The leader speaks to the loss of honor: "Am I to come back to my country not reckoned to be worth three hundred pieces" (22.59.18)? In a scene reminiscent of the appeal by the Sabine women to spare their fathers and bothers (1.13.2), the assembled people, including the women, plead with the senators to ransom "their sons, their brothers, and their kinsmen" (22.59.1). Although strong enough to move the Romans to incorporate the foreign Sabines, the appeal is not sufficient to bring the Roman citizens back home.

Titus Manlius Torquatus responds, recasting the *exempla* of the past and the lessons to be learned. The surviving soldiers at Cannae betray what it means to be Roman by failing to be "move[d]" by the "brave examples" of those slaughtered all around them (22.60.14). Torquatus continues, these men "long" for their country at the wrong time, after they have lost their freedom (22.60.15). "Long for your country, while you are free and untainted. No, rather, long for it while it *is* your country, while you live as its citizens (*Liberi atque incolumes desiderate patriam; immo desiderate, dum patria est, dum cives eius estis*)" (22.60.15, trans. modified). The soldiers, furthermore, betray the authority of Rome by not obeying Publius Sempronius, but by listening to Hannibal (22.60.16). These felt meanings come to define citizenship: Absent such a longing, the men "have forfeited [their] status, lost [their] civic rights (*iure civium*), been made slaves of the Carthaginians" (22.60.15). A Rome composed of such citizens, Torquatus continues, would no longer be Rome (22.60.18).

Rome – not only the city, but as it extends into the periphery – must now be reconstituted. It must be refounded as an empire, which Livy models after both Romulus and Camillus. The newly constituted troops are comprised not of the best men, but of slaves (22.57.11–12), criminals, and debtors who, as though Romulus were releasing them from their asylum, will now be given citizenship (23.14.2–4). The men are armed with Gallic spoils from the triumph of Gaius Flaminius. The importance of the weapons is that they compensate for this undistinguished group; they become, as Jaeger suggests, "living reminders of past victories."[96] But there is more at stake. Rome's future does not lie with weapons from the past; it rests on whether Rome can create a common animating impulse from an increasingly diverse population that extends to its periphery.

---

[96] Jaeger 1997, 103.

SECURING AN IMPERIAL LANDSCAPE: MYTHS OF INCLUSION

The struggle of Tiberius Sempronius Gracchus, the consular head of this army, to craft a community in the field reveals the tension at the heart of Roman identity: Its past points to both hierarchies of distinction and birth (remembered in the arms the slaves carry) and the continual need to assimilate new, and not necessarily distinguished, groups into these hierarchies.[97] That is, the terms for inclusion must be continually renewed. Gracchus trains the new men to "recognize" their own ranks in the battlefield (23.35.6). And he breaks down old distinctions to create new ones. Thus, he instructs the legates and tribunes that no reproach for one's previous status can be the cause of discord between the classes: Old soldiers mix with new, freemen with slaves. Everyone whom Rome entrusts with arms will be considered "sufficiently honoured and well-born" (23.35.8). These precepts, given and followed with care, unite the men in *concordia* "so that it was almost forgotten from what status each man had been made a soldier" (23.35.9). One memory is built on another to incorporate new groups into a Roman identity.

Part of the adaptability of the Roman political system lies paradoxically in its hierarchical nature. For a more egalitarian community, such as democratic Athens, membership is an all-or-nothing proposition: Individuals are either inside or outside the protections of the community. But Rome has an elaborate array of distinctions by which groups can be included: the granting of citizenship (with differential access to power), the right to migrate, and the granting of private rights such as intermarriage, inheritance, and the ownership of Roman land.[98] Thus, after the victory at Beneventum, Graachus does two things. First, he fulfills his public promise (*fide publica*) by making the slaves who have fought "all equals by the right of freedom" (24.16.11). But among citizens there are still distinctions. So, after recognizing the equality of freedom, Graachus

---

[97] Kraus points to how Livy "constructs an ever-expanding narrative of ever-expanding power in which descendants learn from ancestors, younger generals from older ones, while the mechanism of the state perpetuates similarity through difference in its series of repeating annual magistracies" (1998, 281; see also Pittenger 2008, 288–91 on triumphs). My suggestion, and it is not contrary to what Kraus is saying, is that part of Livy's narrative repetition involves redefining (and not just reproducing) Roman authority relations.

[98] See Champion, in Hammer, chapt. 19 (forthcoming).

then, fearing the "loss of every distinction between valour and cowardice," marks those who acted cowardly by requiring that they stand while eating and drinking during their time in service (24.16.12). The scene of the feast hosted by the people of Beneventum is painted in the Temple of Liberty: slaves marked as equals by their liberty caps, but distinctions retained by the representation of some standing and some sitting.

The necessity of maintaining some fluidity within Roman society is reinforced in Spain where Gnaeus Scipio and Publius Scipio, brothers commanding separate armies, are killed. Only the leadership of Lucius Marcius, a man whose "station" is nowhere near as noteworthy as the Scipio line (25.37.2), restores the shattered armies. His *auctoritas* comes not from his birth but from his training (under Gnaeus Scipio), his virtue, and his recognition by others that he was elected as commander (25.37.5–6). The soldiers carry out his *imperium* with renewed energy (25.37.7).

Important for the Roman conception of power is its generative capacity: Power can be multiplied "to a potentially infinite number of persons."[99] The advantage of Rome over the singular greatness of Alexander, as Livy suggests, lay in the ability of Rome to continually produce soldiers and commanders with ability and valor (9.17.3). Livy's *History* both reflects on and engages in this act of generation.

---

[99] Richardson 1991, 5.

6 SENECA AND JURISDICTION

Seneca the Younger (Lucius Annaeus Seneca, ca 4 BCE – 65 CE), more than Virgil or Livy, participated in the principate. Elected to the quaestorship, Seneca rose to prominence in his practice of law, his oratorical skills earning the ire of Caligula (Dio 59.19.7–8) and his senatorial career interrupted by his exile to Corsica in 41 CE by Claudius on the charge of adultery with Julia Livilla (Caligula's sister). In 49 CE, at the request of Agrippina the Younger (another sister of Caligula and fourth wife incestuously married to Claudius), Seneca was recalled to tutor the twelve-year-old Nero in rhetoric while also gaining the praetorship (by now an imperial administrative position). Agrippina the Younger would engineer Nero's rise. Seneca would go on to advise the sixteen-year-old new emperor, Nero, for the first eight years of his rule. As Seneca's own influence waned, he requested retirement from his service, offering to turn over the fortune he had amassed (Tac. *Ann.* 14.53–56). The offer was refused, so Seneca spent less and less time in Rome, retreating but unable to escape Nero's reach. He was sentenced to death (forced to commit suicide) after being implicated in the Pisonian conspiracy, a plot to kill Nero, though one that likely did not include Seneca.

It is not hard to explain why Seneca would serve as the *amicus* of the new *princeps*. He would likely have been killed if he refused (Juvenal 5.109). His role allowed him to exhibit his own skills in crafting speeches and hopefully shaping the young leader. He was able, at least for a while, to moderate the "trend toward slaughter" under the early Nero (Tac. *Ann.* 13.2.1). And, in a culture that had always been suspicious of philosophy, Seneca could demonstrate, as he did in one of his early speeches of Nero's reign, that Stoicism was not antithetical to politics (*De clem.* 2.4.2–3).[1]

Despite this proximity to the principate, though, Seneca's contributions to political thought are less clear. Only with great difficulty can one discern in his philosophic works references to contemporaneous events. In fact, his *Epistles* are frequently grouped with his tragedies as literary inventions.[2] Furthermore, it is difficult to figure out how Seneca's philosophical principles inform his political life. Seneca's declaration in *De clementia* (55 or 56 CE) that Nero inherited a state "unstained by blood" (*De clem.* 1.11.3; also 1.1.5), spoken in the wake of Nero's murder of Brittanicus in 55 BCE, Claudius' legitimate son and heir, confirms Griffin's understated judgment of Seneca as never a man of "rigid principle" (also Tac. *Ann.* 13.15.3–5).[3] Griffin, in assessing Seneca's role in Nero's court, writes, "From the start, Seneca assumed responsibility for promoting the ideology of the new regime."[4] Viewed against his actions, Seneca's writings can come across as uncritical, hypocritical, or self-justificatory (see Dio 61.10.2–6).[5] Finally, Seneca in seen as joining so many other Stoics in calling for a withdrawal from political life. Sabine, in his influential interpretation of political thought, sees Seneca as turning away from worldly interests and inward toward "spiritual

---

[1] See Griffin 1976, 140–41.
[2] On the *Epistles* as literary constructs (though Lucilius likely real), see von Albrecht 1989, 114, n. 25; Bourgery 1911; Griffin 1976, p. 349–55, 416–19; Leeman 1951; Maurach 1970, 21; Griffin 1988, 136; Too 1994; Nussbaum 1994, 337; Edwards 1999; Inwood 2005, 346–47. Those seeing historicity (and growing personal relationship with Lucilius) of the *Epistles*: Albertini 1923, 136–46; Grimal 1978, 155–64, 315–27; Müller 1980, 139–42; Wilson 2001.
[3] Griffin 1976, 135. See also Sandbach 1975, 161–62. For a defense of Seneca's own sincerity in the practice of his ethics as proclaimed in the *Epistles*, see Andrews 1930.
[4] Griffin 1976, 133.
[5] Uncritical: Veyne 1987, 45; 2003, 13, 227–30; Brown 1987, 248–51; unphilosophical: Strozier 2002, 162 ("not particularly analytic"); "vapid": Henry and Walker 1963, 108–9; hypocritical: Coleman 1974, 286, n.2; Sandbach 1975, 162; Too 1994; aristocratic: Habinek 1992 = 1998; self-justificatory: Sullivan 1985, 144.

interests."⁶ Littlewood, speaking generally about Seneca's writings, interprets Seneca's declamations of "disengagement and withdrawal from an irredeemably corrupt world" as characteristic of Seneca's "isolationist brand of Stoicism."⁷ By "abandoning the world, the shared locus of human activity and human meaning," Seneca, as Littlewood concludes, "abandoned any conceptual space" for political definition.⁸

The Stoics did talk about politics, though extracting something like political thought from the fragments we have has not always been easy. Both Zeno and Chrysippus wrote their versions of Plato's *Republic*, though even the most identifiable aspect of Stoic politics, the community of sages, remains dramatically incomplete. In any case, by the time we get to Seneca, there is little talk of an exclusive community of the sages. Nor is there much discussion of any other type of political system. Seneca himself notes that the Stoics are better known for their caution (*cautio*) than their courage (*Ep.* 22.7), advising others to avoid provoking the anger of those in power (*Ep.* 14.7) or even taking sides (*Ep.* 14.13). For good reason scholars frequently see the Stoics generally, and Seneca specifically, as substituting morality for politics.

I do not want to understate the interior aspects of Seneca's writings. But I want to suggest that there is a political dimension to this interiority that operates at the intersection of a Roman and Stoic conception of jurisdiction. By jurisdiction I am referring to the right and power to exercise authority over or make judgments about something. Romans were enmeshed in a complex array of overlapping jurisdictions. Law defined one's status: free or slave; type of freedom (either by birth or by

---

⁶ Sabine 1937, 176. Sabine essentially interprets Seneca as paralleling, even anticipating, Christian thought.

⁷ Littlewood 2004, 16. See also Strozier 2002, 164 (interiority as protection from world), 169; Fitch and McElduff 2002, 20; Edwards 1997, 24 (inwards); Cooper and Procopé 1995, xxv–xxvi ("apolitical" and "an inward looking moralist"); Griffin 1976, 8 (surveying scholarship); I. Hadot 1969, 80–1; Momigliano 1969 (orig. 1950), 253, 255 ("His best, most profound, words were about private virtues and intimate feelings"); Ferguson 1958, 137.

⁸ Littlewood 2004, 44. *The Cambridge Companion to the Stoics* (2003), for example, contains no chapter on politics. Seneca as focused on individual morality, see Reydams-Schils 2005, 85; Wolin 2004, 85; Griffin 1976, 210; Coleman 1974, 289: "novel form of moral essay"; I. Hadot 1969, 80–84.

grant of freedom from slavery); type of citizenship (Roman, Latin, or *peregrinus*); independence of the citizen; and of those who were independent, whether they were under guardianship, caretakership, or neither.[9] Law also defined a host of attendant rights and obligations: taxation, marriage, inheritance, ownership, commerce, political office, military service, and civil protections.[10] Seneca continually invokes these juridical aspects of Roman life in his own thought: of common law, statute, guardianship, judgment, imperial decree, imperial edicts, injury, arbiter, authority, law, and duty.[11]

From a Stoic perspective, jurisdiction is tied back to natural law (*lex naturae*; also referred to as *koinos logos*), the organizing basis of nature that unifies all the structures and events of the cosmos.[12] An understanding of what one should do must start with and be informed by not just the limits that nature provides but also how one is constituted (which

---

[9] See Crook 1967, 36; Lintott 1993, 161–67 on citizenship.
[10] On Roman law and society, see Crook 1967 and Johnston 1999.
[11] Habinek, for example, sees Seneca's writings as maintaining the "fixity and stratification of the Roman social system" (1998, 137). Griffin, more sympathetically, contends that Seneca sought to raise "to the level of theory the concepts and standards of Roman society" (2000, 534; also Inwood 1995: provide moral foundation to traditional ethic). Roller argues that Seneca is seeking to ultimately displace an aristocratic ethos with Stoic ethics (Roller 2001, 77–88). Appearances of political language include *ius*: Sen. *Ep.* 3.3 (applied to friendship), 18.1 (license is law), 36.6 (fortune has no jurisdiction), 39.3 (fortune has no jurisdiction), 47.14 (slaves allowed to pronounce judgment), 48.3 (rights of humanity), 57.3 (and fortune), 65.22 (soul bring quarrels to tribunal), 107.6 (apply law to self), 113.30 (push limits of empire), 123.16 (death); statute: see Inwood 2004 and Sen. *Ep.* 63.2, 86.2, 106.2; guardianship: *Ep.* 25.6; judgment: see Düll 1976, 371–77; Inwood 2004, 2005, 152–55; decree: *Ep.* 18.11; edicts: 48.10; 117.30; injury: *Ep.* 47.20; duty: *Ep.* 3.2; 19.5; 19.8; 20.2; 22.3; 22.7; 45.2; 71.28; 74.20; 77.19; 78.20; 86.10; 90.5; 93.4; 94.5; 94.33; 94.37; 95.41 (human relations generally); 99.6,19; 101.1, 3; 102.6; 103.3; 114.23; 120.2; 120.11; 122.2; 122.3; arbiter: *De ben.* 3.7.5; authority: *Ep.* 11.9; 25.6; 29.3; 30.7; 55.5; 71.7; 94.27; 115.3; court proceedings: *De ot.* 1.17.7–18.1; *De ira* 3.5.3. Also 307–15 below.
[12] See, for example, Sen. *De prov.* 1.3; 5.7; *De ben.* 4.7.1; *Ep.* 65.12; DL 7.135, 139, 156. Thus, all branches of philosophic knowledge – logic, ethics, and physics – blend together (DL 7.40). For a helpful discussion of the range of ways in which natural law is used in Stoicism generally and Seneca specifically, see Inwood 2005, 224–48; also Sen. *De ira* 2.27.2; *De prov.* 1.2; 5.6–7 (obedient to law); *Ep.* 30.11 (equitable); 65.19 (order); 77.12 (fixed); 117.19; 101.7; 107.6–12; 123.16; *Nat. quaest.* 3.15.3, 3.16.4, 3.29.3, 3.29.7; *Cons. Helv.* 6.8).

will figure prominently in our nature as social beings).[13] One's recognition of and obedience to such laws underlies the Stoic notion of piety and, for Seneca, tranquility (Sen. *Ep.* 92.3; also *De ira* 3.6.1; Stob. 2.7.5b12 P = *SVF* 3.604: piety). By way of reason one evaluates what is to be sought and avoided, recognizes what is under and not under one's control, and endures when falling under another's power.[14] In our obedience to natural law we are citizens of the cosmic city, which encompasses the entire universe (Sen. *De ot.* 4.1).

In reconciling these two forms of jurisdiction, that of the specific and the cosmic city (Sen. *De ot.* 4.1), the Stoics taught obedience to the jurisdiction of the state since the state, like all events and circumstances, is an expression of nature's purpose.[15] Moreover, since politics is considered an indifferent activity, an activity that does not affect the only true good of human life, moral goodness (*kalon* = *honestum*), nothing the state does can affect one's moral being. The Stoics disagreed, however, about one's involvement in politics. Zeno says that the wise man will engage in politics unless something prevents him (Sen. *De ot.* 3.2). Chrysippus advises not to enter politics if the conditions are not suitable (Sen. *De ot.* 8.1–4). Athenodorus of Tarsus says it is always right to withdraw from politics (Sen. *De tranq.* 3.2). And Stobaeus reports the view of politics as a preferred indifferent (Stob. 2.7.11m P = *SVF* 3.686), one that is consistent with our nature as social beings even if the state is imperfect.

Seneca wrestles with all of these issues, seeing political involvement as consistent with our social nature (Sen. *De ot.* 8.1–4;

---

[13] For a discussion of controversies surrounding the relationship between the Stoic causal universe and freedom (or responsibility), see Bobzien 1998. Whether persuasive or not, the Stoics distinguished between antecedent (external) causes and principal (inner) causes, and identified inner causes as the primary cause of human actions, to salvage a notion of personal responsibility (see Cic. *De fato* 18.41–42).

[14] I take up more fully the Stoic foundation of jurisdiction and judgment in Seneca's thought below. On the relationship between reason and natural law for the Stoics, see also Chapt. 1, 36–38, Chapt. 8, 361–66 (Epictetus), and 371–81 (Marcus Aurelius); On the cosmic city, see Chapt. 1, 42, Chapt. 8, 376–79, and below, 315–20.

[15] Diogenes Laertius reports that Stoics also never relax penalties fixed by law (7.123) or, as Stobaeus reports, show tolerance (Stob. 2.7.11d P = *SVF* 3.640). See Brunt 1975, 9.

De tranq. 3.7), but one in which we can adjust "our effort according as the state shall lend itself to us" (*De tranq.* 5.4; also 4.1).[16] But the problem that Seneca poses runs deeper than this choice. The succession of emperors – Augustus, Tiberius, Caligula, Claudius, and Nero – had fundamentally altered the nature of jurisdiction by organizing the principate increasingly around, and as subordinate to, the will of the sovereign. Against the backdrop of the complex array of laws and rules that regulated the administration of Rome's vast territory was the reality of the principate that, as Seneca writes, was "hampered by no bonds" (*De ben.* 3.7.5).[17] Seneca is writing from his own experience of the principate that witnessed the maleability of the criteria that oriented public conduct. Individuals rose and fell (and sometimes rose again only to fall again), were exiled or executed based on contrived crimes and manipulated trials, or simply murdered on behalf of those responsible for the law.

For the empirical approaches of Seneca and the Stoics, the laws of nature that serve as the basis of value and the impetus for conduct acquire authority over our actions by way of our senses as we observe models, make comparisons, identify patterns, and affirm judgments that form our character. By destroying the stability of these cues, the principate makes one's relationship to the political world and one's relationship to oneself increasingly unrecognizable and unknowable. The result for Seneca is what the Stoics mean by insanity: the breakdown of sense as one must make choices and bear the consequences of those choices in a world in which everything can mean its opposite.[18] More than asking whether to be involved in politics or abstain (and on what basis to

---

[16] On Seneca's view of political involvement, see Griffin 2000, 556–58; Braund 2009, 65–66.

[17] See Lintott 1993, 22, 111–60. On the continuing function of the senate into the second century, see Talbert 1987. Macmullen describes the networks of relationships, more than any impartial procedures, by which "an imperial administration of only a few hundred" could rule an empire (1988, 121). These relationships could provide stability over time. But if they become corrupt or undependable then there is no place else to turn.

[18] The opposite of *mania* (= *insania*) is typically *phronesis* (or sense) (see Graver 2007, 116–20).

abstain), Seneca shows that each choice implicates one in a version of madness, as either an excessive aversion to the world or a desire for it.

Seneca does not abandon a notion of political jurisdiction but redeploys it to restore the boundaries by which one knows oneself and orients oneself to the world. Suggestive of the orienting role jurisdiction plays in Seneca's thought is his declaration, "For it is to the senses that you and yours have entrusted the decision (*arbitrium*) of things to be sought and things to be avoided" (*Ep.* 124.3, trans. modified), learning to refuse to be under the "jurisdiction" (*arbitrium*) ((*De clem.* 1.24.2; *Ep.* 13.1) of that which is alien to us, that which is not akin to us.[19] *Arbitrium*, along with such related legal terms as *iudex, iudicium,* and *iudicare* that figure prominently in Seneca's works, takes on meanings of judgment, authority, and power that are all aspects of jurisdiction.[20] That one has the right and power leads to another question: By what criteria does one exercise jurisdiction? Cicero, for example, shows how Quintus

---

[19] *arbitrium*: *Ep.* 4.8: other yields power of life and death; 17.6: endurance against falling under emperor's power; 71.37: bring passions under our control; 73.10: control of own time; 85.13: endings in our control, and enduring when falling under another's power; 110.20: food and water under another jurisdiction; 124.3: evaluating what is to be sought and avoided.

[20] Inwood notes that one finds in Seneca's use of the language of judging (employing such terms as *iudex, iudicium,* and *iudicare*) "an intriguing, influential, and creative exploitation of this notion in the service of his own moral philosophy" (Inwood 2005, 203). Inwood argues that judgment (*iudicium*) and decision (*arbitrium*) give self-command a character of a mental-event like a courtroom (Inwood 2005, 152–53; see *De ira* 2.22.4). Inwood is addressing a debate about whether Seneca reflects a departure from orthodox Stoicism, particularly in his conception of the will (*voluntas*). Where orthodox Stoicism understands the will as the choices resulting from psychological and physiological causes, such as lax tension of the soul (Chrysippus SVF 3.473, part = LS 65T), Seneca begins to make room for a notion of the will as a more distinct psychological force, one in which wanting has become "a reflective, internalized action" (Inwood 2005, 152). Pohlenz argues for a Senecan emphasis on a vital will, or a will as a distinct psychological force central to moral progress (1948–49, 1.319–20; 1965, 344–46). He is followed by I. Hadot 1969, 162–64; Voelke 1973, 171–79; and Dihle 1982, 134–35, 142 (135: "vague volunteerism"). Rist 1969, 224–30, argues for continuity between Seneca and orthodox Stoicism, though the language is "innovative" in connecting moral character with desires (Rist 1994, 187). Inwood 2005, 132–56, argues that the distinctiveness of Seneca does not lie in *voluntas* but in other indirect aspects of Seneca's thoughts that talk about the association of self-command with self-control (rather than with causation by one's own desires).

Scaevola, the pontifex maximus, would attach great weight to the phrase, "as good faith requires," in his exercise of jurisdiction (*arbitrium*) in deciding the obligations of parties to each other (Cic. *De off*. 3.17.70). Livy has Fabius admonish people for exercising *arbitrium* in war as though they were in peace (Livy 24.45). Jurisdiction gets used beyond simply the context of law, as when Lucretius describes how the *arbitrium* of what lies within individual bodies compels motion in the body (Lucr. 2.281) or when Sulpicius refers to Antonius' claim that an art lies outside the *arbitrium* of opinion (Cic. *De orat*. 1.23.108). For Seneca, to know thyself, the Socratic injunction that finds such resonance with the Stoics, is ultimately understood not as an issue of contemplation or introspection but of jurisdiction. To render a judgment (*iudicium*) that accords with reason (*Ep*. 92.11–13) requires that one restore the boundaries by which one can view oneself.

DE CLEMENTIA AND JURISDICTION

The principate, as we saw in Chapter 4, was increasingly organized around and subordinated to the will of the sovereign. With the rise of Augustus, the initiative associated with the people and the authority associated with the senate "would be carried out under Augustus' *auctoritas*," tying the significance and political meaningfulness of actions increasingly to the approval of the emperor.[21] As Rudich notes, "In appearance, Augustus preserved all traditional institutions intact, but transformed them by and large into channels of personal power while building up alongside them a centralized officialdom of his own."[22] Pliny would comment on how everything depends on the will of one man, a sentiment voiced earlier by Seneca and then by Tacitus.[23] It is as though

---

[21] Galinsky 1996, 13; also Wieacker 2006, 21–28.
[22] Rudich 1993, xvii; also Lintott 1993, 168–74 on the developing role of the emperor in replacing the senate "as the source of benefits" to provincial clients (174).
[23] See Pliny *Ep*. 3.20.12; Sen. *De clem*. 1.5.1; Tac. *Ann*. 1.12.3. Ideology of *corpus imperii*: Goodyear 1972, 180; Häussler 1965, 273–57; Beranger 1953, 218–37. On the visual language that now focused on the image of the emperor, see Zanker 1988.

DE CLEMENTIA AND JURISDICTION

Appius Claudius, in his attempted legal abduction of Verginia, had become the *exemplum* of imperial jurisdiction (see Chapt. 5, 256–57).

We do not see lawlessness. In fact, it is under the principate that one sees the growing prestige of the jurists who, though focused primarily on issues of civil law, issued interpretations of law to magistrates, judges, or private parties, drafted legal documents, and aided litigants in navigating court procedures, eventually working to rationalize the vast workings of imperial law. Augustus would even designate a group of jurists as qualified to issue opinions with the emperor's authority and other jurists would serve in administrative posts.[24] And local systems of law continued to operate or were blended with imperial law, although provincial administration was often corrupt or incompetent and the ability of redress was difficult.[25] But as the importance of magistrates, assemblies, and the senate waned as independent sources of edicts and legislation, a variety of ways were developed by which emperors could create legal rules: administrative orders (*edicta*); judicial decisions on individual cases by the emperor that establish precedents (*decreta*); answers to questions of law submitted by individuals (*rescripta*); and instructions issued by the emperor or his officers (*mandata*).[26] Moreover, through his domestic tribunal "the emperor assumed jurisdiction not only over matters affecting him personally, such as conspiracies, but also over common-law crimes," which he could transfer from ordinary judicial authorities at his discretion.[27] The *princeps* was not bound by any rules that governed criminal procedures. And he could define the offense and the penalty.

Each emperor did not use this jurisdiction in the same way. Augustus employed his jurisdiction to bring order to the empire and arguably to instill a new cultural orientation to Rome. Tiberius (14–37 CE), upon

---

[24] Mousourakis 2007, 101.
[25] On the blending of Roman law and local custom, see Humfress 2013, focusing on the third century CE and after. On provincial administration, see Brunt 1959, 554–558; Griffin 1976, 240–41. What is noteworthy is the reach of the *princeps* into the provinces (Brunt 1959, 556–59). As Brunt writes, in talking about Nero's actions toward the provinces, "The crimes and caprices of an autocrat and his favourites, though at first sight affecting a narrow circle, determined the destinies of millions" (1959, 559).
[26] Mousourakis 2007, 102–10.   [27] Mousourakis 2007, 131.

being elevated to *princeps*, spoke on behalf of the rule of law, often referred public matters to the senate, and seemed genuinely frustrated with the willing subservience of the nobility (see Tacitus' discussion in Chapter 7). So, too, did Claudius (41–54 CE) in succeeding Caligula (37–41 CE), and then Nero (54–68 CE) (Suet. *Nero* 10.1). But in each case, this jurisdiction becomes more arbitrarily employed and the reach of the *princeps* penetrates deeper into all aspects of life. As Griffin writes of Claudius, "One of the worst Claudian abuses was the increase of the Emperor's jurisdiction at the expense of the ordinary tribunals and magistrates," a "passion for litigation" ridiculed by ancient sources for "irregularity in procedure through haste and folly" as well as "encouraging the venality of pleaders by making all cases turn on the influence of advocates with him."[28] Seneca, upon assuming his position in Nero's court, parodies the arbitrariness, cruelty, and excesses of Claudius' reign in *Apocolocyntosis*. Nero, like the emperors who preceded him, promised better: He would rule "according to the principles of Augustus" and would miss no opportunity to demonstrate his *liberalitas* (generosity), *clementia* (mercy), and even his *comitas* (civility) (Suet. *Nero* 10.1; Tac. *Ann.* 13.4.2–5.1; 13.11.2). Seneca even describes Nero as one who sought the return of *leges* to Rome (*De clem.* 1.1.4)

There is at least some plausibility to Seneca's belief that Nero might restore the boundaries of judgment and action. In Tacitus' recounting of Nero's ascension speech to the senate and praetorian guard, written by Seneca, Nero emphasizes the restoration of senatorial prerogatives and the reassertion of the boundary between household and state interests (*Ann.* 13.4.2; also Dio 61.3).[29] Seneca may have hoped for (or sought to assure the public of) a return of law as something to which individuals could appeal and authority could be accountable.[30] And at least early in his reign Nero chose cases that personally concerned him or in which he could demonstrate his diligence, concern with corruption, or clemency.[31] But his appeal to the practice of mercy, unique in Stoic texts, points to the reality of the legal system. Where legal action is bound by procedure,

---

[28] Griffin 1976, 108.   [29] On this hope, see Braund 2009, 11–16.
[30] On *De clementia* as meant to assure the public, see Griffin 1976, 138–41.
[31] Griffin 1976, 110–14.

the emperor is not.[32] Seneca's *De clementia* (55–56 CE), written in the first years of Nero's rule, thus, is an attempt to assert a notion of jurisdiction by way of nature (e.g., 2.7.3).

Seneca's opening line suggests how much jurisdiction had changed. In describing *De clementia* as a "mirror" that will "reveal you to yourself" (1.1.1), Seneca is drawing on a traditional Stoic trope of displaying one before oneself, as well as on the Greco-Roman "mirror of princes" genre of providing advice to kings.[33] But he is also pointing to how nothing except the emperor defines the limits of jurisdiction. As Seneca portrays Nero's conversation with himself:

> Have I of all mortals found favour with Heaven and been chosen to serve on earth as vicar of the gods? I am the arbiter of life and death for the nations [compare to *Ep.* 4.8]; it rests in my power (*in mea manu positum est*) what each man's lot and state shall be; by my lips Fortune proclaims what gift she would bestow on each human being; from my utterance peoples and cities gather reasons for rejoicing; without my favour and grace no part of the wide world can prosper; all those many thousands of swords which my peace restrains will be drawn at my nod; what nations shall be utterly destroyed, which banished, which shall receive the gift of liberty, which have it taken from them, what kings shall become slaves and whose heads shall be crowned with royal honour, what cities shall fall and which shall rise – this it is mine to decree (*De clem.* 1.1.2).

---

[32] See for example Wirszsubski 1968, 132–36; Brunt 1977, 109–12.

[33] Seneca's *De clementia* is in the tradition of Hellenistic treatises on kingship, though he modifies this tradition by focusing on a specific virtue, *clementia*, rather than general characteristics of rule (Griffin 1976, 149; also Braund 2009, 17–30, with discussion of other influences, including the panegyrical and philosophical essay). On the Hellenistic influence, see Griffin 1976, 143–46 and Adam 1970, 12–19. There has been some controversy about whether *De clementia* is primarily about jurisdiction and the *princeps'* role as *iudex* (Adam 1970, 20–24) or is primarily political (Büchner 1970, 204–8, 221–23). The extreme views, as Griffin points out, miss both the frequent examples of criminal trials as well as instances, such as the treatment of enemies, that lie outside purely judicial concerns (Griffin 1976, 151). My suggestion here is that *De clementia* is an attempt to identify some basis limiting the unconstrained jurisdiction of the *princeps*, an ability to act (as the opening section attests) in every aspect of life.

The language is extraordinary, setting up what will be for Seneca a later critique of despotism by way of its association with Fortune. But for now, in the mirror provided by Seneca, Nero's only *exemplum* appears as a copy of himself (*De clem.* 1.1.6) and the only danger is that he forgets himself (1.1.7).[34]

Seneca's characterization of the *princeps*' jurisdiction is often interpreted as an articulation of the ideology of the *princeps*.[35] Griffin suggests, for example, that in saying to Nero, "You are the soul of the state and the state is your body" (1.5.1), Seneca is providing "a historical justification of the Principate."[36] Around the *princeps* is a "discordant, factious, and unruly" multitude that will destroy itself and others if unbridled (1.1.1; also 1.3.5; 1.6.1).[37] The body is the "servant of the soul": the body is "larger and more showy," but the soul works invisibly to rule the "vast throng" (1.3.5). As such, the *princeps* provides the "bond by which the commonwealth is united" (1.4.1), without which the "fabric of mightiest empire will fly into many parts" (1.4.2). Thus, whether a *rex* (surprisingly used, given its meaning to a Roman audience) or a *princeps*, the power (*vis*) of the ruler is ultimately an expression of individual virtue.[38] The soul's power (*vis*) lies in the harmony it brings to the self; the *imperium* of the *princeps* lies in the propriety and glory that he provides to the political body (1.3.3; also 1.7.2).

Seneca additionally compares the *princeps*' authority to a father's *potestas*, a comparison also supportive of the ideology of the *princeps* that takes on an invidious form for Tacitus (see Chapt. 7: Tacitus). To some extent, the image continues with the previous image of the *princeps* as the soul of the political body. In this case, the people are not the body but related by flesh and blood (1.14.3). And the image contains some of the same implications: it is total and unchecked power (a *dominus*) (1.3.5) that aims with care and moderation toward the correction of his children

---

[34] Seneca will later provide an extended biography of Augustus (1.9.1–10.4), although noting there is no comparison to Nero (1.11.1).
[35] Griffin 1976, 129–71.   [36] Griffin 1976, 139; 2005, 541–42.
[37] Wallace-Hadrill discusses the *scelus*, or wrong doing, that marks humanity (1982, 30).
[38] Griffin suggests that Seneca's use of *rex* is meant for his audience to concentrate "on the reality rather than the forms" of rule (1976, 147; 2005, 542).

(1.14.1–2). The people are entrusted to the *pater patriae* as wards (*tutelae*), a legal category of guardianship (1.18.1).³⁹

There is no real Stoic basis for conceiving of the state as the body of the sovereign, though it is a claim, as I will argue, that Seneca uses to buttress another point.⁴⁰ And although the Stoics had no objection to monarchy, I want to suggest that when Seneca contends that nature "conceived the idea of king" (1.19.2), he is less making an argument on behalf of kingship and more on behalf of nature. That is, Seneca's point is not to justify kingship by way of nature but to define its jurisdiction within nature's *ius* and *lex*, or right and law, in a political environment defined both by the unruly behavior of the people and the unruled behavior of the emperor (1.18.2; 1.19.1; just kingship as best: *De ben.* 2.20.2). Seneca defines this jurisdiction by way of *clementia*.⁴¹

Griffin notes, "Seneca's *clementia* bears a very ambiguous relation to law."⁴² Seneca recognizes that mercy, which is "the moderation which remits something from the punishment that is deserved and due," is inconsistent with a Stoic notion of justice that always gives what is due (*De clem.* 2.3.2; also *Ep.* 88.29–30; earlier in Cic. *De inv.* 2.54.164). The call for mercy, as remitting some of a punishment, also runs contrary to a Stoic association of statutory law with just penalties. But as Griffin suggests, "The Stoic rule about keeping to the penalties prescribed by law was becoming useless in a system where, increasingly, it was legal for the judge to decide the penalties and where for many charges handled no precisely appropriate law existed."⁴³ The system is no longer characterized by laws with fixed penalties (or the rule of law) but by the impulses

---

³⁹ See Roller 2001, 244.
⁴⁰ Griffin notes how the metaphor of mind and body is used by the Stoics to describe the relationship between divine reason and the world, and how this metaphor is then used by Cicero to describe the relation between the laws and the state, but does not suggest an incongruity between Stoic usages and Seneca's (Griffin 2000, 537). For the Stoics, the sage's soul is part of the state to the extent that each soul is part of nature's reason. We are, as Seneca will write more in a Stoic vein, "the parts of one great body," which is not the *princeps* but nature (*Ep.* 95.52). And the sage's soul would be coextensive with the soul of the state only in a community of sages, each sage acting in conformity or harmony (*homologia = concordia*) with nature (*Ep.* 94.68).
⁴¹ On the meaning of *clementia*, see Braund 2009, 30–44.
⁴² Griffin 1976, 160.   ⁴³ Griffin 1976, 163.

of the *princeps* and those acting on his behalf.⁴⁴ There is now the sober (and un-Stoic) recognition that "the letter of the law" is not a guide to what is *aequo* and *bono*, fair and good (2.7.3; also 1.2.1). So Seneca looks for a standard in mercy as a guide to what is fair and good, a standard that originates in war as a gesture toward the defeated enemy and given prominence by Julius Caesar as a form of personal benefaction toward Roman citizens in his struggle to win back opponents in the civil war.⁴⁵ It is a standard that, as Braund notes, "was a concomitant of the monarchical power concentrated in the hands of the Roman *princeps*."⁴⁶ To show *clementia* is "testimony of absolute power."⁴⁷

Seneca's appeal, thus, is not to law but to Nero's "natural impulse" toward good deeds and words, which he seeks to shape into a "principle" (2.1.2). Seneca makes mercy into the just response that contrasts between pity and severity. Too much mercy becomes pity (*misericordia*) that is not only a failing because it "succumbs to the sight of others' ills" (2.4.4) but can also result in "confusion and an epidemic of vice" (1.2.2). Pity runs contrary to the "calm, unshaken appearance" of the sage and inhibits "the discernment of fact" (2.5.4–6.1). The other extreme, *severitas*, or cruelty, not only exceeds the boundaries (*fines*) of humanity (1.25.2) but also, when it becomes pleasurable, points to insanity (1.25.2; 2.4.2).

Seneca derives the principle of mercy from *oikeiōsis* (= *commendatio* [Cicero], *conciliari* and the reflexive *sibi conciliari*), which (as we saw in Chapter 1) means appropriation, attachment, or a natural affection for what belongs to oneself. In part *oikeiōsis* points to how humans, like all animals, have a natural sense of or feeling for their constitution, able to manipulate their bodies and limbs without difficulty (*Ep.* 121.5–6). As Seneca writes, "This function they exercise immediately at birth. They come into the world with this knowledge; they are born full-trained" (*Ep.* 121.6). Seneca describes how all beings endeavor "to carry out their natural motions," even when those motions are difficult (thus further

---

⁴⁴ Griffin points out that trials before the *princeps* were no longer bound to a fixed, legal penalty (1976, 162). On *clementia* as contrary to the rule of law, see Wirszubski 1968, 150–53.
⁴⁵ Braund 2009, 35.   ⁴⁶ Braund 2009, 32; also Augustus *RG* 34.2.
⁴⁷ Braund 2009, 32; also Wirszubski 1968, 151.

rejecting the Epicurean view that we are motivated by pleasure): A turtle on its back will wave its feet to right itself because he "misses his natural condition" just as a child will labor to walk even though falling in the effort (*Ep.* 121.8). Although animals or children (or even an adult) cannot explain why they feel what they do or what moves them to act in a particular way, all beings "must necessarily have a feeling of the principle which they obey and by which they are controlled" (*Ep.* 121.12). In the case of humans, to be adapted to one's constitution means to exist not just as living beings but also as reasoning ones (*Ep.* 121.14).

Oikeiōsis is not just a natural awareness but also an "inborn affection for our body" (*Ep.* 14.1; also 121.14; also Cic. *De fin.* 3.5.16). This affection expresses itself most fundamentally as an impulse toward self-preservation, which means that "I gauge all my actions with reference to my own welfare" and look "out for myself before all else" (*Ep.* 121.14, 17; also DL 7.85). "Impulses towards useful objects, and revulsion from the opposite, are according to nature; without any reflection to prompt the idea, and without any advice, whatever, Nature has prescribed, is done" (*Ep.* 121.21). The hen does not fear the goose but runs from the hawk, not from experience, but possessed of a "presentiment of harm" (*Ep.* 121.19). Furthermore, all beings are provided with the skills or capabilities to do that according to their constitution: a spider can weave a web just as a bee can build a comb (*Ep.* 121.22). And humans are born with the impulse to virtue (Sen. *Ep.* 120.4; *Stob.* 2.7.5b8 P = *SVF* 1.566) that begins as the most basic impulse for self-preservation.

To be conscious of oneself as a reasoning being means that one cares for oneself (*Ep.* 121.17), but also that one perceives other humans as related (*Ep.* 5.4; 121.14). We are social beings, drawn to and caring for what is related (*De clem.* 1.3.2; *Ep.* 9.17; Cic. *De fin.* 3.20.66; DL 7.123; *De ben.* 4.17.2: urge toward loving one's parents or children just as one is moved to love oneself). Seneca signals early on in *De clementia* this emphasis on a care for that which is kin, arguing that no virtue befits our social nature meant for the common good more than mercy (1.2.2). Seneca hints later at a Stoic vision of society that is not harsh but concerned with "mutual help," kindness, gentleness, and a concern for the common good (see 2.4.3; also 1.3.2).

It is by way of *oikeiōsis* that the seemingly disparate images of a body and father used by Seneca also connect to *clementia*. Seneca makes clear the relationship when he writes, "you are the soul of the state and the state your body, you see, I think, how requisite is mercy; for you are merciful to yourself when you are seemingly merciful to another" (1.5.1). And similarly, in talking about the interest of a father in his children, Seneca notes, "Slow would a father be to sever his own flesh and blood" (1.14.3). Seneca's appeal is to the jurisdiction of nature by which the emperor would exercise care and affection for others as beings related to oneself.

Seneca is not appealing simply to abstraction; there are practical rules of governing that derive from *oikeiōsis*, as well. People will respond out of their own desire for self-preservation. It is "their own safety that men love" (1.4.1). But severity that is "constant and sharp and brings desperation arouses the sluggish to boldness, and urges them to stop at nothing" (1.12.4–5). Ultimately, the ruler is "safer" (1.11.4) who gains the "love of his countrymen" (1.19.6).[48]

THE FORMATION OF CHARACTER AND THE MAKING OF MADNESS

Seneca may have had some reason to hope that Nero would restore the boundaries of judgment and action. In the first few years of his reign, Nero even acted with restraint.[49] But by 64 CE the hope had passed (Tac. *Ann.* 15.35.1) and Seneca withdrew (or attempted to withdraw) from political life. Perhaps he imagined, as he had written in *De otio* (likely written before 62 CE), that "safe retreat" from a corrupt state might be possible (*De ot.* 3.4; also *De tranq.* 5.5). But his *Epistles* (written perhaps from 62–64 or 63–64 CE), are far less optimistic, suggesting the near

---

[48] On the role of love in Stoic community, see Schofield 1991 who takes up Athaneus' claim that love inspires mutual commitment that allows the state to remain free (Schofield 1991, 50). Schofield notes that the Stoics do not spend time developing the notion of political freedom and that while love may add to security of the city, it is not the same for the Stoics as freedom (Schofield 1991, 54–55).

[49] Griffin 1976, 170.

impossibility of escape.⁵⁰ What emerges in these later writings is a characterization of the principate as despotic, one in which the boundaries of jurisdiction – the jurisdiction of law, propriety, value, and morality – are continually subverted. In response Seneca offers a nuanced, even sympathetic, exploration of the complexities not just of leading a moral life, but also a dutiful one (remembering that duty in this context refers to making appropriate choices of indifferent goods [*kathēkonta*]). The power of Seneca's writings lies neither in his portrayal of the sage nor in his recitation of traditional Stoic maxims by which one acquires wisdom, both of which he does,⁵¹ but in his treatment of the struggle of the individual to navigate in a despotic world, where one is faced with the untenable choice between recognition and retreat, both of which, Seneca will argue, make one unrecognizable to oneself.

By the self the Stoics are referring to the gradual development of the individual from rudimentary self-preservation to moral being (Cic. *De fin.* 3.6.20–21; Sen. *Ep.* 120).⁵² What begins as an instinctive or non-rational differentiation between things conducive to and not conducive to our preservation gradually develops a more rational foundation so that we begin to perform appropriate acts (*kathēkonta* = *officia*). That process is by no means obvious. By way of both preconceptions (*prolēpseis* = *praesumptiones*) and conceptions (*ennoiai* = *notiones*) (Aetius 4.11.1–4 = LS 39E), we are able to sort through and organize the myriad impressions we encounter through our senses. For Chrysippus a preconception is a "general notion" that comes by nature, including things (as we saw in our discussion of *oikeiōsis*) like what is harmful, what is

---

⁵⁰ For the dating of his *Epistles*, see Griffin 1976, 316. Her suggestion that "Seneca's recipe for security in the Letters is philosophical retirement," though, is too tidy. The list of qualifications about how to withdraw (as well as Seneca's own attempt to withdraw) suggest the impossibility of the task.

⁵¹ Notably *De brevitate vitae*, *De tranquillitate animi*, and *De otio* for theoretical discussions and applications of the conduct of the *sapiens*. Griffin notes that the *Epistles* contain so much advice with different qualifications and cautions, particularly for the *proficientes*, individuals in-between total *imperfecti* and the *sapientes*, that it is difficult to identify "a consistent and coherent system" (1976, 324).

⁵² Such awareness (Sen. *Ep.* 121) "may be said to *create* a proper self (an I) that will constitute an unchangeable point of view from which everything *outside* that self will henceforth be seen" (Engberg-Pedersen 1990b, 70).

appropriate, and what is akin.[53] Where preconceptions are acquired through a natural process, conceptions are stored thoughts (thus a kind of impression) that are developed either through instruction or through our own experiences (Plut. *De comm. not.* 1084f; Aetius 4.11.1–4 = LS 39E; Sen. *Ep.* 120.4). Conceptions are not empirical generalizations. Rather, they are, in Brittain's phrase, "criteria of truth" that we have an innate capacity to form, but that require sense-experiences in which we develop that capacity and the content of those concepts.[54] Over time we develop the ability to reason about these experiences, recognizing what is according to nature, and learning to weigh and evaluate indifferent goods to decide which actions are appropriate for one's particular disposition and situation (*Ep.* 92.3; also *De ira* 3.6.1; DL 7.107–8).[55] In Seneca's threefold guide to practical ethics (for the non-sage who cannot comprehend the universe in its totality), one must first decide the proper function and worth of each thing, then regulate one's impulses accordingly, then bring into harmony one's impulses with actions (*Ep.* 89.14). Vogt quite rightly notes the connection between *oikeiōsis* and the development of appropriate acts: "the most relevant evaluative and normative notions that nature makes us acquire grow out of concepts of the useful and harmful, that which belongs to us and is alien to us, and that which we should be doing."[56] These acts may include honoring one's parents, taking care of one's health, exercising, and engaging in civic association (see DL 7.107; Cic. *De fin.* 3.20.66), each of which derives from our affection for that which is kin: our bodies, our family, our neighbors, other citizens, and then humanity, all of whom share our rational nature.

---

[53] See DL 7.54; 7.85: first impulse; Sen. *Ep.* 120.4: nature gives us disposition toward privileging goodness. The status of preconceptions is debated. See generally Vogt 2008, 165, fn 14 and Brittain 2005. Also Sandbach 1930, 48 (ingrained); Inwood 2005, 271–301 (acquired through sensory experience guided by natural tendency to focus on the good).

[54] Brittain 2005, 177; also Long 1986, 124. Cooper does not differentiate between preconceptions and conceptions, arguing that concepts are natural in that "we do not reach them by calculating or inferring anything in any way, for example, from our experiences; we just naturally, given our experiences of, and with, the world around us, form the relevant concepts" (2004, 214).

[55] Helpfully, see Vogt 2008, 173–78 who is following Brittain 2002.

[56] Vogt 2008, 185.

We not only begin to act consistently, but with continued practice we experience a critical change in the disposition of the soul: We no longer perform appropriate acts for the advantage they bring to us or those akin to us but begin to value a pattern of behavior (Stob. 2.7.11m P = SVF 3.366).[57] As Seneca writes, a person "is not a wise man until his mind is metamorphosed into the shape of that which he has learned" (*Ep.* 94.48; also 120.10: cannot help but act rightly). That is, we do not value the goods or the consequences, which the Stoics classify as "indifferent"; we value morally perfect actions (*katorthōmata*), performing the right actions for the right reason with the right disposition (e.g., acting justly, showing self-restraint, acting sensibly, being benevolent and joyful).[58] The only end of human life is moral goodness (*kalon* = *honestum*); a "life in agreement with nature," as Zeno writes, "which is the same as a virtuous life" (DL 7.87).[59] Such morally perfect actions, achievable by the rare sage (Sen. *De cons. sap.* 7.1: achievable), depend only on virtue, the disposition of the soul to act in perfect harmony with our nature as reasoning beings (see Cic. *De fin.* 3.6.21; 3.10.33; Stob. 2.7.5b1 P = SVF 3.262; 2.7.6e P = SVF 1.554; also SVF 1.202; Sen. *Ep.* 5.4; 66.6; 76.9–10; 95.57; DL 7.87–89, 97–98). Between things that are good (*agathon* = *bonum*) and evil (*kakon* = *malum*), the only actions of absolute value or disvalue because they set in motion or sustain what is in accord with virtue or with vice (DL 7.94, 104; Sen. *Ep.* 87.36), lies the vast realm of indifferent goods, goods that

---

[57] Frede argues that we recognize and admire the wisdom displayed in these acts (1999, 90).

[58] See Stob. 2.7.11e P = SVF 3.501–2 for a discussion of right acts. For some (Kidd 1978, 248–49; Inwood 1999b, 698), *katorthōmata* are a perfected form of *kathēkonta* (though it should be emphasized that appropriate actions are not necessarily right actions: see DL 7.88). Others (Vogt 2008, 62) see in Stoicism a definitional break: *kathēkonta* are concerned with the choice of indifferent goods, not moral ones. Stobaeus reports the definition of a *katorthōmata* as a "complete appropriate act" (*teleion kathēkon*) (Stob. 2.7.11a P).

[59] Chryssipus in DL 7.87–88, adding nature refers both to human nature and the nature of the whole; Stob. 2.7.5b3 P = SVF 3.264, 2.7.6a P = SVF 1.179; 1.552; 3.12; 3.20; 3.44; 3.57: range of definitions provided by the Stoics; Sen. *De ben.* 5.12.5. For a helpful discussion of the differing (or evolving) accounts in Stoicism between reason, virtue, and happiness, see Schofield 2003, 240–46.

contribute neither to happiness nor unhappiness (Cic. *De fin.* 3.6.21; DL 7.104; Stob. 2.7.7 P = *SVF* 3.118).

We derive knowledge of the good, as Seneca writes, from what can be grasped by the senses (*Ep.* 124.6; also Chapt. 8, 360–66 for a more technical discussion of Stoic psychology).[60] That knowledge is neither automatic nor easily derived from general observations. Cicero, for example, reports that for the Stoics honorable action is natural, in that we are inclined to choose it, but "is not one of the primary natural attractions" (Cic. *De fin.* 3.6.22). So too for Seneca, "Nature could not teach us this [knowledge [*notitia*] of that which is honorable] directly; she has given us the seeds of knowledge, but not knowledge itself" (Sen. *Ep.* 120.4; also Stob. 2.7.5b3 P = *SVF* 3.264). The virtues grow out of innate preferences: prudence from a desire to understand; justice from our natural sociability; and courage and temperance from desires for mastery and order (Cic. *De off.* 1.4.11–5.17). And one learns from others, observing models of behavior and making comparisons (Sen. *Ep.* 120.4, 9; also 109.2). Cicero, for example, lists a number of sources of education, including parent, nurse, teacher, poet, and the stage (Cic. *De leg.* 1.17.47). Even the wise man, as Stobaeus reports, uses "his practical experiences with regards to life" to do all things well (Stob. 2.7.11g P = *SVF* 3.567; also 2.7.11i P = *SVF* 3.567).

Just as the external world provides patterns of virtue, so it can seduce with its charms, inviting us to hand over any control of ourselves to the rule of license. Laudatory patterns of behavior that surround us conceal failings (Sen. *Ep.* 120.5, 8). The influence of good models can as easily become the appeal of bad models: "the familiar friend, if he be luxurious, weakens and softens us imperceptibly; the neighbour, if he be rich, rouses our covetousness; the companion, if he be slanderous, rubs off some of his rust upon us, even though we be spotless and sincere" (*Ep.* 7.7; also 94.53–54). And we can be corrupted either by bad teaching when we are still young or by being seduced by the "counterfeit of good": pleasure (Cic. *De leg.* 1.17.47).

---

[60] Frede 1999, 74–5: naturally acquire a notion of the good that motivates us; Inwood 2005, 271–301: notion of good acquired through sensory experience that is guided by natural tendency to focus on the good.

THE FORMATION OF CHARACTER AND THE MAKING OF MADNESS

Facing these sorts of challenges is part of the honing of character. When "many difficulties have confronted us on this side and on that, and have occasionally even come to close quarters with us" (*Ep.* 13.1), in struggling against "opposition and difficulty" (*De clem.* 1.24.2; *Ep.* 13.1), one learns how to recognize what is under and not under one's control. So when Seneca exclaims, "We are mad, not only individually, but publicly" (*Non privatim solum, sed publice furimus*), he is employing a notion of madness that Cicero associates with having lost power (*potestas*) over oneself because of fear, pain, lust, or wrath (*Ep.* 95.30; Cic. *Tusc.* 3.5.11). To have *potestas* requires a sense of limits: limits on what others can do to you and limits on what you yourself can do that one learns through the "experience of customs and laws" (Stob. 2.7.11k P = *SVF* 3.677). In Stobaeus' account, madness is an ignorance of oneself and what accords with oneself that renders the impulses "unstable and agitated" (Stob. 2.7.5b13 P = *SVF* 3.663).

There is a famous Stoic saying that anyone who is not a sage is mad (DL 7.124; Cic. *Tusc.* 3.5.11; *Acad.* 2.44.136). That saying, like many Stoic paradoxes, is meant to highlight a truth: Sense lies in acting according to reason (which only the sage does); madness lies in not knowing the value or importance of things. Certainly Seneca, like other Stoics, recognizes degrees of madness (describing, for example, the different types of treatments and punishments for those whom are medically mad, and thus become something less than human). Seneca is not talking about medical madness; he is portraying how the repeated experience of a passion or passions, the continual physiological alteration of the *pneuma*, alters the physiological state of the soul (creeping into the bones and sinews of the body) until the vices are "hardened and chronic" (*Ep.* 75.11; also Cic. *Tusc.* 3.2.4; 4.10.24–11.25; 4.13.29,).[61] Over time, as Graver notes, "when an agent has, on several different occasions, assented to the same evaluation of some particular object-type, he begins to form a more extensive system of beliefs linking that positive or negative evaluation to

---

[61] Cicero initially translates *pathos* as *morbus* but then revises that translation to *perturbatio*: *De fin.* 3.10.35. See Graver 2007, 121–25 on how emotions can be causes in Stoicism.

numerous other opinions he happens to hold."[62] What emerges is a sickness (*aegrotatio* = *nosēma*) or, more severely, a disease (*morbus* = *arrōstēma*) of the soul (and corresponding aversions).[63] A sickness is an "intense belief, persistent and deeply rooted, which regards a thing that is not desirable as though it were eminently desirable" (Cic. *Tusc.* 4.11.26; Stob. 2.7.10c P = SVF 3.395, 402, 408, 413). A disease is sickness in conjunction with weakness, a proneness of one's own disposition (Cic. *Tusc.* 4.13.29; Stob. 2.7.10e P = SVF 3.421). The corresponding aversions are intense beliefs, incorrectly held, about what is to be avoided. There is in addition defectiveness (*vitiositas*), which is "a habit or a disposition which is throughout life inconsistent and out of harmony with itself" (Cic. *Tusc.* 4.13.29). The result of this hardening of false beliefs is comparable to the medical conditions of *melancholia* (arising from an excess of black bile) or *feritas* (brutishness).[64] The problem of madness is that it is unbounded (*Ep.* 39.5); there are no limits to what can be imagined, what can be desired or feared, and what one will do to realize one's desires or avoid one's fears.[65] Seneca lays out the characteristics of madness: One is "devoid of self-control, forgetful of decency, unmindful of ties, persistent and diligent in whatever it begins, closed to reason and counsel, excited by trifling causes, unfit to discern the right and true" (*De ira* 3.1.2).

For Seneca, the principate had fundamentally altered one's sense of jurisdiction, the ability of the mind to distinguish between the "boundaries" (*modi*) of truth (*Ep.* 13.9) and the boundlessness of the imagination. One practices (because one is taught) fear or desire until these excessive impulses become part of one's disposition. The individual no longer learns the proper limit (*modus*) of action because the experience of the

---

[62] Graver 2002, 152.
[63] On the ambiguity in Stoicism of whether emotions are diseases (since one is a motion, the other a disposition), see Rabel 1981. Rist argues that the passions are diseases for the Stoics (1969, 26–27). I will suggest that for Seneca the passions are disturbances that over time can become diseases.
[64] See Graver 2007, 120–25.
[65] The Stoics frequently compare madness to dreams in which our relaxed pneumatic tension leads us to accept the images as real (see DL 7.158).

political world teaches the opposite (*Ep.* 95.30).⁶⁶ One does not assign real worth (*aestimatio*) to humans but assigns it to worthless things (*Ep.* 87.5; 115.8; *De ira* 3.34.2). One craves false glory (*Ep.* 94.64) or public applause (*Ep.* 59.15). One "fears those whom [one] ought to love" (*Ep.* 123.16). Or one comes to associate pleasure with cruelty. Seneca's political thought lies in his exploration of a political world that had created the condition of insanity by subverting the categories of worth, leaving one with choices that invariably implicate one in madness: an aversion to the world or a desire for it.

DESPOTISM: CREATING INSANITY

Other than in the *Apocolocyntosis* and other scattered references to Claudius, Seneca really does not refer a lot to or make judgments about other *principes*. In Griffin's assessment, "Seneca's references to the *principes* are moral in that they concentrate on the virtues and vices of the men, not on 'policies.'"⁶⁷ But Seneca does provide a powerful reading of the political world of the principate, one that locates its political implications by way of a politicized reading of Fortune.

Fortune seems like an unlikely choice for Seneca's critique of politics since Chance (*casus*) and Fortune (*fortuna*) are, for the Stoics, "merely a matter of human ignorance" about "the overall order of nature."⁶⁸ In typically Stoic prose, Seneca declares that one must become reconciled to what Fortune has given them (*De tranq.* 10.4; also 11.2; *De cons. sap.* 8.3). The claim, as it related to the larger question of Fate, involved the Stoics in centuries of debate. Seneca seems at one point to evince some of the irresolution of the debate:

---

[66] For the early Stoics conditions such as *melancholia* can undermine or even destroy virtue by destroying the ability for the individual to know with any certainty (see DL 7.118, 127).

[67] Griffin 1976, 217.

[68] Frede 2003, 183–84. On determinism in Stoic philosophy generally, see also Bobzien 1998. In Seneca, see *De prov.* 6.1; *Ep.* 101.5: "Time does indeed roll along by fixed law, but as in darkness; and what is it to me whether Nature's course is sure, when my own is unsure?"

> Whether the truth, Lucilius, lies in one or in all of these views, we must be philosophers; whether Fate binds us down by an inexorable law, or whether God as arbiter of the universe has arranged everything, or whether Chance drives and tosses human affairs without method, philosophy ought to be our defence. She will encourage us to obey God cheerfully, but Fortune defiantly; she will teach us to follow God and endure Chance (*Ep.* 16.5).

Seneca sidesteps the issue: "But it is not my purpose now to be led into a discussion as to what is within our own control (*iuris nostri*), — if foreknowledge is supreme, or if a chain of fated events drags us along in its clutches, or if the sudden and the unexpected play the tyrant (*dominor*) over us" (*Ep.* 16.6).

Of interest is Seneca's association of Fortune with the political language of *iuris* and *dominor*. *Dominor*, the verbal form of *dominus*, means to master or have dominion over something and carries an increasingly negative connotation as it moves from describing household rule and the rule of inanimate things to political rule (see Virg. *G* 1.154). Cicero, for example, writes of how a king is transformed into a despot (*dominus*) when he turns to a mastery (*dominatus*) that is less just (Cic. *De rep.* 2.26.47–48).[69] For Seneca, the *dominus*, at home and in politics, is associated with "monstrous greed," cruelty toward his slaves (formerly citizens) (*Ep.* 47.2–4), and an unquenchable desire to extend one's rule over new territories and people (*Ep.* 113.30; 119.8). There is no limit on the *ius* of the *dominus*.

There are two obvious reasons why Seneca might compare the despot to Fortune. First, the vicissitudes of Fortune, like the actions of the despot, might seem arbitrary to those against whom it moves. But that association still hinges on an idea that it is the people who do not understand what is, in fact, an ordered and purposeful universe. Second, Fortune, like the despot, removes events from our control, becoming our sovereign master. But when Seneca associates Fortune with *iuris nostri* in *Epistle* 16, Seneca seems less interested in how Fortune treats us and more in how it transforms us. The despotic world emerges as a liquid landscape in which everything, including oneself, can become something else.

---

[69] See also Cic. *De rep.* 1.33.50; 2.19.34.

DESPOTISM: CREATING INSANITY

Fortune can favor us. Seneca depicts Fortune, like the *princeps* holding a festival, as handing out the dole and distributing honor, wealth, and influence (*honor, divitia, gratia*) (*Ep.* 74.7). Fortune elevates us when it elects us and gives us fame and recognition (*Ep.* 118.3). But Fortune can also destroy us. To some extent, this claim simply follows on the Stoic injunction against either desiring or fearing events that we cannot control (see *Ep.* 37.4). But in the connection to politics, Fortune looms more ominously, subverting the value of things. Like a bad tempered master, Fortune moves with capricious glee (*Ep.* 4.4), attacking more violently those who shine most brilliantly (*Ep.* 91.4). The political tactics of Fortune also change: "She does not always attack in one way, or even with her full strength; at one time she summons (*advocat*) our own hands against us; at another time, content with her own powers, she makes us of no agent (*sine auctore*) in devising perils for us. No time is exempt; in the midst of our very pleasures there spring up causes of suffering" (*Ep.* 91.5). In the movement of Fortune, "Everything is slippery, treacherous, and more shifting than any weather (*Nihil non lubricum et fallax et omni tempestate mobilius*). All things are tossed about and shift into their opposites" (*Ep.* 99.9).

Fortune transforms into chattel everything that falls under its *dominium*: "money, person, position," which are made "weak, shifting, prone to perish, and of uncertain tenure" (*Ep.* 66.23). The gifts of Fortune that we think we hold are like "snares" that trap us (*Ep.* 8.3). The heights of eminence that we achieve end in a fall (*Ep.* 8.4). And in another image, Seneca describes how our possessions so weigh on us that they can crush us (*Ep.* 76.31). The power of Fortune lies in its ability to destroy whatever it elevates.

In this despotic realm, those "clad in purple" are no more than actors whom fortune has clothed with inherited estates, titles, and other deceptions (*Ep.* 76.32). Under Fortune's jurisdiction, it becomes almost impossible to identify the true value (*aestimatio*) of a man (*Ep.* 76.32). Even more difficult is identifying the true value of oneself since Fortune places one under the judgment of another (*alieni arbitrium*) (*Ep.* 74.1; also *Ep.* 31.10). Seneca at one point offers the orthodox Stoic view that one can only avoid such a sentence by fixing a "limit" on the goods one seeks according to the bounds of nature's law (*Ep.* 15.11; 25.4) and placing oneself "beyond the jurisdiction" (*extra ius dicionemque*) of chance (*Ep.* 39.3). Thus, although Fortune "decides" (*iudico*) the results, as Seneca continues in this language of jurisdiction, "I do not allow her to pass sentence upon myself" (*Ep.* 14.16). Governed by reason, we achieve *libertas* (*Ep.* 37.4; 51.9; also *De const. sap.* 9.2–5; 19.2 on sage; *De vita beata* 3.4; 4.5), not only because we are in harmony with nature, but also because we are aware of ourselves at all points, clear about how we got to where we are (*Ep.* 37.5; also 22.11). Seneca suggests on a number of occasions (and eventually takes) the route of suicide. In talking about the terrible torture a tyrant can inflict, Seneca offers the advice, "Slavery is not hardship when, if a man wearies of the yoke, by a single step he may pass to freedom."[70] Thus Seneca applauds Cato: "the freedom which it [the sword] could not give to his country it shall give to Cato" (*De prov.* 2.10).

However much Seneca understood Epicurus' injunction, "'Think on death (*Meditare mortem*),'" as bidding us to "think on freedom (*meditari libertatem*)" (*Ep.* 26.10), Seneca's apparent "obsession" with suicide, as Rist characterizes it, seems to give way to a genuine attempt to navigate this world.[71] But where one stands – by what jurisdiction one acts – is made extraordinarily difficult in a world that perverts the political, legal, and social markers by which Romans define and orient themselves.

BRUTISHNESS: THE POLITICS OF ENTERTAINMENT

Seneca's critique is not just that of the *princeps* but of a larger cultural environment fostered by and supportive of this despotic realm. Seneca notes, "of all the agencies which coerce and master our minds, the most effective are those which can make a display" (*Ep.* 14.6). That display

---

[70] *Cons. Marc.* 20.3; also *De prov.* 6.7;; *Ep.* 12.10; also 22.5–6; 26.10; 66.13; 70.14–16; 77.6; in Stoic context: DL 7.130; *De fin.* 3.18.60; Plut. *De stoic. rep.* 1042d. Rist sees this freedom as entirely negative and different from the claims of earlier Stoics who allowed suicide when nature commanded (1969, 248–49). Inwood views suicide as freedom for Seneca because it is an assertion of one's own control over one's life and death (2005, 302–21). Stobaeus reports that the Stoics allowed for suicide for the wise, but does not connect it to freedom (Stob. 2.7.11m P = *SVF* 3.758).

[71] Rist 1969, 246.

occurs in the "huge parade" of increasingly elaborate and violent forms of spectacle entertainments (*Ep.* 14.4). These spectacles – including gladiatorial contests, beast hunts, *naumachia*, and criminal punishments – occur in the most public of arenas, replacing the Forum as the locus of acculturation.

Scholars have seen the spectacles as producing a "discourse" and "rhetorical effect" that was supposed to play "an important role in the moralization and maintenance of Roman social roles and hierarchical relations."[72] Gladiatorial contests were presented as lessons in the fundamental Roman values of courage, endurance, and discipline (see *De tranq.* 11.4–5; *De cons. sap.* 16.2).[73] The arena also "solidif[ied]" symbols that associated the emperor and the empire with mythology, divinity, and conquest, a focus on the emperor that often came at the expense of elite status.[74] And for the people, the arena provided a venue for popular expression. As Edmondson notes, "After the decline of republican political institutions, they represented almost the only remaining opportunities for political debate between plebs and *princeps*."[75]

Debate is too strong a term. The spectacles were opportunities for the people to express their satisfaction or dissatisfaction and for the emperor to demonstrate his magnanimity and closeness to the people. But the people seemed genuinely reluctant to embrace attempts to return even minimal powers to them. Caligula's gesture to restore elections to the people's assembly in 38 CE, for example, was such a failure that he rescinded it the following year. There was no longer a public good that oriented these institutions, nor a sense of efficacy that animated them. Public expression had found its register in the shared pleasure of consumption.[76]

---

[72] Gunderson 1996, 115, 139.   [73] Toner 1995, 68.   [74] Auguet 1994, 106.
[75] Edmondson 1996, 72. See also Wiedemann 1992, 176–77; Tengström 1977, 54.
[76] See Hammer 2010 on the consuming aspects of these spectacles. These spectacles, Plass argues, were a "special, institutionalized form" of "conspicuous consumption at Rome, fed not merely by economic resources but, more dramatically, by copious supplies of blood" (Plass 1995, 50). "The maintenance of the emperor's role," as Millar notes, "demanded not only a constant outflow of gifts, but the giving of them in a magnanimous and dignified manner" (Millar 1977, 136). Also Millar 1977, 140; Wistrand 1992, 63; Potter 1996, 131.

It is around this spectacle of consumption that some see the elites as defining or reasserting themselves. Toner argues that the elites may have tried to establish a "new hegemony" by incorporating lower class pleasure into elite culture.[77] Gunderson characterizes the arena as affirming elite identity through the "illustrative spectacle" of gladiatorial strength, courage, and endurance[78] as well as by delineated seating and dress.[79] The aristocracy could demonstrate their taste, self-control, and power to subject the bodies of the lower class to the gaze of the upper class.[80] As Seneca writes, "it shows greater self-control to refuse to withdraw oneself and to do what the crowd does, but in a different way, – thus neither making oneself conspicuous nor becoming one of the crowd" (*Ep.* 18.4; *De tranq.* 14.3). And Habinek suggests that it is around taste that Seneca seeks to affirm aristocratic and hierarchical sentiments that emphasize privilege and distinction (albeit based on criteria of achievement rather than birth).[81]

But Seneca is doing more than advocating for a new aristocracy. When he decries the change in status relations, he is pointing, not unlike Tacitus later, to the subversion of the political categories of governance in which there are neither reliable markers of authority nor limits to its jurisdiction. The spectacles parody the processes by which individuals receive honors, riches, and influence (*Ep.* 74.7). Seneca describes the frenzied scene of the emperor tossing gifts into the stands:

> showering down honours, riches, and infuence upon this mob of mortals; some of these gifts have already been torn to pieces in the hands of those who try to snatch them, others have been divided up by treacherous partnerships, and still others have been seized to the great detriment of those into whose possession that have come. Certain of

---

[77] Toner 1995, 125.   [78] Gunderson 1996, 139.
[79] On seating, see Fredrick 2002, 243–47; Edmondson 1996; Gunderson 1996, 123–26; Rawson 1987.
[80] On the control of the gaze, see Fredrick 2002, 246.
[81] Habinek 1992; also Shaw 1985; and Roller 2001, 272–86. On growing conflicts in status relations between birth and achievement, and between insider and outsider status, see Shaw 1985, 25–26 and Habinek 1998, 137–38. Roller 2001, 107–8, argues that Seneca seeks to shift "the arena of competition," from winning high military honors, which are less accessible to the elite, to places like the arena and the centumviral court.

BRUTISHNESS: THE POLITICS OF ENTERTAINMENT

these favours have fallen to men while they were absent-minded; others have been lost to their seekers because they were snatching too eagerly for them, and, just because they are greedily seized upon, have been knocked from their hands (*Ep.* 74.7).

The desire for political favors appears more like the scramble for the coins at public games, one's cravings excited when so few gifts are awaited by so many (*Ep.* 74.9). The spectators become impassioned and are torn apart as they "look back now in this direction and now in that," even more excited as they must grab for the few gifts that are awaited by all (*Ep.* 74.8).

As if to feed this insatiable appetite, the Roman games emerge as an almost frantic succession of consumption. Seneca describes attending a mid-day exhibition that he thought would provide respite "from the slaughter of their fellow-men" (*Ep.* 7.3). But there was no pause; in fact, the exhibition became "pure murder" (*Ep.* 7.3). No helmets or shields, just the call by the spectators for death. So that there is no cessation in pleasure, "In the morning they throw men to lions and the bears; at noon, they throw them to the spectators" (*Ep.* 7.4). And the spectators "grow angry with gladiators" that they are not glad to die, transforming "themselves into enemies, in looks, in gesture, and in violence" (*De ira* 1.2.4).

The spectacles overwhelm the spectator with "forgetfulness" of that which is honorable (*Ep.* 95.33). One enters a world in which standards of behavior appear as fantasy: The spectators are "deceived by imaginary blows" and "pacified by the pretended tears of those who beg forgiveness" so that "mock resentment is removed by a mock revenge" (*De ira* 1.2.5). Absent any limits, Seneca writes, humans now "seek *voluptas* from every source" (*Ep.* 95.33).[82] Seneca also uses *voluptas* to describe the pleasure that hidden technologies bring to the eyes and ears (*Ep.* 88.22). Only now Seneca spells out the implications of a world judged by the standards of consumption: Nothing that feels good is considered bad. And nothing is excluded from making one feel good, including the "satisfying spectacle" of seeing "man made a corpse"

---

[82] See also Walters who explores how the spectator was able to "use the bodies of the deviants for their own pleasure" (1998, 365).

(*Ep.* 95.33). As Seneca writes, "Man, an object of reverence in the eyes of man, is now slaughtered for jest and sport" (*Ep.* 95.33). This brutishness (*feritas*) is a form of insanity in which anger has become a disposition so that one's behavior has no relationship to events. Seneca comments that we have reached "the farthest limit of insanity, when cruelty has changed into pleasure and to kill a human being now becomes a joy" (*De clem.* 1.25.2; also 2.4.2; on Caligula, *De ira* 3.18.3–4: torture for pleasure). Brutality transgresses all natural and human bounds,[83] leading one to invent instruments and seek ways to inflict ever-greater amounts of cruelty (*De clem.* 1.25.2), undermining the traits of sympathy and sociability, the natural basis of a community sense (*sensus communis*) (see *Ep.* 5.4).

It is not that the community simply observes the gladiators; it is that the people take on the characteristics of the gladiatorial games. As Seneca writes:

> Among those whom you see in civilian garb there is no peace; for a slight reward any one of them can be led to compass the destruction of another; no one makes gain save by another's loss; the prosperous they hate, the unprosperous they despise; superiors they loathe, and to inferiors are loathsome; they are goaded on by opposite desires; they desire for the sake of some little pleasure or plunder to see the whole world lost (*De ira* 2.8.2).

Seneca draws out the comparison: "They live as though they were in a gladiatorial school – those with whom they eat, they likewise fight. It is a community of wild beasts, only that beasts are gentle toward each other and refrain from tearing their own kind, while men glut themselves with rending one another (*Ferarum iste conventus est, nisi quod illae inter se placidae sunt morsuque similium abstinent, hi mutua laceratione satiantur*)" (*De ira* 2.8.3). The social education that one receives breaks down one's natural sense of kinship, turning one against the other not out of fear (as it is for Hobbes) but pleasure. In this savage environment, in which the

---

[83] In similarly transgressing the boundaries of nature in the interest of consumption, the Romans dig out gold and silver that nature has hidden away (Sen. *Ep.* 94.57) and that will not endure (*Ep.* 95.73).

community has become mad, one is left, as Seneca writes, to either "imitate or loathe the world" (*Ep.* 7.7).

AVERSION: HIDING FROM THE WORLD

The Stoics were no strangers to hardship. Seneca's *On firmness*, for example, serves as a comprehensive catalogue of all the hardships that can be met with *patientia*, endurance (*De cons. sap.* 2.2–3; 3.2). As Seneca writes, "By this mark [of the striking of hardship] I will show you the wise man" (*De cons. sap.* 3.3; also *De cons. sap.* 2.6). At times, Seneca's advice seems to evince little of the complexity of living in a corrupt world. Seneca remarks that the individual must have both the ability to change and to endure (*De tranq.* 14.1). And the mind must be withdrawn from events external to it: "Let it have confidence in itself, rejoice in itself, let it admire its own things, let it retire as far as possible from the things of others and devote itself to itself, let is not feel losses, let it interpret kindly even adversities" (*De tranq.* 14.2). Yet, when one thinks of the corruption of current affairs, "the mind is plunged into night" (*De tranq.* 15.1). One must drag oneself into the light (*De tranq.* 2.5).

The world Seneca is describing is one in which criminality has become a mode of political action. Seneca notes the "moral topsy-turvey" (*Ep.* 95.29): "We check manslaughter and isolated murders; but what of war and the much-vaunted crime of slaughtering whole peoples?" (*Ep.* 95.30). Cruelty (*saevus*), a term often associated with lawless tyranny, is now "practised in accordance with acts of senate and popular assembly, and the public is bidden to do what is forbidden to the individual" (*Ep.* 95.30: *ex senatus consultis plebisque scitis saeva exercentur et publice iubentur vetata privatim*).[84] One practices fear or desire until these excessive impulses become part of one's disposition, one's reactions bearing little relationship to the world.

To escape the madness of a political world without boundaries, the individual might seek stillness in some private existence. One must

---

[84] Lawless tyranny: Livy 34.32.3.

"[keep] still – talking very little with others, and as much as may be with yourself" (*Ep.* 105.6).⁸⁵ Seneca counsels Lucilius "to canvass (*petere*) for nothing, and to pass by all the elections (*comitia*) of Fortune" in order to achieve *libertas*, a political term that requires paradoxically that one somehow absent oneself from politics (*Ep.* 118.3).

Seneca writes of his own "seclusion" that he sought out of "apprehension" (*timor*) and "weariness" (*lassitudo*) (*Ep.* 56.9). And he allows us to peer into the recesses of this despotic quiet where individuals, haunted by fear, "shrink into dark corners," burying their secrets deep in their heart and distrusting even themselves (*Ep.* 3.4). In fact, Seneca refers to this retreat as banishment (*Ep.* 55.5). In such seclusion one then enters a similarly boundless terrain of the imagination. The products of one's imagination (for all but the sage) lack any limits or any standard by which to judge what is real because we are prone by habit to exaggerate (*augere*), imagine (*fingere*), and anticipate (*praecipere*) pain and sorrow (*Ep.* 13.5, 7; also 16.9). But perhaps most troubling is that such solitude produces, even in a better sort of person, a false quiet (*quies*) (*Ep.* 3.5). This quiet has a "pretence of soundness" (*sanitas*) (*Ep.* 56.10), one that is actually "slackness and langor" (*dissolutio et languor*) (*Ep.* 3.5).⁸⁶ The individual who flees from human affairs ends up living like a "frightened and sluggish animal" in which even "sluggishness" (*inertia*) assumes "an air of authority (*auctoritas*) with us" (*Ep.* 55.5; also *De tranq.* 2.6). One finds oneself under the jurisdiction of one's vain and limitless imaginings.

Seneca recalls the image of Vatia, a wealthy praetorian and descendent of a politically active family, who knew "how to hide" from the treachery of Tiberius's court (*Ep.* 55.4). People assume that "a person has found leisure who has withdrawn from society" (*Ep.* 55.4). Except for the wise man, though, one cannot find solace in seclusion: "Does he who is a victim of anxiety know how to live for himself?" (*Ep.* 55.5). The Roman juridical subject cannot just retreat from politics when there is no jurisdiction to put in its place: no authority to guide them, no duties

---

⁸⁵ On the Senecan idea of stillness, see Too 1994, 220–21.
⁸⁶ The alternative of retreat to the country is explored, as well, in Senecan drama. See *Thy.* 401–3, 455, 468; *Her.* 159–85; and Fitch and McElduff 2002, 37–38.

that bind them to others, and no discourse to enliven them. In this absence of movement one risks succumbing to the authority of *inertia*.[87]

UNGOVERNED DESIRE

Seneca writes in *De tranquillitate animi*, "For it is the nature of the human mind to be active and prone to movement" (*De tranq.* 2.11). Such a solitary existence is particularly unendurable for a mind interested in public affairs and desiring action (*De tranq.* 2.9; also 3.7–8). Indeed, genius requires an excited mind (*De tranq.* 17.10). Seneca, thus, calls for his audience to rouse themselves to action and emerge into view from their "uncontrollable sluggishness" (*inertia*) (*Ep.* 56.8).

Politics had always been the path by which the Roman elites could measure themselves against the achievements of their ancestors. So deeply enmeshed is the importance of recognition in Greek and Roman society that even the Stoics (if we are to believe Cicero's account) were compelled, under the criticism of Carneades, to change their opinion that fame had no value other than as something useful and to declare that good fame (*bona fama*) was "preferred and desirable for its own sake" (Cic. *De fin.* 3.17.57). A man of "good breeding and liberal education could desire to have the good opinion of his parents and relatives, and of good men in general, and that for its own sake and not for any practical advantage" (Cic. *De fin.* 3.17.57).

So, too, Seneca engages in a lengthy defense of *claritas* (renown), *fama* (fame), and *gloria* (glory), terms that overlap in their meaning. Renown (*claritas*), Seneca argues in employing a political vocabulary, does not need many votes (*multa suffragia*) but can be satisfied by the judgment (*iudicium*) of one good man (*Ep.* 102.11). In fact, *claritas* requires only the silent judgment, and not the actual words, of a good man (*Ep.* 102.14–15, 17). *Gloria*, which Seneca characterizes as "the shadow of virtue" that "will attend virtue even against her will" (*Ep.* 79.13), requires the judgments of the many (*Ep.* 102.17). However, the judgment of one good

---

[87] On references to Vatia's life as a living death, see Motto and Clark 1993, 115–24 and Henderson 2004, 73–77.

man "practically amounts" to being thought well by all good men since their judgment of what is true will be identical (*Ep.* 102.12). But even that shadow can lag behind, delayed by the envy and ignorance of one's contemporaries (*Ep.* 79.13). *Fama*, unlike *gloria*, requires the voices of many and, thus, has an even more tenuous existence (*Ep.* 102.17; also 102.13). *Fama*, for example, barely comes to Socrates, Cato, Democritus, and Rutilius, almost resulting in the loss of our knowledge of their virtue, innocence, and worth (*Ep.* 79.14).[88]

The problem of recognition is that one ends up playing to others. One's sociability, in fact, leads one to take cues from others, potentially altering the terms of approbation and condemnation. When one person is "overwhelmed by disaster, the rest are overwhelmed by fear, and the possibility that they may suffer makes them as downcast as the actual sufferer" (*Ep.* 74.4). Similarly, one is easily seduced, like the siren songs, by the allure of others (*Ep.* 31.2). Seneca admits, "There are things which, if done by the few, we should refuse to imitate; yet when the majority have begun to do them, we follow along – just as if anything were more honourable because it is more frequent! Furthermore, wrong views, when they have become prevalent, reach, in our eyes, the standard of righteousness" (*Ep.* 123.6). So powerful is the majority that "even Socrates, Cato, and Laelius might have been shaken in their moral strength by a crowd that was unlike them" (*Ep.* 7.6–7). Not just the majority, but also those who immediately surround us can easily lead us to celebrate vice as virtue, rashness as bravery, moderation as sluggishness, and cowardice as prudence (*Ep.* 45.7).

The problem of despotism is not just that the *princeps* becomes the arbiter of ideals; it is that the populace takes on "the temper of kings (*reges*)" (*Ep.* 47.20). One does not learn about boundaries; one becomes implicated, whether wittingly or unwittingly, in a world devoid of limits. It is not that one is powerless. As Seneca notes, even if given great power (*magna potentia*), one would make ungoverned (*inpotenter*)

---

[88] Roller, too, notes the ambiguity in Seneca's sense of the role or importance of the external witness (2001, 82–88). Roller interprets it as Seneca translating Stoic ideas into what would have been commonsense understandings by Romans (2001, 87). I take more seriously the importance of the external audience to Seneca.

use of it (*Ep.* 42.3). One's soul is "torn asunder" (*distraho*) or "pulled to pieces" (*discerpo*) by the struggle between ambition, anger, and pleasure (*Ep.* 51.8), a tearing apart that Tacitus will later associate with the emergence of Tiberius.[89] Like kings, the people are "driven into wild rage by our luxurious lives, so that whatever does not answer to our whims arouses our anger" (*Ep.* 47.19). And coinciding with the legal development of the *princeps* becoming an injured party, so individuals "insist" that they have "received an injury" (*iniuria*) so that they "may inflict them" (*Ep.* 47.20).[90] In the practice of political life, friends conspire against friends (*Ep.* 101.15); *delatores* (or accusers) make informing on others into a path of power; political functionaries, as they thirst to become lords of many, become slaves of the desire for more (*Ep.* 9.22); and enemies, or even those who by chance are associated with enemies, die in dungeons (*Ep.* 55.3). In *De beneficiis*, Seneca describes (in language that comes surprisingly close to descriptions later by Tacitus) how under Tiberius "there was such a common and almost universal frenzy for bringing charges of treason, that it took a heavier tool of the lives of Roman citizen than any Civil War; it seized upon the talk of drunkards, the frank words of jesters; nothing was safe – anything served as an excuse to shed blood, and there was no need to wait to find out the fate of the accused since there was but one outcome" (*De ben.* 3.26.1). When not terrifying, politics borders on parody: candidates offering bribes, employing agents, "wearing down their hands with the kisses of those to whom they will refuse the least finger-touch after being elected"; others struggling for honors, triumph in war, permanent power, riches, and marriage (*Ep.* 118.3–4). However much one may strive to counter the hope, envy, hatred, fear, and contempt that motivates individuals to do evil (*Ep.* 105.1), ultimately one is left with the admonition not to "trust the countenance of those you meet" (*Ep.* 103.2). Individuals will lie in wait, not striking when first encountering another, but delighting in the prospect of ruining another (*Ep.* 103.2).

In the visual culture of Rome, appearing before others serves as an important mechanism by which the individual "incorporated others into

---

[89] See Tacitus: Tiberius and mother tear state apart (*distraho*) (*Ann.* 1.4.5).
[90] MacMullen 1988, 139.

himself or herself as witnesses and ideals."[91] Yet, as Seneca writes, we are never free of concern "if we think that every time anyone looks at us he is always taking our measure" (*De tranq.* 17.1). The trap of despotism is that it requires that individuals take on different guises, sometimes to be seen, sometimes not to be seen (and to make sure to avoid being seen trying not to be seen) (*Ep.* 14.7). The metaphor that Seneca uses, like the metaphor that Tacitus will employ, is that of the theater. Seneca writes of how one must wear one's different masks and play different parts in life's drama. Edwards, for example, relates Seneca's "fascination with the slipperiness of the self, his urge to dramatize tensions within the self," to Neronian Rome and "Seneca's own place in the Neronian court." Rome under Nero, Edwards argues, required that one be able to assume different roles and dissimilate one's feelings, not unlike the stage-acting that had become so much a part of Nero's reign.[92] But the mask seems problematic not just as a way of hiding but of appearing. The challenge, as Seneca tells Lucilius, is to maintain a continuously recognizable character so that people are able to praise (*laudari*) you or at least to identify (*adgnosci*) you (*Ep.* 120.22; also 80.7). Yet, recognition can easily require "trickery" – a sort of acting – because the people "will withhold their approval if they do not recognize you as one of themselves" (*Ep.* 29.11). As Seneca warns Lucilius, in continuing the theatrical image, "if I see you applauded by popular acclamation, if your entrance upon the scene is greeted by a roar of cheering and clapping, – marks of distinction meet only for actors, – if the whole state, even the women and children, sing your praises, how can I help pitying you?" (*Ep.* 29.12). The person who lives under a mask "cannot be happy and without anxiety" (*De tranq.* 17.1).

For Romans, who are inextricably connected to their political role, the price of recognition is a self that can no longer be recognized. The applause of the crowd elevates the individual, but the "heights of power" look like "a sheer precipice." (*Ep.* 94.73; also *De tranq.* 10.5). "Hence they are exhausted and disturbed whenever they look down the abrupt steep of their greatness (*Itaque exanimantur et trepidant, quotiens*

---

[91] Barton 2002, 222. On flattery in Seneca, see Roller 2001, 108–24.
[92] Edwards 1997, 35.

despexerunt in illud magnitudinis suae praeceps)" (Ep. 94.73, trans. modified). In a play on words, Seneca remarks that what appears weighty (*graves*) in the eyes of others weighs more heavily (*gravior ... incubat*) on those who ascend to these heights (*Ep.* 94.74; also *De tranq.* 2.5). This weightiness plays itself out in another image in which the weight of cargo can make a shifting ship more unstable (*Ep.* 28.3). The instability is heightened by the ship that continually shifts in its purpose (*De tranq.* 2.6). The Stoic takes on weight – the weight of political duty, tradition, and recognition – that is more perilously tossed to and fro by the shifting estimation and judgment of the world (*Ep.* 26.6; 95.57–58). On the sea one capsizes; on a mountain one plummets, terrified at the height and exhausted from trying to keep one's balance, living a life of restless aimlessness (*inquietus inertia*) (*De tranq.* 12.3). The fate of recognition, like the fate of invisibility, as suggested by both *exanimare* and *incubare*, is exhaustion and death.

RESTORING JURISDICTION

We know from our discussion of Livy, as well as the emphasis by the Stoics on appearing before oneself, about the centrality of vision in the fashioning of ethical conduct. The imagination becomes the visual record by which one orients oneself in the world. But where Livy seeks to recall a set of felt meanings that have receded, though perhaps not entirely disappeared, Seneca has no such luxury. There is no recourse by which one can easily restore vision because of the subversion of the markers by which one orients oneself politically.

Underlying the tension in Seneca's thought between recognition and retreat is his sense of the deeply human desire to appear, not just as affirmation of greatness but also as confirmation of existence. He speaks of the pleasure of a letter that brings one real traces (*vera ... vestigia*) and real marks (*veras notas*) of an absent friend (*Ep.* 40.1). "For that which is sweetest when we meet face to face is afforded by the impress of a friend's hand upon his letter, – recognition (*Nam quod in conspectu dulcissimum est, id amici manus epistulae impressa praestat, agnoscere*)" (*Ep.* 40.1). Striking in Seneca's statement is the importance he places on recognition as something that is embodied. Images of friends "only refresh the memory and lighten our longing by a solace that is unreal" (*Ep.* 40.1). What is real – what reveals (*ostendo*) itself to us – is the physical traces of another's being (*Ep.* 40.1; also *Ep.* 31.1).

Seneca is speaking within a Roman culture that placed extraordinary emphasis on visibility. Roman character was always on display: as *exempla* to be emulated, as *decorum* by which such virtues as fortitude and courage could be seen by others, as the imagined gaze of others in orienting behavior and defining one's sense of worth.[93] Seneca describes to Lucilius how we should live "as if we lived in plain sight of all men" (*Ep.* 83.1). Seneca, thus, promises Lucilius that he will inform him "by letter what I am doing, and in what sequence" as he watches himself and reviews each day (*Ep.* 83.2). As Long notes, in identifying how we bring ourselves into view, "Our natures are such that we fashion our own selves, and correct self-fashioning requires the interrogative and reflective task."[94] This image of artistic making has less to do with the "dandyism" that has been attributed to Foucault[95] and more to do with the care of the self as a form of "looking."[96] Seneca's *Epistles*, whether real or written as a fiction, emulate a process of education in which there is the trace of the teacher watching, guiding, responding, and prodding the student to train one's sight so that one learns to see oneself in a way that allows one to make judgments about one's relationship to the world.[97]

---

[93] On the role of the imagined gaze of others in defining one's sense of worth, see Kaster 2005, 35–65.

[94] Long 1996, 281. As Seneca writes, "all art is but imitation of nature" (*Ep.* 65.3).

[95] Hadot 1992, 230. See also Thacker 1993.

[96] Foucault 2005, 10, 217. On Foucault and Seneca, see Hammer 2008. I am leaving aside here Foucault's claim about the distinctiveness of the imperial tradition (and Seneca) in this care of the self. As this chapter demonstrates, I do not agree with Foucault that this care of the self results in anything like an "individualism" (see Foucault 1990, 3.41–43, 93–95). Gill argues against a turn toward "a new focus on individuality or subjectivity" in Hellenistic and Roman thought (2008, 364).

[97] On the connection of *oikeiōsis* to seeing, including seeing oneself, see Pembroke 1971, 118–19; Engberg-Pedersen 1990b, 42–46, 95; Vogt 2008, 183–84.

So Seneca begins with a Roman world that has made someone like Lucilius into a "nobody" (*pusillus*) (*Ep.* 44.1) and with materials, however humble, by which to begin fashioning a somebody (*Ep.* 85.40; also 31.11). Playing upon a long discourse that associates noble birth with gold and silver, Seneca looks to a humbler raw material: clay. As Seneca reminds Lucilius, when men were closest to the gods in the Golden Age, they, too, were made from clay (*Ep.* 31.11). Seneca, thus, begins to fashion an alternate, philosophic genealogy, one that does not look to pedigrees (*stemma*) nor associates nobility with "a hall full of smoke-begrimed busts" (*fumosis imaginibus*) (*Ep.* 44.1, 5; also *De ben.* 3.28.2: all share noble parentage of heaven). Socrates, for example, was not an aristocrat. Cleanthes served as a laborer. And philosophy made Plato a nobleman (*Ep.* 44.3). A "noble mind is open to all men" and is the way in which "we may all gain distinction" (*nobiles*) (*Ep.* 44.2, trans. modified).[98] But the process of gaining distinction is hardly elevated: It (like the craft of ancient art) requires labor to shape the soul (*Ep.* 50.5).[99] As Seneca reminds Lucilius, in drawing a comparison to a building, some dispositions are "pliable and easy to manage, but others have to be laboriously wrought out by hand" and the materials exhausted in preparing the foundation (*Ep.* 52.6).

The individual, whose mind is distorted with error and confusion (*Ep.* 94.5), can no more begin shaping oneself than the novice artisan can begin sculpting clay. Both need patterns and practice. Seneca, thus, points to precepts (*praecepta*) as a necessary beginning point for training the mind, both when the mind is young and tender and when it has become used to vices (*De ira* 2.18.1–36.6). Precepts have been seen by a number of scholars as constituting (with *decreta*, or principles) a system of fixed moral rules.[100] But the range of Seneca's topics and writings

---

[98] Seneca, furthermore, rejects the view that "only young minds are moulded" and that an older man, thus, "cannot be re-shaped" (*Ep.* 25.2). On Seneca's use of the imagery of social status in talking about Stoicism, see Roller 2001, 275–86.

[99] As Veyne notes, "*Style* does not mean distinction here; the word is to be taken in the sense of the Greeks, for whom an artist was first of all an artisan and a work of art was first of all a work" (1993, 7).

[100] Kidd 1978 provides an early argument for how *praecepta* and *decreta* constitute a system of moral rules. See Chapt. 1: Cicero, fn. 31, for different interpretations of natural law in Stoicism.

points to a role of moral instruction and guidance that goes beyond any formalized moral injunctions. His discussions continually reference the situational nature of decisions. As Seneca writes, the value of advice may depend on "the time, or the place, or the person" (*Ep.* 94.35; also 71.1; 94.14–16). The individual must not only account for different circumstances but must also know oneself, accounting for one's own natural disposition (*Ep.* 94.51; also 94.27). The prescriptions are not fixed; rather, as Seneca notes, advice "should 'grow while we work,'" developing increasing complexity that reflects the range of situations we encounter and experiences we have (*Ep.* 71.1; also 94.32).[101] And precepts do not have the character of a law. As Seneca says of gratitude, for example, there are no legal procedures, no judge, nor jury by which one could decide the appropriateness of gratitude (*De ben.* 3.7.1–3.8.4); it frequently relies on common sense (*sensus communis*) (1.12.3). Furthermore, unlike law, which frightens (*Ep.* 94.37), precepts can act as "a sort of exhortation" (*Ep.* 94.25), more like a companion to discuss and bring before the mind what risks being lost or confused (*Ep.* 94.26; also 94.55).

Against the isolating and deadening effects of *inertia*, this companion "engages the attention and rouses us, and concentrates the memory, and keeps it from losing grip" (*Ep.* 94.25). It can refresh memory (*Ep.* 94.21, also 94.25) and add "new points of view" (*Ep.* 94.30). And if one's "natural disposition has not been crushed," precepts can restore or give strength to the soul (*Ep.* 94.31) by lending support. To combat restless aimlessness where the mind frantically pursues what is of no real value, *praecepta* can chasten and scold, helping to check the emotions or give pause in order to rein in the insane (*insanus*) individual (*Ep.* 94.36, 47). Precepts can also go "straight to our emotions" (*adfectus*), fanning the spark of virtue that nature implants in the soul (*Ep.* 94.28–29). But the biggest work of *praecepta* involves helping one to see (*videre*) by giving guidance and practice in sorting the "jumbled mass" of matter into "proper classes" (*Ep.* 94.19, 21, 29, 32; also 38.2; also *De ira* 2.2.2: strengthen mind). One can start with what might be before one's eyes (*Ep.* 94.25; also 94.37; 95.34–35), over time learning

---

[101] See Kidd 1978, 255–56; Inwood 1999a, 104–5 on the relationship between katorthomic (moral) *decreta* and kathekontic (appropriate) *praecepta*.

and practicing patterns for how one reasons about choices (see esp. *De ben.* 4.10.1–2). One might be reminded of Cicero's suggestion that the senses can be trained, like an artist's, to see in the shadows and discern what others cannot see (Cic. *Acad.* 2.7.20). Paralleling the emergence of the individual from the shadowy netherworld of despotism, Seneca notes how teaching precepts functions much like the advice a physician gives to a recovering patient (one healed by *decreta*) not to "expose your weak vision to a dangerous glare; begin with darkness, and then go into half-lights, and finally be more bold, accustoming yourself gradually to the bright light of the day" (*Ep.* 94.18, 20). Unlike for Plato where one leaves the world of shadows and enters the light of truth, for Seneca the world, and one's place in that world, acquires illumination and clarity.

For Seneca, precepts are not enough since "advice concerning a portion of life" is not sufficient "without having first gained a knowledge of the sum of life as a whole" (*Ep.* 94.1; also 95.12). Where *praecepta* can give guidance about "what" to do, *decreta* (principles or doctrines) give us knowledge of "why" (*Ep.* 94.11). *Decreta* are formal principles based on and integrated into a philosophic system (*Ep.* 94.2, 4, 15; also Stob. 2.7.5b4 P).[102] They less issue prescriptions than convey the "inevitable laws of the universe," bringing to mind the "sense of [one's] own condition" (*Ep.* 94.7–8).[103] In one image Seneca associates *decreta* with the sap from a trunk that give life to the branches (the *praecepta*) (*Ep.* 95.64; also 95.64: like heart). What *decreta* do is give the "whole of life" to *praecepta* (95.12; see *Ep.* 95.59), providing assurance to things that are "adrift in our minds" by giving certainty to that which is hidden (*Ep.* 95.61–62).

The relationship between *praecepta* and *decreta* was likely part of a discussion in Stoicism since Seneca directs his comments to Aristo, a dissenting student of Zeno, who held that precepts are redundant (and thus not a necessary branch of philosophy) since individuals can fashion what to do in particular cases from knowledge of *decreta* (*Ep.* 94.2). But as Seneca writes, *decreta*, one's state of mind (*habitus*), and *praecepta* are

---

[102] See Kidd 1978, 253; Mitsis 1993. [103] See especially Inwood 1999a, 119.

"creative of" and "resultant from" the other (*Ep.* 94.49). One's judgments are strengthened by following one's duties, which precepts assist in carrying out (*Ep.* 94.34). And *decreta* help one fulfill these duties "in the proper way" (*Ep.* 95.40).

To find additional models of authority, one can also look to the "huge multitude" of maxims and quotations that are "scattered about in profusion" and need only "to be picked up" (*Ep.* 33.6). But there is a limit to the use of such passages. The builder, like the moral being, cannot live in imitation of another. Fearful of stunting the moral maturation of Lucilius, Seneca, in *Epistle* 33, eschews the further use of "extracts and quotations" or "mottos" (*Ep.* 33.3, 4). Seneca will continue to draw on the words of other philosophers; he will neither seek to encapsulate wisdom in a phrase nor attribute that wisdom to a particular source. That pedagogy seems to have a fairly explicit political reference. To have our words under "the leadership and commanding authority of one alone" is to replicate despotism in one's thoughts (*Ep.* 33.4). But, as Seneca writes, in giving legal standing to the self, "We Stoics are not subjects of a despot (*rex*); each of us lays claim to oneself (*sibi quisque se vindicat*)" (*Ep.* 33.4, trans. modified). *Vindico* is suggestive here of jurisdiction, referring to making a legal claim to something as one's own (Cic. *De rep.* 1.17.27; 1.32.48; *De off.* 1.7.22; *Brut.* 58.212; Caesar *BG* 7.1; *BC* 1.22; Livy 3.45.11; 3.46.3; 3.46.7; 3.46.8; 3.48.5). To lay claim to oneself is the essence of Roman *libertas*. To place oneself in a free condition requires initiative: One must both initiate one's standing to act and actually act. The individual must eventually "lean on himself" (*Ep.* 33.7).

> Take command, and utter some word which posterity remembers. Put forth something from your own stock...Remembering is merely safeguarding something entrusted to the memory; knowing, however, means making everything your own; it means not depending upon the copy and not all the time glancing back at the master.
>
> *Impera et dic, quod memoriae tradatur. Aliquid et de tuo profer .... Meminisse est rem commissam memoriae custodire. At contra scire est et sua facere quaeque nec ad exemplar pendere et totiens respicere ad magistrum* (*Ep.* 33.7–8).

Only then, as Seneca combines an aesthetic with legal image, can one fashion (*facio*) one's own guardianship (*tutela*) (*Ep.* 33.10).

In a traditional Roman context, the individual would appoint a guardian (*custos*) in order to have "someone whom you may look up to, someone who you may regard as a witness (*iudex*) of our thoughts" (*Ep.* 25.5; also 6.5: *exempla*).[104] But in an age in which authority is corrupted in crime and *exempla* confuse *ambitio* with *virtus* (*Ep.* 94.66–68), that guardian must be refashioned from history and memory.[105] The past, thus, is not just a record of instruction; it is formed into a companion, as an internalized voice and image so that you live "as if he were watching you" (*Ep.* 11.8; also 11.9–10; 25.5–6; 39.1–2; 55.8–11; 62.2–3). Seneca, therefore, tells Lucilius to "set as a guardian (*custos*) over yourself the authority (*auctoritas*) of some man, whether your choice be the great Cato, or Scipio, or Laelius, – or any man in whose presence even lost individuals would check their bad impulses" (*Ep.* 25.6, trans. modified; also 94.55; similarly, 94.52, 59: *advocatus*; 94.8, 10, 72: *monitor*).[106] One might also look to philosophers who, because they are our ancestors, provide the measure for conduct that is worthy (*Ep.* 44.3). Socrates stands out, as he is appropriated by the Stoics: During the reign of the Thirty Tyrants, he consoled, encouraged, scolded, and "for those who wanted to imitate him, he carried round with him a great example, as he moved a free man amid thirty masters" (*De tranq.* 5.2). So, too, as Seneca's own evaluation of Caesar changed to associate him less with *clementia* and more with servitude, a trajectory that follows Seneca's growing sense of his own despotic environment, Cato assumes prominence for standing "alone against the vices of a degenerate state that was sinking to destruction beneath its very weight," staying "the fall of the republic to the utmost that one man's hand could do to draw it back" (*De cons. sap.* 2.2; compare *De ira* 2.23.3; 3.30.4 to *Ep.* 71.9: ruin of *res publica*; 94.65; 95.70–71).[107] In reconceptualizing the relations of

---

[104] Mayer describes Seneca's exemplary figures as "a sort of guardian angel" (Mayer 1991, 167). On the use of *exempla* in Seneca, see Turpin 2008.
[105] On the problem of *exempla* for Seneca, see Roller 2001, 88–97.
[106] See also *Ep.* 11.10; 24.3–6; 42.7–8; 104.21; 104.27.
[107] On the changing attitude of Seneca toward Caesar, see Griffin 1976, 184–94. Griffin describes Seneca as speaking "more like a senator, and less like a political theorist" in

authority that inhere in despotism, Seneca is careful to note that these men of authority "are not our masters (*domini*), but our guides (*duces*)" (*Ep.* 23.11; also 33.4 and 80.1).

Seneca's point is not that an imagined companion is just like a real companion.[108] Rather, the fashioning of a companion follows from Seneca's warnings about secluding oneself, hidden not only from the gaze of others, but also from oneself. In such invisibility lies lawlessness, which we can understand most basically as an inability to act according to a set of limits or boundaries. Seneca's letters, thus, seek to make one present to oneself by way of an imagined other.[109] Drawing on a theatrical image, Seneca tells Lucilius that each becomes enough of an audience for the other (*Ep.* 7.11). "I see you," Seneca writes in this moment of recognition, "and at this very moment I hear you" (*Ep.* 55.11). Combining a theatrical with a juridical image, Seneca tells Lucilius, "Play the part, first of accuser, then of judge, last of intercessor (*accusatoris primum partibus fungere, deinde iudicis, novissime deprecatoris*)" (*Ep.* 28.10). In this sensual appropriation by the imagination, time and distance are gathered together into the conversation with oneself as another. As a result, as Seneca writes, "I have begun to be a friend to myself" and thus can "never be alone" (*Ep.* 6.7). At the point at which "you have respect for yourself," and thus are ready to care for yourself, you can send away your guardian (*Ep.* 25.6) and plead your case to yourself (*De ira* 3.36.3; or *De ira* 2.22.4: plead the cause of an absent person against yourself).

But such presentness cannot occur only in the imagination because, as we have seen, one can easily be lost in its boundlessness. There must be tangibility – a way of leaving behind the contours of the self. For Seneca, this tangibility is comprised, at least in part, by writing (*Ep.* 84.2, 5). Writing, as Foucault suggests, is an exercise of thought that "reactivates

---

his growing regret for the Republic (1976, 194). I'm not completely sure what is encompassed in this notion of a political theorist. I understand Seneca's later characterization of Caesar as enslaving (and the pairing with Cato) as coinciding with Seneca's growing sense of the struggle to restore jurisdiction under despotism.

[108] The creation of companionship is an aspect of Seneca's thought that has been frequently noticed. See, for example, Edwards 1997, 30. References in Seneca include *Ep.* 6.7; 24.17; 25.4–5; 26.7; 27.1; 28.10; 35.2; 78.21.

[109] On the self in dialogue with the self in a Greek context, see Gill 1996.

what it knows, calls to mind a principle, a rule, or an example, reflects on them, assimilates them, and in this manner prepares itself to face reality."[110] Writing leaves behind the physical traces of oneself by which one can be recognized by others and by oneself (*Ep.* 40.1; 83.1). It gives body (*corpus*) to what one has read, heard, and practiced (*Ep.* 84.2), gathering together and giving shape to the bits and pieces that comprise experience and memory so that one can begin to restore jurisdiction and lay claim to oneself.[111]

There is a corresponding renewal of rhetoric, and one that suggests the relationship between sanity and community life. As a response to the disjuncture between worth and acclaim, one should not speak with the audience in mind (as in rhetoric) but with the self in view (*Ep.* 20.1).[112] In contrast to the "heedless flow" of speechmaking, words should be chosen "deliberately," weighed because they are "worth weighing" (*Ep.* 40.11–13). And as a break from the falsity created by despotism one must feel what one says and be "wedded to it" (*Ep.* 75.3). We must "say what we feel, and feel what we say" so that speech can "harmonize with life" (*Ep.* 75.4). From the slipperiness of the self in which one always takes on different guises, through this new rhetoric "man has fulfilled his promise who is the same person both when you see him and when you hear him" (*Ep.* 75.4).

CITIZENSHIP AND COMMUNITY LIFE

Schofield (among others) argues that over time Stoic theorizing moves away from a "preoccupation with the *polis*" and toward simply the "moral potentialities of man considered as man, not as citizen."[113] Schofield is referring to the development in Stoicism from Zeno's community of sages to Chrysippus' doctrine of a cosmic city. The idea of the cosmic

---

[110] Foucault 1997, 209.
[111] Time had become a moral, rather than simply a physics, problem for the Stoics. See Goldschmidt 1953, 55–73; Rist 1969, 273–88; and Motto and Clark 1993, 54–64.
[112] Foucault 2005, 406.
[113] Schofield 1991, 102–3; also Reydams-Schils 2005, 85.

city grows out of Diogenes the Cynic's description of himself as a citizen of the universe, developed further by Cicero who describes the world as the city that is inhabited by gods and men who live by justice and law.[114] The language appears in Seneca when he states that one's cosmic citizenship makes one free by right of nature (*iure naturae*) even if not by right of Roman citizenship (*Nat. quaes.* 3.pref.16; also *De ot.* 4; *Ep.* 28.4). That freedom derives from one's ability to legislate for oneself, to enact what should and should not be done, according to right reason (which is sanity).[115] The language of the cosmic city, as Schofield points out, "attempts to retain community and citizenship while removing all contingency – such as physical proximity or mutual acquaintance – from the notion of citizenship."[116] As some indication of this, Seneca does not discuss the expansion of Roman citizenship as a means to the realization of a universal city.[117]

Much of what I have sought to demonstrate in this chapter is the continual awareness by Seneca of contingency to human affairs, both in his own life and in his refusal to seek philosophic recourse in an ideal community. We can begin to get at how contingency figures into Seneca's discussion of the cosmic city by way of a passage from Stobaeus that contrasts living in a city to living as a rustic (*agroikos*). For Stobaeus to live as a rustic means to have "a lack of experience of the customs and laws of the city" (Stob. 2.7.11k P = *SVF* 3.677). Living by the laws of the city means, as we have seen, to live according to the common laws that have their foundation in nature. Nature is important in this formulation, but so are customs, the informal ways in which one learns habits of action.[118] As part of one great, universal body where we are created from the same source and for the same end, we have, as Seneca writes, duties (*officia*) that arise from our mutual affection toward others (*Ep.* 95.52), reciprocal relationships judged not by laws (*De ben.* 3.8.1–4; 3.15.1–4)

---

[114] Cic. *De nat. deor.* 2.62.154; *De leg.*1.7.23; Stob. 2.7.11i P = *SVF* 1.587: definition of a city; Sen. *De ben.* 7.1.7; 6.23.6: *imperium*; Schofield 1991, 61.
[115] Schofield 1991, 68; Cooper 2004, 212–13. Also *Ep.* 75.1; freedom comes from being the "subject of my conduct"; having power over oneself (also DL 7.121).
[116] Schofield 1991, 103.   [117] Griffin 1976, 249–50.
[118] As we have noted, *lex* and *mos maiorum* are inextricably connected to each other (see Meier 1980, 45–51, 155–57; Wieacker 1988, 353–54; Hölkeskamp 2010, 12–22).

but by a community sense (*sensus communis*) (*De ben.* 1.12.3). Seneca's elaboration of these social relations has a strikingly Roman feel. Criticizing Chrysippus for having "very little to say about the duty itself of giving, receiving, and returning" (*De ben.* 1.3.8), Seneca notes that this duty "constitutes the chief bond of human society" (*De ben.* 1.4.2; also 6.41.2; *De ira* 1.5.3).[119] Seneca is talking about *beneficia*, which are technically distinct from *officia*. Duties (*officia*) are aspects of social obligations while benefits (*beneficia*) are not dictated by a specific obligation (*De ben.* 1.6.1).[120] But they are both aspects of a more general responsibility toward others that includes *humanitas*, or kindliness (*Ep.* 71.28; 88.30: *humanitas*; 93.4; 95.51: on duties generally).[121]

Seneca does not write in the same way or with the same level of detail that Cicero does in *De officiis*. And, as Griffin catalogues, in *De beneficiis* Seneca omits discussions of a range of exchange relationships in Roman society, including benefits given to the masses.[122] But in an age characterized by the isolating effects of despotism, Seneca is less offering a manual than cultivating a social disposition. Like Lucretius and Cicero before, he comments on the comparative minuteness and transitoriness of all mortal communities (*Nat. quaest.* 1.pref. 8–10).[123] But it is a perspective more in keeping with Cicero, meant to cultivate a particular view of the types of relationships and social benefits that define the individual as a community being. Seneca takes this larger view in his discussion of slaves, for example, suggesting a fundamental human equality:

> Kindly remember that he whom you call your slave sprang from the same stock, is smiled upon by the same skies, and on equal terms with yourself breathes, lives, and dies. It is just as possible for you to see in him a free-born man as for him to see in you a slave (*Ep.* 47.10).

Individuals, as Seneca continues, should be valued and associated with "according to their character, and not according to their duties"

---

[119] Especially helpful here is Inwood 2005, 65–94 on *De beneficiis*, who demonstrates how Seneca reconciles "the rigoristic and purely ethical dogma of the school" with "the realities of social and political life (2005, 91). See also Griffin 2013.
[120] Griffin 2013, 27–28.   [121] Griffin 2013, 45.   [122] Griffin 2013, 74–81.
[123] For some of the political aspects of Seneca's *Naturales quaestiones*, see Hine 2006.

(*Ep.* 47.15; also *De ben.* 3.18; 3.21.22).[124] But the interactions that Seneca imagines are not cosmic; they are local, imagining, for example, how the *domus* (household) could be seen as a miniature *res publica* in which slaves could attain honors and participate in self-government (*Ep.* 47.14).

Philosophy, as Seneca comments, teaches how to give and receive benefits well (*Ep.* 73.9).[125] Although short of a community of the wise, the outcome of these interactions is that both the community and the individual can be bettered, reinforcing what Griffin sees as "the social side of being *civilis*."[126] It is advice aimed at the Roman elite. But for Seneca the implications are more general: "The service of a good citizen is never useless; by being heard and seen, by his expression, by his gesture, by his silent stubbornness, and by his very walk he helps" (*De tranq.* 4.6; see also *Ep.* 47.16 on associating with slaves).[127]

Seneca delineates the different types of benefits that one can provide to another. Of foremost importance are benefits that are necessary for life (how we are able to live it or ought to live it) (*De ben.* 1.11.1), such as saving a person from a tyrant or from an enemy, or protecting another's liberty or chastity, or saving another's kin, without which one would feel robbed of life (*De ben.* 1.11.4). The next type of benefits are those that are useful, such as money to attain a certain standard or living, or office and advancement (*De ben.* 1.11.5). The final type of benefits are those that provide pleasure, which should be special precisely because they are not given frequently, may not be abundant, are carefully chosen for the occasion, and can last (*De ben.* 1.11.5; 1.12.1). In choosing something that endures, the additional benefit is that the object, as it is before their eyes, "brings up the thought of its giver and impresses it upon their mind" (*De ben.* 1.12.1).

In talking about benefits, Seneca is speaking from within a Roman social system in which hierarchical social bonds are formed through the exchange of objects and services. In this exchange, one shows *gratia*, or

---

[124] On Seneca's views on slavery, see Griffin 1976, 256–85.
[125] On the philosophical backdrop to Seneca's discussion of benefits, see Griffin 2013, 15–29.
[126] Griffin 2013, 11.
[127] Inwood 2005, 81: "The sage becomes not a paradox, but a practically relevant and useful component in the advice given about real social relations."

favor or regard for social position (*honor*) and friendship; the recipient in turn show *gratus*, or gratitude for the favor received. By receiving and returning benefits and showing and receiving gratitude, Seneca is not referring to the actual material gifts – money or a political office, for example – which are the "marks" of services (*De ben.* 1.5.2). The benefit is the "goodwill" of one who bestows it (*De ben.* 1.5.2; 1.5.5), or the "spirit" or "intention" (1.6.1), which is a "province of the mind" (1.5.2). A benefit is "the act of a well-wisher who bestows joy and derives joy from the bestowal of it, and is inclined to do what he does from the prompting of his own will" (*De ben.* 1.6.1; force and fear negate choice: *De ben.* 2.18.7). What matters is the character of the giver (*De ben.* 1.9.1) and, to some extent, the receiver (*De ben.* 1.10.5). That is, benefits are not absolute acts but always proportionate: One might endanger oneself to save a worthy man who is being robbed, but one only needs shout for help if it is an unworthy person (*De ben.* 1.10.5). A benefit is thus immune from fortune; it cannot perish, like the thing given, since it is a virtuous act (*De ben.* 1.5.3). Moreover, as a virtuous act the benefit is a good whereas what is done or given is an indifferent (*De ben.* 1.6.2). The pleasure of gratitude derives not from thinking about what has been received "as of him from whom it was received" (*De ben.* 1.15.4; 3.17.3). Seneca even seeks to direct the competitive aristocratic culture "to surpass in deed and spirit" those who have conferred benefits on us (*De ben.* 1.4.3; also 1.4.4: "honorable rivalry"). In a Roman world defined by hierarchies of reciprocal relationships, Seneca is attempting to identify the enduring bond, something more than pure instrumentality or naked self-interest, by which one can engage in the contingent relationships of community life.[128]

It is not that Seneca abandons the notion of cosmic citizenship. Seneca accepts the canonical Stoic view that through friendship the wise can practice virtue (*Ep.* 9.8; 109.1; 109.2–3). But he grounds this citizenship in the real interactions between human beings. Gratitude, as Seneca

---

[128] On the relationship of Seneca's conception to a Roman conception of benefits, see Griffin 2000, 548–51; 2013, who sees Seneca as "raising to theory" these tradtional ideals (2013, 63; also 74) and Roller 2001, 77–88, who sees Seneca as fundamentally challenging these traditional values.

suggests, underlies the "unity of the human race" upon which our survival depends (*De ben.* 4.18.4). In our fellowship (*societas*) with others we acquire "dominion over all creatures," extending our "sovereignty to an element not his own" (*De ben.* 4.18.3).

Seneca does not offer a vision of political institutions. Nor, though, is cosmic citizenship an abstraction. In the vastness of the imperial landscape, individuals have no choice but to encounter each other and to have relationships that extend well beyond one's intimate or local associations. In claiming the world as one's country one can engage in human interaction (*commercium*) "with the whole earth," giving us a "wider field for our virtue" (*De tranq.* 4.4). One needs *societas* for the material benefits it provides. But *societas* survives because of the intangible and enduring traces of gratitude that bind each to the other.

7 TACITUS: THE POLITICAL PSYCHOLOGY OF DESPOTISM

≉≉≉≉≉≉≉≉≉

Virgil, writing as Rome emerged from decades of violence, could envision the possibility of a new founding, a restored Golden Age of Rome, or at least some measure of peace. Livy, writing while Augustus was at least making gestures toward the republican past, could imagine the possibility of reanimating a Roman republican spirit. And Seneca could perhaps convince himself of his importance as a Stoic advisor in guiding and moderating the young Nero. But the legacy of savage cruelty, decadence, and incompetence that spanned the emperors from Tiberius to Domitian (81–96 CE) could support no such hope for Tacitus (Publius [or Gaius] Cornelius Tacitus, 56 – 117 CE). A "new factor," Martin writes, had imposed itself on the structure of historiography: "the reign of the individual emperor."[1] The theme that Martin and others see as guiding Tacitus' *Annals* (*Annales*) is the figure of the cruel and decadent tyrant.[2]

---

[1] Martin 1981, 104.
[2] Martin 1981, 142–43. So Benario sees Tacitus as affirming the necessity of the principate, "provided the emperor was good" (1972, 19). Kapust locates Tacitus' works with in an epideictic tradition of providing moral lessons by way of praise and blame (Kapust 2011, 150–51, 162–70). The focus on the personality of the emperor can be seen, for example, in debates about the nature of Tiberius. Tiberius as dissembling hypocrite: Marsh 1931, 14; Pippidi 1944, 37; Walker 1952, 238–39; Alexander 1954, 356–57; Syme 1958, 422–23; Martin 1981, 113; Gill 1983, 486; Sinclair 1995, 82; Griffin 1995, 36;

Rome had known tyrants before. Tacitus, in fact, opens the *Annals* with an account of the different experiences of concentrated power:

> The City of Rome from its inception was held by kings; freedom and the consulship were established by L. Brutus. Dictatorships were taken up only on occasion, and neither did decemviral power remain in effect beyond two years, nor the military tribunes' consular prerogative for long. Not for Cinna nor for Sulla was their lengthy domination, and the powerfulness of Pompeius and Crassus passed quickly to Caesar, the armies of Lepidus and Antonius to Augustus, who with the name of princeps took everything, exhausted as it now was by civil dissensions, under his command (*Ann.* 1.1.1).

Tacitus does not suggest that Augustus was more depraved than Appius Claudius, nor that Tiberius, particularly in the beginning of his reign, was crueler than Sulla (see *Hist.* 2.38). What marks the difference is their duration. Tacitus' language continually draws attention to the temporary nature of each of these earlier tyrannical moments, their duration limited by opposition, whether of the people, the senate, or other leaders.[3] What is so striking about the principate is the exhaustion from which it emerges, or what Eder describes as "the eerie silence" that accompanies its rise: a prideful aristocracy willing to continuously degrade itself; a noisy people rendered compliant; political institutions made into empty forms; and little inclination by anyone to change things.[4] These perplexities lead Tacitus to a diagnosis that something more enduring had penetrated into Roman political life. It is not the big moments, though, that Tacitus recounts. Rather, Tacitus' characterizes his *Annals* as *parva*

Boesche 1996, 87–109. More complex portrait of Tiberius: Tarver 1902, 294–319; Rogers 1943; Syme 1958, 426–29; Levick 1976, 75–8; Woodman 1998, 69; Seager 2005. As Tacitus writes in his obituary of Tiberius, "he erupted into crimes and degradations alike when at last, with his shame and dread removed, he had only himself to rely on" (*Ann.* 6.51.3). Quoted passages from *The Annals* are from Woodman, unless otherwise noted.

[3] See Goodyear 1972, 92–93: decemviral power actually lasted into the third year, though legal power only lasted two years; the military tribunes actually lasted from 444–367 BCE, "oscillating with consulship or dictatorship down to 406, thereafter almost unbroken" (Goodyear 1972, 93).

[4] Eder 1990, 74; also Raaflaub and Samons 1990, 450–54.

forsitan et levia memoratu, "little things perhaps, and things petty to remember" out of which "movements of vast changes often take their rise" (*Ann.* 4.32.2, my translation).

The acceptance of the principate is often attributed to the peace it lent after so many decades of violence and strife. In reconstructing the political world of the early principate, scholars sometimes lend it a certain normalcy, identifying formal structures of power, the operation of laws and institutions, the seemingly normal material interests that continued to motivate individuals, and the belief in the authority and legitimacy of imperial rule. When Tacitus views the principate from the experience of Domitian, he is referencing a far less visible, far more experiential, way in which the principate alters the cues by which individuals and groups develop their political attitudes, dispositions, and aspirations.[5] The calm is not evidence of normalcy but a symptom of sickness.

Tacitus is formulating an argument that is premised on what might be called political psychology. By "psychological" I do not mean it as a synonym for "character," as it is frequently used.[6] Instead, Tacitus is exploring the transformation in collective perceptions, emotions, moods, preferences, motivations, and calculations that serve as the impetus for political action. More than leading us to make judgments about the merits of individuals, Tacitus' account is meant to tell us something about the effects of circumstances, both past and present, on how individuals understand and navigate through a despotic world. In this regard, Tacitus' psychology is as much political as it is individual as he is

---

[5] Wirszurbski 1968, 160: "Perhaps the most striking feature of Tacitus' attitude to the Principate and to liberty is the fact that his estimate of the former and his idea of the latter are not determined solely, nor even primarily, by constitutional considerations."

[6] On the association of psychology with character, see Alexander 1952, 327 (little relation to what is called psychological today); Alexander 1954, 352–57; Miller 1964, 293; Häussler 1965; Martin 1981, 215; Mellor 1993, 70–71. Henry and Walker question Tacitus' reputation as an "acute psychologist" since his description of individual motivation and behavior is "entirely lacking in subtlety and penetration" (1963, 106). Luce attempts to shift scholarly focus from what he describes as the "almost exclusive concentration on the constancy of character" to what he calls "behavior": the ways in which an individual "acts and reacts" in response to the circumstances in which one finds oneself (Luce 1986, 156).

engaged in an exploration of the consequences of the gradual perversion and disintegration of the stable cues by which individuals orient themselves politically.[7]

We can perhaps better contextualize Tacitus' political psychology by way of Celsus (25 B.C.E–50 C.E), who is credited with compiling one of the most important and comprehensive medical treatises of the early imperial era, *De medicina*. Celsus reflects a movement toward a more scientific approach to medicine, less a form of philosophy than a study of the causes and treatment of physical as well as psychological disturbances. Describing the method of medicine, Celsus writes that one needs "to lay open the bodies of the dead and to scrutinize" the innards to obtain "a knowledge of hidden causes involving diseases" so that one can know how to care for them (Cels. pro. 23, 14).

So Tacitus also performs a vivisection of the political body to understand the malady of despotism. What emerges is a description of the motions (*motus*) of history that correspond to the almost imperceptible alterations of the collective spirit (*Ann.* 4.32.2; 1.2.1).[8] Despotism appears as something akin to a wasting disease (*tabes*) or to what Celsus and the Greeks call *atrophia*.[9] Striking for our interpretation of Tacitus is that *atrophia* has two contradictory causes, both of which seem operative in the political body that has succumbed to despotism. *Atrophia*, according to Celsus, is brought about by excessive desire in which the patient consumes more than he ought or by excessive dread in which the patient

---

[7] Von Fritz writes, there is "a problem not only of the psychology of Tiberius and of other individual emperors but also of the political psychology of the institution of the Principate itself that is to a large extent independent of the personal psychological equation both of the emperors and of Tacitus" (1957, 79); also Betensky 1978, 420; B. Williams 1990, 154–56. Cousin notes the instances of Tacitus' use of words that reflect the psychological response to the insecurity and unrest of the time: *pertimescere* 2, *pavescere* 8, *tristitia* 14, *timor* 16, *maestitia* 17, *maestus* 31, *pavere* 32, *pavidus* 33, *anxius* 33, *tristis* 39, *trepidus* 39, *timere* 44, *metuere* 57, *terror* 75, *pavor* 81, *metus* 402 (Cousin 1969, 121).

[8] Compare to Cels. pro. 15: *inflammatio talem motum efficit, qualis in febre est*. For Tacitus' conception of the state as a biological organism, see Havas 1991.

[9] On the use of *tabes*, see, for example, *Ann.* 1.53.2; 11.6.2; 12.50.2; 12.66.1 and Cels. 3.22.1. For a discussion of the practice of ancient psychology, see Roccatagliata 1986.

consumes less (Cels. 3.22.1). Combined, these forces set the political body against itself, leading to the gradual exhaustion of the animating impulses of Roman political life (e.g., *Ann.* 1.1.1).

Tacitus (like Seneca before) is talking about the loss of political bearings: one's sense of the clarity by which institutions and norms transmit expectations, channel ambition, and recognize accomplishments. These markers lose their objectivity, or the sense that they have an existence and meaningfulness apart from the individual, as they become increasingly indistinguishable from the emperor's will. With the progress of despotism, every marker – whether distinctions of legal and illegal, honorable and dishonorable, or trustworthy and untrustworthy – can mean its opposite. As Tacitus takes us inside the individual while the individual attempts to navigate through this unknowable and unreliable realm, we see the consequences of this transformation of the political landscape as ambition is replaced with melancholy, delirium, and servility. Tacitus' diagnostic starting point, to which we turn first, is the primitive societies of the Germans and Britons where the markers by which one navigates through community norms are in their most uncorrupted forms.

PRIMITIVE SOCIETIES

There is by now a long-standing tradition in ancient discourse that traces the genealogy of societies back to some primitive starting point.[10] That comparison serves a complex set of purposes in Roman thought, whether to trace the corruption of morals from a more innocent Golden Age (culminating in Augustine's notion of human fallenness from Eden), to identify our natural (as opposed to cultural) dispositions as does Lucretius, to romanticize a simpler existence as does Virgil in the *Eclogues*, or to highlight the increasing complexity, as well as the costs, brought about

---

[10] On the role of discussions of primitive times in ancient society, see Jens 1956, 349–52; Syme 1958, 125–26; Edelstein 1967; Wallace-Hadrill 1982, 19–36; Heilmann 1989. On *Germania* as mirror of Rome, see Syme 1958, 48, 126; Dudley 1968, 221; Dorey 1969; Mellor 1993, 14–16, 62; O'Gorman 1993; Rives 1999; Benario 1999; Haynes 2003, 13.

by human innovation as does Virgil in the *Aeneid*. Tacitus' earlier writings on the Germans and Britons, an anthropology of primitive society, provide the backdrop to his later discussion of the malady of despotism. In a digression in the third book of the *Annals* that refers back to primitive societies, Tacitus makes this connection, using the language of disease to describe how Rome is now afflicted by "the infinite number and variety of laws" (*multitudinem infinitam ac varietatem legum*) of his time. Tacitus' language, as Woodman and Martin point out, parallels Seneca's characterization of medical treatments as simpler in earlier societies until "by degrees it reached its present stage of complicated variety" (*paulatim ... in hanc pervenit tam multiplicem varietatem*) (*Ann.* 3.25.2; Sen. *Ep.* 95.15).[11] Tacitus' claims also recall Celsus who reports that "complex" forms of medicine were not needed in primitive times because individuals were not spoiled by indolence or luxury (Cels. pro. 5).[12] Now, Seneca writes, as did Celsus before, defenses need to be established that are all the more powerful because of the greater violence that attacks us (Sen. *Ep.* 95.14–15; also Cels. pro. 5).

Tacitus is exploring the operation of human sentiments in their most basic form, looking at the ways in which perceptions, ideas, memories, and habits orient individuals and communities to what is proper and improper. Tacitus' anthropology is not like Lucretius', an exploration of, and attempt to return to, what is natural. Rather, culture is always a part of human experience. Communities arrange experiences and judgments of those experiences from which individuals take their cue. They do this by providing collective memories that precede the life of the individual, as well as establishing laws, customs, and institutions that prescribe and proscribe conduct, creating habits that connect succeeding generations. And societies transmit concepts and ideas, the lived meanings that we saw with Livy, that provide linkages between different experiences.

As a profile of political psychology, these primitive tribes serve as a psychological starting point for tracing the course of despotism as it

---

[11] Woodman and Martin 1996, 239. *Laboro* is frequently used of disease. See Woodman and Martin 1996, 236 and Langslow 2000, 199.

[12] Also, "Plain vices could be treated by plain cures (*remedia simplicia*)" because bodies were still strong and unspoiled by luxury (Sen. *Ep.* 95.14).

breaks down the categories – and thus disorients the sentiments – by which individuals orient themselves politically. These early societies were not more natural or more innocent. What differentiates them from contemporary societies is that the norms and expectations of community life were more transparent.[13] One knew what the community expected and the types of actions that would yield rewards or punishments. Thus, Tacitus emphasizes the norms of reciprocity and equal exchange (*Germ.* 21.1), the clarity of the criteria for selection of kings and military leaders (*Germ.* 7.1), and the ability of commanders to lead by example (*Germ.* 7.1; 13.3–4). Important matters were brought before a public assembly, deliberation occurred with people who were "incapable of pretence," and decisions were made by people who were free from "illusion" (*Germ.* 22.4). The incentive to courage lay in the proximity of one's kin both in the organization of the squadrons and in the closeness of loved ones to battle so that the soldier could hear "the wailing voice of women and the child's cry" and be seen and praised by those he "covets most" (*Germ.* 7.3–4). Punishments were proportionate to the crime (*Germ.* 12.2; also 21.1). Shame was still operative (*Germ.* 6.6). And in social life there was "no arena with its seductions, no dinner-tables with their provocations to corrupt them. Of the exchange of secret letters men and women alike are innocent; adulteries are very few for the number of the people" (*Germ.* 19.1). In striking contrast to the interactions in imperial Rome, people spoke "without craft and cunning, and expose in the freedom of the occasion the heart's previous secrets" (*Germ.* 22.4).

What undermines this spirit, fostering both passivity and softness, is the loss of *libertas* that comes with Roman conquest (*Agric.* 11.4, of both the Britons and Gauls). Though at first resisting this servitude (*Agric.* 13.1), one learns to love the pleasure of inaction, distorting the perceptions of rewards and punishments so that individuals trade freedom for pleasure under the guise of progress (see *Agric.* 21.1). Such was the lot of the Britons who, Tacitus notes with bitter irony, under the corrosive influence of the Romans "gave the name of 'culture'"

---

[13] On Tacitus' purpose in writing the *Germania*, see Timpe 1989 (arguing against the work as either simply a moral treatise or political tract); Rives 1999; and Benario 1999.

(*humanitas*) to their servitude (*Agric.* 21.2). Introduced to rhetorical training, adopting the toga, "little by little the Britons went astray into alluring vices: to the promenade, the bath, the well-appointed dinner table" (*Agric.* 21.2).

Tacitus is drawing a comparison between the slow descent into servitude by the Britons and the Romans, who have similarly succumbed to *inertia* (*Agric.* 3.1).[14] Although Tacitus suggests that in some communities laws may reverse the course of despotism (*Ann.* 3.26.2), the sickness to which Rome has succumbed admits of no easy remedy. Laws, at first aimed at protecting liberty and maintaining *concordia*, become the forceful way of advancing one's perverted (*prava*) ends, aimed to advance oneself or to destroy another (*Ann.* 3.27.1).[15] As Tacitus observes, "with the infection in the state at its peak, the number of laws was at its greatest" (*Ann.* 3.27.3), heightening the disorganization of the political markers of Roman society. The *remedia* introduced by Pompeius, for example, the chosen healer of society, turned out to be more burdensome (*graviora*) than the ailment (*Ann.* 3.28.1).[16] As sole consul, he established a new court and proceedings (the *lex Pompeia de vi*), ostensibly to prosecute swiftly individuals responsible for recent disturbances (such as the murder of Clodius, the burning of the senate house, and the ensuing riots), but in reality to eliminate Milo, a political rival.[17] Pompeius also established the *lex de ambitu*, a law that retroactively as well as prospectively punished electoral corruption, especially bribery. The use of the law to advance one's own political interests served only to highlight the jumbling of norms: "all acts of the basest nature passed with impunity, and many of honesty led to extermination" (*Ann.* 3.28.1). With the outbreak of civil war, neither right (*ius*) nor

---

[14] Helpfully, see Liebeschuetz 1966; Lavan 2011.
[15] *Pravus* also said of Sempronius Gracchus (*Ann.* 1.53.3); of the Parthian view of Vonones (*Ann.* 2.2.4); of Piso's confession (*Ann.* 3.16.4); of the depravity of Roman wives (*Ann.* 3.34.3); of the depravity of the nobility and the sickness of the age (*Ann.* 3.65.1); of Junius Rusticus (*Ann.* 5.4.1); and of Agrippina's charge against Nero's preceptors (*Ann.* 12.41.3).
[16] On *corrigere* in medicine, see Woodman and Martin 1996, 255. On *gravis* in medicine, see Celsus pro. 39; 1.3.1.
[17] See Gruen 1995, 224–35; Habicht 1990, 58–9; Morstein-Marx 2004, 3–4.

custom (*mos*) remained, returning Rome to a now corrupt form of primitive society (*Ann.* 3.28.1).[18]

The rule of one man in the figure of Octavian, at least in the eyes of some, appeared as the new *remedium*, bringing about *quies*, or calm, to the disordered community (*Ann.* 1.9.4–5). Tacitus' language recalls the task of a physician who aims, as Celsus writes, toward the quiet of the spirit (*ad quietem animi*) of a disturbed patient (see Cels. 3.18.5). And to some extent Augustus brings this quiet. He restores the rule of law by reappointing an urban praetor and invalidating illegal acts of the triumvirate.[19] He attends to the material needs of the populace.[20] And, as Galinsky argues, he speaks to the "revitalization of the mores of the *res publica*."[21]

For Tacitus, though, the *quies* created by Augustus recalls an unhealthy calm that gradually spreads throughout the community. What lies beneath the surface is, simply put, madness that results from the loss of stable markers by which one can navigate through the political realm. These markers are of two types: institutions to which individuals can appeal and cultural norms by which individual ambition is channeled and achievement recognized. Augustus quiets the people with cheap corn, a purchase of tyranny, to recall Livy, that Spurius Maelius had attempted unsuccessfully in the Republic (*Ann.* 1.2.1; Livy 4.15.6). He calms the army through gifts (likely the promise of land upon discharge) (*Ann.* 1.2.1).[22] He entices everyone "with the sweetness of inactivity" (*Ann.* 1.2.1). And he concentrates the functions of the senate, magistracy, and legislature into his own person, silencing the most outspoken, either on the battlefield or through proscription lists,[23] and subduing the rest who prefer safety to the danger of the old order (*Ann.* 1.2.1). Perhaps the most telling quiet from Tacitus' perspective is the silence and falsification of history that occurs as historians became enfeebled, whether because of

---

[18] Compare to Tacitus' statement that for the Germans, "good habits" (*boni mores*) had more force than "good laws elsewhere" (*alibi bonae leges*) (*Germ.* 19.5; also *Ann.* 3.26.1).
[19] Eder 1990, 103. See also Lacey 1996, 210 and Nicolet 1984.
[20] Nicolet 1984.   [21] Galinsky 1996, 8.   [22] See Goodyear 1972, 104.
[23] On proscriptions, see Syme 1939, 187–201.

the growth of *adulatio*, cringing flattery, or dread (*metus*) (*Ann.* 1.1.2).[24] As Tacitus writes in opening his *Histories*, after Actium the truth of history is impaired "because men were ignorant of politics as being not any concern of theirs; later, because of their passionate desire to flatter; or again, because of their hatred of their masters" (*Hist.* 1.1).[25]

From a psychological perspective, the temper of the quiet that comes over the Roman citizenry seems more like political paralysis than tranquility. Like paralysis, as Celsus writes, individuals "drag out a miserable existence, their memory lost also," so no living memories of the Republic remains. Few are left "who had seen the Republic" (Cels. 3.27.1A; *Ann.* 1.3.7). Gone with these memories is a republican disposition of equality that combines vigor and restraint (*Ann.* 1.4.1).[26] In the place of these orienting memories is the body and will of Augustus, the *pater patriae* (as formalized in 2 BCE), the father of the country, to whom everyone looks (*Ann.* 1.4.1).[27]

Tacitus' language, as it manipulates the image of the benevolence of the Augustan age, recalls a notion that has its origin in Aristotle: the emperor as *dominus*, the despotic head of the household.[28] As Tacitus insinuates through the murmurings of those opposed to Augustus's rule, "devotion to his parent" was merely the pretext for the "desire for dominion" (*Ann.* 1.10.1). By the time of Tiberius, as Tacitus implies, the spirit of despotism had set in: there "was a rush (*ruo*) into servitude"

---

[24] *Adulatio* ascribed to Oriental despotisms: Livy 9.28.4. The extent and nature of censorship under Augustus are assessed by Raaflaub and Samons 1990, 436–47. Galinsky provides a rather sympathetic account of the flourishing of art, literature, and expression under Augustus (1996, 225–87, 370); Rudich points to the sheer uncertainty of navigating what was permitted and prohibited in the early principate (2006). Tacitus provides an account of the prosecution of Cremutius Cordus by clients of Sejanus for publishing annals praising M. Brutus (*Ann.* 4.33).

[25] Translation Moore.

[26] See also *Ann.* 3.26.2: "equality was cast aside." On Tacitus' use of *aequalitas* in a political context, see Wirszubski 1968, 116; Goodyear 1972, 118.

[27] The state, in fact, became legally the "parent of everyone," inheriting the property of childless households (*Ann.* 3.28.3). Augustus would also appropriate the private religious cults to make himself *Pater Patriae* (Lacey 1996, 5, 13, 169–89). On the model of emperor as father, see Stevenson 1992.

[28] See, for example, *Ann.* 1.3.2; 1.4; 1.10.1. On the use of *dominus* by Tacitus to describe imperial rule, see Benario 1964 and Fontana 1993.

by consuls, senators, and knights: "the more illustrious each was, the more false and frantic" (*Ann.* 1.7.1). The hastiness and ruin denoted by *ruo* contrasts sharply with, and occurs under the guise of, quiet, justifying Tacitus' own aim to look beneath the surface (*introspicere*) of events not just to highlight the hypocrisy of the era but to diagnose the malady of despotism (*Ann.* 4.32.2).[29]

As these markers become progressively subsumed under the will of the sovereign, there are two primary choices that face people who must navigate through this realm. Both choices result in forms of madness. The first choice, which is played out in the mutinies that open the *Annals*, is to rage like a madman against the arbitrary decisions, the cruelties, and the disingenuousness of the sovereign until one ultimately collapses from exhaustion. The second choice is servility. The path to power, recognition, and status (and often survival) lay in the ability to cater to the whims of the emperor. Since those whims are themselves unstable and unknowable, servility fosters its own form of insanity in which what one says and how one acts becomes increasingly disconnected from any communication of meaning or feeling. It is in the institutionalization of terror, though, that the sentiments of honor, friendship, and liberty – the central animating impulses of Roman political life – are finally dissolved.

UNMEDIATED POLITICS

What makes despotism so insidious (and so maddening) is that it does not just parade as unabashed illegality or cruelty; it often operates under the guise of law and custom. Thus, what some commentators see as Tacitus' begrudging recognition that institutions were still operative is in fact a more subtle argument about the unpredictability of these forms. Tiberius spoke on behalf of the rule of law (*Ann.* 3.69.2–6), he frequently employed Augustan precedent (1.77.1–3; 4.37.1–38.3; 6.3.1–3),[30] he recognized ancient liberties (*Ann.* 1.7.3; 4.6), he often referred public

---

[29] See Lana 1989 for Tacitus' distinctive use of *introspicere*.
[30] On Tiberius' use of Augustan precedent, see Cowan 2009.

matters to the senate (see, for example, *Ann.* 4.6.2), he rejected extravagance, even his own (*Ann.* 3.52–54), and he seemed genuinely frustrated with the subservience of the nobility (see *Ann.* 2.38.1; 3.35.1; 3.65.3).[31] Tiberius "handed out honors," as Tacitus notes, "by paying regard to the nobility of ancestors, brilliancy of soldiering, and illustrious qualities at home" (*Ann.* 4.6.2).

But the continuities are deceptive. Eder, in pointing to continuities between the Republic and the early principate, suggests that one can understand the principate as "the formation of a social and political power based on personal relationships and dependencies," relationships that had always been central to the politics of republican Rome but were now "carried to extremes."[32] What makes these relationships so extreme is that they are no longer mediated through meaningful institutional forms. The senate and the people had been rendered "ineffective and unarmed" (*Ann.* 1.46.1). The senate, in Tacitus' words, had become an *imago antiquitatis*, a shadow of its past (see *Ann.* 3.60.1).[33] And the tribunes discovered, as Julius Agricola realized, that "to be passive was to be wise" (*Agric.* 6.3). Thrasea, for example, warns Arulenus Rusticus that to exercise the veto would be "an empty initiative, of no advantage to the defendant and ruinous to the intervener" (*Ann.* 16.26.5).[34] Although the imperial powers maintained a constitutional form, they were organized around, and subordinated to, the will of the sovereign.

One sees the nod to customary forms played out with heightened anxiety. For example, Tiberius' attempt to encourage debate in a senate

---

[31] Thus, I think that Dunkle makes Tacitus' portrait of Tiberius too stereotypical (Dunkle 1971, 17–18).

[32] Eder 1990, 83–4. On continuities of Augustus' reign with the earlier republican system, see Introduction; Raaflaub 1987, 41–45; and Galinsky 1996.

[33] See Ginsburg 1981, 87–95; 1993; Marshall 1975, 15–16: Tacitus' treatment of the senate; Ginsburg 1981, 124–26 (fn. 27–34): Tiberius's continual intrusions into senate affairs; Eck 1984: limitations of senatorial self-representation; Talbert 1987, 172–4: infrequency of senatorial disagreement with the emperors. Confirming evidence of the irrelevance of senatorial careers: the difficulty of finding candidates for quaestorships, tribuneships, and aedileships (Levick 1985, 60). Tiberius laments the difficulty of finding suitable people to fill governorships (*Ann.* 6.27.3).

[34] There are examples of tribunes intervening. See, for example, *Ann.* 1.77.1–3: Haterius Agrippa intervening against proposals allowing praetors to beat actors.

where no one would speak his mind made more poignant, as Tacitus observes, the "traces of dying freedom" (*Ann.* 1.74.5; also 3.35.2; 4.6.1; 4.7.1). When Tiberius declares that he will vote in the prosecution of Granius Marcellus, hoping to instill equity in judgments, Piso asks in what order the emperor would vote: "If first, I shall have something to follow; if after everyone else, I am afraid lest I dissent improvidently" (*Ann.* 1.74.5).

Piso expresses the anxiety, more than any fear, of navigating through public institutions and processes that appear incoherent and insincere. As Brunt points out:

> Fear can hardly account for servility before Tiberius' last years. The explanation may lie partly in the equivocal position of the 'first man in the state'. All real power was in his hands, and yet he professed to be an accountable minister. How could men be sure when he was seeking advice for form's sake, or sincerely wished for counsel and was prepared to act in accordance with the general wish?[35]

By the time of Tiberius, as Asinius Gallus would make clear in his appeal to Tiberius in the early days of the *princeps*' accession to office, "the body of the state was one and needed to be ruled by the mind of one individual" (*Ann.* 1.12.3).[36]

The result of this association of the political body with the body of the emperor is not the powerlessness of other groups but a lack of gradations in the ability to express or negotiate power. Groups could affirm and groups could vent, but there were few other avenues that they can or might want to take. Accompanying this loss of any mediating function by institutions is the transfer to the will of the sovereign of the mechanisms of political recognition and power by which the highest rewards – wealth, honor, and status – are defined and earned. In sharp contrast to the German tribes where the rules, expectations, and enforcement of those expectations were transparent, in despotism one encounters a

---

[35] Brunt 1984, 444.
[36] Ideology of *corpus imperii*: Beranger 1953, 218–37; Häussler 1965, 273–57; Goodyear 1972, 180. See also Pliny *Ep.* 3.20.12: everything depends on will of one man and Sen. *De clem.* 1.5.1 (and chapt. 8): the emperor is the "soul of the state and the state your body." On the visual language that now focused on the image of the emperor, see Zanker 1988.

political landscape where public categories of true and false, right and wrong, just and unjust, protected and unprotected, legal and illegal, and honorable and dishonorable have no reality apart from the emperor's will, making it impossible for individuals to know, understand, make inferences about, or predict the boundaries of political conduct.

In talking about changes in norms and institutions, Tacitus directs our attention to the disorienting effects of the loss of these institutional and cultural forms of mediation. Two different, seemingly contradictory, responses occur: frenzied and unsustainable outcry and enfeebled and corrupted servility. Both responses are, in fact, symptoms of the same ailment. Tacitus gives us images of both: the armies abroad driven to mutiny, and the elites at home succumbing to servility. In both cases, everyone ends up mixed together in a political form that appears radically egalitarian. Beneath the carefully maintained hierarchies of status, Tacitus exposes the leveling quality of despotism in the primary language available to him: as the willingness of the elites to take on the attributes of mass behavior. If there is a helpful image, it is of politics becoming theatrical in the same way that theater in Rome becomes political. However much the theater, like politics, retained the forms of a status hierarchy, it becomes the most raucous and the most servile of forums.

The mutinies: The breakdown of trust

The mutinies in Pannonia and Germany provide some insight into the disorienting effects of an unmediated politics. The episodes are commonly read as inviting comparison between Germanicus and Tiberius, whether of Germanicus as the heroic leader to the villainous Tiberius, or as more critical of such popular leaders as Germanicus for allowing *licentia* in catering to the mob.[37] Woodman, for example, sees these

---

[37] Ross 1973, 226–27. Ross is following Shotter 1968. For the tradition of Germanicus as hero (or exemplary leader), see Walker 1952, 9, 118–19; Mendell 1970, 30; Daitz 1960, 37; Koestermann 1963, 39; Syme 1958, 418; Dudley 1968, 100; Mellor 1993, 75–76; Williams 1997; Kapust 2011, 168. More ambiguous treatments of Germanicus's heroism are offered by Goodyear 1972, 239–41; B. Williams 1990, 141–45; and Pelling 1993.

episodes as more critical of Germanicus than is often assumed, but broadens his diagnosis of the extent of the turmoil. In drawing on a Roman historiographic tradition of brothers fighting on behalf of Rome, Tacitus announces that something is amiss: Rather than successfully integrating new territory into Rome, as did Tiberius Nero and Claudius Drusus at the end of Livy's *History*, Drusus and Germanicus "are obliged to combat mutiny in their own ranks."[38] The mutinies, Woodman argues, appear as "detailed and comprehensive case studies of collective madness" that require drastic forms of leadership.[39]

Rowe, quite in contrast, portrays the Pannonian and German mutinies as a form of political interaction in which the soldiers employed the "formal tools their political culture provided": They assembled, began constructing a *tribunal*, engaged in "oratory and response," selected ambassadors, made collective decisions, and issued their demands.[40] Rowe observes, "From a disinterested perspective, the same mutinies appear remarkable for their orderliness. Soldiers deliberated in assemblies, made moderate demands, and demonstrated a keen grasp of the political system to which they belonged."[41] Speaking generally about the soldiers as an imperial constituency, Rowe concludes, the military camps appeared "like poleis" and the soldiers, perhaps unique in imperial Rome, had developed a "participatory political culture centered on the *contio*."[42]

The political forms that Rowe points to, however, are precisely the problem; they make all the more apparent the absence of trustworthy institutional mechanisms for mediation. But where Woodman and others focus primarily on leadership responses to the resulting disorder, I believe that Tacitus is using the episodes to associate that madness with an unmediated politics. However much political forms may be emulated, they are characterized more by widespread distrust in them. The result is a political realm with extraordinary volatility that ebbs and flows with the passions of the crowd and the ability of leaders to inflame or subdue this fervor. It is theater with political forms as its props.

---

[38] Woodman 2006a, 324.　[39] Woodman 2006a, 325.
[40] Rowe 2002, 163.　[41] Rowe 2002, 162.　[42] Rowe 2002, 172.

Tacitus signals this perverse theatricality when he introduces Percennius, the instigator of the mutiny among the Pannonian legions, who was a "leader of a theatrical claque" in his early years. With his experience of stage rivalries and his "provocative tongue," he is able "to stir up (*miscere*) crowds with his actorish enthusiasm" (*Ann.* 1.16.3). Tacitus describes his influence:

> On impressionable minds, uncertain about what the precise condition of soldiering after Augustus would be, he exerted a gradual influence in nightly dialogues or when day had turned to evening, and when the better men had slipped away, he trooped all the basest ones together. At length, with others too now ready to serve the mutiny, his questions took on the style of a public meeting: why, in the fashion of slaves, were they obedient to a few centurions and even fewer tribunes? (*Ann.* 1.16.3–17.1)

The scene, as it manipulates Roman tropes, recalls both Livy's portrayal of Brutus' appeal to the enslavement of the Romans by the Tarquins and Sallust's description of Catiline's disingenuous summons to the conspirators. The crowd responds with approval "from a variety of incentives, some remonstrating about the marks of their beatings, others their white hair, most of them their worn-out coverings and naked bodies" (*Ann.* 1.18.1). The soldiers employ a series of political forms, notably constructing a tribunal, but they are forms, as Tacitus is careful to note, that are constructed in a state of madness (*furor*) (*Ann.* 1.18.2). Blaesus, the commander, pleads on behalf of mediation, arguing that naming deputies and providing them instructions is better than "mutiny (*seditio*) and disruption (*turba*)" (*Ann.* 1.19.2). Although Blaesus brings momentary calm, he cannot establish long-term, procedural resolution: the decision – affirmed through a shout – to choose Blaesus' son as an envoy only demonstrates to the soldiers that "necessity had extracted what they would not have achieved through moderation" (*Ann.* 1.19.5).

What emerges through Tacitus' account is the sheer instability of these political interactions: the mutiny reignited; attempts to suppress the mutiny through terror by leading some of the mutineers to jail to be beaten; and the crowd shouting abuse at the leaders and then rising up, aroused variously by odium, sympathy, alarm, and indignation, to free the deserters and criminals condemned for capital offenses. The freed prisoners then mix (*misceo*) almost immediately with the crowd (*Ann.* 1.21.3). *Misceo* is a suggestive word here, meaning to mix or mingle, sometimes for good (like marriage) but often denoting an unnatural confusion.[43] In this case, the confusion is compared to a fever that burns hotter as the mutiny finds new leaders to address the turbulent crowd, "agitated as they were" (*Ann.* 1.22.1).[44] Vibulenus, a common soldier, now becomes a leader, further inflaming the crowd through the most corrupt forms of rhetoric: He lies about the death of his brother, weeps and strikes his face and breast, and then fawns at the feet of each man until he "provoked so much consternation and resentment that some of the soldiers bound the gladiators who were among Blaesus' slaves, some the rest of his establishment, while others poured out to look for the body" (*Ann.* 1.23.1).

But there is nothing sustainable, precisely because there is nothing trustworthy or predictable, in the interactions. Tiberius, though "reclusive and especially given to concealing all the grimmest matters," sends Drusus to the camp, but with "no particularly fixed instructions" (*Ann.* 1.24.1). What Drusus encounters are the tattered forms of imperial order: soldiers are unkempt, the military standards are not displayed, and the crowd greets Drusus with an angry roar. Turmoil, rather than traditional dignity and order, mar the *adlocutio*, the formal imperial address to the troops.[45] More than that, though, are the fluctuating emotions: "a frightening roar and suddenly quiet; in accordance with their different emotions they were panicked and terrifying (*atrox clamor*

---

[43] See *Ann.* 1.7.1: Tiberius mixes tears with joy, regrets with adulation; 1.16.3: Percennius stirs crowd; 1.18.2: mixing of legions; 1.54.2: Augustus mixes in the pleasures of the crowd; 1.64.1: mingling of cries in battle; 3.22.2: Tiberius confuses symptoms of anger and mercy; 3.67.4: Silanus, desperate under criminal attack, mingles reproaches with petitions; 4.51.2: confusion of battle because of inability to distinguish friend from foe. *Misceo* forms the root, as well, for *promiscuus*, an indiscriminate mixing.

[44] See Woodman 2006a, 315.

[45] On the *adlocutio*, see Campbell 1984, 72–76. Compare the image of the camps with Polybius' account of the orderly arrangement of the camps (Polyb. 6.31.1–14).

et repente quies; diversis animorum motibus pavebant terrebantque)" (*Ann.* 1.25.2).

What really provokes an outburst and points to this issue of an unmediated politics is when Drusus suggests that there are proper institutional mechanisms that obligate both the emperor and the troops for addressing the grievances.[46] When Drusus appeals to the jurisdiction (*arbitrium*) of the senate and his father, an assertion that such mechanisms actually exist, he is interrupted with a tumultuous shout (*Ann.* 1.26.1). The soldiers exclaim (not inaccurately), "It was obviously a novelty that the Commander should refer only the benefits of soldiers to the senate: was the same senate therefore to be consulted each time reprisals or battles were declared?" (*Ann.* 1.26.3). It is only an eclipse that leads the troops to believe the gods are against them, halting a further outbreak of violence. What is striking, though, is how Drusus chooses to take advantage of this chance event by sending popular officers to the tents of the soldiers to make them "mutually suspicious" so that the collectivity, once united in its outcry, would be separated again: recruit from recruit, veteran from veteran, legion from legion (*Ann.* 1.28.6).

The German mutinies are portrayed in similarly tumultuous terms: fury (*Ann.* 1.31.1), delirium (1.31.3), frenzy (1.32.1), and paroxysms of rage (1.32.1), spoken in "indistinguishable utterances" that the soldiers attribute to exhaustion (1.35.1–2). The anger again unifies the men, only absent mechanisms for collective expression the unity once again appears more as a disordered mixing. When Germanicus returns to address the troops, they "seemed thoroughly disorganized" (*permisceo*) (*Ann.* 1.34.3; also 1.18.2). They are separated neither by company nor rank. And, just as the Pannonian troops respond to Drusus' letter from Tiberius as a farce, even though the letter was real, the German troops detect that the letter given to them promising the resolution of the grievances is a fabrication and demand, instead, immediate action (*Ann.* 1.37.1). The actual difference between a real

---

[46] Similarly, Ash notes that in Tacitus' recounting of civil wars in the *Histories*, "soldiers on all sides gradually develop a mistrust of their immediate commanding officers" (1999, 168).

letter and a forgery turns out to be of little consequence, particularly since, as Tacitus later observes, Tiberius would simply cancel any promises that had been made (*Ann.* 1.78.2). But Tacitus poses a striking juxtaposition in passing and one to which we will turn. Against the backdrop of rebellious troops are the senate and commons, feeble and helpless (*Ann.* 1.46.1), already given sufficient sedative to prepare them for their servitude (*Ann.* 1.46.3).

Back at home: Fostering servility

Of course the people are not completely placid. There are moments in which the urban plebs, too, express themselves collectively.[47] Absent formal institutions of political expression, though, the site of such outbursts was often the theater where, as Tacitus comments, "the common people have the greatest license" (*Hist.* 1.72; also *Ann.* 3.36.1).[48] The characteristic of license for Tacitus is its leveling quality as distinctions and recognition of rank and status give way to resentment and abuse against good people (*Ann.* 3.36.1). Just as the murmurings of the soldiers escalate into mutiny in Pannonia and Germany, so at about the same time in Rome the disorderliness of the theater (*theatri licentia*) "erupted more seriously now," leading soldiers, including members of the praetorian guard, to suppress the expressions of public dissent (*Ann.* 1.77.1). In other examples of such collective license, Lepida excites the audience attending the Games, who "shouted savage execrations" against Quirinius for having accused Lepida of attempting to poison him (*Ann.* 3.23.1). The theatrical factions had gotten to be so "mutinous" in whipping up the people to a pitch of "outrage and violence" that Tiberius bans actors from Italy (*Ann.* 4.14.3). High corn prices nearly end in rioting with demands made by the populace in the theater for several days "with more license against the Commander than was customary" (*Ann.* 6.13.1). And Claudius

---

[47] On forms of mass unrest in the principate, see Yavetz 1969, chapts. 2, 5; Bollinger 1969, 50–71; Gilbert 1976, 71–79; Nippel 1995, 85–90; Kienast 1999, 201–3.

[48] For the importance of the theater as the primary forum of political expression, see Veyne 1990: 398–403; Nippel 1995, 87; Potter 1996, 144; Beacham 1999, 160–61.

reprimands the crowd for its insolence in mocking individuals of rank, including a consular (*Ann.* 11.13.1).

These collective bodies, both of the army and the urban plebs, are not powerless.[49] Emperors frequently address the troops to both gauge opinion and establish a personal and imperial relationship with the army.[50] Tiberius is quite rightly concerned that Germanicus' relationship to the troops could imperil his own rule (see, for example, *Ann.* 1.31.1; 1.35.3; 1.52.1).[51] The people, too, are able to bring pressure on imperial rule (see *Ann.* 2.87.1; 5.4.2). Tiberius, always bothered by the crowds (*Ann.* 6.13.1), struggles to find ways to effectively limit popular displays, both in the street (*Ann.* 1.8.5–6) and in the theater (*Ann.* 1.77; 4.14.3). And other members of the imperial family would bask in the collective (and similarly undifferentiated) affirmations of imperial authority: Germanicus' son, Nero (*Ann.* 3.29.3), Claudius (*Ann.* 12.7.1: affirming Claudius' incestuous marriage), the young Nero (*Ann.* 11.11.2), and Octavia (*Ann.* 14.61).

But such outbursts become the rare collective expressions of the community. Tacitus more frequently shows how this unmediated politics creates a disjointed and enfeebled public discourse. Tacitus' description of the public reception of Tiberius' words upon assuming the throne reveals how disconnected discourse had become from expressions of purpose or meaning. Tacitus depicts a public realm bereft of the language by which people communicate understanding:

> More in such a speech was impressive than credible; and Tiberius' words, even on matters which he was not for concealing, were – whether by nature or habit – always weighed and obscure; but on that occasion, when he was striving to hide his feelings deep down, their extra complication led to uncertainty and ambiguity. But the fathers, whose one dread was that they seemed to understand, poured out complaints, tears, and vows.

---

[49] I disagree with Bartsch that Tacitus presents a view of the emperor as controlling and manipulating the crowds, without the crowd being able to exert control (1994, 24–26). On the need for even absolute rulers to respond to and anticipate forms of collective expression, see Levick 1967, 230 and Rowe 2002.

[50] Campbell 1984, 18.   [51] See Shotter 1968, 195–96.

> *Plus in oratione tali dignitatis quam fidei erat; Tiberioque, etiam in rebus quas non occuleret, seu natura sive adsuetudine, suspensa semper et obscura verba; tunc vero nitenti ut sensus suos penitus abderet, in incertum et ambiguum magis implicabantur. At patres, quibus unus metus si intellegere viderentur, in questus, lacrimas, vota effundi* (*Ann.* 1.11.2–3, trans. modified).

In a despotic world where liberty is feared and flattery detested, words, facial expressions, and gestures have to be adjusted to betray no trace of one's thoughts (*Ann.* 2.87.1; also *Ann.* 3.65.2; 13.4.1 ; 13.16.4). Thus, one's expression conveys the nonsensical ramblings of an insane person: tears mixed with delight, grief with adulation (*lacrimas gaudium, questus adulationem miscebant*) (*Ann.* 1.7.1; see Cels. 3.18.2).[52] Only the dead, through books written as make-believe wills, could speak truthfully (*Ann.* 14.50.1).

Whether talking about the outbreak of mutiny or the servility of the aristocracy, Tacitus continually conveys the mutual suspicion and anxiety that animates public interactions. Anything said, as Syme notes, "evaded verification and tended to be discredited."[53] Political discourse and debate, consequently, were replaced by rumors that were born of fear, hate, and distrust (see *Ann.* 1.4.2; 1.25.2; 3.19.2; 4.11.2; 13.26.1). Public orations, the way in which the elite constituted themselves as free citizens, were replaced by inconsequential private recitations that rendered speech "cold and lifeless."[54] One spoke only at great risk, and then without much effect, lending to Roman politics the continued guise of tranquility.[55] The populace could only give itself "permission for concealed utterances against the princeps or for suspicious silence" (*Ann.* 3.11.2; also 3.19.2). And the senate demonstrated a continual unwillingness to debate, decide, initiate and take responsibility, until

---

[52] Tiberius, too, is able to "overturn and exchange the signs of anger and clemency" (*Ann.* 3.22.2). On the growing variance between "gesture" and "feeling," see Betensky 1978; also Rudich 1993, xxii.
[53] Syme 1958, 365.   [54] See Dupont 1997, 49.
[55] Saxonhouse 1975, 56. See also Syme 1939, 483; Henderson 1990, 192; Fontana 1993; Rudich 1993, xxx–xxxii ("rhetoricized mentality"); Edwards 1994, 92–93; and Boesche 1996, 88–95.

"trained to love" vice, they made crimes into "eminent virtues" (*Hist.* 1.5; also *Ann.* 14.14; 14.60.1).[56] Even as flattery became the public discourse of choice, the coerced insincerity of praise only heightened the emperor's insecurity and deepened his contempt for the elite. As Tacitus would remark, in language that plays on the imbalances that contribute to disease, the absence (*nulla*) or excess (*nimia*) of sycophancy in a corrupt society is equally dangerous (*Ann.* 4.17.1; also *Hist.* 1.85; see for example Cels. 1.3.2).

Tacitus is making an argument about the two primary responses that groups may take in this form of unmediated politics in which individuals lack appeal, recourse, or protection. One could join the unsustainable and risky voices of protest.[57] Or one could join in affirmations of the emperor's will, a will marked by increasing depravity. The path to power in imperial Rome lay in becoming part of the court: a personal retainer or advisor who, like Sejanus, could come to know and cater to the urges of the emperor.[58] The new political man, like Sejanus, was at once cringing and insolent, outwardly modest but possessing "a lust for acquiring supremacy," and skilled at concealing himself (*Ann.* 4.1.3). For Macro, as well, who played a role in bringing down Sejanus, "the falseness of hypocrisy had nevertheless been a lesson well learned in his grandfather's lap" (6.45.3). To everyone else, one did not ask why the emperor had elevated one person and not another, or why the emperor had made a particular decision. The gods, as Terentius remarks (with the full force of Tacitus' irony), "have given [to the emperor] the supreme judgment of

---

[56] See, for example, *Ann.* 3.31.2–4: senate engages in trivial quarrel; 3.35.1: Tiberius's abmonition for senate's failure to act; 13.26.1: debate governed by fear; 14.45: ineffectual protest; 14.64.3: senate's willingness to approve crime.

[57] See Levick 1985, 62. The options open to individual forms of protest were fairly limited and appeared more as opting out of things, a largely passive and ineffective form of protest (see *Ann.* 14.12.2; 16.21).

[58] Examples of *equites* who saw more power in the emperor's service rather than in a senatorial career include Maecenas and C. Sallustius Crispus (*Ann.* 3.30). Mela "abstained from seeking office, having the inverted ambition that as a Roman equestrian he might match consulars in powerfulness. At the same time he believed that a shorter way to acquiring money was through the procuratorships for administering the princeps' business" (*Ann.* 16.17.3). See Mommsen 1905, 4.311; Syme 1939, 385; Talbert 1987, 77–80; Levick 1985, 63.

affairs; to us is left the glory of compliance" (*obsequii gloria*) (*Ann.* 6.8.4). Virtue, honor, and glory stood as the true obstacles to advancement.[59] In the competition for recognition, the aristocracy willingly accepted servility as the path to power, status, and wealth (see, for example, *Ann.* 1.2.1; 14.15.5).

Despotic equality and political spectacle

The competition that once elevated the nobility now produces a perverse equality among the different ranks of society in their expressions of both opposition to and affirmation of imperial rule.[60] We get some sense of the blurring lines of rank and behavior in the prosecution of Cn. Piso when the senate joins with the frenzied people in "ferocious cries" and in expressing every "hostility and savagery" against the defendant (*Ann.* 3.15.2; also 6.7.3: "lowest denouncements"). Freedmen are disrespecting, even threatening, their patrons (*Ann.* 13.26.2). In the later Pisonian conspiracy against Nero, Tacitus emphasizes how "among people of different lineage, rank, age, and sex, rich and poor, everything was contained in silence" (*Ann.* 15.54.1).[61] Although the outlets of expression differ initially – the elites, as we will see, would have the courts as their circus – ultimately the aristocracy comes to inhabit even the spectacle of the theater.

In comparison to the aristocratic suspicion of the theater in the Republic (*Ann.* 14.20), Tacitus describes the experience under Nero: "Neither nobility nor age nor the holding of offices served as a hindrance to anyone's practicing the art of a Greek or Latin actor, right down to gestures and rhythms which were quite unmanly. Indeed illustrious ladies too gave grotesque performances" (*Ann.* 14.15.1–2; also 14.14; 15.37).[62] Every

---

[59] High rank, for example, was a cause for attack by Nero. See *Ann.* 13.1; 15.35; 16.7. So was virtue (*Ann.* 16.21.1; 16.23.1).

[60] This perverse equality occurs even as the social order continued to be enforced in theatrical seating (see Zanker 1988, 149–52; Edwards 1993, 110–13; Edmondson 1996, 84–95).

[61] On the Pisonian conspiracy, see Rudich 1993, 87–112.

[62] On the nearly unavoidable moral complicity in despotism, see Liebeschuetz 1966, 133–34.

incentive existed for corruption. Coins were distributed, "which the good were to spend from compulsion, the profligate from self-glorification" (*Ann.* 14.15.2). Among these competitors of vices, few would be left behind, including the emperor who would appear on stage before an audience now supplemented with centurions, tribunes, and the newest corps of Roman knights (*Ann.* 14.15.3–4; also 14.20.4).[63] "And for days and nights they resounded with applause, calling the princeps's good looks and voice by divine designations: as if because of some excellence of theirs, they lived brilliant and honored lives" (*Ann.* 14.15.5).

The gradations and boundaries of political life that define Roman society dissolve as Nero treats the "whole City as his own house" (*Ann.* 15.37.1). Like the scrutinizing of words and facial expressions that accompanies public discourse, leading to a breakdown in public meaning, so there is a similar scrutinizing of participation in the spectacles. One now feared to be missing from Nero's spectacles "since many people openly (and more in secret) were on hand to examine the names and faces, the eagerness and sourness, of the assembly" (*Ann.* 16.5.2). Tacitus' image of the theatricality of politics, as depicted in the mutinies, now comes full circle: Nero becomes the leader of the theatrical claque, roaming the streets in disguise and giving license to inflict injuries on men and women of distinction (*Ann.* 13.25.1–2), surrounding himself with soldiers and gladiators to encourage brawls (*Ann.* 13.25.3), mirroring fighting in the games with fighting in the stands (*Ann.* 13.25.4), all to the raucous applause of the aristocracy. As the boundaries of fantasy and reality dissolve, Rome becomes enveloped in "a world of unreality," to use Woodman's words, a world in which individuals take their cues increasingly from the unknowable will of the emperor.[64]

---

[63] See also *Hist.* 1.4; Yavetz 1969, 115, 124; Sullivan 1985, 40–41; Beacham 1999, 200–1.

[64] Woodman 1993, 127. See also MacDonald 1965, 177 (Domus Aurea as disorienting); Betensky 1978, 420 (everything "staged"); Edwards 1994, 92–93 (inversion of real and unreal); Beacham 1999, 228 (the city as a "stage set"); Haynes 2003, 23–24, 31; Bartsch 1994, 47. Also Sen. *Nat. quaes.* 1.16–17 (illusion).

THE PSYCHOLOGY OF TERROR

Tacitus is moving us toward understanding the political psychology of despotism, a world in which no stable markers exist by which one can orient action. We have already seen how the gradual elimination of mediating functions makes political expression more vulnerable (since expression appears as personal rather than institutional) and political action more volatile (because of the immediacy of the interactions). But what really marks despotic rule and enforces this unreality is the institutionalization of terror. Beginning with Tiberius terror was formalized in procedures, sanctioned by state rewards, and carried out through state institutions. Tacitus' language, as many have suggested, likely exaggerates the actual number of persons executed by Tiberius.[65] Certainly the numbers do not compare with modern standards of slaughter. The effect of terror, though, is not measured by a body count alone but by how it insinuates its way into and ultimately corrodes the forces of honor, liberty, and friendship, arguably the central animating and binding principles of Roman political life.[66]

The disorienting effect of terror occurs in Rome because it rises within and is sanctioned by state institutions. We saw this misuse of the legal system with the legal abduction of Verginia (see Chapt. 5, 256–57). Sulla had made the systematic prosecution of enemies into a political tool. Augustus had followed this model in prosecuting political opponents, though the extent is unknown.[67] Importantly, Augustus expanded the

---

[65] Suetonius places the number of prosecutions in 33 CE, described by Tacitus as *immensa strages*, at no more than twenty individuals (Suet. *Tib.* 61; *Ann.* 6.19.2). Walker calculates that eighteen individuals were executed for treason during Tiberius's rule (1952, 84–5, 263–70). There is, however, a substantial increase in suicides after 31 CE (Walker 1952, 84). Rutledge argues that the *delatores* played only a "limited part in curtailing the freedoms of others" in the early principate (2001, 4).

[66] See Tac. *Hist.* 1.15: "*Fidem, libertatem, amicitiam, praecipua humani animi bona.*"

[67] On the use of proscriptions as a form of "legal murder," see Syme 1939, 187–201 (quote from 187). For a review of the evidence of opposition to Augustus, see Raaflaub 1987 and Raaflaub and Samons 1990. On opposition to Nero, see Rudich 1993. For a broader discussion of the extent of opposition, and the responses of the emperors, see the contributions to Adalberto and van Berchem 1987, *Opposition et résistances à l'empire d'Auguste à Trajan*.

lex maiestatis, the law of majesty, once a republican concept used to prosecute public misdeeds, to include libels against leading men and women.[68] The culmination, though, of the institutionalization of terror occurs when Tiberius broadens the *lex maiestatis* to include intimations deemed hostile to the emperor, an emperor, as Tacitus notes, driven by insatiable suspicion.[69] At that point institutions and norms become transformed into instruments of the emperor's will and the occupation of *delator*, or informant, becomes a "form of life" (*Ann.* 1.74.1), bringing money into the treasury as well as rewards for the prosecutors.[70] Tacitus' point is not that *delatores* act out of motives unknown in Rome before; it is that despotism functions by playing upon traditional motivations – the desire for honor, trust, and influence, for example, or the defense of the household – to ultimately undercut the stability of those markers for political behavior and to transfer the enforcement of those markers increasingly to the *princeps*. One of the key advantages of *maiestas* prosecutions, and suggestive of the loss of any institutional mediation, is that it gave easier access to evidence acquired from slaves under torture, evidence that could be used to prosecute other crimes in which a defendant so charged would not have access to counsel.[71]

Suggestive of this destabilizing of political forms, Tacitus describes the *delatores* as exhibiting *audacia*, a term often associated with

---

[68] Bauman 1974, 14–15, 25–51; Levick 1985, 56; Raaflaub and Samons 1990, 444; Rutledge 2001, 37–39, 44–46. On the inconsistency of the use of this term and the types of crimes associated with the term by literary sources, including Tacitus, see Bauman 1974, 1–24.

[69] Tacitus traces the source of the *maiestas* prosecutions back to Tiberius' own troubled soul, which had been excited (*asperavere*) by satires of his life and character (*Ann.* 1.72.4). On *asperare* in medicine, see Cels. 4.5.6; Langslow 2000, 175, 305.

[70] Necessity of prosecutions for treasury: Levick 1985, 56–7; advancement, see Rutledge 2001, 20–53; the continued rewards for informers, see *Hist.* 1.2; *Ann.* 1.74.2; and Rudich 1993. Rutledge argues that the *delatores* were actually acting according to traditional Roman motivations and, in fact, would have been "readily appreciated by their republican forebears" (Rutledge 2001, 53). In fact, as Rutledge observes, "In their larger social context, then, *delatores* are merely an instrument by which the moral fabric of Caesar's household is maintained, and Caesar's role as head of that *familia* is in essence an extension of the *patria potestas* underlying higher magisterial offices preexisting in the Republic" (Rutledge 2001, 65).

[71] Bauman 1974, 55–59, 93.

sedition.⁷² In this case, the sedition is not the violent overthrow of the political body but an ailment that feeds on or eats away (*exedo*) the vitals of the community (*Ann.* 2.27.1; 6.7.3; also 1.73.1; 1.75.1; 2.28.3; 4.30.3; 4.52.4; 4.66.1).⁷³ In fact, the *delatores* become like the physician as purveyor of disease, an image Tacitus associates with the final decades of the Republic. As Tacitus writes, the "antagonisms, accusations, hatreds, and injustices were being fostered simply in order that the rottenness of the forum would bring money to advocates in the same way as the virulence of disease brought rewards for doctors" (*Ann.* 11.6.2).

The *delatores* penetrate into every aspect of human interaction.⁷⁴ Calpurnius Piso, for example, is charged with holding "private conversation" against Tiberius (*Ann.* 4.21.2). A son prosecutes his father (*Ann.* 4.28). Domitius Afer accuses his mother, Claudia Pulchra (*Ann.* 4.52). Titius Sabinus, still in sorrow over the death of Germanicus, denounces in grief (to Latiaris) both Sejanus and Tiberius in what he believes to be the security of friendship but is in fact a trap (*Ann.* 4.68.2). As Tacitus remarks more generally, "whether in the forum or at a dinner party, men were censured because each individual was frantic to forestall someone else in marking out a defendant" (*Ann.* 6.7.3). No conversation – even those that never occurred – and no relationship – even the most intimate ones – were safe from the new "guardians" of the

---

⁷² *Audacia* can connote reckless courage or boldness (see, for example, *Ann.* 1.38.2). In the late Republic it is applied to individuals who display recklessness and unscrupulousness aimed at overthrowing the existing order (*Ann.* 4.1.3; 4.10.2; with 4.67.3). The term is also applied to the stirrings of a slave war in Italy or the potential turbulence that threatens to overturn a community whenever the emperor or magistrates are absent (*Ann.* 4.27.2; 6.11.2). See Wirszubski 1961, 14; Wood 1986, 37–39; and Kaster 2005, 55.

⁷³ Related, Keitel sees Tacitus using images of civil war to describe the mutinies and the actions of the nobles and the *delatores* (1984, 317–25). *Exedere* in medical terminology, see Langslow 2000, 197.

⁷⁴ On the continued and pernicious role of the informers in subsequent reigns, see *Ann.* 11.5.1: Claudius; *Ann.* 14.48; 16.7–35: Nero; *Hist.* 1.2: Nero; *Agric.* 2.3: Domitian. As Levick writes, "The Emperor might be induced to renounce *maiestas*, for example; so with Gaius, Claudius, and (tacitly) Nero. What that meant is not clear. Not the repeal of the Lex, which was never re-enacted; nor did the Senate suspend the statute; the state could not do without it" (1985, 57).

constitution (*Ann.* 4.30.2). Even women were not safe. Those who "could not be charged with taking over the state, were indicted for their tears" (*Ann.* 6.10.1). So Vitia, the mother of Fufius Germinus, is executed because she wept for the killing of her son (*Ann.* 6.10.1). The eyes of the friends and relatives of all those executed for complicity with Sejanus are checked for sorrow, as well (*Ann.* 6.19.3). The indiscriminate mixing of the mutiny and then of the theater now becomes the image of ruined lives: "The wreckage stretched indefinitely – every sex, every age, illustrious, ignoble, scattered, or heaped" (*Ann.* 6.19.2).[75]

The immediate effect of terror is to kill, but its importance, as we have seen already with Seneca, lies in breaking down the categories by which people orient themselves: public and private, friend and enemy, virtue and vice, best and worst, thought and expression.[76] This it does in two ways. First, terror levels, removing any distinctions that define the norms of elite behavior. Tacitus at one point characterizes his history as an account not of great deeds – the traditional topic of Roman historiography – but of "savage orders, constant accusations, deceitful friendships, the ruin of innocents and always the same reasons for their extermination" (*Ann.* 4.33.3). A telling moment occurs when the aristocracy becomes like a mob, the worst elements bringing down the best. In describing how Mamercus Scaurus, an ex-consul, Junius Otho, a praetor, and Bruttedius Niger, an aedile, simultaneously charge Gaius Silanus with treason, Tacitus points to the distortion, even inversion, of the traditional norms of aristocratic honor (*Ann.* 3.66.1).[77] Scaurus, in Tacitus' characterization, dishonors his illustrious ancestor (Marcus Scaurus). Junius Otho, elevated to the senate from his crude beginnings as a schoolteacher, defiles even these lowly origins through his shamelessness and audacity (*Ann.* 3.66.3). And Bruttedius' ambition, which sought rapid advancement through imperial ranks, "sent to the bottom (*pessum*) many good men"

---

[75] Keitel 1984, 307 interprets this passage as invoking an image of the captured city.
[76] See Barthes' evocative discussion of death in Tacitus' *Annals* (1982).
[77] On *corripio* in medical terminology, see Woodman and Martin 1996, 459, 260. The inversion of the moral order in which individuals are honored for their vices becomes the standard of society under subsequent emperors. See *Ann.* 14.3; 14.13; 14.15; 14.59; 14.62; 14.64; 15.50.

(*Ann.* 3.66.4).⁷⁸ Other accusers would join in: first a former quaestor, then his legate, and then the most fluent rhetoricians who pressed the case against Junius Otho. So too under the prosecution of Cossutianus Capito, who saw the opportunity to settle old scores, Nero would "extirpate virtue itself by killing Thrasea Paetus and Barea Soranus," both of whom had become opponents of the regime (*Ann.* 16.21.1).⁷⁹

Terror not only levels but also isolates. Tacitus' discussion of Libo's trial, for example, is less a court document and more an exploration of the profound disorientation and growing sense of isolation perpetrated by the prosecutions.⁸⁰ Tacitus' discussion becomes a veritable compendium of different types of public and private cues, all of them lost. Libo is betrayed by his closest friend. He is honored by Tiberius with a praetorship and invitations to dinner, an event in Roman society associated with confirming power relations and forging social bonds,⁸¹ even while the emperor secretly encourages the prosecution. There are no nonverbal cues. As Tacitus notes, Tiberius buries his anger, shows no strangeness in his expression, and no disturbance in his speech (*Ann.* 2.28.2; also of Claudius, 11.38.3: betrays no "human emotion").⁸² Libo, thus, cannot detect in Tiberius's expression a sense of the extent of danger, even appealing to the emperor who responds with unmoved expression

---

⁷⁸ On *pessum* in medical vocabulary, see Cels. 5.21.
⁷⁹ On Tacitus' use of Thrasea as an *exemplum* of *virtus*, see Turpin 2008, 378–89.
⁸⁰ In other ancient versions, Libo is portrayed as a plotter who is suspected of seeking to overthrow Tiberius (Valleius 2.130; Suet. *Tib.* 25; Sen *Ep.* 70.10; also Marsh 1926, 294–96). See Rogers 1952, 285 on Tacitus' accounts of treason trials. The discovery of the *Tabula Siarensis* and the *Senatus Consultum de Cn. Pisone Patre*, both of which deal with affairs surrounding the death of Germanicus and the trial of Piso, suggest that Tacitus (at least in the case of Piso) is generally accurate in his account. See Eck, Caballos, and Fernández 1996, 289–98; Woodman and Martin 1996, 114–18; Flower 1996, 246–54; 1999, 110–15; Griffin 1997b, 258–61; Talbert 1999, 95–6. For a survey of the controversy surrounding Tacitus' use of the *acta senatus*, specifically, and his accuracy, generally, see Talbert 1987, 326–34. Häussler 1965 more generally makes an argument for Tacitus' objectivity and detachment as an historian.
⁸¹ On Roman dinner parties under the principate, see Roller 2001, 135–46. Such examples by Tacitus shows the limitations on the "negotiation" of social exchange, specifically conviviality, by which aristocrats could "constrain" or play a part in constructing the emperor's authority (Roller 2001, 129, 173).
⁸² On *condo* in medical terminology, see Cels. 3.25.3.

(*immoto...vultu*) (*Ann.* 2.29.2). Law provides no guide, either, since Tiberius invents "a new jurisprudence" in the course of the proceedings, ordering Libo's slaves to be sold to the treasury agent so that they could testify against him (*Ann.* 2.30.3).[83] Nor is there recourse in family. Libo wanders from house to house to seek support from his wife's relatives but is refused until "exhausted by dread and illness" (*metu et aegritudine fessus*) (*Ann.* 2.29.2). Even while Libo prepares one last feast, soldiers surround his home, making themselves seen and heard as he sits at his table. So tormented is Libo by his banquet that he commits suicide (*Ann.* 2.31.1). The sense of the sheer arbitrariness of the proceedings is reinforced when the trial continues "with the same assertiveness" until Tiberius can claim, in a moment of inconsequential magnanimity, that he would have spared Libo's life if he had not hastened to kill himself (*Ann.* 2.31.3; similarly, see 16.11.3).[84]

Like Libo, Silanus is left "on his own, and ignorant of advocacy, and in a state of dread (which cripples even practiced eloquence)" (*Ann.* 3.67.2). And King Archelaus, whom Tiberius seeks to punish for perceived slights while exiled earlier in Rhodes, is ultimately broken, not by the fictitious charges of treason, but through "tension" combined with the weariness of his age (*Ann.* 2.42.3). Tacitus describes the general psychological state as the terror progresses: Everyone was "tense and panicked" (*Ann.* 4.69.3). Later cases yield the same results. Tacitus ends his discussion of 33 CE with the starvation of Asinius Gallus (6.23.1), Drusus Caesar, who survives for a time by eating the stuffing from his bed (6.23.2), Agrippina (6.25.1), and Cocceius Nerva (6.26.2). These cases, as Woodman comments, highlight a reversal by Tiberius in the aim of his actions to starve rather than feed his people (compare to Tiberius' earlier response to a food crisis at 2.87).[85] What was so terrifying was that Tiberius no longer hid the crimes, reading out the allegations against the dead (6.24.3). Tacitus comments on how Petronius

---

[83] Dio suggests that selling a master's slaves to the treasury so that they could testify against their master was practiced, in fact, by Augustus (Dio 55.5).
[84] See also *Ann.* 15.35.3 when Nero declares in his "usual speech" that he would have granted clemency to Torquatus Silanus, who committed suicide when his condemnation appeared imminent.
[85] Woodman 2006b, 188.

refuses to tolerate "the delay in his fear or hope" that normally accompanies the anticipation of the emperor's cruelty, as well as the desperate flattery that accompanies one's suicide (*Ann.* 16.19.1). Time did nothing to soften reprisals: Tiberius punished "vague or bygone matters as though they were of extreme seriousness and recent" (6.38.1). The senate, too, alternates between their habitual sadness and terror as they preside over the new round of prosecutions by Nero (*Ann.* 16.29.1). Even reporting the "servile passivity and so much blood wasted at home," as Tacitus comments on his own writing, "wear[ies] the spirit and numb[s] it with sorrowfulness" (*Ann.* 16.16.1).

The true measure of Rome's slide into despotism is the loss of liberty. In part, there is the loss of formal guarantees of liberty since there are no longer laws that can be known, but only everchanging wants that must be obeyed. And there is no longer the *libertas* that is associated with "command of the people" (*Ann.* 6.42.2). But the most serious loss of liberty is the loss of the will to speak – the paralysis of the spirit.[86] Wirszubski writes, "It appears that by libertas Tacitus understands, not the freedom of the citizen to determine his own destiny and the destiny of his country, nor the constitutional safeguards of the citizen's rights, but merely the courage to preserve one's self-respect in the face of despotism and amidst adulation."[87] It is a *libertas*, as Wirszubski continues, that is "sustained by consciousness, not of what one is entitled to, but of what one owes to one's own dignity."[88] Tacitus remarks on how Thrasea's "free-speaking" on one measure in the senate "exploded the servitude of others," leading the senators to pass a decree to limit the punishment of Antistius who was convicted of *maiestas*, even maintaining resolve in the face of Nero's anger (*Ann.* 14.49.1, 3). And in talking about Seneca's end, Tacitus makes clear the juxtaposition of Seneca's "free speaking" with "servitude" (*Ann.* 15.61.1). But it is a consciousness noteworthy by its exceptional nature that is undermined as the bonds of trust that connect one person to another are broken.

---

[86] On fear as a "physiological reaction" that paralyzes the body, see Shklar 1987, 84.
[87] Wirszubski 1968, 166. On the connection of servitude to passivity in Tacitus, see Lavan 2011.
[88] Wirszubski 1968, 166.

Tacitus describes how terror dissolves these bonds. In describing the "wreckage" of those prosecuted for their association with Sejanus, Tacitus emphasizes as well how one was taught to not act by any feelings for the dead:

> Nor were relatives or friends allowed to stand by, to shed tears or even to gaze for too long, but the guards posted round, intent on each person's sorrow, escorted the putrefying bodies until they were dragged into the Tiber, where, floating about or beached on the banks, no one dared either cremation or contact. The dealings (*commercium*) which are the human lot had fallen to the power of dread and, as savagery swelled, pity was banished (*Ann.* 6.19.3).

Commercium, as we saw earlier with Seneca, is associated with communication and fellowship that occurs between humans. When the stable props by which one orients oneself no longer exist, the individual mind, as Celsus writes, is placed at the mercy of "vain imaginings," a form of insanity that expresses itself variously as sadness, hilarity, rebellious violence, and melancholy (Cels. 3.18.3; 3.18.10).[89] As Tacitus writes of Domitian's reign, the unleashing of the informers "deprived us even of the give and take of conversation" (*Agric.* 2.3). Prevented from normal outlets of expression, people stop acting from compassion (*Ann.* 6.19.3) or any collective impulse (see *Ann.* 4.12.1), except for punctuated moments of frenzy. The "energetic" perished and those who survived did so without ever "opening their lips" (*Agric.* 3.3). "Shackled" by silence, eloquence becomes feeble and breaks down (*Dial.* 39.1–2). One survived by slipping into a melancholic existence, neither accepting nor defying, but wasting away.[90] Recounting Domitian's rule, Tacitus describes how

---

[89] Henderson, for example, writes, "It will not be the mere performance — the 'score' — of Tiberian or Neronian Treason Trials that we are to consider, it is the (anti-)logic in its re-oriented functioning around the *persona* of the Emperor that we are to trace from its inception. In the new Order, there is *no* 'Trial'; it is a matter of the tyrant's (however benign) perception of how threatened he feels, of how the sum adds up in confirming his grasp of power ('Should it be generosity, liquidation or menace *this time?*): power as power over meaning, *Wor(l)d-Power*. The misnomer *maiestas* destabilizes Roman discourse. Systematically. Into pieces" (1990, 177).

[90] See Jens 1956 who traces Tacitus' growing sense of the impossibility of individuals under imperial rule not slipping into listlessness. Syme remarks, "It was the acute consciousness of personal insecurity and political impotence that depressed and

listlessness (*inertia*) acquires a "subtle charm" that comes over us until "the languor we hate at first we learn to love" (*Agric.* 3.1: *subit quippe etiam ipsius inertiae dulcedo, et invisa primo desidia postremo amatur*). Tacitus' recounting of Octavia's brief life provides perhaps the most poignant image of the anxiety of existence under despotism:

> And the girl, in the twentieth year of her age, amid centurions and soldiers, already released from life by the presentiment of evil, could nevertheless not yet rest in death. Subsequntly, after an interval of a few days, she was ordered to die, although she testified that she was now a widow and no more than a sister, and she invoked the Germanici, whom they had in common, and finally the name of Agrippina, during whose lifetime she had sustained a marriage admittedly unhappy but exempt from extermination. She was restrained with bonds, and the veins in all her limbs were severed; and because her blood, staunched by panic, trickled too slowly, she was executed by means of the steam from an extra-hot bath. And there was the addition of a more frightful savagery, in that her head, amputated and carried into the City, was seen by Poppaea (14.64.1–2).

Individuals are suspended, succumbing to a deathlike existence in the struggle to survive, the brutality of the death a reminder to others.

POLITICAL THOUGHT AND THE RESTORATION OF SANITY

But Tacitus does not end on this note of irresolution. His portrayal of Thrasea's suicide, the final episode we have of the *Annals*, betrays none of that anxiety but points, instead, to future generations whose spirit might be strengthened "with steadfast examples" (*Ann.* 16.35.1). But what are those examples? It is not simply disobedience, which may do little to benefit the community (*Agric.* 42.4) and has even less to do with Tacitus' praise of Agricola, who served faithfully under Domitian. What

> perverted the morale of the aristocracy. There was no field left them now for action — or even for display" (Syme 1939, 504).

makes Thrasea, like Agricola, so important is that they do not succumb to the disorientation caused by the altered world of despotism. It is not accidental that the memory of Thrasea is joined with Agricola (*Agric.* 2.1). The power of despotism lies in how it transforms the habits and mores of a people. The "majority," as Tacitus recounts, "are taught by what happens to others" (*Ann.* 4.33.2), experiences that under despotism systematically deny the cues by which one can orient oneself. The altered political world of despotism is one in which few men are able to "distinguish the honorable from the baser" (*Ann.* 4.33.2) because there is no longer the public practice of judgment. Tacitus' *Dialogue on Oratory* is precisely an exploration of the choices facing the orator: whether to disappear by withdrawing from public life, to risk disappearing by imprudently speaking with integrity, or to seem to appear by cravenly molding one's rhetoric to flatter the Court.[91] Historiography, too, becomes disconnected from public discourse. As Tacitus writes in opening his *Histories*, after Actium historiography no longer conveys anything (1.1).

The weakness of despotism is that it must extinguish the memory of succeeding ages to effectively deny experience and expression. As Tacitus remarks of life under Domitian, "we should have lost memory itself as well as voice, had forgetfulness been as easy as silence (*memoriam quoque ipsam cum voce perdidissemus, si tam in nostra potestate esset oblivisci quam tacere*)" (*Agric.* 2.3). Memory leaves its traces, which are difficult to completely expunge. The challenge of destroying all traces of memory is suggested by the case of Cremutius Cordus, who is charged with publishing a history that praises Brutus and Cassius and, more damagingly, lists the authors of the proscriptions (*Ann.* 4.34–35). Memory, Cremutius declares to the senate, is enshrined in history (*Ann.* 4.35.2). Indeed, even with Cremutius's condemnation, self-starvation, and the burning of his books, copies of his account remained, "concealed and published"

---

[91] On Tacitus as arguing for a prudential model of oratory, see Kapust 2011, 111–42; also Turpin 2008, 399, on learning how to understand relationships with an emperor; Strunk 2010. Dressler 2013 argues for much greater indeterminacy in the meaning of the *Dialogue*.

(*Ann.* 4.35.4).[92] Veiled in the quiet of the despotism, genius punished grows in authority, eventually testifying against the malady of the age (*Ann.* 4.35.5).

"*Nunc demum redit animus* (Now at last spirit returns)" (*Agric.* 3.1, trans. modified). Tacitus' words stand out for their poignancy, sounding as defiant as they do hopeful. When Tacitus breaks the silence, he is puncturing the unreality of despotism that is fostered in fear, timidity, and isolation. The first duty of history, as Tacitus remarks, is to provide a record of this past "to prevent virtues from being silenced and so that crooked words and deeds should be attended by the dread of posterity and infamy" (*Ann.* 3.65.1; also *Ann.* 4.33). In reversing the imperceptible ways in which individuals suffer from the vain imaginings of a despotic realm, Tacitus' historiography is not simply diagnostic or evaluative, but curative.[93]

---

[92] Augustus instituted public bonfires to burn offensive literature (Syme 1939, 486). Both Augustus and Tiberius prosecuted Cassius Severus, a man "hated and feared for his bitter tongue and incorrigible love of independence" (Syme 1939, 486; *Ann.* 1.72.3; 4.21.3). Domitian executes, among others, Junius Rusticus for publishing eulogies of men killed by him, in turn banishing philosophers from the city and from Italy (Suet. *Domitian* 10.1; 10.3–4). And individuals could be legally removed from memory (*Ann.* 2.32: Libo Drusus; 3.17–18: Piso; 3.76: Brutus and Cassius; 11.38: Messalina). On the practice of *damnatio memoriae*, see Flower 2006).

[93] There is a wide range of different assessments of Tacitus' historiography. Syme places Tacitus' vocation in the context of a senatorial tradition in which, mature in his years and exhausted from political battle, he retired to assert "a personal claim to glory and survival" (Syme 1970, 2). Fornara connects Tacitus to the "bitter diagnostic style" of Sallust. Tacitus, as a senatorial historian in the age of empire, plays the role of "judge and jury" of the "tyrannous and base government[s]" under the emperors (Fornara 1983, 76, 118–19). O'Gorman sees Tacitus as engaged in part of a larger struggle between senatorial and imperial history over historical memory. O'Gorman emphasizes, in particular, the attempt by Tacitus to undermine dynastic attempts to "naturalise hereditary power" (2000, 106). She points to the disjunction between the real and ideal as serving as an "ironic commentary" on the "position of the historian" (O'Gorman 2000, 182). Marincola sees Tacitus as probing "beneath the surface" to "inquire into the truth behind the appearances of domestic policies at Rome" (Marincola 1997, 95). Haynes suggests, "However, looking down into the abyss, as Tacitus does, means understanding that there is no Truth, no historical necessity, outside of the symbolic" (2003, 13; also 20–21). Sinclair argues similarly that Tacitus' "procedure of 'looking beneath the surface'" is an attempt "to enlarge his reader's understanding of social reality by rending the veil of deception that

If Tacitus' writings fly in the face of traditional modes of historiographic method, it may have a great deal to do with this task of restoring the lost sentiments of a political self. He is a political thinker in an age of insanity. The treatment of insanity, as Celsus writes, requires that the mind of the patient be "slowly and imperceptibly" turned from vain imaginings to something more real (Cels. 3.18.11; see also 1.3.2). There are a variety of ways in which such changes may be effected, but all of them aim at prompting the patient to recall whatever glimmers of sanity might remain. Fears must be allayed and hope put forward (Cels. 3.18.10, 18); one's "interest" might be "awakened" by recalling activities that once excited the individual, such as having a patient read who likes literature (Cels. 3.18.11); patients should be "pressed to recite anything they can remember" (Cels. 3.18.11); and the spirit, in the case of melancholy, should be agitated (Cels. 3.18.22).

Referencing a traditional aesthetic of Roman oratory, Tacitus has Marcus Aper remark that like the human body, so in speech there can be "no beauty" where "the veins are prominent, or where one can count the bones: sound healthful blood must fill out the limbs, and riot over the muscles, concealing the sinews in turn under a ruddy complexion and a graceful exterior" (*Dial.* 21.8). That grace may have been used at one time by Roman orators to convey beauty; now it is used to disguise ugliness. In his asymmetrical, often jarring syntax that highlights pretext, juxtaposes truth and falsehood, and emphasizes the discordant relationship between events, Tacitus wants to peel away the skin of the political body to see the tortured soul.[94] His writings are meant to agitate, prod, provoke, and awaken the community from its despotic slumber. As Walker writes, "*in the style*, there is a conscious artistry, a development of all the potentialities of words to startle, impress, fascinate and move the listener."[95] Henderson describes the *Annals* as a "discursive clash

---

surrounds so much of political life" (Sinclair 1995, 63). Kapust sees Tacitus as writing a "rhetorical history" that teaches prudence (Kapust 2011, 144; also Turpin 2008 on use of *exempla*).

[94] See Boissier 1906, 22–23; Walker 1952, 57–66; Klingner 1955, 193; Syme 1958, I.199; Martin 1981, 214–35; Goodyear 1981, 185–87; Henderson 1990, 193–94; Sinclair 1995; Kraus and Woodman 1997, 110–11; O'Gorman 2000, 4–10.

[95] Walker 1952, 53.

between language and desire, meaning and power, challenging any civic mentality to suffer, probe and resist the draining away of Rome from itself that unwinds from first to last."[96] These "striking" moments might then be remembered and passed on to others (*Dial.* 20.4), reversing the course of despotic amnesia.

One commentator describes Tacitus' thought as "hardly that of a political theorist" but of a "good citizen shocked at the abuse of power."[97] Tacitus' contribution to political thought is much more significant than that. He makes visible an invisible reality: the mental map by which one navigates the political terrain. The problem of despotism, as Tacitus suggests, is that it isolates a person from the stable props by which one can confirm one's impressions and anticipate reactions. The political theorist becomes like the physician, treating what is akin to insanity, seeking not to create a different world but to restore sensations to one's political life.

[96] Henderson 1990, 194.   [97] Mendell 1970, 68.

8 MARCUS AURELIUS AND THE *COSMOPOLIS*

Seneca and Tacitus' respective journeys into the disorienting effects of Roman politics under a succession of cruel and corrupt despots can hardly prepare one for Marcus Aurelius (Marcus Aelius Aurelius Verus, 121–180 CE), who is as close to a philosopher-king as the ancient world would allow: emperor (161–180 CE) and Stoic who left behind his *Meditations* (*Eis heauton*, or *To himself*), a journal of his thoughts and spiritual exercises.[1] We are not alone in that fascination; his reputation was widespread, his rule elevated by some to that of a god.[2] What we are to make of Marcus as a political thinker, though, is another matter. One could analyze his philosophic contributions, like one might Plato or Aristotle's. But we will be disappointed. Philosophy in ancient times did not necessarily rest on novelty but on a practice in which one incorporated the lessons of one's teachers into one's own life. There is little to suggest that Marcus' thoughts were particularly systematic, though there are distinctive points of emphasis.[3]

---

[1] On categorizing his type of writing, see Brunt 1975; Rutherford 1989, 8–21; Hadot 1998.

[2] For example, "Vita Marci," in *Historia Augusta* 19.12. On Marcus Aurelius' reputation in antiquity, see Stertz 1977.

[3] See Long 1986, 115; Sandbach 1975, 176.

One might also look at the influence of Stoicism on his political actions, an approach, although not to the same extent as with Seneca, that yields ambiguous results. A philosophy oriented to action in the world should be able to show results. But what those results should be is not entirely clear. Stoicism was not a reformist philosophy but one that identified happiness as the conformity of the will to fate (e.g., Epict. 1.12.17). We would not expect to see a radical program aimed at some ideal. As Marcus famously writes, "You should not hope for Plato's ideal state, but be satisfied to make even the smallest advance, and regard such an outcome as nothing contemptible" (9.29). He could as easily have said Zeno's republic, a Stoic community of sages.[4] Perhaps Marcus nibbled at the edges of employing Stoic ideas: His judgments seem scrupulously written and, not surprisingly, attentive to precedent; there is a stress on "humanity" in his writings; philosophical schools seemed to flourish under his reign; and in his personal life Marcus seemed to alter the criteria for possible suitors for his daughter.[5] But even that is not completely satisfactory. Women were still seen as akin to possessions.[6] And Marcus engaged in the persecution of the Christians, resulting notably in the martyrdom of Justin and the executions at Lyons.[7] As Stanton rather pointedly concludes, "The real Marcus Aurelius seems to be basically a Roman rather than a Stoic" whose "Stoic philosophy, like his opium addiction, serves as insulation against the discomfort of the Roman frontiers and the realities of Roman politics."[8]

Setting aside the gratuitous judgment about opium usage that is based on rather ambiguous historical data,[9] I want to highlight what is seen as the choice between being a Stoic and being a Roman. Michel Foucault has also suggested that one can identify two opposite phenomena that emerge in Roman culture as a reaction against the vastness of the Roman empire. On the one hand, "there is an accentuation of everything that

---

[4] See DL 7.32–33; Schofield 1991, 22–56; though for Zeno it is a city that exists, as Vogt argues (2008, 66–67).
[5] Precedent: Williams 1976, 78–82; humanity: Williams 1976, 81–82; philosophic schools: Oliver 1981; daughter: Reydams-Schils 2005, 152–53. On Marcus' position as emperor as carrying out detailed fulfillment of duty, see Brunt 1975, 23–26.
[6] For Epictetus, women were common, but allocated, property (Epict. 2.4.8).
[7] Rutherford 1989, xvii.   [8] Stanton 1969, 587.   [9] See Hadot 1998, 250–57.

allows the individual to define his identity in accordance with his status and with the elements that manifest it in the most way," such as physical bearing, clothing, and signs of generosity.[10] On the other hand, there is the philosophic attitude exemplified by the Stoics that consists "in defining what one is purely in relation to oneself."[11]

But we have seen that these two methods of orienting oneself are actually more connected. For the Stoics, we are always members of both a cosmic and earthly city. And while the realms are distinct in their moral value, they are never completely separate in the actual experience of living. Seneca, for example, draws on and reinterprets the Roman juridical identity by way of Stoicism as a way of orienting oneself in a political system that had lost reliable standards of conduct or connection between action and consequences. Similarly, what makes Marcus Aurelius' political thought interesting is not whether his Stoicism departs from or isolates himself from Roman culture but how his philosophy engages it. Where Foucault sees an intensification of the relation to the self, Marcus reorients that individual through a relation to the world.[12] Marcus' Stoicism is neither a philosophy of detachment nor a justification for the status quo, both criticisms traditionally made of Stoicism, but a much more complex re-imagining, by way of Roman culture, of one's place in a *cosmopolis*.

EPICTETUS

Marcus Aurelius' Stoicism owes its greatest debt to Epictetus (55–135 CE) who, as Hadot writes, "dominated the entire second century."[13] Marcus' immediate acquaintance with Epictetus came by way of Junius Rusticus (later Prefect of the City, 162–68 CE), who passed on Epictetus' *Discourses* from his own library (*Medit.* 1.7). To a certain extent, we do not do Marcus Aurelius any favors by asking to whom he is most similar, if only because it does not allow his thought to stand on its own. Furthermore, other influences are readily evident, not the least of which is Plutarch's

---

[10] Foucault 1990, 3.85. [11] Foucault 1990, 3.85.
[12] Foucault 1990, 3.86. [13] Hadot 1998, 11.

moralizing use of literature (for example, 10.34; 11.6), Heraclitus' aphoristic style and emphasis on the dynamic, unstable flux of nature (for example, 4.43; 4.46; 6.17; 7.19; 9.28; 10.33.4: transitoriness; 12.21; 12.23), the extensive literature on good kings (esp. 1.16), the Cynics' focus on "the inner self together with its opinions" as the only thing that matters (see 2.15; 11.6.2; 12.22), and a nod toward Epicurean atomism (4.3.2; 6.4; 6.10; 6.24; 7.32; 8.17; 8.25; 9.28; 10.6; 10.7.2; 11.3; 11.18.1; 12.24).[14] And Marcus has his own points of departure from Epictetus: in Marcus' uncertainty about the nature of God (for example, 9.28; 12.14), in his emphasis on the *daimōn*, and, as I will suggest, in his understanding of the *kosmos* as a *polis*.[15] Nonetheless, Epictetus is a good starting point, not only giving us an opportunity to acquaint ourselves with Epictetus but also helping us orient Marcus' thought. Some of this summary will overlap with the earlier discussion of Stoicism in Chapter 1 and 6, but with the focus on Epictetus and Marcus Aurelius.

Epictetus was born in Hierapolis in Phrygia (in modern Turkey) and was brought to Rome as a slave of Epaphroditus, a freedman and *a libellis* (an official in charge of petitions) for Nero. He was allowed to attend the classes of Musonius Rufus, the most prominent Stoic teacher of the time. After being freed by Epaphroditus, Epictetus opened his own school in Rome but was expelled with other philosophers by Domitian in 93–94. He went to Nicopolis in Epirus where he opened another school, though, like Socrates, wrote nothing. What we know comes in large part from Arrian of Nicomedia's notes from classroom exercises (more than from systematic philosophic treatises).

For the Stoics, as we saw with Cicero and Seneca, we are part of a unified, rational nature, ourselves possessing a unified soul that is organized by reason (e.g., *Medit.* 7.9; 7.23; 8.34; 9.6.1; 11.21; 12.30; contrast to Posidonius who employs Plato's tripartite soul). As Epictetus writes, "the true nature of God" is "intelligence (*nous*), knowledge (*epistēmē*), right reason (*logos orthos*)" (Epict. 2.8.2), with which humans have been endowed. Where animals perceive and respond reactively to nature

---

[14] Plutarch: Rutherford 1989, 27–28; Heraclitus: Rutherford 1989, 31; Asmis 1989, 2247; Cynics: Asmis 1989, 2245.
[15] God: Rutherford 1989, 245; *daimōn*: Rutherford 1989, 237–38.

(according to their nature), our response to the environment is regulated by reason through the directing principle (*hēgemonikon*) of the soul (*Medit.* 8.7; 10.38). Reason is not a separate faculty of the soul, such as one sees in Plato's tripartite scheme, but defines its structure. Stated slightly differently, everything we see and do and everything we understand derives from choices of our reasoning soul (Epict. 1.6.14–15; 1.28.20; 2.8.6–8).

We are continually receiving data from the external world that we must sort through. The goal of Stoicism is to move one toward conformity with the rational structures of the universe, bringing one into harmony with nature (Epict. 1.4.18; 1.6.21; 1.7.2; 1.7.5; 3.15.13). The goal is difficult precisely because we can know only what we experience. There is no Platonic apprehension of the Forms, nor even an unmediated relationship with some objective reality; there are only impressions, our interpretation of the external world by which we form judgments about how to act (*Medit.* 5.10: error always possible).

The beginning of philosophy, as Epictetus announces, is the consciousness of one's weakness and impotence in one's interpretation of things of real consequence (Epict. 2.11.1; see *Medit.* 1.7). Although theory is important, it is only a beginning point "for in theory there is nothing which holds us back from following what we are taught, but in the affairs of life there are many things which draw us away" (Epict. 1.26.3). What theory needs is "the man to bear witness to the arguments by his acts" (Epict. 1.29.56). The emphasis is thus on philosophy as a practice of daily life in which one sees oneself (*Medit.* 11.1), examines oneself (*Medit.* 5.11; 11.1), watches over oneself (*Medit.* 11.9), "rehearse[s]" the lessons, "write[s] [them] down daily," "exercise[s]" them (Epict. 1.1.25; 3.8.1; 3.12.5), molds oneself (*Medit.* 11.1), and "digest[s]" them (Epict. 3.21.2; also *Medit.* 10.31.2; 10.37). The practice of philosophy is the training of one's relationship to the external world, a relationship organized by assent, desire, and impulse, practices that correspond to a body that senses, a soul that desires, and an intelligence that establishes principles of conduct (*dogmata*) (*Medit.* 3.16.1; also 2.2). Marcus is following Epictetus when he characterizes a rational nature as operating properly "when it never gives its assent to a false or doubtful impression, directs its impulses only to actions that further the common good, and limits its desires and aversions only to things that are within its power" (8.7).

The cornerstone of the practice of philosophy is the training of one's power of assent (*sunkatathesis* = *adsensio*) to a representation (*phantasia* = *visum* [also *species*]), a judgment about the objective accuracy of a perception. For the Stoics, perception is the process by which the *pneuma*, flowing from the sensed object, stimulates the senses and transmits an image or "presentation" (*phantasia*) to the command center or directing principle (*to hēgemonikon* = *principale*/ *mens*).[16] All sensory stimuli do not create images, only those that make an "imprint" or "impression."[17] Things "stand outside the door, keeping themselves to themselves, without knowledge of or message about themselves" (9.15). The foundation of all judgment is how a representation appears to the individual. A thought occurs when a person combines information about the present object with stored images, including memories of past experiences, reactions and evaluations of those experiences, and inferences made from those images.[18] How we act depends, in turn, on our own assessment of the validity of the presentation, or "assent" (*sunkatathesis* = *adsensio*), and in turn on the "impulse" (*hormē* = *impetus*) that leads us to "pursue or avoid" that external thing.[19] As Epictetus writes, "The measure of man's every action is the impression of his senses": whether it is formed rightly (and thus blameless) or wrongly (and thus paying the penalty) (Epict. 1.28.10). Everything, as Marcus says at several points, turns on value-judgment (*hupolēpsis*) (*Medit.* 2.15; 12.22; 12.26). The soul "takes its colouring" from its *phantasiai* (*Medit.* 5.16). Disturbances arise from the *hupolēpsis* that is within us (*Medit.* 4.3.4). Through practice one learns to withhold assent and strip one's response to a representation of all subjective elements, all the incorrect messages one gives it, analyzing the event in its entirety and in terms of its material, cause, and objective (Epict. 3.2.5; 3.12.14–15; *Medit.* 3.11; 5.13; 8.26, 29; 8.49; 9.7; 9.37; 10.35; 12.8–10; 12.18). Stoic writings are filled with exhortations to systematically strip away one's

---

[16] On the difficulties of translation, see Sandbach 1971; von Staden 1978; Frede 1992; Nussbaum 1994, 327; Long 1996, 271.
[17] von Staden 1978, 97. See also Hahm 1978, 84–85.
[18] See Long 1996, 247; Frede 1987, 152–57; Sandbach 1971; Cic. *Acad.* 2.7.21.
[19] Long 1996, 245.

own preconceptions and concerns so that an event can be described in its factuality. The aim of the training of assent, as Hadot has argued, is truth, though a truth, as we have seen, that is always mediated by one's impressions and thus always subject to error (*Medit.* 9.1.2).[20]

Where assent is an affirmation by the reasoning soul of the accuracy of an impression, how well it accords with the nature's truth, desires (*orexeis*) and aversions (*ekkliseis*) are affective states that correspond (literally) to movements of the soul. The focus here is on the passions (*pathē*), which are not separate aspects of the soul but false judgments about the status of a representation (whether it is good or bad) and about the appropriate response to that status (whether it is then to be feared, etc.). There are four categories of passions that correspond to movements of the soul: appetite (*epithumia*), which is a longing or reaching for some future good; fear (*phobos*), which is a recoiling from some future perceived harm; pleasure (*hēdonē*), which is a swelling of the soul in response to some apparent good; and distress (*lupē*), which is a contraction in response to some apparent evil.

One aims to bring the movement of the soul into accord with a proper evaluation of the impression (Epict. 3.2.1; 2.17.15; *Medit.* 8.7; 9.7).[21] What is the meaning of a political promotion that has been denied to me? I might lament the loss of prestige or the opportunity for political influence. I might fear that I could lose my current job. Or I might plot my revenge. In the training of desire, one strips away false evaluations that are based on assigning improper value and responses to things: worrying about a future that one cannot control, for example, or desiring externals that have no ethical value. In the training of desire, one frees oneself from the hold of passions (*Medit.* 1.9.3; 2.5; 3.6.2), eliminating the judgment that one is harmed (4.7), and learning to accept what nature has willed as just (see *Medit.* 4.10; 10.2). To desire something other than what may happen is to refute the rational order of the universe (Epict. 2.2.35: never fail to get what you wish; 2.2.21: adapt to whatever comes;

---

[20] See Hadot 1998, 234–35.
[21] Hadot argues that Epictetus and Marcus Aurelius are distinct among Stoics in distinguishing three functions of the guiding principle, adding desire to assent and impulse (1998, 128).

Medit. 12.5). Desire must be trained to embrace one thing: that which has fallen to one by destiny (Epict. 1.12.15; *Medit.* 7.20; 7.37; 8.34; 12.1.1). As Hadot notes, "Everything that happens to me is destined for me, in order to give me the opportunity to consent to what God wants for me, in precisely this moment, and in precisely this form."[22] Marcus Aurelius observes, in talking about the different things that nature might prescribe for us, such as sickness and disability or some good fortune, "For when we say that these things 'fit' us, we are talking like the masons when they say that squared blocks fit in walls or pyramids, because they fit in with one another in a particular structural arrangement" (*Medit.* 5.8.1).

The reasoning soul regulates one's response to the environment in a third way, and that is by training the impulses (*hormai*), which direct one's actions toward external things. This is the faculty of initiative and choice by which one makes use of external impressions (Epict. 1.1.12; *Medit.* 8.16; 8.26; 9.7). If the training of desire is learning to live according to "universal nature" in which one embraces "what happens to you" then the training of the impulses is learning to live according to how one's living nature directs "what you must do on your own account" (*Medit.* 7.55; see DL 7.86–89), a direction that is in accord with nature and implanted in us by reason. As Marcus writes, "Observe what your nature requires of you, in so far as you are merely governed by physical nature, and then do it and accede willingly, if your nature as a living creature will suffer no damage. Next you must observe what your nature as a living creature requires of you, and accept that fully, if your nature as a rational living creature will suffer no damage." (*Medit.* 10.2; also 4.48).

For Epictetus the only true good or virtue (*aretē*) is that which depends on rational agency (*prohairesis*) or choice (Epict. 1.22.9; 2.16.1; 3.3.8). Any goods not directly related to moral choice are classified as indifferent (*adiaphora*) (Epict. 1.30.3). Although material things, including life itself, are indifferent, their usage is not (Epict. 2.6.2). Their usage – one's relationship to one's parents, friends, and country, for

---

[22] Hadot 1998, 162.

example – must derive from moral purpose (Epict. 2.22.20). Furthermore, even though there is only one true good, reason can nonetheless help us differentiate value (*axia*) and orient our actions towards what is appropriate (*kathēkonta*), which are actions that are consistent with reasoning nature and with our own character (Epict. 1.2.7; 1.6.15; 2.23.8–15; 2.23.34–35; 3.2.4; 3.21.5; *Medit.* 7.55; 7.75; 12.32). It is in this latter claim, or at least in the emphasis, that Marcus seems most to depart from Epictetus. Marcus will repeat that joy (*euphrosunē*) lies in the conformity of the soul to nature (8.26). But that nature contains a civic element – a notion of community, justice, and love – that is interpreted as a type of power with which we are endowed and for which we are responsible for enacting.

FREEDOM AND MANLINESS

For Epictetus, a former slave, the political realm looms not surprisingly as the site of enslavement that seeks to rule over one by controlling one's body (Epict. 1.9.15–17; 1.18.17) or by getting the individual, in the desire to be seen and praised, to forego one's principles (Epict. 1.10.1–6). Epictetus (and the Stoics generally) held that nothing material – "neither death, nor exile, nor toil, nor any such thing" – can be "the cause of our doing or of our not doing, anything, but only our value-judgments (*hupolēpseis*) and principles of action (*dogmata*)" (Epict. 1.11.33, trans. modified; also 2.6.15; *Medit.* 8.1). What we control is our *prohairesis*, our basic choice of principle that directs judgments about impressions (Epict. 1.12.35; 1.17.22: assenting to truth).[23] Freedom is "the power of independent action" (DL 7.121), which is ultimately the power of moral choice against the backdrop of political coercion. In assent to reason and nature lies serenity and freedom (Epict. 1.4.6; 1.4.18–19).

To understate the situation fairly significantly, Marcus is not a slave. The nephew of Antoninus' wife, he was adopted by the emperor Antoninus at the request of Hadrian to ensure succession. He was raised to

---

[23] Sandbach points out that Epictetus is the first known Stoic to make the term into a technical one (Sandbach 1975, 165).

the status of Caesar at the age of eighteen, becoming emperor at the age of thirty-nine (161 CE) when he then selected his adoptive brother, Lucius Verus, to share power. It was a tumultuous time in the Empire: the invasion of the Parthians in the eastern provinces (161); flooding of the Tiber (161); earthquakes at Cyzicus (161) and at Smyrna (178); a devastating plague that many see as a turning point in the collapse of the empire (166);[24] threatened invasions from the Marcomanni and the Quadi (a Germanic tribe) to the north (166–75); and the rebellion of Avidius Cassius in the east (175).

Marcus presents us with a view of politics that is threatening less because of coercion and more because of the seduction of fame and power and the vicissitudes of political turmoil. Marcus recalls the times of Vespasian, or of any emperor for that matter: "people marrying, bringing up children, falling sick, dying, fighting wars, feasting, trading, working the land, flattering, putting on airs, suspecting their fellows, hatching plots, praying for the death of others, grumbling at their present lot, falling in love, piling up fortunes, lusting for high office or a crown" (4.32.1). One clamors for fame from those whom one has "never seen and will never see" (6.18), grovels to those one dislikes (11.14), and caters to the mob in seeking adulation (1.16.3). The man who needs "praise from the crowd" or who fears he will lose to others what he most prizes, Marcus writes, cannot be free (6.16.3; also 1.16.3). One pursues something that is empty: a "re-echo [of] your name" (8.44). Similarly the individual who is ruled by the desires that arise from the immediacy of the senses is like a puppet, no different from a wild beast or, as Marcus adds, Nero (3.16.1).

Marcus shares with Epictetus a view of freedom (*eleutheria*) that lies in a retreat into oneself (4.3.1, 4) or a gathering of oneself into oneself (7.28; 8.48: citadel). For the Stoics, even though we are blended with others, nature allows us to isolate ourselves and keep things in our own power (7.67; 5.5). What depends on us – what lies in our control – is how we receive the world (7.68; 5.20; 11.11) and how we act in it (5.20; 8.16). We are to strip ourselves of everything that is exterior (or indifferent) to

---

[24] See Gilliam 1961 for the debate and evidence.

us: concerns about what other people are saying and doing (3.4.1; 8.46); passions (6.16.3); involuntary emotions (5.26); past and future (2.14; 3.7; 7.8); and superstition (1.16.3). It is a notion of freedom tied to *apatheia* (6.16.3; 11.18.10), self-mastery (*to kratein heatou*) (1.15.1; 8.48), and self-sufficiency (*autarkia*) (6.16.3; 3.5; yet 7.7).

For Marcus, though, there is a public dimension to this self-mastery: excellence that is filtered through the lens of Roman manliness. In referring to images of masculinity in his *Meditations*, Brunt suggests that "far from being pre-occupied with the need to overcome the fear of physical danger, when Marcus gives 'manliness' any specific content, he declares it to lie in conquering the weakness of irascibility."[25] Not only does Marcus give content to this manliness, but he also redefines it away from the competitiveness and violence that had long ago doomed the Republic.

The Stoics had always seen bodily movements as betraying internal movements of the soul. The body does not disguise one's character (see 2.16); rather, the body displays it. The good man (*ho agathos*) "reveals these qualities" in his voice and eyes (11.15; also 7.24; 7.31; 7.37) and sees these "images of the virtues shining forth in the character of those around us" (6.48). As this Stoic emphasis on bodily dispositions is interpreted by way of a Roman notion of *decorum*, though, these trained habits of the body are more explicitly tied to one's social role, given to individuals by nature and circumstance. The maleness of the association of life with work (*ergon*) or art (*technē*), the adaptation of action "to the purpose for which it has been produced" (6.16.2; also 5.1.2; 6.14; 6.35; 6.40; 6.55; 8.19), is made clear when Marcus asks, "What is your profession (*technē*)? 'To be a good man (*agathon*)'" (11.5, trans. modified). Or as he writes earlier, "At every hour devote yourself in a resolute spirit, as befits a Roman and a man, to fulfilling the task in hand" (2.5).

The characteristics associated with this role contrast with the womanly virtues of docility, affection, and unaffectedness (1.17.7) or the abject condition of a slave (9.40). So Marcus, after enjoining himself to look within (7.59), continues, "One's body too should hold firm and

---

[25] Brunt 1974, 7.

not droop, whether in motion or at rest; for what the mind achieves for the face, by ensuring that it preserves an intelligent and decorous expression, should be required likewise of the body as a whole. But all of this should be attended to without affectation" (7.60). Nor should one be affected in speech and action: "do not attempt to embellish your thoughts by dressing them up in fine language; avoid excessive talk and superfluous action" (3.5; also 8.30). In this way, "The art of living is more like the wrestler's art than the dancer's" in that one "must stand ready and firm to meet whatever happens to it, even when unforeseen" (7.61). As Marcus writes, in joining together images of manliness and rule, "let the god within you be the overseer of one who is manly and mature, a statesman, a Roman, and a ruler" (3.5).

But Marcus also seeks to redefine the Roman image of masculinity. To be methodical, calm, and consistent is associated with manliness (1.16.9; also 6.30.2). Manliness is listed among such goods as wisdom, temperance, and justice (5.12; also 3.6; 3.11.2). A good man is able to forego pleasure if it does not come, but able to enjoy it if it is present (8.10). To be tempted by lust or anger is not masculine (*andrikon*) (2.10). To be mild and have a gentle disposition is to be "more human (*anthrōpikōteron*)," which is also "more manly (*arrenikōteron*)" (11.18.10; also 11.15; 1.16.1, of Antonius). Such a man "possesses strength (*ischuos*), nerve (*neurōn*) and manly courage (*andreias*)" (11.18.10, trans. modified). We are like soldiers storming the rampart (7.7). Or, in another image, we are like masters of our own house (8.56).

This mastery does not eventuate in *imperium* or *dominium*, the traditional avenue of Roman power, but in the Greek *dunamis*. As Marcus writes, "For the nearer a man comes in his mind to *apatheia*, the nearer he comes to strength (*dunamis*)" because he does not succumb or surrender to the passions (11.18.10). The power (*dunamis*) is one implanted by nature, a power of living (11.16) and of display (5.5) in which the maker is at hand to work on the self (6.40). It is a power of nature "to generate the necessary substances and transformations and successions" (9.1.4). But this manliness turns on a paradox: Freedom, as a generative power, lies in being self-made slaves. "One who flees from his master is a runaway slave; now the law is our master, and one who departs from it is therefore a runaway slave" (10.25).

Marcus is addressing the decadence, violence, and competitiveness that had nearly bankrupted the nobility and given rise to the despotisms of the *principes*, manifest in the cruel rule of Domitian. Marcus' emphasis on self-mastery addresses a problem endemic in Roman politics, one that we already saw explored by Sallust; namely, that *virtus* had lost any moorings so that each person becomes the interpreter of both the ends and methods of political life. Sallust can only appeal to ancestral tradition. Marcus starts with these traditions, including in his dedications in Book 1 his debt to Severus for having introduced him to Thrasea, Helvidius, Cato, Dion, and Brutus, who by now had become Stoic martyrs who had opposed the tyrannical consolidation of power.[26]

We already know Cato by way of Sallust: an austere political leader who was renowned for his principled stands and ultimately his own suicide in opposition to Caesar's assertion of power. Brutus would plot the assassination of Caesar. Thrasea Paetus (whom we encountered by way of Tacitus) had refused to support a proposal in the senate to celebrate the death (in fact the murder) of Agrippina. His passive opposition in refusing to endorse Nero's crimes led to his forced suicide. Helvidius Priscus, like Thrasea, was a defender of the power of the senate and an outspoken critic of the authority of the *princeps*. In Epictetus' recounting:

> When Vespasian sent him word not to attend a meeting of the Senate, he answered, "It is in your power not to allow me to be a member of the Senate, but so long as I am one I must attend its meetings." "Very well then, but when you attend, hold your peace." "Do not ask for my opinion and I will hold my peace." "But I must ask for you opinion." "And I must answer what seems to me right." "But if you speak, I shall put you to death." "Well, when did I ever tell you that I was immortal? You will do your part and I mine. It is yours to put me to death, mine to die without a tremor; yours to banish, mine to leave without sorrow." (Epict. 1.2.19–21)

He ultimately was banished and executed.

---

[26] Marcus apparently conferred with the senate and people (Hadot 1998, 300).

Traditions are not enough, though. The heroes of old, as Marcus reminds himself, are obsolete: "For all things are swift to fade and become mere matter for tales, and swiftly too complete oblivion covers their every trace" (4.33; also 3.10: no knowledge of self; 4.19; 7.6; 7.21). It is not that memory is irrelevant, though. What these examples have in common is that they are lives of self-mastery lived politically. Their political relevance is suggested in the following sentence when he describes the importance of a government founded on equality (*isonomia*), equity (*isotēs*), and freedom of speech (*isēgoria*), and of "a monarchy which values above all things the freedom (*eleutheria*) of the subject" (1.14). This is not the language of political fulfillment. Rather, it is a view of politics that mirrors the impartial order of nature, one in which each is equal in obedience to the Law (4.4), equity derives from a recognition of worth (4.32.2), and a realm that values freedom as moral choice and expression (3.6). What endures – what is worth remembering and even enacting politically – are the eternal principles, even as they appear in others, by which one comes to know oneself (e.g., 3.10; 5.24; 11.26). One locates oneself not in tradition but, as we will see, in the infinite expanse of time and space that defines the cosmos.

CONTEMPLATION

The practice of philosophy, the ability to bring oneself into conformity with nature, requires, as Marcus Aurelius writes, that one "look down from a height" (*Medit.* 9.30; also 7.48; 11.1.2; 12.24). Marcus Aurelius is invoking an image by now familiar in ancient political thought, whether Plato's "Myth of Er," Plato's philosopher who visits the city in body only (*Theaet.* 173e; allusion to 174b in *Medit.* 10.23), Cicero's "Dream of Scipio," or Lucretius' philosopher looking down at the scramble for power. Rutherford sees Marcus as sharing this "perennial motif in ancient philosophic writing" in order "to illustrate the isolation and superior vision of the philosopher."[27] Marcus, though, stakes out a distinctive

---

[27] Rutherford 1989, 155.

perspective, one that we can begin to understand in juxtaposition to the Platonic, Ciceronian, and Lucretian models.

For Plato, Lucretius, and Cicero, the cosmic perspective reveals a disjuncture between human existence and the universe, creating a sense in which the individual does not quite belong. The philosopher must be coaxed to return to earth: One blinks, unable to see, in Plato's cave; one is promised a reward in fulfilling one's thankless political duties in Scipio's dream; and one must scratch out an existence, returning to the hopeless drudgery of *labor* in Lucretius' nature. So too, as we will see in the next chapter, individuals are for Augustine "pilgrims in a foreign land," beings with eternal souls who find themselves temporally bound. Salvation lies elsewhere: in contemplation of the Forms, in a return to the cosmos, in the practiced distance of the philosopher, or in Heaven.

Marcus' language seems to share with these approaches a perspective that diminishes one's earthly existence, making one realize one's own insignificance (4.3.3; 6.36.1; 9.28.2; 9.32; 12.24). "Everything material disappears very swiftly into the universal substance, and swiftly too every cause is re-absorbed in the universal reason, and very swiftly the memory of everything is buried in eternity" (*Medit.* 7.10). The vastness of the ebb and flow of the universe makes "all that is highly prized in life" appear "hollow, putrid, and trivial; puppies snapping at one another, little children bickering, and laughing, and then all at once in tears" (*Medit.* 5.33). There is little that is new or distinct: all of history, "the whole court of Hadrian, say, or of Antoninus, the whole court of Philip, or Alexander, or Croesus; for in every case the play was the same, and only the actors were different" (*Medit.* 10.27; also 4.32.1–2; 6.46: like theater). We appear as a speck, a point between "the expanse of time that stretches before our birth" and the "equally boundless time that will follow after our dissolution" (9.32; also 4.36; 12.32). Rist sees Marcus as "so overwhelmed by man's puny strength on the cosmic scene that none of man's actions appears more than trivial."[28] Rutherford contends, for example, that "the *Meditations* go further than either Cicero or Plutarch in condemnation of the human world and of mortal pursuits."[29]

---

[28] Rist 1969, 286.
[29] Rutherford 1989, 21; also Asmis 1989, 2240: more contempt for body than Stoics.

Rutherford attributes this position to "their author's loneliness and isolation."[30] Where "Epictetus, concentrating on the life of the world, is content," Rutherford argues, "the disillusionment of Marcus seeks a purer and higher existence beyond this mortal sphere."[31]

I agree that there is a searching desire for belonging in Marcus' writing, but it is one that does not locate salvation in some higher realm. Where these other cosmic perspectives serve to distance one from earthly life, Marcus inverts the claim: The person who lacks such a comprehensive view is like an alien or wanderer in the world (2.17; 4.29: alien in universe; 10.8.2: adrift; 2.13.6: recalling Epict.). "He who does not know what the universe is does not know where he is" (8.52). Rather than locating salvation in something that comes after life, for Marcus this comprehensive view serves as our salvation in life (*sōtēria biou*) by orienting us in time and space (12.29; also 7.2.1; 7.47).

Contemplation and time

The problem of time is in part a problem of flux: For Marcus we live in a Heraclitan universe in which everything is change. "There is a stream of things entering into being, and time is a raging torrent; for no sooner does each thing enter our sight then it has been swept away, and another is passing in its place, and that too will be swept away" (4.43; also 4.46; 6.17; 7.19; 9.28; 10.33.4; 12.21; 12.23). The problem, or at least a problem, is where one locates oneself in that rushing torrent that expands infinitely into the future and into the past. Time for the Stoics does not have the ontological status of "being."[32] Furthermore, the Stoics argue that there is no logical moment called "the present" since any moment of time can be divided still further (see Chrysippus in *SVF* 2.509; also Plut. *De comm. not.* 1081c-1082a). Time, though, and the present, is "something."[33] For Marcus, and he agrees with Chrysippus here, the present has duration, if only experientially (Chrysippus in *SVF* 2.509; *Medit.* 6.36).

---

[30] Rutherford 1989, 121. [31] Rutherford 1989, 248, for example, Epict. 3.13.16.
[32] See Reydams-Schils 2005, 29. [33] Reydams-Schils 2005, 29.

So what is one to see and do in imagining oneself in the flow of infinite time? How does one simply not get lost? What does one retrieve from this exercise in thought? In part, in reflecting on the distant past and future, one does not see a disorienting confusion but (contrary to Heraclitus) sameness; the continuation of "the present rhythm of events" (7.49) brought about because of a "rational conjunction" of everything (4.45). But within this flow of time we also locate ourselves; we are given an allotment, a beginning and ending point (2.6; 3.10). Even amidst this cosmic vastness, this proportion is special: We are part (*meros*) of this cosmos (2.4). And if one does not use that time "to clear the fog from your mind, the moment will be gone, as you are gone, and never be yours again" (2.4; also 4.17).

That realization carries weight (*baros*) (8.36; also 4.50). In the exercise of thought one learns how to break up time into smaller and smaller spans (8.36; 11.2), creating boundaries around the moment (8.36). In doing this, we transform the experience of the present from a burden to initiative by attending to things that relate to oneself (3.4.3). It is the present, and not the past or future, that belongs to us precisely because it is in the present that we are conscious of ourselves as initiating and acting. What we possess, and what is harnessed by attention to the present, is the power (*dunamis*) of living (11.16), which is the ability to direct oneself to some aim according to nature (2.7). In contrast, "its own form of movement on every occasion is not granted to a cylinder, nor to water, nor to fire, nor to anything else that is governed by nature or irrrational soul" (10.33). But *nous* and *logos* can carry its way "through everything (as fire moves upwards, or a stone downwards, or a cylinder down an incline)" (10.33; see also Chrysippus in Cic. *De fato* 19.43). The present, thus, emerges as the realm of freedom precisely because no "hindrances" can be placed on "my impulses or my disposition" nor on my "power to act with reservation" in which I can adapt when obstacles present themselves (5.20; also 8.32; 8.35; 8.41; 8.48).[34]

---

[34] Also Hadot 1998, 119.

Contemplation and space

Just as through contemplation we are summoned to a smaller and smaller moment of time, so too we are reoriented in space. The reorientation is most frequently understood as a retreat into the self (4.3.1, 4; also 3.4.3). Nussbaum, speaking generally about the Stoics, sees them as denying any sort of value to us as social beings.[35] Reydams-Schils points to "Epictetus's radical emphasis on self-reliance" and the tendency in "Roman Stoic accounts [to] either hesitate to list among the external indifferents the people with whom we have bonds or do so only under specific conditions."[36] Hadot characterizes the individual as erecting a citadel.[37] Rutherford suggests of the *Meditations*, "there is much more attention given to the mind as a retreat, which must be made into a fortress."[38] Asmis describes how Marcus "yearns for detachment."[39] And Foucault, as we have seen, has influentially interpreted the Stoic cultivation of the self as a relation to oneself.[40]

Marcus at times employs this language of a retreat into the self (4.3.1, 3; also 3.4.3). But his relationship to space involves a more ambitious projection outward. Looking at oneself from the perspective of nature, from this cosmic stance, "means from the perspective of the self's relation to a world that is the product of immanent divine agency."[41] But that relationship is also to the "earthy elements" of the humors that form our "composite being" by which we are always pulled back to the earth (11.20.2; also 10.7.2). That is, any contemplation of oneself must always comprehend one as a sentient being.

There are several implications of this claim that bear on the issue of belonging. We are, genealogically speaking, of one image and likeness (see 8.34). For Marcus Aurelius, that which is eternal is matter in transition, set in motion by Reason or driven by the impulse of Reason (6.15; 8.50; 9.3.1; 9.19; 10.11; 10.18; 12.21). As Marcus enjoins, "Constantly think of the universe as a single living being, comprised of a single substance and a single soul" and "how it accomplishes all things

---

[35] Nussbaum 1994, 362. [36] Reydams-Schils 2005, 59. [37] Hadot 1998.
[38] Rutherford 1989,124. [39] Asmis 1989, 2244.
[40] See Foucault 1990b, 1997a, 2005. [41] Reydams-Schils 2005, 42.

through a single impulse" (*Medit.* 4.40; also 7.9). Reincarnation appears as an eternal return: Everything is changed into universal substance or dispersed (6.4; 10.7), forming an unbroken cycle in which spirit, cleansed of "the defilement of our earthly existence" (7.47), returns to earth to regenerate things coming into being (4.44–46; 9.14; 10.37; Epict. 2.1.18). We come from recycled spirit that is diffused into the universe and then transformed into *logos spermatikos*, seminal reason that is then transmitted through the sperm and blood (4.21.1; also 4.14).[42]

Furthermore, as one comprehends the unity of universal Reason, one sees "how all things in the universe are bound up together and interrelated" (6.38; also 7.9). Marcus reminds himself "how close is the kinship which unites each human being to the human race as a whole, for it arises not from blood or seed but from our common share in reason (*nou koinōnia*)" (12.26; see Epict. 1.9.1). Each of us is a limb of a common body, created to work together in harmony (7.13). Marcus' claim rests upon a Stoic view in which common elements in nature "strive to rejoin their kind," with higher levels of association corresponding with higher forms of rationality, from inanimate matter to irrational creatures and finally to rational creatures who form political communities, friendships, households, gatherings, and agreements (9.9). The measure of the superiority of that which shares in intelligence is its eagerness "to mix and coalesce with its own kind" (9.9.1).

Ultimately, in speaking the language most familiar to the Romans, Marcus suggests that one belongs in this world as a political being: "As Antoninus, my city and fatherland is Rome; as a human being, it is the universe" (6.44). The *kosmos* appears as the highest *polis* of which all other cities are "mere households" (3.11.2; also 4.4). The idea can be traced back to the early Cynics and Stoics who envisioned this *polis* as an ideal community of sages along the later line of Augustine's city of God, a community organized by justice and bound to God but mixed with the earthly city.[43] What makes the cosmos a real city in the Stoic sense is that it is comprised of people living according to law and justice (see Chapt. 6, 315–20).[44] For Epictetus, the *kosmos* as a state is important in assigning authority and obedience to the whole over the

---

[42] See Reydams-Schils 2005, 123–25.
[43] See Schofield 1995a; Obbink 1999.   [44] Obbink 1999, 189.

part (Epict. 2.10.4–6; 4.1.154).[45] So too, for Marcus the *kosmos* is the only community in which we are regulated by a common law, motivated by a common interest (*sumpheron*) (6.45) and oriented by justice.[46] Justice for Marcus is the root of virtues because it rests on constancy (like rational nature itself) in apportioning things according to worth (see 4.32.2; 8.7; 9.1.1; 11.10). Employing a conventional Stoic view, Marcus sees justice (and his own behavior) as acting to benefit one's "fellows according to their deserts and in no way to do them harm" (9.1.1; also 3.11; 4.26; 10.5; 12.1.1). To act unjustly is to act impiously because one acts contrary to divine intelligence, which has "subordinated, co-ordinated, and assigned to each the lot that is owing to it" (5.30; also 5.8.2–3; 9.1.1–4).

For Marcus, this city is not just comprised of the community of sages, but is more inclusive, related more to his overarching concern with belonging. Marcus gives a cosmic take on Nicias' words to his troops, "you yourselves, wherever you settle down, are a city already" (Thuc. 7.77), claiming, "what matter whether you live here or there, if everywhere you live in this great city of the universe?" (10.15). We are all "working together to a single end," namely acceptance of the rational order of the universe (6.42; also 6.39; 9.23; 10.2; Epict. 2.10.4–6). Going well beyond Epictetus, Marcus argues that to be rational is to be *koinōnikos* (social) and *politikon* (civic), directing our actions toward others (*Medit.* 3.4; 6.30.1; 9.42.5; 10.2; 11.18.1; 11.20; 12.30). We "have come into the world for the sake of one another" (*Medit.* 4.3.2). To be without a *polis* is to be torn from the unity of the universe and the "concord" of others (9.23; also 2.16; 8.34; 11.8). The person without a *polis* is like a *xenos*, an alien who has no understanding of his surroundings, or a *phugas*, an exile from reason, or a *ptōchos*, a beggar who must depend on others (4.29; also 9.23: destroys concord [*sumphōnia*]; 11.8; 12.1.2). It is precisely this lack of a civic dimension that underlies Marcus' dislike of the Christians as being unpatriotic (3.16.2). Referring more generally to the divisions and turmoil in society, Marcus notes that "only the intelligent creatures have forgotten

---

[45] See Stanton 1968, 186.
[46] Also 12.36: "under its laws equal treatment is meted out to all"; 4.4: we are citizens because of law that is common.

this eagerness and inclination to come together, and it is here alone that one fails to find this confluence of like with like" (9.9.3).

What Marcus develops, and this anticipates Augustine, is the nature of this bond, which is comprised not just of obedience to reason but also of love (*philos*) for one's neighbor (11.1.2; also 6.39; 7.13; 7.31). To live according to universal nature requires that we "welcome what is presently assigned" to one (10.11), which includes love of those "among whom your lot has fallen" (6.39). In part, this love encompasses the entirety of the universe. Giving a Stoic interpretation to a passage from Euripides, Marcus writes, "'The earth loves (*erāi*) showers, and the holy ether loves (*erāi*) [to fall in showers].' And the universe loves (*erāi*) to create whatever is to be; so I will say to the universe, 'Your love is my love too.' Is that not also implied in the expression, 'This loves to (*philei*) come about?" (10.21). It is a conception of the natural relationship and order of things that is bound together as love. This love also derives from *oikeiōsis*, a natural attraction of similar things, something shared by all living beings (2.13; also 7.13; 10.21; also Chapt. 1 and 6). And it derives, as well, from an attraction to the beautiful, a sense of love (as *erōs*), as Schofield suggests, that plays a part in Zeno's *Republic* (from what we can reassemble of it) in fostering friendship and community (see 2.1).[47] But Marcus also contends that a being "strives" toward "that for the sake of which each being has been constituted and for which it was made," which is fellowship (5.16; also 9.27; 9.42.5; 11.1.2). Rational beings are not just *koinōnikoi* but are impelled by "the feeling of common fellowship" (*to koinōnikon pathos*)" (12.30).

The language is surprising since *pathē* are comprised for the Stoics of false assent that is contrary to nature (see 1.9.3; 2.5.2). The closest we get in Stoic thought is *eupatheiai* (= *constantiae*), or good affective states that correspond to three of the passions: instead of appetite, there is wish (*boulesis* = *voluntas*); instead of fear there is caution (*eulabeia* = *cautio*); and instead of pleasure there is joy (*chara* = *gaudium*). Throughout the *Meditations*, Marcus mentions a number of these good states: *emphrōn* (prudence), the "attention needed to apprehend each object with due

---

[47] Schofield 1991, 46.

accuracy, and freedom from negligence"; *sumphrōn* (sympathy), "the willing acceptance of all that is allotted to you by universal nature"; *huperphrōn* (high-mindedness), "the elevation of the thinking part of you above the smooth or violent agitations of the flesh" (10.8.1; also 5.9); good grace (*eumeneia*) (7.3; 8.51.2; 9.11); pity (*eleēnōn*) (2.13; 7.26); considerateness (*eugnōmosunē*) (5.9); and thankfulness (8.8, criticizing those who are *acharistos*).[48]

Marcus uses *pathē* in another context that may be instructive here. He suggests that a broadened view of the universe is not dispassionate but entices our admiration (3.2.1) and our passion (*pathē*) for the processes of the universe (3.2.2). In a sense, we are training ourselves to see differently, a seeing that (in Stoic physiology) operates as a *phantasia* that translates into an impulse. One is reminded of Epictetus' evocative passage, "God has brought man into the world to be a spectator of Himself and of His works, and not merely a spectator, but also an interpreter" (Epict. 1.6.19). We are to train our desire "to work or take your rest as the reason of the city requires" (9.12; 11.37). This passion is properly directed as love, not love in which the mind becomes *sumpathēs* with the flesh (7.65), the descensive part of us, but love directed by its own *dunamis* at the sight derived from this new perspective (12.3). It is love that appears more like an extension (like a ray of sun): extending straight out, entering whatever cracks it encounters, and never slipping away or sinking down when it meets an obstacle (8.57). It does not violently impact or shrink away, "but stand(s) firm and illuminate(s) the object that receives it" (8.57). Marcus' language is striking and stands in dramatic contrast to conceptions of the self (articulated most fully by Hadot) as a "citadel."[49] We may seek invulnerability from outside, but we also project ourselves outward with nature's power.

---

[48] Engberg-Pederson notes the many occasions in which Marcus talks about good affective states (Engberg-Pedersen 1998, 306–7, 322–26; Irwin 1998, 225) or our natural affections (1.9.3).

[49] The title of Hadot 1998.

THE *DAIMŌN*

These conceptions of manliness, fellowship, and love are integrated into Marcus' conception of the *daimōn*. Mention of a *daimōn* can be traced back to Socrates, where it appears as an ever-present guiding voice. There is evidence that early Stoic thought posited "external demons of non-human origin."[50] Diogenes Laertes reports that the early Stoics held that there are *daimones* "who are in sympathy with mankind and watch over human affairs" (DL 7.151; see also Epict. 2.5.18 talking about Socrates). For Seneca, a divine power is implanted in humans "in order that we may have a nearer knowledge of divinity" (*Ep.* 41.5; also 66.22). Seneca also gives this divinity life: it "associates with us, but still cleaves to its origin"; it "turns its gaze and strives to go" toward its source; and "it concerns itself with our doings only as a being superior to ourselves" (*Ep.* 41.5). For Epictetus, God places a *daimōn* next to and within each person that serves as a protecting comrade (*parastatēs*) who both watches over us and is entrusted to our care (Epict. 1.14.12).

Hadot describes the *daimōn* as "nothing but mythical, imaginative expressions, intended to render the Stoic conceptions of Reason and Destiny more alive and personal."[51] Reydams-Schils sees it as embodying "a much more radical continuity between human and divine reason and, as such, indicates the very fluidity of the boundary between the one and the other."[52] For Asmis, the *daimōn* "forms the basis of his ethics. More clearly and emphatically than any predecessor, Marcus regards the intellectual soul within each human being as a divinity."[53] It is an ethic, I will suggest, that is organized around a recast notion of piety.

Marcus calls the conformity of the soul to nature piety. One is impious who offends the will of the gods by acting in opposition to nature (9.1.1). Not unexpectedly, Marcus understands piety as the obligation to pay due respect to and obey a higher authority. Marcus' *daimōn* appears as the authority of nature implanted in us (see 3.6.2; 3.7). It is a particle given by the gods to serve as one's "overseer (*prostatēs*) and guide (*hēgemonia*)" (5.27). Or it is like "the overseer of one who is manly and

---

[50] Algra 2007, 372. [51] Hadot 1998, 159–60.
[52] Reydams-Schils 2005, 44. [53] Asmis 1989, 2243.

mature, a statesman, a Roman, and a ruler, who has taken his post as one who is awaiting the signal for his recall from life and is read to obey without need of an oath or another man as his witness" (3.5). Impiety is not just a failure to observe some external authority; it is the failure to care for (or love) this element of the divine by keeping it untainted, or without *hubris* (*anubristos*) (3.12; also 2.1; 3.6.2; 3.8; 3.12; 3.16.2; 8.45.2; 9.2). That is, piety is a responsibility to nature that is ultimately a personal responsibility toward oneself (see 9.4; also 3.13).

In this same way we can understand the civic dimension of love. We are made to care for ourselves and to put body inclinations to our own use (7.55.2; see Chapts. 1 and 6 on *oikeiōsis*). As Epictetus writes, no one is dearer to me than me (Epict. 3.4.10). But the care for oneself is not an isolated venture. The care for oneself is a care for one's *daimōn*, which is the embrace of the being of things (10.21). Love is not premised on sacrifice or on a sense of one's own incompleteness but on an embrace of being. In dramatic contrast to interpretations of Marcus' thought as reflecting loneliness and isolation, his *Meditations* seek to join us with others, recognizing in them a fellowship, as we are joined with ourselves, overcoming our own alienation. In training or directing our desires to love one's own nature we love others (11.4; also 7.13). It is a similar type of love, as it is mediated through Christ, that will reach its fullest Roman expression in Augustine.

9 AUGUSTINE: POLITICAL THOUGHT AS CONFESSION

We rarely encounter St. Augustine of Hippo's (Aurelius Augustinus, 354–430 CE) political thought in its Roman context, either reading him by way of the Platonists or "from a critical distance," as one political theorist writes, to "reassess and modify effects of the Augustinian legacy on the present."[1] His connection to Rome seems most apparent in biographical accounts of his early years: the son of a pagan father, Patricius, and Christian mother, Monica; inspired to a life of philosophy by his reading of Cicero's *Hortensius* at the age of 19; trained in law and ambitiously pursuing an imperial career as rhetor; appointed as chair of rhetoric in Milan, the seat of the imperial court, in 384; and himself renowned for his skills in a culture in which spectators would fill coliseums to listen to orators compete for *fama*. With Augustine's conversion to Christianity in 386, though, he is seen as entering a separate cultural and historical stream from pagan Rome, indifferent to the survival and hostile to the ethics of the Roman state. In his embrace of "the Bible and the Christian tradition," Coleman writes, he is seen as breaking decisively from the "perverse human fantasy of self-perfection, self-sufficient omnipotence and self-dependent autonomy" associated with

---

[1] Connolly 1993, xviii. For example, Morford notes that Augustine "developed the most extended system of philosophy in Latin prose," but then does not discuss Augustine, ending *The Roman Philosophers* with Marcus Aurelius (2002, 12).

ancient ethics.² In his view of Roman history, Markus contends, "Augustine speaks of Rome as an outsider."³

Even Augustine's philosophic orientation is seen as more Greek than Roman, indebted most of all to the neo-Platonists and Stoic interpretations of Plato. Coleman, for example, notes, "Augustine appropriated an amalgam of ancient philosophies whose principle ingredient was Platonism."⁴ Gregory sees Augustine's conception of love as navigating between "'ethically responsible' Stoicism and 'spiritual' Platonism," though it is unclear to whom he attributes either of these approaches.⁵ Wetzel argues that throughout his entire career Augustine remains true to the Stoic ideal of the "convergence of virtue, autonomy, and happiness in wisdom."⁶ Stead mentions only Cicero's *Hortensius* as an influence on Augustine.⁷ O'Connell does not even accept that, rejecting any substantive influence of Cicero.⁸ And Jaeger characterizes the city of God as a christianized Plato's republic.⁹ But Augustine's relationship to, and critique of, Rome is more textured: Far from being an outsider, Augustine is engaged in a critical exploration with Roman political thinkers about this Roman past.¹⁰

In saying this, one should not underestimate Augustine's debt to Plato and his Stoic interpreters.¹¹ Augustine finds recourse in Plato's notion of the eternal, unchanging, and perfect Form of the Good that is beyond the senses but gives form to all things (*De lib. arb.* 2.17.45.174). He follows Plato in using mathematics as an example of intelligible structures that

---

² Coleman 2000, 293; also Harding 2008.   ³ Markus 1988, 57.
⁴ Coleman 2000, 296; also 304–10; Stead who mentions only Cicero's *Hortensius* as an influence on Augustine (1994, 219–20); Jaeger 1943, 2.77; Cary 2005, 3; Wetzel 1992, placing it in the context of Stoicism; Figgis 1963, 34–35; O'Connell 1968 (Plotinus); Djuth 1990 (Stoics).
⁵ Gregory 2008, 38–39.   ⁶ Wetzel 1992, 11.   ⁷ Stead 1994, 219–20.
⁸ O'Connell 1968, 3–4.   ⁹ Jaeger 1943, 2.77.
¹⁰ Markus recognizes these "authentically Roman" feelings by Augustine (1988, 57). But I think he understates how the tensions in Augustine's thought emerge from this Roman context rather than from careless, or unthought, inconsistencies. Harding 2008 seeks to demonstrate how Augustine is engaged in a critique of Roman ideals from within rather than from an outside, sacral perspective.
¹¹ *Civ. Dei.* 8.4; *Conf.* 8.2; also Armstrong 1972 on Augustine's relationship to Christian Platonism.

are known by the reasoning mind apart from senses (*De lib. arb.* 2.8.20.79–2.8.24.95; *Solil.* 1.8.15). He categorizes wisdom as discernment of the highest good (*De lib. arb.* 2.9.27.104–108; 2.10.29.119; 2.13.36.141–142). Like Plato he defines the ultimate good as knowing and imitating God (*Civ. Dei.* 8.8; 10.1), though he sees Plato's god as one who is solitary and noncommunicative (*Civ. Dei.* 9.1; 10.3). He even flirts with the possibility of an earthly sage in his fusing of neo-Platonism with his newly discovered Christianity during his retreat with a small philosophic circle, including his mother, to a friend's rural estate at Cassiciacum in 386. And, as Wetzel argues, Augustine, like Plato, retains confidence in the power of knowledge for personal transformation.[12] That knowledge emerges as "grace's irresistibility," which Wetzel interprets as Augustine's "attempt to salvage Platonism's naïve and uninformed confidence in the power of knowledge to motivate."[13]

But Plato and the Stoics take us only so far. Augustine's writings abound with such Roman authors as Sallust, Cicero, Virgil, Livy, Varro, and Seneca, learned during his Roman education in law and rhetoric at the University of Carthage. These authors, though, serve as more than a backdrop to or a point of rejection for Augustine's Christianity; they fundamentally orient his thought.[14] Recent scholarship has begun exploring how Augustine writes within a Roman rhetorical tradition, modeling his writings at Cassiciacum (*Contra academicos, De beata vita, De ordine*, and *Soliloquia*) after Cicero's dialogues, his sermons as therapies of the soul, and the role of the statesman in promoting a just society.[15] Kolbet, for example, contends that Augustine admired Cicero for having "employed his mastery of the cultural idiom to point readers like Augustine to an ideal higher than the culture itself" (see, for example, *De doc. Chr.* 4.17.34; 4.18.35; 4.19.38).[16] Virgil's poetry, which moved him to tears as a youth and which many see as decisively rejected by Augustine to be replaced by reason, was recited amidst the philosophic discussions

---

[12] Wetzel 1992, 6.   [13] Wetzel 1992, 9.
[14] Though he is sharply critical of these authors, e.g., *Conf.* 1.13: rejects Virgil of youth.
[15] Dialogues: Kolbet 2010, 88–105; Foley 2003; Conybeare 2006, 24–27, though pointing to other possible genre influences; therapies: Kolbet 2010, 3, 7, 71; statesman and just society: Dodaro 2004, 6–26, 182–214.
[16] Kolbet 2010, 71; so too St. Ambrose: Kolbet 2010, 73–80.

at Cassiciacum (*Contra acad.* 1.5.14; 2.4.10; 3.1.1; *De ord.* 1.7.26), used to explore notions of grammar and rhythm (see *De musica*), and underlies his sense of the role of the emotions in orienting individual and collective action.[17] His distinctive notion of the will is seen as derived, at least in part, from a hermeneutic tradition of Roman jurisprudence as well as "general Latin usage."[18] Augustine is similarly steeped in a Roman historiographic tradition, looking to the past as much for *exempla* as prophecy. He praises Varro for "storing and preserving" the sacred elements of the past "in the memory of good citizens" (*Civ. Dei.* 6.2). He invokes familiar exemplars of sacrifice, gratitude, fortitude, and fidelity: Brutus, Torquatus, Mucius, Curtius, Decii, Marcus Pulvillus, Marcus Regulus, Lucius Valerius, Cincinnatus, and Fabricius (*Civ. Dei.* 5.18). And Rome itself stands as a model of great sacrifice, endurance, and accomplishment that puts to shame those serving the city of God who "do not cling to the virtues that they clung to in serving the glory of the earthly city" (*Civ. Dei.* 5.18; also 5.14; 5.17).

But it is in his exploration and extension of Roman themes that we can more fully appreciate Augustine's relationship to Roman political thought. Humans are wanderers, like Virgil's exiles, in search of a home. But one cannot escape this earth into a realm of speechless contemplation; instead, one finds comfort and sorrow in a world that is as imperfect and as violent as it is loved, one that we know and can talk about through our senses. For Augustine, humans are not creatures moved by reason but by love and emotion. Communities, thus, can neither mirror an *eidos* nor aim toward a divine law; instead, they are defined by the bonds of affection that are formed from memory, habit, and experience. Augustine brings to a culmination the suspicion of theory that characterizes Roman political thought: autochthonous foundings, typologies of regimes, abstract conceptions of the state and individual, perfectibility, and political models of reasoned discourse and self-knowledge that are silent in the face of the complexities of our political situatedness. Augustine's political thought continues the Roman encounter with the ubiquity of violence, the

---

[17] See MacCormack 1998. *Civ. Dei.* 5.12; 10.27; 14.5; 14.9 (emotion as part of being human); *Conf.* 1.20; 3.4; 5.8; 10.27.
[18] Dihle 1982, 143.

imperfection of institutional structures, and the unavoidability of corruption. But he adds to it an ethos of confession: Human communities, held together by bonds of affection that are forged in memory and experience, can only endure if there is a type of love that inspires humility (a recognition of our incompleteness), forgiveness (a recognition of the incompleteness of others), and compassion (a recognition of the consequences of that incompleteness). Ultimately, though, he departs from his Roman past in claiming that it is God and neither philosophy nor politics that can make such endurance possible.

DESIRE AND ATTACHMENT

Augustine shares (though as we will see, dramatically revises) the ethical assumptions by now commonplace in ancient political thought: that all things exist for some end; that we are uniquely endowed with reason; that we are moved by knowledge; and that we are beings oriented to the end of happiness (*beatitudo*) (*Civ. Dei.* 19.1). Conceptually connecting human psychology to ontology by way of a unifying framework that explains the motion or movement of everything, Augustine argues that all beings are oriented by love (*amor*), or a desire or impulse (*impetus*) that Augustine understands as a motion of the soul (*motus animi*), directed toward possessing that which fulfills or satisfies one's being (*De trin.* 13.4.7; also *De trin.* 9.2.2). Augustine characterizes that satisfaction to which all beings move as peace (*pax*), or "a tranquillity of order" (*Civ. Dei.* 19.13; also 12.5; 19.14; 3.9).

When Augustine speaks about being (*essentia*), he is employing a conventional hierarchy based on the awareness or consciousness of the being, a scale ascending from merely existing to living to understanding (*esse vive intellegere*) (*Civ. Dei.* 12.2; on hierarchy, see *De lib. arb.* 1.7.16.54–56; 2.3.7.22). Even the lowest forms of being, inanimate objects that are "without any sensation or life," have a "kind of impulse" (*quidam adpetitus*) to seek their "proper place in the order of nature" (*Civ. Dei.* 11.28). So oil poured into water rises to the top; water poured into oil sinks to the bottom (*Conf.* 13.9). The argument extends to beings with sensation but not consciousness. A tree, though unable to love by any "conscious motion" (*sentiente motu*, trans. modified), "might in a way appear to pursue the aim of becoming more productive and bountifully fruitful" (*Civ. Dei.* 11.28). A body, too, "tends toward its proper peace, and by the plea of its weight, so to speak, demands a place of rest" (*Civ. Dei.* 19.12). In the deterioration of a corpse, "no matter what other things it is mixed with, no matter what transformation or permutation it undergoes, it still finds itself among the same laws that are everywhere diffused for the preservation of every mortal species, and act as peacemakers in that they match the parts that belong together" (*Civ. Dei.* 19.12).

The peace or well-being (*sufficiens bonum*) of an irrational animal, comprised of a body and life-giving spirit (*anima*), is a life that accords with its sensuality: love (*amor*) of a carnal life, which consists of healthy components of its body and the satisfaction of its appetites (*Civ. Dei.* 11.28; 13.23; 19.14). Unlike non-animal beings, animals have a type of awareness, an internal sense of themselves as sensing (*De lib. arb.* 2.4.10.38), allowing them to direct and judge the bodily senses (*De lib. arb.* 2.5.12.48; *De vera relig.* 29.53). An animal looks to a noise, for example, straining to hear or cocking the ears to identify danger or locate prey. "For just as animals, by avoiding pain (*dolor*), show that they love bodily peace, and by pursuing pleasure (*voluptas*) in order to satisfy the wants of their appetites show that they love peace of soul, so by their shunning death they give a sufficient indication how great is their love of the peace that harmonizes soul and body" (*Civ. Dei.* 19.14). The preservation of species similarly occurs through a sort of peace: "by cohabitation, by begetting, bearing, suckling and rearing their young" (*Civ. Dei.* 19.12).

The peace that defines the aim of human beings is happiness (*beatitudo*). As Augustine writes, framing an assumption of ancient political philosophy in the language of desire, "the happiness that a rational being craves as his proper goals," a craving that derives from one's origin, is premised on two conditions: that it is enjoyed continuously and that one is certain of its continued enjoyment (*Civ. Dei.* 11.13; also *Civ. Dei.* 19.1; *De beata vita* 2.10; *De lib. arb.* 1.4.10.30; *Conf.* 10.21). Augustine defines that final good as "the finished state in which [the being] is brought to complete perfection" (*Civ. Dei.* 19.1).

What we perceive and desire is not an artifact of natural properties (such as oil and water separating) or of instinct (as it might be with animals) but of the will (*voluntas*) or attention of the mind (*animi intentio*), a faculty of the rational soul (*animus*). In our relationship to the exterior world, the will both directs our senses to an object and converts that object into an image that is impressed on the mind (*De trin*. 11.2.2; 12.15.25). Once impressed on the mind, the will makes sense of that object – what it is and how we are supposed to respond to it – by an internal operation that combines memory (part of our irrational soul that stores past images as well as affections associated with those images: *Conf*. 10.14) with understanding or comprehension (*intellectus*) by which images are compared, combined, organized, extended, and evaluated (*De trin*. 13.20.26; also *Conf*. 10.8; 10.11; 10.15).[19]

The operation of the mind is not a tidy one: as one brings forth memory, one must contend with "forgetfulness" by which experiences are "swallowed up and buried" as well as sort through and draw together (*cogo*) (*Conf*. 10.11) memories that "rush out in troops," disordered and confused (*Conf*. 10.8). When one speaks of Carthage, Augustine notes, "I seek for what to say within myself, and find an image of Carthage within myself; but I received this through the body, that is, through the sense of the body, since I was present there in the body, and have seen and perceived it with my senses, and have retained it in my memory, that I might find the world about it within myself" (*De trin*. 8.6.9; also 13.1.4). As Hannah Arendt writes, the attention of the mind (*animi intentio*) "unites our sense organs with the real world in a meaningful way, and then drags, as it were, this outside world into ourselves and prepares it for further mental operations, to be remembered, to be understood, to be asserted or denied."[20]

Augustine has actually introduced a subtle and important claim: The activity of seeking that underlies every human action is a desire to obtain, to make something one's own. The desire "which is latent in seeking, proceeds from one who seeks, remains as it were in suspense,

---

[19] Augustine thus rejects the Greek notion of the will as a "byproduct of cognition" (Dihle 1982, 125).

[20] Arendt 1978, 2.100. See *De trin*. 8.6.9; 9.6.10; 11.2.2.

and only comes to rest in the goal towards which it is directed, when that which is sought has been found and is united with him who seeks" (*De trin.* 9.12.18). *Voluntas*, as Rist characterizes it, "is a love which has been accepted or consented to."[21] The desire for food is a desire to ingest it. The way in which we make sense of the world similarly involves directing our attention in order to make sensation into something understandable, transforming what is outside into something within us. When we hear an unfamiliar word, we desire to know what it is, transforming it from a mere sound into something signifying something, into an idea conveyed to the mind (*De trin.* 10.1.2). The report of a beautiful thing moves us to outwardly yearn to see and enjoy that thing, since we have a sense of what it will look like from other beautiful bodies we have seen, while there is something within us that gives approval (*De trin.* 10.1.1). The love of another is born from a knowledge that arises from within oneself as we look for particular characteristics, and enjoy them, in another. And to know oneself is a form of inquiry, a desire to find, or to discover, or (like a birth) to bring forth what is already within us (*De trin.* 9.12.18). This is not the homogenizing love of a universal soul: What our will loves, what we have made a part of us, makes each of us different.

We cannot love what we do not know (*De trin* 1.1.1; 13.4.7; 13.5.8; *Conf.* 1.1). As embodied beings (*Civ. Dei.* 1.13), we know the world through our senses. It is through our bodies that we experience pleasure and pain (*De lib. arb.* 2.5.12.49). It is through our bodily senses, as we have seen, that we "change and transform" what we experience "into ourselves," into something, including our memory, that is part of us (*De lib. arb.* 2.7.19.72). And it is through our bodies that we communicate with each other and are able to teach and guide others.

For Augustine there is nothing wrong with loving this world; in fact, Augustine continually evinces a fondness for earthly life:

> Certainly you love only the good because the earth is good by the height of its mountains, the moderate elevation of its hills, and the evenness of its fields; and good is the farm that is pleasant and fertile; and good is the house that is arranged throughout in symmetrical

---

[21] Rist 1994, 177.

proportions and is spacious and bright; and good are the animals, animate bodies; and good is the mild and salubrious air; and good is the food that is pleasant and conducive to health; and good is health without pains and weariness; and good is the countenance of man with regular features, a cheerful expression, and a glowing color; and good is the soul of a friend with the sweetness of concord and the fidelity of love; and good is the just man; and good are riches because they readily assist us; and good is the heaven with its own sun, moon, and stars; and good are the angels by their holy obedience; and good is the lecture that graciously instructs and suitably admonishes the listener; and good is the poem with its measured rhythm and the seriousness of its thoughts. (*De trin.* 8.3.4)[22]

But our embodiment creates an almost chaotic relationship to our surroundings and to ourselves. Because they are bodies that it loves, the mind cannot draw those bodies into its incorporeal nature except by fastening together images, "which it has made out of itself, and forces them into itself" (*De trin.* 10.5.7; also *Conf.* 10.8). So strong is the "force of love" that "the mind draws in with itself those things upon which it has long reflected with love, and to which it has become attached by its devoted care, even when it [the mind] returns in some way to think of itself" (*De trin.* 10.5.7).

The mind can err in two ways in this process. First, taking aim at the materialist approaches of Epicureanism, Stoicism, and Cynicism, Augustine argues that the mind errs when it binds itself to these images so strongly that it regards itself "as something of this kind," as a body or as something corporeal – as atoms, or blood, or earthly elements (*De trin.* 10.6.8).

Second, and more problematically, the mind errs in celebrating its own power in being able to make the world its own. In the activity of making sense of things, we turn tangible things into intangible representations so that our mind can operate on them: associating, combining, extrapolating, and judging. Through the act of the will in which we

---

[22] For Arendt, our love of eternity necessarily results in a hatred of the self and the temporal earth (1996, 27).

direct our attention and turn something outside into something inside us, we seem to possess the universe: "the heaven, the earth, the sea, and whatever I could perceive in them" (*Conf.* 10.8). Rather than seeking knowledge (*scientia*), "the action by which we use temporal things well" (*De trin.* 12.14.22; *De trin.* 12.12.17: "cognition of temporal and changeable things"; 11.3.6), the will seeks its end in the love of experiencing, excelling, and handling things that are perceived through the body, or what Augustine refers to as *cupiditas* (*De trin.* 12.10.15). The will "snatches the deceptive images of corporeal things from within and combines them together by empty thought, so that nothing seems to it to be divine unless it be of such a kind of this; covetous of its own selfish possessions it becomes prolific in errors and, prodigal of its own selfish goods, it is emptied of strength" (*De trin.* 12.10.15).[23] We in essence substitute the something that God has created with the nothing that we have created in our fantasies. It is this movement toward nothing that for Augustine is what it means to sin.

That sensuality is in turn reinforced and endorsed by custom and habits of the mind, memories that orient our will (*Conf.* 7.17; 10.40; *De doc. Chr.* 1.9.9). In confusing the world with our fantasies, the soul becomes entangled in these images, "which it has fixed in memory, foully defiled by the fornication of the phantasy" (*De trin.* 12.9.14). We take the order of the world and turn it into "confused multitudes of phantasies, which contradict one another" (*Conf.* 7.17) that we must navigate like a ship in a storm-tossed sea (*Civ. Dei.* 5.22). We "conceive better things" with our minds but search for them with our "eyes in inappropriate places" (*De lib. arb.* 3.5.14.51). As Augustine writes in *De libero arbitrio*:

> Lust dominates the mind and drags it back and forth, despoiled of the richness of virtue, poor and needy; at one moment taking falsehoods for truths and even making a practice of defending them, at another rejecting what it had previously accepted and nonetheless rushing to other falsehoods; not withholding its assent and often in dread of clear lines of argument; now despairing of the whole enterprise of finding the truth, lingering deep within the shadows of foolishness; now

---

[23] On the influence of Plotinus: Kolbet 2010, 83.

struggling towards the light of understanding but again falling back from it due to exhaustion (*De lib. arb.* 1.11.22.77).

The process is incremental: Through the "slippery movement" of minute actions of the will, guided by "the perverse desire of becoming like a God," of recreating the world in our own image through our fantasies, we instead arrive "at a likeness to the beasts" (*De trin.* 12.11.16). "But through the desire of proving his own power (*potestas*), man by his own will falls down into himself, as into a sort of center" (*De trin.* 12.11.16).

The image is striking because it points to a fundamental rejection of the individual as a sovereign being, one able to master oneself and one's will in relationship to one's environment. For Augustine that center is an empty space, a falling into an absence that insures one's own unhappiness. That unhappiness is manifest in two ways, both related to absence. First, one cannot be happy when one loves what is "unworthy of his love" (*De trin.* 13.8.11). For animals, a life of sensuality is proper. For humans, who possess both a body and rational soul, a life lived only in pursuit of sensual pleasures is a life unworthy of our humanity (for example, *De lib. arb.* 1.8.18.64). We end up being ruled by what we should rule (*De lib. arb.* 1.15.33.113; *Conf.* 10.6). In turning from our created nature, in "basely and perversely crav[ing] a lower thing," we desire "less being" (*Civ. Dei.* 12.6).

Second, happiness is associated with obtaining what one wills. Or conversely, one cannot be happy if one "wills something that he does not have" (*De trin.* 13.8.11). Yet, if we associate happiness not just with the possession of temporal things but also with the attainment of what we imagine those temporal things to be, then we are always clinging to absence, living in fear that what we have (which is nothing) will be lost or what we desire (which is also nothing) will never be obtained. The fear of losing the fantasy of what one loves propels one into a vicious cycle in which individuals will do anything to "try to remove hindrances so that they may securely attach themselves to these things to be enjoyed" (*De lib. arb.* 1.4.10.30). The result is "a life full of crime and wickedness, a life which is better called death" because it leads us to embrace absence (*De lib. arb.* 1.4.10.30). *Cupiditas*, in short, belies our mortality. We strive for happiness to obtain what we will, yet we associate happiness either with something that lies outside our will or with what we will wrongly (*De trin.* 13.5.8).

THE LIMITS OF *VIRTUS*

The solution proposed in ancient philosophic discourse to *cupiditas* is *virtus*. The Stoics, to recall, argue that virtues, which aim to perfect our rational soul, are the only human good. The Stoic turns inward, mastering through reason one's sensory responses to one's environment, finding happiness in wisdom. The "happiness of proud mortals" that derives from the practice of these virtues, as Augustine writes in summarizing the Stoic approach, is that "He wills, therefore, what he can, since he cannot have that which he wills" (*De trin.* 13.7.10). For the Stoics the invulnerability of the soul rests on our ability to strip away all that is peripheral and accidental so that we come to see and know ourselves in our essence, as agents of nature's reason (*De beata vita* 4.25).

Augustine recognizes the role these virtues play in controlling *cupiditas*. Virtues are learned ways of using the gifts of nature, which Augustine understands as regulating one's dispositions of love. True virtue is loving well. *Temperantia* (which is Augustine's translation of *sophrosunē*), the highest of virtues for Augustine, is giving love wholeheartedly to God, which means to direct our desires to things as they are created. The purpose is to restrain what Augustine calls the perverted pleasures (*delectationes pravae*) (*De trin.* 14.9.12; also *De lib. arb.* 1.13.27.89; *Civ. Dei.* 11.25: *fructus* and *usus*; 19.14) or the "lusts (*libidines*) of the flesh lest they win the consent of the mind" (*Civ. Dei.* 19.4). *Temperantia*, thus, brings us "into harmony with things of greater spiritual beauty and more unfading delight" rather than celebrating the enjoyment of our own sensuality (*Civ. Dei.* 12.8; *De beata vita* 4.31). *Fortitudo* teaches us to bear with whatever adversity may fall upon us, teaching patience in the attainment of love (*De trin.* 13.7.10; *De lib. arb.* 1.13.27.89). *Prudentia* helps us navigate through conflicting *phantasia* by guarding us against mistakes in choosing the objects of love (*De trin.* 14.9.12; *De lib. arb.* 1.13.27.89). And justice (*iustitia*) is a proper arrangement of love, keeping us from desiring what does not properly belong to us by requiring that we submit to proper rule and order (*De trin.* 14.9.12).

In his early philosophic writings during his retreat at Cassiciacum (386–87), between his conversion while professor of rhetoric at Milan and his baptism into the church (387), Augustine evinces this Stoic belief in the ability to attain invulnerability.[24] Through a Senecan scrutinizing of the self, making oneself visible to oneself, Augustine would teach his small school of followers at Cassiciacum that all impulses can be subject to reason (*Solil.* 1.14.24).[25] Through wisdom one can obtain happiness (*De beata vita* 4.33)

But in a striking replay of Cicero's own unresolved grief after the death of his daughter, Augustine's therapy of the soul after the death of his mother in 387 would similarly fall short (*Civ. Dei.* 19.4; *Conf.* 9.11–13; see also *Conf.* 2.9; 4.8; 6.16; *Ep.* 84.1). To imagine "wisdom's immunity from grief rests on the illusion that knowledge can somehow remove the sage from time"[26] and from sin (*Civ. Dei.* 14.9), that one can occupy a vantage point in which s/he is able to exist purely in the present, grasping the totality of things in one unified, atemporal, motionless, and immutable vision (*Civ. Dei.* 11.21; *Conf.* 11.31).[27] Even in Christ, humans "feel fear and desire, pain and gladness while they live in God's fashion" (*Civ. Dei.* 14.9; also 14.8).[28]

Augustine's exploration of the perplexity of time, which departs from Aristotle's understanding of time as a problem of physics, is meant precisely to grapple with the ethical implications of our temporal nature.[29] When Augustine asks what time is, his concern is the human experience of time. We cannot experience the future, nor can we experience the past; we can only experience the present, which exists as a kind of stretching of the present: as perceived, as anticipated, and as remembered (*Conf.* 11.13; 11.20; 11.23; 11.26; 11.28). To the extent that we are

---

[24] Colish 1990, 216; Byers 2003, 433–48; Foley 2003, 179, though not drawing the connection to Stoicism; see, for example, *Solil.* 1.10.17; 1.14.24.
[25] See Kolbet 2010, 100.   [26] Wetzel 1992, 10.   [27] Wetzel 1992, 40.
[28] See also Dodaro 2004, 194–95, on rejection of Stoic *apatheia*.
[29] See Ricoeur's illuminating discussion (1984, 3–30).

able to hold in our mind the past (as memory), the future (as expectation), and the present (as things perceived), we approximate God in His ever-presentness (on life without distraction, see *Conf.* 11.29; on grasping at once, see *Conf.* 11.31). Where God stands outside time, though, in our embodiment we are composed in time. What time introduces is the chasm between God and humans, between "eternal things" and the unstable "motions of things past and to come" (*Conf.* 11.11; also 11.7; also *De vera relig.* 22.43). Even our sense of the present is an illusion since "no time is all at once present" (*Conf* 11.11). What it means to be in time is to come into and pass out of existence, to tend "not to be," to be associated with non-Being (*Conf.* 11.14).

For Augustine, as important as the virtues are in orienting our love to that which has eternal value, they reveal their own incompleteness because they cannot remove us from time. We are torn apart by an internal war (*bellum intestinum*) in which we are unable to do what we would wish, in which our will bears the weight of our history and habits (*Civ. Dei.* 19.4). For Augustine, Stoic happiness amounts to brave misery: endurance in time (*De trin.* 13.7.10). The Stoic allowance of suicide, referring to the example of Cato, serves as the exclamation point for Augustine: "What a happy life, that seeks the help of death to end it" (*Civ. Dei.* 19.4). For Augustine ancient philosophy generally founders on a contradiction: it ultimately abandons "the first and greatest commandment of nature," which even these schools uphold, "that a man should be brought into harmony with himself and therefore instinctively avoid death" (*Civ. Dei.* 19.4). Augustine's rhetoric soars in pointing to a philosophic tradition that betrays itself: "Mighty is the power in these evils" that so defeats nature that we now long for the death that we sought to avoid (*Civ. Dei.* 19.4).

The Stoic goal of *apatheia* is for Augustine wrongly conceived. Our minds are emotional, not in the sense of the disordered disturbances that act against reason, but in the sense of our will as animated by love.[30] "To have a past," as Wetzel observes, is "to admit grief into wisdom."[31]

---

[30] Act against reason: see Gregory 2008, 278–79; Scrutton 2005: 169–77; *Civ. Dei.* 14.9, 16; animated by love: Burnell 2005, 62.
[31] Wetzel 1992, 109.

"But if any man has no sorrow in his heart either when he suffers himself or when he imagines such suffering, his case is certainly far from miserable, for he thinks himself happy precisely because he has lost all human feeling to boot" (*Civ. Dei.* 19.7). To banish all love for earthly things – and this is the inadequacy of Stoicism for Augustine – is in essence to die.[32]

The more Augustine would follow the Stoic logic of scrutinizing himself to conform to the image of nature's reason, the more inscrutable he appeared. For Augustine we can never completely know ourselves because we are not comprised of a will that carries out the dictates of reason and directs action, but of two antagonistic wills that aye or nay, each without a clear antecedent or cause.[33] The sheer unknownness of the will derives from its inextricable relationship to memory and understanding, themselves formed from the imprint of experience. Our will, as Augustine writes, possesses "its own kind of knowledge which cannot be there without memory and understanding" (*De trin.* 15.21.41; also *Conf.* 11.18). Furthermore, the will is always situated; we cannot know our will without our will since it is the will that directs us to explore it. We cannot know with certainty why we do something nor can we even comprehend what we are doing without images or words, both artifacts of experience and culture. I cannot even know that I will be the same person tomorrow that I am today (*Civ. Dei.* 19.5) precisely because what I am is comprised of a complex amalgam of experiences, memories, habits, affections, dispositions, and of course reason, all of which shape, both consciously and subconsciously, one's will. Its own complex historicity as well as its embodied location is implicated in any self-examination and remains, like Socrates' *daimōn*, hidden from us.

The Socratic injunction to know oneself requires the ability to continually subject the self to examination, to root out all the prejudices, unexamined assumptions, and habits so that one's desires and appetites can be ruled by reason. There is for Plato a political implication: Politics is modeled on the soul, as the parts are brought into their natural harmony by the rule of reason. For Augustine, the scrutinizing of the

---

[32] Babcock 1991, 45.
[33] Contra Dihle 1982, 143: "sheer volition." See also Arendt 1978, 2.92–96.

self does not result in being able to live by one's own reason but entails a recognition of one's own incompleteness, both in what can be known and how one is governed (*De trin.* 10.5.7). There is a political corollary: Politics is not the rule of universal reason but the organization of historically rooted desire.

AUGUSTINE'S CRITIQUE OF ROME: THE ORGANIZATION OF DESIRE

Augustine's discussion of Roman politics follows from this ontology of love. In his discussion of politics, Augustine eschews writing a traditional history (*Civ. Dei.* 3.18), at least in part because of the divergent interests of pagans and Christians in the past.[34] Roman historians looked to the past for an account of the political, social, military, and economic events and deeds in order to understand the course of change, bestow fame, and provide *exempla*. Christians, given their millennial hopes, had more interest in fitting a redemptive narrative into historical events and even of foretelling a Christian empire (particularly after 380 CE when Christianity becomes the official religion of the empire), an Augustan *pax Romana* given a theological foundation (importantly, St. Ambrose, Origen, Eusebius, Theodosius).[35] By the time Augustine writes *City of God* (*De Civitate Dei*), after the sacking of Rome in 410 by Alaric and the Visigoths, "the idea of a Christian Empire, as an achieved institutional reality" had vanished.[36] Augustine's explicit reason for looking to

---

[34] Momigliano 1963, 79–99.
[35] Markus 1988, 3; also Rist 1994, 208–10, 216–36. By the third century, Christianity had come to be seen by Romans as not only an exclusive sect, but also one, given their millennial hopes, that had little interest in the survival of the Roman state. We already get some sense of this with Marcus Aurelius' reference to the Christians as traitors, a notion reinforced by their refusal to subscribe to the state cult of *sol invictus*, the cult of the unconquered Sun, meant to include the different pagan sects in Rome. In the fourth century, Christianity had not only been recognized by Constantine in 313 in the Edict of Milan, himself converting to Christianity, but also had become the official religion of the empire under Theodosius I in 380, its opposition to pagan Rome marked by the controversial removal of the altar of Victory from the Curia in 383.
[36] Markus 1988, 39.

Roman history and Roman authors is to exonerate the Christians from blame for Rome's fall.

But Rome plays a larger role in Augustine's argument, one that points not to his divergence from but his affinity with Roman political thought.[37] Written as Rome's *res publica* was disintegrating under the forces of factionalism, violence, and dynastic competition, Cicero famously defines a *res publica* as a *res populi*, a people united in fellowship "by a common sense of right and a community of interest" (*Civ. Dei.* 19.21). In no less dire a circumstance, as Rome is sacked, Augustine redefines a *res publica* as a "large gathering of rational beings united in fellowship by their agreement (*concordia*) about the objects of their love" (*Civ. Dei.* 19.24).

We lose sight of how closely this definition tracks a Roman sensibility. Augustine's claim that a *res publica* cannot be a community of justice because we can never give God His due is consistent with a Stoic view of a true city and true citizenship as including only the virtuous who live and govern themselves according to nature's law, the law of reason (DL 7.32–33; Cic. *Acad.* 2.44.136). But in Augustine's modification of the definition, a *res publica* is a people oriented by attachments or feelings.[38] Roman political thought operates in this register: in describing the disorienting and enervating effects of a loss of attachments; in invoking the language of tradition, care, homelessness, and love; and in locating the affective underpinnings of such concepts as authority and liberty. When Augustine invokes Sallust in his discussion of Rome, he is not just using the Roman historian as vindication of Rome's prior corruption; he is extending Sallust's analysis of politics as the organization of desire. Where Sallust seeks resolution in the restoration of tradition, though,

---

[37] See also Harding 2008, 66–70 and Augustine's relationship to Roman historiography.
[38] Barrow 1950, 21–22: Augustine does not talk about the *res publica* since it is an organization of material assets; Burt 1999, 68: society as a "moral union of two or more persons striving for a common good by cooperative activity," though this misses the affective aspect of Augustine's definition; R. Williams 1987, 59–60: Augustine's redefinition is ironic in order to critique society; Markus 1988, 65: more neutral conception of relationship of society to justice; Dodaro 2004: 17, 26: point is a focus on Christ.

Augustine points ultimately to the intractable dilemmas of political life.[39] We are social beings who cannot find happiness in society.

The primary mechanism by which the Romans organized desire was by way of glory, the favorable judgment of others. "This glory they most ardently loved (*ardentissime dilexerunt*). For its sake they chose to live and for its sake they did not hesitate to die. They suppressed all other desires (*cupiditates*) in their boundless desire (*cupiditas*) for this one thing" (*Civ. Dei.* 5.12). Suppress does not quite do justice to the passage; the word used, *premo*, carries the meaning here of shaping through pressure, not the suppression of desire but its organization by way of a stronger desire. What moves this desire, what directs it, arises precisely out of our social nature: the love of praise (*amore laudis/ laudis aviditas*) (*Civ. Dei.* 5.13; 5.12) and fear of shame (*inglorius*) (*Civ. Dei.* 5.12). One wants to be seen and talked about.

Praise was directed toward two actions: liberty (*libertas*) and dominion (*imperium*). "In short, since they held it shameful for their native land to be in servitude, and glorious for it to rule and command, their first passion to which they devoted all their energy was to maintain their independence; the second was to win dominion" (*Civ. Dei.* 5.12). The passion for *libertas* operated first within the community, born of their experience of kingship (*Civ Dei.* 5.12). Pointing to Rome's peculiar historical trajectory (an important issue since political forms are not abstractions, but grow out of particular contexts), he notes that the "royal state was regarded not as a mark of a proper ruler, nor that of a benevolent adviser, but rather as the arrogance of a tyrant" (*Civ. Dei.* 5.12). It was in that time, in the years following the expulsion of the Tarquins, when the memory of kingship was still fresh, that Rome "performed so many marvellous deeds, which were no doubt praiseworthy and glorious as men judge things" (*Civ. Dei.* 5.12).

---

[39] Von Heyking argues incorrectly that Augustine exposes the corruption of early Rome that Sallust "masked" (2001, 42). It is hard to mask what one states explicitly, as does Sallust (see Chapt. 3). And the claim understates a deeper level of compatibility in their understanding of the organization of community life. On Sallust and Augustine, see Harding 2008, 61–63.

But how men judge things sets in motion a dynamic in which no end is ever complete. One judges by way of one's temporally constituted senses, which measure the fulfillment of love quantitatively: by the amount of the desired object that is acquired. In the case of glory, which one measures by the "marvellous deeds" that are seen and admired (*Civ. Dei.* 5.12), liberty by itself is not enough to sate the passion for glory; the measure of marvellous (*mirandus*) deeds is still grander once beheld by more people. So Rome coupled the love of liberty with a thirst for dominion (*dominatio*), a love of reigning and commanding and subjugating (*regnandi atque imperandi et subjugandi*) extolled by Virgil, as Augustine notes (*Civ. Dei.* 5.12). Even then, though, conquest was justified in the name of liberty. Rome grew in size, driven by the necessity of defending life and liberty (*Civ. Dei.* 3.10).

The organization of desire requires not only direction – what is the object of love – but also a path – the means by which it is pursued or how is it practiced. As Augustine notes, "The hero and the coward alike desire" honor, glory, and power, "but the former, that is, the hero, climbs by the honest path" (*Civ. Dei.* 5.12). The other "'pushes ahead by treachery and deceit,' wishing to appear good though he is not" (*Civ. Dei.* 5.19, citing Sallust). Augustine follows Sallust in identifying the role of fear – in this case, the fear of approbation – in channeling the pursuit of glory by the former path rather than the latter. But Augustine supplements Sallust's discussion (though in a very Roman way) by connecting fear to love: One fears losing what one loves. Fear focuses one's efforts, reminding one of what matters, which for the Romans was glory associated with liberty.

We might recall, for example, Livy's account of the Romans huddled on the Capitol as they watched their city destroyed, suddenly reminded of, and made resolute in defense of, the liberty they had squandered. For Augustine, the experience of the Tarquins and the fear of their return lead the patricians to act "with justice and moderation" toward the plebs (*Civ. Dei.* 5.12; 3.17). But once the memory of tyranny recedes and the threat finally ends with the war with Etruria, "the patricians treated the plebeians as if they were slaves, scourged them tyrannically, drove them from their land and exercised power alone, excluding all others. The one class was bent on being masters, the other refused to be slaves" (*Civ. Dei.* 5.12; also 2.18; 3.16), giving rise to discord that ended only from "fear of a treacherous peace, as long as Carthage remained standing" (*Civ. Dei.* 2.18). "For then once more they felt the pressure of a good terror; a new and greater anxiety restrained their restless spirits from those disturbances and recalled them to domestic harmony" (*Civ. Dei.* 5.12; also 3.17). With the defeat of Carthage and the "lust for power" no longer "repressed by fear" (*Civ. Dei.* 1.31), *concordia* gives way to civil strife and then bloody proscriptions. One can hear the Sallustian lament in Augustine's words: "What a sea of Roman blood the social wars, the servile wars, the civil wars poured out! How great the area of Italy that they devastated and made desolate!" (*Civ. Dei.* 3.23; also 3.28; also said of the Gracchan period: 3.24). As glory becomes more fraudulently sought, Caesar being Augustine's example, the controlling effect of praise and blame are weakened, undermining the relationship between merit and public judgment: Praise could be purchased through bribes and inflated by the hypocrite and bad deeds could be disguised through deceit (*Civ. Dei.* 5.12). Unrestrained by glory and liberty forgotten, love expresses itself as passion for domination (*libido dominandi*) in which men, "worn out and tired," become subjected to "the yoke of slavery" (*Civ. Dei.* 1.30; also 2.22; 3.21). Rome begins to use "the words glory and victory" to "veil the truth" that they are ruled by the "lust for mastery" (*Civ. Dei.* 3.14).

The difference between *libertas* and *dominatio* is a difference in the power attributed to the will. *Libertas*, which Augustine (consistent with an entire Roman tradition) associates with sovereignty, exists in the consent of mind to move itself to action or restrain from action (*De trin.* 12.12.17). Political liberty, thus, derives from a similar sovereignty, the ability to will and act together. There are limits built into this notion of liberty: A free community must have obedience to the laws of one's own making, for example, or, for the Stoics, a recognition of what the will cannot will. The problem arises when the mind "wills to enjoy its own power" (*De lib. arb.* 3.25.76.262), when it loves its own power (*De trin.* 12.9.14; 12.11.16). Rome's decline arises from the association of liberty with the absence of any "nuisance or impediment" to one's will (*Civ. Dei.* 2.20). Augustine's discussion of Rome, thus, reveals the communal implications of the soul's belief in its own power.

Libertas (and *felicitas*) find expression no longer in a community united by a common affection (ultimately in our love, as an act of will, of obeying the *lex aeterna*, the eternal law), but in lust that "dominates" the mind (*De lib. arb.* 1.11.22.77). Augustine's discussion of lust trades largely on the language of dominion: *subdo*, *dominator*, and *servilis* (*Civ. Dei.* 2.20; 4.3).

> [The] reign of desires savagely tyrannizes and batters a person's whole life and mind with storms raging in all directions. On this side fear, on that desire; on this side anxiety, on that spurious enjoyment; on this side torment over the loss of something loved, on that ardor to acquire something not possessed; on this side sorrows for an injury received, on that the burning to redress it. Whichever way one turns, greed can pinch, extravagance squander, ambition enslave, pride puff up, envy twist, laziness overcome, stubbornness provoke, submissiveness oppress – these and countless others throng the realm of lust, having the run of it (*De lib. arb.* 1.11.22.78).

The object of love – one's own will rather than Rome's liberty – has consequences for the organization of community life. Wealth is used "to make weaker men" into subjects, the rich misusing the poor "to minister to their pride," leaders desiring that their subjects be "abject," and provinces made subservient and servile (*Civ. Dei.* 2.20). What the people imagine as liberty, as Augustine riffs at one point, is "an abundant supply of public prostitutes," lavish houses and banquets, indecent theaters, bloody games, and "unclean spirits" (*Civ. Dei.* 2.20, 29).

It is more than Rome becoming decadent, the ending point of most scholarly discussions of Augustine's critique. It is that license is used to bind people to the state, to create *ordo* by organizing desire, justified under the guise of religion (*Civ. Dei.* 4.32). Most telling are the Roman spectacle entertainments, the games that originated in celebration of the various gods (2.27; 6.7).[40] These spectacles become the primary form of

---

[40] Scholarship differs as to whether Augustine's critique of Roman religion arises from a failure to recognize the importance of civic religion for political society (Voegelin 1952, 87) or that his criticisms were actually based on "outdated" concerns that would not fundamentally disrupt Roman civic order (Fortin 1996, 2: 94–97), or both (von

public education: "the mingled obscenities and atrocities, the disgraceful crimes, real or imaginary, of the gods, have been publicly and openly advertised," presented "for all to see, put forward as models to be imitated" (*Civ. Dei.* 2.26; 6.7). The lessons are reinforced through the "applause of a great multitude," drowning out the barely audible words of decency that are spoken by a few (*Civ. Dei.* 2.26). In fact, Roman conquest simply becomes a version of the gladiatorial games, writ large. "Or does it make a difference," Augustine writes, "that there was no arena, though battlefields much wider than an arena were filled with the corpses, not of two gladiators, but of multitudes belonging to two peoples, and that those contests were not bounded by an amphitheatre but by the whole world, and that it was an impious spectacle upon which those then alive gazed – as will their descendants so long as the report of it is handed down" (*Civ. Dei.* 3.14). Like the training of *virtus*, so these spectacles train one to take pleasure in suffering (*Civ. Dei.* 2.27) and to imitate these deeds (*Civ. Dei.* 2.27), drowning out any natural feeling (*sensus*) for decency (*Civ. Dei.* 2.26) and overrunning "the manly practices of the fatherland" (*Civ. Dei.* 1.31; also 2.9; 6.7; Chapt. 6, 296–301).

THE HUMAN CONDITION

Augustine's analysis of Rome's fall points to the intractable dilemmas of our social and political existence. In his conception of politics Augustine is more Sallust and Cicero than he is either Plato or Stoic. Politics neither mirrors an *eidos* nor aims toward a divine law.[41] It is not "natural" in the sense of conforming to a cosmic order but, according to Augustine's notion of "dual providence," is an aspect of providence as the result of

---

Heyking 2001, 44). Augustine hardly minced words in his critique of the religious foundations of Roman society and, as Rome is collapsing, is hardly concerned with undermining the Roman civic order (von Heyking 2001, 44). Religion plays a role in organizing desire. The measure of success is how well it attains the end of peace. There will always be a tension between religion and politics since, for Augustine, politics invariably involves one in decisions that do not necessarily have a spiritual foundation or justification.

[41] See Markus 1988, 88–89 on Augustine's changing position.

human wills operating freely.[42] Nor though, and this will be discussed later, is politics merely a coercive mechanism for controlling sin. Rather, humans, like all beings, are endowed with what Augustine describes as "certain good things that befit this life," namely, temporal peace (*pax temporalis*) (*Civ. Dei.* 19.13), which consists of "personal health and preservation and fellowship (*societas*) with one's kind" (*Civ. Dei.* 19.13). The desire for peace underlies all forms of association, from the household to the city to a cadre of thieves to even oneself (as maintaining the order of one's body) (*Civ. Dei.* 19.12).[43] As Augustine notes, things "could not exist if there were not some sort of peace to hold them together" (*Civ. Dei.* 19.13; also *De lib. arb.* 1.15.32.108).

This natural peace is not simply coercive but takes on the Roman language of agreement (*consensio*), concord (*concordia*), and rule (*imperium*).[44] The peace of the irrational soul is "an ordered repose of the appetites" (*Civ. Dei.* 19.13). The peace of the rational soul is the "ordered agreement (*consensio*) of knowledge and action" (*Civ. Dei.* 19.13). Peace in the household is an ordered agreement "concerning command and obedience" (*Civ. Dei.* 19.13). "Earthly peace" is "an ordered agreement of mind" (*Civ. Dei.* 19.13) or a "merging of human wills in regard to the things that are useful for this mortal life" (*Civ. Dei.* 19.17). We organize, make temporal laws (*De lib. arb.* 1.6.14–48; 1.15.32.108), even fight wars with the goal of peace.

A social life is a necessary part of human life that requires temporal laws that prescribe "the right by which peace and human intercourse are preserved" (*De lib. arb.* 1.15.32.108). These goods include the body (with goods valued differently for different skills), *libertas*, close

---

[42] Markus 1988, 91–93.

[43] See Deane 1963, 235: peace is the highest end of the state; also Rist 1994, 212–13.

[44] Cary contends that Augustine does not include "peace of the earthly city" on the list, suggesting that the exclusion is because the "members of the earthly city belong to the category of 'the unhappy,' who are in a state of perturbation rather than tranquility" (2005, 21). It is certainly the case that the wretched (*miseri*) are not in a state of peace. Augustine is talking, though, about how all things desire peace. Included in this list are agreements among men, the basis of political relationships. *Consensio* is used by Cicero to refer to general agreement (*Tusc.* 1.13.30) and friendship (*De amic.* 6.20: *caritate consensio*).

relationships, the state, honor and praise, and property (things we control by right) (*De lib. arb.* 1.15.32.109–110). But social life is an unstable good precisely because we are separated by the experience of our own senses (*De lib. arb.* 2.7.15.59): "we sense our own senses themselves individually, so that I do not sense your sense nor you mine" (*De lib. arb.* 2.7.19.72). Nor can we know "the hearts of those with whom we choose to be at peace, and even if we could know them today, in any case we know not what they may be like tomorrow" (*Civ. Dei.* 19.5; 15.7; *Conf.* 10.21).[45]

Augustine knew all too well from his rhetorical training the impossibility of the hearer being able to know whether the words are true or whether the speaker knows or believes what he is saying. That is, we cannot know the mind of the speaker from the words spoken (*De mag.* 13.42; *Conf.* 11.2: "chair of lying"; 10.3). Augustine, quoting Cicero, identifies the precarious state of human affairs shrouded in deceit: "'No ambushed foes are harder to detect than those who mask their aim with a counterfeit loyalty or under the guise of some close tie" (*Civ. Dei.* 19.5; citing Cic. *Ver.* 2.1.13). The larger the community, the more people included, "the more does its forum teem with lawsuits both civil and criminal, even though its calm be not disturbed by the turbulence, or more often the bloodshed, of sedition and civil wars. Cities are indeed free at times from such events, but never from the threat of them" (*Civ. Dei.* 19.5; also 15.4: "divided against itself"). Even legal judgments are fraught with error since one "cannot look into the consciences of those whom they judge" (*Civ. Dei.* 19.6), leading to the paradoxical situation of torturing the innocent to protect them from being judged guilty. The human condition is precarious, not because we are constantly seeking to dominate the other, but because the "dark places" of the heart make it impossible for us to read or know the other person. As Augustine writes, so the judge "has both tortured an innocent man in order to learn the truth and put him to death without learning it" (*Civ. Dei.* 19.6).

Augustine is making a larger argument about the nature of language that goes beyond simply saying it can be used deceptively. For

---

[45] See also Arendt 1958, 244.

Augustine, words by themselves are only letters and sounds that comprise signs that signify things. Between the word (*verba*) and the actual thing (*res ipsa*) being signified is the *dicibile*: what is understood in a word and held in the mind (*De doc. Chr.* 2.1.1; 4.5.7). We learn words through a complex interplay between the individual, other individuals, and the world in which we absorb by seeing and doing and hearing how to identify and communicate about the world and ourselves (e.g., *De mag.* 10.33; *De doc. Chr.* 2.2.3). When we learn and use words, we become implicated in a web of significations in which words are merely signs that can be explained only by way of other signs, not only opening a gap between names and what they signify but also between our knowledge of the words and our knowledge of the speaker (*De mag.* 3.6; 4.8; 4.9; 8.23; *Conf.* 1.8).[46] We might be able to show something without words – building a table, for example – but cannot impart understanding of why or for what purpose we are doing it, or even what is being signified and how it is related (through signs) to other activities. As Augustine writes, "To use words to treat of words is as complicated as to rub fingers together and expect someone else to distinguish which fingers tingle with warmth and which help others to tingle" (*De mag.* 5.14). To simply see or be told something is not sufficient to understand the experience. Augustine is suggesting that to understand something requires the experience of it, either through sense-perception or through the mind, an experience that can never be adequately communicated to or understood by another. (*De mag.* 11.37; 12.39–40). As Burnyeat notes, Augustine "has no argument for the thesis that knowledge requires firsthand learning." Rather, he is identifying the "great gap between the epistemic position of an eyewitness who watches an event with his own eyes and that of the jury later."[47]

Augustine takes the argument still further: No one can teach another knowledge (*scientia*), which Burnyeat glosses to mean understanding

---

[46] Bearsley 1983; Burnyeat 1987, 3; contrary to Wittgenstein 1958, 77 that words correspond to things for Augustine. On signs, see Jackson 1969. On the Stoic and Epicurean influences on Augustine's notion of language as well as his departure from them, see Rist 1994, 25–30.

[47] Burnyeat 1987, 20; also Rist 1994, 30, 33–34.

(*intellegere*). One can communicate information, but one cannot make someone understand.[48] By that he means that lacking some understanding already (including understanding of the words), we listen or speak in vain (*De mag.* 13.41). Words cannot communicate the invisible, either what resides in another or in oneself.

Augustine sounds a note reminiscent of Seneca. One is not just caught in moments of frenzy; one exists in a state of insanity (*dementia*) precisely because there are no reliable markers by which one can navigate one's social life. So one may feel obligated by duty (*officium*) to serve in political life, yet, like the judge who is required by law to torture an innocent man without learning the truth, one is compelled by imperfect law to make judgments that harm others not from evil intent but from ignorance (*Civ. Dei.* 19.6). One might celebrate the "bond of peace" imposed by the Roman empire that gave commonality to isolated communities by providing a universal language, yet it is a commonality achieved at the cost of "human slaughter and bloodshed" (*Civ. Dei.* 19.7). One might strive for peace, yet be drawn into social and civil wars, either to try to achieve calm or out of fear (*Civ. Dei.* 3.10: "just wars"; *Civ. Dei.* 5.15: Roman expansion). One can seek refuge in friendship from the distresses of human society, striving after "a spiritual embrace in the way of faith" (*De trin.* 9.6.11). Yet, one can easily mistake "a foe for a friend or a friend for a foe" (*Civ. Dei.* 19.8). Still more terrifying is that friendship itself may be changed "into perfidy, malice and villainy" (*Civ. Dei.* 19.8). And the more friends one has and the more scattered they are the more one fears some evil will befall them: "hunger, warfare, disease, captivity, and the unimaginable sufferings of slavery" (*Civ. Dei.* 19.8). It is precisely the comfort of such friendships that "consumes our hearts" when we imagine their suffering (*Civ. Dei.* 19.8). Ultimately, any peace we know on earth is incomplete and imperfect: It provides "solace of our wretchedness" rather than "positive enjoyment of blessedness" and "remission of sins" rather than "perfection of virtues" (*Civ. Dei.* 19.27). What this means politically, as we will see in the final section, takes on considerably more nuance than is often admitted into his thought.

---

[48] See Burnyeat 1987, 7–8; Rist 1994, 42, 46.

WISDOM AND *CARITAS*

We are moved by love, yet our love of earthly things, our attachments to a temporal order, can never bring us the tranquility we desire. Driven by our own sense of incompleteness, the answer to this longing is not the subordination of desire, but its orientation to *caritas*, a love of the eternal. Augustine draws from Plato (by way of the Stoicized Platonism of Cicero and the neo-Platonism of Plotinus) the notion of wisdom as knowledge of the eternal structures of the universe that give form to the world (e.g., wisdom: *De lib. arb.* 2.9.27.104–108; 2.10.29.119; 2.13.36.141–142; gives form: *De lib. arb.* 2.16.44.171; 2.17.45.174; *Contra acad.* 3.18.41).[49] There is no doubt about the hierarchy: We are to direct our image of these higher impressions (*De lib. arb.* 3.25.74.256; *De beata vita* 4.33) to "a better and truer life" by which we can judge temporal things (*De trin.* 11.5.8; also 12.2.2). Given our embodied nature, though, in which our will is inextricably tied to both the temporal and eternal, Augustine is considerably less sanguine than Plato about the attainment of that wisdom.[50]

In *On the trinity*, composed between 413 and 416 CE,[51] Augustine engages in his fullest and most sophisticated treatment of the nature of wisdom. The central question motivating the work arises from Augustine's epistemology and psychology that share with Roman political thought an emphasis on vision as the most important way in which one understands and orients oneself. For Augustine, we cannot love what we cannot know and we cannot know what we cannot see. "When we believe in any corporeal things, of which we have heard or read but have not seen, our mind must represent them to itself as something with bodily features and forms, just as it occurs to our thoughts; now this image is either false or true" (*De trin.* 8.4.7; *De ut. cred.* 13.28).

Yet, the eternal structure and truth of things, of which we are commanded to believe (*De trin.* 13.1.3) and for which we yearn, are

---

[49] Plotinus: Kolbet 2010, 80–85.
[50] See also Conybeare 2006, 156–62, who shows Augustine's reluctance to "relinquish his situation in the body" in even such writings, such as *Soliloquia*, that are heavily influenced by Plato.
[51] Or 399 to 419 CE for Stead 1994, 221.

"far removed from the body" and from speech (*De lib. arb.* 2.11.30.122). There are not forms by which we make sense of things. God, Augustine writes, "is not a body to be sought for with bodily eyes" (*De trin.* 8.4.6). Nor is there language by which we make things sensible. We cannot articulate the experience of the eternal with language "though which men's thoughts are mutually made known" (*De trin.* 10.1.2).

The contrast with Plato is dramatic. Plato's ascent to the realm of eternal Forms, while arduous, is a relief. In fact, the philosopher must be forced to return to the temporal order. For Augustine, though God is the source of true happiness (*beatitudo*), in our ascent "eventually," he writes, "I return in exhaustion to familiar things, so that I am able to say something or other" (*De lib. arb.* 2.11.30.122; also *De trin.* 15.27.50). For Plato, the relation to memory is one of recollection of the eternal Forms that one had encountered in the afterlife. For Augustine, to the extent that there is any such memory, it is of principles (*rationes*) or impressed ideas (*impressae notiones*), such as happiness and truth, that allow us to make judgments and form concepts.[52] For Plato, perfection is reached once we are free from our bodies. For Augustine, following the depiction by Virgil of souls longing to return to their bodies, our souls yearn for our bodies and are made whole again in Heaven (*Civ. Dei.* 20.9, 15; 22.21, 26, 27, 28). Furthermore, if for Plato we are moved by wonder, for Augustine, we are moved more by misery, a sense of our own incompleteness (*Conf.* 10.28). It is a "pragmatic attitude" toward philosophy, characteristic of the Romans: a desire to be released from our pain (*dolor*) and labor (*labor*) (*Conf.* 10.28), have our emptiness filled (*Conf.* 10.31), and be happy.[53]

We are impelled by the desire for God, which means (since we only desire what we know) that we must somehow know Him. What Augustine does is attempt to demonstrate how our knowledge of God is in fact infused in our knowledge of the world (and in our memory: *Conf.* 10.24–27). He does this by way of a distinctive notion of the Trinity, not as different and hierarchically arranged substances (which had driven the debate in the previous centuries) but as a triadic relationship

---

[52] Rist 1994, 31, 76–77.   [53] Arendt 1978, 2.85.

of unity and equality among the parts (see *De doc. Chr.* 1.5.5). Because we are created in the image of God, this triadic relationship is duplicated in our understanding of the world and ourselves, giving us glimpses, however faintly, of the divine Trinity.

The desire for the corporeal: the trinity of sensation, perception, and attention

So Augustine begins his own ascent, reasoning from the sensible to the insensible, asking "by what likeness or comparison with known things can we believe?" (*De trin.* 8.5.8).[54] We love justness (*De trin.* 8.6.9), for example, or a friend (*De trin.* 8.8.12), or beauty, or are "enkindled with love" for the Apostle Paul because of the life he lived (*De trin.* 8.9.13). We love these things, "not because we hear it from some others, but because we see it within ourselves" (*De trin.* 8.9.13), as "memorials" to be contemplated (*De mag.* 12.39). These external forms serve as *exempla* that by themselves cannot teach but excite something within us. Sounding thoroughly Roman, Augustine writes, "Thus the love for this form, according to which they are believed to have lived, causes us to love the life of these men; and their life thus believed arouses a more fervent love for this same love" (*De trin.* 8.9.13). This love is "a kind of life which binds or seeks to bind some two together, namely, the lover and the beloved" (*De trin.* 8.10.14). It is in the recognition of things we know – the love of a friend or the life of an Apostle – that we can begin to "ascend even from here and to seek for those higher things, insofar as it is granted to man" (*De trin.* 8.10.14). In that ascent we continue to be moved by the "hope of acquiring" that which we desire (*De trin.* 10.1.2), an act of making something our own through understanding.

Our knowledge of the world, as we have seen, occurs through the triadic relationship of sensation, perception, and attention, a relationship of equality and unity in which the external world is made a part of us through our attention. Even in the case of the Apostle Paul, for example, one is excited by an image, wanting to bind oneself to it. Augustine

---

[54] Also *De ord.* 1.8.23: you feel, you believe, you understand.

extends this inquiry to knowledge of intangible things, asking what it means for the mind (*mens*) to know and love itself. The question belies a Stoic assumption that we are born with self-awareness and self-love, a notion of *oikeiōsis* that underlies the development of the individual (for example, *De trin.* 9.4.7). What it means to love oneself is for Augustine "to desire to help oneself to enjoy oneself" (*De trin.* 9.2.2).

The desire for the incorporeal: the trinity of intellect, memory, and will

Given the perplexity of the mind seeking "passionately" to know itself when it does not yet know itself (*De trin.* 10.3.5), Augustine raises a series of interpretive possibilities about the status of that knowledge. What keeps the mind from desiring a false representation of itself? Or does it see "in the reason of the eternal truth" how beautiful it would be to know oneself, and thus seek that happiness (*De trin.* 10.3.5)? Or does it possess some remembrance of its blessedness that directs it to continue the path to truth?

What the mind knows (that moves it to seek to know itself) is several things: The mind knows that it is seeking itself (*De trin.* 10.3.5); it knows that it lives (*De trin.* 10.4.6); and it knows that it is a mind (otherwise it would not know to seek itself) (*De trin.* 10.4.6). Just as the mind "gathers the knowledge of corporeal things through the bodily senses, so it gains the knowledge of incorporeal things through itself, since it is incorporeal" (*De trin.* 9.3.3). But there is a difference. The mind does not know itself by seeing many minds (as one might know a tree), since it cannot see those minds. Nor can the mind see itself. "For not as the eye of the body sees other eyes and does not see itself, so does the mind know other minds and does not know itself" (*De trin.* 9.3.3). That is, we do not see the power by which we know; we know a mind from itself and attribute that mindedness to others (*De trin.* 9.6.9).

Unlike a body, in which "the part is less than the whole in the extension of place" (*De trin.* 10.7.9), the mind is always whole, always present, and knows itself through itself. The mind should not seek itself as though it were absent (like one might seek to discover a new land or know a word); rather, it should withdraw itself from those sensible things that it added to itself and discern itself as always present (*De trin.* 10.8.11; 10.9.12). The injunction to "know thyself" is not to acquire or to uncover; it is to be present to oneself (*De trin.* 10.9.12). It is to know oneself as one who lives, remembers, understands, wills, thinks, knows, and judges (*De trin.* 10.10.14; also *Conf.* 10.6).

It is in this exploration of the soul (*animus*) that Augustine finds the closest analog to the operation of the Trinity. Of this list of things of which the mind is certain, Augustine focuses on the activity of *cogitatio* – the trinity of intellect (*mens*), memory (*memoria*), and will (*voluntas*) – in which the will combines and directs the memory about what to retain and forget and directs the intellect about what to choose for understanding. "When the mind, therefore, sees itself through thought, it understands itself and recognizes itself; consequently, it begets this, its own understanding and its own knowledge" (*De trin.* 14.6.8). Knowing, remembering, and willing are distinct but "mutually referred to each other" in a relationship of equality: "not only is each one comprehended by each one, but all are also comprehended by each one" (*De trin.* 10.11.18). I remember that I have memory, understanding, and will; I understand that I have understanding, will, and memory; and I will that I will, remember, and understand. Our relation to ourselves, our desire to know ourselves, is an act of love (as a binding act of the will). "Behold! the mind, therefore, remembers itself, understands itself, and loves itself; if we perceive this, we perceive a trinity, not yet God indeed, but now finally an image of God" (*De trin.* 14.8.11).

The desire for God: The trinity of wisdom, eternity, and happiness

We begin to grasp the truth of God as "a word" (*verba*) within ourselves, one that we try to express (however incompletely) through our voice and bodily movements to convey that truth to the listener (*De trin.* 9.7.12; *De doc. Chr.* 1.13.13). Augustine's reference to a word is striking, positioning him between his nuanced understanding of the cultural context of words as signs, as we have seen, and a theological tradition of the word as *Logos*. Words cannot communicate the invisible. Nor can they make one understand. Yet, Augustine is using words, and he learns from (and continually invokes) the words of Christ, St. Matthew, and St. Paul. The words that Augustine is describing do not fill "a determined space of time with their syllables" (*De trin.* 9.10.15). They are not words that correspond to a thing that can be seen. Rather, they are words that "bid us look for things" (*De mag.* 11.36). They are words that lead us to explore, to examine, to inquire into things that are not immediately visible, to understand how words bring to mind God's providential design (see *De mag.* 1.2).[55] "We listen to Truth which presides over our minds within us, though of course we may be bidden to listen by someone using words," namely Christ as the true teacher (*De mag.* 11.38; *Conf.* 11.6). It is not words, though, that teach; it is "the things themselves which inwardly God has made manifest to him," which we see through our own inward eye (*De mag.* 12.40). We cannot know everything at once; rather, "when he is questioned about the parts which compose the whole, he is induced to bring them one by one into the light" (*De mag.* 12.40). We encounter the universe as corporeal beings but are able to ask questions to inquire, to judge, and to begin to grasp the invisible that made the visible (*Conf.* 10.6).

We do not and cannot see God; we see Him as in a mirror, as an image that appears in us (or "we see through a glass darkly": *Conf.* 10.5). In attempting to understand how we can comprehend the incomprehensible, Augustine returns to how a word is transformed from a sound into an image so that we can see it even when the word is unspoken. "For the sight of thought is very similar to the sight of knowledge" (*De trin.* 15.11.20).[56] Speaking within a cultural tradition that privileged vision, Augustine proceeds by analogy: "For just as our word in some way becomes a bodily sound by assuming that in which it may be

---

[55] Also Kolbet 2010, 148.
[56] For criticisms of this transference of empirical vision into thought, see Markus 1964, 87. Stead expresses some dismay (from the perspective of a philosopher) that Augustine not only focuses on vision, but "brings together accounts of ordinary bodily sight, and other operations which at least involve visual imagery, with remarks about the mind which is said to 'see' in a purely metaphorical sense" (Stead 1994, 226). I follow Burnyeat: "Both philosophers are in fact saying the very opposite, that knowledge or understanding is of the connections between things, of things only as parts of a whole interrelated system; that is why, like empirical vision, it involves seeing things for oneself" (Burnyeat 1987, 22).

manifested to the senses of men, so the Word of God was made flesh by assuming that in which He might also be manifested to the senses of men" (*De trin.* 15.11.20). The true word, Augustine writes, is the word "that belongs to no language" but comes only from the knowledge "from which it is born" (*De trin.* 15.12.22; also 15.15.24; also *Conf.* 10.6). The Word of God is born from a different kind of knowledge than the words we use; it is not formed from experience but known before anything was created (*De trin.* 15.13.22). This turning of our love toward God, thus, is a form of recollection, a turning of the mind to its origins. The Word is Christ, born from God. And as it is born from God, it cannot be mistaken and cannot lie (*De trin.* 15.15.22).

We begin to comprehend the divine Trinity through its correspondence with other trinities that Augustine identifies, but with some differences. God exists as a trinity of eternity (*aeternitas*), wisdom (*sapientia*), and happiness (*beatitudo*) that is divinely established in the mind and can be recalled by the roughly corresponding trinity of the memory of an inner word that we have never thought before, beheld by understanding latent in memory, and embraced by love directed toward understanding (*De trin.* 15.21.40). It is not that one sees the image of God, as one might see the image of a tree; it is that individuals "look upon their mind as an image" and "refer what they see to Him, whose image it is, and also to see by conjecturing that which they now see through the image by beholding, since they cannot yet see face to face" (*De trin.* 15.23.44). In directing our vision inward, we are to behold as if in a mirror, not occupying a commanding presence outside us (like viewing from a watchtower), but are to see Him as we are ourselves transformed, "changed from one form into another," passing from "an obscure form to a bright form" (*De trin.* 15.8.14).

Without trying to resolve the theological difficulties of the Holy Trinity, one can hear the Roman resonance in the Holy Trinity of the Father, the Son, and the Holy Spirit as a unity of the father (a Roman association of fathers with memory), the son (begotten as the redeeming Word who submits himself completely to the father), and love (a gift that binds each to the other) (e.g., *De trin.* 15.23.43). The Holy Spirit is not something separate from the Father and Son but is the love that binds

Father to Son, that gives unity to difference, and is the gift of love that comes to us from the Father and Son, as well.[57]

The transformation of desire: grace and *caritas*

In a complete reversal of Stoicism, Augustine argues that one must believe before one can know and that knowledge of the Word can only come by way of grace (see *De ut. cred.* 9.21–22). Only God can prepare the will by directing our attention to what we are supposed to see and hear, to prepare our will so that it can be bound to God. "True knowledge" resides in us "as a word" conceived "in love" (*De trin.* 9.7.12; 9.8.13). Thus, one must live by faith (*fides*) in the unseen since we cannot "see as yet our good" (*Civ. Dei.* 19.4). The foundation of faith and of knowledge is not human reasoning but divine authority (*De trin.* 13.9.12; *De ut. cred.* 8.20; 9.21; .16.34). Faith, thus, as Wetzel states, is "consent to the knowledge that love of God brings."[58]

Augustine's language of transformation follows his psychology: When we love something our happiness comes from making it a part of us. We are transformed by the objects we desire, whether from the nutrition we receive from food, the words we learn to describe the world, or the memories that orient our will. We do not replace desire but form it as *caritas*. *Caritas* "joins our word with the mind from which it is born," binding itself with them "in an incorporeal embrace" (*De trin.* 9.8.13). Stated slightly differently, love ultimately unifies the will.

The transformative love associated with God fundamentally reorients the nature of our craving. For corporeal things, "what is conceived by desiring is born by attaining" (*De trin.* 9.9.14); for incorporeal things, to love is to attain (*De trin.* 9.9.14). When we crave a body, we crave a part, a body among other bodies, that is less than the whole in the extension of place (*De trin.* 10.7.9). But *caritas* does not extend in space; it is "the undifferentiated love of fellow-members" that derives from God and is extended as one has loving partners (*Civ. Dei.* 15.5). Through *latreia*, which Augustine translates as *servitus* or *cultus Dei*, we worship that

---

[57] See Peters 1993, 66–67. [58] Wetzel 1992, 203.

which dwells "in the united heart of all and in each one separately" (*Civ. Dei.* 10.3). The love of God is the love of the other that one sees in oneself, "the same love by which it loves itself" (*De trin.* 9.4.5). This is not simply the sort of abstract love characteristic of Stoicism, but a recognition of another as "participating in the luminous beauty of God."[59] The love of the other is strikingly conversational: If I see someone who has suffered in defense of faith, "I approach him, address him, engage him in conversation, express my affection for him in whatever words I can; and in turn I wish that the same affection should be brought about in him and expressed towards me; and since I cannot discern so quickly and investigate his innermost heart thoroughly, I strive after a spiritual embrace in the way of faith" (*De trin.* 9.6.11). I may find out through conversation that I had misjudged the man, to which my love changes from the purpose of finding pleasure to "the purpose of providing help" in changing that man into one who is just (*De trin.* 9.6.11).

This love is also generative: "Let him love his brother and he will love the same love" (*De trin.* 8.8.12). Those who refuse "to share this possession with another will not have it at all" (*Civ. Dei.* 15.5). Thus, love is transformed from that which is finite, depleting, and exclusive to that which is infinite, generative, and inclusive. In one, in loving we want what others have; in the other, in loving we gain what others are. In one, the satisfaction of love is to possess it; in the other it is to share it (a relationship). And in one, we love what is less than us; in the other our love is tied to something greater than us.[60]

ROMAN RESONANCES IN AUGUSTINE'S POLITICAL THOUGHT

Given our discussion so far it is not surprising that attempts to tease out an Augustinian politics have yielded an array of contradictory interpretations. His argument is seen as everything from a realist assessment of

---

[59] Gregory 2008, 44.
[60] There is a large literature on *caritas* (= *agape*) as a social ethic. Important for my thinking are Outka 1972; Elshtain 1981; Gregory 2008.

politics as unrelated to virtue to a political Augustinism in which politics is connected to salvation, from a liberal pluralism and skepticism to an anti-liberal authoritarianism, from a feminist ethic to patriarchal domination, from an anti-political dimension in its indifference to current political structures to a Christian-infused ethic that saves (or even replaces) politics, and from classical to medieval to even modern in its orientation.[61] Augustine's brilliance is evidenced in attempts to re-occupy his thought, in Connolly's words, drawing out its implications for our own thinking about democracy.[62] My interest here is less to show how Augustine can occupy our home than to help him occupy his own by drawing out the Roman influence on his thought, helping us clarify in the process some of the distinctive aspects of Roman thought.

Perhaps the most influential reading of Augustine's politics is a realist interpretation. Realism generally, and I will distinguish where I differ from this approach, operates from two premises. First, in our disobedience to a moral order, our nature is expressed as a lust for mastery and domination, an *animus dominandi*.[63] Second, in the irrecoverableness of that moral order politics is sovereign. By that, the realists mean that politics is not modeled after, subordinate to, or an embodiment of, an ideal. Rather, earthly politics is organized by its own ends. The "purpose of the state and of its coercive machinery was to deal with the disorganisation and conflict resulting from the Fall."[64] At its best politics is remedial, not as a realm of human realization (as it is in the classical

---

[61] Realism: Niebuhr 1953, 145–46; Deane 1963, 66; Figgis 1963; political Augustinism: see survey in de Lubac 1989; Sabine 1937, 192; liberal pluralism: Markus 1988, 166–78; Weithman 1991; Gregory 2008; scepticism: Oakeshott 1975, 84; anti-liberal: Cochrane 1940, 249; Schall 1984, 47–51; White 1994; religious coercion: Figgis 1963, 78; Brown 1964; Rist 1994, 239–45; von Heyking 2001, 240–53 (authoritarianism from Roman law); anti-political: Barr 1962; R. Williams 1987; TeSelle 1988, 92–93; Rist 1994, 254 (community of households as ideal); feminist ethic: Børresen 1990; Conybeare 2006, 195–202; Elshtain 1981, 73; Rist 1994, 112–31; patriarchal: Pagels 1989; Christian-infused ethic: Schlabach 1994 (302: "nonviolence toward the truth"); Milbank 1990; White 1994; von Heyking 2001; Elshtain 1995; T. Smith 2005; classical/ medieval: Breyfogle 2005, 217–18.

[62] W. Connolly 2004, 510.

[63] *animus dominandi*: Morgenthau 1946, 192–96; Markus 1988, 93–94.

[64] Markus 1988, 84.

ideal) but as a way of restraining human sin and "minimis[ing] disorder."[65] Augustine's vision, Markus writes, "springs from a sense of conflicting purposes, of uncertainties of direction and of tensions unresolvable in society."[66] For Deane, "Politics is a realm in which fallible, sinful men work out imperfect, precarious solutions to recurring difficulties and tensions."[67] It is a deeply tragic conception of existence in which no resolution is possible on this earth to "tension, strife and disorder," a tragic conception "for which ancient philosophy, in Augustine's view, could find no room."[68]

The contrast to ancient philosophy is confined to a particular reading of Plato and Aristotle. Whatever the merits of that reading, though, this tragic conception is hardly unfamiliar to Augustine's own Roman past.[69] When Augustine equates kingdoms with robbery, he is speaking from within a Roman political tradition, now at the end of its story, that continually grappled with the tragic dimensions and limits of its own power: whether a founding mired in violence, a conception of glory that would turn citizen against citizen until the Republic was destroyed, a tradition of manly liberty that would give way to hypocrisy and sycophancy, or ultimately a city that would crumble, just as it had destroyed so many cities before. There is a sober realism in Augustine's thought, born of his understanding of the sheer complexity of human existence. Augustine's romp through Varro's categorization of the 288 different ways in which philosophers have attempted to understand what one means by, and how to attain, happiness points to the implausibility of attempts to systematize politics (*Civ. Dei.* 19.1). Augustine, in some sense, reflects the culmination of – even provides the psychological premises for – Roman political thought's resistance to perfectibility. We are embodied beings who are largely unknown to each other as well as ourselves, comprised of a variety of memories, habits, thoughts, experiences, inclinations, and impulses that exist at various levels of consciousness and unconsciousness but ultimately define who we are.

---

[65] Markus 1988, 84; also Deane 1963, 7, 223–24. [66] Markus 1988, 177.
[67] Deane 1963, 222. [68] Markus 1988, 83.
[69] On challenges to this reading, see Gregory 2008, 87–89.

Wandering

The realist conception that culminates in a negative, coercive politics resolves too neatly the ambiguity of Augustine's and, more generally, Roman political thought. Markus, for example, suggests that Augustine's political neutrality, his seeming indifference to the institutional forms of politics, derives from a sense of the citizens of the city of God as pilgrims (*peregrini*) in a foreign land (for example, *Civ. Dei.* 1.1; 1.9; 1.15; 1.35; 10.7; 19.18).[70] The translation as "pilgrim" is itself problematic, drawing on a later derivation of *peregrinus*, as an identifiable people on a purposeful journey to a holy place or land. Although there is that language of journey in Augustine, we do not have to read a later notion of pilgrim back into Augustine; Augustine's sensibility is that of a Virgilian quest for a home, only without giving us refuge on this earth (for example, *De doc. Chr.* 1.33.36; also Stoic: Sen. *Ep.* 120.18: use world "like a foreign visitor hastening on his way").

The sense of wandering informed the Roman imagination: a community founded by a displaced people (Virgil; *Civ. Dei.* 3.14) and populated by refugees (Livy; *Civ. Dei.* 5.17). This identity is fundamentally different from the Greek and Jewish experiences, the Greeks depicting themselves as born of the land, the Israelites as returning to their land. For the Romans, there is nothing natural, fixed, or visible about who is included as Roman or even where it is located. In these ambiguities Augustine betrays the imperial context in which citizenship expanded with empire through acts of incorporation so that anyone, at some point, could potentially be Roman.

From this past we can read much of the sense of searching that informs Augustine's thought. Augustine describes his own quest as like Aeneas' *errores* (*Contra acad.* 1.5.14; also *Conf.* 1.13), a striving that never finds completeness on this earth. Augustine speaks of "remembering Jerusalem, with my heart lifted up towards her; Jerusalem my country, aye, Jerusalem my mother," yearning for when "all that is of me from this dispersed and disordered estate" will be gathered together (*Conf.* 12.16).

---

[70] Markus 1988, 67, 74–75, 83. Markus variously translates these terms as pilgrim and foreigner.

The desperate longing for a home gets transformed in Augustine's psychology to a desire to possess for oneself, to "know who we were and where we were" (*Civ. Dei.* 6.2) on a land that is not one's own (*Civ. Dei.* 16.24; 19.14). Even in his discussion of Cacus, the cave-dwelling giant, Augustine writes that "all that he desired was peace unmolested by any, a peace whose calm was untroubled by any man's violence or the fear of it" (*Civ. Dei.* 19.12).

The city of God and the earthly city are communities that bear the mark of this status. Although the true home of the saved lies in the city of God (*civitas Dei*), a city whose orientation in love (as *caritas*) is mutually exclusive to the earthly city, the place where they reside as embodied beings is as aliens in the earthly city, a term that refers both to the visible cities we inhabit and to an invisible orientation of depraved love (*cupiditas*).[71] Where the Israelites knew who they were as they wandered in the desert, there is no longer such clarity. Jerusalem serves as a vision of peace, Babylon as a vision of confusion, but they are now mingled (*En. Psalmos* 65.2; *De doc. Chr.* 3.34.49), everyone residing in the earthly city and assuming various responsibilities and duties. The citizens of the city of God appear as members of the Church as well as officials of the state (*Civ. Dei.* 11.1; 19.26; 20.5; 20.9), those who serve the state potentially joining "the roster" of the city of God (*Civ. Dei.* 2.29). One cannot even know with any certainty who possesses the truth (*De ut. cred.* 7.16). Markus captures the ambiguity: "For the citizen of the heavenly city, concerns for the *saeculum* is the temporal dimension of his concern for the eternal city."[72] What emerges, as Brown writes, is "the idea of a man,

---

[71] Gregory distinguishes between the earthly city and earthly societies (Gregory 2008, 52), though I can find no such distinction in Augustine. Augustine refers to our actual habitation on earth in different terms, such as human kingdoms (*regna humana*) (*Civ. Dei.* 5.1) and earthly kingdoms (*regna terrena*) (*Civ. Dei.* 5.12; 5.25; 6.1), but also as a *civitas terrena* (*Civ. Dei.* 5.1; 5.14; 5.16; 5.18; 5.19; 10.25; 14.18; 19.17). Augustine is clear, for example, in characterizing the Roman heroes as citizens of a *civitas terrena* (*Civ. Dei.* 5.14). I find persuasive Markus' claim that Augustine translates the African church's view (influenced by Tertullian and Cyprian, out of which the Donatists also emerge) of a pure Church that is in opposition with the world into eschatological, but not sociological, categories (Markus 1988, 120–27; also Rist 1994, 228–29).

[72] Markus 1988, 102.

placed as a stranger in an uncomprehending land, a man whose virtue lies in a tension towards something else, in hope, in faith, in an ardent yearning for a country that is always distant, but made ever-present by the quality of his love, that 'groans' for it."[73] But it is a tension that Augustine models after Rome's past. Augustine's *peregrini* appear as Aeneas' "wandering and fugitive kingdom" (*Civ. Dei.* 3.14). Like Romulus who populated the city by establishing it as an asylum where "any man might seek refuge and be free from guilt," the city of God similarly offers "citizens for the eternal city" a refuge, bringing them "together by a promised amnesty for all and sundry crimes" (*Civ. Dei.* 5.17). The heavenly city is not a people, but, like Rome, "summons citizens from all peoples, and gathers an alien society of all languages" (*Civ. Dei.* 19.17).

To a certain extent Markus is correct in suggesting that for Augustine our alien status creates a distance from the earth.[74] Our relationship to the things of the earth is as something to use (*uti*), in contrast with our relationship to God as something to enjoy (*frui*) (*De doc. Chr.*1.4.4; 1.5.5; *Civ. Dei.* 5.16). The earth appears as a source of continual trial and as a place to be endured (*Civ. Dei.* 1.29). Augustine does not offer a theory of the state, as many have noted. Nor does he provide systematic comparisons of different regime types. In fact, so malleable is Augustine's institutional conception of politics that it can encompass everything from slavery to Spartacus' slave revolt (*Civ. Dei.* 4.5) and from a band of robbers to a kingdom (*Civ. Dei.* 4.4; 4.5). But Augustine is not being indifferent, nor does he view all political forms as equally bad.[75] He is speaking from within a Roman political tradition and reflecting on a Roman past that continually grappled with the bonds of community life.

Dominion

Augustine's beginning point of thinking about communities is with the dominion (*dominor*) humans were given over the irrational creatures. As we were made in God's image, we were not created to hold dominion

---

[73] Brown 1972, 323–24.
[74] Markus 1988, 67, 74–75, 83; also Brown 1967, 325; Elshtain 1995, 96.
[75] Rist 1994, 230–39, 305: equally bad; Markus 1988, 55: neutral.

over other rational creatures (*Civ. Dei.* 19.15). Augustine notes, "So it was that the first just men," Abel being the first, "were established as shepherds of flocks, rather than as kings of men" (*Civ. Dei.* 19.15; so Abel as shepherd). It is in our fallen state, though, that dominion is justified: a fact of existence from the perspective of humanity; a just order from the perspective of God's plan (*Civ. Dei.* 19.15). Augustine reports what was at that time a common view of the derivation of the word *servus* from *servare* (to preserve) "from the fact that those who by the law of war might have been put to death, when preserved by their victors, became slaves, so named from their preservation" (*Civ. Dei.* 19.15). Like those saved in war in fighting "to defend his sin," so humanity is like the vanquished, saved from eternal death but humbled by being placed in a state of bondage (*Civ. Dei.* 19.15). Slavery as a punishment is "ordained by that law which bids us to preserve the natural order and forbids us to disturb it" (*Civ. Dei.* 19.15).[76]

Slavery is not something to which Augustine is simply indifferent. Slavery is not part of the cosmic order; it is not an institution that models some divine order or that identifies the master as in some sense naturally superior. It is natural only in the sense that it is a result of human arrangements, a moment of one individual having power over another, in a fallen world. He expresses gratitude for God's mercy in saving Rome from the savagery and threatened slavery of Radagaisus, king of Goths (though it turns out that God was saving his punishment of Rome for later) (*Civ. Dei.* 5.23). He also describes the slave trade as a wicked kind of commerce (Divjak *Ep.* 10). In any case, we would not accept Augustine's willingness to accommodate slavery as a form of order. But what emerges from our fallen state for Augustine is less the problem of slavery than the misplaced notion of freedom that is associated with dominion (and doing what one wants: *Civ. Dei.* 2.20).[77] Augustine quotes Peter, "'For by whom a man is vanquished, to him is he also bound as a slave'"

---

[76] Rist interprets Augustine in this way (1994, 236–39). As Rist argues, "since we are all justly slaves and dependent on God's mercy, we need have few qualms about the 'social' implications of the implementation of that mercy or about how God's ways are worked out in our fallen society" (1994, 252).

[77] See Marshall 2012.

(*Civ. Dei.* 19.15, quoting 2 *Peter* 2.19). That is, enslavement shows up in pride and lust for ruling over another (*Civ. Dei.* 19.14). Augustine summarizes the point in the preface of *City of God*: when the earthly city "seeks for mastery, though the nations are its slaves, [it] has as its own master that very lust for mastery" (*Civ. Dei.* 1.pref).

There is a fundamental warning about the nature of earthly power. On the one hand, Augustine seems to affirm a conception of power as zero-sum, one associated with realist and neo-realist interpretations of politics: One can only increase power at the expense of someone else's power. Thus, Augustine talks about how Rome rose to power, initially through justified wars and later through unjustified ones, in which Rome had to either defend its power against the encroachment of others or expand its power by conquering others (*Civ. Dei.* 4.15). On the other hand, Augustine identifies the tyrannical impulse that underlies this zero-sum conception of power: Peace is possible only when it is concentrated in the hands of a few (or one). Or stated slightly differently, the tyrannical impulse arises when the will "wants to be in its own power" (*De lib. arb.* 2.19.53.199). It is an impulse that lies at the heart of the founding of the earthly city (*Civ. Dei.* 15.5), whether Cain's murder of his brother out of envy or Romulus' murder of his brother to remove a rival. It is the impulse to power that drives the extractive politics of distribution that made the state poor but private citizens rich (*Civ. Dei.* 5.12). And it resides in the relentless quest for empire, an erroneous desire "to rule lastingly over those whom it was able to subjugate victoriously" (*Civ. Dei.* 15.4). There is a kind of earthly peace that can be achieved when "no one remains to resist it" (*Civ. Dei.* 15.4). But it is one, as the Roman empire demonstrates, that is necessarily temporary, often begetting "new misery" and adding to the old (*Civ. Dei.* 15.4).

Justice

This predatory and ultimately self-destructive conception of power must be tempered by justice (*Civ. Dei.* 4.4). Many commentators, especially realists, point to Augustine's rejection of the possibility of a just community, and in fact the lack of any progressive agenda, as a rejection of a goal of justice in a community. But for Augustine, and for such realists as

Morgenthau and Markus, the goal of justice will always be as imperfect as it is necessary because it is the foundation of how Augustine sees communities as ordered.[78] Justice is an order according to what is due, one for Augustine that has less to do with law than with an orientation of love. Augustine resembles the Stoics in seeing our social existence as embedded in relationships of love, each with its form of rule, that radiate out from ourselves, family, neighbors, citizens, and human society (*Civ. Dei.* 19.3; 19.14; *De doc. Chr.* 1.26.27; 1.28.29).[79] We are bound to each other through a similar nature and "feeling of kinship" (*Civ. Dei.* 12.22). But he departs from the Stoics in characterizing the objects of our love as *usus*, as uses (for example, *De doc. Chr.* 1.22.20). Interpreted from our post-Kantian vantage point, commentators see Augustine as instrumentalizing relationships, as treating people as means rather than as ends. But *usus* has a much broader set of meanings than simply use, encompassing a practice or a relationship with something.[80] Christ, for example, in his mortality appears as an *usus* (*De doc. Chr.* 1.14.13; 1.17.16). For God, we are *usus* (*De doc. Chr.* 1.32.34: in His use He references His own goodness). What it means for something to be an *usus* is to employ it to obtain the deserving object of our love (*De doc. Chr.* 1.4.4). In loving the world properly, we love it for God, understanding the invisible things of God by way of the visible things before us (*De doc. Chr.* 1.4.4).[81] In loving our neighbor, in our use of our neighbor, we love his blessedness and turn ourselves and the other toward that blessedness.[82] That is, in loving, like in our love of Christ, we experience a "transformation of affections" through acts "of charity and self-giving" (*De doc. Chr.* 1.17.16; 1.22.21; 1.34.38).[83] Charity takes on a very specific meaning. It is not just giving but proper loving that orients all the other virtues (*De doc. Chr.* 3.10.16).[84] In our use of our neighbors, we model how God uses

---

[78] Markus 1988, 44: imperfect justice is not the same as injustice; Morgenthau 1960: trying to be just, 61–67.

[79] See O'Donovan 1980, 121–23 on the tension between universal neighbor-love and special brother-love.

[80] See Baer 1996.   [81] See Rist 1994, 164–66 on use-love.

[82] Baer 1996, 57.   [83] Baer 1996, 55–56.

[84] On charity as the unifying virtue, see Langan 1979.

human beings as a type of care, one that turns us toward God (*De doc. Chr.* 1.11.11: the Way).[85]

Though borrowing from the Stoics and neo-Platonists, Augustine's sensibility is more on the lines of Cicero's brand of Stoicism wrapped in pragmatism. Whatever immutable laws may govern our relationships, their particular expression and institutional form appear in communities by way of negotiation, as an "ordered agreement" (*concordia*) guided by two principles: that one harm no individual and that one "help every man that he can" (*Civ. Dei.* 19.14). What organizes this agreement is command (*imperium*) and obedience (*oboedio*), but unlike what many realists claim, it is oriented by a particular bond: "those who are concerned for others give commands" while "those who are objects of concern obey" (*Civ. Dei.* 19.14). Or as Augustine writes in a similar vein, a just relationship is "to be led by those who love us" and "to lead those whom we love" (*Civ. Dei.* 10.3). Even in the case of mastery, command is not self-regarding but guided by mercy (*misericordia*) for others (*Civ. Dei.* 19.14) and compassion (*clementia*) (*Civ. Dei.* 1.7).

The affective bonds of community life

What connects Augustine to Roman political thought is a shared insight that institutions are not the key to community life. It is perhaps a surprising claim since the Romans are best known to us for their laws and institutions. But Augustine's notion of a *civitas* comes out of a Roman tradition, articulated most fully by Cicero and Livy, that defined communities by the affective ties that are born of history and experience. It is a striking aspect of scholarship that discussions of Augustinian love rarely get placed in their Roman political context. Noting the lack of any institutional forms, Figgis argues that the language of *civitas* in Augustine isn't really political, nor does it bear a relationship to a *res publica*, but is more like a society for Augustine.[86] Barr minimizes this language, noting, "To call it a 'city' is of course a literary figure."[87] Markus notes that when Augustine speaks about authority and coercion,

---

[85] von Heyking 2001, 202.   [86] Figgis 1963, 51.   [87] Barr 1962, 213.

"he always does so in a vocabulary of persons rather than of institutions," his conception of the state dissolving "into a kind of atomistic personalism."[88] Markus attributes this tendency to Augustine's need to empty the state of any eschatological significance, leaving only the categories of the two cities intact.[89] Gregory connects the idea of an "affective organization" to "Christian *padeia* (sic) and *askesis*."[90] Arendt follows a neo-Platonic reading of Augustine in separating these affective elements from politics in such a way that this sort of abstract love "thrusts the other out of the world."[91]

Such readings miss the highly contextual, earthbound ways in which love is manifest in Roman political thought. As we saw with Cicero, and is in fact critical to Augustine's conception, a *civitas* or *res publica*, whether of earth or God (*Civ. Dei.* 2.21), is not an institutional form but a relationship of people, a *societas*, or joining of *socii* (see *En. Psalmos* 9.8; *De urb. exc.* 6). That relationship (like our relationship to God, for Augustine) requires belief in the invisible. Against the darkness of the human heart (as Arendt accurately interprets Augustine), there must be trust (*fides*), a faith in the invisible bonds of duty and in an orientation of love that underlies relations of authority and bind a people together (*De ut. cred.* 12.26). "If trust of this kind were to disappear from human affairs, who would not be aware of the confusion and appalling upheaval which would follow?" (*De fid. inv.* 2.4).

It is as though Augustine could not conceive of community, including the city of God, outside the language of *civitas* (see *Civ. Dei.* 19.5). There is no comparable language of *civitas* in Aristotle's conception of the soul. Nor is there in Plato, where the reincarnation of souls is a lonely voyage through the heavens. The closest we have in Plato is Socrates' recounting of the philosophic discourse that may await him with his death, but the language is not even vaguely political. The political language is apparent immediately when Augustine opens the *City of God* by invoking a new

---

[88] Markus 1988, 149.   [89] Markus 1988, 151.   [90] Gregory 2008, 274.
[91] Arendt 1996, 96. Arendt associates the relevance of community in Augustine with "the factuality of history and to the past as such" (1996, 99). She revises this interpretation later, suggesting that the plurality of the human condition, the foundation of politics for Arendt, is affirmed and motivated by love for Augustine (Arendt 1993, 139). On Arendt's interpretation of Augustine, see Hammer 2000.

founder (*conditor*) (*Civ. Dei.* 1.pref; also 11.1; 12.4). Founders give form. Drawing on Aristotle's categories, Augustine identifies two kinds of forms: a form that is applied externally to physical substances, such as the work of a craftsman, and a form that has "inherent efficient causes" derived from an intelligent nature that gives form to all things without itself being formed. Romulus and other founders are like craftsmen who are able to give form to a city through their "will, plan and power" (*voluntas consilium imperium*) (*Civ. Dei.* 12.26). God is the one efficient cause, but nevertheless appears in the thoroughly Roman role as the one "craftsman, creator, and founder" (*artifex, creator, conditor*) of the universe (*Civ. Dei.* 12.26).

Like Rome, the city of God is organized by affection, but one, unlike other earthly cities, founded on true justice in which the goal of every action is the attainment of heavenly peace (*Civ. Dei.* 19.17). In this heavenly peace citizens live justly in faith, serving both God and one's neighbors since "the life of a city is certainly a social life" (*Civ. Dei.* 19.17; also 19.19). There is a striking social element to this heavenly city, as though Augustine's Romanness would not permit inactivity. "No man ought to be so completely inactive as not to think of his neighbour's advantage, nor so active as to neglect the contemplation of God" (*Civ. Dei.* 19.19; also works: 19.27). The only true city, the city of God or as he says at one point, the *res publica* of Christ (*Civ. Dei.* 2.21), is one in which "God rules an obedient city according to his grace" in such a way that "in all men who belong to this city and who obey God the soul commands the body and the reason faithfully commands the vices in a system of law" (*Civ. Dei.* 19.23). Roman conceptions of authority penetrate his thought: Even in his early writings, Augustine assumes that Christ's *auctoritas* necessarily accompanies *ratio* (*Contra acad.* 3.20.43),[92] a relationship of authority that grows stronger in his later work. Augustine employs Roman jurisprudential language, as well, in talking about God's providence as governor or helmsman (*gubernet*) (*Civ. Dei.* 15.27).[93] The peace of the heavenly city, as Augustine writes, is "a perfectly ruled (*imperandi*) and fully

---

[92] See Conybeare 2006, 38.   [93] See von Heyking 2001, 135.

concordant fellowship in the enjoyment of God and in mutual enjoyment by union with God" (*Civ. Dei.* 19.13).

We are beings who are made happy by hope (*spes*), an anticipation of perfection in which there will be nothing more to endure (*Civ. Dei.* 19.4; also 19.20).[94] Hope is the assurance "that vision will follow right looking" (*Solil.* 1.6.13), that one will see what had before been invisible (*Civ. Dei.* 19.27). It is with God that the gifts of nature of both the body and the soul will be restored to perfection and made everlasting (*Civ. Dei.* 19.10) and that virtue – our learned ways of using the gifts of nature – will not struggle against vice but be complete in obedience to God and possession of peace (*Civ. Dei.* 19.10). And it is a realm that brings to perfection the yearnings of Roman political thought: a realm of *securitas* (freedom from anxiety), *libertas* (which Augustine defines as our obedience to God), and *beatitudo finalis* (final happiness) "that knows no devouring end" (*Civ. Dei.* 19.10).

Politics as confession

Whatever the perfection that awaits us, Augustine ultimately articulates a politics that confesses its own inadequacy. Confession is an act of discovering the self (*Conf.* 10.37) that also attempts to communicate what is within us. That is, confession is not private but is performed before others (*Conf.* 10.4), revealing or, stating it in a more Roman way, putting on display what is in our heart (*Conf.* 10.3: no ear is at another's heart).[95] In that moment of confession, with the "medicine of repentance" (*Civ. Dei.* 15.7), we are given the power (through grace) to reorient our desires away from the fantasy of mastery and possession, away from a zero-sum conception of power based on *cupiditas*, and toward power as *caritas*, a love of the eternal but also a love of others as distinct aspects of the eternal (see, for example, *De trin.* 9.8.13).

Lest we immediately discount the importance of confession as hopelessly unrealistic, what he is pointing to is actually the beginning of realism (that the realists seem to have forgotten). The act of confession is a

---

[94] Markus identifies hope as the centerpiece of Augustine's thought: 1988, 83, 169.
[95] See also *Contra acad.* 2.7.17 on dialogues as *spectaculum* and Conybeare 2006, 42–59).

statement that we are not creatures who know: We do not know the past, we do not know each other, and we can only inadequately communicate ourselves. We are capable of both deceiving and being deceived (*Conf.* 4.1). Our starting point is humility.[96] Our confession is a deceptively simply one: "I don't know" (*nescio*) (see *De ord.* 2.6.19; also *Conf.* 1.6). The point is that in our fallen state we cannot achieve mastery because we cannot know or control everything. The power of confession is that it relaxes the grip of habit by acknowledging that our notion of what is good or what we should do may be premised on old habits of thought that we accept as knowledge. As Schlabach writes, "To be right, all further acting must involve a willing that is strong in awareness of its own weakness."[97] Faced with challenges to ideas, we question ourselves rather than dismiss or turn against the challenge.

I count Hans Morgenthau, one of the founders of what has become known as political realism, as among a handful of political scientists to get it right. I say this, recognizing that I am reading Morgenthau against the realists and neo-realists who almost uniformly simplify or ignore the vast range and complexity of his thought. Not his critics but his supporters turn Morgenthau's confession about the limits of power into a celebration of the acquisition of power, his sense of fallenness from a moral order (and Morgenthau believed a moral order existed) into an embrace of amoralism, his view of the mystery and darkness of the human heart into a rational science of calculation and prediction,[98] his sensitivity to the plurality of human experiences and political forms into a reductionist account of interest, his humility into arrogance, his sense of a politics inextricably tied to culture into one abstracted from any affective context, and a view of politics as allowing the flourishing of different ends to one whose only aim is the containment of evil.[99] For Morgenthau, "It is, then, the predicament of trying to be just that we are too ignorant, too selfish, and too poor to do what justice demands of us."[100] We are moral beings who do not know how to be moral. "Thus,

---

[96] On humility in Augustine, see Schlabach 1994. [97] Schlabach 1994, 317.
[98] This notion of calculability emerges later in Morgenthau and Thompson 2001, 4.
[99] See Morgenthau 1946; 1948; 1960; 1970; 2004.
[100] Morgenthau 1970, 67.

we are condemned by the nature of justice, and our own, to give and to receive too little or too much, or at least to be ignorant of whether we have received and given too little or too much. In the eyes of man, the accounts of justice never square. Yet we must try to square them."[101]

Augustine's recourse to a politicized eternity brings Roman political thought to a close. I say Roman because if Augustine had been a Greek he would have likely ended in a very different place, one that emphasized reason more than affection, perfectibility more than fallenness, and ascetic withdrawal more than embeddedness. Augustine's tragic conception of politics comes out of a Roman experience that never retreated from an awareness of its own origins in homelessness, the violence that both forged and divided the Republic, and the loss of the *libertas* it prized most. Augustine's political thought is the culmination of Roman thought precisely because it offers neither an escape nor a retreat from our own care for a political world that is as flawed as it is dear.

[101] Morgenthau 1970, 67.

BIBLIOGRAPHY

Abizadeh, Arash. 2007. "On the Philosophy/Rhetoric Binaries: Or, is Habermasian Discourse Motivationally Impotent?" *Philosophy and Social Criticism* 33: 445–472.

Ackermann, Erich. 1979. *Lukrez und der Mythos*. Wiesbaden: Franz Steiner Verlag.

Adalberto, Giovanni and Denis van Berchem. Eds. 1987. *Opposition et resistances a l'Empire d'Auguste a Trajan*. Vandoeuvres-Genève: Fondation Hardt.

Adam, Traute. 1970. *Clementia Principis*. Stuttgart: Ernst Klett.

Agamben, Giorgio. 2005. *State of Exception*. Translated by Kevin Attell. University of Chicago Press.

Alberti, Antonina. 1995. "The Epicurean Theory of Law and Justice." *Justice and Generosity*. Edited by André Laks and Malcom Schofield. Cambridge University Press, 161–190.

Albertini, Eugéne. 1923. *La Composition dans les ouvrages philosophiques de Sénèque*. Paris: E. de Boccard.

Alexander, William. 1952. "The 'Psychology of Tacitus." *Classical Journal* 47: 326–28.

———1954. *The Tacitean 'non liquet' on Seneca*. Berkeley: University of California Press.

Alfonsi, Luigi. 1961. "Cicerone filosofo." In *Marco Tullio Cicerone. Scritti (commemorativi pubblicati nel bimillenanio della morte)*. Rome: Centro di Studi Ciceroniani, Istituto di Studi Romani, 177–85.

Algra, Keimpe. 1997. "Lucretius and the Epicurean Other: On the Philosophical Background of DRN V. 1011–1027." In *Lucretius and his Intellectual*

Background. Edited by K.A. Algra, M.H. Koenen, P.H. Schrijvers. Amsterdam: Royal Netherlands Academy of Arts and Sciences, 141–50.

———2007. "Stoics on Souls and Demons: Reconstructing Stoic Demonology." In *Body and Soul in Ancient Philosophy*. Edited by Dorothea Frede and Burkhard Reis. University of Hamburg Press, 359–387.

Allen, Barry. 1993. *Truth in Philosophy*. Cambridge, MA: Harvard University Press.

Allen, Danielle. 2004. *Talking to Strangers: Anxieties of Citizenship since Brown v. Board of Education*. University of Chicago Press.

Anderson, Benedict. 1983. *Imagined Communities: Reflections on the Origin and Spread of Natonalism*. London: Verso.

Anderson, W.D. 1955. "Venus and Aeneas: The Difficulties of Filial *Pietas*." *Classical Journal*. 50: 233–238.

Anderson, William. 1969. *The Art of* The Aeneid. Englewood Cliffs: Prentice Hall.

Ando, Clifford. 2000. *Imperial Ideology and Provincial Loyalties in the Roman Empire*. Berkeley: University of California Press.

———2011. *Law, Language, and Empire in the Roman Tradition: Empire and After*. Philadelphia: University of Pennsylvania Press.

Andrews, Alfred. 1930. "Did Seneca Practise the Ethics of His Epistles?" *Classical Journal* 25: 611–25.

Annas, Julia. 1993. *The Morality of Happiness*. Oxford University Press.

———1995. "Aristotelian political theory in the Hellenistic period." *Justice and Generosity*. Edited by André Laks and Malcolm Schofield. Cambridge University Press, 74–94.

———1997. "Cicero on Stoic Moral Philosophy and Private Property." In *Philosophia Togata I: Essays on Philosophy and Roman Society*. Edited by Miriam Griffin and Jonathan Barnes. Oxford: Clarendon, 151–173

Arena, Valentina. 2010. "Invocation to Liberty and Invective of *Dominatus* at the End of the Republic. *Bulletin of the Institute of Classical Studies*. 50: 49–73.

———2012. Libertas *and the Practice of Politics in the Late Roman Republic*. Cambridge University Press.

———forthcoming. "Informal Norms, Values, and Social Control in the Roman Participatory Context." In *A Companion to Greek Democracy and the Roman Republic*. Edited by Dean Hammer. Oxford and Malden, MA: Wiley- Blackwell.

Arendt, Hannah. 1958. *The Human Condition*. University of Chicago Press.

———1963. *On Revolution*. New York: Penguin.

———1968. *Between Past and Future*. Enlarged Edition. New York: Penguin.

———1978. *The Life of the Mind*. New York: Harvest.

———1982. *Lectures on Kant's Political Philosophy*. Edited by Ronald Beiner. University of Chicago Press.

———1993. *Was ist Politik?: Fragmente aus dem Nachlaß*. Edited by Ursula Ludz. München: Piper.

———1996. *Love and Saint Augustine*. Edited by Joanna Vecchiarelli Scott and Judith Chelius Stark. University of Chicago Press.

———2005. *The Promise of Politics*. Edited by Jerome Kohn. New York: Random House.

Armstrong, A. Hillary. 1972. "Neoplatonic Valuations of Nature, Body and Intellect." *Augustinian Studies* 3: 35–59.

Armstrong, David. 1995. "The Impossibility of Metathesis: Philodemus and Lucretius on Form and Content in Poetry." In *Philodemus and Poetry: Poetic Theory and Practice in Lucretius, Philodemus, and Horace*. Edited by Dirk Obbink. Oxford University Press, 210–32.

Armstrong, John. 1997. "Epicurean Justice." *Phronesis* 42: 324–34.

Arnold, Edward. 1911. *Roman Stoicism*. Cambridge University Press.

Ash, Rhiannon. 1999. *Ordering Anarchy: Armies and Leaders in Tacitus' Histories*. Ann Arbor: University of Michigan Press.

Asmis, Elizabeth. 1982. "Lucretius' Venus and Stoic Zeus." *Hermes* 110: 458–70.

———1983. "Rhetoric and Reason in Lucretius." *American Journal of Philology* 104: 36–66.

———1984. *Epicurus' Scientific Method*. Ithaca: Cornell University Press.

———1989. "The Stoicism of Marcus Aurelius." *ANRW* II. 36.3, 2228–2252.

———1991. "Philodemus's Poetic Theory and 'On the Good King' According to Homer." *Classical Antiquity* 10: 1–45.

———1992. "An Epicurean Survey of Poetic Theories (Philodemus *On Poems* 5, Cols. 26–36)." *Classical Quarterly* 42: 395–415.

———1995. "Epicurean Poetics." In *Philodemus and Poetry: Poetic Theory and Practice in Lucretius, Philodemus, and Horace*. Edited by Dirk Obbink. Oxford University Press, 15–34.

———1996. "Lucretius on the Growth of Ideas." *Epicureismo greco e romano*. Edited by Gabriele Giannatoni and Marcello Gigante. Napoli: Centro di studio del pensiero antico, Vol. 2, 763–78.

———2004. "The State as a Partnership: Cicero's Definition of *Res Publica* in His Work *On the State*." *History of Political Thought* 25: 569–99.

———2005. "A New Kind of Model: Cicero's Roman Constitution in *De Republica*." *American Journal of Philology* 126: 327–416.

———2008a. "Cicero on Natural Law and the Laws of the State." *Classical Antiquity* 27: 1–33.

———2008b. "Lucretius' New World Order: Making a Pact with Nature." *Classical Quarterly* 58: 141–157.

Astin, A.E. 1967. *Scipio Aemilianus*. Oxford: Clarendon.

Atkins, E.M. 1990. "'*Domina et Regina Virtutum*': Justice and *Societas* in *De Officiis*." *Phronesis* 35: 258–89.

———2000. "Cicero." In *The Cambridge History of Greek and Roman Thought*. Edited by Christopher Rowe and Malcolm Schofield. Cambridge University Press, 477–516.

Auguet, Roland. 1994 (orig. 1972). *Cruelty and Civilization: The Roman Games*. London: Routledge.

Augustine. 1912. *Confessions*. Translated by William Watts. Cambridge, MA: Harvard University Press.

———1963. *Augustine: Earlier Writings*. Translated by John Burleigh. Philadelphia: Westminster Press. Contains translations of *Soliloquia, De magistro, De libero arbitrio, De vera religione, De utilitate credendi, De natura boni*, and *De fide et symbolo*.

———1968. *City of God*. Translated by David Wiesen. Cambridge, MA: Harvard University Press.

———2010a. *Faith in the Unseen*. Translated by Michael Campbell. In *Trilogy on Faith and Happiness*. Edited by Boniface Ramsey. Hyde Park: New York City Press,.

———2010b. The Happy Life. Translated by Roland Teske. In *Trilogy on Faith and Happiness*. Edited by Boniface Ramsey. Hyde Park: New York City Press.

———2010c. *On the Free Choice of the Will, On Grace and Free Choice, and Other Writings*. Edited and translated by Peter King. Cambridge University Press.

Aurelius, Marcus. 2011. *Meditations*. Translated by Robin Hard. Oxford University Press.

Austin, R.G. 1986. *Aeneidos: Liber Sextus*. Oxford University Press.

Babcock, William. 1991. "Cupiditas and Caritas: The Early Augustine on Love and Human Fulfillment." In *The Ethics of St. Augustine*. Edited by Babcock. Atlanta: Scholars Press, 39–66.

Bacon, Helen. 1986. "The *Aeneid* as a Drama of Election." *TAPA* 116: 305–34.

———2001. "Mortal Father, Divine Mother: *Aeneid* VI and VIII." In *Poets and Critics Read Vergil*. Edited by Sarah Spence. New Haven: Yale University Press, 76–85.

Badian, Ernst. 1958. *Foreign clientelae (264–70 BC)*. Oxford: Clarendon.

———1962. "From the Gracchi: to Sulla (1940–59)." *Historia* 11: 197–245.

———1966. "The Early Historians." In *Latin Historians*. Edited by T.A. Dorey. New York: Basic Books, 1–38.

———1967. *Roman Imperialism in the Late Republic*. Pretoria: Communications of the University of South Africa.

———1986. "The Young Betti and the Practice of History." In *Costituzione romana e crisi della repubblica: Atti del convegno su Emilio Betti*. Edited by Giuliano Crifò. Napoli: Edizioni Scientifiche Italiane, 73–96.

———1993. "Livy and Augustus." In *Livius: Aspekte seines Werkes*. Edited by Wolfgang Schuller. Konstanz: Universitätsverlag Konstanz, 9–38.

———1996. "*Tribuni Plebis* and *Res Publica*." In Imperium Sine Fine: *T. Robert S. Broughton and the Roman Republic*. Edited by Jerzy Linkerski. Stuttgart: Franz Steiner Verlag, 187–213.

Baer, Helmut. 1996. "The Fruit of Charity: Using the Neighbor in *De Doctrina Christiana*." *Journal of Religious Ethics* 24: 47–64.

Bailey, Cyril. 1928. *The Greek Atomist and Epicurus*. Oxford: Clarendon.

———1940. "The Mind of Lucretius." *The American Journal of Philology* 61: 278–91.

———1947. *Titus Lucretius Carus, De Rerum Natura*. 3 vols. Oxford: Clarendon.

———1949. *Lucretius: Annual Lecture on a Master Mind*. London: Geoffrey Cumberlege.

Balot, Ryan K. 1998. "Pindar, Virgil, and the Proem to *Georgic 3*." *Phoenix* 52: 83–94.

Balsdon, J.P.V.D. 1960. "*AUCTORITAS, DIGNITAS, OTIUM.*" *Classical Quarterly* n.s. 10: 43–50.

———1979. *Romans and Aliens*. London: Duckworth.

Baraz, Yelena. 2012. *A Written Republic: Cicero's Philosophical Politics*. Princeton University Press.

Barnes, Jonathan. 1996. "Epicurus: Meaning and Thinking." *Epicureismo greco e romano*. Vol. 1. Edited by Gabriele Giannantoni and Marcello Gigante. Napoli: Centro di studio del pensiero antico, 197–220.

———1997. "Roman Aristotle." *Philosophia Togata II: Plato and Aristotle at Rome*. Edited by Barnes and Miriam Griffin. Oxford: Clarendon, 1–69.

Barr, Robert. 1962. *The Two Cities in Saint Augustine*. Québec: Presses de l'université Laval.

Barrow, R.H. 1950. Introduction to St. Augustine. *The City of God*. London: Faber and Faber.

Barthes, Roland. 1982. "Tacitus and the Funerary Baroque." In *A Barthes Reader*. Edited by Susan Sontag. New York: Hill and Wang, 162–66.

Barton, Carlin. 2002. "Being in the Eyes: Shame and Sight in Ancient Rome." In *The Roman Gaze: Vision, Power, and the Body*. Edited by David Fredrick. Baltimore: Johns Hopkins University Press, 216–35.

Bartsch, Shadi. 1994. *Actors in the Audience: Theatricality and Doublespeak from Nero to Hadrian*. Cambridge, MA: Harvard University Press.

Batstone, William. 1988. "The Antithesis of Virtue: Sallust's Synkrisis and the Crisis of the Late Republic." *Classical Antiquity* 7: 1–29.

———1994. "*Georgics* 1.181: *Inludunt* and the Scope of Vergilian Pessimism." *Classical Philology* 89: 261–68.

———1997. "Virgilian didaxis: value and meaning in the *Georgics*." In *The Cambridge Companion to Virgil*. Edited by Charles Martindale. Cambridge University Press, 125–44.

Bauman, Richard. 1974. *Impietas in Principem*. München: C.H. Beck.

———1983. *Lawyers in Roman Republican Politics*. München: C.H. Beck.

———1985. *Lawyers in Roman Transitional Politics*. München: C.H. Beck.

———1989. *Lawyers and Politics in the Early Roman Empire*. München: C.H. Beck.

Bayet, Jean. 1954. "Lucrèce devant la pensée grecque." *Museum Helveticum* 11: 89–100.

Beacham, Richard. 1999. *Spectacle Entertainments of Early Imperial Rome*. New Haven: Yale University.

Bearsley, Patrick. 1983. "Augustine and Wittgenstein on Language." *Philosophy* 58: 229–36.

Becker, Trudy. 1997. "Ambiguity and the Female Warrior: Vergil's Camilla." *Electronic Antiquity* 4.

Bell, Andrew. 1997. "Cicero and the Spectacle of Power." *Journal of Roman Studies* 87: 1–22.

Bell, Kimberly. 2008. "*Translatio* and the Constructs of a Roman Nation in Virgil's *Aeneid*." *Rocky Mountain Review* 62: 11–24.

Benario, Herbert. 1964. "Tacitus and the Principate." *Classical Journal* 60: 97–106.

———1972. "*Imperium* and *Capaces Imperii* in Tacitus." *American Journal of Philology* 93: 14–26.

———1989. *The Classical Association of the Middle West and South: A History of the First Eighty Years*. Greenville: Classical Association of the Middle West and South.

———1999. *Tacitus, Germany, Germania*. Warminster: Aris & Phillips.

Benhabib, Seyla. 1996. "Toward a Deliberative Model of Democratic Legitimacy." *Democracy and Difference: Contesting the Boundaries of the Political*. Edited by Benhabib. Princeton University Press, 67–94.

Béranger, Jean. 1953. *Recherches sur l'aspect idéologique du principat*. Basel: Verlag Friedrich Reinhardt AG.

Berlin, Isaiah. 1969. "Two Concepts of Liberty." In *Four Essays on Liberty*. Oxford University Press, 118–72.

Betensky, Aya. 1978. "Neronian Style, Tacitean Content: The Use of Ambiguous Confrontations in the *Annals*." *Latomus* 37: 419–435.

Bettini, Maurizio. 2011. *The Ears of Hermes: Communication, Images, and Identity in the Classical World*. Translated by William Short. Columbus: Ohio State University Press.

Beye, Charles Rowan. 1963. "Lucretius and Progress." *Classical Journal* 58: 160–69.

Bickerman, Elias. 1952. "*Origines Gentium*." *Classical Philology* 47: 65–81.

Bignone, Ettore. 1945. *Storia della letteratura Latina*. Vol. 2. Firenze G.C. Sansoni.

Bleicken, Jochen. 1998. *Augustus: Eine Biographie*. Berlin: Alexander Fest Verlag.

———1990. *Zwischen Republik und Prinzipat: Zum Charakter des zweiten Triumvirats*. Göttingen: Vandenhoeck and Ruprecht.

Bleisch, Pamela. 1999. "The Empty Tomb at Rhoeteum: Deiphobus and the Problem of the Past in *Aeneid* 6.494–547." *Classical Antiquity* 18: 187–226.

Blickman, Daniel. 1989. "Lucretius, Epicurus, and Prehistory." *Harvard Studies in Classical Philology* 92: 157–91.

Blundell, Mary Whitlock. 1990. "Parental Nature and Stoic οἰχείωσις." *Ancient Philosophy* 10: 221–242.

Bobzien, Susanne. 1998. *Determinism and Freedom in Stoic Philosophy*. Oxford: Clarendon.

Boesche, Roger. 1996. *Theories of Tyranny from Plato to Arendt*. University Park: Pennsylvania State University Press.

Boissier, Gaston. 1906. *Tacitus and Other Roman Studies*. Translated by W.G. Hutchison. N.Y.: G.P. Putnam's Sons.

Bollinger, Traugott. 1969. *Theatralis licentia: Die Publikumsdemonstration an den öffentlichen Spielen im Rom des früheren Kaiserzeit und ihre Bedeutung im politischen Leben*. Winterthur: Verglag Hans Schellenberg.

Bonds, William. 1978. *Joy and Desire in the* Aeneid*: Stoicism in Vergil's Treatment of Emotion*. Diss. Pennsylvania.

Bonjour, Madeleine. 1975. *Terre natale: études sur une composante affective du patriotisme romain*. Paris: Belles lettres.

Børresen, Kari. 1990. "In Defense of Augustine: How *Femina* is *Homo*." In *Collectanea Augustiniana*. Edited by Bernard Bruning. Louvain: Leuven University Press, 411–28.

Bourgery, Abel. 1911. "Les lettres a Lucilius: sont-elles de vraies lettres?" *Revue de philologie* 35: 40–55.

Bourke, Vernon. 1992. *Augustine's Love of Wisdom: An Introspective Philosophy*. Purdue University Press.

Bourne, Frank. 1977. "Caesar the Epicurean." *Classical World* 70: 417–32.

Bowra, C.M. 1933. "Aeneas and the Stoic Ideal." *Greece & Rome* 3: 8–21.

———1952. "Orpheus and Eurydice." *Classical Quarterly* n.s. 2: 113–26.

Boyancé, Pierre. 1941. "*Cum Dignitate Otium*." *Revue des études anciennes* 43: 172–91.

Boyd, Barbara. 1987. "*Virtus Effeminata* and Sallust's Sempronia." *TAPA* 117: 183–201.

Boyle, A.J. 1972. "The Meaning of the *Aeneid*: A Critical Inquiry." *Ramus* 1: 63–90, 113–51.

———1979. "*In Medio Caesar:* Paradox and Politics in Virgil's *Georgics*." *Ramus* 8: 65–86.

———1986. *The Chaonian Dove: Studies in the* Eclogues, Georgics *and* Aeneid *of Virgil*. Leiden: Brill.

Bradley, Anthony. 1969. "Augustan Culture and a Radical Alternative: Vergil's *Georgics*." *Arion* 8: 347–58.

Braund, Susanna. Ed. 2009. *Seneca:* De Clementia. Oxford University Press.

Bremmer, J.N. 1987. "Romulus, Remus and the Foundation of Rome." In *Roman Myth and Mythology*. Edited by J. N. Bremmer and N.M Horsfall. London: Institute of Classical Studies, 25–48.

Brennan, Tad. 1996. "Reasonable Impressions in Stoicism." *Phronesis* 41: 318–34.

Breyfogle, Todd. 2005. "Toward a Contemporary Augustinian Understanding of Politics." In *Augustine and Politics*. Edited by John Doody, Kevin Hughes, and Kim Paffenroth. Lanham: Lexington Books, 217–36.

Briggs, Jr., W.W. 1981. "Virgil and the Hellenistic Epic." *ANRW* II. 31.2: 948–984.

Bright, David. 1971. "The Plague and the Structure of *De rerum natura*." *Latomus* 30: 607–32.

Bringmann, Klaus. 1971. *Untersuchungen zum späten Cicero*. Diss. Marburg. Göttingen: Vandenhoeck & Ruprecht.

Brittain, Charles. 2001. "Rationality, Rules and Rights." *Apeiron* 34: 247–67.

———2002. "Non-rational Perception in the Stoics and Augustine." *Oxford Studies in Ancient Philosophy* 22: 253–308.

———2005. "Common Sense: Concepts, Definitions and Meaning In and Out of the Stoa." In *Language and Learning*. Edited by Dorothea Frede and Brad Inwood. Cambridge University Press, 164–209.

Brown, Peter. 1964. "St. Augustine's Attitude to Religious Coercion." *Journal of Roman Studies* 54: 107–16.

———1967. *Augustine of Hippo*. Berkeley: University of California Press.

———1972. "Political Society." In *Augustine: A Collection of Critical Essays*. Edited by R.A. Markus. Garden City, New York: Anchor Books, 311–35.

———1987. "Late Antiquity." In *A History of Private Life: I. From Pagan Rome to Byzantium*. Edited by Paul Veyne. Translated by Arthur Goldhammer. Cambridge: Belknap, 235–312.

Brown, Robert. 1995. "Livy's Sabine Women and the Ideal of *Concordia*." *TAPA* 125: 291–319.

Brunt, P.A. 1959. "The Revolt of Vindex and the Fall of Nero." *Latomus* 18: 531–59.

———1962. "The Army and the Land in the Roman Revolution." *Journal of Roman Studies* 52: 69–86.

———1965. "*Amicitia* in the late Roman Republic." *Proceedings of the Cambridge Philological Society* n.s. 2, 191: 1–20.

———1966. "The Roman Mob." *Past and Present* 35: 3–27.

———1971a. *Italian Manpower: 225 B.C. –A.D. 14*. Oxford: Clarendon.

———1971b. *Social Conflicts in the Roman Republic*. New York: W.W. Norton and Company.

———1974. "Marcus Aurelius in his *Meditations*." *Journal of Roman Studies* 64: 1–20.

———1975. "Stoicism and the Principate." *Papers of the British School at Rome* 43: 7–35.

———1977. "*Lex de Imperio Vespasiani*." *Journal of Roman Studies* 67: 95–116.

———1978. "*Laus imperii*." In *Imperialism in the Ancient World*. Edited by P.D.A. Garnsey and C.R. Whittaker. Cambridge University Press, 159–91.

———1982. "*Nobilitas* and *Novitas*." *Journal of Roman Studies* 72: 1–17.

———1983. "Princeps and Equites." *Journal of Roman Studies* 73: 42–75.

———1984. "The Role of the Senate in the Augustan Regime." *Classical Quarterly* 34: 423–44.

———1986. "Cicero's *Officium* in the Civil War." *Journal of Roman Studies* 76: 12–32.

———1988. *The Fall of the Roman Republic: And Related Essays*. Oxford: Clarendon.

Buchheit, Vinzenz. 1963. *Vergil über die Sendung Roms*. Heidelberg: Carl Winter.

———1972. *Der Anspruch des Dichters in Vergils* Georgika. Darmstadt: Wissenschaftliche Buchgesellschaft.

Büchner, Karl. 1956. *P. Vergilius Maro: Der Dichter der Römer*. Stuttgart: Alfred Druckenmüller Verlag.

———1970. "Aufbau und Sinn von Senecas Schrift über die Clementia." *Hermes* 98: 203–23.

———1983. "Vera vocabula rerum amisimus: Thukydides und Sallust über den verfall der Wertbegriffe." In *Hommages a Robert Schilling*. Edited by Hubert Zehnacker and Gustave Hentz. Paris: Société d'Édition les Belles Lettres, 253–61.

Burck, Erich. 1964. *Die Erzählungskunst des T. Livius*. Berlin: Weidmannsche.

———1991. "Livius und Augustus." *Illinois Classical Studies* 16: 269–81.

Burckhardt, Leonhard. 1990. "The Political Elite of the Roman Republic: Comments on Recent Discussion of the Concepts *Nobilitas* and *Homo Novus*." *Historia* 39: 77–99.

Burgess, J.F. 1971. "*Pietas* in Virgil and Statius." *Proceedings of the Virgil Society* 11: 48–60.

Burnell, Peter. 2005. *The Augustinian Person*. Washington D.C.: Catholic University of America Press.

Burnyeat, M.F. 1987. "The Inaugural Address: Wittgenstein and Augustine *De Magistro*." *Proceedings of the Aristotelian Society. Supplementary Volumes* 61: 1–24.

Burt, Donald. 1999. *Friendship and Society: An Introduction to Augustine's Practical Philosophy*. Grand Rapids: Eerdmans.

Byers, Sarah. 2003. "Augustine and the Cognitive Causes of Stoic 'Preliminary Passions' (*Propatheiai*)." *Journal of the History of Philosophy* 41: 433–448.

Cabisius, Gail. 1984/1985. "Social Metaphor and the Atomic Cycle in Lucretius." *Classical Journal* 80: 109–20.

Cairns, Francis. 1989. *Virgil's Augustan Epic*. Cambridge University Press.

Calhoon, Cristina. 1997. "Lucretia, Savior and Scapegoat: The Dynamics of Sacrifice in Livy 1.57–59." *Helios* 24: 151–69.

Campbell, Gordon. 2003. *Lucretius on Creation and Evolution: A Commentary on* De Rerum Natura, *Book Five, Lines 772–1104*. Oxford University Press.

Campbell, J.B. 1984. *The Emperor and the Roman Empire, 31 BC-AD 235*. Oxford: Clarendon.

Camps, W.A. 1969. *An Introduction to Virgil's* Aeneid. Oxford University Press.

Canfora, Luciano. 1993. *Vita di Lucrezio*. Palermo: Sellerio.

Canning, Joseph. 1996. *A History of Medieval Political Thought (300–1450)*. New York: Routledge.

Cape, Robert. 1995. "The Rhetoric of Politics in Cicero's Fourth Catilinarian." *American Journal of Philology* 116: 255–77.

Cape, Robert. 1997. "Persuasive history: Roman rhetoric and historiography." In *Roman Eloquence: Rhetoric in Society and Literature*. Edited by William Dominik. London: Routledge, 175–88.

Caranci, Luciana Alfano. 1988. *Il mondo animato di Lucrezio*. Napoli: Loffredo Editore.

Carlyle, Robert Warrand and Alexander James Carlyle. 1950 (orig. 1936). *A History of Mediaeval Political Theory in the West*. Edenburgh: William Blackwood and Sons.

Carter, J.M. 1972. "Cicero: Politics and Philosophy." In *Cicero and Virgil: Studies in Honour of Harold Hunt*. Edited by John Martyn. Amsterdam: Adolf M. Hakkert, 15–36.

Cary, Phillip. 2005. "United Inwardly by Love: Augustine's Social Ontology." In *Augustine and Politics*. Edited by John Doody, Kevin Hughes, and Kim Paffenroth. Lanham: Lexington Books, 3–33.

Celsus. 1971. *On Medicine*. Translated by W.G. Spencer. Cambridge, MA: Harvard University Press.

Chambers, Simone. 1996. *Reasonable Democracy: Jürgen Habermas and the Politics of Discourse*. Ithaca: Cornell University Press.

Champion, Craige. 2004. *Cultural Politics in Polybius's Histories*. Berkeley: University of California Press.

———forthcoming. "Interstate Relations, Federal States, Colonization, and Empire during the Roman Republic." In *A Companion to Greek Democracy and the Roman Republic*. Edited by Dean Hammer. Oxford and Malden, MA: Wiley- Blackwell.

Chaplin, Jane. 2000. *Livy's Exemplary History*. Oxford University Press.

Chilton, C.W. 1962. "The Epicurean Theory of the Origin of Language: A Study of Diogenes of Oenoanda, Fragments X and XI (W)." *American Journal of Philology* 83: 159–67.

Cicero, Marcus Tullius. 1913. *On Duties*. Translated by Walter Miller. Cambridge, MA: Harvard University Press.

———1914. *On Ends*. Translated by H. Rackham. Cambridge, MA: Harvard University Press.

———1952. *Orator*. Translated by H.M. Hubbell. Cambridge, MA: Harvard University Press.

———1996. *Laelius on Friendship*. Translated by William Armistead Falconer. Cambridge, MA: Harvard University Press.

———1996. *On the Orator*. Translated by E.W. Sutton. Cambridge, MA: Harvard University Press.

———1996. *Tusculan Disputation*. Translated by J.E. King. Cambridge, MA: Harvard University Press.

———2000. *Academics*. Translated by H. Rackham. Cambridge, MA: Harvard University Press.

———2000. *On the Laws*. Translated by Clinton Walker Keyes. Cambridge, MA: Harvard University Press.

———2000. *On the Republic*. Translated by Clinton Walker Keyes. Cambridge, MA: Harvard University Press.

———2001. *Letters to Friends*. Translated by D.R. Shackleton Bailey. Cambridge, MA: Harvard University Press.

Cichorius, Conrad. 1922. *Römische Studien*. Leipzig: Teubner.

Cizek, Eugen. 1992. "À propos de la poétique de l'histoire chez Tite-Live." *Latomus* 51: 354–64.

Claassen, Jo-Marie. 1999. *Displaced Persons: The Literature of Exile from Cicero to Boethius*. Madison: University of Wisconsin Press.

Clark, Anna. 2007. *Divine Qualities: Cult and Community in Republican Rome*. Oxford University Press.

Clarke, M.L. 1956. *The Roman Mind: Studies in the History of Thought from Cicero to Marcus Aurelius*. Cambridge, MA: Harvard University Press.

Classen, C. Joachim. 1968. "Poetry and Rhetoric in Lucretius." *TAPA* 99: 77–118.

———1986. "Einleitung." In *Probleme der Lukrezforschung*. Edited by Classen. Hildesheim: Georg Olms Verlag.

———1989. "Die Peripatetiker in Cicero's *Tuskulanen*." In *Cicero's Knowledge of the Peripatos*. Edited by William Fortenbaugh and Peter Steinmetz. New Brunswick: Transaction, 186–200.

Clausen, Wendell. 1964. "An Interpretation of the *Aeneid*." *Harvard Studies in Classical Philology* 68: 139–47.

———2002. *Virgil's Aeneid: Decorum, Allusion, and Ideology*. *Beiträge zur Altertumskunde* 162. Munich and Leipzig: K.G. Saur.

Clay, Diskin. 1983. *Lucretius and Epicurus*. Ithaca: Cornell University Press.

Coby, J. Patrick. 1999. *Machiavelli's Romans: Liberty and Greatness in* The Discourses on Livy. Lanham: Lexington Books.

Cochrane, Charles. 1940. *Christianity and Classical Culture: A Study of Thought and Action from Augustus to Augustine*. Oxford: Clarendon.

Cole, Thomas. 1967. *Democritus and the Sources of Greek Anthropology*. Chapel Hill: American Philological Association.

———1998. "Venus and Mars (*De Rerum Natura* 1.31–40)." In *Style and Tradition: Studies in Honor of Wendell Clausen*. Edited by Peter Knox and Clive Foss. Stuttgart: Teubner, 3–15.

Coleman, Janet. 2000. *A History of Political Thought: From Ancient Greece to Early Christianity*. Oxford: Blackwell.

Coleman, Robert. 1974. "The Artful Moralist: A Study of Seneca's Epistolary Style." *Classical Quarterly* 24: 276–89.

Colish, Marcia. 1971. "The Idea of Liberty in Machiavelli." *Journal of the History of Ideas* 32: 323–50.

———1990. *The Stoic Tradition from Antiquity to the Early Middle Ages*. 2nd Ed. 2 vols. Leiden: E.J. Brill.

Collingwood, R.G. 1946. *The Idea of History*. Oxford: Clarendon.

Colman, John. 2012. *Lucretius as Theorist of Political Life*. New York: Palgrave Macmillan.

Commager, Jr., H.S. 1957. "Lucretius' Interpretation of the Plague." *Harvard Studies in Classical Philology* 62: 105–18.

Conley, Duane. 1981. "The Stages of Rome's Decline in Sallust's Historical Theory." *Hermes* 109: 379–82.

Connolly, Joy. 2001. "Picture Arcadia: The Politics of Representation in Vergil's *Eclogues*." *Vergilius* 47: 89–116.

———2007. *The State of Speech: Rhetoric and Political Thought in Ancient Rome*. Princeton University Press.

———2009. "Virtue and Violence: The Historians on Politics." In *The Cambridge Companion to the Roman Historians*. Edited by Andrew Feldherr. Cambridge University Press, 181–94.

———2010. "Vergil and the Challenge of Autocracy." In *A Companion to Vergil's* Aeneid *and its Tradition*. Edited by Joseph Farrell and Michael Putnam. Oxford: Wiley-Blackwell, 404–17.

Connolly, William. 1993. *The Augustinian Imperative: A Reflection on the Politics of Morality*. Newbury Park: Sage.

———2004. "Response: Realizing Agonistic Respect." *Journal of the American Academy of Religion* 72: 507–11.

Conte, Gian. 1986. *The Rhetoric of Imitation: Genre and Poetic Memory in Virgil and Other Latin Poets*. Ithaca: Cornell University Press.

Conti, Marina. 1982. "Spunti politici nell' opera di Lucrezio. *Rivista di cultura classica e medioevale* 24: 27–46.

Conybeare, Catherine. 2006. *The Irrational Augustine*. Oxford University Press.

Cook, Albert. 1994. "The Angling of Poetry: The Nature of Lucretius." *Arethusa* 27: 193–222.

Cooper, John. 2004. "Knowledge." In *Nature and the Good: Essays on Ancient Philosophy*. Princeton University Press.

Cooper, John and J.F. Procopé. 1995. *Seneca, Moral and Political Essays*. Cambridge University Press.

Corbeill, Anthony. 2004. *Nature Embodied: Gesture in Ancient Rome*. Princeton University Press.

Cornell, T.J. 1975. "Aeneas and the Twins: The Development of the Roman Foundation Legend." *Proceedings of the Cambridge Philological Society* 21: 1–32.

———1986. "The Value of the Literary Tradition Concerning Archaic Rome." In *Social Struggles in Archaic Rome: New Perspectives on the Conflict of the Orders*. Edited by Kurt Raaflaub. Berkeley: University of California Press, 52–76.

———1995. *The Beginnings of Rome: Italy and Rome from the Bronze Age to the Punic Wars (c. 1000- 264 BC)*. London: Routledge.

———2001. "Cicero on the Origins of Rome." In *Cicero's Republic*. Edited by J.G.F. Powell and J.A. North. London: Institute of Classical Studies, 41–56.

Cotton, Hannah and Alexander Yakobson. 2002. "*Arcanum Imperii*: The Powers of Augustus." In *Philosophy and Power in the Graeco-Roman World: Essays in Honour of Miriam Griffin*. Edited by Gillian Clark and Tessa Rajak. Oxford University Press, 193–209.

Cousin, Jean. 1969. "Rhetorik und Psychologie bei Tacitus im Hinblick auf seine DEINVSIS." In *Tacitus*. Edited by Viktor Pöschl. Wege der Forschung, vol. 97. Darmstadt: Wissenschafltiche Buchgesellschaft.

Cowan, Eleanor. 2009. "Tacitus, Tiberius, and Augustus." *Classical Antiquity* 28: 179–210.

Cox, W. 1986. "Lucretius." In *Probleme der Lukrezforschung*. Edited by Joachim Classen. Hildesheim: Georg Olms Verlag, 221–35.

Crawford, Michael. 1978. *The Roman Republic*. Cambridge, MA: Harvard University Press.

Crook, John. 1967. *Law and Life of Rome*. Ithaca: Cornell University Press.

Crowther, N.B. 1983. "Greek Games in Republican Rome." *L'Antiquité classique* 52: 268–73.

Daitz, Stephen. 1960. "Tacitus' Technique of Character Portrayal." *American Journal of Philology* 81: 30–52.

Daraki, Maria. 1986. "Michel Foucault's Journey to Greece." *Telos* 67: 87–110.

Daube, David. 1938. "*Societas* as Consensual Contract." *Cambridge Law Journal* 6: 381–403.

———1969. *Roman Law*. Edinburgh University Press.

Davidson, Arnold. 1990. "Spiritual Exercises and Ancient Philosophy: An Introduction to Pierre Hadot." *Critical Inquiry* 16: 475–82.

———1994. "Ethics as Ascetics: Foucault, the History of Ethics, and Ancient Thought." In *Foucault and the Writing of History*. Edited by Jan Goldstein. Oxford: Blackwell, 63–80.

Davidson, James. 2009. "Polybius." In *Cambridge Companion to the Roman Historians*. Ed. Andrew Feldherr. Cambridge University Press, 123–136.

Davies, J.C. 1971. "Was Cicero Aware of Natural Beauty." In *Greece & Rome*, 2nd series, 18: 152–65.

Dawson, Doyne, 1992. *Cities of the Gods: Communist Utopias in Greek Thought*. Oxford University Press.

Deane, Herbert. 1963. *The Political and Social Ideas of St. Augustine*. New York: Columbia University Press.

Deininger, Jürgen. 1985. "Livius und der Prinzipat." *Klio* 67: 265–72.

Dekel, Edan. 2012. *Virgil's Homeric Lens*. New York: Routledge.

De Lacy. 1939. "The Epicurean Analysis of Language." *American Journal of Philology* 60: 85–92.

———1957. "Process and Value: An Epicurean Dilemma." *TAPA* 88: 114–26.

———1964. "Distant Views: The Imagery of Lucretius 2." *Classical Journal* 60: 49–55.

De Ligt, Luuk. forthcoming. "Economic Life: Production, Trade, and Consumption in the Roman Republic." In *A Companion to Greek Democracy and the Roman Republic*. Edited by Dean Hammer. Oxford and Malden, MA: Wiley-Blackwell.

De Lubac, Henri. 1989. "'Political Augustinism.'" In *Theological Fragments*. Trans. by Rebecca Howell Balinski. San Francisco: Ignatius Press, 235–86.

De Ste. Croix, G.E.M. 1981. *The Class Struggle in the Ancient Greek World from the Archaic Age to the Arab Conquests*. Ithaca: Cornell University Press.

De Zulueta, Francis. Ed. 1953. *The Institutes of Gaius*. Oxford: Clarendon.

Dench, Emma. 2005. *Romulus' Asylum: Roman Identities from the Age of Alexander to the Age of Hadrian*. Oxford University Press.

DeWitt, Norman. 1954. *Epicurus and His Philosophy*. Minneapolis: University of Minnesota Press.

Diano, Carlo. 1974. *Scritti Epicurei*. Firenze: Leo S. Olschki.

Didymus, Arius. 1999. *Epitome of Stoic Ethics*. Edited by Arthur Pomeroy. Atlanta: Society of Biblical Literature.

Dihle, Albrecht. 1982. *The Theory of Will in Classical Antiquity*. Berkeley: University of California Press.

Dingel, Joachim. 1974. *Seneca und die Dichtung*. Heidelberg: Carl Winter Universitätsverlag.

Divjak, Johannes. 1981. *Sancti Aureli Augustini Opera, Epistolae ex Duobus Codicibus Nuper in Lucem Prolatae*. Corpus Scriptorum Ecclesiasticorum Latinorum 88. Vienna: Hoelder-Pichler-Tempsky.

Djuth, Marianne. 1990. "Stoicism and Augustine's Doctrine of Human Freedom after 396." *Collectanea Augustiniana*. Edited by Joseph Schnaubeit and Frederick Van Fleteren. New York: Peter Lang, 387–401.

Dodds, Muriel. 1929. *Les récits de voyages: sources de l'Esprit des lois de Montesquieu*. Paris: Librairie Ancienne Honoré Champion.

Dodaro, Robert. 2004. *Christ and the Just Society in the Thought of Augustine*. Cambridge University Press.

Donaldson, Ian. 1982. *The Rapes of Lucretia: A Myth and its Transformations*. Oxford: Clarendon.

Dondin-Payre, Monique.1981. "'*Homo nouus*: Un slogan de Caton à César?" *Historia* 30: 22–81.

Dorey, T.A. 1969. "'Agricola' and 'Germania.'" In *Tacitus*. Edited by Dorey. London: Routledge, 1–18.

Dougherty, Carol. 1998. "It's Murder to Found a Colony." In *Cultural Poetics in Archaic Greece: Cult, Performance, Politics*. Edited by Carol Dougherty and Leslie Kurke. Oxford University Press, 178–98.

Douglas, A.E. 1965. "Cicero the Philosopher." In *Cicero*. Edited by T.A. Dorey. London: Routledge and Kegan Paul, 135–70.

———1995. "Form and Content in the Tusculan Disputations." In *Cicero the Philosopher: Twelve Papers*. Edited by J.G.F. Powell. Oxford: Clarendon, 197–218.

Dressler, Alex. 2013. "Poetics of Conspiracy and Hermeneutics of Suspicion in Tacitus's *Dialogus de Oratoribus*." *Classical Antiquity* 32: 1–34.

Drexler, Hans. 1957. "Res publica." *Maia* 9: 247–81.

———1958. "Res publica." *Maia* 10: 3–37.

Drogula, Fred. 2007. "*Imperium*, *Potestas*, and the *Pomerium* in the Roman Republic." *Historia* 56: 419–52.

Drumann, W. 1919. *Geschichte Roms*. Leipzig: Verlag von Gebrüder Borntraeger.

Drummond, Andrew. 1995. *Law, Politics and Power*. Stuttgart: Franz Steiner Verlag.

Dudley, Donald. 1968. *The World of Tacitus*. London: Secker and Warburg.

Dué, Casey. 2000. "Tragic History and Barbarian Speech in Sallust's *Jugurtha*." *Harvard Studies in Classical Philology* 100: 311–25.

Dugan, John. 2005. *Making a New Man: Ciceronian Self-Fashioning in the Rhetorical Works*. Cambridge University Press.

Düll, Rudolf. 1976. "Seneca iurisconsultus." *ANRW* II.15. Edited by Hildegard Temporini and Wolfgang Haase. Berlin: Walter de Gruyter, 364–80.

Dumézil, Georges. 1969. *Idées romaines*. Paris: Gallimard.

———1980. *Camillus: A Study of Indo-European Religion as Roman History*. Edited by Udo Strutynski. Translated by Annette Aronowicz and Josette Bryson. Berkeley: University of California Press.

Dunkle, J. Roger. 1967. "The Greek Tyrant and Roman Political Invective of the Late Republic." *TAPA* 98: 151–71.

———1971. "The Rhetorical Tyrant in Roman Historiography: Sallust, Livy and Tacitus." *Classical World* 65: 12–20.

Dupont, Florence. 1997. "*Recitatio* and the Reorganization of the Space of Public Discourse." In *The Roman Cultural Revolution*. Edited by Thomas Habinek and Alessandro Schiesaro. Cambridge University Press, 44–59.

Dyck, Andrew. 2004. *A Commentary on Cicero, De Legibus*. Ann Arbor: University of Michigan Press.

Dyson, Julia. 1994. "*Georgics* 2.503–12: The Temple's Shadow." *Vergilius* 40: 3–18

———1996. "*Caesi Iuvenci* and *Pietas Impia* in Virgil." *Classical Journal* 91: 277–86.

———1997. "*Fluctus Irarum, Fluctus Curarum*: Lucretian *Religio* in the *Aeneid*." *American Journal of Philology* 118: 449–57.

Dyson, R.W. 2001. *The Pilgrim City: Social and Political Ideas in the Writings of St. Augustine of Hippo*. Woodbridge: Boydell.

Eagleton, Terry. 1990. *The Ideology of the Aesthetic*. Oxford: Basil Blackwell.

Earl, Donald. 1960. "Political Terminology in Plautus." *Historia* 9: 235–43.

———1961. *The Political Thought of Sallust*. Cambridge University Press.

———1962. "Terence and Roman Politics." *Historia* 11: 469–85.

———1967. *The Moral and Political Tradition of Rome*. Ithaca: Cornell University Press.

———1972. "Prologue-form in Ancient Historiography." *ANRW*. Edited by Hildegard Temporini, Wolfgang Haase, Joseph Vogt, Victor Ehrenberg, and Ursula Vogt. 1.2: 842–56.

———1982. "Sallust (86–35 B.C.)." *Ancient Writers: Greece and Rome*. Vol. 2 of 2. Edited by T. James Luce. New York: Charles Scribner's Sons, 621–41.

Eck, Werner. 1984. "Senatorial Self-Representation: Developments in the Augustan Period." In *Caesar Augustus: Seven Aspects*. Edited by Fergus Millar and Erich Segal. Oxford: Clarendon, 129–67.

Eck, Werner, Antonio Caballos, and Fernando Fernández. 1996. *Das senatus consultum de Cn. Pisone patre*. München: C.H. Beck'sche Verlagsbuchhandlung.

Edelstein, Ludwig. 1966. *The Meaning of Stoicism*. Cambridge, MA: Harvard University Press.

———1967. *The Idea of Progress in Classical Antiquity*. Baltimore: Johns Hopkins University Press.

Eder, W. 1986. "The Political Significance of the Codification of Law in Archaic Societies: An Unconventional Hypothesis." In *Social Struggles in Archaic Rome: New Perspective on the Conflict of the Orders*. Edited by Kurt Raaflaub. Berkeley: University of California Press, 262–300.

———1990. "Augustus and the Power of Tradition: The Augustan Principate as Binding Link between Republic and Empire." In *Between Republic and Empire: Interpretations of Augustus and His Principate*. Edited by Kurt Raaflaub and Mark Toher. Berkeley: University of California Press, 71–122.

Edmondson, J.C. 1996. "Dynamic Arenas: Gladiatorial Presentations in the City of Rome and the Construction of Roman Society during the Early Empire." In *Roman Theater and Society: E. Togo Salmon Papers I*. Edited by William Slater. Ann Arbor: University of Michigan Press, 69–112.

Edwards, Catharine. 1993. *The Politics of Immorality in Ancient Rome*. Cambridge University Press

———1994. "Beware of Imitations: Theatre and the Subversion of Imperial Identity." In *Reflections of Nero: Culture, History & Representation*. Edited by Jas Elsner and Jamie Masters. Chapel Hill: University of North Carolina Press, 83–97.

———1997. "Self- Scrutiny and Self- Transformation in Seneca's Letters." *Greece & Rome*, 2nd series, 44: 23–38.

———1999. "The Suffering Body: Philosophy and Pain in Seneca's Letters." In *Constructions of the Classical Body*. Edited by James Porter. Ann Arbor: University of Michigan Press, 252–68.

Edwards, Mark. 1960. "The Expression of Stoic Ideas in the *Aeneid*." *Phoenix* 14: 151–65.

Egermann, Franz. 1932. *Die Proömien zu den Werken des Sallust*. Sitzungsberichte. Vol. 214. Wein: Hölder-Piehler-Tempsky A.G., 1–87.

Eisenhut, Werner. 1973. *Virtus Romana: Ihre Stellung im römischen Wertsystem*. München: Wilhelm Fink Verlag.

Elder, J.P. 1954. "Lucretius 1.1–49." *TAPA* 85: 88–120.

Ellis, Ellen. 1927. "Political Science at the Crossroads." *American Political Science Review* 21: 773–91.

Elshtain, Jean Bethke. 1981. *Public Man, Private Woman: Women in Social and Political Thought*. Princeton University Press.

———1995. *Augustine and the Limits of Politics*. University of Notre Dame Press.

Engberg-Pedersen, Troels. 1990a. "Stoic Philosophy and the Concept of the Person." In *The Person and the Human Mind: Issues in Ancient and Modern Philosophy*. Edited by Christopher Gill. Oxford: Clarendon, 109–35.

———1990b. *The Stoic Theory of Oikeiosis: Moral Development and Social Interaction in Early Stoic Philosophy*. Aarhus University Press.

———1998. "Marcus Aurelius on Emotions." In *The Emotions in Hellenistic Philosophy*. Edited by Julia Sihvola & Troels Engberg-Pederson. Dordrecht: Kluwer, 305–337.

Erler, Michael. 1997. "Physics and Therapy: Meditative Elements in Lucretius' *De rerum natura.*" In *Lucretius and his Intellectual Background.* Edited by K.A. Algra, M.H. Koenen, and P.H. Schrijvers. Amsterdam: Royal Netherlands Academy of Arts and Sciences, 79–92.

———2002. "Epicurus as *Deus Mortalis*: *Homoiosis Theoi* and Epicurean Self-Cultivation." In *Traditions of Theory: Studies in Hellenistic Theology, Its Background and Aftermath.* Edited Dorothea Frede and André Laks. Leiden: Brill, 159–81.

Ernout, Alfred and Léon Robin. 1962. *Lucrèce, De Rerum Natura, Commentaire exégétique et critique.* 2nd ed. 3 vols. Paris: Soc. d'Éd. Les Belles Lettres.

Erskine, Andrew. 1990. *The Hellenistic Stoa: Political Thought and Action.* Ithaca: Cornell University Press.

———1997. "Cicero and the Expression of Grief." In *The Passions in Roman Thought and Literature.* Edited by Susanna Morton Braund and Christopher Gill. Cambridge University Press, 36–47.

Euben, J. Peter. 2001. "The Polis Globalization, and the Politics of Place." In *Democracy and Vision: Sheldon Wolin and the Vicissitudes of the Political.* Edited by Aryeh Botwinick and William Connolly. Princeton University Press, 256–89.

———2003. *Platonic Noise.* Princeton University Press.

Fantham, Elaine. 1972. *Comparative Studies in Republican Latin Imagery.* University of Toronto Press.

———1973. "*Aequabilitas* in Cicero's Political Theory and the Greek Tradition of Proportional Justice." *Classical Quarterly* 23: 285–90.

———2004. "Liberty and the People in Republican Rome." *TAPA* 135: 209–29.

———2004b. *The Roman World of Cicero's* De Oratore. Oxford University Press.

Farrell, Joseph. 1986. "The Distinction between *comitia* and *concilium.*" *Athenaeum.* Studi Periodici di Letteratura e Storia dell' Antichità 64: 407–38

———1991. *Vergil's* Georgics *and the Traditions of Ancient Epic: The Art of Allusion in Literary History.* Oxford University Press.

Farrington, Benjamin. 1953a. "Second Thoughts on Epicurus." *Science and Society* 17: 326–39.

———1953b. "*Vita Prior* in Lucretius." *Hermathena* 81: 59–62.

———1966 (orig. 1939). *Science and Politics in the Ancient World.* 2nd ed. New York: Barnes and Noble.

———1967. *The Faith of Epicurus*. New York: Basic Books.

Farron, Steven. 1981. "The Death of Turnus Viewed in the Perspective of its Historical Background." *Acta Classica* 24: 97–106.

———1982. "The Abruptness of the End of the *Aeneid*." *Acta Classica* 25: 136–41.

———1985. "Aeneas' Human Sacrific." *Acta Classica* 28: 21–33.

———1986. "Aeneas' Revenge for Pallas as a Criticism of Aeneas." *Acta Classica* 29: 69–83.

Feeney, Denis. 1983. "The Taciturnity of Aeneas." *Classical Quarterly* n.s. 33: 204–19.

———1984. "The Reconciliation of Juno." *Classical Quarterly* n.s. 34: 179–94.

———1986. "History and Revelation in Vergil's Underworld." *Proceedings of the Cambridge Philological Society* 212: 1–24

———1991. *The Gods in Epic: Poets and Critics of the Classical Tradition*. Oxford University Press.

Feldherr, Andrew. 1997. "Livy's Revolution: Civic Identity and the Creation of the *res publica*." In *The Roman Cultural Revolution*. Edited by Thomas Habinek and Alessandro Schiesaro. Cambridge University Press, 136–57.

———1998. *Spectacle and Society in Livy's History*. Berkeley: University of California Press.

Ferguson, John. 1958. *Moral Values in the Ancient World*. London: Methuen.

Ferrary, Jean-Louis. 1982. "Le idee politiche a Roma nell'epoca repubblicana." *Storia delle idee politiche economiche e sociali* 1: 723–804.

———1984. "L'Archeologie du *de re Publica* (2, 2, 4–37, 63): Ciceron Entre Polybe et Platon." *Journal of Roman Studies* 74: 87–98.

———1995. "The Statesman and the Law in the Political Philosophy of Cicero." In *Justice and Generosity*. Edited by André Laks and Malcolm Schofield. Cambridge University Press, 48–73.

Festugière, A.J. 1956 (orig. 1946). *Epicurus and His Gods*. Translated by C.W. Chilton. Cambridge, MA: Harvard University Press.

Figgis, John. 1963. *The Political Aspects of St. Augustine's "City of God."* Gloucester, MA: Peter Smith.

Finley, M.I. 1983. *Politics in the Ancient World*. Cambridge University Press.

Fitch, John and Siobhan McElduff. 2002. "Construction of the Self in Senecan Drama." *Mnemosyne* 55: 18–40.

FitzGerald, William. 1951. "Pietas Epicurea." *Classical Journal* 46: 195–99.

Flower, Harriet. 1996. *Ancestor Masks and Aristocratic Power in Roman Culture.* Oxford: Clarendon.

———1999. "Piso in Chicago: A Commentary on the APA/AIA Joint Seminar on the *Senatus Consultum de Cn. Pisone Patre.*" *American Journal of Philology* 120: 99–115.

———2004. "Spectacle and Political Culture in the Roman Republic." In *The Cambridge Companion to the Roman Republic.* Edited by Harriet Flower. Cambridge University Press, 322–43.

———2006. *The Art of Forgetting: Disgrace and Oblivion in Roman Political Culture.* Chapel Hill: University of North Carolina Press.

———2010. *Roman Republics.* Princeton University Press.

Foley, Michael. 2003. "The Other Happy Life: The Political Dimensions to St. Augustine's Cassiciacum Dialogues." *Review of Politics* 65: 165–83.

Fontana, Benedetto. 1993. "Tacitus on Empire and Republic." *History of Political Thought* 14: 27–40.

Fontana, Benedetto, Gary Nederman, and Gary Remer. 2004. "Introduction: Deliberative Democracy and the Rhetorical Turn." In *Talking Democracy: Historical Perspectives on Rhetoric and Democracy.* Edited by Fontana, Nederman, and Remer. University Park: Penn State University Press, 1–15.

Fornara, Charles. 1983. *The Nature of History in Ancient Greece and Rome.* Berkeley: University of California Press.

Forsythe, Gary. 2005. *A Critical History of Early Rome: From Prehistory to the First Punic War.* Berkeley: University of California Press.

Fortin, Ernest. 1996. "Augustine and Roman Civil Religion," in *Classical Christianity and the Political Order: Refelections on the Theologico – Political Order.* Vol. 2. Edited by Brian Benestad. London: Rowman & Littlefield, 85–106.

Fott, David. 2009. "How Machiavellian is Cicero?" In *The Arts of Rule: Essays in Honor of Harvey C. Mansfield.* Edited by Sharon Krause and Mary Ann McGrail. Lanham: Lexington, 149–65.

Foucault, Michel. 1990a. *The History of Sexuality. Vol. 1 An Introduction.* Translated by Robert Hurley. New York: Vintage.

———1990b. *The History of Sexuality. Vol. 3 The Care of the Self.* Translated by Robert Hurley. New York: Vintage.

———1997a. "The Ethics of the Concern for Self as a Practice of Freedom." In *Ethics: Subjectivity and Truth*. Vol. 1. Edited by Paul Rabinow. New York: Free Press, 281–302.

———1997b. "Self Writing." In *Ethics: Subjectivity and Truth*. Vol. 1. Edited by Paul Rabinow. New York: Free Press, 207–222.

———2005. *The Hermeneutics of the Subject: Lectures at the Collège de France 1981–1982*. Edited by Frédéric Gros. Translated by Graham Burchell. New York: Palgrave.

Fowler, D.P. 1997 (orig. 1989). "Lucretius and Politics." *Philosophia Togata 1: Essays on Philosophy and Roman Society*. Edited by Miriam Griffin and Jonathan Barnes. Oxford: Clarendon, 120–50.

Fowler, W. Warde. 1911. *The Religious Experience of the Roman People*. London: Macmillan.

Foxhall, Lin. 1998. "Pandora Unbound: A Feminist Critique of Foucault's History of Sexuality." In *Rethinking Sexuality: Foucault and Classical Antiquity*. Edited by David Larmour, Paul Miller, and Charles Platter. Princeton University Press, 122–37.

Frede, Dorothea. 1989. "Constitution and Citizenship: Peripatetic Influence on Cicero's Political Conceptions in the *de re publica*." In *Cicero's Knowledge of the Peripatos*. Edited by William Fortenbaugh and Peter Steinmetz. New Brunswick: Transaction, 77–100.

———1992. "The Cognitive Role of *Phantasia* in Aristotle." In Essays on Aristotle's *De Anima*. Edited by Martha Nussbaum and Amélie Oksonberg Rorty. Oxford: Clarendon, 279–95.

———2003. "Stoic Determinism." In *The Cambridge Companion to the Stoics*. Edited by Brad Inwood. Cambridge University Press, 179–205.

Frede, Michael. 1987. "Philosophy and Medicine in Antiquity." *Essays in Ancient Philosophy*. Minneapolis: University of Minnesota Press, 225–242.

———1987. "Stoics and Skeptics on Clear and Distinct Impressions." *Essays in Ancient Philosophy*. Minneapolis: University of Minnesota Press, 151–76.

———1999. "On the Stoic Conception of the Good." In *Topics in Stoic Philosophy*. Edited by Katerina Ierodiakonon. Oxford: Clarendon, 71–94.

Fredrick, David. 2002. "Mapping Penetrability in Late Republican and Early Imperial Rome." In *The Roman Gaze: Vision, Power, and the Body*. Edited by David Fredrick. Baltimore: Johns Hopkins University Press, 236–64.

Friedlander, Paul.1939. "The Epicurean Theology in Lucretius' First Prooemium (Lucr. I.44–49)." *TAPA* 70: 368–79.

———1941. "Pattern of Sound and Atomistic Theory in Lucretius." *American Journal of Philology* 62: 16–34.

Frier, Bruce. 1985. *The Rise of the Roman Jurists: Studies in Cicero's* Pro Caecina. Princeton University Press.

Fronda, Michael. forthcoming. "The Emergence of Participatory Communities: Why Roman Republicanism? Its Emergence and Nature in Context." In *A Companion to Greek Democracy and the Roman Republic.* Edited by Dean Hammer. Oxford and Malden, MA: Wiley- Blackwell.

Furley, David. 1967. *Two Studies in the Greek Atomists.* Princeton University Press.

———1982. "Lucretius." In *Ancient Writers: Greece and Rome.* Vol. 2. Edited by T. James Luce. New York: Charles Scribner's Sons, 601–20.

———1986. "Lucretius and the Stoics." In *Probleme der Lukrezforschung.* Edited by Carl Joachim Classen. Hildesheim: Georg Olms Verlag, 75–95.

———1989. *Cosmic Problems: Essays on Greek and Roman Philosophy of Nature.* Cambridge University Press.

Gabba, Emilio. 1979. "Per un'interpretazione politca del De Officiis di Cicerone." *Rendiconti dell'Accademia dei Lincei.Classe di Scienze morali, storiche, filologiche,* 34: 117–141.

———1984. "The Historians and Augustus." In *Caesar Augustus: Seven Aspects.* Edited by Fergus Millar and Erich Segal. Oxford: Clarendon, 61–88.

Gaertner, Jan. 2008. "Livy's Camillus and the Political Discourse of the Late Republic." *Journal of Roman Studies* 98: 27–52.

Gale, Monica. 1994. *Myth and Poetry in Lucretius.* Cambridge University Press.

———2000. "Virgil on the Nature of Things: The *Georgics.*" In *Lucretius and the Didactic Tradition.* Cambridge University Press.

———2003. "Poetry and the Backward Glance in Virgil's *Georgics* and *Aeneid.*" *TAPA* 133: 323–52.

Galen. 1972, 1988, 1999. *De Placitis Hippocratis et Platonis.* In Kidd and Edelstein, *Posidonias.*

Galinsky, Karl. 1988. "The Anger of Aeneas." *American Journal of Philology* 109: 321–48.

———1996. *Augustan Culture: An Interpretive Introduction*. Princeton University Press.

Garnsey, Peter. 2007. *Thinking About Property: From Antiquity to the Age of Revolution*. Cambridge University Press.

Garsten, Bryan. 2009. *Saving Persuasion: A Defense of Rhetoric and Judgment*. Cambridge, MA: Harvard University Press.

Gebhard, Elizabeth. 1996. "The Theater and the City." *Roman Theater and Society: E. Togo Salmon Papers I*. Edited by William Slater. Ann Arbor: University of Michigan Press, 113–27.

Geertz, Clifford. 1973. "The Politics of Meaning." *The Interpretation of Cultures*. New York: Basic Books, 311–26.

Gelzer, Matthias. 1962. "Die Nobilität der römischen Republik." *Kleine Schriften*. Vol. 1. Wiesbaden: Franz Steiner Verlag, 17–135.

———1969. *Nobilität der römischen Republik*. London: Basil Blackwell.

Getty, Robert. 1950. "Romulus, Roma, and Augustus in the Sixth Book of the Aeneid." *Classical Philology* 45: 1–12.

Giancotti, Francesco. 1959. *Il preludio di Lucrezio*. Messina: Casa Editrice G. D'Anna.

Gilbert, Rolf. 1976. *Die Beziehungen zwischen Princeps und stadtrömischen Plebs im frühen Principat*. Bochum: Studienverlag Dr. N. Brockmeyer.

Gildenhard, Ingo. 2007. *Paideia Romana: Cicero's* Tusculan Disputations. Cambridge: Cambridge Philological Society.

———2011. *Creative Eloquence: The Construction of Reality in Cicero's Speeches*. Oxford University Press.

Gill, Christopher. 1983. "The Question of Character-Development: Plutarch and Tacitus." *Classical Quarterly* 33: 469–487.

———1985. "Ancient Psychotherapy." *Journal of the History of Ideas* 46: 307–325.

———1987. "Two Monologues of Self-Division: Euripides, *Medea* 1021–80 and Seneca, *Medea* 893–977." In *Homo Viator: Classical Essays for John Bramble*. Edited by Michael Whitby, Philip Hardie, and Mary Whitby. Bristol: Bristol Classical Press, 25–37.

———1996. *Personality in Greek Epic, Tragedy, and Philosophy: The Self in Dialogue*. Oxford: Clarendon.

———2000. "Stoic Writers of the Imperial Era." In *The Cambridge History of Greek and Roman Political Thought*. Edited by Christopher Rowe and Malcolm Schofield. Cambridge University Press, 597–615.

———2006. *The Structured Self in Hellenistic and Roman Thought*. Oxford University Press.

———2008. "The Self and Hellenistic-Roman Philosophical Therapy." In *Vom Selbst-Verstandnis in Antike und Neuzeit*. Edited by Alexander Arweiler and Melanie Möller. Berlin: Walter de Gruyter, 359–80.

Gillespie, Stuart and Philip Hardie. 2007. "Introduction." In *Cambridge Companion to Lucretius*. Edited by Gillespie and Hardie. Cambridge University Press. 1–17.

Gilliam, J.F. 1961. "The Plague under Marcus Aurelius." *American Journal of Philology* 82: 225–51.

Ginsburg, Judith. 1981. *Tradition and Theme in the* Annals *of Tacitus*. Salem: The Ayer Company.

———1993. "*In Maiores Certamina*: Past and Present in the Annals." In *Tacitus and the Tacitean Tradition*. Edited by T.J. Luce and A.J. Woodman. Princeton University Press.

Glidden, David. 1979. "*Sensus* and Sense Perception in the *De rerum natura*. "*California Studies in Classical Antiquity*. 12:155–81.

Glucker, John. 1978. *Antiochus and the Late Academy*. Göttingen: Vandenhoeck and Ruprecht.

———1988. "Cicero's Philosophical Affiliations." In *The Question of "Eclecticism": Studies in Later Greek Philosophy*. Edited by John Dillon and A.A. Long. Berkeley: University of California Press, 34–69.

Goldmann, Frank. 2002. "Nöbilitas als Status und Gruppe-Überlegungen zum Nobilitätsbegriff der römischen Republik." In *Res publica reperta*. Edited by Jörg Spielvogel. Stuttgart: Franz Steiner Verlag, 45–66.

Goldschmidt, Victor. 1953. *Le système Stoïcien et l'idée de temps*. Paris: Librairie Philosphique J. Vrin.

Goodwin, Jeff, James Jasper, and Francesca Polletta. 2001. "Introduction: Why Emotions Matter." In *Passionate Politics: Emotions and Social Movements*. Edited by Goodwin, Jasper, and Polletta. University of Chicago Press, 1–24.

Goodyear, F.R.D. 1968. "Development of Language and Style in the *Annals* of Tacitus." *Journal of Roman Studies* 58: 22–31.

———1972. *The* Annals *of Tacitus, Books 1–6*. Vol. 1. Cambridge University Press.

———1981. *The* Annals *of Tacitus, Books 1–6*. Vol. 2. Cambridge University Press.

Görler, Woldemar. 1995. "Silencing the Troublemaker: *De Legibus* 1.39 and the Continuity of Cicero's Scepticism." In *Cicero the Philosopher*. Edited by J.G.F. Powell. Oxford: Clarendon, 85–113.

Gottschalk, H.B. 1996. "Philosophical Innovation in Lucretius." In *Polyhistor: Studies in the History and Historiography of Ancient Philosophy*. Edited by Keimpe Algra, Peter van der Horst, and David Runia. Leiden: E.J. Brill, 231–40.

Graver, Margaret. 2002. *Cicero on the Emotions:* Tusculan Disputations *3 and 4*. University of Chicago Press.

———2007. *Stoicism and Emotion*. University of Chicago Press.

Green, William. 1942. "The Dying World of Lucretius." *American Journal of Philology* 63: 51–60.

Gregory, Eric. 2008. *Politics and the Order of Love: An Augustinian Ethic of Democratic Citizenship*. University of Chicago Press.

Grethlein, Jonas. 2006. "*Nam Quid ea Memorem*: The Dialectrical Relation of *Res Gestae* and *Memoria Rerum Gestarum* in Sallust's *Bellum Jugurthinum*." *Classical Quarterly* 56: 135–48.

Griffin, Jasper. 1979. "The Fourth *Georgic*, Virgil, and Rome." *Greece & Rome*, 2nd series, 26: 61–80.

Griffin, Miriam. 1968. "Seneca on Cato's Politics: *Epistle* 14, 12–13." *Classical Quarterly* 18: 373–75.

———1976. *Seneca: A Philosopher in Politics*. Oxford: Clarendon.

———1988. "Philosophy for Statesmen: Cicero and Seneca." In *Antikes Denken-Moderne Schule: Beiträge zu den antiken Grundlagen unseres Denkens*. Edited by H.W. Schmidt and P. Wülfing. Heidelberg: Carl Winter Universitätsverlag, 133–150.

———1995. "Tacitus, Tiberius and the Principate." In *Leaders and Masses in the Roman World: Studies in Honor of Zvi Yavetz*. Edited by I. Malkin and Z.W. Robinsohn. Leiden: E.J. Brill, 33–57.

———1997a. "Philosophy, Politics, and Politicians." In *Philosophia Togata I: Essays on Philosophy and Roman Society*. Edited by Miriam Griffin and Jonathan Barnes. Oxford: Clarendon, 1–37.

———1997b. "The Senate's Story." *Journal of Roman Studies* 87: 249–63.

———2005. "Seneca and Pliny." In *The Cambridge History of Greek and Roman Political Thought*. Edited by Christopher Rowe and Malcolm Schofield. Cambridge University Press, 532–58.

———2013. *Seneca on Society: A Guide to* De Beneficiis. Oxford University Press.

Grimal, Pierre. 1978. *Seneca: Macht und Ohnmacht des Geistes*. Darmstadt: Wissenschaftliche Buchgesellschaft.

Gruen, Erich. 1984. *The Hellenistic World and the Coming of Rome*. Berkeley: University of California Press.

———1992. *Culture and National Identity in Republican Rome*. Ithaca: Cornell University Press.

———1995 (orig. 1974). *The Last Generation of the Roman Republic*. Berkeley: University of California Press.

———1996. *Studies in Greek Culture and Roman Policy*. Berkeley: University of California Press.

Gunderson, Erik. 1996. "The Ideology of the Arena." *Classical Antiquity* 15: 113–51.

Gurd, Sean. 2012. *Work in Progress: Literary Revision as Social Performance in Ancient Rome*. Oxford University Press.

Gurval, Robert. 1995. *Actium and Augustus: The Politics and Emotions of Civil War*. Ann Arbor: University of Michigan Press.

Habermas, Jürgen. 1996. *Between Facts and Norms: Contributions to a Discourse Theory of Law and Democracy*. Translated by William Rehg. Cambridge, MA: M.I.T. Press.

Habicht, Christian. 1990. *Cicero the Politician*. Baltimore: Johns Hopkins University Press.

Habinek, Thomas. 1989. "Science and Tradition in *Aeneid* 6." *Harvard Studies in Classical Philology* 92: 223–55.

———1990. "Sacrifice, Society, and Vergil's Ox-born Bees." In *Cabinet of the Muses, Essays in Honor of T. G. Rosenmeyer*. Edited by Mark Griffith and Donald Mastronarde. Atlanta: Scholars Press, 209–23.

———1992. "An Aristocracy of Virtue: Seneca on the Beginnings of Wisdom." In *Beginnings in the Classical Literature*. Edited by Francis Dunn and Thomas Cole. Yale Classical Studies 24. Cambridge University Press, 187–203.

———1994. "Ideology for an Empire in the Prefaces to Cicero's Dialogues." *Ramus* 23: 55–67.

———1997. "The Invention of Sexuality in the World-City of Rome." In *The Roman Cultural Revolution*. Edited by Habinek and Alessandro Schiesaro. Cambridge University Press, 23–43.

―――1998. *The Politics of Latin Literature: Writings, Identity, and Empire in Ancient Rome*. Princeton University Press.

Habinek, Thomas and Alessandro Schiesaro. 1997. "Introduction." In *The Roman Cultural Revolution*. Edited by Habinek and Schiesaro. Cambridge University Press, xv–xxi.

Hadot, Ilsetraut. 1969. *Seneca und die griechisch-römische Tradition der Seelenleitung*. Berlin: Walter de Gruyter.

Hadot, Pierre. 1992. "Reflections on the notion of 'the cultivation of the self.'" In *Michel Foucault, Philosopher*. Edited by Francois Ewald. Translated by Timothy Armstrong. New York: Routledge, 225–31 (= Hadot 1995).

―――1995. *Philosophy as a Way of Life: Spiritual Exercises from Socrates to Foucault*. Edited by Arnold Davidson. Translated by Michael Chase. Oxford: Blackwell.

―――1998. *The Inner Citadel: The* Meditations *of Marcus Aurelius*. Translated by Michael Chase. Cambridge, MA: Harvard University Press.

Hahm, David. 1978. "Early Hellenistic Theories of Vision and the Perception of Color." In *Studies in Perception: Interrelations in the History of Philosophy and Science*. Edited by Peter Machamer and Robert Turnbull. Columbus: Ohio State University Press, 60–95.

Hallett, Judith, and Marilyn Skinner. Eds. 1997. *Roman Sexualities*. Princeton University Press.

Hamilton, John. 2013. *Security: Politics, Humanity, and the Philology of Care*. Princeton University Press.

Hammer, Dean. 2000. "Freedom and Fatefulness: Augustine, Arendt and the Journey of Memory." *Theory, Culture & Society* 17: 83–104.

―――2002a. "Hannah Arendt and Roman Political Thought: The Practice of Theory." *Political Theory* 30: 124–149. Reprinted in *Hannah Arendt: Critical Assessments of Leadings Philosophers*. Edited by Garrath Williams. London: Routledge, 2006.

―――2002b. *The* Iliad *as Politics: The Performance of Political Thought*. Norman: University of Oklahoma Press.

―――2004. "Ideology, the Symposium, and Archaic Greek Politics," *American Journal of Philology* 125: 479–512.

―――2006. "Bourdieu, Ideology, and the Ancient World." *American Journal of Semiotics* 22: 85–106.

———2008. *Roman Political Thought and the Modern Theoretical Imagination.* Norman: University of Oklahoma Press.

———2009. "What is Politics in the Ancient World?" In *Blackwell Companion to Greek and Roman Political Thought.* Edited by Ryan Balot. Oxford: Blackwell.

———2010. "Roman Spectacle Entertainment and the Technology of Reality," *Arethusa* 43: 63–86.

Hardie, Philip. 1986. *Virgil's* Aeneid*: Cosmos and Imperium.* Oxford: Clarendon.

———1992. "Augustan Poets and the Mutability of Rome." In *Roman Poetry and Propaganda in the Age of Augustus.* Edited by Anton Powell. Bristol: Bristol Classical Press, 59–82.

Harding, Brian. 2008. *Augustine and Roman Virtue.* London: Continuum.

Harris, H.A. 1968–69. "The Games in *Aeneid* V." *Proceedings of the Virgil Society* 8: 14–26.

Harrison, E.L. 1984. "The *Aeneid* and Carthage." In *Poetry and Politics in the Age of Augustus.* Edited by Tony Woodman and David West. Cambridge University Press, 95–115.

Harrison, S.J. 1990. "Some Views of the *Aeneid* in the Twentieth Century." In *Oxford Readings in Vergil's* Aeneid. Edited by S.J. Harrison. Oxford University Press, 1–20.

Häussler, Reinhard. 1965. *Tacitus und das historische Bewusstsein.* Heidelberg: Carl Winter Universitätsverlag.

Havel, Václav. 1991. *Open Letters: Selected Writings 1965–1990.* Edited by Paul Wilson. New York: Alfred A. Knopf.

Havas, László. 1991. "Éléments du biologisme dans la conception historique de Tacite." *ANRW*. Edited by Wolfgang Haase and Hildegard Temporini, Part 2: Principat vol. 33.4. Berlin: Walter de Gruyter, 2949–2986.

Haynes, Holly. 2003. *The History of Make-Believe: Tacitus on Imperial Rome.* Berkeley: University of California Press.

Heath, John. 1994. "The Failure of Orpheus." *TAPA* 124: 163–96.

Heilmann, Willibald. 1989. "'Goldene Zeit' und geschichtliche Zeit im Dialogus de oratoribus. Zur Geschichtsauffasung des Tacitus." *Gymnasium* 96: 385–405.

Heinze, Richard. 1903. *Virgils epische technik.* Leipzig: B.G. Teubner.

———1924. "Ciceros 'Staat' als politische Tendenzschrift." *Hermes* 59: 73–94.

———1925. "*Auctoritas.*" *Hermes* 60: 348–66.

Hemker, Julie. 1985. "Rape and the Founding of Rome." *Helios* n.s. 12: 41–47.

Henderson, John. 1990. "Tacitus/ The World in Pieces." In *The Imperial Muse: Flavian Epicists to Claudian*. Edited by A.J. Boyle. Bendigo: Aureal Publications, 167–210.

———2004. *Morals and Villas in Seneca's Letters: Places to Dwell*. Cambridge University Press.

Henry, Denis and B. Walker. 1963. "Tacitus and Seneca." *Greece & Rome*, 2nd series, 10: 98–110.

Herington, C.J. 1966. "Senecan Tragedy." *Arion* 5: 422–71.

Herrmann, Léon. 1956. "Catulle et Lucrèce." *Latomus* 15: 465–80.

Hine, Harry. 2006. "Rome, the Cosmos, and the Emperor in Seneca's *Natural Questions*." *Journal of Roman Studies* 96: 42–72.

Hock, Rudolph. 1988. "Servile Behavior in Sallust's *Bellum Catilinae*." *Classical World* 82: 13–24.

Hölkeskamp, Karl-Joachim. 1987. *Die Entstehung der Nobilität*. Stuttgart: Franz Steiner Verlag.

———1993. "Conquest, Competition and Consensus: Roman Expansion in Italy and the Rise of the *Nobilitas*." *Historia* 42: 12–39.

———1995. "*Oratoris maxima scaena*: Reden vor dem Volk in der politischen Kultur der Republik." In *Demokratie in Rom? Die Rolle des Volkes in der Politik der römischen Republik*. Edited by Martin Jehne. Stuttgart: Franz Steiner Verlag, 11–49.

———2000. "The Roman Republic: Government of the People, by the People, for the People?" *Scripta classica Israelica* 19: 203–23.

———2004. *Senatus Populusque Romanus: Die politische Kultur der Republik-Dimensionen und Deutungen*. Stuttgart: Franz Steiner Verlag.

———2010. *Reconstructing the Roman Republic: An Ancient Political Culture and Modern Research*. Translated by Henry Heitmann-Gordon. Princeton University Press.

Holton, James. 1963. "Marcus Tullius Cicero." In *History of Political Philosophy*. Edited by Leo Strauss and Joseph Cropsey. Chicago: Rand McNally and Co., 130–50.

Honoré, Tony. 1981. *Emperors and Lawyers*. London: Duckworth.
———1982. *Ulpian*. Oxford: Clarendon.
Hopkins, Keith. 1965. "Elite Mobility in the Roman Empire." *Past and Present* 32: 12–26.
Hopkins, Keith and Graham Burton. 1983. "Political succession in the late Republic (249–50 B.C.)." In Hopkins. *Death and Renewal*. Cambridge University Press, 31–119.
Horowitz, Maryanne Cline. 1998. *Seeds of Virtue and Knowledge*. Princeton University Press.
Horsfall, Nicholas. 1976. "Virgil, History and the Roman Tradition." *Prudentia* 8: 73–89.
———1990. "Virgil and the Conquest of Chaos." In *Oxford Readings in Vergil's Aeneid*. Edited by S.J. Harrison. Oxford University Press, 466–77.
———1991. "Virgil and the Poetry of Explanations." *Greece & Rome*, 2nd series. 38: 203–11.
———1996. "The Cultural Horizons of the *Plebs Romana*." *Memoirs of the American Academy in Rome* 41: 101–19.
How, W.W. 1930. "Cicero's Ideal in His *de Republica*." *Journal of Roman Studies* 20: 24–42.
Howes, J.R. 1972. "Cicero's Moral Philosophy in the *De Finibus*." In *Cicero and Virgil: Studies in Honour of Harold Hunt*. Edited by John Martyn. Amerserdam: Adolf M. Hakkert, 37–59.
Hubbard, Thomas. 1998. *The Pipes of Pan: Intertextuality and Literary Filiation in the Pastoral Tradition from Theocritus to Milton*. Ann Arbor: University of Michigan Press.
Hulliung, Mark. 1983. *Citizen Machiavelli*. Princeton University Press.
Humfress, Caroline. 2013. "Laws' Empire: Roman Universalism and Legal Practice." *New Frontiers: Law and Society in the Roman World*. Edited by Paul J. de Plessis. Edinburgh University Press, 73–101.
Humphrey, Nicholas. 2006. *Seeing Red: A Study in Consciousness*. Cambridge: Belknap Press.
Hunt, H.A.K. 1954. *The Humanism of Cicero*. Melbourne University Press.
Hutchinson, G.O. 2001. "The Date of *De Rerum Natura*." *Classical Quarterly* n.s. 51: 150–62.
Inwood, Brad. 1985. *Ethics and Human Action in Early Stoicism*. Oxford: Clarendon.

———1993. "Seneca and psychological dualism." In *Passions and Perceptions: Studies in Hellenistic Philosophy of Mind, Proceedings of the Fifth Symposium Hellenisticum*. Edited by Jacques Brunschwig and Martha Nussbaum. Cambridge University Press, 150–83.

———1995. "Seneca in His Philosophical Milieu." *Harvard Studies in Classical Philology* 97: 63–76.

———1999a. "Rules and Reasoning in Stoic Ethics." In *Topics in Stoic Philosophy*. Edited by Katerina Ierokiakonou. Oxford: Clarendon, 95–127.

———1999b. "Stoic Ethics." In *The Cambridge History of Hellenistic Philosophy*. Edited by Keimpe Algra, Jonathan Barnes, Jaap Mansfeld and Malcom Schofield. Cambridge University Press, 675–705.

———Ed. 2003. *The Cambridge Companion to the Stoics*. Cambridge University Press.

———2004. "Moral Judgment in Seneca." In *Stoicism: Traditions and Transformations*. Edited by Steven Strange and Jack Zupko. Cambridge University Press, 76–94.

———2005. *Reading Seneca: Stoic Philosophy at Rome*. Oxford University Press.

Irwin, T.H. 1998. "Stoic Inhumanity." In *The Emotions in Hellenistic Philosophy*. Edited by Juha Sihvola and Troels Engberg-Pedersen. Dordrecht: Kluwer, 219–241.

Jackson, Darrel. 1969. "The Theory of Signs in St. Augustine's *De doctrina christiana*." *Revue des Études Augustiniennes* 15: 9–49.

Jaeger, Mary. 1997. *Livy's Written Rome*. Ann Arbor: University of Michigan Press.

———1999. "Guiding Metaphor and Narrative Point of View in Livy's AB VRBE CONDITA." In *The Limits of Historiography: Genre and Narrative in Ancient Historical Texts*. Edited by Christina Kraus. Leiden: Brill, 169–95.

Jaeger, Werner. 1943. *Paideia: The Ideals of Greek Culture*. Translated by Gilbert Highet. Oxford University Press.

Jed, Stephanie. 1989. *Chaste Thinking: The Rape of Lucretia and the Birth of Modern Humanism*. Bloomington: Indiana University Press.

Jehne, Martin. Ed. 1995. *Demokratie in Rom?: Die Rolle des Volkes in der Politik der römischen Republik*. Stuttgart: Franz Steiner Verlag.

Jehne, Martin and Rene Pfeilschifter. Eds. 2007. *Herrschaft ohne Integration? Rom und Italien in republikanischer Zeit*. Frankfurt am Main: Verlag Antike.

Jenkyns, Richard. 1985. "Pathos, Tragedy, and Hope in the *Aeneid*." *Journal of Roman Studies* 75: 60–77.

———1989. "Virgil and Arcadia." *Journal of Roman Studies* 79: 26–39.

———1998. *Virgil's Experience: Nature and History; Times, Names, and Places*. Oxford University Press.

Jens, Walter. 1956. "*Libertas* bei Tacitus." *Hermes* 84: 331–52.

Johnson, W.R. 1965. "Aeneas and the Ironies of *Pietas*." *Classical Journal* 60: 360–64.

Johnson, W.R. 1976. *Darkness Visible: A Study of Vergil's* Aeneid. Berkeley: University of California Press.

Johnston, David. 1999. *Roman Law in Context*. Cambridge University Press.

Johnston, Patricia. 1980. *Vergil's Agricultural Golden Age: A Study of the Georgics*. Leiden: E.J. Brill.

Jones, A.H.M. 1951. "The *Imperium* of Augustus." *Journal of Roman Studies* 41: 112–19.

———1960a. "The Elections under Augustus." *Studies in Roman Government and Law*. Oxford: Basil Blackwell, 29–50.

———1960b. "I Appeal unto Caesar." *Studies in Roman Government and Law*. Oxford: Basil Blackwell, 51–65.

———1960c. "Imperial and Senatorial Jurisdiction in the Early Principate." *Studies in Roman Government and Law*. Oxford: Basil Blackwell, 69–98.

Jope, James. 1989. "The Didactic Unity and Emotional Import of Book 6 of *De Rerum Natura*." *Phoenix* 43: 16–34.

Joshel, Sandra. 1992. "The Body Female and the Body Politic: Livy's Lucretia and Verginia." *Pornography and Representation in Greece and Rome*. Edited by Amy Richlin. Oxford University Press, 112–30.

Jufresa, Montserrat. 1996. "Il tiempo e il sapiente Epicureo." In *Epicureismo greco e romano*. Vol. 1. Edited by Gabriele Giannantoni and Marcello Gigante. Napoli: Centro di studio del pensiero antico, 287–98.

Kajanto, Iiro. 1957. *God and Fate in Livy*. Turku: Turun Yliopiston Kustantama.

Kapust, Daniel. 2008. "On the Ancient Uses of Political Fear and its Modern Implications." *Journal of the History of Ideas* 69: 353–73.

———2011. *Republicanism, Rhetoric, and Roman Political Thought: Sallust, Livy, and Tacitus*. Cambridge University Press.

Kaster, Robert. 1997. "The Shame of the Romans." *TAPA* 127: 1–19.

———2005. *Emotion, Restraint, and Community in Ancient Rome.* Oxford University Press.

Keaveney, Arthur. 1982. *Sulla: The Last Republican.* London: Croom Helm.

———2007. *The Army in the Roman Revolution.* London: Routledge.

Keitel, Elizabeth. 1984. "Principate and Civil War in the *Annals* of Tacitus." *American Journal of Philology* 105: 306–325.

Keith, A.M. 2000. *Engendering Rome: Women in Latin Epic.* Cambridge University Press.

Kelly, Christopher. 1980. *Ruling the Later Roman Empire.* Cambridge, MA: Harvard University Press.

Kennedy, D.F. 1992. "'Augustan' and 'Anti-Augustan': Reflections on Terms of Reference." In *Roman Poetry and Propaganda in the Age of Augustus.* Edited by Anton Powell. Bristol: Bristol Classical Press, 26–58

Keohane, Nannerl. 1972. "Virtuous Republics and Glorious Monarchies: Two Models in Montesquieu's Political Thought." *Political Studies* 20: 383–96.

Keppie, L. 1996. "The Praetorian Guard Before Sejanus." *Athenaeum* 84: 101–24.

Kerferd, G.B. 1971. "Epicurus' doctrine of the soul." *Phronesis* 16: 80–96.

Kidd, I.G. 1971. "Posidonius on Emotions." *Problems in Stoicism.* Edited by A.A. Long. London: Athlone Press, 200–15.

———1978. "Moral Action and Rules in Stoic Ethics." In *The Stoics.* Edited by John Rist. Berkeley: University of California Press, 247–58.

Kidd, I.G. and L. Edelstein (on volume 1). Eds. 1972, 1988, 1999. *Posidonius.* 4 vols. Cambridge University Press.

Kienast, Dietmar. 1999. *Augustus: Prinzeps und Monarch*, 3rd edition. Darmstadt: Wissenschaftliche Buchgesellschaft.

Kinsbury, Benedict, and Benjamin Straumann. 2009. "Reflections on the Roman Foundations and Current Interpretations of the International Political and Legal Thought of Grotius, Hobbes, and Pufendorf." In *The Philosophy of International Law.* Edited by Samantha Besson and John Tasioulas. Oxford University Press, 33–51.

Kinsey, T.E. 1964. "The Melancholy of Lucretius." *Arion* 3: 115–30.

Kleve, Knut. 1986. "*Id facit exiguum clinamen.*" In *Probleme der Lukrezforschung.* Edited by Carl Joachim Classen. Hildesheim: Georg Olms Verlag, 125–29.

Klindienst Joplin, Patricia. 1990. "Ritual Work on Human Flesh: Livy's Lucretia and the Rape of the Body Politic." *Helios* 17: 51–70.

Klingner, Friedrich. 1955. "Beobachtungen über Sprache und Stil des Tacitus am Anfang des 13. Annalenbuches." *Hermes* 83: 187–200.

———1967. *Virgil:* Bucolica, Georgica, Aeneis. Zurich: Artemis Verlag.

———1986. "Philosophie und Dichtkunst am Ende des zweiten Buches des Lucrez." In *Probleme der Lukrezforschung.* Edited by Carl Joachim Classen. Hildesheim: Georg Olms Verlag, 383–412.

Knauer, Georg. 1964. "Vergil's *Aeneid* and Homer," *Greek, Roman, and Byzantine Studies.* 5: 61–84.

Knox, Peter. 1997. "Savagery in the *Aeneid* and Virgil's Ancient Commentators." *Classical Journal* 92: 225–33.

Koebner, R. 1951. "Despot and Despotism: Vicissitudes of a Political Term." *Journal of the Warburg and Courtauld Institutes* 14: 275–302.

Koestermann, Erich. 1963. *Cornelius Tacitus,* Annalen Band *1,* Buch *1–3.* Heidelberg: Carl Winter Universitätsverlag.

Kohns, Hans Peter. 1974. "*Consensus iuris – communio utilitatis.*" *Gymnasium* 81: 485–98.

———1976. "*Prima causa cocundi.*" *Gymnasium* 83: 209–14.

Kolbet, Paul. 2010. *Augustine and the Cure of Souls.* University of Notre Dame Press.

Konstan, David. 1986. "Narrative and Ideology in Livy: Book 1." *Classical Antiquity* 5: 198–216.

———1989. "What is New in the New Approaches to Classical Literature?" In *Classics: A Discipline and Profession in Crisis?* Edited by Phyllis Culham and Lowell Edmunds. New York: University Press of America, 45–49.

———1994. *Sexual Symmetry: Love in the Ancient Novel and Related Genres.* Princeton University Press.

———1996. "Friendship from Epicurus to Philodemus." In *Epicureismo o greco e romano.* Vol. 1. Edited by Gabriele Giannanton and Marcello Gigante. Napoli: Centro di studio del pensiero antico, 386–96.

———2008. *A Life Worthy of the Gods: The Materialist Psychology of Epicurus.* Las Vegas: Parmenides.

Kraus, Christina. 1994a. Livy. *Ab urbe condita.* Book VI. Cambridge University Press.

———1994b. "'No Second Troy': Topoi and Refoundation in Livy, Book V." *TAPA* 124: 267–89.

———1998. "Repetition and Empire in the AB VRBE CONDITA." In *Style and Tradition: Studies in Honor of Wendell Clausen.* Edited by Peter Knox and Clive Foss. Stuttgart: Teubner, 264-83.

———1999. "Jugurthine Disorder." In *The Limits of Historiography: Genre and Narrative in Ancient Historical Texts.* Edited by Kraus. Leiden: Brill, 217-47.

Kraus, Christina, and A.J. Woodman. 1997. *Latin Historians.* Oxford University Press.

Kries, Douglas. 2003. "On the Intention of Cicero's De Officiis." *Review of Politics* 65: 375-93.

Lacey, W.K. 1996. *Augustus and the Principate: The Evolution of the System.* Leeds: Francis Cairns.

Laidlaw, W.A. 1968. "Otium." *Greece & Rome*, 2nd series, 15: 42-52.

Laistner, M.L.W. 1947. *The Greater Roman Historians.* Berkeley: University of California Press.

Lau, Dieter, 1975. *Der lateinische Begriff Labor.* München: W. Fink.

Lana, Italo. 1989. "*Introspicere* in Tacito." *Orpheus* 10: 26-57.

Langan, John. 1979. "Augustine on the Unity and the Interconnection of the Virtues." *Harvard Theological Review* 76: 81-95.

Langslow, D.R. 2000. *Medical Latin in the Roman Empire.* Oxford University Press.

———1975. *Der lateinische Begriff Labor.* München: W. Fink.

Lavan, Myles. 2011. "Slavishness in Britain and Rome in Tacitus' *Agricola*." *Classical Quarterly* 61: 294-305.

Leach, Eleanor. 1993. "Absence and the Desire in Cicero's *De Amicitia*." *Classical World* 89: 3-20.

Lee, M. Owen. 1979. *Fathers and Sons in Virgil's* Aeneid: Tum Genitor Natum. Albany: State University of New York Press.

Lee-Stecum, Parshia. 2008. "Roman *refugium*: refugee narratives in Augustan versions of Roman pre-history." *Hermathena* 184: 69-91.

Leeman, A.D. 1951. "The Epistolary From of Sen. Ep. 102." *Mnemosyne* 4th series, 4: 175-81.

Lendon, J.E. 1997. *Empire of Honour: The Art of Government in the Roman World.* Oxford: Clarendon.

———2002. "Historical Thought in Ancient Rome." *A Companion to Western Historical Thought.* Edited by Lloyd Kramer and Sarah Maza. Oxford: Blackwell, 60-77.

―――――2009. "Historians without History: Against Roman Historiography." In *The Cambridge Companion to the Roman Historians*. Edited by Andrew Feldherr. Cambridge University Press, 41–61.

Levene, D.S. 1993. *Religion in Livy*. Leiden: E.J. Brill.

―――――1997. "Pity, Fear and the Historical Audience: Tacitus on the Fall of Vitellius." *The Passions in Roman Thought and Literature*. Edited by Susanna Morton Braund and Christopher Gill. Cambridge University Press, 128–49.

―――――2000. "Sallust's Catiline and Cato the Censor." *Classical Quarterly* 50: 170–91.

Levick, Barbara. 1967. "Imperial Control of the Elections under the Early Principate: *Commendatio, Suffragatio*, and '*Nominatio*'." *Historia* 16: 207–30.

―――――1976. *Tiberius the Politician*. London: Thames and Hudson.

―――――1982. "Morals, Politics, and the Fall of the Roman Republic." *Greece & Rome*, 2nd series, 29: 53–62.

―――――1985. "The Politics of the Early Principate." *Roman Political Life: 90 B.C.- A.D. 69*. Edited by T.P. Wiseman. Exeter: University of Exeter, 45–68.

Lieberg, G. 1994. "Das Methodenkapitel in Ciceros Staat (*Rep.* 2, 11, 21–22)." *Mnemosyne* 4th series. 47: 12–32.

Liebeschuetz, W. 1966. "The Theme of Liberty in the *Agricola* of Tacitus." *Classical Quarterly* 16: 126–139.

―――――1967. "The Religious Position of Livy's History." *Journal of Roman Studies* 57: 45–55.

Lind, J.R. 1986. "The Idea of the Republic and the Foundations of Roman Political Liberty." *Studies in Latin Literature and Roman History*. Vol. 4. Edited by Carl Deroux. Bruxelles: Revue D' Etudes Latines, 44–108.

Linderski, Jerzy. 1993. "Roman Religion in the Livy." *Livius: Aspekte seines Werkes*. Edited by Wolfgang Schuller. Konstanz: Universitätsverlag Konstanz, 53–70.

Lintott, Andrew. 1972. "Imperial Expansion and Moral Decline in the Roman Republic." *Historia* 21: 626–38.

―――――1993. *Imperium Romanum: Politics and administration*. London: Routledge.

―――――1997. "The Theory of the Mixed Constitution at Rome." In *Philosophia Togata I: Essays on Philosophy and Roman Society*. Edited by Miriam Griffin and Jonathan Barnes. Oxford: Clarendon, 70–85.

———1999. *The Constitution of the Roman Republic*. Oxford: Clarendon.
Littlewood, C.A.J. 2004. *Self-Representation and Illusion in Senecan Tragedy*. Oxford University Press.
Livy. 1998. *History of Rome*, translated by B.O. Foster. Cambridge, MA: Harvard University Press.
Lloyd, A.C. 1978. "Emotion and Decision in Stoic Psychology." In *The Stoics*. Edited by John Rist. Berkeley: University of California Press, 233–46.
Long, A.A. 1971. "*Aisthesis, Prolepsis* and Linguistic Theory in Epicurus." *Bulletin of the Institute of Classical Studies of London* 18: 114–33.
———1977. "Chance and Natural Law in Epicureanism." *Phronesis* 22: 63–88.
———1986. *Hellenistic Philosophy: Stoics, Epicureans, Sceptics*. 2nd ed. Berkeley: University of California Press.
———1995a. "Cicero's Plato and the Aristotle." *Cicero the Philosopher: Twelve Papers*. Edited by J.G.F. Powell. Oxford: Clarendon, 37–61.
———1995b. "Cicero's politics in *De officiis*." In *Justice and Generosity*. Edited by André Laks and Malcolm Schofield. Cambridge University Press, 213–40.
———1996. *Stoic Studies*. Berkeley: University of California Press.
Long, A.A. and D.N. Sedley. 1987. *The Hellenistic Philosophers*. 2 vols. Cambridge University Press.
Longrigg, James. 1963. "Philosophy and Medicine." *Harvard Studies in Classical Philology* 67: 147–75.
Lorca, Andrés Martínez. 1996. "Lucrecio: Una critica ilustrada a la religión popular." *Epicureismo greco e romano*. Vol. 2. Edited by Gabriele Giannantoni and Marcello Gigante. Napoli: Centro di studio del pensiero antico, 851–64.
Lowrie, Michèle. 2005. "Vergil and Founding Violence." *Cardozo Law Review* 27: 945–76.
———2007. "Sovereignty before the Law: Agamben and the Roman Republic." *Law and Humanities* 1: 31–55.
———2008. "Cicero on Caesar or *Exemplum* and Inability in the Brutus." In *Vom Selbst-Verstandnis in Antike und Neuzeit*. Edited by Alexander Arweiler and Melanie Möller. Berlin: Walter de Gruyter, 131–54.
———2009. "*Auctoritas* and Representation: Augustus' *Res gestae*." In *Writing, Performance, and Authority in Augustan Rome*. Edited by Lowrie. Oxford University Press, 279–308.

———2010a. "Rom immer wieder gegründet." In *Übertragene Anfänge: Imperiale Figurationen um 1800*. Edited by Tobias Döring, Barbara Vinken, and Günter Zöller. München: Wilhelm Fink, 23–49.

———2010b. "Spurius Maelius: Dictatorship and the Homo Sacer." In *Citizens of Discord: Rome and Its Civil Wars*. Edited by Brian Breed, Cynthia Damon, and Andreola Rossi. Oxford University Press, 171–85.

———2010c. "Vergil and Founding Violence." In *A Companion to Vergil's* Aeneid *and its Tradition*. Edited by Joseph Farrell and Michael Putnam. Oxford: Wiley-Blackwell, 391–417.

———2013. "Foundation and Closure." *The Door Ajar: False Closure in Classical Antiquity*. Edited by Farouk Grewing and Benjamin Acosta-Hughes. Heidelberg: Winter Verlag.

———forthcoming. "*Rege incolumi*: Orientalism and Security at *Georgics* 4.212."

Luce, T.J. 1965. "The Dating of Livy's First Decade." *TAPA* 96: 209–240.

———1971. "Design and the Structure in Livy: 5.32–55." *TAPA* 102: 265–302.

———1977. *Livy: The Composition of his History*. Princeton University Press.

———1986. Tacitus' Conception of Historical Change: The Problem of Discovering the Historian's Opinions." In *Past Perspectives: Studies in Greek and Roman Historical Writing*. Edited by I.S. Moxon, J.D. Smart, and A.J. Woodman. Cambridge University Press, 143–57.

Lucretius. 1975. *On the Nature of Things*. Translated by W.H.D. Rouse. Cambridge, MA: Harvard University Press.

Lyne, R.O.A.M. 1983. "Vergil and the Politics of War." *Classical Quarterly* 33: 188–203.

———1987. *Further Voices In Vergil's* Aeneid. Oxford: Clarendon.

MacCormack, Sabine. 1998. *The Shadows of Poetry: Vergil in the Mind of Augustine*. Berkeley: University of California Press.

MacDonald, William Lloyd. 1965. *The Architecture of the Roman Empire*. New Haven: Yale University Press.

Mackay, Christopher. 1963. "Hero and Theme in the *Aeneid*." *TAPA* 94: 157–66.

———2004. *Ancient Rome: A Military and Political History*. Cambridge University Press.

MacKay, L.A. 1962. "Sallust's *Catiline:* Date and Purpose." *Phoenix* 26: 181–94.

MacKendrick, Paul. 1989. *The Philosophical Books of Cicero.* New York: St. Martin's Press.

Macmullen, Ramsay. 1980. "How Many Romans Voted?" *Athenaeum* 58: 454–7.

———1988. *Corruption and the Decline of Rome.* New Haven: Yale University Press.

MacQueen, Bruce. 1981. *Plato's Republic in the Monographs of Sallust.* Chicago: Bolchazy Carducci Publishers.

Manent, Pierre. 1998. *The City of Man.* Translated by Marc LePain. Princeton University Press.

Manin, Bernard. 1987. "On Legitimacy and Political Deliberation." Translated by Elly Stein and Jane Mansbridge. *Political Theory* 15: 338–68.

Mansfield, Harvey. 1996. *Machiavelli's Virtue.* University of Chicago Press.

Manuwald, Bernd. 1980. *Der Aufbau der lukrezischen Kulturentstehungslehre.* Mainz: Franz Steiner.

Marcus Aurelius. 1916. *Meditations.* Translated by C.R. Haines. Cambridge, MA: Harvard University Press.

Markus, R.A. 1964. "Augustine." In *A Critical History of Western Philosophy.* Edited by D.J. O'Connor. Glencoe: Free Press, 79–97.

———1988. *Saeculum: History and Society in the Theology of St. Augustine.* 2nd ed. Cambridge University Press.

Marincola, John. 1997. *Authority and Tradition in Ancient Historiography.* Cambridge University Press.

Marković, Daniel. 2008. *The Rhetoric of Explanation in Lucretius'* De rerum natura. Leiden: Brill.

Marsh, Frank. 1926. "Tacitus and Aristocratic Tradition." *Classical Philology* 21: 289–310.

———1931. *The Reign of Tiberius.* Oxford University Press.

Marshall, A.J. 1975. "Tacitus and the Governor's Lady: A Note on *Annals* III.33–34." *Greece & Rome* 22: 11–18.

Marshall, Stephen. 2012. "Taking Liberty behind God's Back: Mastery as the Central Problem of Slavery." *Polity* 44: 155–81.

Martin, Ronald. 1981. *Tacitus.* Berkeley: University of California Press.

Martindale, Charles. 1993. *Redeeming the Text: Latin Poetry and the Hermeneutics of Reception*. Cambridge University Press.

Matthes, Melissa. 2000. *The Rape of Lucretia and the Founding of Republics*. University Park: Penn State University Press.

Maurach, Gregor. 1970. *Der Bau von Senecas Epistulae morales*. Heidelberg: Carl Winter Universitätsverlag.

Mayer, R.G. 1991. "Roman Historical *Exempla* in Seneca." *Sénèque et la prose latine: neuf exposés suivis de discussions*. Edited by Pierre Grimal. Vandoeuvres-Genève: Fondation Hardt, 141–76.

McClure, Kirstie. 1997. "The Odor of Judgment: Exemplarity, Propriety, and Politics in the Company of Hannah Arendt." In *Hannah Arendt and the Meaning of Politics*. Edited by Craig Calhoun and John McGowen. Minneapolis: University of Minnesota Press, 53–84.

McDonnell, Myles. 2006. *Roman Manliness: Virtus and the Roman Republic*. Cambridge University Press.

McGushin, Patrick. 1964. "Virgil and the Spirit of Endurance." *American Journal of Philology* 85: 225–53.

McLeish, Kenneth. 1972. "Dido, Aeneas, and the Concept of *Pietas*." *Greece &Rome*, 2nd series, 19: 127–53.

McNay, Lois. 1992. *Foucault and Feminism*. Boston: Northeastern University Press.

Meier, Christian. 1965. "*Populares*." *RE Suppl*. 10: 549–615.

———1980. *Res Publica Amissa: Eine Studie zu Verfassung und Geschichte der späten römischen republik*. 2nd Edition. Wiesbaden: Franz Steiner Verlag GMBH.

Mellor, Ronald. 1981. "The Goddess Roma." In *ANRW*. Edited by Wolfgang Haase and Hildegard Temporini. 2.17.2: 950–1030.

———1993. *Tacitus*. New York: Routledge.

Mendell, Clarence. 1970. *Tacitus: The Man and His Work*. Hamden: Archon Books.

Mette, Hans Joachim. 1961. "Livius und Augustus." *Gymnasium* 68: 269–85.

Meyer, Eduard. 1922. *Caesars Monarchie und das Principat des Pompeius*. Stuttgart: J.G. Cotta'sche Buchhandlung Nachfolger.

Milbank, John. 1990. *Theology and Social Theory: Beyond Secular Reason*. Oxford: Blackwell.

Miles, Gary. 1980. *Virgil's* Georgics: *A New Interpretation*. Berkeley: University of California Press.

———1986. "The Cycle of Roman History in Livy's First Pentad." *American Journal of Philology* 107: 1–33.

———1995. *Livy: Reconstructing Early Rome*. Ithaca: Cornell University Press.

Millar, Fergus. 1966. "The Emperor, the Senate, and the Provinces." *Journal of Roman Studies* 56, parts 1 & 2: 156–66.

———1973. "Triumvirate and Principate." *Journal of Roman Studies* 63: 50–67.

———1977. *The Emperor in the Roman World (31 B.C. – A.D. 337)*. London: Duckworth.

———1984. "The Political Character of the Classical Roman Republic, 200–151 B.C." *Journal of Roman Studies* 74: 1–19.

———1986. "Politics, Persuasion, and the People Before the Social War (150–90 B.C.)." *Journal of Roman Studies* 76: 1–11.

———1998. *The Crowd in Rome in the Late Republic*. Ann Arbor: University of Michigan Press.

———2002. *The Roman Republic in Political Thought*. Hanover: University Press of New England for Brandeis University Press.

Miller, N.P. 1964. "Dramatic Speech in Tacitus." *American Journal of Philology* 85: 279–96.

———1977. "Tacitus' Narrative Technique." *Greece & Rome* 24: 13–22.

Miller, Paul. 1998. "Catullan Consciousness, the 'Care of the Self,' and the Force of the Negative in History." In *Rethinking Sexuality: Foucault and Classical Antiquity*. Edited by David Larmour, Paul Miller, and Charles Platter. Princeton University Press, 171–203.

Minyard, J.D. 1985. *Lucretius and the Late Republic: An Essay in Roman Intellectual History*. Leiden: E.J. Brill.

Mitchell, Richard. 1986. "The Definition of *patres* and *plebs*: An End to the Struggle of the Orders." *Social Struggle in Archaic Rome: New Perspectives on the Conflict of the Orders*. Edited by Kurt Raaflaub. Berkeley: University of California Press, 130–174.

———1990. *Patricians and Plebeians: The Origin of the Roman State*. Ithaca: Cornell University Press.

Mitchell, T.N. 1984. "Cicero on the Moral Crisis of the Late Republic." *Hermathena* 136: 21–410.

Mitsis, Phillip. 1988. *Epicurus' Ethical Theory: The Pleasures of Invulnerability*. Ithaca: Cornell University Press.

———1993. "Seneca on Reason, Rules, and Moral Development." In *Passions and Perceptions: Studies in Hellenistic Philosophy of Mind, Proceedings of the Fifth Symposium Hellenisticum*. Edited by Jacques Brunschwig and Martha Nussbaum. Cambridge University Press, 285–312.

———1994."The Early Stoic Theory of Natural Law." in *Hellenistic Philosophy*. Vol. 2. Edited by K.J. Boudouris. Athens: International Center for Greek Philosophy and Culture, 130–40.

Moles, John. 1993. "Livy's Preface." *Proceedings of the Cambridge Philological Society* 39: 141–68.

Momigliano, Arnaldo. 1941. "Review: Benjamin Farrington, Science and Politics in the Ancient World." *Journal of Roman Studies* 31: 149–57.

———1942. "Camillus and Concord." *Classical Quarterly* 36: 111–120.

———1963. "Pagan and Christian Historiography in the Fourth Century A.D." In *The Conflict between Paganism and Christianity in the Fourth Century*. Edited by Momigliano. Oxford: Clarendon, 79–99.

———1969. "Seneca between Political and Contemplative Life." *Quarto contributo alla storia degli studi classici e del mondo antico*. Rome: Edizioni di Storia e Letteratura, 239–56.

———1986. "The Rise of the *plebs* in the Archaic Age of Rome." In *Social Struggles in Archaic Rome: New Perspectives on the Conflict of the Orders*. Edited by Kurt Raaflaub. Berkeley: University of California Press, 175–197.

———1989. "The Origins of Rome." *Cambridge Ancient History*. 2nd edition, vol. 7, pt. 2. Edited by F.W. Walbank, A.E. Astin, M.W. Frederiksen, and R.M. Ogilvie. Cambridge University Press, 52–112.

Mommsen, Theodor. 1869. *Römische Geschichte*. Berlin: Weidmannsche Buchhandlung.

———1887–8. *Römisches Staatsrech*. Leipzig: Verlag von S. Hirzel.

———1905. *Gesammelte Schriften*. Vol. 4 Berlin: Weidmannsche Buchhandlung.

———1996. *A History of Rome under the Emperors*. Edited by Barbara and Alexander Demandt, translated by Clare Krojzl. London: Routledge.

Monti, Richard. 1981. "Lucretius on Greed, Political Ambition and Society: de rer. nat. 3.59–86." *Latomus* 40: 48–66.

Moorton, Richard. 1989. "The Innocence of Italy in Vergil's *Aeneid*." *American Journal of Philology* 110: 105–30.

Morford, Mark. 2002. *The Roman Philosophers: From the Time of Cato the Censor to the Death of Marcus Aurelius*. London: Routledge.

Morgan, Llewelyn. 1999. *Patterns of Redemption in Virgil's* Georgics. Cambridge University Press.

Morgenthau, Hans. 1946. *Scientific Man Versus Power Politics*. University of Chicago Press.

———1948. *Politics among Nations*. New York: Alfred A. Knopf.

———1958. *Dilemmas of Politics*. Chicago: University of Chicago Press.

———1960. *The Purpose of American Politics*. New York: Alfred A. Knopf.

———1970. *Truth and Power*. New York: Praeger.

———2004. *Political Theory and International Affairs. Hans J. Morgenthau on Aristotle's* The Politics. Edited by Anthony Lang, Jr. London: Praeger.

Morgenthau, Hans and Kenneth Thompson. 2001. *Politics among Nations*. 6th ed. New Delhi: Kalyani.

Morley, Neville. 2007. "Civil War and Succession Crisis in Roman Beekeeping." *Historia* 56: 462–70.

Morstein-Marx, Robert. 1995. *Hegemony to Empire: The Development of the Roman Imperium in the East from 148 to 62 B.C*. Berkeley: University of California Press.

———2004. *Mass Oratory and Political Power in the Late Roman Republic*. Cambridge University Press.

———forthcoming. "Persuading the People in the Roman Participatory Context." In *A Companion to Greek Democracy and the Roman Republic*. Edited by Dean Hammer. Oxford and Malden, MA: Wiley-Blackwell.

Morstein-Marx, Robert, and Nathan Rosenstein. 2006. "The Transformation of the Republic." In *A Companion to the Roman Republic*. Edited by Morstein-Marx and Rosenstein. Oxford and Malden, MA: Wiley-Blackwell, 625–37.

Most, Glenn. 2001. "Memory and Forgetting in the *Aeneid*." *Vergilius* 47: 148–70.

Motto, Anna Lydia and John Clark. 1993. *Essays on Seneca*. New York: Peter Lang.

Mouritsen, Henrik. 1998. *Italian Unification: A Study in Ancient and Modern Historiography*. London: University of London Institute of Classical Studies.
———2001. *Plebs and Politics in the Late Roman Republic*. Cambridge University Press.
———forthcoming. "The Incongruence of Power: The Roman Constitution in Theory and Practice." In *A Companion to Greek Democracy and the Roman Republic*. Edited by Dean Hammer. Oxford and Malden, MA: Wiley- Blackwell.
Mousourakis, George. 2007. *A Legal History of Rome*. London: Routledge.
Müller, Gerhard. 1977. "Die Finalia der sechs Bücher des Lucrez." In *Lucrèce*. Genève: Fondation Hardt, 197–231.
Müller, Wolfgang. 1980. "Der Brief als Spiegel der Seele." *Antike und Abendland* 26: 138–57.
Münzer, Friedrich. 1920. *Römische Adelsparteien und Adelsfamilien*. Stuttgart: J.B. Metzlersche Verlagsbuchhandlung.
Murley, Clyde. 1947. "Lucretius, *De Rerum Natura*, Viewed as Epic." *TAPA* 78: 336–46.
Murray, Gilbert. 1945. "The Future of Greek Studies." *Journal of Hellenic Studies* 65: 1–9.
Nappa, Christopher. 2005. *Reading after Actium: Vergil's* Georgics, *Octavian, and Rome*. Ann Arbor: University of Michigan Press.
Narducci, Emanuele. 1997. "Perceptions of Exile in Cicero: The Philosophical Interpretation of a Real Experience." *American Journal of Philology* 118: 55–73.
Nederman, Cary. 1988. "Nature, Sin and the Origins of Society: The Ciceronian Tradition in Medieval Political Thought." *Journal of the History of Ideas* 49: 3–26.
———1993. "Humanism and Empire: Aeneas Sylvius Piccolomini, Cicero and the Imperial Ideal." *Historical Journal* 36: 499–515.
———2000a. "Machiavelli and Moral Character: Principality, Republic and the Psychology of *Virtù*." *History of Political Thought* 21: 349–64.
———2000b. "Rhetoric, Reason, and Republic: Republicanisms – Ancient, Medieval, and Modern." In *Renaissance Civic Humanism: Reappraisals and Reflections*. Edited by James Hankins. Cambridge University Press, 247–69.

---. 2000c. "War, Peace, and Republican Virtue: Patriotism and the Neglected Legacy of Cicero." In *Instilling Ethics*. Edited by Norma Thompson. Lanham: Rowman and Littlefield, 17–29.

Nethercut, William. 1971–1972. "The Imagery of the *Aeneid*." *Classical Journal* 67: 123–43.

Nicgorski, Walter. 1984. "Cicero's Paradoxes and His Idea of Utility." *Political Theory* 12: 557–78.

---. 1991. "Cicero's Focus: From the Best Regime to the Model Statesman." *Political Theory* 19: 230–51.

Nicholas, Barry. 1962. *An Introduction to Roman Law*. Oxford: Clarendon.

Nichols, James. 1976. *Epicurean Political Philosophy: The* De Rerum Natura *of Lucretius*. Ithaca: Cornell University Press.

Nicolet, Claude. 1980. *The World of the Citizen in Republican Rome*. Translated by P.S. Falla. Berkeley: University of California Press.

---. 1983. "Polybe et la 'constitution' de Rome: aristocratie et démocratie." In *Demokratia et aristokratia: A propos de Caius Gracchus: mots grecs et réalités romaines*. Paris: Publications de la Sorbonne, 15–35.

---. 1984. "Augustus, Government, and the Propertied Classes." In *Caesar Augustus: Seven Aspects*. Edited by Fergus Millar and Erich Segal. Oxford: Clarendon, 89–128.

---. 1993. "The Citizen: The Political Man." *The Romans*. Edited by Andrea Giardina. Translated by Lydia Cochrane. University of Chicago Press, 16–54.

Niebuhr, Reinhold. 1953. *Christian Realism and Political Problems*. New York: Charles Scribner's Sons.

Nippel, Wilfried. 1980. *Mischverfassungstheorie und Verfassungsrealität in Antike und Früher Neuzeit*. Stuttgart: Klett-Cotta.

---. 1995. *Public Order in Ancient Rome*. Cambridge University Press.

North, J.A. 1990a. "Democratic Politics in Republican Rome." *Past and Present* 126: 3–21.

---. 1990b. "Politics and Aristocracy in the Roman Republic." *Classical Philology* 85: 277–87.

Nugent, S. Georgia. 1994. "*Mater* Matters: The Female in 'Lucretius' *De Rerum Natura*." *Colby Quarterly*. 30:179–205.

Nussbaum, Martha. 1989. "Mortal Immortals: Lucretius on Death and the Voice of Nature." *Philosophy and Phenomenological Research* 50: 303–51.

———1994. *The Therapy of Desire: Theory and Practice in Hellenistic Ethics*. Princeton University Press.

———1996. "Patriotism and Cosmopolitanism." In *For Love of Country*. Edited by Joshua Cohen. Boston: Beacon, 2–17.

———1997. "Kant and Stoic Cosmopolitanism." *Journal of Political Philosophy* 5: 1–25.

———2000. "Duties of Justice, Duties of Material Aid: Cicero's Problematic Legacy." *Journal of Political Philosophy* 2: 176–206.

Nussbaum, Martha, and Juha Sihvola. Eds. 2002. *The Sleep of Reason: Erotic Experience and Sexual Ethics in Ancient Greece and Rome*. University of Chicago Press.

Oakeshott, Michael. 1975. *On Human Conduct*. Oxford University Press.

Oakley, S.P. 1997. *A Commentary on Livy, Books VI–X: Volume 1: Introduction and Book 6*. Oxford University Press.

Obbink, Dirk. 1996. "Epicurus on the Origin of Poetry in Human History." In *Epicureismo greco e romano*. Vol. 2. Edited by Gabriele Giannanton and Marcello Gigante. Napoli: Centro di studio del pensiero antico, 683–700.

Obbink, Dirk. 1999. "The Stoic Sage in the Cosmic City." In *Topics in Stoic Philosophy*. Edited by Katerina Ierodiakonon. Oxford: Clarendon, 178–95.

———2002. "'All Gods are True' in Epicurus." In *Traditions of Theology: Studies in Hellenistic Theology, Its Background and Aftermath*. Edited by Dorothea Frede and André Laks. Leiden: Brill, 183–221.

O'Connell, Robert. 1968. *St. Augustine's Early Theory of Man, A.D. 386–391*. Cambridge: Belknap.

O'Donovan, Oliver. 1980. *The Problem of Self-Love in St. Augustine*. New Haven: Yale University Press.

Ogilvie, R.M. 1965. *A Commentary on Livy: Books 1–5*. Oxford: Clarendon.

O'Gorman, Ellen. 1993. "No Place like Rome: Identity and Difference in the *Germania* of Tacitus." *Ramus* 22: 135–54.

———2000. *Irony and Misreading in the* Annals *of Tacitus*. Cambridge University Press.

Oliver, James. 1968. *The Civilizing Power: A Study of the Panathenaic Discourse of Aelius Aristides Against the Background of Literature and Cultural Conflict*. Philadelphia: American Philosophical Society.

———1981. "Marcus Aurelius and the Philosophical Schools at Athens." *American Journal of Philology* 102: 213–25.

Otis, Brooks. 1963. *Virgil: A Study in Civilized Poetry.* Oxford: Clarnedon.

Outka, Gene. 1972. *Agape: An Ethical Analysis.* New Haven: Yale University Press.

Pagels. Elaine. 1989. *Adam, Eve, and the Serpent.* New York: Vintage.

Pangle, Thomas. 1998. "Socratic Cosmopolitanism: Cicero's Critique and Transformation of the Stoic Ideal." *Canadian Journal of Political Science* 31: 235–62.

Pantzerhielm Thomas, S. 1936. "The Prologues of Sallust." *Symbolae osloenses* 15–16: 140–62.

Parker, Victor. 2004. "*Romae omnia venalia esse.* Sallust's Development of a Thesis and the Prehistory of the Jugurthine War." *Historia* 53: 408–23.

Parry, Adam. 1963. "The Two Voices of Virgil's *Aeneid.*" *Arion* 2: 66–80.

———1972. "The Idea of Art in Vergil's *Georgics.*" *Arethusa* 5: 35–52.

Paterson, Jeremy. 1985. "Politics in the Late Republic." In *Roman Political Life: 90 BC-AD 69.* Edited by T.P. Wiseman. Exeter: University of Exeter, 21–43.

Patin, Henri. 1868. "Du poëme *De La Nature*: L'Antilucrèce chez Lucrèce." *Études sur la poésie latine* 1: 117–37.

Paul, G.M. 1966. "Sallust." In *Latin Historians.* Edited by T.A. Dorey. New York: Basic books.

———1984. *A Historical Commentary on Sallust's* Bellum Jugurthinum. Liverpool: Francis Cairns.

Pauw, Dirk. 1991. "The Dramatic Elements in Livy's History." *Acta Classica* 34: 33–49.

Pavlock, Barbara. 1985. "Epic and Tragedy in Vergil's Nisus and Euryalus Episode." *TAPA* 115: 207–24.

Peirce, Charles. 1960. "Some Consequences of Four Incapacities." *Collected Papers of Charles Andrew Peirce.* Edited by Charles Hartshorne and Paul Weiss. Vol. 5. Cambridge: Belknap, 156–189.

Pelling, Christopher. 1993. "Tacitus and Germanicus." In *Tacitus and the Tacitean Tradition.* Edited by T.J. Luce and A.J. Woodman. Princeton University Press, 59–85.

Pembroke, S.G. 1971. "*Oikeiōsis.*" In *Problems in Stoicism.* Edited by A.A. Long. London: Athlone Press, 114–49.

Penella, Robert. 1990. "*Vires/ Robur/ Opes* and *Ferocia* in Livy's Account of Romulus and Tullus Hostilius." *Classical Quarterly* 40: 207–13.

Penwill, J.L. 1994. "Image, Ideology, and Action in Cicero and Lucretius." *Ramus* 23: 68–91.

Perkell, Christine. 1978. "A Reading of Virgil's Fourth *Georgic*." *Phoenix* 32: 211–21.

———1989. *The Poet's Truth: A Study of the Poet in Virgil's* Georgics. Berkeley: University of California Press.

———2001. "Vergil Reading His Twentieth-Century Readers A Study of *Eclogue* 9." *Vergilius* 47: 64–88.

———2002. "The Golden Age and Its Contradictions in the Poetry of Vergil." *Vergilius* 48: 3–39.

Peters, Ted. 1993. *God as Trinity: Relationality and Temporality in Divine Life*. Lousville: Westminster Press.

Petersen, Hans. 1961. "Livy and Augustus." *TAPA* 92: 440–52.

Pettit, Philip. 1993. "Negative Liberty, Liberal and Republican." *European Journal of Philosophy* 1: 15–38.

———1996. "Freedom as Antipower." *Ethics* 106: 576–604.

———1997. *Republicanism: A Theory of Freedom and Government*. Oxford University Press.

———2002. "Keeping Republican Freedom Simple: On a Difference with Quentin Skinner." *Political Theory* 30: 339–56.

Philippson, Robert. 1910. "Die Rechtsphilosophie der Epikureer." *Archiv für Geschichte der Philosophie* 23: 284–446.

Pina Polo, Francisco. 1996. *Contra Arma Verbis: Der Redner Vor Dem Volk in der Späten Römischen Republik*. Stuttgart: Franz Steiner Verlag.

Pippidi, D.M. 1944. *Autur de Tibère*. Bucaresti: Institutal di Istorie universala "N. Iorga."

Pitkin, Hanna. 1988. "Are Freedom and Liberty Twins?" *Political Theory* 16: 523–52.

Pittenger, Miriam. 2008. *Contested Triumphs: Politics, Pageantry, and Performance in Livy's Republican Rome*. Berkeley: University of California Press.

Plasberg, Otto. 1926. *Cicero in seinen Werken und Briefen*. Leipzig: Dieterich'sche Verlagsbuchhandlung.

Plass, Paul. 1995. *The Game of Death in Ancient Rome: Arena Sport and Political Suicide*. Madison: University of Wisconsin Press.

Platter, Charles. 1995. "*Officium* in Catullus and Propertius: A Foucauldian Reading." *Classical Philology* 90: 211–24.

Pocock, J.G.A. 1972. "Languages and their Implications: The Transformation of the Study of Political Thought." In *Politics, Language, and Time*. Edited by Pocock. London: Methuen.

———1975. *The Machiavellian Moment: Florentine Political Thought and the Atlantic Republican Tradition*. Princeton University Press.

———1985. "State of the Art." In *Virtue, Commerce, and History*. Edited by Pocock. Cambridge University Press.

Pohlenz, Max. 1948–49. *Die Stoa: Geschichte einer geistigen Bewegung*. 2 vols. Göttingen: Vandenhoeck and Ruprecht.

Pöschl, Viktor. 1936. *Römischer staat und griechisches staatsdenken bei Cicero*. Darmstadt: Wissenschaftliche Buchgesellschaft, reprinted 1983.

———1940. *Grundwerte römischer Staatsgesinnung in den Geschichtswerken des Sallust*. Berlin: Walter de Bruyter.

———1961. "The Poetic Achievement of Virgil." *Classical Journal* 56: 290–99.

———1962. *The Art of Vergil: Image and Symbol in the* Aeneid. Translated by Gerda Seligson. Ann Arbor: University of Michigan Press.

Posidonius. 1972, 1988, 1999. Edited by I.G. Kidd and L. Edelstein (on vol. 1). 4 vols. Cambridge University Press.

Posner, Eric. 2010. "The Constitution of the Roman Republic: A Political Economy Perspective." John M. Olin Program in Law and Economic Working Paper. Website: http://www.law.uchicago.edu/files/file/540-327-eap-rome.pdf.

Potter, David. 1996. "Performance, Power and Justice in the High Empire." *Roman Theater and Society: E. Togo Salmon Paper I*. Edited by William Slater. Ann Arbor: University of Michigan Press, 129–59.

———1999. "Political Theory in the *Senatus Consultum Pisonianum*." *American Journal of Philology* 120: 65–88.

Powell, Anton. 1992. "The *Aeneid* and the Embarrassments of Augustus." In *Roman Poetry and Propoganda in the Age of Augustus*. Bristol: Bristol Classical Press, 141–74.

Powell, J.G.F. 1995. "Introduction: Cicero's Philosophical Works and their Background." In *Cicero the Philosopher: Twelve Papers*. Edited by J.G.F. Powell. Oxford: Clarendon, 1–35.

———2001. "Were Cicero's Laws the Laws of Cicero's *Republic*?" In *Cicero's Republic*. Edited by Powell and J.A. North. London: Institute of Classical Studies, 17–39.

Puliga, Donatella. 1983. "Χρονοσ ε θανατοσ ιν Επιψυρο." *Elenchos* 4: 235–60.

Purcell, Nicholas. 1995. "On the Sacking of Carthage and Corinth." In *Ethics and Rhetoric: Classical Essays for Donald Russell on his Seventy-Fifth Birthday*. Edited by Doreen Innes, Harry Hine, and Christopher Pelling. Oxford: Clarendon, 133–48.

Putnam, Michael. 1970. *Virgil's Pastoral Art: Studies in the* Eclogues. Princeton University Press.

———1979. *Virgil's Poem of the Earth: Studies in the* Georgics. Princeton University Press.

———1995. *Virgil's* Aeneid: *Interpretation and Influence*. Chapel Hill: University of North Carolina Press.

———2001. "The Ambiguity of Art in Virgil's *Aeneid*." *Proceedings of the American Philosophical Society* 145: 162–83.

———2011. *The Humanness of Heroes: Studies in the Conclusion of Virgil's* Aeneid. Amsterdam University Press.

Quinn, Kenneth. 1968. *Virgil's Aeneid: A Critical Description*. London: Routledge.

Quint, David. 1993. *Epic and Empire: Politics and Generic Form From Virgil to Milton*. Princeton University Press.

Raaflaub, Kurt. 1974. *Dignitatis Contentio*. München: C.H. Beck'sche Verlagsbuchhandlung.

———1986a. "The Conflict of the Orders in Archaic Rome: A Comprehensive and Comparative Approach." In *Social Struggles in Archaic Rome: New Perspective on the Conflict of the Orders*. Edited by Raaflaub. Berkeley: University of California Press, 1–57.

———1986b. "From Protection and Defense to Offense and Participation: Stages in the Conflict of the Orders." In *Social Struggles in Archaic Rome: New Perspective on the Conflict of the Orders*. Edited by Kurt Raaflaub. Berkeley: University of California Press, 198–243.

———1987. "Grundzüge, Ziele und Ideen der Opposition gegen die Kaiser IM 1. JH.N. CHR: Versuch einer Standortbestimmung." In *Opposition et resistances a l'Empire d'Auguste a Trajan*. Edited by Giovanni Adalberto and Denis van Berchem. Vandoeuvres-Genève: Fondation Hardt, 1–63.

———1993. "Politics and Society in Fifth-Century Rome." *Bilancio Critico su Roma arcaica fra monarchia e repubblica, in memoria di Ferdinando Castagnoli*. Edited by M.A. Levi. Rome: Accademia Nazionale dei Lincei, 129–57.

———2004. *The Discovery of Freedom in Ancient Greece*. Translated by Renate Franciscono. University of Chicago Press.

———2010. "Poker um Macht und Freiheit: Caesars Bürgerkrieg als Wendepunkt im Übergang von der Republik zur Monarchie." In *Zwischen Monarchie und Republik: Gesellschaftliche Stabilisierungsleistungen und politische Transformationspotentiale in den antiken Stadtstaaten*. Edited by Bernhard Linke, Mischa Meier, and Meret Strothmann. Stuttgart: Franz Steiner Verlag, 163–86.

———forthcoming. "Why Greek Democracy? Its Emergence and Nature in Context." In *A Companion to Greek Democracy and the Roman Republic*. Edited by Dean Hammer. Oxford and Malden, MA: Wiley- Blackwell.

Raaflaub, Kurt, and L.J. Samons II. 1990. "Opposition to Augustus." *Between Republic and Empire: Interpretations of Augustus and His Principate*. Edited by Kurt Raaflaub and Mark Toher. Berkeley: University of California Press, 417–454.

Rabel, Robert. 1981. "Diseases of Soul in Stoic Psychology." *Greek, Roman, and Byzantine Studies* 22: 385–93.

Radford, Robert. 2002. *Cicero: A Study in the Origins of Republican Philosophy*. Amsterdam: Rodopi.

Rahe, Paul. 2000. "Situating Machiavelli." In *Renaissance Civic Humanism: Reappraisals and Reflections*. Edited by James Hankins. Cambridge University Press, 270–308.

Rainer, J. Michael. 1997. *Einführung in das römische Staatsrecht*. Darmstadt: Wissenschaftliche Buchgesellschaft.

Rawson, Elizabeth. 1972. "Cicero the Historian and Cicero the Antiquarian." *Journal of Roman Studies* 62: 33–45.

———1975. *Cicero: A Portrait*. Ithaca: Cornell University Press.

———1976. "The Ciceronian Aristocracy and is Properties." In *Studies in Roman Property*. Edited by M.I. Finley. Cambridge University Press, 85–102.

———1985. *Intellectual Life in the Late Roman Republic*. Baltimore: Johns Hopkins University Press.

———1987. "*Discrimina Ordinum*: The *Lex Julia Theatralis*." Papers of the British School at Rome 55: 83–114.

———2005. "Seneca and Pliny." In *The Cambridge History of Greek and Roman Political Thought*. Edited by Christopher Rowe and Malcolm Schofield. Cambridge University Press, 532–58.

Reed, J.D. 2007. *Virgil's Gaze: Nation and Poetry in the* Aeneid. Princeton University Press.

———2010. "Vergil's Roman." In *A Companion to Vergil's* Aeneid *and its Tradition*. Edited by Joseph Farrell and Michael Putnam. Oxford and Malden, MA: Wiley-Blackwell, 66–79.

Reitzenstein, Richard. 1917. *Die Idee des Principats bei Cicero und Augustus*. Nachrichten von der königlichen Gesellschaft der Wissenshaften zu Göttingen, phil.-hist. Klasse, 339–436.

———1924. "Zu Cicero *de re publica*." *Hermes* 59: 356–62.

Remer, Gary. 1999. "Political Oratory and Conversation: Cicero versus Deliberative Democracy." *Political Theory* 27: 39–64.

———2004. "Cicero and the Ethics of Deliberative Rhetoric." In *Talking Democracy: Historical Perspectives on Rhetoric and Democracy*. Edited by Benedetto Fontana, Cary Nederman, and Gary Remer. University Park: Penn State University Press, 135–61.

Reydams-Schils, Gretchen. 2005. *The Roman Stoics: Self, Responsibility, and Affection*. University of Chicago Press.

Richard, J. C. 1986. "Patricians and Plebeians: The Origin of a Social Dichotomy." In *Social Struggles in Archaic Rome: New Perspectives on the Conflict of the Orders*. Edited by Kurt Raaflaub. Berkeley: University of California Press, 105–129.

Richardson, J.S. 1991. "*Imperium Romanum*: Empire and the Language of Power." *Journal of Roman Studies* 81: 1–9.

Ricoeur, Paul. 1984. *Time and Narrative*. Vol. 1. Trans. by Kathleen McLaughlin and David Pellauer. University of Chicago Press.

Rist, John. 1969. *Stoic Philosophy*. Cambridge University Press.

———1978. "The Stoic Concept of Detachment." In *The Stoics*. Edited by John Rist. Berkeley: University of California Press, 259–72.

———1994. *Augustine: Ancient Thought Baptized*. Cambridge University Press.

Rives, J.B. 1999. Tacitus. *Germania*. Oxford: Clarendon.

Roccatagliata, Giuseppe. 1986. *A History of Ancient Psychiatry*. New York: Greenwood Press.

Rogers, Robert. 1943. *Studies in the Reign of Tiberius: Some Imperial Virtues of Tiberius and Drusus Julius Caesar*. Westport: Greenwood Press.

———1952. "A Tacitean Pattern in Narrating Treason-Trials." *TAPA* 83: 279–311.

Roller, Matthew. 2001. *Constructing Autocracy: Aristocrats and Emperors in Julio-Claudian Rome*. Princeton University Press.

———2009. "The exemplary past in Roman historiography and culture." In *The Cambridge Companion to the Roman Historians*. Edited by Andrew Feldherr. Cambridge University Press, 214–30.

———2010. "Demolished Houses, Monumentality, and Memory in Roman Culture." *Classical Antiquity* 29: 117–80.

Rose, Peter. 1995. "Cicero and the Rhetoric of Imperialism: Putting the Politics Back into Political Rhetoric." *Rhetorica* 13: 359–99.

Roselaar, Saskia. 2012. *Processes of Integration and Identity Formation in the Roman Republic*. Leiden: Brill.

Rosivach, V.J. 1980. "Latinus' Genealogy and the Palace of Picus (*Aeneid* 7.45–9, 170–91)." *Classical Quarterly n.s.* 30: 140–52.

Ross, David. 1987. *Virgil's Elements: Physics and Poetry in the* Georgics. Princeton University Press.

———1998. "Images of Fallen Troy in the *Aeneid*." In *Style and Tradition: Studies in Honor of Wendell Clausen*. Edited by Peter Knox and Clive Foss. Stuttgart: Teubner, 121–29.

Ross, Jr., D.O. 1973. "The Tacitean Germanicus." *Yale Classical Studies* 23: 209–27.

Rossbach, Otto. 1882. "De Senecae Dialogis." *Hermes* 17: 365–76.

Rowe, Greg. 2002. *Princes and Political Cultures: The New Tiberian Senatorial Decrees*. Ann Arbor: University of Michigan Press.

Rudich, Vasily. 1993. *Political Dissidence under Nero: The Price of Dissimulation*. London: Routledge.

———2006. "Navigating the Uncertain: Literature and Censorship in the Early Roman Empire." *Arion* 3rd series. 14: 7–28.

Rutherford, R.B. 1989. *The Meditations of Marcus Aurelius: A Study*. Oxford: Clarendon.

Rutledge, Steven. 2001 *Imperial Inquisitions: Prosecutors and Informants from Tiberius to Domitian*. New York: Routledge.

Ryberg, Inez. 1958. "Vergil's Golden Age." *TAPA* 89: 112–31.

Sabine, George. 1937. *A History of Political Theory*. New York: Henry Holt and Co.

Sabine, George, and Stanley Smith. 1976 (orig. 1929). "Introduction." *On the Commonwealth*. Indianapolis: Bobbs-Merrill Co., 1–102.

Saller, Richard. 1984. "*Familia, Domus*, and the Roman Conception of the Family." *Phoenix* 38: 336–55.

Sallust. 1921. *The War with Catiline and The War with Jugurtha*. Translated by J.C. Rolfe. Cambridge University Press.

———1992. *The Histories*. 2 vols. Translated and commentary by Patrick McGushin. Oxford: Clarendon.

Sandbach, F.H. 1930. "ΕΝΝΟΙΑ and ΠΡΟΛΕΨΙΣ in the Stoic Theory of Knowledge." *Classical Quarterly* 24: 44–51

———1940. "*Lucreti Poemata* and the Poet's Death." *Classical Review* 54: 72–77.

———1971. "Phantasia Kataleptikē." In *Problems in Stoicism*. Edited by A.A. Long. London: Athlone Press, 9–21.

———1975. *The Stoics*. New York: W.W. Norton and Company.

Sandel, Michael. 1996. *Democracy's Disconnect: America in Search of a Public Philosophy*. Cambridge University Press.

Saxonhouse, Arlene. 1975. "Tacitus' *Dialogue on Oratory*: Political Activity under a Tyrant." *Political Theory* 3: 53–68.

Scanlon, Thomas. 1980. *The Influence of Thucydides on Sallust*. Heidelberg: Carl Winter Universitätsverlag.

———1998. "Reflexivity and Irony in the Proem of Sallust's *Historiae*." In *Studies in Latin Literature and Roman History*. Vol. 9. Edited by Carl Deroux. Bruxelles: Latomus, 186–224.

Schall, James. 1984. "St. Augustine and Christian Political Philosophy." In *The Politics of Heaven and Hell: Christian Themes from Classical, Medieval, and Modern Political Philosophy*. Lanham, MD.: University Press of America, 39–66.

Schellhase, Kenneth. 1976. *Tacitus in Renaissance Political Thought*. University of Chicago Press.

Schiavone, Aldo. 1977. "Classi e politica in una società precapitalistica: il caso della Roa repubblicana." *Quaderni di storia* 9: 33–69.

———2012 (orig. 2005). *The Invention of Law in the West*. Translated by Jeremy Carden and Antony Shugaar. Cambridge, MA: Harvard University Press,

Schiesaro, Alessandro. 1997. "The boundaries of knowledge in Virgil's *Georgics*." In *The Roman Cultural Revolution*. Edited by Thomas Habinek and Schiesaro. Cambridge University Press, 63–89.

———2007a. "Didaxis, Rhetoric, and the Law in Lucretius." In *Classical Constructions*. Edited by S.J. Heyworth with P.G. Fowler and S.J. Harrison. Oxford University Press, 63–90.

———2007b. "Lucretius and Roman politics and history." In *The Cambridge Companion to Lucretius*. Edited by Stuart Gillespie and Philip Hardie. Cambridge University Press, 41–58.

Schindel, Ulrich. 1983. "Livius philosophus?" In *Livius: Werk und Rezeption. Festschrift für Erich Burck zum 80. Geburtstag*. Edited by Eckard Lefèvre and Eckart Olshausen. München: C.H. Beck, 411–419.

Schlabach, Gerald. 1994. "Augustine's Hermeneutic of Humility: An Alternative to Moral Imperialism and Moral Relativism." *Journal of Religious Ethics* 22: 299–330.

Schmal, Stephen. 2001. *Sallust*. Hildesheim: Georg Olms Verlag.

Schmidt, P.L. 1978–79. "Cicero's Place in Roman Philosophy: A Study of His Prefaces." *Classical Journal* 74: 115–27.

Schofield, Malcolm. 1991. *The Stoic Idea of the City*. Cambridge University Press.

———1995a. "Cicero's Definition of *Res Publica*." In *Cicero the Philosopher: Twelve Papers*. Edited by J.G.F. Powell. Oxford: Clarendon, 63–83.

———1995b. "Two Stoic approaches to justice." In *Justice and Generosity*. Edited by André Laks and Malcolm Schofield. Cambridge University Press, 191–212.

———1999. *Saving the City: Philosopher-Kings and Other Classical Paradigms*. London: Routledge.

———2000. "Epicurean and Stoic Political Thought." In *The Cambridge History of Greek and Roman Political Thought*. Edited by Christopher Rowe and Malcolm Schofield. Cambridge University Press, 435–56.

———2002. "Academic Therapy: Philo of Larissa and Cicero's Project in the *Tusculans*." In *Philosophy and Power in the Graeco-Roman World: Essays in Honour of Miriam Griffin*. Edited by Gillian Clark and Tessa Rajak. Oxford University Press, 91–109.

———2003. "The School, from Zeno to Arius Didymus." In *The Cambridge Companion to the Stoics*. Edited by Brad Inwood. Cambridge University Press, 233–56.

———2005. "Epicurean and Stoic political thought." In *The Cambridge History of Greek and Roman Political Thought*. Edited by Christopher Rowe and Malcolm Schofield. Cambridge University Press, 435–56.

———forthcoming. "Liberty, Equality, and Authority: Theory and Practice in the Later Roman Republic. In *A Companion to Greek Democracy and the Roman Republic*. Edited by Dean Hammer. Oxford and Malden, MA: Wiley- Blackwell.

Schrenk, Lawrence. 1994. "Cicero on Rhetoric and Philosophy: *Tusculan Disputations*." *Ancient Philosophy* 14: 355–60.

Schrijvers, P.H.1970. *Horror ac divina voluptas*. Amsterdam: Adolf M. Hakkert.

———1974. "La pensée de Lucrèce sur l'origine du langage (*DRN*. V 1019–1090)." *Mnemosyne* 4th series, 27: 337–64.

———1996. "Lucretius on the Origin and Development of Political Life (*De Rerum Natura* 5.1105–1160)." *Polyhistor: Studies in the History and Historiography of Ancient Philosophy*. Edited by Keimpe Algra, Peter van der Horst, and David Runia. Leiden: E.J. Brill, 220–30.

Schur, Werner. 1934. *Sallust als Historiker*. Stuttgart: Verlag W. Kohlhammer.

Scrutton, Anastasia. 2005. "Emotion in Augustine of Hippo and Thomas Aquinas: A Way Forward for the Im/passibility Debate?" *International Journal of Systematic Theology* 7: 169–77.

Scullard, H.H. 1973. *Roman Politics, 220–150 BC*. 2nd ed. Oxford: Clarendon.

Schwartz, Eduard. 1897. "Die Berichte ueber die Catilinarische Verschwoerung." *Hermes* 32: 554–608.

Seager, Robin. 2005. *Tiberius*. 2nd edition. Oxford: Blackwell.
Sedley, David. 1981. "Review: The End of the Academy." *Phronesis* 26: 67–75.
———1998. *Lucretius and the Transformation of Greek Wisdom*. Cambridge University Press.
———2003. "The School, from Zeno to Arius Didymus." *The Cambridge Companion to the Stoics*. Edited by Brad Inwood. Cambridge University Press, 7–32.
Segal, Charles. 1986. *Language and Desire in Seneca's Phaedra*. Princeton University Press.
———1990. *Lucretius on Death and Anxiety: Poetry and Philosophy in De Rerum Natura*. Princeton University Press.
Seider, Aaron. 2013. *Memory in Vergil's Aeneid: Creating the Past*. Cambridge University Press.
Seneca. 1928. "On Clemency." "On Anger." "On Firmness." In *Moral Essays*. Translated by John Basore. Cambridge, MA: Harvard University Press.
———1932. "On Tranquillity of Mind." "On Consolation to Marcia." In *Moral Essays*. Translated by John Basore. Cambridge, MA: Harvard University Press.
———1935. "On Benefits." In *Moral Essays*. Translated by John Basore. Cambridge, MA: Harvard University Press.
———1971. *Natural Questions*. Translated by Thomas Corcoran. Cambridge, MA: Harvard University Press.
———1996. *Epistles*. Translated by Richard Gummere. Cambridge, MA: Harvard University Press.
Serres, Michel. 1991. *Rome: The Book of Foundations*. Translated by Felicia McCarren. Stanford University Press.
Shackleton Bailey, D.R. 1986. "*Nobiles* and *Novi* Reconsidered." *American Journal of Philology* 107: 255–60.
Shaw, Brent. 1985. "The Divine Economy: Stoicism as Ideology." *Latomus* 44: 16–54.
Sherwin-White, A.N. 1956. "Violence in Roman Politics." *Journal of Roman Studies* 46: 1–9.
———1982. "The *lex repetundarum* and the Political Ideas of Gaius Gracchus." *Journal of Roman Studies* 72: 18–31.
Shklar, Judith. 1987. *Montesquieu*. Oxford University Press.

Shotter, D.C.A. 1968. "Tacitus, Tiberius and Germanicus." *Historia* 17: 194–214.

Sinclair, Patrick. 1995. *Tacitus the Sententious Historian: A Sociology of Rhetoric in* Annales *1–6*. University Park: Penn State University Press.

Skinner, Quentin. 1978. *The Foundations of Modern Political Thought. Vol. 1. The Renaissance*. Cambridge University Press.

———1981. *Machiavelli*. New York: Hill and Wang.

———1988. "Motives, Intentions, and the Interpretation of Texts." In *Meaning and Context: Quentin Skinner and his Critics*. Edited by J. Tully. Cambridge: Polity.

———1989. "The State." In *Political Innovation and Conceptual Change*. Edited by Terence Ball, James Farr, and Russell Hanson. Cambridge University Press, 90–131.

———1990a. "Machiavelli's *Discorsi* and the Pre-Humanist Origins of Republican Ideas." In *Machiavelli and Republicanism*. Edited by Gisela Bock, Quentin Skinner, and Maurizio Viroli. Cambridge University Press, 121–41.

———1990b. "The Republican Ideal of Political Liberty." In *Machiavelli and Republicanism*. Edited by Gisela Bock, Quentin Skinner, and Maurizio Viroli. Cambridge University Press, 293–309.

———1996. *Reason and Rhetoric in the Philosophy of Hobbes*. Cambridge University Press.

———1998. *Liberty before Liberalism*. Cambridge University Press.

Sklenář, R. 1998. "*La République des Signes*: Caesar, Cato, and the Language of Sallustian Morality." *TAPA* 128: 205–20.

Small, Jocelyn. 1976. "The Death of Lucretia." *American Journal of Archaeology* 80: 349–60.

Smith, Philippa. 1995. "A Self-Indulgent Misuse of Leisure and Writing? How Not to Write Philosophy: Did Cicero Get it Right?" In *Cicero the Philosopher: Twelve Papers*. Edited by J.G.F. Powell. Oxford: Clarendon, 301–323.

Smith, R.R.R. 2002. "The Use of Images: Visual History and Ancient History." In *Classics in Progress: Essays on Ancient Greece and Rome*. Oxford University Press, 59–102.

Smith, Thomas. 2005. "The Glory and Tragedy of Politics." In *Augustine and Politics*. Edited by John Doody, Kevin Hughes, and Kim Paffenroth. Lanham: Lexington Books, 187–213.

Smolenaars, J.J.L. 1987. "Labour in the Golden Age: A Unifying Theme in Vergil's Poems." *Mnemosyne* 4th series, 40: 391–405.

Snell, Bruno. 1960. *The Discovery of the Mind in Greek Philosophy and Literature*. New York: Dover.

Sorabji, Richard. 2000. *Emotion and Peace of Mind: From Stoic Agitation to Christian Temptation*. Oxford University Press.

Spence, Sarah. 1988. *Rhetorics of Reason and Desire: Vergil, Augustine, and the Troubadours*. Ithaca: Cornell University Press.

Spurr, M.S. 1986. "Agriculture and the *Georgics*." *Greece & Rome*, 2nd series, 33: 164–87.

Stacey, Peter. 2007. *Roman Monarchy and the Renaissance Prince*. Cambridge University Press.

Stadter, P.A. 1972. "The Structure of Livy's History." *Historia* 21: 287–307.

Stahl, Hans-Peter. 1981. "Aeneas – An 'Unheroic' Hero?" *Arethusa* 14: 157–77.

Stanley, Keith. 1965. "Irony and Foreshadowing in *Aeneid* I, 462." *American Journal of Philology* 86: 267–77.

Stanton, G.R. 1968. "The Cosmopolitan Ideas of Epictetus and Marcus Aurelius." *Phronesis*.13: 183–95.

———1969. "Marcus Aurelius, Emperor and Philosopher." *Historia* 18: 570–87.

Stead, Christopher. 1994. *Philosophy in Christian Antiquity*. Cambridge University Press.

Steel, C.E.W. 2001. *Cicero, Rhetoric, and Empire*. Oxford University Press.

Stehle, Eva. 1974. "Virgil's *Georgics*: The Threat of Sloth." *TAPA* 104: 347–69.

Steinmetz, Peter. 1989. "Beobachtungen zu Ciceros philosophischem Stankpunkt." In *Cicero's Knowledge of the Peripatos*. Edited by William Fortenbaugh and Peter Steinmetz. New Brunswick: Transaction, 1–22.

Stemmler, Michael. 2000. "*Auctoritas exempli*: Zur Wechselwirkung von kanonisierten Vergangenheitsbildern und gesellschaftlicher Gegenwart in der spätrepublikanischen Rhetorik." In *Mos mairum: Untersuchungen zu den Formen der Identitätsstiftung und Stabilisierung in der römischen Republik*. Edited by Bernhard Linke and Michael Stemmler. Stuttgart: Franz Steiner Verlag, 141–205.

Stertz, Stephen. 1977. "Marcus Aurelius as Ideal Emperor in Late-Antique Greek Thought." *Classical World* 70: 433–39.

Stevenson, Tom. 2005. "Readings of Scipio's Dictatorship in Cicero's *De Re Publica* (6.12)." *Classical Quarterly* 55: 140–52.

Stevenson, T.R. 1992. "The Ideal Benefactor and the Father Analogy in Greek and Roman Thought." *Classical Quarterly* 42: 421–36.

Stewart, Douglas. 1972. "Morality, Mortality, and the Public Life: Aeneas the Politician." *The Antioch Review* 32: 649–64.

Strasburger, Hermann. 1968. *Zur Sage von der Gründung Roms.* Heidelberg: Carl Winter.

——1983. "Livius über Caesar: Unvollständige Überlegungen." In *Livius: Werk und Rezeption: Festchrift für Erich Burck zum 80. Geburtstag.* Edited by Eckard Lefèvre and Eckart Olshausen. München: C.H. Beck, 265–91.

Straumann, Benjamin. 2011. "Constitutional Thought in the Late Roman Republic." *History of Political Thought* 32: 280–92.

Strauss, Leo. 1964. *The City and Man.* University of Chicago Press.

——1968. "Notes on Lucretius." In *Liberalism Ancient and Modern.* New York: Basic Books, 76–139.

Striker, Gisela. 1995. "Cicero and Greek Philosophy." *Harvard Studies in Classical Philology* 97: 53–61.

——1996. "Origins of the concept of natural law." In *Essays on Hellenistic Epistemology and Ethics.* Cambridge University Press, 209–20.

Strozier, Robert. 2002. *Foucault, Subjectivity, and Identity: Historical Constructions of Subject and Self.* Detroit: Wayne State University Press.

Strunk, Thomas. 2010. "Offending the Powerful: Tacitus' *Dialogus de Oratoribus* and Safe Criticism." *Mnemosyne* 4th series 63: 241–67.

Sullivan, J.P. 1985. *Literature and Politics in the Age of Nero.* Ithaca: Cornell University Press.

Sumi, Geoffrey. 2005. *Ceremony and Power: Performing Politics in Rome between Republic and Empire.* Ann Arbor: University of Michigan Press.

Summers, Kirk. 1995. "Lucretius and the Epicurean Tradition of Piety." *Classical Philology* 90: 32–57.

Süss, Wilhelm. 1966. *Cicero: Eine Einführung in seine philosophischen Schriften (mit Ausschluß der staatsphilosophischen Werke).* Weisbaden: Franz Steiner Verlag.

Syme, Ronald. 1939. *The Roman Revolution.* Oxford University Press.

——1958. *Tacitus,* 2 vols. Oxford: Clarendon.

———1959. "Livy and Augustus." *Harvard Studies in Classical Philology* 64: 27–87.

———1964. *Sallust*. Berkeley: University of California Press.

———1970. *Ten Studies in Tacitus*. Oxford: Clarendon.

Tacitus. 1970. *Agricola. Germania. Dialogus*. Translated by M. Hutton and W. Peterson. Revised by R.M. Ogilvie, E.H. Warmington, and M. Winterbottom. Cambridge, MA: Harvard University Press.

———1994. *Annales*. Edited by Henrich Heubner. Stuttgart: B.J. Teubner.

———1996. *The Histories*. Translated by C.H. Moore. Cambridge, MA: Harvard University Press.

———2004. *The Annals*. Translated by A.J. Woodman. Indianapolis: Hackett.

Talbert, Richard. 1987. *The Senate of Imperial Rome*. Princeton University Press.

———1999. "Tacitus and the *Senatus Consultum de Cn. Pisone Patre*." *American Journal of Philology* 120: 89–97.

Tan, James. 2008. "*Contiones* in the Age of Cicero." *Classical Antiquity* 27: 163–201.

Tanner, R.G. 1972. "Cicero on Conscience and Morality." In *Cicero and Virgil: Studies in Honour of Harold Hunt*. Edited by John Martyn. Amsterdam: Adolf M. Hakkert, 87–112.

Tarrant, Harold. 1985. *Scepticism or Platonism? The Philosophy of the Fourth Academy*. Cambridge University Press.

———1997. "Poetry and Power: Virgil's Poetry in Contemporary Context." In *The Cambridge Companion to Virgil*. Edited by Charles Martindale. Cambridge University Press, 169–87.

Tatum, W. Jeffrey. forthcoming. "The Practice of Politics and the Unpredictable Dynamics of Clout in the Roman Republic." In *A Companion to Greek Democracy and the Roman Republic*. Edited by Dean Hammer. Oxford and Malden, MA: Wiley- Blackwell.

Tarver, J.C. 1902. *Tiberius the Tyrant*. Westminster: Archibald Constable and Co., Ltd.

Taylor, Lily Ross. 1918. "Livy and the Name Augustus." *Classical Review* 32: 158–61.

———1949. *Party Politics in the Age of Caesar*. Berkeley: University of California Press.

———1966. *Roman Voting Assemblies: From the Hannibalic War to the Dictatorship of Caesar*. Ann Arbor: University of Michigan Press.

Taylor, Margaret. 1947. "Progress and Primitivism in Lucretius." *American Journal of Philology* 68: 180–94.

Tengström, Emin. 1977. "Theater und Politik im Kaiserlichen Rom." *Eranos* 75: 43–56.

TeSelle, Eugene. 1988. "Toward an Augustinian Politics." *Journal of Religious Ethics* 16: 87–108.

Thacker, Andrew. 1993. "Foucault's Aesthetics of Existence." *Radical Philosophy* 63: 13–21.

Thomas, Richard. 1982. *Lands and People in Roman Poetry: The Ethnographical Tradition*. Cambridge: Cambridge Philological Society Supplement

———1988. *Virgil: Georgics*. 2 vols. Cambridge University Press.

———2001. "The *Georgics* of Resistance: From Virgil to Heaney." *Vergilius* 47: 117–47.

———2001. *Virgil and the Augustan Reception*. Cambridge University Press.

———2004–2005. "Torn Between Jupiter and Saturn: Ideology, Rhetoric and Culture Wars in the *Aeneid*." *Classical Journal* 100: 121–47.

Thury, Eva. 1987. "Lucretius' Poem as a Simulacrum of the *Rerum Natura*." *American Journal of Philology* 108: 270–94.

Timpe, Dieter. 1989. "Die Absicht der *Germania* des Tacitus." *Beiträge zun Verständnis der* Germania *des Tacitus, Vol. I: Bericht über die Kolloquien der Kommission für die Altertumskunde Nord-und Mitteleuropas in Jahr 1986*. Edited by Herbert Junkuhn and Dieter Timpe. Göttingen: Vandenhoeck and Rubrecht, 106–127.

Toll, Katharine. 1991. "The *Aeneid* as an Epic of National Identity: *Italiam Laeto Socii Clamore Salutant*." *Helios* 18: 3–14.

———1997. "Making Roman-Ness and the *Aeneid*." *Classical Antiquity* 16: 34–56.

Toner, J.P. 1995. *Leisure and Ancient Rome*. Cambridge: Polity.

Too, Yun Lee. 1994. "Educating Nero: A Reading of Seneca's Moral Epistles." In *Reflections of Nero: Culture, History, and Representation*. Edited by Jas Elsner and Jamie Masters. Chapel Hill: University of North Carolina Press, 211–24.

Townend, Gavin. 1965. "Imagery in Lucretius." In *Lucretius*. Edited by D.R. Dudley. New York: Basic Books, 95–114.

Tracy, Catherine. 2008–2009. "The People's Consul: The Significance of Cicero's Use of the Term 'Popularis.'" *Illinois Classical Studies* 33–34: 181–99.

Treggiari, Susan. 1979. "Sentiment and Property: Some Roman Attitudes." In *Theories of Property: Aristotle to the Present*. Edited by Anthony Parel and Thomas Flanagan. Waterloo: Wilfrid Laurier University Press, 53–85.

———2003. "Ancestral Virtues and Vices: Cicero on Nature, Nurture and Presentation." In *Myth, History and Culture in Republican Rome: Studies in honour of T.P. Wiseman*. Edited by David Bruand, Christopher Gill, and Timothy Peter Wiseman. University of Exeter Press, 139–64.

Tuck, Richard. 1999. *The Rights of War and Peace: Political Thought and the International Order From Grotius to Kant*. Oxford University Press.

Turpin, William. 1994. "*Res Gestae* 34.1 and the Settlement of 27 B.C." *Classical Quarterly* 44: 427–37.

———2008. "Tacitus, *exempla*, and the *praecipuum munus annalium*." *Classical Antiquity* 27: 359–404.

Vanderbroeck, Paul. 1987. *Popular Leadership and Collective Behavior in the Late Roman Republic (ca. 80–50 B.C.)*. Amsterdam: J.C. Gieben.

Vander Waerdt, P.A. 1987. "The Justice of the Epicurean Wise Man." *Classical Quarterly n.s.* 37: 402–22.

———1994a. "Philosophical Influence on Roman Jurisprudence? The Case of Stoicism and Natural Law." In *ANRW*. Edited by Wolfgang Haase and Hildegard Temporini. II.36.7: 4851–4900.

———1994b. "Zeno's *Republic* and the Origins of Natural Law." In *The Socratic Movement*. Edited by Vander Waerdt. Ithica: Cornell University Press.

Vasaly, Ann. 1987. "Personality and Power: Livy's Depiction of the Appii Claudii in the First Pentad." *TAPA* 117: 203–226.

———1993. *Representation: Images of the World in Ciceronian Oratory*. Berkeley: University of California Press.

———2009. "Characterization and Complexity: Caesar, Sallust, and Livy." In *The Cambridge Companion to the Ancient Historians*. Edited by Andrew Feldherr. Cambridge University Press, 245–60.

Vernant, Jean-Pierre. 1991. "A 'Beautiful Death' and the Disfigured Corpse in Homeric Epic." In *Mortals and Immortals: Collected Essays*. Edited by Froma Zeitlin. Princeton University Press, 50–74.

Veyne, Paul. 1987. "The Roman Empire." *A History of Private Life. I. From Pagan Rome to Byzantium.* Edited by Paul Veyne, translated by Arthur Goldhammer. Cambridge, MA: Belknap Press, 5–234.

———1990. *Bread and Circuses: Historical Sociology and Political Pluralism.* Edited by Oswyn Murray. Translated by Brian Pearce. New York: Penguin.

———1993. "The Final Foucault and His Ethics." *Critical Inquiry* 20: 1–9.

———2003. *Seneca: The Life of a Stoic.* New York: Routledge.

Virgil. 2000. *Eclogues. Georgics. Aeneid.* Translated by H.R. Fairclough. Cambridge, MA: Harvard University Press.

Viroli, Maurizio. 1990. "Machiavelli and the Republican Idea of Politics." In *Machiavelli and Republicanism.* Edited by Gisela Bock, Quentin Skinner, and Maurizio Viroli. Cambridge University Press, 143–71.

———1992. *From Politics to Reason of State: The Acquisition and Transformation of the Language of Politics 1250–1600.* Cambridge University Press.

———1998. *Machiavelli.* Oxford University Press.

Vlastos, Gregory. 1946. "On the Pre-History of Diodorus." *American Journal of Philology* 67: 51–59.

———1986. "Minimal Parts in Epicurean Atomism." In *Probleme der Lukrezforschung.* Edited by Carl Joachim Classen. Hildesheim Georg Olms Verlag, 97–123.

Voegelin, Eric. 1952. *The New Science of Politics.* University of Chicago Press.

———1975. *From Enlightenment to Revolution.* Edited by John Hallowell. Durham: Duke University Press.

———1997. *Hellenism, Rome, and Early Christianity.* Vol. 1 of *History of Political Ideas.In The Collected Works of Eric Voegelin.* Vol. 19. Ed. Athanasios Moulakis. Columbia: University of Missouri Press.

Voelke, André-Jean. 1973. *L'idée de volonté dans le stoïcisme.* Paris: Presses Universitaires de France.

Vogt, Katja. 2008. *Law, Reason, and the Cosmic City: Political Philosophy in the Early Stoa.* Oxford University Press.

Volkmann, Hans. 1958. *Sullas marsch auf Rom.* Munich: R. Oldenbourg.

von Albrecht, Michael. 1989. *Masters of Roman Prose from Cato to Apuleius: Interpretative Studies.* Translated by Neil Adkin. Leeds: Francis Cairns.

———2004. *Wort und Wandlung: Senecas Lebenskunst.* Leiden: Brill.

von Fritz, Kurt. 1943. "Sallust and the Attitude of the Roman Nobility at the Time of the Wars against Jugurtha (112–105 B.C.)." *TAPA* 74: 134–68.
———1957. "Tacitus, Agricola, Domitian, and the Problem of the Principate." *Classical Philology* 52:73–97.
von Heyking, John. 2001. *Augustine and Politics as Longing in the World.* Columbia: University of Missouri Press.
von Staden, Heinrich. 1978. "The Stoic Theory of Perception and its 'Platonic' Critics." In *Studies in Perception: Interrelations in the History of Philosophy and Science.* Edited by Peter Machamer and Robert Turnbull. Columbus: Ohio State University Press, 96–136.
———2000. "Body, Soul, and Nerves: Epicurus, Herophilus, Erasistratus, the Stoics, and Galen." In *Psyche and Soma: Physicians and Metaphysicians on the Mind-Body Problem from Antiquity to Enlightenment.* Edited by John Wright and Paul Potter. Oxford: Clarendon, 79–116.
von Ungern-Sternberg, Jürgen. 1986. "The Formation of the 'Annalistic Tradition': The Example of the Decemvirate." In *Social Struggles in Archaic Rome: New Perspectives on the Conflict of the Orders.* Edited by Kurt Raaflaub. Berkeley: University of California Press, 77–104.
———1998. "Die Legitimitätskrise der römischen Republik." *Historische Zeitschrift* 266: 607–24.
von Wilamowitz-Moellendorff, Ulrich. 1982. *History of Classical Scholarship.* Translated by Alan Harris. Baltimore: Johns Hopkins University Press.
Walbank, F.W.A. 1943. "Polybius on the Roman Constitution." *Classical Quarterly* 37: 73–89.
———1960. "History and Tragedy." *Historia* 9: 216–34.
———2002. *Polybius, Rome and the Hellenistic World: Essays and Reflections.* Cambridge University Press.
Walker, Andrew. 1993. "*Enargeia* and the Spectator in Greek Historiography." *TAPA* 123: 353–77.
Walker, B. 1952. *The Annals of Tacitus: A Study in the Writing of History.* University of Manchester Press.
Wallace-Hadrill, Andrew. 1982. "The Golden Age and Sin in Augustan Ideology." *Past and Present* 95: 19–36.
———1988. "The Social Structure of the Roman House." *Papers of the British School at Rome* 56: 43–97.

———1990. "Roman Arches and Greek Honours: The Language of Power at Rome." *Proceedings of the Cambridge Philological Society*. 36: 143–81.

Wallace-Hadrill, Andrew. 1997. "Mutatio morum: The Idea of a Cultural Revolution." In *The Roman Cultural Revolution*. Edited by Thomas Habinek and Alessandro Schiesaro. Cambridge University Press, 3–22.

———2008. *Rome's Cultural Revolution*. Cambridge University Press.

Walsh, P.G. 1955. "Livy's Preface and the Distortion of History." *American Journal of Philology* 76: 369–83.

———1958. "Livy and Stoicism." *American Journal of Philology* 79: 355–75.

———1961. *Livy: His Historical Aims and Methods*. Cambridge University Press.

———1966. "Livy." *Latin Historians*. Edited by T.A. Dorey. New York: Basic Books, 115–42.

Walters, Jonathan. 1998. "Making a Spectacle: Deviant Men, Invective, and Pleasure." *Arethusa* 31: 355–67.

Ward, Allen. 2004. "How Democratic was the Roman Republic?" *New England Classical Journal* 31: 101–19.

Wardman, Alan. 1982. *Religion and Statecraft Among the Romans*. London: Granada.

Warren, James. 2007. "Lucretius and Greek philosophy." In *Cambridge Companion to Lucretius*. Edited by Stuart Gillespie and Philip Hardie. Cambridge University Press, 19–32.

Waters, K.H. 1970. "Cicero, Sallust and Catiline." *Historia* 19: 195–215.

Watson, Alan. 1968. *The Law of Property in the Later Roman Republic*. Oxford: Clarendon.

Watson, Gerard. 1971. "The Natural Law and Stoicism." In *Problems in Stoicism*. Edited by A.A. Long. London: Athlone Press, 216–38.

———1988. "Discovering the Imagination: Platonists and Stoics on phantasia." *The Question of "Eclecticism": Studies in Later Greek Philosophy*. Edited by John Dillon and A.A. Long. Berkeley: University of California Press, 208–33.

Webb, Ruth. 1997. "Imagination and the Arousal of the Emotions in Greco-Roman Rhetoric." In *The Passions in Roman Thought and Literature*. Edited by Susanna Morton Braund and Christopher Gill. Cambridge University Press, 112–27.

Weithman, Paul. 1991. "Toward an Augustinian Liberalism." *Faith and Philosophy* 8: 461–80.
West, David. 1969. *The Imagery and Poetry of Lucretius*. Edinburgh University Press.
Wetzel, James. 1992. *Augustine and the Limits of Virtue*. Cambridge University Press.
Wheeler, Marcus. 1952. "Cicero's Political Ideal." *Greece & Rome* 21: 49–56.
Wieacker, Franz. 1988. *Römische rechtsgeschichte*. München: C.W. Beck.
———2006. *Römische rechtsgeschichte*. München: C.W. Beck.
White, Michael. 1994. "Pluralism and Secularism in the Political Order: St. Augustine and Theoretical Liberalism." *University of Dayton Review* 22: 137–53.
———2012. *Political Philosophy: An Historical Introduction*. 2d ed. Oxford University Press.
White, Nicholas. 1979. "The Basis of Stoic Ethics." *Harvard Studies in Classical Philology* 83: 143–78.
White, Peter. 1993. *Promised Verse: Poets in the Society of Augustan Rome*. Cambridge, MA: Harvard University Press.
White, Stephen. 1995. "Cicero and the Therapists." In *Cicero the Philosopher: Twelve Papers*. Edited by J.G.F. Powell. Oxford: Clarendon, 219–46.
Wiedemann, Thomas. 1992. *Emperors and Gladiators*. London: Routledge.
———2000. "Reflections of Roman Political Thought in Latin Historical Writing." In *The Cambridge History of Greek and Roman Political Thought*. Edited by Christopher Rowe and Malcolm Schofield. Cambridge University Press, 517–531.
Wigodsky, Michael. 1972. *Vergil and Early Latin Poetry*. Wiesbaden: Franz Steiner Verlag.
Wilhelm, Robert. 1982. "The Plough-Chariot: Symbol of Order in the *Georgics*." *Classical Journal* 77: 213–30.
Wilkinson, L.P. 1963. "Virgil's Theodicy." *Classical Quarterly* n.s. 13: 75–84.
———1966. "Virgil and the Evictions." *Hermes* 94: 320–24.
———1969. *The* Georgics *of Virgil: A Critical Survey*. Cambridge University Press, reprinted as Norman: University of Oklahoma Press, 1997.
Williams, Bronwyn. 1990. "Reading Tacitus' Tiberian *Annals*." In *The Imperial Muse: Flavian Epicist to Claudian*. Edited by A.J. Boyle. Bendigo, Australia: Aureal Publications, 140–66.

Williams, Gordon. 1955. "Review of *Tite-Live, Histoire Romaine*." *Journal of Roman Studies* 45: 227–229.

Williams, Mary Frances. 1997. "Four Mutinies: Tacitus *Annals* 1.16–30; 1.31–49 and Ammmianus Marcellinus *Res Gestae* 20.4.9–20.5.7; 24.3.1–8." *Phoenix* 51: 44–74.

Williams, R.D. 1960. *P. Vergili Maronis Aeneidos liber tertius: edited with a commentary*. Oxford: Clarendon.

———1964. "The Sixth Book of the *Aeneid*," *Greece & Rome* 11: 48–63.

———1981. "The Shield of Aeneas." *Vergilius* 27: 8–11.

———1990. "The Purpose of the *Aeneid*." In *Oxford Readings in Vergil's Aeneid*. Edited by S.J. Harrison. Oxford University Press, 21–36.

Williams, Raymond. 1979. *Politics and Letters: Interviews with New Left Review*. London: NLB.

Williams, Rowan. 1987. "Politics and the Soul: A Reading of the *City of God*." *Milltown Studies* 19/20: 55–72.

Williams, Wynne. 1976. "Individuality in the Imperial Constitutions: Hadrian and the Antonines." *Journal of Roman Studies* 66: 67–83.

Williamson, Callie. 2005. *The Laws of the Roman People: Public Law in the Expansion and Decline of the Roman Republic*. Ann Arbor: University of Michigan Press.

Willis, William. 1941. "Athletic Contests in the Epic." *TAPA* 72: 392–417.

Wilson, Marcus. 2001. "Seneca's *Epistles* Reclassified." In *Texts, Ideas, and the Classics: Scholarship, Theory, and Classical Literature*. Edited by S.J. Harrison. Oxford University Press, 164–187.

Wirszubski, Chaim. 1954. "Cicero's *CVM DIGNITATE OTIVM*: A Reconsideration." *Journal of Roman Studies* 44: 1–13.

———1961. "*AVDACES*: A Study in Political Phraseology." *Journal of Roman Studies* 51: 12–22.

———1968. *Libertas as a Political Idea at Rome During the Late Republic and Early Principate*. Cambridge University Press.

Wiseman, T.P. 1971. *New Men in the Roman Senate 139 B.C.-A.D. 14*. Oxford University Press.

———1979. *Clio's Cosmetics: Three Studies in Greco-Roman Literature*. Totowa, N.J.: Rowman and Littlefield.

———1985. "Competition and Co-operation." In *Roman Political Life: 90 B.C.-A.D. 69*. Edited by Wiseman. University of Exeter, 3–19.

———1986. "Monuments and the Roman Annalists." In *Past Perspectives: Studies in Greek and Roman Historical Writing*. Edited by I.S. Moxon, J.D. Smart and A.J. Woodman. Cambridge University Press, 87–100.

———1987. *Roman Studies: Literary and Historical*. Liverpool: Francis Cairns.

———1994. "The Origins of Roman Historiography." In *Historiography and Imagination: Eight Essays on Roman Culture*. University of Exeter Press, 1–22.

———1995. *Remus: A Roman Myth*. Cambridge University Press.

———2002. "Roman History and the Ideological Vacuum." In *Classics in Progress: Eight Essays on Ancient Greece and Rome*. Edited by Wiseman. Oxford University Press, 285–310.

———2009. *Remembering the Roman People: Essays on Late-Republican Politics and Literature*. Oxford University Press.

Wistrand, Magnus. 1992. *Entertainment and Violence in Ancient Rome: The Attitudes of Roman Writers of the First Century A.D.* Göteborg: Acta Universitatis Gothoburgensis.

Wittgenstein, Ludwig. 1953. *Philosophical Investigations*. Translated by G.E.M. Anscombe. New York: Macmillan.

———1958. *The Blue and Brown Books*. New York: Harper & Row.

Wolin, Sheldon. 2004 (orig. 1960). *Politics and Vision*. Expanded Edition. Princeton University Press.

Wood, Neal. 1967. "Machiavelli's Concept of *Virtù* Reconsidered." *Political Studies* 15: 159–72.

———1983. "The Economic Dimension of Cicero's Political Thought: Property and State." *Canadian Journal of Political Science* 16: 739–56.

———1986. "*Populares* and *Circumcelliones*: The Vocabulary of 'Fallen Man' in Cicero and St. Augustine." *History of Political Thought* 7: 33–51.

———1988. *Cicero's Social and Political Thought*. Berkeley: University of California Press.

———1995. "Sallust's Theorem: A Comment on 'Fear' in Western Political Thought." *History of Political Theory* 16: 174–89.

———2004. *Tyranny in America: Capitalism and National Decay*. London: Verso.

Woodman, A.J. 1988. *Rhetoric in Classical Historiography: Four Studies*. London: Croom Helm.

———1993. "Amateur Dramatics at the Court of Nero: *Annals* 15.48.74." In *Tacitus and the Tacitean Tradition*. Edited by T.J. Luce and Woodman. Princeton University Press, 104–28.
———1998. *Tacitus Reviewed*. Oxford: Clarendon.
———2006a. "Mutiny and Madness: Tacitus, *Annals* 1.16–49." *Arethusa* 39: 303–29.
———2006b. "Tiberius and the Taste of Power: The Year 33 in Tacitus." *Classical Quarterly* 56: 275–89.
Woodman, A.J. and R.H. Martin. 1996. *The* Annals *of Tacitus. Book 3*. Cambridge University Press.
Wormell, D.E.W. 1965. "The Personal World of Lucretius." In *Lucretius*. Edited by D.R. Dudley. New York: Basic Books, 35–67.
Wright, M.R. 1995. "Cicero on Self-Love and Love of Humanity in *De Finibus* 3." In *Cicero the Philosopher*. Edited by J.G.F. Powell. Oxford: Clarendon.
Yakobson, Alexander. 1999. *Elections and Electioneering in Rome: A Study in the Political System of the Late Republic*. Stuttgart: Franz Steiner Verlag.
Yavetz, Zvi. 1963. "The Failure of Catiline's Conspiracy." *Historia* 12: 485–99.
———1969. Plebs *and* Princeps. Oxford: Clarendon.
Young, Iris. 1996. "Communication and the Other: Beyond Deliberative Democracy." In *Democracy and Difference: Contesting the Boundaries of the Political*. Edited by Seyla Benhabib. Princeton University Press, 120–35.
Zanker, Paul. 1988. *The Power of Images in the Age of Augustus*. Translated by Alan Shapiro. Ann Arbor: University of Michigan Press.
Zetzel, James. 1972. "Cicero and the Scipionic Circle." *Harvard Studies in Classical Philology* 76: 173–79.
———1989. "*Romane Memento:* Justice and Judgment in *Aeneid* 6." *TAPA* 119: 263–84.
———1996. "Natural Law and Poetic Justice: A Carneadean Debate in Cicero and Virgil." *Classical Philology* 91: 297–319.
———2001. "Citizen and Commonwealth in *De Re Publica* Book 4." In *Cicero's Republic*. Edited by J.G.F. Powell and J.A. North. London: Institute of Classical Studies, 83–97.

———2003. "Plato with Pillows: Cicero on the Uses of Greek Culture." In *Myth, History and Culture in Republican Rome: Studies in honour of T.P. Wiseman*. Edited by David Braund and Christopher Gill. University of Exeter Press, 119–38.

Ziegler, Konrat. 1966. *Das hellenistische Epos*. Leipzig: B.G. Teubner.

INDEX LOCORUM

Aelius Aristides
  Panath.
    27, 240
Aetius
  4.11.1–4 = LS 39E, 287
Alexander of Aphrodisias
  SVF 2.936, 36
  SVF 3.32, 36
Appian
  BC
    12, 14
Arist.
  NE
    1167a–1167b, 48
    1177b, 141
  Pol.
    1288b, 33
    1334a6–8, 148
Arusianus Messius
  484.19, 154
Aug.
  Civ. Dei.
    1.pref., 423, 427
    1.1, 419
    1.7, 425
    1.9, 419
    1.13, 389
    1.15, 419
    1.29, 421
    1.30, 148, 401
    1.31, 148, 401, 403
    1.35, 419

    2.9, 403
    2.18, 148, 150, 400
    2.20, 401–2, 422
    2.21, 426–7
    2.22, 401
    2.26, 403
    2.27, 403
    2.29, 402, 420
    3.9, 386
    3.10, 400, 407
    3.14, 401, 403, 419, 421
    3.16, 400
    3.17, 177, 400–1
    3.18, 397
    3.21, 401
    3.23, 401
    3.24, 401
    3.28, 401
    4.3, 402
    4.4, 421, 423
    4.5, 421
    4.15, 423
    4.32, 402
    5.1, 420
    5.12, 385, 399–400, 420, 423
    5.13, 399
    5.14, 385, 420
    5.15, 407
    5.16, 420–1
    5.17, 385, 419, 421
    5.18, 385, 420
    5.19, 400, 420

Aug. (cont.)
  5.22, 391
  5.23, 422
  5.25, 420
  6.1, 420
  6.2, 385, 420
  6.7, 403
  8.4, 383
  8.8, 384
  9.1, 384
  10.1, 384
  10.3, 384, 416, 425
  10.7, 419
  10.25, 420
  10.27, 385
  11.1, 420, 427
  11.13, 387
  11.21, 394
  11.25, 393
  11.28, 386
  12.2, 386
  12.4, 427
  12.5, 386
  12.6, 392
  12.8, 393
  12.22, 424
  12.26, 427
  13.23, 387
  14.5, 385
  14.8, 394
  14.9, 385, 394–5
  14.16, 395
  14.18, 420
  15.4, 405, 423
  15.5, 415–16, 423
  15.7, 405, 428
  15.27, 427
  16.24, 420
  19.1, 386–7, 418
  19.3, 386, 424
  19.4, 394–5, 415, 428
  19.5, 396, 405, 426
  19.6, 405, 407
  19.7, 396, 407
  19.8, 407
  19.10, 428
  19.12, 387, 404, 420
  19.13, 404, 428
  19.14, 386–7, 393, 420, 423–5
  19.15, 422–3
  19.17, 404, 420–1, 427
  19.18, 419
  19.19, 427
  19.20, 428
  19.21, 398
  19.23, 427
  19.24, 398
  19.26, 420
  19.27, 407, 427–8
  20.5, 420
  20.9, 409, 420
  20.15, 409
  22.21, 409
  22.26, 409
  22.27, 409
  22.28, 409

Conf.
  1.1, 389
  1.6, 429
  1.8, 406
  1.13, 384, 419
  1.20, 385
  2.9, 394
  3.4, 385
  4.1, 429
  4.8, 394
  5.8, 385
  6.16, 394
  7.17, 391
  8.2, 383
  9.11–13, 394
  10.3, 405, 428
  10.4, 428
  10.5, 413
  10.6, 392, 412–14
  10.8, 388, 390
  10.11, 388
  10.14, 388
  10.15, 388
  10.21, 387

10.24–27, 409
10.27, 385
10.28, 409
10.31, 409
10.37, 428
10.40, 391
11.2, 405
11.6, 413
11.7, 395
11.11, 395
11.13, 394
11.14, 395
11.18, 396
11.20, 394
11.21, 405
11.23, 394
11.26, 394
11.28, 394
11.29, 395
11.31, 394–5
12.16, 420
13.9, 386
Contra acad.
  1.5.14, 385, 419
  2.4.10, 385
  2.7.17, 428
  3.1.1, 385
  3.18.41, 408
  3.20.43, 427
De beata vita
  2.10, 387
  4.25, 393
  4.31, 393
  4.33, 394, 408
De doc. Chr.
  1.4.4, 421, 424
  1.5.5, 410, 421
  1.9.9, 391
  1.11.11, 425
  1.13.13, 412
  1.14.13, 424
  1.17.16, 424
  1.22.20, 424
  1.22.21, 424
  1.26.27, 424

1.28.29, 424
1.32.34, 424
1.33.36, 419
1.34.38, 424
2.1.1, 406
2.2.3, 406
3.10.16, 424
3.34.49, 420
4.5.7, 406
4.17.34, 384
4.18.35, 384
4.19.38, 384
De fid. inv.
  2.4, 426
De lib. arb.
  1.4.10.30, 387, 392
  1.6.14–48, 404
  1.7.16.54–56, 386
  1.8.18.64, 392
  1.11.22.77, 392, 402
  1.11.22.78, 402
  1.13.27.89, 393
  1.15.32.108, 404
  1.15.32.109–110, 405
  1.15.33.113, 392
  2.3.7.22, 386
  2.4.10.38, 387
  2.5.12.48, 387
  2.5.12.49, 389
  2.7.15.59, 405
  2.7.19.72, 405
  2.8.20.79–2.8.24.95, 384
  2.9.27.104–108, 384, 408
  2.10.29.119, 384, 408
  2.11.30.122, 409
  2.13.36.141–142, 384, 408
  2.16.44.171, 408
  2.16.45.174, 408
  2.17.45.174, 383
  2.19.53.199, 423
  3.5.14.51, 391
  3.25.74.256, 408
  3.25.76.262, 401
De mag.
  1.2, 413

Aug. (cont.)
  3.6, 406
  4.8, 406
  4.9, 406
  5.14, 406
  8.23, 406
  10.33, 406
  11.36, 413
  11.37, 406
  11.38, 413
  12.39, 410
  12.39–40, 406
  12.40, 413
  13.41, 407
  13.42, 405
De ord.
  1.7.26, 385
  1.8.23, 410
  2.6.19, 429
De trin.
  1.1.1, 389
  3.9.12, 415
  8.3.4, 390
  8.4.6, 409
  8.4.7, 408
  8.5.8, 410
  8.6.9, 388, 410
  8.8.12, 410, 416
  8.9.13, 410
  8.10.14, 410
  9.2.2, 386, 411
  9.3.3, 411
  9.4.5, 416
  9.4.7, 411
  9.6.9, 411
  9.6.10, 388
  9.6.11, 407, 416
  9.7.12, 412, 415
  9.8.13, 415, 428
  9.8.14, 415
  9.10.15, 413
  9.12.18, 389
  10.1.1, 389
  10.1.2, 389, 409–10
  10.3.5, 411
  10.4.6, 411
  10.5.7, 390, 397
  10.6.8, 390
  10.7.9, 411, 415
  10.8.11, 412
  10.9.12, 412
  10.10.14, 412
  10.11.18, 412
  11.2.2, 388
  11.3.6, 391
  11.5.8, 408
  12.2.2, 408
  12.9.14, 391, 401
  12.10.15, 391
  12.11.16, 392, 401
  12.12.17, 391, 401
  12.14.22, 391
  12.15.25, 388
  13.1.3, 408
  13.1.4, 388
  13.4.7, 386, 389
  13.5.8, 389, 393
  13.7.10, 393, 395
  13.8.11, 392
  13.20.26, 388
  14.6.8, 412
  14.8.11, 412
  14.9.12, 393
  15.8.14, 414
  15.11.20, 413
  15.12.22, 414
  15.13.22, 414
  15.15.22, 414
  15.15.24, 414
  15.21.40, 414
  15.21.41, 396
  15.23.43, 414
  15.23.44, 414
  15.27.50, 409
De urb. exc.
  6, 426
De ut. cred.
  7.16, 420
  8.20, 415
  9.21, 415

9.21–22, 415
12.26, 426
13.28, 408
16.34, 415
De vera relig.
  22.43, 395
  29.53, 387
En. Psalmos
  9.8, 426
  65.2, 420
Ep.
  10 (Divjak), 422
  84.1, 394
Solil.
  1.6.13, 428
  1.8.15, 384
  1.10.17, 394
  1.14.24, 394
Augustus
RG
  1, 23
  34, 284

Bell. Afr.
  22.2, 160

Caesar
BC
  1.22, 160, 312
BG
  7.1, 312
Cels.
  pro. 5, 326
  pro. 14, 324
  pro. 15, 324
  pro. 23, 324
  pro. 39, 328
  1.3.1, 328
  1.3.2, 342, 356
  3.18.2, 341
  3.18.3, 352
  3.18.5, 329
  3.18.10, 352, 356
  3.18.11, 356
  3.18.18, 356
  3.18.22, 356

3.22.1, 324–5
3.25.3, 350
3.27.1A, 330
4.5.6, 346
5.21, 349
Chrysippus
  SVF 2.509, 373
  SVF 2.974 = Cic. De fato 19.43, 374
  SVF 3.314 = LS 67R, 37
  SVF 3.324, 42
  SVF 3.473 = LS 65T, 277
Cic.
  Acad.
    1.11.41, 238
    2.7.20, 311
    2.7.21, 236, 363
    2.10.30, 238
    2.26.84, 29
    2.31.99–32.104, 29
    2.44.136, 42, 291, 398
  Att..
    1.19.10, 28
    2.1.8, 35, 72
    2.7.4, 57
    7.3.2, 76
    7.11.1, 45
    12.13.1, 81
    12.14.3, 81
    12.15, 80–1
    12.18.1, 80–1
    12.28.2, 80–1
    12.38a.1, 81
    12.40.2, 81
  Balb.
    2.6, 90
  Brut.
    56, 198
    212, 67, 312
  Caec.
    25.70, 60
    26.73–75, 60
  Cat.
    1.3, 67–8
    1.4, 67
    2.22, 159

Cic. (cont.)
   2.26, 134
   3.10, 28
   3.14–15, 27
   3.23–27, 27
   3.26, 88
   4.13, 28
   4.22, 31, 89
   4.22–23, 91
Cluent.
   53.146, 74
   53.147, 55
De amic.
   6.20, 404
   13.47, 81
De div.
   1.14.24, 79
   2.14.33, 36
De fato
   18.41–42, 275
   19.43, 374
De fin.
   1.18.57–58, 135
   2.14.45, 88
   3.5.16, 285
   3.5.16–17, 38
   3.6.20, 38
   3.6.20–21, 287
   3.6.21, 38, 289–90
   3.6.21–22, 38
   3.6.22, 290
   3.10.33, 38, 289
   3.10.35, 291
   3.17.57, 303
   3.18.60, 296
   3.19.62–63, 38
   3.19.64, 88
   3.20.66, 285, 288
   4.5-7, 81
   4.7.17–18, 77
   5.4.11, 141
   5.23.65, 40
   5.23.65–66, 35
   5.23.66, 40
   De Imperio Cn. Pompei

   1.2, 59
   5.13, 90
   6.14, 88
   7.17, 88
   7.17–18, 88
   7.19, 88
   11.31–32, 91
   13.36–39, 90
   14.40–41, 90
   24.69, 59
De inv.
   1.1.1, 71–2
   1.2.2, 74–5
   1.2.2–3, 34, 73
   1.2.3, 74
   1.4.5, 72
   1.30.48, 75
   1.34.58, 79
   1.53.101, 73
   1.53.101–2, 73
   1.55.106, 73
   2.4.12, 71
   2.5.17–18, 73
   2.52.157, 74
   2.52.157–58, 71
   2.53.160, 40
   2.54.164, 283
   2.56.169, 41
De leg.
   1.5.16, 35, 87
   1.5.17, 36
   1.6.18, 36
   1.6.18–19, 36–7
   1.6.19, 33, 40, 58
   1.7.23, 35, 87, 316
   1.9.26–27, 36
   1.10.28, 31
   1.10.30, 33, 36, 38
   1.11.31, 63
   1.11.32, 87
   1.12.33, 41
   1.13.35, 35, 47
   1.13.38–39, 29
   1.13.39, 99
   1.15.42, 33, 40

1.15.42–43, 39
1.16.43–44, 39
1.16.44, 36
1.17.47, 63, 290
1.18.48–49, 41
1.20.54, 29
1.21.55, 29
1.22.59, 36
1.23.61, 87
1.24.62, 44
2.1.3, 75, 82, 84
2.2.4, 75, 82, 84
2.2.5, 88
2.4.8–9, 36
2.5.11, 58
2.5.11–12, 40
2.17.42, 27
2.17.44, 130
3.1.3, 88
3.6.14, 34
3.7.17, 54
3.9.19, 63
3.10.23, 59
3.10.24, 35
3.12.28, 53, 57, 76
3.15.33, 59
3.19.44, 58
De nat. deor.
  1.4.9, 80
  1.30.85, 108
  1.42.117, 132
  2.31.78–79, 87
  2.44.115, 36
  2.59.147, 141
  2.61.153, 141
  2.62.154, 87, 316
De off.
  1.1.2, 29
  1.2.5, 44
  1.2.6, 29
  1.3.8, 38
  1.4.11, 37, 60
  1.4.11–5.17, 290
  1.4.12, 34, 38–9, 61
  1.5.15, 38

1.6.18, 29, 43
1.6.19, 44
1.7.20, 40, 48, 61, 65
1.7.21, 60–1
1.7.22, 43, 61–2, 88, 312
1.7.23, 41, 43, 52
1.7.24, 61
1.8.25, 62, 64
1.8.26, 61, 64
1.9.28, 41
1.10.21, 40
1.10.31, 47
1.10.32, 41
1.10.33, 42
1.11.34, 90
1.11.35, 90
1.11.36, 90
1.12.38, 88
1.13.39, 90
1.13.41, 43, 88
1.14.42, 43
1.14.45, 42–3, 88–9
1.15.46, 43–4
1.15.47–48, 89
1.15.49, 42
1.16.50, 43
1.17.53, 31, 46, 88
1.17.53–54, 88
1.17.53–58, 61
1.17.54, 31, 46
1.17.54–55, 88
1.17.55–56, 46
1.17.57, 46, 88
1.17.58, 88
1.19.62, 44
1.19.63, 44
1.19.64, 44
1.22.76, 67
1.22.78, 27
1.23.79–80, 27, 74
1.25.85, 53, 59
1.26.92, 62
1.27.94, 44
1.27.96, 44
1.27.98, 44

Cic. (cont.)
   1.28.99, 44, 59
   1.28.100, 31, 41
   1.28.100–101, 44
   1.29.102, 44
   1.31.110–33.120, 45
   1.31.111, 44
   1.31.114, 44
   1.34.124, 45, 53, 59
   1.35.126, 84
   1.41.146, 84
   1.41.147, 59
   1.41.149, 31
   1.43.153, 34, 39, 43–4
   1.44.156, 44
   1.44.157, 31, 44
   1.44.157–158, 34
   1.44.158, 39, 44, 61
   1.45.159, 34, 38
   2.2.6, 86
   2.2.7–8, 29
   2.3.10, 41
   2.4.13–14, 41
   2.4.15, 35, 41
   2.5.16, 31
   2.5.18, 38
   2.7.23, 42
   2.7.24, 63
   2.8.27, 89–90, 154
   2.8.28, 92
   2.8.28–29, 90
   2.8.29, 66
   2.8.62, 42
   2.9.32, 42
   2.9.33, 51
   2.11.40, 41, 47
   2.12.41–42, 55
   2.20.70, 42
   2.21.72, 43
   2.21.73, 60, 64
   2.22.78, 60, 64, 66
   2.22.79, 64
   2.23.81–82, 66
   2.23.83, 64
   2.23.89, 57
   2.24.84, 62, 66
   2.24.85, 64, 66, 88
   2.24.87, 62
   3.1.2, 66
   3.2.6, 17
   3.3.11, 41
   3.4.16, 78
   3.4.20, 41
   3.4.23, 41
   3.5.21, 65
   3.5.21–23, 36
   3.5.22, 61, 66
   3.5.22–23, 61
   3.5.23, 62, 65
   3.5.23–24, 66
   3.6.26, 31, 41
   3.6.28, 39, 46
   3.6.31, 41
   3.10.42, 86
   3.17.69, 88
   3.17.70, 48, 52, 278
   3.23.83, 66
   3.30.110, 41
  De optimo genere oratorum
   1.3, 74
   5.15, 74
  De orat.
   1.1.1, 86
   1.3.9, 77
   1.3.12, 73, 75
   1.5.17, 72
   1.5.17–18, 71
   1.5.18, 73
   1.8.33, 74
   1.12.50–51, 71
   1.14.60, 71–2
   1.23.108, 278
   1.34.156–57, 73
   1.34.157, 73
   1.42.188, 55
   1.46.202, 27, 72
   1.48.211, 78
   1.51.223, 73

1.51.223–52.224, 72
1.52.223, 74
1.52.223–53.227, 72
1.58.249, 79
2.12.51–16.70, 237
2.24.102, 70
2.30.132, 67
2.31.134, 67
2.39.164–66, 67
2.38.159, 72
2.43.184, 75
2.44.86, 237
2.44.185–86, 71
2.45.189, 73
2.45.190, 72
2.46.192–93, 73
2.50.197, 72
2.56.214, 72
2.57.216, 72
2.87.257, 236
3.1.2, 74
3.1.4, 55, 66
3.5.19, 33
3.14.54, 74
3.17.62–3.18.68, 29
3.17.64, 77
3.18.66, 81
3.19.69–73, 29
3.28.109, 71
3.29.113, 71
3.40.160, 236
3.41.163, 236
3.50.195, 86
3.59.222, 72
3.59.223, 72
De rep.
  1.2.2, 81
  1.2.3, 34, 78
  1.6.10, 106
  1.7.12, 34, 78
  1.17.26–29, 79
  1.17.27, 312
  1.20.33, 32
  1.25.39, 34–5

  1.25.40, 34
  1.26.41, 35
  1.27.43, 51, 63
  1.28.44, 51
  1.29.45, 76
  1.31.47, 54, 63
  1.32.27, 312
  1.32.48, 55, 58
  1.32.49, 55
  1.33.50, 63, 294
  1.34.51, 57, 59
  1.34.51–52, 53, 59
  1.34.52, 76
  1.34.53, 63–4
  1.40.62, 64
  1.42.65, 64
  1.42.67, 56
  1.43.67, 64
  1.44.68, 63–4, 66
  1.45.69, 63
  2.1.2, 34–5
  2.2.4, 240
  2.4.7, 62
  2.4.7–8, 62
  2.7.13, 50
  2.9.15, 51, 76
  2.9.16, 131
  2.11.21, 50
  2.11.22, 32, 35
  2.12.23, 50–2
  2.13.25, 52
  2.14.26, 62
  2.14.27, 131
  2.17.31, 52
  2.17.32, 52
  2.18.33, 62
  2.19.34, 294
  2.21.33, 52
  2.21.37, 34
  2.22.33, 40
  2.22.39, 49
  2.22.39–40, 12
  2.23.43, 50–1, 54–5
  2.25.46, 53

Cic. (cont.)
   2.26.47, 51
   2.26.47–48, 294
   2.26.48, 47, 53
   2.28.50, 35, 50–1, 53, 63
   2.28.51, 76
   2.29.51, 78–9
   2.30.52, 32
   2.32.56, 50, 53, 59
   2.33.57, 36, 50, 53
   2.33.58, 53
   2.34.59, 53
   2.37.63, 255
   2.39.66, 32–3
   2.42.69, 73
   2.43.69, 48
   3.3.5, 78
   3.4.7, 36
   3.8.13, 39
   3.9.16, 39
   3.10.17, 39
   3.11.18, 40
   3.13.23, 39
   3.22.33, 38, 87
   3.25.37, 50–1
   3.25.38, 56
   3.26.38, 50
   3.31.43, 30, 51, 63
   3.32.44, 55
   3.33.45, 53, 59, 64
   4.3.3, 34
   5.1.2, 79, 85
   5.3.5–4.6, 76
   5.6.8, 57, 79
   6.3.3, 77
   6.13.13, 79
   6.17.17–18.19, 82
   6.19.20, 77
   6.24.26, 82
   6.26.28, 82
   6.26.29, 79, 81–2
Fam.
   1.8.2, 47
   1.9.21, 86
   2.12.2, 78
   3.7.5, 28
   7.12, 95
   12.12.1, 95
   15.19.2, 95
Flac.
   24–26, 88
Font.
   21, 88
Leg. agr.
   2.1.3–2.2.5, 19
   2.9.22–11.29, 59
   2.11.28, 50
   2.17.45–46, 50
   2.35.95, 62
Marc.
   22, 198
Mil.
   80, 68
Mur.
   66, 16
Orat.
   17.55, 72
   34.120, 82
Par. stoi.
   34, 56
Phil.
   1.5.12, 65
   1.7.16, 49
   1.7.18, 49
   1.8.19, 49
   1.9.21–22, 66
   1.10.25, 49
   1.10.26, 49
   1.15.36, 59
   1.15.37, 59
   2.3.5, 47
   2.3.6, 49
   2.4.9, 47
   2.34.85, 59
   2.42.109, 49
   2.44.113, 78–9
   2.45.115, 59
   3.4.8, 55

3.5.12, 55
Pis.
   1.1-2, 16
Q. fr.
   2.9.3, 108
   3.5.1-2, 78
   3.5.2, 45
Quinct.
   3.11, 46
Rab.
   12.33, 68
Rosc.
   8.24, 46
Sest.
   6.15, 57
   9.20, 57
   15.34, 172
   22.49, 45
   34.73, 157
   35.75, 169
   36.69, 69
   36.77, 69
   39.84, 69
   39.86, 69
   42.91-92, 69
   45.96-98, 18
   45.98-46.98, 86
   46.98-99, 57
   54.115, 59
   55.117, 59
   56.120-21, 59
Top.
   2.9, 61
Tusc.
   1.1.1, 83
   1.13.30, 404
   1.14.31, 82, 85
   1.14.32, 82
   1.14.33, 84
   1.19.44, 81
   1.19.44-45, 77
   1.20.45, 80, 83
   1.20.47, 84
   1.24.57, 33

   1.25.62, 82-3
   1.26.64-65, 77
   1.28.68, 83-4
   1.28.69, 83
   1.30.74-1.31.76, 77
   1.31.76, 80
   1.37.90, 82
   2.1.1, 2
   2.18.42, 81
   2.21.48, 81
   2.24.58, 81
   3.1.2, 236
   3.2.3, 85
   3.2.4, 85, 291
   3.3.6, 80
   3.5.11, 236, 291
   3.10.23, 237
   3.14.30, 141
   3.15.33, 144
   3.17.36, 81
   3.17.36-37, 38
   3.23.55, 80
   3.29.72, 80
   3.31.76, 80
   3.32.77, 80
   4.1.1, 82-3
   4.2.3, 84-5
   4.3.6, 108
   4.10.23, 237
   4.10.23-11.27, 237
   4.10.24-11.25, 291
   4.11.26, 292
   4.13.29, 291-2
   4.13.31, 84
   4.23.51, 28, 69, 82
   4.28.60, 80
   4.28.61, 81
   4.29.63, 80
   4.35.74, 80
   4.38.83, 80
   5.2.5, 80, 82-3
   5.3.9, 86
   5.4.10, 82-3
   5.4.11, 29

Cic. (cont.)
   5.23.66, 77, 85
   5.23.105, 77
   5.23.111, 77
   5.23.115, 77
   5.24.69, 82
   5.25.70, 82
   5.25.71, 80, 82
   5.25.72, 82, 85
   5.28.81, 141
   5.36.103–4, 87
   5.36.105, 85
   5.37.108, 87
   5.39.114, 75
  Ver.
   2.1.13, 405

Dio
  55.5, 350
  59.19.7–8, 271
  61.10.2–6, 272
  61.3, 280
Diog. Oen.
  fr. 9 (Smith), 236
  fr. 56 (Smith), 105
Dion. Hal.
  Ant. Rom.
   2.7–29, 240
   4.19.2–3, 12
   21.2, 12
DL
  7.32–33, 42, 359, 398
  7.40, 274
  7.45–46, 236
  7.48, 238
  7.49–50, 236
  7.54, 288
  7.85, 285, 288
  7.86–89, 365
  7.87, 289
  7.87–88, 37, 289
  7.87–89, 38, 289
  7.88, 36, 38, 289
  7.94, 289

  7.97–98, 38, 289
  7.104, 289
  7.107, 288
  7.107–8, 38, 288
  7.116, 81
  7.118, 293
  7.121, 316, 366
  7.123, 275, 285
  7.124, 291
  7.127, 293
  7.130, 83, 296
  7.134, 36
  7.135, 274
  7.136, 36
  7.139, 274
  7.148–49, 36
  7.148–49, 41
  7.151, 380
  7.156, 274
  7.158, 292
  7.173, 45
  10.34, 98
  10.32, 101, 238
  10.120, 107
  10.121, 107
  10.123–37, 99
  10.136–37, 100

Ennius
  fr. 156 Sk, 15
Epic.
  Her.
   37, 103
   37–38, 127
   38, 101
   38–39, 116
   39–40, 97
   40–41, 97
   42, 98
   45, 98
   46, 110
   46–48, 99
   46–53, 236
   49, 111

50, 111
50–51, 104
51, 111
52, 101
62, 101
63, 98
64, 98
75–76, 105
77, 131
78, 103
80, 103
82, 102
83, 103
KD
  3, 99
  5, 135
  6, 95
  7, 106
  12, 103
  14, 106
  18, 104
  20, 102, 104
  23, 101
  24, 101
  28, 106
  32–33, 135
  34, 136
  36–38, 135
  40, 106
Men.
  23–24, 130
  122, 99
  124–25, 105
  124–27, 105
  127, 144
  128, 99
  128–129, 99
  129, 98–9
  130, 105
  131, 99–100
  132, 99, 103
  133, 105
Pyth.
  85, 103

85–88, 103
116, 103
Vat.
  23, 106
  28, 106
  34, 106
  39, 106
  52, 106
  56, 106
  58, 106
  61, 106
  66, 106
  78, 106
Epict.
  1.1.12, 365
  1.1.25, 362
  1.2.7, 366
  1.2.19–21, 370
  1.4.6, 366
  1.4.18, 362
  1.4.18–19, 366
  1.6.14–15, 362
  1.6.15, 366
  1.6.19, 379
  1.6.21, 362
  1.7.2, 362
  1.7.5, 362
  1.9.1, 376
  1.9.15–17, 366
  1.10.1–6, 366
  1.11.33, 366
  1.12.15, 365
  1.12.17, 359
  1.12.35, 366
  1.14.12, 380
  1.17.22, 366
  1.18.17, 366
  1.22.9, 365
  1.26.3, 362
  1.28.10, 363
  1.28.20, 362
  1.29.56, 362
  1.30.3, 365
  2.1.18, 376

Epict. (cont.)
  2.2.21, 364
  2.2.35, 364
  2.4.8, 359
  2.5.18, 380
  2.6.2, 365
  2.6.15, 366
  2.8.2, 361
  2.8.6–8, 362
  2.10.4–6, 377
  2.11.1, 362
  2.11.3–18, 104
  2.16.1, 365
  2.17.9, 104
  2.17.15, 364
  2.22.20, 366
  2.23.8–15, 366
  2.23.34–35, 366
  3.2.1, 364
  3.2.4, 366
  3.2.5, 363
  3.3.8, 365
  3.4.10, 381
  3.8.1, 362
  3.12.5, 362
  3.12.14–15, 363
  3.13.16, 373
  3.15.13, 362
  3.21.2, 362
  3.21.5, 366
  4.1.154, 377
Eusebius.
  Praep. Evang.
    15.15.3–5 = SVF 2.528 = LS 67L, 42

Florus
  1.33.1, 148
  1.34.18, 148
  1.47.1, 148

Gaius
  Inst.
    1.1, 36
    1.19, 79
    1.48, 51
    1.52, 51
    3.149–50, 46
    3.151, 46
    3.154, 47
    3.157, 47
    3.195, 47
    4.82, 79
Gal.
  De plac.
    F. 162.8–9, 245
    F. 164.53–54, 236
    F. 165.26–28, 236
    F. 169.114–17, 236
    F. 169.224–27, 236
Gellius
  9.12.15, 177

Historia Augusta
  19.12, 358
Hor.
  Ep.
    1.6, 141
  Ode
    3.14.13–16, 198
    4.5.25–8, 198
    4.15, 202

Juvenal
  5.109, 271

Laudatio Turiae
  2.25, 23
Livy
  pref. 4, 238
  pref. 5, 229
  pref. 9, 236–8
  pref. 10, 237–8
  pref. 12, 238
  1.4.9, 240
  1.5.7, 240
  1.6.3, 240
  1.7.2, 240
  1.8.2, 241, 243
  1.8.5, 240–1
  1.8.6, 240–1
  1.9.6, 240

1.9.14, 241
1.9.15, 241
1.10.4–5, 241
1.11.2, 241
1.11.4, 241
1.13.2, 241
1.13.4, 241
1.13.5, 241
1.13.6, 241
1.18.4, 242
1.19.1, 242
1.32.2, 242, 267
1.43.10, 12
1.47.6–7, 243
1.49.3, 245
1.49.4, 243, 245
1.49.5, 243
1.51.1, 243
1.52.4, 243
1.52.6, 243
1.56.7, 245
1.56.8, 245
1.58.4, 245
1.58.5, 246
1.59.3, 245
1.59.4, 245–6
1.59.8, 246
1.59.9, 246
1.59.11, 246
2.1.1, 246
2.1.2, 242
2.1.4, 254
2.1.6, 246
2.1.7, 247
2.1.8, 247
2.1.9, 247, 254
2.1.11, 250
2.2.5, 247
2.2.7, 248
2.7.7, 249
2.7.11, 249
2.23–24, 10, 249
2.29.9, 253
2.30.2, 253
2.32–33, 10

2.33.1, 248
2.33.1–2, 250
2.32–33, 249
2.52.2, 253
2.52.3, 254
3.13.4, 248
3.31.7, 247
3.31.8, 254
3.33.8, 254
3.33.10, 254
3.34.1, 254
3.34.2, 254
3.34.3, 247
3.34.8, 254
3.36.1, 254
3.36.4, 255
3.36.5, 255
3.36.6, 255
3.36.7–9, 255
3.36.8, 255
3.37.8, 255
3.38.1, 255
3.38.2, 255
3.38.8, 255
3.38.10, 255
3.38.11, 255
3.39.3, 256
3.39.4, 256
3.41.4, 256
3.44.4, 257
3.44.8, 256
3.44.9, 256
3.45.4, 256
3.45.8, 248, 256
3.45.11, 257, 312
3.46.1, 256
3.46.2, 256
3.46.3, 312
3.46.7, 312
3.46.8, 312
3.47.4, 256
3.48.3, 236
3.48.5, 257, 312
3.48.9, 257
3.49.1, 257

Livy (cont.)
  3.49.6, 257
  3.50.2–3, 257
  3.50.7, 257
  3.50.10, 257
  3.50.13, 258
  3.52.2, 258
  3.52.5, 258
  3.53.9, 257
  3.54.7, 258
  3.55.4, 248
  3.55.4–7, 258
  3.55.10, 248
  3.56.4, 257
  3.56.5–6, 248
  3.56.8, 257
  3.56.10–13, 248
  3.61.1, 258
  3.65.7, 250
  3.65.11, 247, 250
  4.5.1, 247
  4.5.2, 247
  4.6.11, 247
  4.13.4, 251
  4.15.6, 329
  4.16.1, 251
  4.20.7, 232, 259
  4.30.16, 249
  4.48.6, 248
  4.53.4, 248
  5.6.2, 260
  5.6.8, 260
  5.7.10, 250
  5.33.11, 236, 259
  5.36.1, 259
  5.37.3, 259
  5.37.4–5, 259
  5.37.7, 259
  5.37.8, 259
  5.38.1, 259
  5.38.3–4, 259
  5.38.5, 259
  5.38.7–8, 259
  5.39.1, 259
  5.41.4, 259
  5.42.3, 260
  5.42.4, 260
  5.42.8, 260
  5.44.2, 260
  5.44.6, 260
  5.46.5, 260
  5.46.6, 260
  5.48.3, 259, 261
  5.49.7, 261
  5.51.3, 261
  5.51.4, 261
  5.52.2–3, 261
  5.52.5, 261
  5.52.7, 261
  5.52.8, 261
  5.52.12, 261
  5.53.1, 261
  5.53.7, 261
  5.53.9, 261
  5.54.3, 261
  5.55.1, 261
  6.11.6, 251
  6.15.5, 252
  6.15.13, 252
  6.18.14, 252
  6.19.7, 252
  6.20.10, 252
  6.20.11, 252
  6.21.5, 249
  6.22.4, 249
  6.27.6, 247
  6.34–42, 249
  6.37.4, 11, 247, 249–50
  6.37.11, 247
  6.37.11–12, 247
  6.38.5, 248
  6.42.9–11, 11
  7.2.2, 239
  7.19.10, 249
  7.32.14, 253
  7.33.3, 247
  7.38.5–10, 251
  7.39.14–17, 251
  7.40.1, 252

7.40.2, 252
7.40.3, 253
7.40.6, 253
7.40.7–8, 253
7.40.11–14, 253
8.5.6, 263
8.5.8, 263
9.17.3, 270
9.28.4, 330
9.46.12–13, 249
10.9.1, 249
10.37.9, 248
21.17.4, 249
22.3, 238
22.4.1, 264
22.6.9, 264
22.6.12, 264
22.7.5, 264
22.7.6, 264–5
22.8.4, 264
22.11.6, 264
22.12.11–12, 238
22.12.12, 265
22.13.11, 264–5
22.14.1, 264
22.14.4–14, 265
22.14.6, 264
22.23.4, 264
22.27.3, 265
22.32.5, 264
22.38, 238
22.39.1, 238
22.54.8, 265
22.55.6–8, 266
22.57.1, 264
22.57.3, 264
22.57.11–12, 268
22.59.1, 268
22.59.18, 267
22.60.14, 268
22.60.15, 268
22.60.16, 268
22.60.18, 268
22.61.10, 264
23.4.6, 265

23.4.7, 266
23.5.9, 266
23.6.1, 266
23.6.3, 266
23.6.4, 266
23.7.1–2, 266
23.7.3, 266
23.7.5, 266
23.14.2–4, 268
23.22.5, 263
23.22.8, 263
23.32.9, 265
23.35.6, 269
23.35.8, 269
23.35.9, 269
24.16.11, 269
24.16.12, 270
25.37.2, 270
25.37.5–6, 270
25.37.7, 270
26.13.16, 267
26.16.8, 267
26.16.10, 267
26.16.11, 267
26.16.12, 267
26.16.13, 267
27.5.16, 249
30.43.2–3, 249
33.25.7, 249
33.46.1, 255
34.32.3, 301
38.45.5, 249
38.50.5–8, 247
40.34.4–6, 130
42.9–11, 250
Lucr.
  De rer. nat.
    1.1, 118
    1.4, 118
    1.8, 118
    1.11, 118
    1.19, 118
    1.20, 118
    1.23, 118
    1.40–43, 95

Lucr. (cont.)
   1.41–43, 117
   1.44–49, 117
   1.57, 118
   1.58–59, 115
   1.63, 120, 130
   1.65, 130
   1.66–67, 96, 120
   1.70–79, 104, 120
   1.79, 132
   1.83, 130
   1.84–101, 130
   1.102–3, 130
   1.104–5, 130
   1.107, 130
   1.107–9, 132
   1.110, 132
   1.112, 129
   1.136–39, 93
   1.146, 112
   1.146–48, 112
   1.147, 114
   1.148, 113
   1.151, 130
   1.156–57, 123
   1.159–214, 116
   1.169–71, 123
   1.169–73, 115
   1.172, 123
   1.173, 123
   1.221–24, 116
   1.223–24, 98
   1.237, 119
   1.240, 124
   1.263–64, 116
   1.302, 120
   1.304, 101
   1.335–39, 97
   1.420, 97
   1.422–25, 101
   1.455–58, 117
   1.459–63, 143
   1.465–66, 143
   1.526–39, 97
   1.584–86, 124
   1.584–98, 125
   1.586, 120
   1.586–87, 124
   1.595, 124
   1.600–614, 97
   1.699–700, 101
   1.716–41, 109
   1.814–15, 115
   1.923, 109, 118
   1.926–27, 109
   1.936–42, 113
   1.948–50, 113
   1.950, 138
   1.995–97, 97
   1.998–1000, 124
   1.1023, 121
   1.1023–25, 119
   1.1109–10, 118
   2.7–14, 94
   2.7–19, 141
   2.10–13, 133
   2.12–13, 138
   2.17–19, 99
   2.18–19, 94
   2.19, 96
   2.34–39, 133
   2.75–76, 116
   2.84–85, 115
   2.85–87, 115
   2.109, 120
   2.110, 120
   2.116–22, 115
   2.118–19, 120
   2.120, 115
   2.124–32, 128
   2.126–27, 134
   2.178–79, 98
   2.262–87, 98
   2.281, 278
   2.286, 123
   2.289–93, 102
   2.406–7, 113
   2.437, 113
   2.467, 113
   2.550, 120

INDEX LOCORUM

2.552, 120
2.563–64, 120
2.569–72, 116
2.584–98, 116
2.586, 124
2.586–87, 124
2.614–15, 130
2.646–51, 117
2.711–17, 115
2.920, 120
2.935–36, 120
2.937–43, 98
2.944–62, 134
2.956, 120
2.989–90, 119
2.1013–22, 113
2.1024–25, 113
2.1028, 119
2.1029, 119
2.1035, 119
2.1037, 119
2.1047, 119–20
2.1065, 120
2.1091, 120
2.1122–27, 134
2.1128–43, 116
2.1136–37, 134
2.1138–43, 134
2.1139–43, 116
2.1144–45, 134
2.1150, 117, 119
3.1, 138
3.28–30, 119
3.39, 112
3.55–58, 142
3.59–61, 134
3.62–63, 138
3.64, 127
3.70, 133–4
3.70–71, 128, 133
3.78, 128
3.79, 127
3.83–84, 133
3.83–86, 134
3.91, 112

3.136–46, 98
3.161–62, 98
3.231–35, 98
3.241–45, 98
3.253–55, 134
3.262–65, 123
3.264–65, 123
3.283–85, 123
3.322, 141
3.334, 123
3.378–79, 133
3.558–59, 123
3.674–76, 123
3.679–85, 123
3.971, 134
3.980–83, 132
3.992–94, 132
3.995–1002, 132
3.995–1023, 133
3.1723, 138
3.1737, 138, 142
3.1740–41, 138
4.11–25, 113
4.176–82, 113
4.197, 111
4.217, 111
4.244–49, 111
4.313, 112
4.337–52, 112
4.338, 112
4.343, 112
4.343–45, 114
4.348–52, 112
4.478–85, 101
4.483–614, 101
4.489, 123
4.622–26, 113
4.663–67, 134
4.665–69, 112
4.669–70, 113
4.671, 113
4.722, 111
4.722–822, 236
4.750–51, 111
4.802–3, 111

Lucr. (cont.)
   4.804–5, 111
   4.812–13, 111
   4.816–17, 111
   4.834–42, 122
   4.851–52, 122
   4.995–98, 128
   4.1097–1100, 127
   4.1161–1240, 129
   5.7, 133
   5.18, 113
   5.41–42, 129
   5.43–44, 113, 129
   5.43–48, 120
   5.44, 113, 120
   5.49–50, 120
   5.57, 120
   5.66, 116
   5.73, 129
   5.87, 120
   5.87–90, 125
   5.88, 129
   5.91–103, 119
   5.95–96, 116
   5.98, 116
   5.109, 116
   5.132–33, 98
   5.165–69, 117
   5.187, 115
   5.187–91, 115
   5.194, 119
   5.198–99, 115
   5.200–34, 115
   5.239, 116
   5.242–46, 116
   5.257–60, 116
   5.304–17, 116
   5.310, 120
   5.311, 133
   5.314–15, 133
   5.330–31, 119
   5.336–37, 93
   5.357–58, 116
   5.380–95, 120
   5.419–20, 115
   5.422–25, 115
   5.426, 120
   5.436, 115
   5.440, 115
   5.440–42, 120
   5.559–60, 98
   5.820, 122
   5.829–32, 116
   5.829–33, 117
   5.855–78, 123
   5.858, 126
   5.924, 120
   5.925–1104, 129
   5.925–52, 126
   5.932, 121
   5.937–38, 121, 126
   5.938, 126
   5.958–59, 121
   5.960–61, 126
   5.961, 126
   5.966, 126
   5.969, 121
   5.969–81, 121
   5.977–81, 126
   5.982–86, 127
   5.1000–1, 128
   5.1007–8, 126
   5.1008, 128
   5.1013–18, 122
   5.1019, 122
   5.1023, 122
   5.1025, 122
   5.1028–29, 124
   5.1033, 124
   5.1087, 124
   5.1087–90, 124
   5.1105–1457, 129
   5.1110–11, 126
   5.1111, 126
   5.1114–16, 126
   5.1119, 127
   5.1120–22, 128
   5.1123, 128
   5.1124, 128
   5.1128, 128

5.1134, 127
5.1141, 133
5.1143–44, 135
5.1147, 135
5.1151, 136
5.1154, 137
5.1155, 137
5.1165, 129
5.1169–82, 129
5.1169–87, 131
5.1172, 131–2
5.1175, 131–2
5.1183–87, 129
5.1185–86, 129
5.1186–87, 131
5.1188, 132
5.1194–95, 132
5.1195, 132
5.1198–1202, 131
5.1203, 141
5.1204–17, 129
5.1207, 130
5.1218, 130
5.1218–19, 132
5.1218–25, 136
5.1218–40, 129
5.1222, 132
5.1223, 132
5.1233–35, 143
5.1234–35, 133
5.1236–40, 129, 132
5.1276–80, 133
5.1305–7, 128
5.1361–62, 128
5.1432–33, 127
5.1432–35, 128
6.1, 138
6.1–3, 135
6.12–16, 138
6.15, 120
6.24, 113, 138
6.36, 138
6.41, 113
6.42, 113
6.54–55, 129

6.64–66, 125
6.65–66, 124
6.68, 113
6.381–82, 129
6.535–56, 139
6.557–76, 139
6.601–7, 138
6.639–41, 139
6.651, 139
6.652, 139
6.653–54, 139
6.657–664, 139
6.663, 139
6.665–72, 139
6.667, 139
6.668, 139
6.669, 139
6.769–72, 140
6.770, 139
6.922, 139
6.1093–96, 139
6.1158–60, 138
6.1222, 142
6.1222–23, 140
6.1230–34, 140
6.1236, 140
6.1239–41, 140
6.1240–41, 142
6.1243–44, 142
6.1245, 140
6.1246, 142
6.1278–80, 140

Marcus Aurelius
Medit.
  1.7, 360, 362
  1.9.3, 364, 378–9
  1.14, 371
  1.15.1, 368
  1.16, 361
  1.16.1, 369
  1.16.3, 367–8
  1.16.9, 369
  1.17.7, 368
  2.1, 378, 381

Marcus Aurelius (cont.)
 2.2, 362
 2.4, 374
 2.5, 364, 368
 2.5.2, 378
 2.6, 374
 2.7, 374
 2.10, 369
 2.13, 378–9
 2.13.6, 373
 2.14, 368
 2.15, 361, 363
 2.16, 368, 377
 2.17, 373
 3.2.1, 379
 3.2.2, 379
 3.4, 377
 3.4.1, 368
 3.4.3, 374–5
 3.5, 368–9, 381
 3.6, 369, 371
 3.6.2, 364, 380–1
 3.7, 368, 380
 3.8, 381
 3.10, 371, 374
 3.11, 363, 377
 3.11.2, 369, 376
 3.12, 381
 3.13, 381
 3.16.1, 362, 367
 3.16.2, 377, 381
 4.3.1, 367, 375
 4.3.2, 361, 371, 377
 4.3.3, 372, 375
 4.3.4, 363, 367, 375
 4.4, 371, 376–7
 4.7, 364
 4.10, 364
 4.14, 376
 4.17, 374
 4.19, 371
 4.21.1, 376
 4.26, 377
 4.29, 377
 4.32.1, 367
 4.32.1–2, 372
 4.32.2, 377
 4.33, 371
 4.36, 372
 4.39, 373
 4.40, 376
 4.43, 361, 373
 4.44–46, 376
 4.45, 374
 4.46, 361, 373
 4.48, 365
 4.50, 374
 5.1.2, 368
 5.5, 367
 5.8.1, 365
 5.8.2–3, 377
 5.9, 379
 5.10, 362
 5.11, 362
 5.12, 369
 5.13, 363
 5.16, 363, 378
 5.20, 367, 374
 5.24, 371
 5.26, 368
 5.27, 380
 5.30, 377
 5.33, 372
 6.4, 361, 376
 6.10, 361
 6.14, 368
 6.15, 375
 6.16, 368
 6.16.2, 368
 6.16.3, 367–8
 6.17, 361, 373
 6.18, 367
 6.24, 361
 6.30.1, 377
 6.30.2, 369
 6.35, 368
 6.36, 373
 6.36.1, 372
 6.38, 376
 6.39, 377–8

INDEX LOCORUM

6.40, 368–9
6.42, 377
6.44, 376
6.45, 377
6.46, 372
6.48, 368
6.55, 368
7.2.1, 373
7.3, 379
7.6, 371
7.7, 368–9
7.8, 368
7.9, 361, 376
7.10, 372
7.13, 376, 378, 381
7.19, 361, 373
7.20, 365
7.21, 371
7.23, 361
7.24, 368
7.26, 379
7.28, 367
7.31, 368, 378
7.32, 361
7.37, 365, 368
7.47, 373, 376
7.48, 371
7.55, 365–6
7.55.2, 381
7.59, 368
7.60, 369
7.61, 369
7.65, 379
7.67, 367
7.68, 367
7.75, 366
8.1, 366
8.7, 362, 364, 377
8.8, 379
8.10, 369
8.16, 365, 367
8.17, 361
8.19, 368
8.25, 361
8.26, 363, 365–6

8.29, 363
8.30, 369
8.32, 374
8.34, 361, 365, 375, 377
8.35, 374
8.36, 374
8.41, 374
8.44, 367
8.45.2, 381
8.46, 368
8.48, 367–8, 374
8.49, 363
8.50, 375
8.51.2, 379
8.52, 373
8.56, 369
8.57, 379
9.1.1, 377, 380
9.1.1–4, 377
9.1.2, 364
9.1.4, 369
9.2, 381
9.3.1, 375
9.4, 381
9.6.1, 361
9.7, 363–5
9.9, 376
9.9.1, 376
9.9.3, 378
9.11, 379
9.12, 379
9.14, 376
9.15, 363
9.19, 375
9.23, 377
9.27, 378
9.28, 361, 373
9.28.2, 372
9.29, 359
9.30, 371
9.32, 372
9.37, 363
9.40, 368
9.42.5, 377–8
10.2, 364–5, 377

Marcus Aurelius (cont.)
  10.5, 377
  10.6, 361
  10.7, 376
  10.7.2, 361, 375
  10.8.1, 379
  10.11, 375, 378
  10.15, 377
  10.18, 375
  10.21, 378, 381
  10.23, 371
  10.25, 369
  10.27, 372
  10.31.2, 362
  10.33, 374
  10.33.4, 361, 373
  10.34, 361
  10.35, 363
  10.37, 362, 376
  10.38, 362
  11.1, 362
  11.1.2, 371, 378
  11.2, 374
  11.3, 361
  11.4, 381
  11.5, 368
  11.6, 361
  11.6.2, 361
  11.8, 377
  11.9, 362
  11.10, 377
  11.11, 367
  11.14, 367
  11.15, 368–9
  11.16, 369, 374
  11.18.1, 361, 377
  11.18.10, 368–9
  11.20, 377
  11.20.2, 375
  11.21, 361
  11.26, 371
  11.37, 379
  12.1.1, 365, 377
  12.1.2, 377
  12.3, 379
  12.8–10, 363
  12.14, 361
  12.18, 363
  12.21, 361, 373, 375
  12.22, 361, 363
  12.23, 361, 373
  12.24, 361, 371–2
  12.26, 363, 376
  12.29, 373
  12.30, 361, 377–8
  12.32, 366, 372
  12.36, 377

Oros
  5.8.2, 148

Philod.
  Against the Sophists
    4.9–15, 103
  On Music
    4, col. 18.16–19, 109

Plato
  Laws
    716c–d, 141
  Phaed.
    81a–84b, 141
  Phaedr.
    245c–249a, 141
  Rep.
    358e–359b, 40
    431d–432a, 48
    500c–501b, 141
    613a–b, 141
  Theaet.
    173e, 371
  Tim.
    41d–47c, 141
    90c–d, 141

Pliny
  Ep.
    3.20.12, 278, 333
  NH
    7.121, 130
    33.150, 148

INDEX LOCORUM

Plut.
  Cato Mai.
    22.4, 2
    22.4–5, 2
    23.1, 2
    27, 148
  De comm. not.
    1081c–1082a, 373
    1084f, 288
    1084f–1085a, 236
  De stoic. rep.
    1042d, 296
  De tranq.
    465f-466a, 106
  De virt. Alex.
    329a–b, 42
  Non posse suav.
    1086f–1087a, 107
    1092e–1096c, 107
  Tib. Gr.
    10.2, 13
    12.1–44, 14

Polyb.
  6.9.13, 8
  6.14.1–12, 8
  6.18, 48
  6.18.2, 8, 148
  6.18.7, 8
  6.31.1–14, 337
  6.43.2, 8
  6.50.6, 8
  6.51.5–6, 8
  6.53, 16
  6.57.1, 8
  6.57.5, 148
  31.25, 148
  32.13.6, 148
  38.21–22, 148

Quint.
  Inst.
    6.2.29, 239
    6.2.29–30, 236
    55.10.13, 15

Sal.
  Cat.
    pref. 3, 2
    1.1, 155, 157
    1.1–4, 162
    1.2, 155
    1.3–4, 155, 165
    1.4, 155
    2.8, 155
    3.2, 162, 174
    3.3–4, 157
    4.2, 162, 176
    5.1–5, 157
    5.6, 157
    6.2, 150, 152
    6.5, 151–2, 156
    6.6, 151
    6.7, 151
    7.1, 152
    7.2, 151
    7.3, 152
    7.3–6, 152
    8.5, 145, 176
    9.1, 150
    9.1–5, 152
    10.1, 154
    10.4, 154
    10.5, 152
    11.1–2, 154
    11.2, 154
    11.2.8, 155
    11.3, 156
    11.4, 156, 178
    11.5–6, 158
    11.5–7, 156
    11.6, 158
    11.7, 156
    12.1, 154
    13.3, 157, 159
    13.5, 157
    14.1–3, 133
    14.2, 157
    14.4–5, 157
    14.5, 157

INDEX LOCORUM

Sal. (cont.)
  15.5, 157
  16.1–2, 157
  16.4, 157
  17.2, 160
  17.5, 160
  20.1, 159–60
  20.2–3, 158
  20.3, 160
  20.4, 160
  20.6, 160
  20.8, 160
  20.13, 160
  21.2, 160–1
  29.2–3, 67
  29.3, 176
  30.4, 154
  31.3, 28
  34.1, 176
  36.4, 176
  37.5, 157
  37.6, 157
  38.3, 147, 176
  39.4, 165
  44.5, 47
  51.1–4, 162
  51.4, 162
  51.15, 162
  51.20, 95
  51.21–23, 163
  51.27, 163
  51.34, 156
  51.37–38, 163
  51.39–40, 163
  51.40, 163
  51.43, 176
  52.4, 163
  52.5, 159
  52.9, 163
  52.10, 165, 176
  52.11, 157, 165
  52.19, 162–3
  52.21, 162
  52.22, 164
  52.23, 159
  52.28, 162
  52.30–31, 163
  52.36, 163
  53.5, 161
  54.1, 161
  54.2, 164
  54.3, 164–5
  54.6, 164–5
  61.8–9, 165

Hist.
  1.3 McGushin = Aug. *Civ. Dei.* 2.18, 150
  1.8 McGushin, 149
  1.10 McGushin = Aug. *Civ. Dei.* 2.18, 150
  1.12 McGushin = Gellius 9.12.15, 177
  1.14 McGushin = Arusianus Messius 484.19, 154
  1.48.7 McGushin, 177
  1.48.10 McGushin, 177
  1.48.20 McGushin, 176
  1.48.27 McGushin, 177
  1.55.24 McGushin, 157
  1.67.3 McGushin, 177
  1.77.1 McGushin, 177
  1.77.3 McGushin, 160
  2.47.5 McGushin, 165
  3.34.1 McGushin, 176
  3.34.13 McGushin, 177
  3.34.15 McGushin, 176
  3.34.19 McGushin, 177
  3.34.21 McGushin, 177
  3.34.26 McGushin, 176
  3.34.27 McGushin, 178
  3.48.3 McGushin, 164
  4.48.8 McGushin, 176

Jug.
  1.3, 166
  3.2, 176
  3.2–3, 174–5
  4.1, 145, 174
  4.3, 145
  4.5, 150, 166, 174

4.5–6, 145
4.6, 150, 166, 174
4.6–7, 174
4.7, 167, 174
5.1, 175–6
5.4, 176
5.7, 167
6.1, 166
6.3, 149, 166
7.5, 166
7.7, 167
8.1, 167
8.2, 156, 167
9.2, 176
10.4, 167
10.6, 150
13.5, 168, 176
13.6, 168
13.7, 168
14.1, 168
14.4, 168
14.7, 168
14.8, 176
14.17, 168
14.23, 168
15.2, 168
15.5, 169
16.2–3, 169
16.5, 169
20.6, 169
21.4, 176
22.2, 169
24.10, 168
26.3, 169
27.1, 169
27.2, 176
27.3, 169, 176
28.4–5, 169
29.1, 169
29.5, 169
30.3, 176
31.1, 176
31.2, 170
31.3, 178
31.5, 170

31.8, 177
31.9, 178
31.10, 170
31.11, 170, 178
31.12, 154, 170
31.14, 170
31.17, 170
31.20, 178
33.3, 176
34.2, 176
35.10, 154, 173
39.3, 176
40.1, 176
40.2, 178
40.3, 170
41.2, 176
41.3, 154
41.5, 149, 176
41.7–8, 153
41.9, 149, 173
42.1, 175
42.4, 178
42.4–5, 178
44.1, 172
44.3, 172
44.4–5, 178
44.5, 170, 172
45.1, 178
45.1–3, 175
45.2, 172
45.2–4, 171
51.1, 175
63.2, 171
63.4, 176
63.6–7, 171
64.1, 152
64.2, 171
64.5–6, 171
65.2, 176
65.4–5, 171
66.2, 176
84.1, 176
85.4, 172
85.12, 172
85.14, 172

INDEX LOCORUM

Sal. (cont.)
  85.15, 173
  85.21, 172
  85.29–30, 172
  85.38, 172
  86.2, 172
  87.1, 172
  87.1–3, 173
  88.4, 172
  95.3, 173
  111.1, 176
  112.3, 176
SE
  Adv. math.
    7.166–89, 29
    7.211–16, 101
  Pyr.
    2.63, 113
Sen.
  Cons. Helv.
    6.8, 274
    10.8, 3
  Cons. Marc.
    20.3, 296
  De ben.
    1.3.8, 317
    1.4.2, 317
    1.4.3, 319
    1.4.4, 319
    1.5.2, 319
    1.5.3, 319
    1.5.5, 319
    1.6.1, 317, 319
    1.6.2, 319
    1.9.1, 319
    1.10.5, 319
    1.11.1, 318
    1.11.4, 318
    1.11.5, 318
    1.12.1, 318
    1.12.3, 310, 317
    1.15.4, 319
    2.18.7, 319
    2.20.2, 283
    3.7.1–3.8.4, 310

    3.7.5, 274, 276
    3.8.1–4, 317
    3.15.1–4, 317
    3.17.3, 319
    3.18.3, 318
    3.21.22, 318
    3.26.1, 305
    3.28.2, 309
    4.7.1, 274
    4.10.1–2, 311
    4.17.2, 285
    4.18.3, 320
    4.18.4, 320
    5.12.5, 289
    6.23.6, 316
    6.41.2, 317
    7.1.7, 316
  De clem.
    1.1.1, 281–2
    1.1.2, 281
    1.1.4, 280
    1.1.5, 272
    1.1.7, 282
    1.2.1, 284
    1.2.2, 284–5
    1.3.2, 285
    1.3.3, 282
    1.3.5, 282
    1.4.1, 282
    1.4.2, 282
    1.5.1, 278, 282
    1.6.1, 282
    1.7.2, 282
    1.9.1–10, 282
    1.11.1, 282
    1.11.3, 272
    1.14.1–2, 283
    1.14.3, 282
    1.18.1, 283
    1.18.2, 283
    1.19.1, 283
    1.19.2, 283
    1.24.2, 277, 291
    1.25.2, 284, 300
    2.1.2, 284

2.3.2, 283
2.4.2, 284, 300
2.4.2–3, 272
2.4.3, 285
2.4.4, 284
2.5.4–6.1, 284
2.7.3, 281, 284
De cons. sap.
  2.2, 313
  2.2–3, 301
  2.6, 301
  3.2, 301
  3.3, 301
  7.1, 289
  8.3, 293
  9.2–5, 296
  16.2, 297
  19.2, 296
De ira
  1.2.4, 299
  1.2.5, 299
  1.5.3, 317
  2.2.2, 310
  2.8.2, 300
  2.8.3, 300
  2.18.1–36.6, 309
  2.22.4, 277, 314
  2.23.3, 313
  2.27.2, 274
  3.1.2, 292
  3.5.3, 274
  3.6.1, 275, 288
  3.18.3–4, 300
  3.30.4, 313
  3.34.2, 293
  3.36.3, 314
De ot.
  3.2, 106, 275
  3.4, 286
  4.1, 275
  4.1–2, 316
  8.1–4, 275
De prov.
  1.2, 274
  1.3, 274

  2.10, 296
  5.6–7, 274
  5.7, 274
  6.1, 293
  6.7, 296
De tranq.
  2.5, 301, 307
  2.6, 302, 307
  2.9, 303
  2.11, 303
  3.2, 275
  3.7, 276
  3.7–8, 303
  4.1, 276
  4.4, 320
  4.6, 318
  5.2, 313
  5.4, 276
  5.5, 286
  10.4, 293
  10.5, 306
  11.2, 293
  11.4–5, 297
  12.3, 307
  14.1, 301
  14.2, 301
  14.3, 298
  15.1, 301
  17.1, 306
  17.10, 303
De vita beata
  3.4, 296
  4.5, 296
Ep.
  3.2, 274
  3.3, 274
  3.4, 302
  3.5, 302
  4.4, 295
  4.8, 277, 281
  5.4, 285, 289, 300
  6.5, 313
  6.7, 314
  7.3, 299
  7.4, 299

Sen. (cont.)
   7.6–7, 304
   7.7, 290, 301
   7.11, 314
   8.3, 295
   8.4, 295
   9.8, 319
   9.17, 285
   9.22, 305
   11.7, 45
   11.8, 313
   11.9, 274
   11.9–10, 313
   11.10, 313
   12.10, 296
   13.1, 277, 291
   13.5, 302
   13.7, 302
   13.9, 292
   14.1, 285
   14.4, 297
   14.6, 296
   14.7, 273, 306
   14.13, 273
   14.16, 296
   15.11, 295
   16.5, 294
   16.6, 294
   16.9, 302
   17.6, 277
   18.1, 274
   18.4, 298
   18.11, 274
   19.5, 274
   19.8, 274
   20.1, 315
   20.2, 274
   22.3, 274
   22.5–6, 296
   22.7, 273–4
   22.11, 296
   23.2, 81
   23.11, 314
   24.3–6, 313
   24.17, 314
   25.2, 309
   25.4, 295
   25.4–5, 314
   25.5, 313
   25.5–6, 313
   25.6, 274, 314
   26.6, 307
   26.7, 314
   26.10, 296
   27.1, 314
   28.3, 307
   28.4, 316
   28.10, 314
   29.3, 274
   29.11, 306
   29.12, 306
   30.7, 274
   30.11, 274
   31.1, 308
   31.2, 304
   31.10, 295
   31.11, 309
   33.3, 312
   33.4, 312, 314
   33.6, 312
   33.7, 312
   33.7–8, 312
   33.10, 313
   35.2, 314
   36.6, 274
   37.4, 295–6
   37.5, 296
   38.2, 310
   39.1–2, 313
   39.3, 274, 296
   39.5, 292
   40.1, 307, 315
   40.11–13, 315
   41.5, 309, 380
   42.3, 305
   42.7–8, 313
   44.1, 309
   44.2, 309
   44.3, 309, 313
   45.2, 274

45.7, 304
47.2–4, 294, 308
47.10, 317
47.14, 274, 318
47.15, 318
47.16, 318
47.19, 305
47.20, 274, 304–5
48.3, 274
48.10, 274
50.5, 309
51.8, 305
51.9, 296
52.6, 309
55.3, 305
55.4, 302
55.5, 274, 302
55.8–11, 313
55.11, 314
56.8, 303
56.9, 302
56.10, 302
57.3, 274
59.15, 293
62.2–3, 313
63.2, 274
65.3, 308
65.12, 274
65.19, 274
65.22, 274
66.6, 289
66.13, 296
66.22, 380
66.23, 295
70.10, 349
70.14–16, 296
71.1, 310
71.7, 274
71.9, 313
71.28, 274, 317
71.37, 277
73.9, 318
73.10, 277
74.1, 295
74.4, 304

74.7, 295, 298
74.8, 299
74.9, 299
74.20, 274
75.1, 316
75.3, 315
75.4, 315
75.11, 291
76.9–10, 289
76.31, 295
76.32, 295
77.6, 296
77.12, 274
77.19, 274
78.20, 274
78.21, 314
79.13, 303
79.14, 304
80.1, 314
80.7, 306
82.29–30, 283
83.1, 308, 315
83.2, 308
84.2, 314
84.5, 314
85.13, 277
85.40, 309
86.2, 274
86.10, 274
87.5, 293
87.36, 289
88.22, 299
88.30, 317
89.14, 288
90.5, 274
91.4, 295
91.5, 295
92.3, 275, 288
92.11–13, 278
93.4, 274, 317
94.1, 311
94.2, 311
94.4, 311
94.5, 274, 309
94.7–8, 311

Sen. (cont.)
94.8, 313
94.10, 313
94.11, 311
94.12, 311
94.14–16, 310
94.15, 311
94.18, 311
94.19, 310
94.20, 311
94.21, 310
94.25, 310
94.26, 310
94.27, 274, 310
94.28–29, 310
94.29, 310
94.30, 310
94.31, 310
94.32, 310
94.33, 274
94.34, 312
94.34–35, 310
94.35, 310
94.36, 310
94.37, 274, 310
94.47, 310
94.48, 289
94.49, 312
94.51, 310
94.52, 313
94.53–54, 290
94.55, 310, 313
94.57, 300
94.59, 313
94.64, 293
94.65, 313
94.66–68, 313
94.68, 283
94.72, 313
94.73, 306
94.74, 307
95.12, 311
95.14, 326
95.14–15, 326
95.15, 326

95.29, 301
95.30, 291, 293, 301
95.33, 299–300
95.40, 312
95.41, 274
95.51, 317
95.52, 283, 316
95.57, 289
95.57–58, 307
95.59, 311
95.61–62, 311
95.64, 311
95.70–71, 313
95.73, 300
99.6, 274
99.9, 295
99.19, 274
100.9, 234
101.1, 274
101.3, 274
101.5, 293
101.7, 274
101.15, 305
102.6, 274
102.11, 303
102.12, 304
102.13, 304
102.14–15, 303
102.17, 303–4
103.2, 305
103.3, 274
104.21, 313
104.27, 313
105.1, 305
105.6, 302
106.2, 274
107.6, 274
107.6–12, 274
109.1, 319
109.2, 290
109.2–3, 319
110.20, 277
113.30, 274, 294
114.23, 274
115.3, 274

115.8, 293
117.19, 274
117.30, 274
118.3, 295, 302
118.3–4, 305
119.8, 294
120, 287
120.2, 274
120.4, 285, 288, 290
120.5, 290
120.8, 290
120.9, 290
120.10, 289
120.11, 274
120.18, 419
120.22, 306
121, 287
121.5–6, 284
121.6, 284
121.8, 285
121.12, 285
121.14, 285
121.17, 285
121.19, 285
121.21, 285
121.22, 285
122.2, 274
122.3, 274
123.16, 274, 293
124.3, 277
124.6, 290
Her.
  159–85, 302
Nat. quaest.
  1.pref. 8–10, 317
  3.pref. 16, 316
  1.16–17, 344
  3.15.3, 274
  3.16.4, 274
  3.29.3, 274
  3.29.7, 274
Thy.
  401–3, 302
  455, 302
  468, 302

Stob.
  2.7.5b1 P = *SVF* 3.262, 38, 40, 289
  2.7.5b3 P = *SVF* 3.264, 289
  2.7.5b3 P = *SVF* 3.264, 37, 290
  2.7.5b8 P = *SVF* 1.566, 285
  2.7.5b13 P = *SVF* 3.663, 291
  2.7.5l P = *SVF* 1.68, 48
  2.7.6a P = *SVF* 1.179, 37
  2.7.6a P = *SVF* 1.179, 1.552, 3.12, 3.20, 3.40, 3.57, 289
  2.7.6e P = *SVF* 1.554, 38, 289
  2.7.7 P = *SVF* 3.118, 290
  2.7.8 P = *SVF* 1.230, 38
  2.7.10c P = *SVF* 3.395, 402, 408, 413, 292
  2.7.10e P = *SVF* 3.421, 292
  2.7.11a P = *SVF* 3.500, 38, 289
  2.7.11b P = *SVF* 3.625, 48
  2.7.11d P = *SVF* 3.640, 275
  2.7.11e P = *SVF* 3.501–2, 38, 289
  2.7.11g P = *SVF* 3.567, 290
  2.7.11i P = *SVF* 1.587, 42, 316
  2.7.11i P = *SVF* 3.567, 290
  2.7.11k P = *SVF* 3.677, 291, 316
  2.7.11m P = *SVF* 3.366, 289
  2.7.11m P = *SVF* 3.686, 275
  2.7.11m P = *SVF* 3.758, 296
Suet.
  Dom.
    10.1, 355
    10.3–4, 355
  Nero
    10.1, 280
    52, 2
  Tib.
    25, 349
    61, 345

Tac.
  Agric.
    2.1, 354
    2.3, 347, 354
    3.1, 328, 353, 355
    3.3, 352
    4.3, 2

Tac. (cont.)
  6.3, 332
  11.4, 327
  13.1, 327
  21.1, 327
  21.2, 328
  42.4, 353
  Ann.
    1.1.1, 322, 325
    1.1.2, 330
    1.2.1, 23, 324, 329, 343
    1.3.2, 324
    1.3.7, 330
    1.4, 324
    1.4.1, 330
    1.4.2, 341
    1.4.5, 305
    1.7.1, 331, 337, 341
    1.7.3, 331
    1.8.5–6, 340
    1.9.4–5, 329
    1.10.1, 324, 330
    1.11.2–3, 341
    1.12.3, 278, 333
    1.14.4, 22
    1.15.1, 22
    1.16.3, 336–7
    1.16.3–17.1, 336
    1.18.1, 336
    1.18.2, 336–8
    1.19.2, 336
    1.19.5, 336
    1.21.3, 337
    1.22.1, 337
    1.23.1, 337
    1.24.1, 337
    1.25.2, 338, 341
    1.26.1, 338
    1.26.3, 338
    1.28, 23
    1.28.6, 338
    1.31.1, 338, 340
    1.31.3, 338
    1.34.3, 338
    1.35.1–2, 338
    1.35.2, 324
    1.35.3, 340
    1.37.1, 338
    1.38.2, 347
    1.46.1, 332, 339
    1.46.3, 339
    1.52.1, 340
    1.53.3, 328
    1.54.2, 337
    1.64.1, 337
    1.72.3, 355
    1.72.4, 346
    1.73.1, 347
    1.74.1, 346
    1.74.2, 346
    1.74.5, 333
    1.75.1, 347
    1.77, 340
    1.77.1, 339
    1.77.1–3, 331–2
    1.78.2, 339
    1.81, 22
    2.2.4, 328
    2.27.1, 347
    2.28.2, 349
    2.28.3, 347
    2.29.2, 350
    2.30.3, 350
    2.31.1, 350
    2.31.3, 350
    2.32, 355
    2.38.1, 332
    2.42.3, 350
    2.87, 350
    2.87.1, 340–1
    3.11.2, 341
    3.15.2, 343
    3.16.4, 328
    3.17–18, 355
    3.19.2, 341
    3.22.2, 337, 341
    3.23.1, 339
    3.25.2, 326
    3.26.1, 329
    3.26.2, 328, 330

3.27.1, 328
3.27.3, 328
3.28.1, 328
3.28.3, 330
3.29.3, 340
3.30, 342
3.31.2–4, 342
3.34.3, 328
3.35.1, 332, 342
3.35.2, 333
3.36.1, 339
3.52–54, 332
3.56.2, 20
3.60.1, 332
3.65.1, 328, 355
3.65.2, 341
3.65.3, 332
3.66.1, 348
3.66.3, 348
3.66.4, 348
3.67.2, 350
3.67.4, 337
3.69.2–6, 331
3.74.4, 23
3.76, 355
4.1.3, 342, 347
4.6, 331
4.6.1, 333
4.6.2, 332
4.7.1, 333
4.10.2, 347
4.11.2, 341
4.12.1, 352
4.14.3, 339–40
4.17.1, 342
4.21.2, 347
4.21.3, 355
4.27.2, 347
4.28, 347
4.30.2, 348
4.30.3, 347
4.32.2, 323–4, 331
4.33, 330, 355
4.33.2, 354
4.33.3, 348

4.34–35, 354
4.35.2, 354
4.35.4, 355
4.35.5, 355
4.37.1–38.3, 331
4.51.2, 337
4.52, 347
4.52.4, 347
4.66.1, 347
4.67.3, 347
4.68.2, 347
4.69.3, 350
5.4.1, 328
5.4.2, 340
6.3.1–3, 331
6.7.3, 343, 347
6.8.4, 343
6.10.1, 348
6.11.2, 347
6.13.1, 339–40
6.19.2, 345, 348
6.19.3, 348, 352
6.23.1, 350
6.23.2, 350
6.24.3, 350
6.25.1, 350
6.26.2, 350
6.27.3, 332
6.38.1, 351
6.42.2, 351
6.45.3, 342
6.51.3, 322
11.5.1, 347
11.6.2, 324, 347
11.11.2, 340
11.13.1, 340
11.24.4, 241
11.38, 355
11.38.3, 349
12.7.1, 340
12.41.3, 328
12.50.2, 324
12.66.1, 324
13.1, 343
13.2.1, 272

Tac. (cont.)
    13.4.1, 341
    13.4.2, 280
    13.4.2–5.1, 280
    13.11.2, 280
    13.15.3–5, 272
    13.16.4, 341
    13.25.1–2, 344
    13.25.3, 344
    13.25.4, 344
    13.26.1, 341–2
    13.26.2, 343
    14.3, 348
    14.12.2, 342
    14.13, 348
    14.14, 342–3
    14.15, 348
    14.15.1–2, 343
    14.15.2, 344
    14.15.3–4, 344
    14.15.5, 343–4
    14.20, 343
    14.20.4, 344
    14.45, 342
    14.48, 347
    14.49.1, 351
    14.49.3, 351
    14.50.1, 341
    14.53–56, 271
    14.59, 348
    14.60.1, 342
    14.61, 340
    14.62, 348
    14.64, 348
    14.64.3, 342
    15.35, 343
    15.35.1, 286
    15.35.3, 350
    15.37, 343
    15.37.1, 344
    15.50, 348
    15.54.1, 343
    15.61.1, 351
    16.5.2, 344
    16.7, 343
    16.7–35, 347
    16.11.3, 350
    16.16.1, 351
    16.17.3, 342
    16.19.1, 351
    16.21, 342
    16.21.1, 343, 349
    16.23.1, 343
    16.26.5, 332
    16.29.1, 351
    16.35.1, 353
Dial.
    20.4, 357
    21.8, 356
    39.1–2, 352
Germ.
    7.1, 327
    7.3–4, 327
    12.2, 327
    13.3–4, 327
    19.1, 327
    19.5, 329
    21.1, 327
    22.4, 327
Hist.
    1.1, 330, 354
    1.2, 346–7
    1.4, 344
    1.5, 342
    1.15, 345
    1.72, 339
    1.85, 342
    2.38, 322
Thuc.
    7.77, 377

Varro
  Ling.
    6.86, 10
Velleius Paterculus
    2.1.1, 148
    2.89.3–4, 23
    2.130.3, 349

INDEX LOCORUM

Vir.
  A
    1.1–2, 203
    1.8, 207
    1.10, 223
    1.25–33, 203
    1.32, 203
    1.33, 223
    1.50–63, 192
    1.57, 208
    1.92, 203
    1.132–34, 217
    1.151, 198
    1.153, 208
    1.178, 220
    1.209, 203
    1.247–49, 225
    1.264, 223
    1.275–78, 225
    1.278, 183
    1.286–88, 216
    1.335–71, 219
    1.418–49, 225
    1.421, 224
    1.421–28, 224
    1.454–55, 224
    1.456, 224
    1.460–63, 203
    1.462–64, 205
    1.494, 205, 224
    1.544–45, 214
    1.602, 217–18
    2.3, 207
    2.12, 207
    2.270–80, 204
    2.271–79, 204
    2.298–308, 204
    2.314–17, 204
    2.316, 205
    2.325, 204
    2.355, 205
    2.363–66, 204
    2.430, 203
    2.486–87, 204
    2.536, 211
    2.558, 204
    2.594–95, 205
    2.701–4, 216
    2.707–10, 226
    2.707–9, 215
    2.709–10, 226
    2.717, 215
    2.723–24, 215
    2.771, 205
    2.793, 204
    3.13–69, 225
    3.94, 223
    3.132, 224
    3.132–39, 225
    3.145, 220
    3.160, 223
    3.167–68, 216
    3.333–51, 225
    3.335–36, 217
    3.349–51, 217
    3.354–55, 217
    3.458–59, 223
    3.489, 216
    3.498, 224
    3.503–5, 219
    3.505, 200
    3.590–92, 205
    3.606, 205
    3.613–14, 205
    4.1–5, 219
    4.17–33, 219
    4.101–4, 219
    4.137–39, 218
    4.193–94, 219
    4.194, 208
    4.206–8, 217
    4.272–76, 223
    4.273, 226
    4.341–43, 219
    4.344, 224
    4.347, 219
    4.393–95, 223
    4.395, 219

Vir. (cont.)
   4.396, 226
   4.434, 219
   4.449, 219
   4.467–68, 219
   4.479, 206
   4.498, 206
   4.624, 208
   4.652, 206
   4.658, 206
   4.659, 206
   5.76, 222
   5.94, 215, 222
   5.107, 222
   5.111–13, 217
   5.116–23, 216
   5.146–47, 222
   5.148–50, 222
   5.250–51, 217
   5.288–89, 222
   5.289, 222
   5.289–90, 222
   5.293, 222
   5.340–41, 222–3
   5.576, 216
   5.617, 224
   5.688, 226
   5.692, 226
   5.746–61, 225
   5.748, 219
   5.755–56, 224
   5.755–58, 217
   5.769, 223
   6.27, 204
   6.110–14, 215
   6.176–84, 223
   6.305, 205
   6.337–71, 205
   6.403, 214
   6.444, 207
   6.494–99, 204
   6.608–13, 211
   6.637–59, 227
   6.660–65, 226
   6.663, 227
   6.687–88, 215, 223
   6.689, 215
   6.695–96, 215
   6.701–2, 215
   6.715, 207
   6.721, 227
   6.724–27, 227
   6.730–47, 207
   6.756–892, 227
   6.760–78, 225
   6.769, 214
   6.771, 226
   6.771–72, 226
   6.776, 225
   6.782, 185
   6.794–805, 185
   6.817, 216
   6.822–23, 219
   6.824, 216
   6.842–3, 216
   6.845, 216
   6.847–53, 2
   6.851, 226
   6.851–53, 115
   6.853, 210
   6.878–79, 214
   6.889, 219, 226
   7.46–49, 186
   7.100–1, 183
   7.157–59, 224
   7.174, 183
   7.177, 183
   7.202–4, 186
   7.247, 183
   7.258, 183
   7.290–300, 208
   7.308–22, 208
   7.316, 209
   7.323–40, 209
   7.335, 209
   7.339, 209
   7.341–405, 209
   7.344–45, 209
   7.365–66, 209
   7.366, 209

7.371–72, 220
7.401–3, 209
7.423–24, 209
7.462, 209
7.467, 209
7.483–92, 186
7.510, 203
7.526, 197, 203
7.545, 212
7.551, 197
7.578–79, 210
7.595–97, 220
7.635–36, 203
7.805, 220
7.805–6, 220
7.912–17, 220
8.29, 212
8.184–89, 220
8.314–25, 186
8.316, 200
8.319–20, 218
8.323, 219
8.324–25, 186
8.325, 187
8.333, 219
8.338, 225
8.342, 219
8.347, 225
8.348, 225
8.355–58, 225
8.356, 225
8.358, 225
8.361, 225
8.481–93, 220
8.489, 220
8.489–94, 210
8.493, 220
8.494, 220
8.628, 225
8.630, 225
8.636, 222
8.637, 225
8.650, 225
8.665, 225
8.666, 225

8.676, 225
8.679, 183
8.685–88, 198
8.691, 225
8.696–713, 218
8.722–23, 226
8.730, 225–6
8.730–31, 226
9.133, 220
9.192, 183
9.227, 183
9.293–302, 215
9.357–66, 220
9.390–91, 204
9.446–49, 205
9.482, 206
9.485, 204–5
9.490, 206
9.497, 206
9.603, 218
9.607–8, 218, 223
9.614–15, 218
9.617–20, 217
10.106, 208
10.790–812, 216
10.824, 214
11.5, 223
11.252–95, 220
11.280, 205
11.304, 183
11.346, 183
11.379, 183
11.460, 183
11.507, 220
11.539–69, 220
11.569, 220
11.571–72, 220
11.578–80, 220
11.583–84, 220
11.657, 220
11.662, 220
11.664, 220
11.711, 220
11.778–82, 220
11.804, 221

Vir. (cont.)
    12.54–63, 209
    12.175–94, 211
    12.177, 226
    12.191–92, 226
    12.200, 226
    12.202–5, 211
    12.206–11, 210
    12.209, 219
    12.210, 224
    12.311–17, 211
    12.503–4, 208
    12.596, 210
    12.695, 211
    12.808–42, 211
    12.818–42, 212
    12.823–28, 218
    12.823–29, 217
    12.834–35, 217
    12.838, 217
    12.897–98, 210
    12.946, 206

E
    1.3, 197
    2.38–39, 200
    2.68, 199
    4.4–25, 197
    4.8, 201
    4.18–19, 186
    4.21–22, 186
    4.22, 186
    4.24–25, 186
    4.26–27, 197
    4.29, 186
    4.30, 186
    4.49, 185
    4.51, 185
    5.32–34, 194
    5.58, 187
    5.60, 186
    5.61, 187
    5.62–63, 187
    6.7, 202
    8.28, 186
    8.52, 186
    8.52–3, 186
    8.85–89, 199
    10.51–52, 197

G
    1.1, 194
    1.3, 200–1
    1.60, 192
    1.61–62, 192
    1.95, 200
    1.118–46, 195
    1.121–35, 187
    1.125, 196, 198
    1.125–27, 187
    1.125–28, 186
    1.127, 187
    1.127–28, 195
    1.129, 186
    1.130, 186
    1.145–46, 195, 198
    1.153, 200
    1.154, 294
    1.155, 196
    1.155–61, 198
    1.160, 196
    1.168, 198
    1.171, 192
    1.182, 194
    1.186, 194
    1.197–98, 192
    1.198, 200
    1.199–200, 198
    1.420, 196
    1.424–26, 196
    1.438–39, 196
    1.439, 196
    1.464–65, 196
    1.493–97, 197
    1.500, 198
    1.501, 217
    1.504, 198
    1.511, 198
    2.1, 200
    2.35, 200
    2.35–36, 196
    2.48, 200

2.51–52, 200
2.55, 200
2.61–62, 200
2.61–64, 198
2.77, 200
2.103–4, 186
2.114, 200
2.155, 202
2.226–56, 196
2.279–87, 198
2.415, 201
2.415–19, 201
2.461–68, 198
2.474, 187, 198
2.483–85, 193
2.486, 194
2.486–89, 194
2.490–512, 187
2.490–92, 194
2.493–94, 194
2.505–12, 198
2.526–31, 194
3.16–39, 198
3.26–39, 202
3.46–48, 198
3.242–44, 194
3.288, 196
3.342–43, 194
3.349–83, 192
3.354–55, 194
3.377, 194
3.378–565, 198
3.452–56, 200
3.478–514, 192
4.1–7, 194

4.6, 194
4.67–70, 198
4.67–87, 185, 194
4.95, 194
4.106–7, 196
4.116–48, 201
4.149–50, 195
4.153–57, 194
4.158, 194
4.158–68, 194
4.158–69, 195
4.177, 194
4.203–5, 194
4.205, 194
4.206–9, 195
4.210–18, 198
4.215, 198
4.218, 194
4.220, 195
4.239–50, 200
4.363–67, 201
4.398, 196
4.405–14, 196
4.488, 199
4.489, 192
4.525, 199
4.555–56, 200
4.560–61, 201
4.559–62, 202

Zeno
  SVF 1.158, 36
  SVF 1.176, 36
  SVF 1.179, 141
  SVF 1.202, 38

INDEX

agreements. *See also* treaties
  about property, 59–62
  and trust, 62–67
  as *consensio*, 404
  as *consensus*, 47
  as *societas*, 46–69
Agricola, Cn. Julius, 354
Agrippina the Elder, 350
Agrippina the Younger, 271
Alba, 267
amicitiae defined, 17
Ancus, 62, 242
Annius, 263
Antonius, 19, 28
apatheia, 81, 368–69, 395
Appius Claudius, 254–58, 279, 322
Aristeaus, 191, 201
Aristotle, 1, 28, 32, 34–35, 45, 108, 113, 121, 123, 182, 232, 258, 330, 358, 394, 418, 426
  and Augustine. *See* Augustine: and Aristotle
  and Cicero. *See* Cicero: and Aristotle
  and Livy. *See* Livy: and Aristotle
  and Lucretius. *See* Lucretius: and Aristotle
  and Tacitus. *See* Tacitus: and Aristotle
Asinius Gallus, 350
Athenodorus of Tarsus, 275
auctoritas, 15, 21, 49, 51, 53–54, 57, 59, 64, 66, 160, 171, 270, 278, 302, 313, 427
  See also power
  Augustus, 278
  defined, 51
Augustine
  affection, 385
  agreements, 398, 404, 425
  and Aristotle, 394, 426
  and Cicero, 384, 398, 425
  and Plato, 383, 396, 408–9
  and Sallust, 398, 400
  and Seneca, 407
  and Socrates, 396
  and Stoicism, 383, 390, 394, 396, 398, 408, 415, 424
  and Virgil, 384–85, 419
  assessments of, 382, 416
  auctoritas, 427
  bonds of community, 425
  caritas. *See caritas*
  civitas, 398, 426
  confession, 428–29
  corruption, 402
  cupiditas, 391
  deception, 405
  desire, 385–93, 399–403
  despotism, 402, 423
  dominatio, 400–1
  dominor, 421
  duty, 407
  earthly city, 420, 425
  earthly power, 423
  entertainment, 402
  epistemology, 405, 408–16
  exempla, 385, 410
  fides, 415, 426
  fortitudo, 393
  foundings, 426
  glory, 399
  grief, 394
  heavenly city, 427
  imperium, 399–400, 404, 425, 427–28
  justice, 393, 423
  knowledge, 405
  language, 405, 412–13
  life, 382
  love, 385–93, 395, 408–16, 424
  memory, 388, 391, 409, 412, 414
  ontology, 386
  peace, 404
  perfectibility, 418
  political realism, 430
  potestas, 392, 401

INDEX

Augustine (cont.)
  prudentia, 393
  psychology, 385–93, 415
  res publica defined, 398
  res publica of Christ, 427
  Roman historiography, 385, 397
  sage. *See* sage
  sin, 391
  slavery, 422
  soul, 388
  temperantia, 393
  time, 392, 394–95
  Trinity, 409–16
  trust, 426
  understanding, 412
  virtue, 393–97
  will, 388, 396, 412, 415
  wisdom, 408–16
Augustus, 20, 22–24, 181, 183, 185, 188–89, 191, 206, 210, 216, 232, 242, 248, 276, 278–79, 321–22, 329–30, 345
  and Livy, 232
  and Virgil, 184–86, 188
  power, 19–24
  res publica restituta, 24–25
auxilium, 10

Barea Soranus, 349
beneficia, 89, 316
Brittanicus, 272
Bruttedius Niger, 348
Brutus, Lucius Junius, 120, 244–45, 248, 254, 257, 259
Brutus, Marcus Junius the Younger, 354, 370

Caesar, 27–28, 44–45, 64, 66, 83, 94–95, 145, 161–65, 174, 177, 214, 222, 229, 401
Caligula, 24, 271, 276, 280, 297, 300
Camilla, 219–20
Camillus, 82, 251, 258–62, 265, 268
Campania, 266
Cannae, 265, 267
Capua, 266
caritas, 408, 415, 420, 428
Carneades, 39, 57, 303
Carthage, 62, 146, 148–49, 152–54, 163, 168, 177, 205, 224–25, 255, 262, 266, 384, 388, 401
Cassius, Gaius, 95, 354
Catallus, 187
Catiline, 155–61, 177
  in Cicero. *See* Cicero: Catilinarian conspiracy
  in Sallust. *See* Sallust: Catilinarian conspiracy
  trust, 160
Cato the Elder, 2, 148
Cato the Younger, 157, 161–65, 174, 296, 313, 370

Celsus, 324, 326, 329–30, 352, 356
Chrysippus, 40, 42, 273, 275, 287, 315, 317, 373–74
Cicero
  and Aristotle, 32, 34, 45
  and Caesar, 45, 64, 83
  and Clodius, 27, 64
  and *exempla*, 33
  and Panaetius, 34, 39
  and Plato, 31, 34, 72, 77, 86
  and Polybius, 40, 48
  and Pompeius, 27
  and *res populi*, 31
  and Stoicism, 36–39, 41–45, 61, 79–84, 87, 237
  and the Epicureans, 47, 82
  and Tullia, 80
  assessments of, 28–30
  auctoritas, 49, 51–52, 66
  best state, 31–36
  care, 79, 84
  Catilinarian conspiracy, 27
  cosmopolitanism, 92
  courage, 44
  culture, 84
  decorum, 44
  detachment, 76
  Dream of Scipio, 76–79
  duty, 37–46
  empire, 88
  grief, 80
  ideal statesman, 76–79
  imperium, 49–51
  interest, 40–42
  justice, 39–45
  law (*ius*), 36–40
  law (*lex*), 40, 55, 58
  legacy, 28–30
  libertas, 49, 52–59
  life, 26
  mixed constitution, 48–59
  natural law, 36–40
  natural reason, 47
  New Academy, 29, 70, 237
  oikeiōsis, 39
  oratory. *See* Cicero: rhetoric
  otium, 86
  partnership and mixed constitution, 48–59
  philosophy as practice, 85
  potentia, 68
  potestas, 50–51, 57
  property, 59–62
  regnum, 50
  res publica as partnership (*societas*), 46–69
  res publica defined, 30–31, 35–36

548

response to crisis, 45, 64, 67
rhetoric, 69–76
rhetoric and philosophy, 69–76
rights of war, 90
role of philosophy, 79–87
sage. *See* sage
senatus consultum ultimum, 67–69
social bonds, 42–46
societas, 46–69
trust, 43, 47–48, 52, 57, 59, 62–67
utilitas, 40
view of the people, 58–59, 86
virtue, 41–45
vis, 69, 91
wisdom, 43
Cinna, 95
civitas, 31, 34–35, 40, 48, 87, 176, 420, 425–26
Claudia Pulchra, 347
Claudius, 24, 271, 280, 340, 349
clementia, 188, 190, 206, 214, 278, 280–81, 283, 285–86, 425
clientelae defined, 17
Clodius, 65, 68, 328
Cocceius Nerva, 350
collegia, 13
comitia tributa. *See* Roman republic: *comitia tributa*
concordia, 48, 150–51, 167, 176, 241, 250, 258, 269, 328, 398, 401, 404, 425
consensio, 404
consensus, 47
Constantine the Great, 24
cosmopolitanism. *See* Stoics: city, Seneca: city, Marcus Aurelius: *cosmopolis*, Cicero: cosmopolitanism
Cossutianus Capito, 349
Crassus, Lucius Licinius, 66
Crassus, Marcus Licinius, 28, 95
Cremutius Cordus, 354
cupiditas, 392–93, 399, 420, 428
cursus honorum, 14

decorum, 16, 38, 44, 308, 368
delatores, 305, 346–47
Democritus, 97
despotism, 24–25, 246, 254–55, 287, 304, 306, 311–12, 314–15, 317, 321–26, 328, 330–31, 333, 345–46, 351, 353–55, 357, 402
terror, 345–53
Dido, 203, 206, 208–9, 219, 225
dignitas, 154, 196, 247
defined, 16
in Sallust, 154
Diogenes the Cynic, 316
dominatio, 247, 400–1

Domitian, 24, 321, 323, 352–54, 361, 370
Domitius Afer, 347
Drusus Caesar, son of Germanicus, 350
Drusus, Nero Claudius or Drusus Julius Caesar, son of Tiberius, 335, 337–38
dunamis, 369, 374, 379

Epictetus, 360–66, *See also* Stoics
eleutheria (freedom), 367
life, 361
philosophy as practice, 362
Epicureanism
in Rome, 94–96
politics, 93
Epicurus. *See also* Epicureanism
aistheseis = *sensus*. *See* Epicurus: and perceptions
and Plato, 100, 103
atomism, 97–100
community, 105–7
concepts, 104
consciousness, 100–5
empiricism of, 100
eudaimonia (happy life), 99
feelings, 98
friendship, 106
hedone = *voluptas*. *See* Epicurus: and pleasure
hope, 144
independence (*autarkeia*), 105
justice, 135
language, 105
Nature, 98
opinion, 101
pathe = *sensus*. *See* Epicurus: and feelings
perceptions, 98, 110
pleasure, 98–99
politics, 106
prolepsis = *notitia*. *See* Epicurus: and concepts
role of philosophy, 101–5
sage. *See* sage
soul, 98
time, 105–6
exempla, 16, 33, 71, 145, 163, 174–75, 179, 230, 251, 264–66, 268, 282, 308, 313, 385, 397, 410
in Augustine, 385, 410
in Cicero, 33
in Livy, 230, 251, 264, 266, 268
in Sallust, 174–79
in Seneca, 282, 308, 313

Fabius Maximus, 264
fides, 415, 426
in Augustine, 415, 426
in Cicero, 43, 62, 66
in Lucretius, 124, 131, 142

549

fides (cont.)
   in Sallust, 160, 167, 170
   in Tacitus, 332–39, 346, 351–53
First Constitutional Settlement, 20
First Triumvirate, 28
foedus, 120, 122, 124, 137 See also treaties
fortitudo, 38, 44, 81, 165

Gaius Gracchus, tribune, ,67, 169
   See also Gracchi
Gaius Memmius, 169
Germanicus Julius Caesar, 334, 338
Gracchi, ,165, 175, 401 See also Tiberius
   Gracchus, Gaius Gracchus

Hannibal, 264
happiness, 77, 81, 93, 102–3, 105–6, 117, 126,
   132, 140, 144, 194, 290, 359, 366, 383,
   386–87, 392–95, 399, 409, 411, 415, 418, 428
Helvidius Priscus, 370
honestum, 41, 275, 289 See also Stoics: moral
   goodness
Horace, 187

imperium, 12, 14, 20, 49–50, 88, 133, 149, 154,
   165, 167, 170, 172, 183, 212, 262–63,
   265–66, 270, 282, 369, 399, 427–28
   See also power
intercessio, 10, 248
ius agendi cum plebe, 10, 248
iustitia, 36–37, 39, 62 See also justice

Jugurtha, 175
Julius Caesar. See Caesar
Junius Otho, 349
jurisdiction, 51, 53–55, 123, 125, 273–87, 292,
   295, 298, 302, 307, 312, 315, 338
   See also Tacitus: jurisdiction, Seneca:
   jurisdiction
   Stoicism, 274–75
jurists, 4, 279
justice, 35–36, 39–44, 46–47, 55, 61–62, 73–74,
   83, 89, 122, 133, 135–37, 142, 189, 211, 283,
   290, 316, 366, 369, 376, 393, 398–400, 423,
   427, 429

kathēkon. See also Stoics: appropriate action
   as *officium* (duty), 38
katorthōma, 37, See also Stoics: right action

leges Aelia et Fufia, 14
leges de repetundis, 90
leges Liciniae Sextiae, 11, 249
leges Valeria et Horatia, 258
Lepidus, 176–77, 229

Leucippus, 97
lex de ambitu, 328
lex Hortensia, 11, 249
lex maiestatis, 346
lex Sempronia, 27
lex Sempronia agraria, 13
libertas, 49, 53, 55–57, 83, 160, 170, 247–48, 257,
   296, 302, 312, 327, 351, 367, 399, 401, 405,
   428, 430
   in Livy, 233, 246–49, 257
   in Lucretius, 117
   in Sallust, 160
   in Tacitus, 351
Libo, M. Scribonius Libo Drusus, 349
Livy
   and Aristotle, 232, 258
   and Plato, 232, 239–42, 258
   assessments of, 230
   concordia, 250
   corruption, 233, 249–53, 259
   decemviri, 253–58
   empire, 262–70
   exempla, 230, 251, 264, 266, 268
   felt meanings, 230–34, 250, 253, 255, 258,
      261–62, 266–68, 307
   founding, 239–42, 259, 261
   Gauls compared to Romans, 259–60
   gender, 244–45, 257
   imperium, 262
   inclusion, 262–70
   libertas, 233, 246–49, 257
   political concepts, 230–34
   primitive societies, 259
   principate, 231
   relationship to Augustus, 232
   role of history, 230, 234
   view of the people, 233
   vis, 267
Lucius Marcius, 270
Lucretia, 242–44, 246, 257, 262
Lucretius
   agreements, 120
   and Aristotle, 113
   and Empedocles, 109
   and Ennius, 109
   and Epicurus, 93, 96–107, 114
   and Homer, 109, 117
   and Plato, 114
   and the Republic, 95, 135
   and Thucydides, 138
   assessments of, 93, 107
   atomism, 115–17
   auctoritas, 143
   boundaries of power, 124, 134
   communities as compounds, 133–35

creation, 115–17
despotism, 120, 129
detachment, 93, 141
empire, 134
facultas, 132
gods, 115–20, 131
imperium, 96, 133
jurisdiction, 123
justice, 135–37
law, 135–37
libertas, 117
life, 96
limits of politics, 143
mos maiorum, 96, 133
opinions, 127
perception, 111
pietas, 129–32
piety redefined, 131
plague, 142–43
potestas, 115, 123–25, 129
primitive origins of communities, 121–25
property, 126
role of poetry, 96, 107–14
Roman destiny, 115
sage. See sage
sovereignty, 122, 132
time, 143
trust, 142
vis, 124, 143

Macer, 176–77
maiestas, 133, 170
Mamercus Scaurus, 348
Marcus Antonius. See Antonius
Marcus Aurelius, 24
　and Plato, 359, 371
　and Stoicism, 359
　assessments of, 358
　Christians, 359
　civic aspects, 366, 376–77
　contemplation, 371
　cosmic city. See Marcus Aurelius: *cosmopolis*
　cosmopolis, 360, 376–77
　daimōn, 380–81
　detachment, 375
　dunamis, 369, 374, 379
　eleutheria (freedom), 367, 369
　gender, 366–71
　kratos, 368
　libertas. See Marcus Aurelius: *eleutheria*
　life, 366
　love, 378
　manliness, 366–71
　nature, 375
　oikeiōsis, 381

passions, 364, 379
piety, 380
sage. See sage
salvation, 371–80
soul. See also Marcus Aurelius: *daimōn*
time, 373–75
Marcus Flavius Flaccus, 169
Marius, 64, 66, 95, 155, 171–75
Metellus, 172, 175
Milo, 68, 328
Minucius Rufus, 264
mos maiorum, 15–16, 96, 114, 133, 172, 212, 216

Nero, 2, 24, 271–72, 276, 280, 282, 284, 286,
　306, 321, 340–41, 343–44, 349, 351, 361,
　367, 370
Numa, 52, 62, 242

Octavia, daughter of Claudius, 340, 353
Octavian, ,19, 28, 190, 197, 201–2, 206, 210, 212,
　214, 222, 229, 329 See also Augustus
　given title "Princeps", 20
　given title, "Augustus", 20
oikeiōsis, 60, 284–88, 381, 411

Panaetius, 34
patrician defined, 14
pax, 99, 184, 208, 386, 397, 404
Petronius, C., 350
Philodemus, 109
pietas, 129–31, 170, 184, 188, 211–16, 223, 226
　in Lucretius, 129–32
　in Virgil, 212–28
Piso, C. Calpurnius, 333
Piso, L. Calpurnius, 347
Pisonian conspiracy, 271, 343
Plato, 1, 28, 31, 34–35, 40, 45, 48, 72, 76–78,
　103, 108, 114, 181, 192, 207, 212, 222, 232,
　239–42, 258, 273, 309, 311, 358, 361, 371,
　383–84, 396, 403, 408–9, 418, 426
　and Augustine, 383, 396, 408–9
　and Cicero, 31, 34, 72, 77, 86
　and Epicurus, 100, 103
　and Livy, 232, 239–42, 258
　and Lucretius, 114
　and Marcus Aurelius, 359, 371
　and Sallust, 148
　and Seneca, 309, 311
　and Virgil, 192, 207, 212, 222
plebiscita, 10
political thought
　affective aspects of, 3, 29–30, 42–43, 49, 52,
　62–67, 72, 79–87, 91–92, 96, 118, 148–55,
　183–84, 200–2, 215, 222, 230–34, 240–41,
　243, 250, 252, 258, 261, 266–67, 284–85,

551

288, 317, 378–79, 381, 385–93, 396, 399–400, 402, 408–16, 424, 427, 430
  definition, 4–5
  Roman suspicion of, 1–3, 94, 145, 272
  visual aspects of, 7, 16, 25, 73, 75, 84, 99, 110, 168, 204, 207–8, 224, 226, 231–33, 237, 243, 245, 249–53, 258, 260–61, 305, 307–15, 323, 357, 363, 379, 407–8, 412–14, 424, 426
Polybius, 7–9
  and Cicero. *See* Cicero: and Polybius
Pompeius, 27, 64, 66, 95, 328
populus Romanus
  in Cicero, 58
  in Sallust, 169, 175–79
  in the Republic, 9
potentia, 68, 147, 149, 160, 304
potestas, 20, 50, 52, 55, 57, 67, 123, 282, 291, 392, 401 *See also* power
  and the people, 57
  Augustus, 20
power, 3, 8, 13, 25, 48, 91, 96, 120, 123, 125–26, 244, 418
  in Augustine. *See* Augustine: *auctoritas*, earthly power, *dominor*, despotism, *dominatio, imperium, potestas*
  in Cicero. *See* Cicero: *libertas, auctoritas, potestas, potentia, regnum*, mixed constitution
  in Livy. *See* Livy: and *vis, imperium, libertas*
  in Lucretius. *See* Lucretius: *imperium, facultas, potestas*
  in Marcus Aurelius. *See* Marcus Aurelius: *dunamis, kratos*
  in Sallust. *See* Sallust: *auctoritas*, Sallust: *vis, imperium, potentia*
  in Seneca. *See* Seneca: *potentia, potestas, imperium, vis*, jurisdiction
  in Tacitus. *See* Tacitus: despotism
  in Virgil. *See* Virgil: violence, principate, *imperium*
provocatio, 20, 247
prudentia, 38, 393
Pyrrhic War, 267

Quintus Fabius Maximus, 263, 265

regnum, 50, 247, 251, 282, 304, 312
  See also despotism
res publica
  as *res populi*, 31, 55, 57
  definition, 30, 35
  oaths of loyalty, 23
  restituta, 23
  sovereignty of the people, 10

translation of, 30–31
Roman principate
  army, 22
  continuity with the Republic, 24–25, 332
  entertainment, 296–301, 343–45
  ideology of, 20, 182, 185, 278, 282, 297, 330, 333
  jurisdiction, 278–86
  law, 283, 346
  powers, 19–24, 278–86
  praetorian guard, 23, 339
  public discourse in, 339–42
  senate, 21–22, 332
  spectacle entertainment. *See* Roman principate: entertainment
  the people, 22, 340
  tribunate, 19–20, 22, 183, 332, 344
Roman republic
  campaigning, 13
  comitia centuriata, 12
  concilium plebis, 10, 249
  conflict, 18–19, 166
  contio (contiones), 12–13
  institutions, 8–19
  nobilis (nobilitas), 17–18
  norms, 15–19
  novi homines (new men), 18–19
  optimates, 18
  populares, 18, 160
  populus Romanus, 9
  senate, 15
  sovereignty of the people, 9–11, 58
  tribal assembly, 11–12 *See* Roman republic: *comitia tributa*
  tribunate, 10, 12, 18, 49, 53, 59, 64, 67, 169, 173, 175, 177, 248–49, 252–54, 256–58, 265
Rome
  destiny, 114
  Romulus, 34, 50, 62, 219, 225, 240, 242–43, 259–60, 268, 421, 423, 427

sacrosanctus, 10, 19
sage
  in Augustine, 384, 394
  in Cicero, 42, 44, 76, 78
  in Epicurus, 104
  in Lucretius, 142
  in Marcus Aurelius, 359, 377
  in Seneca, 273, 284, 287–89, 296, 302
  in Stoicism, 42, 273, 289, 291, 315, 376
Sallust
  ambition, 154, 167
  and Aristotle, 148
  and Carthage, 148, 150, 152–54, 177
  and Caesar, 161–65

552

and Cato the Younger, 161–65
and Jugurtha, 165–70
and Marius, 171–74
and Plato, 148
and Polybius, 148
assessments of, 146, 149
auctoritas, 171
Catilinarian conspiracy, 155–61
concordia, 150
corruption, 146, 149, 155, 164, 167–68, 175–76
exempla, 174–79
gender, 159
human nature, 149
imperium, 149, 154, 165, 167, 170, 172
libertas, 160
life, 145
luxury, 158
memory, 146–48, 162–65
metus hostilis, 148–55
mos maiorum, 146, 162–65
organization of desire, 150
potentia, 147, 149, 160
role of history, 174–79
role of political thought, 174–79
time, 163
view of the people, 175–79
virtus, 148, 151–55, 166
vis, 155
wisdom, 151
sapiens. See sage
sapientia, 38, 43, 151
Scipio Aemilianus, 77, 155, 167
secession of the plebs
  first, 10, 249
  second, 258
Second Constitutional Settlement, 20
Second Punic War, 262
Second Samnite War, 266
Second Triumvirate, 19, 229
Sejanus, 342, 347
senatus consultum ultimum, 67
Seneca
  and Nero, 271, 278–86
  and Plato, 309, 311
  and Socrates, 278, 304, 309, 313
  assessments of, 272
  benefits (*beneficia*), 315–20
  citizenship, 315–20
  city, 315–20
  cosmic city. See Seneca: city
  despotism, 276
  duty, 287, 316
  empiricism of, 290
  entertainment, 296–301
  exempla, 282, 308, 313
  fame, 303
  glory, 303
  imperium, 282
  insanity. See Seneca: madness
  jurisdiction, 273, 275, 278–86, 292, 295, 298, 302, 312, 315
  kingship, 283
  life, 271
  madness, 276, 291, 300
  mirror of princes, 281
  moral development, 287–92
  oikeiōsis, 284
  philosophy as practice, 307–15
  politics, 304, 306
  potentia, 304
  potestas, 291
  practical ethics, 288
  precepts (*praecepta*), 309–11
  principate, 271
  principles (*decreta*), 309, 311
  rhetoric, 315
  sage. See sage
  seclusion, 272, 301–3
  slavery, 317
  societas, 320
  spectacle entertainment. See Seneca: entertainment
  suicide, 296
  theater, 306
  theater and politics, 296–301, 305
  vis, 282
Silanus, C. Junius, 348, 350
slavery, 47, 51, 53, 65, 106, 117, 134, 155, 159, 172, 177–79, 241, 243, 245–47, 256–57, 268–69, 274, 294, 296, 305, 337, 346, 350, 361, 366, 368–69, 400, 402, 407, 421–22
Social War, 14, 66, 91, 166, 213, 263, 401
societas
  as partnership, 46–69
  Cicero, 46–69
  defined, 46
  Seneca, 320
sovereignty. See Roman republic: sovereignty of the people
Spurius Carvilius, 263
Spurius Maelius, 251, 329
Spurius Manlius Capitolinus, 251–52
Stoics
  appropriate action (*kathēkon* = *officium*), 38, 287, 366
  assent, 363
  citizenship, 88, 315
  city, 42, 88, 315
  conceptions (*ennoiai* = *notiones*), 287
  cosmic city. See Stoics: city

553

INDEX

Stoics (cont.)
  empiricism of, 276, 290, 362
  fame, 303
  fortune, 293
  freedom, 367
  friendship, 319
  impulses, 365
  indifferent goods, 289, 365
  jurisdiction, 274–75
  justice, 39–42
  king as body, 283
  kingship, 283
  madness, 276, 291
  moral development, 287–92
  moral goodness, 41, 44, 275, 289, 365
  natural law, 36–39, 274
  nature, 36, 284–85, 361
  oikeiōsis. See *oikeiōsis*
  passions, 81, 291, 364, 378
  patientia, 301
  poetry, 109
  politics, 273, 275, 315
  preconceptions (*prolēpseis = praesumptiones*), 287
  right action (*katorthōma = perfectum officium*), 37, 289–90, 366
  sage, 42 See sage
  social bonds, 87
  soul, 37, 289, 361, 363, 365
  virtue, 289, 365
suffragium, 247
Sulla, 59, 64, 66, 95, 155–59, 171, 173, 177, 263, 345

Tacitus
  and Aristotle, 330
  assessments of, 321
  Britons, 326–29
  corruption, 325–31
  despotism, 322–25, 330, 333, 351, 354–55, 357
  Germans, 326–29, 333
  jurisdiction, 334–39, 350
  libertas, 351
  madness, 331
  maiestas prosecutions, 345–53
  memory, 354
  mutiny, 334
  political psychology, 323
  primitive societies, 325–31
  public discourse, 339–42, 354
  role of history, 353–58
  style, 356
  terror, 345–53
  theater, 334
  theater and politics, 295, 334–39, 343–45

Tarquins, 254
  and Lucretius, 120
  in Augustine, 400
  in Cicero, 53
  in Livy, 242–49, 256
  in Virgil, 210, 220
temperantia, 38, 393
Thrasea (Clodius Thrasea Paetus), 332, 349, 354, 370
Tiberius, 24, 305, 322, 331–32, 334, 337, 339, 346–47, 349
Tiberius Gracchus, tribune, ,13, 65, 68–69
  See also Gracchi
Tiberius Sempronius Gracchus, consul, 269
Titius Sabinus, 347
Titus, 24
Titus Manlius Torquatus, 263, 268
treaties
  in Lucretius, 120, 122, 124, 137
  in Virgil, 209–11, 226
trust, ,3, 43, 46–47, 62, 64, 66, 138, 167, 211, 250, 305, 334, 346, 351, 426 See also *fides*
Turnus, 203, 206, 209, 211, 213, 220
tyranny. See despotism

Verginia, 256, 262, 279, 345
Vespasian, 24
Virgil
  agreements, 210
  and Augustus, 188
  and Carthage, 205, 224
  and Homer, 181, 203–4, 210, 225
  and Lucretius, 192–200, 224
  and Plato, 192, 207, 212, 222
  and Stoicism, 192, 205
  Arcadia, 188
  as didactic, 190, 192
  as ideological, 189
  as spiritual, 188
  assessments of, 180, 187–91
  bugonia, 201
  care, 200–2
  corruption, 187
  Corycian gardener, 201
  culture, 200–2
  Eurydice, 198–200
  founding, 202, 212–28
  funeral games, 221
  gender, 208–10, 220
  glory, 195
  Golden Age, 186–93
  Harvard School, 190
  ideal community, 182
  imperium, 182
  labor, 195–203

554

memory, 183, 197–200, 207
mos maiorum, 212, 216
New Historicism, 191
Orpheus, 198–200
pastoralism, 186–93
pietas, 212–28
political escapism, 182
principate, 182
role of poetry, 207–8, 225
shield, 225
time, 197–200, 224

Underworld, 196, 199, 201, 204, 211, 225, 227
violence, 203–12
virtue. *See virtus*
virtus, 16, 37, 126, 149–53, 158, 161, 164–65, 167–68, 172, 197, 313, 370, 393, 403
vis, 91, 123, 143, 155, 226, 267, 282
See also power
voluntas, 378, 388, 427

Zeno, 88, 273, 275, 289, 311, 315, 359, 378

Lightning Source UK Ltd.
Milton Keynes UK
UKHW02f1946150918
328934UK00013B/190/P

9 780521 124089